Cultural Anthropology

Understanding a World in Transition

SHELDON SMITH
University of Wisconsin—LaCrosse

PHILIP D. YOUNG
University of Oregon

ALLYN AND BACON

Boston • London • Toronto • Sydney • Tokyo • Singapore

Series Editor: Sarah L. Kelbaugh
Editor in Chief, Social Sciences: Karen Hanson
Editorial Assistant: Elissa V. Schaen
Executive Marketing Manager: Suzy Spivey
Editorial Production Service: Chestnut Hill Enterprises, Inc.
Manufacturing Buyer: Suzanne Lareau
Cover Administrator: Linda Knowles

Copyright © 1998 by Allyn & Bacon
A Viacom Company
160 Gould St.
Needham Heights, MA 02194

Internet: www.abacon.com
America Online: keyword: College Online

Library of Congress Cataloging-in-Publication Data

Smith, Sheldon,
    Cultural anthropology : understanding a world in transition /
Sheldon Smith, Philip D. Young.
        p.   cm.
    ISBN 0-205-27005-0
    1. Ethnology.   I. Young, Philip D.   II. Title.
GN316.S59   1997
306—dc21   97-28380
                                                    CIP

Printed in the United States of America

10 9 8 7 6 5 4 3 2 1   02 01 00 99 98 97

Photo Credits: Maps drawn by the University of Oregon Geography Department, Andrea Soule; Woodfin Camp & Assoc./p. 22, © Bernard Boutrit/p. 50, © Catherine Karnow/ pp. 70 & 92; p. 72, © Kal Muller/p. 232, © Hulton Deutsch/pp. 146, 312, © Jason Laure/p. 461, © Chuck O'Rear/p. 478, © Frank Fournier; p. 345, The Gamma Liaison Network/p. 27, © Stephanie Welsh/p. 232, Swersey/p. 299, Ralph Gaillarde; Sygma/p. 32 © Jason Bleibtreu/p. 128, Bill Nation/p. 241, Igor Kostin; pp. 42, 173, 186, & 197, Comstock; p. 80, p. 224, 275, 352, & 356, Corbis-Bettmann; pp. 87, 112, 265, & 398, Archive Photos; p. 92, The Granger Collection, New York; pp. 107, 117, 246, 248, & 256, courtesy Murphy Library, University of Wisconsin–La Crosse; p. 122, Motion Picture & Television Photo Archive/ © Gabi Rona; p. 130, Matrix/ © Karen Kausmauski; pp. 138 & 170, National Geographic Society/pp. 138 & 170, Edward S. Curtis/p. 183, James P. Blair/p. 304, O. Louis Mazzatenta/p. 430, Bruce Dale; pp. 150, 159, Bureau of American Ethnology/Smithsonian; pp. 207 & 214, Photographs and Prints Division, Schomburg Center for Research in Black Culture, The New York Public Library, Astor, Lenox, and Tilden Foundations; p. 229, North Wind Picture Archives; p. 266, 284, 384, AP/Wide World Photos; pp. 288 & 328, Impact Visuals/pp. 288 & 328, © Paula Beonstein/p. 471, Ricardo Funari; p. 318, Aurora/ © Robert Caputo; p. 323, Sharon Hutchinson; pp. 165, 331, 337, 478, & 481, © Victor Engelbert; p. 364, © Ed Kashi; pp. 192, 369, 391, 400, & 403, © Wolfgang Kaehler; p. 375, © Eric Valli; pp. 179, 426, DDB Stock Photos/pp. 411 & 416, © H. Huntly Hersch/p. 443, © Suzanne Murphy/p. 447, © Noir Benedicto; p. 422, Magnum Photos; © David Alan Harvey; p. 451, P. Young; pp. 457 & 462, S. Smith.

Contents

Preface

In the years from the end of World War II until the collapse of the Soviet Union, interests around the world were focused on the potential threat of atomic war and the destruction of the planet. That threat has now faded, and our focus has shifted to the more mundane, but equally critical issues of political, economic, demographic and ecological transitions throughout the world. The transitions bring promises and they bring threats. A few short years ago, Americans generally did not know where Bosnia or Rwanda/Burundi were; now they do and the stories these regions tell agonize us. Our portfolio of interests has shifted from global war to much more local issues and problems of human adaptation; these local issues, however, are driven by global change.

Anthropology has a unique contribution to make to the study of global change, for it is the preeminent discipline in the study of culture change through time and space. In the period directly after World War II, anthropologists such as Robert Redfield, George Foster, John Gillin, Oscar Lewis, and Margaret Mead were at the forefront in explaining a changing world, one that described the influence of "modernization" on traditional societies. But with the age of postmodernism the concept of modernization became less relevant as anthropologists began to doubt that modern ideas made life in traditional societies better. Anthropologists, borrowing heavily from the field of literary criticism, turned to critiques of modernity and the objectivity of ethnographic science. Questions of what the true "other" really was came to dominate the discipline for a time. These critiques of ethnography and philosophical musings about "otherness" served one useful purpose. They forced anthropologists to examine carefully both their methods of data collection and their theoretical assumptions.

As so often happens in world history, our world is again going through dramatic and rapid changes, and anthropology has renewed its interest in the study of sociocultural change. These changes are no longer driven by Western technology and culture, but by the global marketplace, which is having a dramatic impact on political and ecological systems around the world. Out of the self–examination precipitated by the postmodern critique has come a renewed theoretical and methodological vigor within the field, precisely what is needed to move into the realm of analysis of global systems.

We have been interested in how anthropology can be used to interpret contemporary global issues since our years in graduate school and before. Both of us lived outside of the United States before we took the plunge to becoming professional students of culture. While we both share interests in the more traditional fields of anthropology, such as prehistory, kinship studies, linguistics, and many other fascinating areas of the discipline, it has been the day-to-day issues of human survival and adaptation that have most intrigued us.

Anthropologists, other social scientists, and historians have increasingly been involved in the analysis of global change, and we have been able to rely on a developing body of theory and case studies to write our textbook. We examine social change by focusing on three major transitions: a globally driven economic transition to capitalism, a political transition that involves democratic reform movements, and an ecological transition to sustained development, which requires a demographic transition to smaller families. These transitions, which can be viewed as empirical changes in systems or ideological shifts in what people believe, often bring a mixed bag of positive and negative outcomes.

Our global approach, with its emphasis on these transitions, allows us to discuss current issues across this changing world. It is common to listen to and read international television and newspaper commentators using the term *transition* to describe international issues such as changes in the political structures of Russia, Bosnia, Mexico, South Africa, but it is also common to have the same concept used by local newspeople to describe changing communities here in the United States. It is just as common to find local journalists in places like Puebla, Mexico, writing articles in the local *Sol de Puebla* that are remarkably "anthropological," examining the impact of international trade on local communities and ecosystems. These concepts, so central to modern cultural anthropology, are now the analytic tools used by international experts, other social scientists, journalists, newscasters, and students of change around the world.

In this book, we take advantage of anthropology's holistic and interdisciplinary approaches in our presentation of a world in transition. The book connects with theoretical points of view found in contemporary economics, political science, geography, psychology, history, global studies, and peace studies. In part we can connect to other disciplines because anthropology has been embraced by these disciplines, and, in turn, anthropology has become increasingly multidisciplinary, absorbing ideas from other disciplines and integrating them into new theoretical perspectives.

One of these perspectives, called political ecology, provides a framework for analyzing the relationship between productive activity, trade, power, and ecological adaptation in both the preindustrial world and in the contemporary world, in traditional societies and modern societies. We utilize this perspective throughout the book, providing the reader with a unified view of how the world works, rather than a collection of topics to learn.

Political ecology combines human (or cultural) ecology and political economy. Human ecology asks questions about adaptation. Its principal concern has been with the interactions between humans and their biophysical environment. A key element in our political ecology approach is the notion that adaptation is a mental process, or what John Bennett has referred to as "minding." Political economy examines questions regarding the institutions of human societies. Its focus has been on the links between productive activity, trade, and the distribution of power in societies. A critical factor in the political economy perspective is the importance of trade, which is an obvious variable for human society in a globalizing age, and a sometimes overlooked factor in connecting societies throughout history and prehistory.

In this book, we also take a regional approach and examine how globalization is transforming societies in six regions of the world. Grounding our discussion in the political ecology framework, we look at the development of American and European societies, Africa, the Middle East, Asia, and Latin America, describing both the age-old adaptations and the contemporary problems facing these regions—problems we read about in our daily newspapers or listen to on the evening newscast. Our political ecology approach highlights the connections between human ecological processes and the political and economic transformations that are occurring in modern states.

Our book also effectively integrates archaeology and history to provide the reader with a sense of continuity from ancient to modern times. This historical context is essential in understanding the dynamics of culture change, ethnic conflict, and indigenous rights issues.

In addition to global, interdisciplinary, holistic, and regional approaches, the text also gives an emphasis to ethnic diversity and ethnic conflict. Chapter 8, "Ethnicity, Ethnic Conflict, and Social Movements," examines the concept of ethnicity and analyzes ethnic conflict and indigenous and ethnic rights movements within the framework of social movements theory. The framework allows us to contextualize social movements, ranging from civil rights movements to indigenous rights movements to ethnonationalism, and to give them meaning in light of global changes. These topics are explored in every regional chapter. While our interest is in current issues, we do not slight traditional topics in anthropology. The first half of the book examines the history of anthropological thought and explores basic questions such as: What is culture? What is community? How do we study culture? How does language influence cultural perception? How do cultural misunderstandings come about? How are distinct types of societies organized? How did the state come into existence? We also examine other traditional topics such as kinship, religion, marriage, systems of production, and exchange within the context of our discussions of bands, tribes, chiefdoms, and states and in the context of case studies presented in the regional chapters.

A unique aspect of the text is Chapter 4, in which we apply our perspective to various facets of American culture. The chapter introduces students to the origins of American culture, the rapid changes it is experiencing, and the major problems it faces going into the third millennium, including such issues as sexuality and minority rights.

The theoretical approach of the text is easily learned, applied, and used. We suggest using an international newspaper, such as the *New York Times*, the *Washington Post*, the *Los Angeles Times*, or, the *Christian Science Monitor* as adjunct reading. The ideas in the book soon mesh with the current events reports, rendering complex global issues comprehensible. In part that is because we integrate current events into the text from the very beginning in the form of case studies and ecological maladaptation boxes. These present the complex political, economic, and demographic shifts involved in the development of ecological issues and problems around the world.

Our text is deliberately brief enough to be suitable for use in a quarter system, yet its content is provocative enough to provide plenty of material for discussion in semester-long courses.

Anthropology has never been an ivory tower discipline, and this is not an ivory tower book. It demands much of students and instructors, but it steps directly into a world with which we must become familiar in the next decades of the new millennium. We have had a great deal of help in our quest. It has been gratifying to find that so many of our colleagues share our interest in an anthropology that deals with transitions we are experiencing.

We wish to thank several individuals who helped along the way, while at the same time absolving them of any responsibility for the final product.

We owe a tremendous debt to Sylvia Shepard, the development editor at Allyn and Bacon, whose hard work, constructive suggestions, editorial insight, and imagination transformed the original manuscript through several iterations into the present text. We stand in awe of her magical talents. Sarah Kelbaugh, Allyn and Bacon's anthropology editor, has guided the book through the various production stages and we are sincerely grateful for all her help.

At the University of Oregon, Harry Wolcott provided insightful comments on the first three chapters and Vernon Dorjahn made his expertise available on the Africa chapter. John Lukacs kindly allowed us to use his picture in Chapter One and helped compose the photo caption. Andrea Soule of InfoGraphics created the original maps to our specifications and altered those from other sources to meet our specific needs. At the University of Wisconsin, La Crosse, Martin Zanger helped with the history of La Crosse, and Ed Hill of the Murphy Library lent his expertise to select photographs on the culture history of La Crosse. Jess Hollenback and Mark Chavalas provided valuable advice on sections dealing with the religions of the Middle East and Asia.

Several colleagues on various campuses served as reviewers of an earlier version of the manuscript and provided many useful comments and suggestions, many of which are reflected in the current text. For their efforts, we sincerely thank: James Armstrong of SUNY at Plattsburgh; Raymond Bucko of Le Moyne College, Syracuse, New York; Charles Ellenbaum, College of Du Page, Glyn Ellen, Illinois; Northhampton, Massachusetts; Paul Magnarella, University of Florida at Gainesville; Richard Moore, Ohio State University, Columbus; Edward Reeves of Morehead State University, Morehead, Kentucky; and Richard Wilk of Indiana University at Bloomington.

Finally, both of us would like to acknowledge our intellectual debts to several individuals who have, knowingly or not, influenced our thinking and the development of our ideas over the years. Patrick Gallagher's charismatic enthusiasm for anthropology strongly influenced Sheldon's choice of an anthropology major at the George Washington University in the early 1960s. John W. Bennett, Distinguished Professor Emeritus at Washington University in St. Louis, has helped keep that interest burning and directed it through almost two decades of professional research, writing, and teaching. The intellectual stimulus for much of this book can be traced to Prof. Bennett's influence as one of the outstanding scholars of contemporary anthropology.

Phil Young spent both his undergraduate and graduate days at the University of Illinois at Urbana, where he was influenced in various ways by an intellectually powerful cast of characters: Joseph B. Casagrande, Julian Steward, Donald Lathrap, Ken Hale, F. K. Lehman, and Oscar Lewis. They are undoubtedly responsible for Phil's lifelong eclecticism. At the University of Oregon, where he has spent most of his career, Phil would like to acknowledge the intellectual stimulation provided over the years by numerous colleagues, but in particular Homer Barnett and Harry Wolcott in the Anthropology Department, Rob Proudfoot in the International Studies Program, and Colette Grinvald, Talmy Givón, and Scott DeLancey in the Linguistics Department.

Studying Anthropology

1

Humankind has met and responded to innumerable crises since the first groups of *Homo sapiens* appeared on Earth. Some responses have been successful—at least for a time, until changing circumstances and new crises required new responses; others have been not so successful or not successful at all. As Marshall Sahlins once said, "Lots of things people do are truly stupid, if understandable, and many cultures have gone to the wall" (1977:221). Will many of the cultures of the twentieth century go to the wall?

Today the peoples of the world face several crises that, with one exception—overpopulation—may not be so different in kind from those of the past but are quite different in magnitude. Among the most serious of our current crises is the unsustainable use of the resources we need for our biological survival as a species. We are seeing massive deforestation, soil erosion, species extinction, rapid depletion of nearly all of the usable resources of the land, the rivers, and the seas, toxic chemical pollution of the air we breathe, the water we drink, and the foods, be they plant or animal, that we consume. Pollution and deforestation in particular seem to be contributing to global warming. Hunger and poverty are becoming more common as the human population that must be supported by dwindling resources continues to increase; and the absolute gap between the well-off and the poor is increasing. To cite one recent statistic: While the world area planted in grain has remained relatively stable since 1970, the number of hectares per capita has steadily decreased since 1950 as the population has increased (Brown, et al. 1996:43). Ideals in our own society that stress equality and equity are becoming further and further removed from the realities of everyday existence for the majority of the world's population. These problems are no longer local, isolated instances; they are worldwide, brought on by the excesses of a global economy in which we are all involved, directly or indirectly, and whether we like it or not. Out of all this is born increasing violence, both structural and unstructured (we will get to what we mean by this later), social, political, and economic oppression, human rights violations in every part of the globe, and for many, feelings of hopelessness and helplessness. Among the most oppressed are those least powerful—the remaining small-scale indigenous societies of the world. Curiously, it is these very people who are fighting back rather than apathetically accepting their lot, while many who are better educated, better informed, and with more power and influence stand anguished, wringing their hands, saying "there's nothing I can do."

Scary, isn't it? But this is not a Doomsday Book; these are just some observations on the current state of the world. The questions are: How did things get to be the way they are; Why do people often collectively make the wrong choices; and, What *can* we do to make them right? We mean by wrong choices those that are ultimately maladaptive, that is, that have consequences that are detrimental rather than beneficial to the society (even though, in the short term, such choices may appear to be beneficial). Economists talk about this in terms of costs versus benefits. Maladaptive choices are generally those in which the long-term costs greatly outweigh the short-term benefits, and the classic problem is that of accurately calculating long-term costs. How can we insure a sustainable future in which all humans may expect humane treatment from their fellows and a reasonably good life? The study of **anthropology** can go a long way toward providing answers to the first question; and these answers can certainly provide sound guidance in seeking answers to the second and third.

A brief modern definition of **anthropology** is the study of humankind. While this definition differs from earlier definitions only in its political correctness, the major concerns of the discipline have shifted significantly as the world has changed, particularly in the latter half of the twentieth century. For example, the traditional preoccupation of **ethnographers** with describing and interpreting kinship terminological systems, descent systems, and rules of marriage and post-marital residence—an understandable focus of interest when studying small-scale societies and communities that, at the time, were relatively isolated socially from the world beyond their boundaries—has seemingly all but disappeared. This is not to say that kinship relations are no longer important, at some level, to the vast majority of the world's societies, including our own (see, e.g., Schneider 1980). Modern cultural anthropologists still consider kinship important to an understanding of the workings of many, if not most, cultures, but kinship studies have been reformulated as studies of gender roles and relations, power, inequality, and difference (Peletz 1995). In general, anthropologists have not so much turned their attention away from studies of societies of intimates (Givón 1979); rather, they have increasingly focused on the larger scale interconnections of communities, regions, and states and the consequences of these for societies of all sizes and cultural persuasions.

Many anthropologists are disturbed by the changes they see in our modernizing world. A year ago I (SS) received a letter from a senior anthropologist, now retired, who felt deeply distressed by changes he had helped bring about in East Africa. (When recounting personal experiences in the text, (SS) after the "I" stands for Sheldon Smith and (PY) stands for Philip Young.) He viewed modernization as a destroyer of traditional communities. There is no doubt that modernization has introduced new ideas that allow (or force) native peoples to become subordinate to the will of outsiders, threaten their customs and their habitats, and have the potential to alter completely their way of life. In this text, we will consider many changes in traditional lifeways from our anthropological perspective, but we must also keep in mind that some people, whose traditions we anthropologists lament the disappearance of, may have a different perspec-

Case Study: Jardín, Colombia, a Personal Account

Recently, I (SS) took a bus from the city of Medellín, Colombia, to the small town of Jardín for a three-month research project. The name *Jardín* means "garden" in Spanish. My first visit to the town was in 1956 when I was sixteen. My memories of Jardín were of a remote, quiet, Andean town of whitewashed walls and red tile roofs set in a valley as green as emeralds. In that year, I attended a Colombian boy's school in Medellín, and joined with a group of Colombian and American friends to buy an old 1935 Ford, which we named the Firebird. We drove the old car on weekends through the towns and villages outside Medellín: La Ceja, Rio Negro, and Jardín. According to custom, young Colombian men used to go to the countryside on *parrandas* (parties) and dance the *bambuco* (a traditional dance) with local girls while their mothers and aunts looked on nervously. In remote communities like Jardín, there were no telephones, no television sets, no radios, and little communication with the world outside except by bus over rutted roads.

During my research project, I became familiar with the town as I collected information on the changes that had occurred in the region since 1956. I was astonished. In 1956 only a few of the wealthiest locals had access to battery-powered short-wave radios. Today most of the middle-class families in the town, and most of the coffee farmers in the countryside, have television sets, VCRs, and boom boxes. People watch reruns of *Dallas* translated into Spanish. A local radio station plays Colombian versions of the Grateful Dead. Television brought soap operas depicting upper-class Colombian culture to the wives of coffee farmers, who, on Saturday nights, now dress up like their favorite actresses and come into downtown Jardín for coffee or a rum drink. No one dances the bambuco in the town's *cantinas* (taverns) anymore, and when I asked about the traditional music I loved so much, young people told me *"ah, esta es la musica de nuestros padres"* (that is the music of our parents). And what did they listen to? American rock-and-roll sung in Colombian Spanish by local rock bands.

In addition, the people of Jardín now face the power of the Medellín and Cali drug cartels. The national and state governments have been strongly influenced by the money of the cartels, and the United States recently sanctioned the government of President Samper due to the flow of drugs from Colombia to the United States. But the people of Jardín have a different perspective than do Americans, who blame drug dealers. Most of the people I interviewed felt that Colombian culture was being corrupted by American demands for drugs, and that until Americans had control over their own problem, the best they could do was to protect their own children from drugs.

I was disturbed by many of the changes since 1956. I missed the traditional music and dances, and I did feel the community was threatened by the power of the "kings of cocaine," as two American writers described them (Gugliotta and Leen 1989). But the people of Jardín did not feel the same. Their attitude was much more realistic and pragmatic. The past was a part of tradition, to be venerated, but not

Jardín, Colombia, in 1984. Jardin is in the heart of the coffee growing region of the province of Antioquia. (Source: S. Smith)

lived, and the gang members from the cartel faced the threat of *"el escopeton"* (the rifleman), one or more locals who targeted drug dealers on the paths around the town at night.

The people of the town use modern technology to protect and preserve their traditions. VCRs and camcorders record the old dances for posterity. People in Jardín watch television to see who is going to win a competition in Bogotá as the best bambuco dancers in the country, but they do not remember the steps. Coffee brokers use computers to study market conditions and try to gauge the best times to buy or sell coffee. American buyers for Starbucks are in constant communication with coffee brokers to find out where the best coffee beans are grown and when to buy. Juan Valdez, who is from this region of Colombia, appears on your television sets advertising fine Colombian coffees.

While rural Colombia is threatened with the homogenization of its popular culture by "media" culture (what shows up on television), modernization does not make Colombian culture disappear. Instead, what is happening is the emergence of a new culture that is neither traditional nor modern but is a patchwork quilt of both. As one shifts the radio dial, stations play traditional folk music or modern rock-and-roll. One cantina in downtown Jardín plays *"El Dueto de Antaño"* (the duet of the past or of yesteryear), while another plays Mexican golden oldies, and a third plays hard rock. Since all three cantinas face the same park, where their loudspeakers are hung from oak trees, a listener can hear expressions of three subcultures at once.

tive on the matter, as illustrated in the personal account in the preceding case study.

What Is Anthropology?

Anthropology is the study of humankind and all its manifestations in all times and places. Anthropologists study the biological, cultural, and psychological aspects of humans. But they do not do it alone. They incorporate and utilize accumulated knowledge from many sources in their search for answers to why humans think and believe and behave in so many diverse ways. There is a sense in which the anthropologist working in the library or the national archives is as much "in the field" as one who is living in a small thatched-roof hut in a tiny tropical forest village several hours (or days) walk from anywhere else. The difference is that the anthropologist in the tropical forest is using living culture carriers as his sources of information and his colleague in the library is making use of the accumulated and recorded cultural wisdom written down by culture carriers of the literate world. Anthropology has been called multidisciplinary or interdisciplinary because it is a discipline that makes use of the collected knowledge of other academic disciplines in a search for a better understanding of the human condition. A medical anthropologist, for example, who makes use of the written documents—and these days, computerized databases—about AIDS, which represent the accumulated knowledge of the western medical community, pores over what epidemiologists have to say, examines the reports of sociologists, social workers, demographers and possibly even political scientists and economists, is using the specialists of these other disciplines as (proxy) informants in much the same way that the anthropologist in the field might interview a native specialist to learn about local beliefs concerning illness and health.

Anthropology as a Science of Process and Connectivity

Anthropology is a fascinating and eclectic discipline that studies all the various forms of human adaptation we call culture change. Most people with just a passing acquaintance with anthropology will be aware of the aspect of anthropology that focuses on the study of biological adaptations and human origins. Thus, most are aware that anthropologists specialize in how humans evolved from an early chimpanzee-like ancestor to modern *Homo sapiens*. But this is only a part of the story. Anthropologists are also interested in culture as an adaptive response to physical habitats and external pressures (such as trade, colonialism, warfare, hegemony) through time. This interest in the adaptive responses of people in very distinct societies over hundreds of thousands of years has led anthropology to be a very broad social science with an unusually holistic world view. This contrasts with the narrower perspectives of the other social sciences.

Eric Wolf, one of the most prominent contemporary American anthropologists, has argued that anthropology is a very special science because it never became highly specialized. Anthropology, sociology, economics, and political science were once parts of a larger science called political economy in the middle of the nineteenth century. Anthropology is the modern heir of political economy,

> a field of inquiry concerned with "the wealth of nations," the production and distribution of wealth within and between political entities and the classes composing them (Wolf 1982:8).

Nineteenth-century intellectuals, such as Saint Simon and August Comte (the father of sociology), by stressing the imitation of the hard sciences, which were already specialized, fostered the breakup of political economy into distinct disciplines. Sociology focused on the study of how close social relationships (solidarity) hold societies together. Economics specialized in the study of how markets work, as though they were disconnected from society. Political science moved in the direction of creating a market model of political process, treating economy and ideology as external "environments," but mostly ignoring anything that is not driven by political decision-making. These specializations in the study of complex processes led to: (1) viewing human social relations (solidarity, markets, political decisions) as "causal in their own right," and (2) viewing categories, such as communities and nation states, as "real." Social relations became causes that were severed from economic, political, and ideological processes and connections. Society and culture were conceptualized as autonomous, self-regulating, and bounded.

Wolf argues that, while anthropology has changed through many schools of thought, it is the primary heir of political economy through its emphasis on "process" and "connectivity." **Process** is the focus anthropologists maintain on the problems of human adaptation to physical habitats (technological changes, impact on the environment), while **connectivity** refers to the "adaptations" between cultures (communication, peace, trade, war). While some anthropologists would like to narrow anthropology to the highly specific ethnographic study of single societies, Wolf argues, quoting Alexander Lesser (1961), that anthropology should view human societies not as closed systems but as open systems that are connected to each other (Wolf 1982:19). Cultures, societies, or nation states should not be viewed as bounded or as self-perpetuated "designs for living." Wolf instead emphasizes the importance of understanding the dynamics of process and connectivity rather than simply creating categories such as *societies, cultures, nations, bands, tribes, chiefdoms, states,* and so forth. Often such categories are misused to explain complex events. Echoing Karl Marx (1964), Wolf prefers an anthropology that stresses laying bare the laws or regularities surrounding the production of wealth (Wolf 1982).

The Subdisciplines of Anthropology

The discipline of anthropology encompasses four major subdisciplines, with specialties within each, and quite a diversity of theoretical perspectives (see Chapter 3). This text is about the subdiscipline of cultural anthropology. Our theme is a common one in the field, that of how and why cultures adapt and change, and by the same token, why cultures often resist change. Our perspective, that is, the way in which we focus our interpretations, relies on **political economy** and **human ecology**. The central ingredient of political economy is **trade**; that of human ecology is **resource utilization**. Both involve **property rights**. It would be difficult—and quite one-sided—to look at one without looking at the other. Both will be considered within the broad framework of culture history, that is, an examination of how cultures in various parts of the world got to be the way they are now, and contemporary processes of globalization. The combination of these two approaches, political economy and human ecology, has come to be called **political ecology.**

The division of anthropology into major subdisciplines in introductory textbooks is not consistent. Some make a twofold division into physical and cultural anthropology and, in turn, subdivide cultural anthropology into archaeology, linguistic anthropology, and ethnology. Others recognize four major subdivisions, and this is the scheme we will follow here. These four are biological anthropology (in the past commonly called physical anthropology), linguistic anthropology, archaeology, and cultural anthropology (also called sociocultural anthropology). In recent decades, **applied anthropology** has begun to emerge as a special field of endeavor and some anthropologists now view applied anthropology as a fifth subdiscipline. Others argue that there is an applied side to each of the four standard subdisciplines. Both views have some validity. The first view is based on applied anthropology as a society of practitioners no matter their subdisciplinary specialization; the second retains the coherence of the subdiscipline and focuses on the distinction between basic and applied research. We will provide separate discussions of applied cultural anthropology below and in Chapter 13.

Biological Anthropology: The Study of Physical Change   Biological anthropology and archaeology are methodologically closer to the natural sciences than linguistic and cultural anthropology. They are also geared to the "long view" of human history, whereas cultural anthropology operates in the "current history" of recent centuries. Biological anthropology, in many respects, closely resembles the field of biology, except that anthropologists focus on human beings, their ancestors, and their primate relatives, and not on other nonhuman life forms. The evolution of *Homo sapiens sapiens* (modern humans) is a major interest of biological anthropologists, as is the range of human biological variation, which itself is a product of evolution. Human evolution is the heart of biological anthropology.

Within the subdiscipline of biological anthropology are three broad but closely related specialties: **Physiological anthropology, paleoanthropology,** and **primatology.**

Physiological anthropology is concerned with the physiological make-up of human beings (and their primate cousins). Anthropologists in this field tend to share many of the interests of human biologists. Their general focus is on how the human body functions and adapts. Medical anthropologists, for example, may work in the tropical areas of Central America, Southeast Asia, and elsewhere trying to find out why certain kinds of diseases occur in the tropics. They may

John Lukacs, paleoanthropologist, examining the teeth of an ancient resident of the archaeological site of Harappa at the on-site field laboratory. One subspecialty in paleoanthropology is the study of human teeth. From teeth, we can learn something about age at time of death, physiological stress during growth and development, differences in dietary patterns (by sex and subsistence pattern), dental occlusion, and nutritional deficiencies. Harappa is one of five major urban centers of Harappan civilization, which flourished in what is now Pakistan and northwest India about 2600 B.C. (Photo source: John Lukacs)

work in highland Peru to find out why certain populations are characterized by aggression and **hypoglycemia** and if there is a relationship between the two. They may study the diet and nutritional status of human populations under various environmental conditions. Or, they may use x-ray technology to find out what was in the digestive tract of a mummified Egyptian pharaoh or the recently discovered Mesolithic Man of the Alps. Some may work like the 1970s TV personality, Quincy, as pathologists specializing in **forensic anthropology.** Often forensic anthropologists are called in by police departments to identify human skeletal remains that may be evidence of a crime. The vast amount of data that anthropologists have accumulated on human biological variation, past and present, is what makes it possible for the forensic anthropologist to decide to what population an individual belonged, and whether the remains are ancient or modern, as well as identifying sex and approximate age. After World War II, the identification of many of the skeletons of American soldiers was done at the Department of Physical Anthropology of the Smithsonian Institute in Washington, D.C. Recently biological anthropologists worked with the government of Argentina to determine how leftist critics were killed during the "dirty war" of a decade ago, and in Bosnia to identify victims of **genocide.**

Paleoanthropology is the aspect of biological anthropology that most people think of as "anthropology." A common response when an anthropologist introduces herself to someone who lacks familiarity with anthropology is "oh, you are one of those people who studies bones, like Richard Leakey." I (SS) clearly remember one time as a young anthropology instructor when some La Crosse city officials asked me to identify what they thought were the bones of an ancient mastodon, but turned out to be those of a recently deceased cow. On another occasion I was asked to identify what local police thought was a human foot. I examined it and not only identified it as human but, more precisely, as that of an adolescent boy or girl. Later, forensic experts in Madison identified it as the foot of a young bear. Since the latter experience, I have avoided trying to do the things that biological anthropologists are trained to do and I stick to my sociocultural interests.

Paleoanthropology is very close in both methods and interests to paleontology, the branch of geology that studies the evolution of early life forms. The focus is on what human fossil remains and those of our primate ancestors can tell us about the evolutionary history of humans. It is not at all unusual to find paleoanthropologists working with paleontologists to recreate the **paleoecology** of a region.

The questions asked by paleoanthropologists usually have to do with human or primate origins and evolution. The term *primate* is applied to the *order* in biological taxonomy that includes all of humanity's ancestors and present-day relatives such as lemurs, monkeys, and apes. Most of the paleoanthropologist's work is done by using methods of excavation closely related to those of archaeology. Paleoanthropologists tend to concentrate on fossil remains, such as the mineralized skeletons of ancient **hominids** (humans and our relatives) and other primates. Because the evidence for human evolution is seen as controversial by some people, paleoanthropologists are often involved in debates with antievolutionists. While the implications of the discoveries of paleoanthropologists are often controversial and hard to understand, the fact of evolutionary change itself is not a matter of controversy among scientists. Like paleontology, paleoanthropology is a fascinating discipline that many nonanthropologists take up as a hobby.

Primatologists may study the comparative anatomy of both living and fossil primates in order to ascertain similarities and differences between us and our primate relatives. Some primatologists study the behavior of living primates in much the same way as ethnographers study human cultures. The major difference is that they cannot ask questions of their subjects. Primate behavior specialists are interested in such questions as the extent to which some forms of behavior common to humans and other primate species may be a result of common biological heritage rather than cultural learning.

Archaeology: The Long View of Culture Change   Archaeology, in many respects, is the oldest subdiscipline of anthropology. Although archaeology also involves the study of human origins and evolution, it differs from paleoanthropology in that the subject matter is not the fossil record, but the **artifacts** that human beings have left behind. Artifacts are those things created by human beings that have definite forms and functions. Archaeology takes the long view of culture change, roughly from three or four million years ago, when the first artifacts appear, to when the historical record takes over and allows us to read about events. **Historical archaeology** is a special subfield of archaeology that examines the sites occupied by human populations during the historic period, and the artifacts these sites contain, in order to supplement the written records of history.

While archaeology is identified most clearly within anthropology with the study of prehistoric cultures, its methods of scientific excavation are often borrowed by other disciplines for research purposes; and its boundaries extend to classical, biblical, and historical archaeology. For example, archaeology has been used recently to excavate early biblical monuments in the Near East and colonial structures in the United States, such as plantations in Georgia and Florida, that are clearly historical. It is an open question here whether these researchers are dabbling in archaeology, anthropology, history, biblical studies, or just what, but the healthy fact that scholars do cross each others' boundaries should remind us just how permeable those boundaries are, how artificial are the definitions of our scientific disciplines, and how important an holistic perspective is to achieving an understanding of why humans do the things they do.

Linguistic Anthropology: A Look into Logic and the Mind   Linguistics is the scientific study of language. **Linguistic anthropology** focuses on the multifaceted relationship between language and culture. It is the anthropologist's way of discerning the logic of other people's reality. It is a way of trying to see things from the **emic** or native point of view, so to speak, whether the natives are hunters and gatherers of the Kalahari desert, Quechua-speaking villagers in the Peruvian Andes, or our next-door neighbors. To paraphrase Pogo, we have met the natives and they are us. The study of languages and the nature of the relationship between the language people speak, their culture, and their thought patterns has long been a part of anthropology. In many respects it really is hard to make a sharp division between linguistic and cultural anthropology.

But the study of language is certainly not now and never has been confined to the field of anthropology. The pretwentieth-century roots of linguistics are to be found in philosophy as well. And today linguistics is a discipline with departmental status in many universities or may be associated with a department of English or Psychology, depending on the history of the institution and the research foci of the linguists. Both linguistics and anthropology have close relationships to the emerging interdisciplinary field of **cognitive science.**

Within the broad field of linguistic anthropology are several divisions of labor. **Comparative linguistics** (also called historical linguistics) focuses on the origins of different languages and the genetic relationships among languages. Linguistic anthropologists such as Floyd Lounsbury, Joseph Greenberg, and Terence Kaufman, each in his own way, have been leaders in this field. **Ethnolinguistics** (also called ethnosemantics) is the study of the ways in which people of different cultures organize, categorize, and classify everything that makes up their world. Brent Berlin, Cecil Brown, and Eugene Hunn are among the outstanding scholars in this field. **Sociolinguists** study the particular ways in which language is used in social interaction to mark, for example, **status** and **role** relationships. The works of William Labov are classics in this field.

There are several reasons why anthropologists, particularly cultural anthropologists, have an interest in linguistics. In a great many societies in which anthropologists do research, the languages are unwritten; that is, there is no tradition of literacy. Under such circumstances, the anthropologist may be the first one to record the language, using a **phonetic** alphabet to record the sounds. Ideally, this is followed by **phonemic** and **morphological** analysis and the compilation of a **lexicon** and a **grammar** of the language, often with the collaboration of a professional linguist.

The anthropologist often becomes the only specialist in the study of a rare language, and even if the language is not rare, he or she may still be among the few to have studied it. Another important reason why the study of linguistics is important to anthropology is that the culture and social organization of a society can be understood only through an understanding of the language, for neither culture nor social organization are directly observable. For example, the way in which people classify their relatives differs significantly from society to society. An anthropologist who does not understand the language will not be able to understand, for example, that among the Ngóbe of Panama, father's brother and mother's brother are perceived as distinct from each other, but a father, his brother, and mother's sister's husband (who would ideally be a father's brother) are perceived as the same kind of social person and accordingly referred to by the same kinship term. This is quite unlike the American kinship system where both father's brother and mother's brother (and sometimes mother's sister's husband and father's sister's husband) are perceived to be the same kind of relative and all are referred to as *uncle*, and father is distinguished (see Figure 1.1). The way kin are classified can provide important clues to the structure and content of certain role relationships within societies.

Finally, linguistics is important to the anthropologist because it is a way to gain some understanding of the workings of the human mind. In the next chapter we will find that a language is a highly specific code that is governed by what may be broad genetically based rules. These rules may have a lot to do with the basic operation of the brain, that is, with cognitive processes, and by studying a language we gain some understanding of the way in which these complex codes work. Furthermore, it appears that many aspects of culture are also governed by rules that parallel rules of language, and, by studying the structure of language, we gain insights into the operation of culture.

Cultural Anthropology: The Anthropology of Current History   The broadest of the subdisciplines of anthropology, in terms of areas of specialization and theoretical perspectives, as well as number of practitioners, is cultural anthropology, also called sociocultural anthropology. It is also the subdiscipline that is least well understood by the well-educated lay person. For thirty years, when asked what I (PY) do for a living, if I have responded "I am a cultural anthropologist," most people on planes, trains, buses, and in the local bars have either responded with "well, that's very interesting," meaning they didn't have the foggiest idea of what

Figure 1.1   **An Example of Ngóbe and American Kin Classification**

Ngóbe classification of males in the parental generation

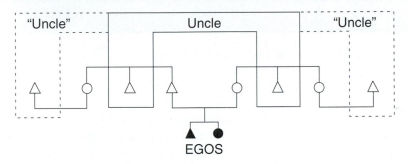

American English classification of males in the parental generation.

I do, or they have asked "Have you dug up any interesting bones lately?" When someone seemed genuinely interested, I took the trouble to explain. For most people, studying living people is something they associate with psychology or sociology, and some feel quite uncomfortable with the very idea that anyone would make a living by studying how other people live.

A Ngóbe family in Panama in 1965. (Source: P. Young)

The term *sociocultural* is a combination of the words **society** and **culture** and is used as a shorthand for the two. To the cultural anthropologist, culture and society are analytically distinct phenomena that are so tightly entwined in real life as to be inseparable. When a cultural anthropologist conducts field research among a particular group of people, the endeavor is called **ethnography** and the researcher an **ethnographer**. When an anthropologist makes a comparison of the features of any two or more societies or cultures, the activity is called **ethnology**, or sometimes comparative ethnography. Such comparisons may be qualitative (looking only for the presence or absence of particular features) or quantitative (for example, counting instances of cooccurrences of two or more features and using statistical methods to determine the degree of significance of resulting correlations).

Among the established specialty fields within cultural anthropology (we are not attempting to name all of them) are **political anthropology** (the study of the emergence and development of public policy), **economic anthropology** (the comparative study of economic systems), **human ecology** (the relationship of cultural systems to physical habitats—also called cultural ecology), **medical anthropology** (applied biological anthropology), **legal anthropology** (comparative law), **ethnoscience** or **cognitive anthropology** (the study of folk taxonomies of human and natural phenomena), the **anthropology of religion** (the comparative study of how humans view the supernatural), and the **anthropology of art** (primarily the study of folk art), to name a few. The essence of almost all of cultural anthropology, regardless of specialization, is the study of social and cultural manifestations of living populations. **Ethnohistory** is a special field of cultural anthropology that attempts to understand the lifeways of past populations through judicious, if tedious, analysis and interpretation of a combination of historical records and archaeological data.

Cultural anthropology is similar to other social sciences, such as sociology, political science, psychology, and economics. However, it is much more general and tends to incorporate aspects of these disciplines. Eric Wolf (1982) has argued that modern cultural anthropology is a type of history, one which differs from history itself through the application of the scientific method. We would call it a social science of current history. By current we mean anything within the last two to three hundred years.

Biological anthropology, then, studies the biological changes in humans over millions of years. Archaeology takes the "long view" of culture change over the last three to four million years. Cultural anthropology is restricted to the recent neighborhood of time, the last two to three hundred years. This is roughly the period within which capitalism has evolved, and much contemporary anthropology examines the impact of capitalism on world societies, although there is certainly much cultural anthropology that deals with many other issues.

The impact of capitalism on the world's societies is a thread running through this book. Many anthropology texts tend to view capitalism as an intrinsically immoral force which disrupts societies. We prefer to view it as one of many forces, albeit a significant one, to which societies adapt. At times the changes are for the better, and at times for the worse. We hold to the point of view that it is preferable for the participant or native to make judgments and not the outsider.

Applied Anthropology: An Emerging Subdiscipline   A distinction can be made between academic and applied cultural anthropology. Academic anthropologists train undergraduate and graduate students and conduct basic research. Applied anthropologists make use of the knowledge anthropology and other disciplines have accumulated in attempts to find solutions to contemporary human problems. The distinction between these two groups is not hard and fast, and many anthropologists do both, teaching for a few years and then doing applied work for a while. While it may often be difficult to sharply distinguish academic from applied research, the distinction is made in many fields of both the social and the natural sciences, and it does have utility.

The role of applied anthropology has grown dramatically since World War II. Applied anthropologists receive much the same ethnographic training as academic anthropologists. Applied anthropologists differ from their academic brothers and sisters in that they are hired to work on practical problems that often require them to develop skills outside of anthropology. Applied anthropologists can be generally thought to work on three different (but obviously related) kinds of problems: economic development, human health, and environmental issues. The former are often referred to as development anthropologists and they are usually trained in some branch of economics or agriculture, although there are several other disciplines that they may try to adapt. The second field is known as medical anthropology. Medical anthropologists usually have some training in medicine or public health and many work in third world countries on various community health problems, such as the diets of young children, population planning, and communicable diseases. The third field is known as eco-logical anthropology (or human ecology or cultural ecology), and is becoming increasingly important as the need becomes more urgent to find solutions to environmental problems. Applied anthropology has become very popular among students who are interested in the discipline but do not want to teach. It is also a viable option in these times when jobs in academic anthropology are hard to find.

Applied anthropology attempts to solve contemporary human problems by using the accumulated knowledge of the discipline. Applied anthropologists often face extremely difficult situations ranging from harsh environments to corrupt governments that hire them but then refuse to give the kind of cooperation needed to solve problems. However, it is becoming increasingly evident to those interested in the problems of third world countries that the work of applied anthropologists is indispensable.

The difference between the cultural anthropologist doing basic research and the applied anthropologist lies in the questions asked. The cultural anthropologist will have an interest in testing some aspect of a scientific theory. This requires being able to spell out the theory clearly and the hypotheses that it suggests. The applied anthropologist, although interested in, and informed by, theory, has greater interest in the resolution of human problems such as hunger, poverty, or the destruction of ecosystems. Back issues of the journals *Human Organization* and *Human Ecology* provide a sampling of the kinds of problems addressed by applied anthropologists: groundwater management in Baluchistan, weight concerns between African American and White female adolescents, the use of family planning among the poor in the United States, the impact of commercial fishing on oceanic ecosystems, common property rights in the state of Kerela, India, deforestation in the Philippines and the Ecuadorean Amazon, pest management in Egypt, mortality in rural Australia, discrimination against Ethiopian Jews in Israel, peacemaking in Mindinao, mental illness in Mexico, the impact of cattle ranching on the little Colorado River Basin, and so on.

While the theories and methods of cultural anthropology form the core of the research effort, the applied anthropologist will need training in other disciplines. Anthropology lends itself to this kind of work because of its holistic (and multidisciplinary) perspective. In the above list, note the importance of the following disciplines: irrigation management (agriculture), sociology, law, forestry management, ethnic studies, conflict resolution, psychology and psychiatry, and animal management. The researchers all started with a core of cultural anthropological knowledge and then reached out to other disciplines for the specific knowledge they needed to be successful. Often applied anthropologists work with specialists in other disciplines as members of a team. Almost all international development work, for example, is done by teams of specialists, not by individuals. Box 1.1 summarizes current trends in the subdisciplines of anthropology.

Linking Basic and Applied Research   Let me (SS) give an example of a project I carried out a decade ago. My brother, Richard, and I have had a lifelong interest in Colombia and both of us have worked in the San Juan River Valley west of

BOX 1.1

Anthropology Dissertation Topics in the 1990s

Biological/Physical. The most current research includes biomolecular data-gathering toward an evolutionary synthesis with paleoanthropology. Dissertations are holistic and experimental, using actualistic studies, tool replication, and microwear analysis. Primate taxonomy and behavior are popular topics.

Archaeology. New PhDs are synthesizing results of past research on individual sites, using supplementary cultural, physical, and linguistic data. Dissertations target political development, land use, migration and ethnoarchaeological patterns within larger geographic regions. Remote sensing, experimental design, and software add excitement to archaeology.

Linguistic. New PhDs emphasize the centrality of speech in society and in multicultural studies. The Native American Language Act has prompted research on endangered languages.

Sociocultural. Today's doctoral students emphasize one or more of four competing viewpoints in their dissertations: (1) science, (2) advocacy, (3) interpretation, and/or (4) postmodernism. To date there has been little synthesis among the four.

Applied. Doctoral research focuses on diverse aspects of health care, agriculture, and economic development. Applied, which includes practitioners from all four subfields of anthropology, is the discipline's growth industry.

(*Source:* Modified from Givens and Jablonski (1995: 306))

Medellín. He wrote his dissertation based on research he did in the valley between 1968 and 1971 (R. Smith 1974). I read his dissertation in 1976 and it raised an interesting issue in applied anthropology: What is the relationship between the ownership of small farms and economic development? I spent the following two years doing library research on the theories behind why large estates (*latifundias* in Spanish) tend to destroy the chance of a region becoming economically developed and why small farms (*minifundias*) tend to help a region become economically developed. This required in-depth reading of the literature on the *latifundia*, but it also drew me to read about the economic development of American small farms. I read literature on economic theory, political theory, and farm management. In 1984, I spent three months in the region. The specific question I had was: Why do small farms tend to promote economic development? My brother had already collected detailed economic data on the farmers of the region. I interviewed a dozen coffee farmers to learn if any significant changes had occurred and learned that none had (but, yes, the Medellín drug cartel was having an impact during my research).

I then spent the following three months tracking coffee investment. What I found was that, unlike large plantation systems and haciendas, local small coffee farmers tend to reinvest part of their profits in their own farms. The farms became more prosperous, and the farmers bought from local middle-class store owners in the town of Jardín. They also invested in two local banks (plantation districts tend not to support banks). These store owners then bought goods from merchants in the city of Medellín, stimulating its economy. The model that finally emerged from my work and that of my brother was one that looks very similar to American farm systems of the Midwest just before the turn of the century, but very different from the hacienda/plantation systems of Guatemala and the rest of Central America (Smith & Smith 1989).

Notice that I used both quantitative data and ethnographic and historical data in my test of a hypothesis (the hypothesis, stated formally, is that small, independent coffee farmers will invest in the local ecosystem to achieve sustained economic development). It is important to realize that humanistic data, such as history, can have great validity in answering a scientific question (this one drawn from agricultural economics).

Culture with a Big "C"

It is fair to say that cultural anthropologists are not in complete agreement about how to define or understand the primary objective of their analysis: **culture**. Exactly what is culture? Culture has been humankind's primary means of adaptation for the past several thousand years, yet it is a concept notoriously difficult to define. We have ceased to change biologically in any significant way, and while there have been a few minor biologically adaptive trends in the last ten thousand years, we adapt to nature through culture, which constantly changes. Culture is often expressed and usually transmitted through language, but it is much more than language. Large-scale complex cultures are usually composed of several different subcultural realities. These **subcultures** may be based on ethnicity (e.g., Mexican Americans), religion (e.g., Catholics or Jews), or even occupation (e.g., longshoremen—see Pilcher 1972).

The classic, and, so far as we know, first anthropological definition of culture was that of Edward B. Tylor who, in 1871, said:

> Culture or Civilization, taken in its wide ethnographic sense, is that complex whole which includes knowledge, belief, art, morals, law, custom, and any other capabilities and habits acquired by man as a member of society (Tylor 1958:1 [1871]).

From this rather all-encompassing beginning, which appears to take in everything, *including* the kitchen sink, the quest for an agreed-on definition of anthropology's central concept has continued. In 1952, Kroeber and Kluckhohn compiled over 150 definitions of culture, provided some historical background on the origin and use of the term, classified the definitions in broad categories, and provided a definition of their own. Their classification contained the following categories: descriptive (emphasis on broad definitions with lists of content); historical (emphasis on tradition); normative (emphasis on rules or ideals); psychological (emphasis on habits and learning); structural (emphasis on patterning); genetic (emphasis on ideas, symbols, culture as product); and finally, incomplete definitions (unsystematic or metaphorical). As Borofsky (1994:3) points out, their own definition of culture seems to have proved too broad and cumbersome and is seldom cited.

Modern definitions of culture are of two general types. The first type is ideational, that is, culture is defined as being purely in the mind; behavior and artifacts are left out, said to be manifestations of culture, but not culture itself. The second type includes the behavioral and material as well as the mental. Definitions of the first type deliberately distinguish internalized mental configurations from the behavior, institutions, and material products that result from them. One is then forced to use a term such as *sociocultural system* in referring collectively to the mental, material, and behavioral; and the phrase, *material culture*, becomes a contradiction in terms. Definitions of the second type, those that include our internalized mental rules for behavior, the behavior itself, and usually the material products of our endeavors as a part of culture with a big "C," although certainly broader in scope (a potential disadvantage), seem more useful (a potential advantage) in that the links among mental rules, behavior, and material culture are stressed and at least part of what we mean by culture is directly observable. We will use a definition of the second type in this book.

Culture is shared knowledge, beliefs and patterns for behavior, the resulting behavior, and the resulting material products. Thus, culture is partly a symbolic phenomenon that exists in the mind; it is a code of sorts that governs the way we act in particular contexts. But by our definition, culture is also partly the patterned behavior that people in a society engage in as a result of shared ideas about what is appropriate. In addition, the shared knowledge of a society's members results in the production of the material goods of a culture, some of which may be purely utilitarian, while others may have purely symbolic meaning, and a whole lot are both useful and symbolic.

Most things that we make are made according to blueprints that we have in our minds. The thing out there, say a 1956 Chevrolet, is a concrete manifestation of an idea that an automobile designer had who worked for the General Motors Company, an idea that caught on and became very popular, but one that is no longer accepted as a design for automobiles. Both the idea and the automobile are a part of American culture. That is, both the idea in the mind and the concrete manifestation of that idea can be considered a part of culture.

When we talk about the culture of the Middle Ages, we are talking about the ideas in the minds of architects, poets, writers, musicians, politicians, farmers, and so on, which are manifested in the material remains of that age. These cultural remains we preserve in museums. Our age will probably rest in the museums of the future, and, speaking of our 1956 Chevrolet, we find that it is already being placed in museums as a relic of the past.

Society has often been confused with culture and vice versa. In many anthropology and sociology texts, the definitions overlap so much that it is hard to distinguish the two. Keesing (1976:568) defines society as, simply, "a population marked by relative separation from surrounding populations and a distinctive culture." This is what we will mean when we refer to society. The members of a society are the carriers of its culture.

What we can observe directly are the manifestations of culture in the form of people's behavior and the things people produce (material culture). We can see two people dancing (social interaction) and we can see the Chevrolet (material culture) but we cannot see the ideas that brought the car into existence or that brought dance steps into being, nor can we directly observe all that there is to know about the cultural significance of dancing or cars in any particular culture. Social institutions such as marriage are also manifestations of culture. While we can observe people getting married, we cannot directly observe the rules of marriage in a society. And we must remember that behavior itself does not always reflect cultural ideals, that is, the way in which people believe they *ought* to behave. It does reflect, in a sense, the playing out of individual understandings of cultural ideals, although we must also bear in mind that any instance of behavior may be a deliberate violation of the cultural rules.

It is important to remember that society and culture are analytically distinguished concepts invented by sociologists and anthropologists in order to communicate about what they are studying. And, while both terms have been introduced to the mass media by sociologists and anthropologists, they are also recent introductions to our language. In a good many societies, the words *culture, society*, and *sociocultural* either do not exist or mean very different things. The word for society in Colombia, *sociedad,* does not refer to a group of people who share a culture, but rather to something like "the moral order," an abstraction of ideal cultural rules, something to live up to. When in Colombia, one must be aware that *sociedad* does not mean "society" in the anthropologist's sense. Ditto for *culture.* The word for culture in Colombian Spanish is *cultura* and refers to high culture: poetry, classical music, ballet, and so on. This use is also the traditional use of the word in the United States, but the word *culture* is slowly being used more and more by sociologists and anthropologists.

Characteristics of Culture

Now that we have defined culture as we will use the term, we need also to examine briefly the main characteristics of culture. Culture is shared, transmitted across generations through learning (not biologically), and patterned. Individual behavior that departs from the accepted cultural norms is idiosyncratic. None of these three major characteristics of culture—shared, learned, and patterned—should be taken to mean that culture is tightly bounded and static or unchanging, and no modern anthropologist would take them to mean this. The fact that cultures change, sometimes slowly, sometimes rapidly, has been known, though not always emphasized, since the early days of anthropology. Perhaps it would be wise to add a fourth characteristic of culture—it is flexible.

Shared

Members of a society do not usually completely share all the beliefs and knowledge that constitute a part of culture. More is likely to be shared in small-scale
societies with relatively few members than in large-scale, complex societies with
hundreds of thousands, or even millions, of members and probably numerous
subcultures. To say that culture is shared is to say that it is an attribute of groups
rather than individuals. What is shared as a part of culture can be described as a
set of central ideas or images or prototypes with their attached symbolic meanings and a permissible range of alternatives. This is what allows people to have a
reasonable set of expectations about the behavior of others in a given social interaction, to recognize permissible deviations from the ideal behavior as well as
culturally inappropriate behaviors. It is also what creates problems in social interaction between members of different cultures where expected behaviors and
the symbolic meaning of them are not the same. Keesing describes these cultural
patterns as "patterns of assumption, perception, and custom," and he provides a
telling example of the misunderstanding that can result in a situation of cross-
cultural interaction:

> A Bulgarian woman was serving dinner to a group of her American husband's
> friends, including an Asian student. After her guests had cleaned their plates, she
> asked if any would like a second helping: A Bulgarian hostess who let a guest go
> hungry would be disgraced. The Asian student accepted a second helping, and
> then a third—as the hostess anxiously prepared another batch in the kitchen.
> Finally, in the midst of his fourth helping, the Asian student slumped to the floor;
> but better that, in his country, than to insult his hostess by refusing food that had
> been offered (1976:1).

Despite the obvious cultural misunderstandings shown in this example, we
should not conclude that different cultures do not share any rules, patterns, expectations, symbolic meanings, or behaviors in common. The modern view is
that cultural boundaries are overlapping and permeable. This is an aspect of
flexibility (see below). Diverse cultures may share common beliefs in the area of
religion, for example. Islam in this respect unites a vast multitude of otherwise
distinct cultures across northern Africa, through the Middle East and into Central Asia, China, Malaysia, Indonesia, and the Philippines. As Lapidus points out
"Though Islam is not often the totality of their lives, it permeates their self-
conception, regulates their daily existence, provides the bonds of society. . ."
(1988:xix).

Learned

Culture is not transmitted from one generation to the next genetically (or biologically). It is passed along across the generations through the complicated cognitive process of learning. Learning takes place through language and observation. Humans are capable of symbolic learning, that is, to put it simply, we can
learn that one thing stands for (symbolizes) something else. Another part of the

Islam unites a vast range of distinct cultures from North Africa to the Philippines.

learning process is the ability to generalize, to discern patterns and formulate rules from specific instances. This is a largely unconscious process; natural language acquisition by children is a good example. While much of the learning that makes up the transmission of culture is from members of older generations to members of younger ones, not all of it is. Parents do learn from their children and grandparents from their grandchildren, although they may be reluctant to admit it. Everyone also learns from their peer groups, members of their own generation. Children, for example, with slightly different (sub)cultural backgrounds, may compare notes and in the process arrive at a new synthesis. This is one of the sources of culture change. Cultural learning in a broad sense is knowledge transmitted among humans—and they need not share the same culture for this to occur. Culture contact is an important source of culture change (see Flexible, below). One of the most intriguing aspects of the learning process is that it is almost always imperfect. Consequently, subtle changes occur in what is understood and how things are done and are passed on. This is another source of culture change. The major sources of culture change are, of course, deliberate alterations in the way things are done that come to be agreed on as useful responses to altered conditions—even though, in the long term, some such changes may turn out to be maladaptive. We will have more to say about culture change in Chapter 3, and most other chapters will contain examples of culture change.

Patterned

To say that there are patterns in culture means that there are agreed-on rules and conventions that people follow or honor in the breach. It means that an outsider can observe repetitive behaviors associated with particular social contexts.

It means that one can consistently recognize the differences between pictorial art forms of contemporary China, for example, and those of the indigenous cultures of the Northwest Coast of North America. Some rules are carried around only in people's heads. This is the only way that culture patterns are maintained in nonliterate societies. It is one of the ways the patterns are maintained in literate societies; the other way is by codification, that is, writing down the rules. Written laws, for example, are a part of U. S. culture. Even when cultural rules and conventions are written down, they are still subject to change, and the rules for making changes may themselves be codified.

Flexible

All cultures change, adapt, in response to altered contexts and circumstances. Change, not equilibrium, is the normal state of cultural systems. One of the significant alterations of context is when two (or more) cultures come in contact with one another. This always results in an interchange of ideas, knowledge, and goods. Not all the new ideas and knowledge or even all the new goods may be acceptable, but the potential is there and culture change of some sort is sure to occur. Culture contact may, and often does, result in a relationship of domination and subordination—and much of this book will examine such relationships. Cultures also change in response to changes in their natural environment. Studies of this kind of change are the classic focus of human or cultural ecology. Such change is not always successful and some cultures may die out as a result. Of course, one might well ask how anyone can know if a culture has become extinct, or has simply been transformed into something else that we do not recognize as a direct descendant of an earlier culture. There is no simple answer to this question.

The Perspective of Anthropology

A perspective is simply a way of looking at things. In addition to the concept of culture itself, the anthropological perspective is informed by three major organizing themes: **holism, comparison,** and the dilemma of **cultural relativism** versus **ethnocentrism**. In addition, there are some concepts that anthropologists stress in presenting their descriptions and interpretations of cultures and societies. These may not be specified in so many words by authors; that is, they may be implicit in what is said, or they may be explicit. Those that we will examine (it would be possible to come up with others) are present in one form or another in most writings of cultural anthropologists. These are the contrast between the concepts of **ideal** and **real culture,** and the contrast between **emic** and **etic** views. We will discuss each, in turn, here, and they will be explicit or implicit in various other places throughout the book. It should be noted that anthropologists are not in complete agreement about the value of these themes to a modern anthropological perspective.

Holism

Holism in anthropology is the view that we must attempt to understand whatever features of culture we are examining within the larger context in which they occur. The operating assumptions here are that different aspects of culture, society, and environment are interrelated, and that what may be enigmatic or puzzling in isolation will be understandable in the larger cultural and environmental context. While simple cause–effect relationships do exist in nature, the holistic view assumes that they are relatively uncommon in cultural systems. (Many biologists, ecologists, and physicists believe simple one cause–one effect relationships are rare in all natural systems.) Holism does not require the belief, attributed to early functionalists, that everything in culture and society is functionally related to everything else. People often compartmentalize bits of knowledge (which reduces psychological stress) and cultures do contain contradictions. It does mean that we think in terms of variables interacting within a system and systems interacting with other systems; that is, that we think in terms of open rather than closed systems. Open systems can be affected by outside forces. Cultures are open systems. The perspective of modern systems ecologists is also holistic. Holism helps us to recognize interdependencies and interrelationships when they exist.

With the emergence of anthropology as modern political economy through the emphasis on connectivity and process, holism has assumed new importance. Sociocultural anthropologists search for the connections between political, economic, ideological, and ecological factors, thus making anthropology a holistic science. The search for connectivity requires that anthropology attend to the findings of other disciplines, such as economics, political science, sociology, psychology, and history. Holism is a major research strategy of modern anthropology. When anthropologists go into the field, they may focus their study on one cultural subsystem: social, political, economic, and so on, but at the same time they try to understand how these various subsystems fit together as they gather their ethnographic data. One of anthropology's major contributions to social science and history is that of *synthesis:* bringing together what other people specialize in studying.

Why is a holistic approach useful? Because most of the contemporary problems of the planet are the consequences of rapid culture change, and the problems we face on the planet are complex phenomena made up of interrelated systems (Smith 1993, 1994). For example, the destruction of the planet's tropical forests is not solely an ecological issue. It is a complex problem made up of political, economic, demographic, and other issues. In Brazil, urban poverty forces people to migrate to the rainforest. The government, which is controlled by a wealthy elite, does not wish to democratize and finds it cheaper to build roads into the Amazon than to deal directly with poverty and overcrowding in urban, and some rural, areas. The institutional constraints needed to protect the rainforest cannot, then, be based strictly on scientific ecological considerations. Brazil is currently going through some important political and economic changes that may begin to address the problems of poverty and the lack of democracy. Political and economic considerations structure government responses. The United Nations can pass all kinds of resolutions to protect nature, and national governments may even agree to conform, but the poor may be unable to comply.

Comparison

While holism promotes the global view, the examination of processes and connections, and the revealing of interrelationships largely within a culture, comparison and the comparative method provide the means for dissecting cultures and societies into components and features and examining similarities and differences in order to construct hypotheses about what such similarities and differences may mean. Comparison appears to be a universal feature of the human thought process. We all make multitudes of comparisons every day, but most of these are implicit or subconscious. Implicit in all ethnographic research is the comparison of features of one's own culture with those of the culture under study. In the process, those that seem strikingly different stand out while those that seem quite familiar tend to recede into the background. This may be one reason why anthropologists have generally had more to say about cultural differences than similarities. Comparison is implicit in all descriptive ethnography; it is the foundation for conveying an understanding of the lifeways of one culture to members of another.

When anthropologists compare two or more cultural features across a sample of several cultures, they are engaging in an explicit form of comparison known as cross-cultural or controlled comparison. This is considered a form of **etic analysis:** The categories or features for comparison are devised or decided on by the researcher. The purpose of such comparison is to come up with hypotheses about possible interrelationships of particular cultural features. For example, is there a relationship between certain types of descent and certain types of postmarital residence such that **patrilocality** and **patrilineality** are found together? And if they are found together most, but not all, of the time, how can the exceptions be explained? This is the method anthropologists use in their attempts to determine how cultural variables are related to one another. Although cross-cultural comparison has yielded some interesting correlations, and continues to be useful in generating hypotheses, there are three problems that one should be aware of in using the method. First, there is the problem of determining whether two features that occur together in different cultures are related functionally or historically. In the past, if one chose a sample of cultures that were geographically distant from one another, the problem of historical borrowing could be (partially) controlled. In today's world, this is not so easy to do.

A second problem is that of insuring that units from which the features are being drawn are themselves comparable. Cross-cultural comparison assumes that the units being compared are distinct cultures. But, as we have already seen, cultures are open systems with permeable and sometimes overlapping boundaries, and their normal state is one of dynamic change rather than static equilibrium. How, then, do we determine that this is Culture A and that is Culture B? And can we compare, for example, tribes and nations?

Third, there is the problem of comparability of data. For example, do all reports of patrilocality refer to exactly the same phenomenon? It should be noted, for example, that some anthropologists use the term *patrilocality* to refer to all instances of postmarital residence where the husband resides with his own kin group and the wife goes to live either in the house of her husband's father or on the lands of the husband's kin; others distinguish living in the husband's father's house from simply living on the lands of the husband's kin and refer to the latter as **virilocality.** Further, is what is being reported by different ethnographers an ideal rule in one instance, in another a generalization based on several attested instances of the practice but without knowing the actual society-wide frequency of the practice, and in a third a normative statement based on high frequency of occurrence in a random sample? Added to these problems is the fact that ethnographies are not identical in their reportage of cultural features. Despite these problems, if used carefully, cross-cultural comparison can yield some significant insights into the workings of cultural systems.

Cultural Relativism versus Ethnocentrism

Simply put, cultural relativism is the view that there is an internal rationale to the beliefs, behaviors, and practices of all cultures and that we should not impose value judgments on the customs of others—at least for a time. It is an argument that we should not judge others by our own standards. Ethnocentrism, on the other hand, is the view that the ways of one's own culture are superior to those of any other and, in fact, the only "correct" ways. Let us briefly examine these views.

There is much discussion in the literature about whether anthropologists should or should not continue to promote cultural relativism, for, historically, anthropology has indeed espoused this view. When I (PY) was in graduate school in the early 1960s, making value judgments about the practices of other cultures was the cardinal sin of anthropology, and discussion was heated about whether anthropologists should involve themselves at all in any applied projects, for this inescapably meant meddling in and changing the ways of others and value judgments were therefore clearly involved. This may be termed the strong version of cultural relativism: No judgments should be made about the morality of the practices of another culture and no efforts should be made—at least not by anthropologists—to change the ways of others. This is a rather naive view, one in part foisted on anthropology by philosophers who insisted on linking cultural relativism to arguments about the existence of universal values, leaving cultural relativists appearing to condone such practices as cannibalism, infanticide, and female genital mutilation. It is doubtful that very many anthropologists ever subscribed to this strong version of cultural relativism, despite the heated arguments over applied anthropology.

The weak version of cultural relativism—the version that we, and we believe most modern anthropologists, accept—argues that our best chance of achieving understanding of the cultures of others is in their own terms and so we should, in the attempt, suspend judgment about whether something that others

This picture of an African girl who has just undergone genital mutilation as a consequence of a cultural custom of Muslim societies raises the provocative question about cultural relativism: Should we, as outsiders be disturbed by this custom? If so, by passing judgment are we "cultural imperialists?"

believe or do is right or wrong, good or bad. In this way we can hope to make sense of what others do in their own terms, that is, achieve an emic view. It is not necessary, in the process, to give up our own values or beliefs or necessarily to approve of all aspects of another culture. But there is a cost to achieving an insider view: The multiple perspectives resulting from cultural relativism make moral and ethical reasoning and judgment more complex. In sum, the strong version of cultural relativism involves refusal to make any value judgments at all; the weak version involves a (temporary) suspension of judgment to facilitate understanding within the cultural context.

"Why should we trust you; you're not like us; you don't believe what we believe; you don't dress and act like we do; you don't even talk like us." Ethnocentrism is the view that one's own culture is superior to all others and that others' ways of believing and doing are wrong or inferior or at the least just plain weird, if harmless. It is the antithesis of cultural relativism. It engenders distrust, sometimes hatred, sometimes violence. It is a view against which anthropologists have always argued, even if they were uncomfortable with the concept of cultural relativism itself. Ethnocentrism is a condition to be transcended if we are to achieve a more humane world; paradoxically, it also seems to be a natural human response to cultural differences. All cultures of which we have records display ethnocentrism to some degree. This does not justify the attitude but it does point out the difficulties in changing it. It seems to be part of the baggage of cultural boundary maintenance and tends to come to the fore under conditions of cultural stress. It is clearly manifest in situations of ethnic conflict. As you proceed through this book, you might think about whether ethnocentrism has increased in the modern world as cultures come into more frequent and intimate contact.

Ideal and Real Culture

Ideal culture embodies what people think they ought to do; **real culture** is what they actually do. In other words, there are ideal rules for behavior, agreed-on by many, and people can often tell you what they are even if they don't personally agree with them. And everyone is aware that no one behaves in conformity with the ideals all the time, sometimes for good reasons, sometimes not. Ethnographers should record both cultural ideals and real behavior. But the matter is not quite this simple, and we will take it up again and examine the complexities in the next chapter in our discussion of field research. For now we will just observe that cultural ideals constitute an emic or insider view because only the people themselves can provide you an account of these—and, again, because cultures are dynamic systems, there may not be complete agreement. If by *real* we mean what the researcher observes, then we can, for the moment, call this an etic view.

Emic and Etic

As we have indicated above, the emic view of things is that of insiders, the members of a culture, and the etic view is that of outsiders, usually but not always scientific observers like anthropologists. Both views have utility. However, the contrast between emic and etic is not as straightforward as simply insider/outsider and has generated controversy among anthropologists about both the utility of the concepts and what they mean. (See T. Headland, K. Pike, and M. Harris, eds., 1990, *Emics and Etics,* for presentations of various points of view.)

Kenneth Pike, a linguist, pointed out that there is a duality to anthropology in that it attempts to state what the native thinks about culture as an insider and at the same time creates a more mechanistic view from the outside that compares the culture studied to other cultures (1954). The first point of view is called **emic analysis** and the second is **etic analysis.** The etic model uses cross-cultural categories to characterize entire societies, often put into an evolutionary or economic perspective. The native often might not recognize the way that his/her culture is described in the second model, but the first description should be familiar.

As an example, in my (SS) study of plantation economies of Central America (1982), I created an economic model of the south coast of Guatemala that showed that large sugar mills called *ingenios* and smaller supplier plantations, called *fincas,* controlled the lives of hundreds of thousands of landless laborers. This was an etic model and borrowed from plantation studies around the world from the Caribbean to Southeast Asia. My etic model connected the local workers to the fincas, the fincas to the ingenios, and these to the world economy. I doubt if any of my consultants would have recognized themselves. Several owners of the fincas who read my study angrily denied their participation in such an exploitative system and were often proud of how they dealt with their own laborers. A *colono,* or resident laborer on a plantation, who thought of himself as being comparatively well off and who looked up to his *patron* as a benefactor would agree, in contrast to migrant workers who competed each day for a job.

An example of an emic model would be a biography of one of the day laborers such as Sidney Mintz's *Worker in the Cane* (1974 [1960]), the poignant story of the life of a sugar worker in Puerto Rico. These two approaches also contrast a "scientific" approach that depends on large models of cultural reality, such as plantation systems, often based on cross-cultural comparison, with a particularistic or one-culture approach such as Mintz's "humanistic" biography, which reads like a novel. While anthropologists often argue that one approach has more value than the other, the two approaches are best seen as complementary. Each approach gives the other greater depth. Ethnographies usually contain something of both.

One of the difficulties of anthropology is that writers sometimes may unconsciously ascribe subjective judgments derived from their own emic model to the views of their subjects. For example, while a sugar cane worker may feel exploited by the owner of a finca, does that mean that "plantation systems" are exploitative? Do "systems" have goals or values? Arguments are **teleological** when goals are ascribed to systems. *Teleological* means to ascribe *telos* or historical goals, to "things." It would appear fair enough to ascribe goals and values to people who are actors but not to the systems within which they act. Thus, plantation systems, capitalist systems, or socialist systems cannot be called "good" or "bad" at the etic level, but it is fair to state that the human actor feels the "system" is good or bad to him or her at the emic level. The emic or insider view may be said to derive from feeling and belief, whereas the etic or outsider view is (or should be) derived from analysis.

Anthropology, Culture Change, and Globalization

Anthropology has long had a tradition of studying culture change. In the period directly after World War II, the study of culture change had as its focus the impact of "modern" societies on "traditional" societies (that is, the impact of technologically advanced societies on those not so advanced). The idea of culture change is itself changing, for we are living through the process of **globalization,** a term that means (among other things) the connecting of every household in the world with every other household through the electronic media. Computers, long-distance telecommunication, the use of satellites, the vanishing cost of transmitting information, industrial robotics, these processes are changing every society in the world. Culture change no longer means the impact of developed societies on developing societies, but the impact of globalization on all the peoples of the world, for better or for worse.

Isolated communities are disappearing. Some anthropologists may lament the disappearance of traditional culture, but the locals do not categorize the world into traditional and modern. They routinely blend elements of both into new patterns. While scholars have long been concerned that traditional cultures would fade as modernization phased out old values, creative cultural systems are emerging that combine the new and the old in sometimes very inventive ways.

At the same time, anthropology is changing. Not only are anthropologists learning how to use computers and the other technologies of the age, but the complex problems being faced by the globalizing world are the kinds of problems anthropologists can work on because of the multidisciplinary perspective of modern anthropology. While the anthropology of forty years ago focused mainly on such topics as kinship relations, descent systems, and residence rules, that is, descriptions of the internal dynamics of cultures, the anthropology of today—and tomorrow—is challenged to find ways to help societies through a variety of transitions to different but satisfying lives. This will by no means be a simple task. There are issues of the environment, of political and economic change, of gender, issues dealing with ethnic relations, and much, much more. The big question is, can anthropology rise to this challenge? Does the knowledge of human lifeways, accumulated mostly through the study of small-scale societies and of village life, provide insight into contemporary problems of complex societies? We believe that it does, and this book will be an elaboration of our view.

This book is about globalization and other transitions. Humans have passed through three great transitions. The first was from an existence based entirely on hunting and food gathering to one in which horticulture, agriculture, and pastoralism dominated and early civilizations developed. This shift may be referred to as the transition from **food extraction** to **food production** and it had profound environmental consequences (to be discussed later). The second transition began with the age of European exploration, *circa* A.D. 1492, that introduced worldwide trade, mercantilism, and monopoly capitalism. Out of this transition emerged the modern world system of the late industrial era. The modern world system was composed of a wealthy European–American core and a poor third world periphery whose resources were monopolized and exploited by the core. The third transition we see as beginning in 1985 when the Soviet Union began to fall apart. This one is hard to describe because we are in the beginning stages. It is a transition in which the monopoly over the resources of the planet by the old First World core is ending and new cores and peripheries are emerging around the world. Many new economic opportunities are opening in both cores and peripheries, but with them come unprecedented threats to ecosystems and human rights. At the same time, electronic technology is fostering the rapid development of a vast network of worldwide communication links that permit information transfer at speeds undreamed of, except by writers of science fiction, even fifteen years ago.

It has been thirty years since my (SS) first introduction to field work in anthropology. In the summer of 1966, I drove down with a team of graduate students to coastal Guatemala where I spent four months doing a detailed study of the plantations around the coastal town of Santa Catalina Siquinala. I began my ethnographic fieldwork by interviewing administrators and workers. I collected census data, economic information, and surveys on the political structure of the south coast.

I learned that half of the workers on the plantation estates were Maya Indians brought down from their cool mountain homes by *contratistas* (contractors) to work off debts incurred during the religious ceremonies of the **cargo system**.

The cargo system is a set of hierarchically arranged positions that entail religious (and in some communities, civil) obligations. These obligations last for one year and every adult male is expected to hold one or more cargos during his lifetime. The obligations include sponsorship of ritual events that are based on both ancient Mayan and Catholic beliefs. Each Maya cargo holder carries a symbolic "cargo" of ritual duties acted out over a year that gives him and his family status in Maya communities. (See Chapter 12 for further discussion of the cargo system.) A man and his wife may, for example, take care of a local Catholic church for the year. Early studies of the cargo system, which I read in graduate school, made it appear indigenous to the Mayan communities. To my surprise, by 1966, the modern cargo system had become integrated into the plantation economy of the coast and Indians had to pay off debts incurred during the ceremonies by working on the hot coastal plantations. The plantations grew sugar cane, most of which was sold to United States corporations in raw form and then refined to become the sugar you put on your breakfast cereal.

My research project became my Master's thesis, and I hoped to return to the coast to expand the work into a Ph.D. But a revolution between the Maya Indians, non-Indian peasants, and the Guatemalan government exploded right in the region where I had done my research. One of the reasons for the violence was exploitation of the workers by plantation owners. In 1982, twenty-six people in the town of Siquinala were killed during a fight between the FAR (Armed Revolutionary Forces) and the government. Some of those killed were Mayan guerrilla fighters, and a few were landowners, many of whom I had interviewed. After years of U. S. support to the Guatemalan government, despite human rights abuses, American diplomats are now trying to negotiate political changes that will end the violence instead of supporting the government in its fight with the FAR. As of 1997, a truce had been declared and the Maya Indians were no longer being systematically targeted by the government. However, this remains an uneasy truce and incidents of violence still occur in the countryside.

The changes in Guatemala symbolize for me the radical changes pressing on modern anthropology. Anthropologists (and other social scientists) refer collectively to the processes and results of changes of roughly the last three decades as first **modernization** and then **globalization**. Whereas, in the classic years of anthropology, roughly from the beginning of this century to the late 1950s, it was possible to find remote Maya communities and to study them as though they had evolved in isolation (an illusion even then), such is no longer possible. To understand the modern Maya, it is necessary to understand their relations with the national government and its connections in turn to other governments, their relationships to transnational corporations in the sugar, cotton, and banana industries, as well as their traditional customs, beliefs, and habits and adaptations the Maya have made to the global economy. This is an example of globalization, of the interconnectivity of societies in the modern world to each other. The term *globalization* must now include the transforming power of computers and mass communication. We are not just connected, but the wiring of the connections is beginning to change the world.

Wolf wrote *Europe and the People Without History* in 1982, just a few years before globalization began to transform the planet. His book examines the world

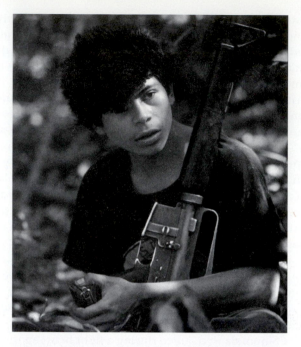

From the 1960 to the early 1990s, indigenous Mayan revolutionaries confronted the Guatemalan army in a bloody civil war. Today, the government and the revolutionaries are working to produce peace.

as it looked during the time period when it was dominated by a Euro-American "core" with a set of peripheries and semi-peripheries that were often called "the third world": Latin America, Asia, and the Middle East. Since 1982, there have been some astonishing changes, among them the slow disintegration of the core, the collapse of the Soviet Union, and the economic transformation of a few third world societies into first world status. The elemental reason for the changes is the coupling of computers and global financial markets. Nation states, such as the United States, Great Britain, and France, no longer have control over the movement of investments and find it increasingly difficult to secure predictable jobs for their citizens. At the same time, investors are demanding that unstable dictatorships, which once functioned with little interest or attention to efficiency, become democratic and capitalistic if they are to attract outside investment. Democratization is occurring in once very undemocratic places ranging from Russia to Chile.

The new changes are having results that are totally unpredictable: The core countries are becoming politically more unstable, including the United States, but also including France, Italy, and Great Britain. New pressures in these countries are producing clashes between ethnic groups that have been at peace for over a generation. In the former periphery, growing economies are putting tremendous pressures on environments. For example, as a part of its economic development, China wishes to create a giant dam system to contain the waters of the Yangtze river in order to create electrical power and prevent flooding, but this threatens to destroy thousands of villages and inflict severe damage on ecosystems. It is becoming obvious that the spread of capitalism requires democracy to protect both human rights and the environment.

There are, then, many problems for anthropologists to study. These problems are global and run the gamut from economic development to ethnic conflict, to human and environmental rights. Cultural anthropologists focused heavily on small-scale traditional societies, at least until the post–World War II era. In the process anthropology accumulated a great wealth of knowledge about the lifeways , social organization, and relationships to nature of these small-scale societies. As these societies become fewer—and less isolated—and anthropology turns more and more to studies of the more complex cultures and subcultures of the industrializing, industrial, and post-industrial world, we should neither abandon nor forget the knowledge gained from these earlier studies. Traditional societies contain some of the only examples available of truly sustainable relationships with nature. The answers to many current dilemmas may very well lie in the accumulated wisdom of these societies of intimates—in their indigenous knowledge, to use the current phrase.

Anthropology is a problem-driven science, but its history is also one of being drawn to classification and the formulation (not without some justification, of course) of categories, such as band, tribe, chiefdom, state, nation, society, clan, lineage, politics, economics, kinship, and ethnicity, that have sometimes undergone a mysterious transformation from categories to explanations. This is an anthropology text that will focus on problems and give short shrift to categories as ends in themselves. However, there is always a need to categorize in science, and, for that matter, in everyday life, so the first part of this book provides the student the categories necessary to our particular brand of anthropological discourse.

In this chapter we have examined the subdisciplines and central concepts of anthropology. In the following two chapters we will explore the methods and theories of modern cultural anthropology; and in the fourth we apply some of these to an examination of culture in America. The second part of the book examines the transitions that have characterized human cultures for the last ten thousand years, but with a special focus on the process of globalization and the impact it is having on modern societies, whether developed or developing. The third part of the book examines many of the problems of human adaptation that are emerging in different regions of the world due to globalization and culture change. At the heart of the book is the proposition that, while the economic transition to capitalism and the political transition to democracy are important, there are other transitions that are equally important and that can get lost, the most basic of which are the recognition of human rights and the rights of nature. Democracy may not protect people from human greed, so democratizing a country that opens rain forests and indigenous peoples to exploitation may not, in the long run, be highly adaptive. The perceived need to preserve jobs in the forest-dependent communities of Oregon may lead to the destruction of the very habitats necessary to create and sustain these jobs. The same is true for fishing communities in the American Northeast.

*S*ummary

Anthropology is a very broad field, overlapping such distinct disciplines as biology, geology, paleontology, history, economics, sociology, philosophy, psychology, the arts, and many other disciplines. Its focus is humankind, which is both defined and studied holistically. A general division of labor is reflected in the four major subdisciplines that we have discussed. Yet most anthropologists are used to wearing several "hats" and maintaining an up-to-date working knowledge of other disciplines and subdisciplines. For example, archaeologists must know considerable biological anthropology and vice versa; applied anthropologists must know quite a lot about economics and ecology; cultural anthropologists should keep up on the work of applied anthropologists, and so on.

While this may seem a little confusing and contradictory, that is only true if one assumes that disciplines should be "pure." However, as we will come to appreciate, human beings are constantly reorganizing and recategorizing their activities and it would be a mistake for students of the human condition not to do the same. In this text, we will focus on issues of "process," "connectivity," and "adaptation." We have deliberately brought in much that is not traditional anthropology—philosophy, history, economics, international issues, and so on—because of our interests in applied anthropology and human ecology. Further, we agree with Eric Wolf's recent critique of the tendency of scholars to territorialize their disciplines and then to define themselves into corners (Wolf 1982). We do not believe it is possible to gain an adequate understanding of the human condition by defining and categorizing alone (although we all do both). It is necessary to focus on problems, processes, and connections.

In the following chapters, we will gain better insights into human culture in its three guises: symbol, behavior, and adaptation. We will see that, while human behavior has a biological basis , it is culture that determines much of what we do and how we do it. The new challenge is to view anthropology as a global discipline with critical relationships to other social sciences and humanities. Anthropologists must continue to develop a multifaceted approach to adaptation. This chapter has argued that anthropology, with its holistic approach, has always borrowed liberally from other disciplines; and we must continue to do so if we are to contribute to an understanding of contemporary human societies and cultures.

The focus of anthropology has always been change. Sometimes culture change is written about through an evolutionary perspective looking for predictive laws. Sometimes it is written about as an anthropology of history, a study of patterns of change. Sometimes writers use the biographies of individuals to describe change over a lifetime. But whatever the anthropologist studies, at the heart of research are our attempts to interpret and explain the shifts in cultural behavior through time. The study of change in the context of the processes of globalization is our central theme in this book. We will examine property rights, modes of production, trade, human–habitat relations, ideology, and the links among them, in an effort to explain some of the primary adaptations humans have made through time and the connections of these to modern culture change.

Key Terms

Anthropology	Hominids
Anthropology of Art	Human Ecology
Anthropology of Religion	Hypoglycemia
Applied Anthropology	Ideal Culture
Artifacts	*Ingenio*
Cargo system	Legal Anthropology
Cognitive Science	Lexicon
Colono	Linguistic Anthropology
Comparative Linguistics	Medical Anthropology
Comparison	Modernization
Connectivity	Morphology
Contratistas	Paleoanthropology
Cultural Relativism	Paleoecology
Culture	Patrilineality
Economic Anthropology	Patrilocality
Emic	*Patron*
Emic Analysis	Phonemics
Ethnocentrism	Phonetics
Ethnographer	Physiological Anthropology
Ethnography	Political Anthropology
Ethnohistory	Political Ecology
Ethnolinguistics	Political Economy
Ethnology	Primatology
Ethnoscience	Process
Etic	Property Rights
Etic Analysis	Real Culture
Finca	Resource Utilization
Food Extraction	Role
Food Production	Society
Forensic Anthropology	Sociolinguitics
Genocide	Status
Globalization	Subculture
Grammar	Teleological
Historical Archaeology	Trade
Holism	Virilocality

Conducting research on any culture and then describing, analyzing, and interpreting your findings is a difficult but fascinating undertaking. There are three major aspects of the endeavor: perspectives on culture; language and culture relations; and fieldwork. In the last chapter we provided an operational definition of culture and discussed some of culture's major characteristics. In this chapter we will examine some perspectives and issues regarding ways to look at cultures or features of them. It is impossible to get an understanding of any culture without also understanding the language; therefore language and its study are included in this chapter. Language is the major (but not the only) form of communication in all human cultures. It is an important means by which culture is transmitted and it is therefore important to understand something about how language functions and how it is related to culture. Fieldwork involves a number of data collection and analysis techniques. We'll begin with perspectives on culture, then have a look at language, and finally discuss fieldwork.

Perspectives on Cultures

Cultures as Adaptive Strategies

John W. Bennett suggests a major component of culture is coping or adaptive strategies (1976, 1993). In this view, mental strategies help us adapt to changes in our local environment and the larger world. Bennett emphasizes the flexibility of culture, a point of view adopted in Chapter 1, and that culture is a dynamic system or set of subsystems with permeable boundaries. Most of what we see happening in the world today confirms this view of cultures as ever-changing systems. Yet this view presents a dilemma to anthropologists who view themselves as sympathizing with societies whose members are fighting to preserve their cultural distinctiveness. In the older view, cultures were seen as, if not unchanging, only very slowly changing. Modernization has produced rapid change in those cultures that anthropologists fondly called traditional and viewed as stable and desirable (with a few exceptions) ways of life. Some scholars reject modernization as a largely negative process and deny that it has benefits for minority cultures. At the same time, however, and with increasing speed, traditional ways of life are disappearing and in their place are appearing new cultures that blend the old and the new. People who are members of traditional cultures are borrowing and inventing new ways to adapt to an ever-changing world.

In this vein, Marshall Sahlins advocates a new historical ethnography that takes into account how cultures incorporate modernization to their own advantage. He notes that Karl Marx argued that modernization destroys all traditional cultures by enculturating native populations to western norms. The error in this argument, says Sahlins, is in conceptualizing culture as *sui generis* (an isolated entity controlled by its own laws). He points out that all cultures are subject to external pressures, natural and social, and that adjustment to such pressures is a normal process. In this regard, he says, no culture is *sui generis*. (1994:387). While cultures of the Pacific Islands may have been dominated by the West in the nineteenth century, and Sahlins questions whether this was ever fully so, they now manipulate modernizing influences and their own past to their advantage when possible:

> Hula schools (*halau hula*) have been flourishing in Hawaii since the early 1970s. Many function under the patronage of Laka, the ancient goddess of hula, are led by inspired teachers (*kemu*), and observe various rituals of training and performance. Hula schools are a significant element of what some participants are pleased to call "the Hawaiian renaissance." . . . The local people articulate with the dominant cultural order even as they take their distance from it, jiving to the world beat while making their own music (Sahlins 1994: 389).

These upbeat commentaries on culture change are in stark contrast to commentaries of a decade ago that lamented the extinction of traditional cultures by Western civilization.

Rather than viewing "modernization" as a wholly negative process in which traditional cultures are consumed by the West, the new assessment is that these cultures are adapting to globalization in ways that were not foreseen by social scientists in the 1970s or early 1980s. Change, it seems, is an ever-present feature of culture despite the static, timeless picture presented by many ethnographies. The **ethnographic present,** so to speak, has always been a fiction and traditional cultures have always been whatever the people themselves conceived them to be at the moment, and changing from one year to the next in response to forces both internal and external. While the pace of cultural change has changed, dramatically in many instances, the fact of change has not. As scientists, we may legitimately (and silently) mourn the passing of ways of life about which we know all too little and the knowledge of which would add to our overall understanding of human capabilities and the human condition. But we must realize that even as we scrupulously record the details of current cultures they are in the process of becoming something new and different—hopefully adaptive successes. In this view, then, adaptive strategies are always altering cultural configurations and cultures are abstractions with very fuzzy boundaries from a continuum of configurations. This highlights the need for anthropologists, when studying cultures, to focus on process and connectivity.

Cultures as Communities

Human beings interact together in social groups that can be observed and studied. It is common to refer to such groups as communities. When we think of a community, the first thing that may come to mind is a bounded geographic space occupied by a group of people. This is only one meaning (or a partial meaning) of the term *community* for social scientists. And even in everyday usage, community does have other meanings. Phrases such as "community of scholars" and "community of nations" are not uncommon.

Communities can be studied through observation and quantification. They are approachable through social science techniques. The anthropologists Conrad Arensberg and Solon Kimball have placed particular emphasis on the importance of the human community in anthropological research (Arensberg and Kimball 1972). For them, community is not a demographic unit nor is it a geographical entity. Kimball and Partridge define community as the "systems of interaction regularities and cultural behaviors which exist within an environmental context" (1979:1). This definition does not, of course, exclude geographically situated demographic units. In short, a community is the symbolically determined way that human beings organize themselves in time and space. Arensberg and Kimball see the community as the most important model of culture:

> We believe the community to be . . . a master institution or master social system;
> a key to society; and a model, indeed, perhaps the most important model of
> culture. . . When we call the community a "master system" or "key" we mean that it
> provides the structure of roles, relationships, and activities embodying this pattern.
> We are impelled to call it a master pattern, master mold, or master system because
> it provides a cell like duplication; a repeated, stable form for the culture in each
> place where that culture occurs and in each generation of its people (1972:x).

We all share in common life in an organized community. When, as children, we begin to move beyond the confines of the family into the larger society, one of the first things we do is to develop a cognitive map of our community. Once you understand how a culture organizes its communities, it is relatively easy to find your way around other communities that you are just visiting. It is that map that is the "master system" to which Arensberg and Kimball referred. Not only that, but you also develop a master plan of all the roles and statuses of your community and how you relate to them as you mature. That knowledge goes into the master map of your community in your brain.

There is a long tradition of community studies in the social sciences and especially in anthropology. Most of the exemplars of this tradition are, in fact, studies of geographically situated communities in the common sense of the term and many, if not most of, these studies assume that the community studied represents a microcosm of the larger culture. From the 1930s until the late 1960s (and continuing today, but less prolifically), anthropologists studied communities, mostly rural, around the world. Such studies included many fine contributions on the organization of American society. For example, Lloyd Warner, an anthropologist who taught at the University of Chicago during this period, did a series called the Yankee City studies. These studies were of a small New England city and attracted a good deal of attention to the study of modern communities. Kimball and Arensberg did research on communities in other regions of the United States that are summarized in the chapter on American society.

Is a community a microcosm of the larger culture in which it is embedded? The answer is, it depends. Long ago, Arensberg (1961) pointed out that, whether one is studying a community as object (as an entity in and of itself) or as a sample from which to generalize about some larger entity, there are four basic issues that must be addressed. First, there is the issue of *representativeness*. By what criteria does one choose a particular community as representative of many, if not most, communities within the larger society? Second is the issue of *completeness*. Given that communities often overlap one another, whether in physical space or in terms of interaction spheres, how does one decide where to construct the boundaries and say this is a part of the community and this is not? Third is the issue of *inclusiveness*. To what extent must the institutions of a given community mirror those of the larger society for it to be considered a fair sample? Fourth, there is the issue of *cohesiveness*. How much cooperation and harmony must there be in order for the selected social group to be considered a community at all? And how much factionalism must there be to mirror conditions in the larger society? None of these issues are easily responded to, and each becomes more complex and more problematic the more complex and subculturally divided the larger society is. Choosing a community of Kayapó horticulturalists in the Amazonian tropical forest as representative, complete, inclusive, and cohesive in regard to Kayapó culture is undoubtedly less problematic than is choosing a community in the United States in order to sample American culture.

Despite these problems and other criticisms of the community study method, the tradition of community study has remained strong in cultural anthropology. Of the many reasons for this, two come readily to mind: The community is a manageable unit for the individual researcher (most anthropological field research is still done by lone individuals), and communities are in many ways the laboratories of the anthropologist. They provide the data for the formulation of hypotheses (that can often be tested using survey methods) and for the testing of hypotheses.

Cultures as Regulators of Time and Space

Another interesting way to look at cultures is as regulators of time and space. This is characteristic of Edward T. Hall, who has produced a series of studies on the topic. All mammals are territorial and have instinctive (biological) spacing mechanisms. Territoriality is the protection of space. It is a means of insuring species propagation and density regulation in a given habitat. The territory provides a framework where there are spaces for the young to learn, to hide, to play, and for adults to acquire food and shelter, and to reproduce. Distance regulation also provides a framework for intraspecies communication and protection against overexploitation of the habitat. Territoriality is often tied to dominance hierarchies, which are worked out through threat and violence among the members of a species who occupy a territory.

In *Understanding Cultural Differences* (1990), Edward and Mildred Hall argue that we are in many ways like our mammalian relatives, but that we organize both space and time according to linguistic and cultural categories. Most of the rules governing time and space regulation are not explicit, but are learned and passed down from one generation to another. The Halls divide up time and space more explicitly in their comparison of predominantly American and European cultures. They look at space regulation in terms of three categories: territoriality, personal space, and the multisensory spatial experience.

They point out that Americans tend to be territorial about places that they label "mine," such as a cook's kitchen or a child's bedroom. In Germany, they say, territoriality is extended to possessions, such as the automobile. Touching a German's car may elicit a response as though the person had been touched. Cultural differences are also evident in spatial arrangements as metaphors for power. German and American businesses reserve the top floors for high-ranking executives. In contrast, French officials occupy a position in the middle surrounded by subordinates. The French sense of power has the individual in the center with lines of power radiating out, rather than at the apex of a hierarchy (Hall and Hall 1990: 10).

Personal space is also culturally defined. Each person is surrounded by invisible "bubbles of space" that expand and contract depending on relations to people nearby, the person's emotional state, cultural background, and the activity being performed. Changes in the bubble that run counter to cultural norms of comfort may evoke aggressive behavior. The Halls point out that in northern Europe the bubbles are very large and people keep their distance (Germany). In southern Europe, the bubbles get smaller as one moves towards the equator. German travelers in southern Europe may feel a sense of entrapment when riding an elevator, bus, or other enclosed vehicle with natives. Notice in the example of the coffee break in Tokyo (see pages 49–50), how the American moved away from the Arab, thinking he was standing too close.

Finally, the Halls note that people perceive space through all of the senses: auditory space is perceived by the ears; thermal space by the skin; kinesthetic space by the muscles; and olfactory space by the nose. This is what they mean by multisensory spatial experience. There are significant cultural differences in the way in which the senses are utilized to program spatial experience. Germans rely heavily on auditory screening, especially when they want to concentrate. French and Italians reject auditory screening and thrive on noisy interruptions; they tune in to what goes on around them. Americans and Germans find French and Italian cities very noisy, while the French and Italians find German and American cities to be cold and aloof. It is easy to understand that such differences are likely to result in cross-cultural misunderstandings.

There are many kinds of time systems. The Halls highlight two as produc-

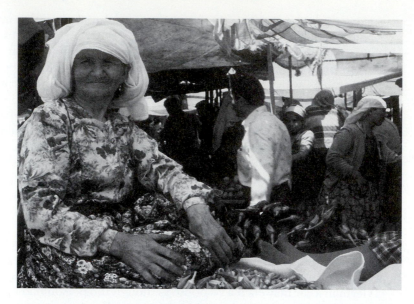

"Crowded" markets like this one have flourished in the Middle East since biblical times.

ing modern cross-cultural misunderstandings: monochronic and polychronic time. *Monochronic* means paying attention to and doing only one thing at a time. Polychronic time means being involved with many things at once. In monochronic cultures, time is experienced in a linear way and is scheduled and compartmentalized, making it possible for a person to concentrate on just one thing at a time. Americans use monochronic time and classify activities by setting priorities. Here people are governed by time and do not like being interrupted. Monochronic time is an artifact of the industrial revolution. German and Swiss cultures are dominated by "the iron hand of monochronic time" (Hall and Hall 1990: 14).

Polychronic time is the antithesis of monochronic. Mexico is a good example of a culture with a polychronic view of time. Two Mexican businessmen standing on a corner talking would prefer to be late for their next appointment than abruptly terminate their conversation before its natural conclusion. Time and schedules are simply not as important as commitments to people.

The Halls see links between the ways in which cultures conceptualize and regulate time, space, and information flow. Monochronic Americans traveling in Mexico may find the use of time and space upsetting. Appointments may mean very little and will be shifted around to accommodate an individual's hierarchy of friends, family, and associates. The Halls believe that millions of dollars have been lost in international business because monochronic and polychronic cultures do not understand one another. They provide the following example:

A French salesman working for a French company that had recently been bought by Americans found himself with a new American manager who expected instant results and higher profits immediately. Because of the emphasis on personal relationships, it frequently takes years to develop customers in polychronic France, and, in family-owned firms, relations with customers may span generations. The American manager, not understanding this, ordered the salesman to develop new customers within three months. The salesman knew this was impossible and had to resign, asserting his legal right to take with him all the loyal customers he had developed over the years. Neither side understood what had happened (Hall and Hall 1990:16–17).

The Halls make a good case for the cultural significance of time and space regulation, but of course there is more than that to cultural differences. Try a small experiment. The next time you are talking with a friend, especially one from another culture, think about personal space and see if you can determine your own and the friend's by moving closer and then further away during the conversation. What does the other person do when you move closer and closer? And how do you feel? What happens as you increase the distance between you and the other person?

Culture, Cognition, and Language

Cultures and Cognition

If we are to understand how the habituation and conditioning that produces cultural patterns takes place, as well as how cultural change occurs, we need to know something about how the human brain stores and processes information. How do culturally distinct coping strategies come into being; how do people internalize the norms of appropriate behavior in communities; and how is knowledge about such cultural phenomena as time and space regulation internalized, if, as the Halls argue, it is largely implicit and seldom consciously taught? Language is our best known means of information storage and processing, but is it the only way we learn our culture? Anthropologists and other social scientists have long referred to the general phenomenon whereby children learn what their parents and others around them know as **enculturation** or **socialization.**

The three major processes of enculturation are observation, practice (participation, repetitious imitation), and language. All are forms of learning. While a great deal of cultural learning undoubtedly takes place through the medium of spoken (and in literate cultures, written) language, it is likely that language as a mechanism for the transmission of cultural knowledge has been overrated, or at the very least, observation and participation have been slighted. We live and function in a literate culture. Much of what we learn is through language. So it is natural for us to think that language is central and observation and participation considerably less important in learning what one needs to know to function effectively in one's culture or, for that matter, to begin to understand another culture. Yet it is well known, for example, that students who learn another language in the classroom do not learn it as rapidly, as thoroughly, nor can they use it as effectively as those who learn it within the cultural context in which it is spoken. Why should this be so? Maurice Block suggests that conceptual thought is not dependent on language (although there is constant interchange between language and conceptual thought once language is developed), that much of our knowledge is nonlinguistic, and that concepts involve implicit networks of meanings that are based on experience (observation and participation) (1994:277–278). For example, learning to play golf, to drive, even to make bread, has a lot to do with observation and practice and may have only minimal language involvement. As anyone who has tried it knows, you don't learn to play golf or to drive by reading the manuals; and you don't learn to make bread—at least not good bread—simply by reading the recipe.

As we shall see in the section below on fieldwork, cultural anthropologists rely heavily on participation and observation as means of learning about other cultures and perhaps what is internalized and conceptualized in this way is at least as important in the production of ethnographic description as what is learned by talking about things in the local language after one learns it. This has been pointedly illustrated by Frederick Barth in his Preface to Robert Pehrson's book, *The Social Organization of the Marri Baluch* (1966). After Pehrson died in the field, Barth set about the task of compiling and analyzing Pehrson's field notes in order to produce the book that Pehrson would have produced had he lived. Barth undertook this task because Pehrson was his friend, they shared professional interests and views, and it was presumed that there were considerable similarities between the Baluch and the Pathan cultures that Barth had studied. But even after memorizing over 200 typed pages of Pehrson's field notes in hopes of achieving some kind of gestalt, Barth's attempts to write up the material in a coherent fashion were frustrated by the diversity of the data and the seeming lack of coherence. Yet Barth reports that Pehrson's field notes were quite detailed and impeccably professional. In desperation, Barth went to Pakistan and spent five weeks living with the Marri. After that brief time in the field, Barth was able to make sense of the notes and write the monograph. What had been missing? Barth reports:

> . . . it is singularly difficult to identify the critical supplementary data. I believe . . . that they are mainly connected with the concrete "stage" or setting in which social life takes place: the sizes of habitations, the uses of space, the physical as well as the conventional opportunities for conversation (Barth in Pehrson 1966:xi).

In other words, despite the attention given to detail in the notes of most anthropologists, much of the context within which social life takes place, is participated in and observed, does not—and perhaps much of it cannot—get recorded in language. Anthropologists have long argued that to really understand a culture you must spend a long time living in it. There is apparently considerable truth in this maxim. However, we should emphasize that it is the interplay between language and other modes of learning that gives us the whole picture.

Characteristics of Language

All humans (with the exception of some born with certain types of genetic abnormalities) have the capacity to use language. This capacity is a part of our evolutionary biological heritage. No other animal has the ability to use, or for that matter, to learn, human language in the way humans learn and use it. This is confirmed rather than disproved by all of the experimental attempts to teach human language (either spoken or sign language) to nonhuman primates. Thus, the ability to use language has a biological base; the ability to communicate in a *particular* language is learned. But to say that languages are learned is not to say that they must be formally taught. In our literate society we tend to think that at least the grammar of a language, and perhaps much of the vocabulary, must be taught in school. But think about the fact that in hundreds of societies, past and present, languages are simply learned by children as they grow up. Formal language training does not occur yet children rapidly become fluent and produce grammatically correct utterances. This attests to the innateness of our language ability.

Among linguists, cognitive scientists, and anthropologists, there is a difference of opinion as to whether language capacity is localized in a separate part of the brain and involves distinct cognitive processes or whether the capacity is more generalized and involves the same cognitive processes as those utilized in nonlinguistic cognition (for example, seeing, hearing, smelling, tasting). The argument is complicated, the evidence is not clear-cut, and we need not resolve the issue here. Regardless of the cognitive processes involved, no one disputes the fact that children do learn languages without formal instruction.

Human languages are incredibly diverse in terms of their surface characteristics, such as the meanings attached to particular sequences of sounds, the inventory of significant sounds themselves, the ways in which sentences are structured, and the types and levels of meaning that may be attached to utterances. Yet, beneath this surface of diversity, all human languages share certain basic characteristics. Charles Hockett calls these universal characteristics of human language "design features" and he originally listed thirteen (1960). Some other animal communication systems contain some of them but no other animal communication system that we know of contains all of them. These features, as modified to a standard list of nine in *Language Files*, are:

1. Mode of communication (vocal-auditory in the case of human and many animal systems);
2. Semanticity (the signals have meaning);
3. Pragmatic function (the communication serves a useful purpose);
4. Interchangeability (ability of individuals to both send and receive messages);
5. Cultural transmission (specific signals are learned rather than genetically transmitted);
6. Arbitrariness (form is not logically related to meaning);
7. Discreteness (complex messages built up out of smaller parts);

8. Displacement (ability to communicate about things not present in space or time); and
9. Productivity (ability to produce an infinite number of novel meaningful messages using a finite number of elements whose individual meanings are arbitrary—this is the feature Hockett termed *duality of patterning*) (Jannedy, Poletto, and Weldon 1994:20–21).

All communication systems contain the first three features; some nonhuman systems contain features four through seven (although there is disagreement about some of these); but only human languages contain eight and nine and only human languages are known to contain all nine. It is these last two features that make human language a truly unique communication system.

People talk and listen, read and write. Linguists analyze the structures of languages into agreed-on components in order to provide descriptions that are comparable. This endeavor is called **descriptive linguistics.** All languages contain a range of discreet sounds called *phones*. The study of these sounds is called *phonetics*. All humans with a normal vocal tract (lips, tongue, oral and nasal cavities, pharynx, larynx, vocal cords, trachea, and lungs) can produce, with practice, the sounds of all human languages. Granted, some sounds, such as the clicks in some African Bantu languages, are notoriously difficult for an English speaker to master. The significant sounds in a language, that is those that make a difference in meaning when speaking, are called *phonemes*. The study of the phonemes of a language is called **phonology.** Some phonemes may be composed of **allophones,** sound variations due to the context of other sounds in which they occur. For example, in English the /t/ sound in [top] is really a [tʰ] sound (aspirated /t/; that is, it has a puff of air following it) while the /t/ in [stop] is unaspirated. (In linguistic analysis, it is customary to use slashes to surround a sound or word rendered phonemically and brackets to surround a sound or word rendered phonetically.) [t] and [tʰ] are allophones of /t/ in English. The phonemes of a language should not be confused with the signs (letters of the alphabet) used to represent them. While the written form of some languages is much closer to a phonemic representation than English is (which is what makes spelling so difficult in English), probably no written language has a writing system that precisely renders its phonemic representation.

All languages combine units of sound into segments that have meaning, called **morphemes.** The study of morphemes is called morphology. **Free morphemes** are what we commonly call words. They can stand alone and have meaning. **Bound morphemes** are those units of meaning that must occur attached to some other morpheme. An example from English is the morpheme *-ed,* as in *finish**ed,*** which carries the meaning *past tense*. In English, bound morphemes occur frequently as prefixes, that is, at the beginning of a word, and as suffixes, at the end of a word. A third type of bound morpheme occurs within a word and is called an **infix**. Infixes are common in some North American Indian languages, such as Navaho. Words are categorized as parts of speech such as nouns, verbs, prepositions, and adjectives.

All languages arrange their words in characteristic ways to form larger units of meaning called sentences, if they can stand independently, and phrases, if they must be part of a sentence. The study of the organization of words into phrases and sentences is called **syntax.** This is what was called grammar when you were being taught "proper" English in school. These larger units of meaning contain systematically arranged parts of speech that are given functional labels such as subject, verb, and object. Different languages arrange these (and other) parts of a sentence in different ways. English declarative sentences, for example, characteristically have the arrangement Subject–Verb–Object, while Ngóbere, the language of the Ngóbe people of Panama, has a Subject–Object–Verb arrangement.

The study of the meaning of words, phrases, sentences, and even larger units of discourse is called **semantics.** The meanings of a word may depend on the context in which it is used, as well as whether it is intended to be taken literally or metaphorically; the same is true of phrases and sentences. The ways in which metaphor is used in different cultures and in different social contexts is itself a topic of much anthropological and linguistic research.

There are many more fascinating details about language that could be addressed, but this is not an introduction to linguistics so we will leave it at this. The student should by now have some sense of the complexity and diversity of human languages as systems of communication. Perhaps it should also be noted that all languages change through time, often in quite systematic ways, and that many of today's languages have common ancestors in the past. The study of language change and the relationships of languages to one another is called historical or comparative linguistics.

We now turn to an as yet unresolved question among anthropologists and linguists, the relation between language and culture.

Figure 2.1 **Like culture, language as a means of communication is quite flexible. Calvin and Hobbes © Watterson. Dist. by Universal Press Syndicate. Reprinted with permission. All rights reserved.**

Calvin and Hobbes
by Bill Watterson

Linguistic Relativity: The Whorfian Hypothesis

The Whorfian hypothesis states that there is a close relationship between the way in which members of a culture perceive their world and the way in which they use their language to communicate their perceptions (their world view). While there seems little doubt that a relationship exists between the categories of a language and those of a culture, Benjamin Lee Whorf went further than most other scholars of his day. He argued that speakers of different languages experience and perceive different realities *because* of the categories of their language. This idea was not entirely original with Whorf, having been suggested in the nineteenth century by Alexander von Humboldt. As proof of his hypothesis, Whorf offered a contrast between several features of English and Hopi. For example, he noted that the Hopi language structures time as cyclical while English structures time as linear. Hopi categorizes action in terms of kind of validity (reporting, expecting, speaking from previous knowledge) and so Whorf called it a "timeless" language; English categorizes action in terms of past, present, and future, thus focusing on time and segmenting it. Whorf also noted other differences between the ways in which Hopi and English categorized reality (1956). He concluded that language influences patterns of thought and therefore of cultural behavior. Such a conclusion is difficult to prove. In addition, more recent work on the Hopi language has shown that it does have ways of expressing not only tense but metaphors for time, units of time including days, number of days, parts of the day, yesterday and tomorrow, days of the week, weeks, months, lunar phases, seasons, and the year (Malotki 1983). Whorf did not have all the information he needed about Hopi to prove his hypothesis. Still, modern anthropologists are interested in the influence of language on behavior.

Most anthropologists today would agree with what we can term a weak version of the Whorfian hypothesis, namely, that languages do express cultural emphases and nuances, but that the relationship goes both ways rather than being of the causal form "language structures cultural reality." The interdependence of language and culture can be seen in the possible misunderstandings that occur when individuals from different cultures attempt to communicate in the language of one or the other.

Language and Cross-Cultural Misunderstanding

Cross-cultural misunderstandings often have their bases in idealized standards of proper behavior. When representatives of different cultures are unaware of each other's cultural expectations, many misunderstandings are possible. Cross-cultural conversations are a good way to illustrate this. The first example below is taken from an account by Elashmawi and Harris (1993). During a business conference at a Tokyo convention center, an American, John Smith, is trying to build a network of personal relations by introducing himself to as many people as possible and engaging them in conversation during coffee breaks. Smith spots two men, one Japanese and the other Arab, and approaches them. The following conversation ensues.

Smith:	Good morning gentlemen. I'm John Smith. (He extends his hand to the Arab man first and then to the Japanese.) Do you mind if I join you?
Mohammed:	(As he shakes Smith's hand with both of his.) Welcome, please join us.
Suzuki:	(He steps backward and bows slightly. He shakes Mr. Smith's hand without saying anything, ready to exchange business cards.)
Mohammed:	Are you enjoying yourself in this wonderful country, Mr. Smith?
Smith:	Oh, sure, its very nice here. What do you do Mr. . . ?
Mohammed:	Mohammed Rageh. I'm from Egypt and the president of my import company. We are here to look at some of the available products and meet our Japanese friends.
Smith:	(Turning to Suzuki.) And your name sir?
Suzuki:	(He silently hands Smith his business card.)
Smith:	(After looking at it quickly.) Oh, you're Mr. Suzuki.
Suzuki:	Yes, Sany Corporation.
Smith:	I see. (Puts Suzuki's card into his pocket and hands each his business card.) Do you have a card Mr. Mohammed?
Mohammed:	(Smiling.) No, I don't carry them with me. Everyone knows me. (Moving closer to John to show his hospitality.) I'm the president.
Smith:	(Stepping back from Mohammed.) Oh, I understand.
Suzuki:	Mr. Smith, you are from the Blackford Company?
Smith:	Yes, I'm the marketing director in charge of the Southwestern Division.
Mohammed:	Well, should we all go have some coffee and enjoy our break time together?
Smith:	I'm sorry, but I have to talk to some other people. Maybe we'll get together later on. It was very nice to meet you. Goodbye.

John Smith walks away to meet more people, not realizing how little he understood about the conversation in which he had just been engaged. Hidden beneath the words were different cultural expectations about both the style of the conversation and the appropriateness of the behavior accompanying it. Smith unknowingly offended both the Arab and the Japanese because of his insensitivity to their cultural expectations. His first blunder occurred when Mohammed asked John about his stay in Japan. John answered abruptly and then asked Mohammed what he did. Arabs like to establish personal relations with someone first before talking about business. Consequently, Mohammed thought John was brusque. The next clash occurred when Smith put away Mr. Suzuki's business card after merely glancing at it. In Japan it is customary to study a business card carefully to determine company name and rank, which are usually not discussed. By putting the card away, John offended Mr. Suzuki. On the other hand, Smith probably interpreted Mr. Suzuki's initial silence as rather standoffish behavior.

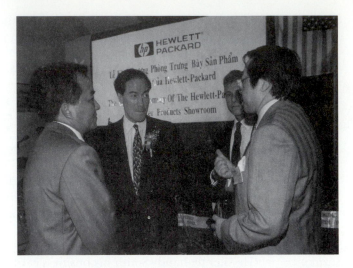

"Oh, you're Mr. Suzuki . . . ." International misunderstandings start with cultural differences.

Next, by moving away from Mohammed when he moved closer, Smith was unknowingly rejecting Mohammed's attempt to be hospitable; and he did so again when he declined to join Mohammed and Suzuki for coffee. Smith was undoubtedly made uncomfortable by Mohammed's closeness. This illustrates what was mentioned above about cultural differences in communication distance. Mr. Smith also offended by stating his own position in his company which probably sounded, at least to Mr. Suzuki, as though he was bragging.

In our second example, taken from Harris and Moran (1987:256), an American working for a transnational company in Greece is trying to follow his democratic cultural ideals, not realizing that his Greek employee has an ideal male standard of conduct called *filotimo*. Filotimo requires Greek men to act manly, to give orders, and also to take them without complaining. But it also means that a "boss" must give orders that are exact and clear.

Verbal Conversation	Attribution
American: How long will it take you to finish this report?	American: I asked him to participate. Greek: His behavior makes no sense. He is the boss. Why doesn't he tell me exactly what he wants?
Greek: I do not know. How long should I take?	American: He doesn't want to be responsible. Greek: I asked him for an order.
American: You are in the best position to analyze time requirements.	American: I press him to take responsibility for his own actions. Greek: What nonsense! I better give him an answer.

Greek: Ten days.

American: He lacks the ability to estimate time. His estimate is totally inadequate.

American: Take fifteen. Is it agreed to?

American: I offer a contract.

Greek: Okay, fifteen days.

Greek: That is an order. I better take it.

(In fact, the report required thirty days, so the Greek, following filotimo and without complaining, worked night and day, but he still needed one more day than the fifteen allotted.)

American: Where is the report?

American: I am making sure he fulfills his contract.
Greek: He is demanding that the report be turned in.

Greek: It will be ready tomorrow.

American: But we agreed it would be ready today.

American: That's what Greeks always say. I must teach him to fulfill his contract.

(Greek hands in his resignation.)

Greek: The stupid incompetent boss! Not only did he give me bad orders, but he doesn't even appreciate that I did a thirty-day job in sixteen days. I can't work for such a bully.

American: Why are Greeks always irresponsible?

Greek: Americans pretend they are fair but they are really brutish.

Figure 2.2 **Even when people are speaking the same language, misunderstandings can occur as a result of differences in cultural and life experiences. Doonesbury. © G. B. Trudeau. Reprinted with permission of Universal Press Syndicate. All rights reserved.**

Doonesbury

BY GARRY TRUDEAU

What these two examples illustrate is that language does not convey the same message for everyone even though the words are the same. Cultural background provides the context for interpretation. Also, language does not convey all of the information that is necessary to understand a message. In both of these examples, misunderstandings might have been avoided if the participants had understood something about each other's cultural expectations. It is not realistic to expect anyone to learn all the nuances of all the cultures with which she or he might come in contact. However, it is reasonable to expect an awareness that there *are* cultural differences that are likely to make a difference.

Two things are essential in any attempt to achieve cross-cultural understanding. First, you must realize that your own culturally based assumptions about human nature and behavior are inherently ethnocentric. Consciously examine your own beliefs and expectations and accept the fact that those of others may be different, but not wrong. Second, try to understand the behavior of someone from another culture within their cultural context (cultural relativism). When approaching a cross-cultural situation, study body language and the response of others to your statements, and be aware of your own reactions. It is possible to mitigate misunderstanding by simply pointing out to members of other cultures that you may have made a mistake, and that perhaps you and others in the group have different values and expectations. A discussion of how two cultures have distinct understandings of human nature is a great learning tool and helps defuse explosive situations.

Doing Ethnography: Fieldwork

Anthropologists play different roles through time when doing research in cultural anthropology. When conducting research in the field, they call themselves **ethnographers** and the studies they produce are called *ethnographies*. The terms are derived from the Greek combining form *éthnos,* meaning "people," and *graphos,* also a Greek term, which means a thing written or drawn. In essence, ethnography means "to write about ethnic groups or people." Ethnographers do detailed studies of different aspects of a peoples' culture, such as kinship systems, economies, political systems, religions, and ideologies. The focus depends on individual theoretical or problem-oriented interests, or the cultural themes of the society under study. That is to say, ethnography is always context-dependent and all ethnographies should be read with this in mind. An ethnography usually contains a description of the findings, often from both an emic and an etic viewpoint, an analysis, which is a "systematic way to identify key factors and relationships among them" (Wolcott 1994:10), and an interpretation of what the data mean within some chosen framework of hypotheses or theories. These components of an ethnography—description, analysis, and interpretation—are not mutually exclusive and often are not sharply separated (or even identified as such) in the writings of ethnographers.

How does one achieve a relatively deep understanding of another culture? Is long-term residence in another society enough? Obviously not. Many Ameri-

Ngóbe men talking with Phil Young during a velorio, *a ceremony which is held approximately 30 days after the death of an individual to honor the memory of the deceased and to formally remove the food restrictions (taboos) which the close relatives have been required to observe during the 30-day period. These restrictions generally include salt and meat. Chiriqui Province, Panama, 1965. (Source: P. Young)*

cans spend years overseas and never really achieve an understanding of the culture that surrounds them. Understanding requires active, systematic effort. It requires long-term field research during which, to the best of one's ability, one suspends one's own beliefs and tries to understand those of others. Learning the ways of another culture is a process that is never complete, often beset with setbacks and difficulties, hopefully none of them insurmountable, and interspersed with comic situations and those that may produce anger. Understanding is achieved slowly. Pieces of information may not fit together in patterns until many weeks or months of patient and often tedious data collection have passed. But when the patterns finally begin to emerge, when glimmers of understanding begin to shine through the darkness, it is an exciting, exhilarating, enlightening experience. As an example of the process of learning in the field, the case study on the following pages presents one of Phil Young's experiences during his initial period of research with the Ngóbe of Panama.

Research Methods

Ethnographers use a wide variety of methods, both qualitative and quantitative, to collect data in the field. The most comprehensive and easiest to understand guide to methods in anthropology, both field methods and analytic methods, both qualitative and quantitative methods, as well as discussions of the realities of ethnographic research, is H. Russell Bernard's *Research Methods in Anthropology: Qualitative and Quantitative Approaches,* 2nd edition (1995). We highly rec-

Case Study: Eating in the Rain

In early 1964, I (PY) arrived in the small Panamanian town of San Felix on the edge of Ngóbe territory. Seven years before, while in the U. S. Army, I had taken a few days leave and visited Ngóbe country. At the end of that brief stay, the people I had met said "Come back and see us." One of them was a man named Jacinto. I wrote a note to Jacinto saying I had returned and was in San Felix. A boy who was going up the mountain to a hamlet near to Jacinto's house agreed to carry the message. Two days later another boy brought Jacinto's reply: "I'm busy working in my fields. What do you want?" Not exactly the enthusiastic greeting I had been anticipating. Although disappointed that Jacinto had not come to town to meet me, I was eager to make arrangements to begin my research. One of the small store owners in San Felix introduced me to Eduardo, a young Ngóbe man from the hamlet of Hato Pilon. I explained to Eduardo that I wished to go far up into the mountains to the hamlet of Cerro Mamita where Jacinto lived. The store owner agreed to rent me a horse and I contracted Eduardo to be my guide.

We arrived at Cerro Mamita during a tropical rainstorm. Both of us were soaked to the skin and then some. A couple of boys came running out of a house and unsaddled the horses. Eduardo indicated to me that the house was Jacinto's. Jacinto came to the doorway, greeted me, and invited me in. After standing near the cooking fire on the floor in the center of the house to dry myself and my clothes, I took the seat I was offered on the bench to the right of the door as one faces out. Men always sit here. Eduardo had remained outside and seated himself on a rock near the house. It was still pouring rain. After some polite conversation, I was served a steaming hot meal by Jacinto's mother. A young girl took a large bowl of food out to Eduardo who was still sitting on the rock. He ate alone in the rain, occasionally conversing with Jacinto, who re-

ommend this book to any students who are contemplating ethnographic research, whether short-term or long-term, and whether overseas or in their own community. Here we will only highlight some of the key aspects of fieldwork.

Literature Search   There are two views about the value of a literature search. One view holds that reading the literature before going to the field will contaminate your own views of what you encounter so you are better off learning everything on your own after arriving in your field location. While there may be some marginal utility in this *tabula rasa* ("clean slate") method for the seasoned professional, there is no benefit to it for the novice. The other view holds that a literature search prior to fieldwork is very important, and it is this view to which we subscribe. There is no sense in spending weeks in the field in order to reinvent the wheel. There is also little to be gained by trying to stick to a narrow review, and a lot to be gained by doing what H. Russell Bernard calls a "snowball sammained inside the house. I asked Jacinto why Eduardo was sitting outside and eating in the rain. The response was less than enlightening: "Because he wants to." Having spent a full day in travel and conversation with Eduardo, I knew he was a rational young man, so this odd behavior puzzled me. I knew there was something more here than met the eye. I didn't know what and at that point had no idea what the right questions might be to ask. But I did not forget the incident.

I successfully made arrangements to live in the hamlet of Cerro Mamita and began my research. (I am leaving out a great many details that are not directly relevant here.) Over the weeks that followed, I collected as much genealogical data as possible. I also collected data on the terms Ngóbe use to refer to kinspersons and on which kinspersons are referred to by which terms. In small-scale societies like that of the Ngóbe, most social relations are based on kinship, so both types of information are essential to understand what is going on. In the course of data collection I found that Jacinto and Eduardo were related by marriage. Eduardo was married to the daughter of Jacinto's mother's sister. I learned that the Ngóbe kin term for a man's mother-in-law (*me*) also refers to her sisters. In other words, a man's wife's mother and her mother's sisters are all considered mothers-in-law by the Ngóbe.

In discussions with Jacinto and others I learned about the Ngóbe practice of mother-in-law avoidance, whereby a son-in-law may never see the face of his mother-in-law, nor enter a house where she is present unless she is appropriately shielded from view, nor speak directly to her. Suddenly Eduardo's seemingly irrational behavior of months before became clear to me. It was completely understandable within the Ngóbe cultural context. Eduardo could not enter the house because one of his mothers-in-law, Jacinto's mother, was present. Of course, he could have sought shelter elsewhere but then he would have been too far from Jacinto's house to participate in the conversation and catch up on the local gossip. All of this was, of course, perfectly obvious to the Ngóbe and their problem on that rainy day long ago was that they couldn't understand why an apparently intelligent adult male like me would ask such a dumb question.

ple" (Bernard 1995). Call someone who has an interest in your question and ask for a list of names of all those he or she knows who might have useful information and network out from that list. Do the same with books and journal articles. Search the stacks in the region where you select a book to find if there are other related topics or texts you could not predict.

The *Annual Review of Anthropology,* which has been published since 1972 (it was a biennial review from 1959–1971), is a good place to start. It contains several hundred review articles on anthropological projects. There are similar reviews for other sciences and social sciences.

Articles in anthropology and related disciplines are published in hundreds of independent journals, some of which are quite obscure and hard to track down. There are many journals published in foreign countries that can only be accessed at the libraries of large research universities. There are also reports published by government agencies and private research foundations.

The task of running down articles from hundreds of journals around the world would be exhausting. Luckily, there is the *Abstracts in Anthropology,* which is found in most university libraries. More sophisticated are the publications of The Institute for Scientific Information in Philadelphia: *Science Citation Index, Social Science Citation Index,* and *Arts and Humanities Citation Index.* Using these indices, it is possible to look up an article published twenty years ago and to find the citations of all those articles that have used the article since then. Furthermore, most universities and colleges have computer terminals that allow on-line searches (the drawback to computer searches is expense; see Bernard 1995 for more information on literature searches).

Participant–Observation   Participant–observation is the method, par excellence, of cultural anthropology. Whatever the other methods an ethnographer may employ in the field, participant–observation will always be prominent. Observing and recording one's observations is something that one can do at the very beginning of field research, even though an understanding of what was observed may not come until much later, as illustrated by Young's experience with the Ngóbe (see the case study). And of course observation continues throughout the time when active participation has become possible. To a certain extent, the participation part requires "going native," that is, doing what the local people do. This is no longer just an anthropological technique. Many researchers from other fields find it necessary to become members of the communities they are researching in order to gain access to information that otherwise is not forthcoming (Bernard 1995).

When I (SS) was in Jardín, Colombia, I worked hard to find some way to participate in the community. It is not as easy as it sounds. One day, talking to the mayor, I asked him if "*mingas*" still existed in Jardín. A *minga* is a cooperative work group traditional to Colombia (and the Andean region). He beamed and pointed to the church and then to the hospital explaining that both had been built through the use of mingas. In great detail he described how the people of the community of Jardín, over several decades, had ascended a local mountain and quarried rock that they carried down to the valley to build both a church and hospital. The mayor then asked if I would like to help the following day working on a minga. I most certainly would! The following morning, I rode in a 1982 Dodge dump truck up to the top of a mountain. I spent the day building a road to a building that housed a TV translator. The translator picked up the TV signal from Medellín and shot it down into the San Juan River valley.

The minga I worked in spent the day carrying rocks from the dump truck to create a small road. It was a very festive event, but hard and muddy labor. The minga was made up of a cross-section of the community: rich, poor, young and old, men and women. I had a chance to experience the very democratic sense of equality in the mountain town of Jardín. When I returned to the town, it was as though I had passed an initiation rite. Thereafter, I could sit in the town square and interview farmers without feeling awkward. For the next several weeks, I was called on to work on other mingas. On one we cut down wild cane to build corrals for a yearly "county fair." In the evenings, I would sit around with the people

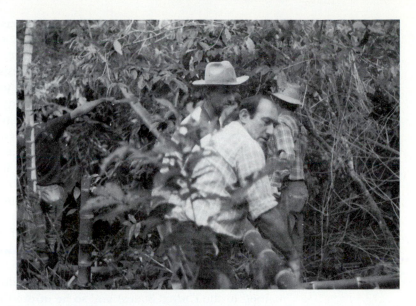

Men cutting wild cane near Jardín, Colombia, in 1984 during a minga. *A minga is a communal work party in which all community members are expected to participate. In the case of heavy work, like cane cutting, the women participate by preparing the food for the workers. (Source: S. Smith)*

I had worked with, sip *aguardiente* (a liquor made from sugar cane) and beer, and pass *cuentos* (stories) about the history of the town. I was particularly interested in the period from 1948 to 1953 when La Violencia occurred, a civil war that turned town against town throughout Colombia and brought on the dictatorship of Rojas Pinilla (I remember Pinilla's portrait on the wall of the boys' school I attended in 1955).

But there are limits to participation. Some will be imposed by the degree to which the people have accepted the anthropologist and by the rules of the culture under study. During my (PY) first few weeks in the field I was never invited to participate in a collective work party and when I asked about doing so I was put off by one excuse or another. After good rapport was established with a number of Ngóbe families and I was incorporated into the kinship network, I had to figure out culturally acceptable ways to refuse such invitations as they became too numerous and began to interfere with my own work. These Ngóbe work parties are all-male activities where heavy work is involved. Because of my integration into family life, I was not asked to accompany the women of nearby households when they went to harvest root crops or collect firewood. In most societies there are some activities in which only women participate and others in which only men participate. In addition to gender, age and status may determine the cultural appropriateness of participation.

Sometimes participation may be viewed as threatening. For example, when I (PY) began my research among the Ngóbe, many men asked me if I was, or was intending to, plant crops. I answered truthfully that I had no intention of farming (honesty is always the best policy), that I was there for other reasons, and I explained my purpose. My response was met with clear signs of relief that I learned later was due to the fact that Panamanians had for years been encroaching on Ngóbe lands. My fluency in Spanish caused most people to categorize me with the Panamanians until they got to know me well.

Finally, some limits should be imposed on participation by the ethnographer. In part this may be to retain a certain degree of objectivity, in part it may be necessary in order to avoid unnecessary physical risks, and in part it may be necessary to spare the feelings of those you are living and working with. Although each field situation is different, sexual liaisons or marriage in the field are not normally recommended (though both have happened), even if they may be culturally appropriate. The field researcher must keep in mind that she or he is a temporary resident and will be going home after a few months. Intimate relationships can make departure difficult both for the researcher and for his or her local partner. At one point during my (PY) work with the Ngóbe, when visiting a nearby hamlet with some of my "brothers," one man, whom I had gotten to know well over the months, decided that I must be lonely (my family had remained in the United States) and so he offered me his daughter in marriage. I politely declined, pointing out that I had a wife in the United States. This response elicited a "so what" from the polygynous Ngóbe and I had to figure another way out of this particular dilemma. I pointed out that I had no sister to exchange and no land and would thus make a poor son-in-law. Even this argument did not completely dissuade the man. My brothers came to my rescue at this point and gently turned the incident into a joking matter, thus giving both father and daughter a graceful way to drop the matter by pretending that the offer had not been a serious one and the joke was on me. I, of course, accepted this interpretation with considerable relief and laughed with the rest (although, so far as I know, the offer had been a serious one).

Learning the Language   In order to be a successful participant observer, to conduct interviews, and to attend to many of the ordinary tasks of daily life in the field, it is necessary to learn the local language. While in some cases and for some purposes it may be possible to get by using a *lingua franca,* a language that is mutually intelligible to you and the people you are working with, it is always preferable to learn the local native language. If an anthropologist is working with a subcultural group in his or her own society, this may involve no more than learning the special vocabulary of the subcultural dialect (and, of course, learning how to use it appropriately). In other cases an anthropologist may find it necessary to learn an unwritten language about which there is little or no prior information. Becoming even marginally fluent may take months of effort and requires that the ethnographer know the fundamentals of linguistics. But in the end the effort expended in learning the local language will return great dividends in terms of the rapport one establishes (people almost everywhere are flattered when an outsider makes the effort to learn their language) and in the richness of the cultural understanding that one achieves.

Interviewing   In this section on interviewing, we review some of the more formal data-collecting methods used by anthropologists in the field. (This section relies on the summary provided by Bernard 1995:209–210.) It should be kept in mind, however, that there is a haphazard quality to anthropological research, dictated by the circumstances of the moment. You never know when you are going to learn something new and it is important to be extremely attentive to small details. People are remarkably interested in providing details about their culture and their own lives to someone who expresses genuine interest and who doesn't cut them off with another question when they are just beginning to elaborate on the last one. It is important to remember that what the researcher may initially view as a digression from the topic the informant may see as an integral part of the tale being told.

All ethnographers conduct interviews in the field. Interviews are of four basic types: informal, unstructured, semi-structured, and structured. Informal interviewing is simply conversations with informants in which no attempt is made to structure or control the content of the conversations. While it can be a rich source of data and provide often unexpected insights and leads to new topics throughout the period of field research, its greatest utility is during the initial stages of participant observation when the researcher is trying to develop a general picture of what the culture is all about, what some of the local do's and don'ts are, and what might be some topics worthy of detailed and more systematic inquiry at a later date.

The unstructured interview is perhaps the most frequently used form of data collection in ethnographic research. It is not simply informal conversation. Both you and your informant know that an interview is being conducted. You provide the topic or theme (and some prompt questions if necessary) and you let your informant talk at his or her own pace. You exercise only minimal control over the responses. For example, you may wish to steer the informant back to the topic if he or she has gone too far off on a tangent. Unstructured interviewing is quite time-consuming. It is appropriate for long-term research and works well when you can interview the same people on many occasions.

In the semi-structured interview a guide is used to insure that a particular set of questions and topics is covered, usually in a specified order. While the interviewer still allows considerable flexibility for responses as in the unstructured interview, the goal is to insure that responses to all topics and questions on the interview guide are elicited. This insures that the responses collected from several respondents can be compared. The semi- structured interview is a good method to use if you are unlikely to have additional opportunities to interview the same people, if you are using several assistants to conduct the interviews, or if your intent is to collect data that is quantifiable. Semi-structured interviews are often used by anthropologists near the end of a period of field research. The questions they contain are based on information obtained from informal and unstructured interviews and participant–observation.

In structured interviewing all informants are asked to respond to identical stimuli. Usually these stimuli are very carefully worded and sequenced questions, but other stimuli include a variety of tasks that informants are asked to perform. Bernard (1995, Chapter 11) provides a detailed account of structured interviewing. The idea in structured interviewing is to carefully control both the stimuli and the circumstances under which they are presented to the respondents. This may be difficult to do under some field conditions. It is the equivalent of the controlled experiments performed by psychologists in laboratories.

Informal, unstructured, and semi-structured interviewing can be done with groups as well as individuals. However, to be effective and produce reliable and valid data, group interviews must be conducted by a highly skilled interviewer, often with one or more assistants.

Surveys   Surveys generally presume a random sample of respondents. They consist of a set of formal questions and are frequently used by sociologists, economists, and political scientists to collect a wide variety of data that is then subjected to various techniques of quantitative analysis in order to derive either hypotheses or conclusions. Oftentimes, when the questions are formulated and administered by members of one culture (or subculture) to members of another, it turns out that at least some of the questions are not culturally sensitive, or are meaningless to the respondents, or are simply not the right questions to ask, and thus the results of such questionnaire surveys may be highly suspect. For example, in a survey administered to the Ngóbe by the Panamanian Ministry of Education in the early 1970s, the Ngóbe respondents were asked what they normally ate for breakfast, lunch, and dinner. Since the Ngóbe do not structure their eating habits around the concept of three meals a day, the results of this attempt to determine what the Ngóbe usually eat were meaningless. Anthropologists who make use of survey questionnaires do so toward the end of their research after they have enough data from other sources to compose a list of meaningful, culturally appropriate, questions. Survey questionnaires that must be administered by an interviewer are a form of structured interview.

Tools of the Trade

Tape Recorders, Cameras, and Camcorders   New technologies have made many new strategies of research possible. Tape recorders have long been used to record interviews, but in the past they were so bulky and conspicuous that they often hindered rather than facilitated research. Now, with recorders equipped with voice activation that will fit in a shirt pocket, people are likely to forget quickly that they are being recorded and will respond with greater spontaneity. However, it is *always* necessary to get permission before using any kind of recording device or camera. To do otherwise is unethical and unprofessional. Some people may feel quite uncomfortable about being recorded or having their picture taken, or not wish it for religious reasons. In the 1960s during research with the Ngóbe, I (PY) found that most Ngóbe did not mind having their picture taken but were totally intimidated by my 22 pound big-as-a-bread-box Butoba tape recorder (state-of-the-art at the time). While some people did timidly consent to be recorded, the usual reaction when I turned the recorder on was that all conversation stopped. When I returned to Ngóbe country in the mid-1970s, hand-held recorders were available, many young Ngóbe owned them, and they were recording each other and me!

Hand-held camcorders with instant playback have replaced the old-fashioned movie camera as the tool of choice in the field. And where there is electricity, television sets are becoming ubiquitous and VCRs quite common. Family and community celebrations and other events can now be easily recorded and then played back to the audience. It is not a bad idea to give a VCR to the community as a gift and leave copies of videotapes so people can watch themselves. One researcher on the Trobriand Islands brought videotapes of the old festivals (originally on film) recorded by Malinowski in the 1920s so young people could watch their grandparents dancing and playing cricket! They could then record their own dancing and playing and compare the two time periods. Here the anthropologist is giving back to people some of their own culture, bits and pieces of which are being lost.

One research method I (SS) have found to be very rewarding is event analysis, a technique developed by Warner, Kimball, and Arensberg to study celebrations (Arensberg & Kimball 1972). I used it to study festivals in the upper Midwest and the day of Corpus Cristi in Colombia. The difficulty of most celebrations is that they include a great many people interacting over a short period of time.

Event analysis requires a good camera or camcorder (or both). In order to carry out the analysis you have to already be accepted as a member of the community and understand local symbolism. In the case of the study of festivals of the Upper Midwest (Smith 1985), I became interested in why there are so many festivals in the part of the country I now live in (La Crosse, Wisconsin). I began by doing library research and discovered that most of the festivals did not occur until after the early 1970s. There is Oktoberfest in La Crosse, Wisconsin, Apple Fest across the Mississippi in La Crescent, Minnesota, Sunfish days in Onalaska, Syttende Mai in several Norwegian towns, Pickle Days, Wadu Shadu, Funfest Days, Fire Department Dance, Black Powder Shoot, Steam Engine Days, and many other colorful celebrations.

I spent two years attending these celebrations, taking photographs of parades and reading the local newspapers. My analysis led to the conclusion that these were celebrations developed by Main Street business owners trying to overcome the impact of malls and interstates (Smith 1985). The celebrations work out the hierarchy of the towns and the symbolism of parades tells people what the participants think is important about their communities. For example, in La Crosse's Oktoberfest (which is a pale imitation of the German model), local men and women are selected to be "Fest Masters." There is a Mister and Mrs. Oktoberfest, and there is real competition over who is selected. Reading a list of participants is like looking at the power structure of the city of La Crosse. But power is not the only thing symbolized. So is commitment to community, traditional values, and the search for answers to community problems. One float in 1985 had the sign "Parents Without Partners" and "Oktoberfest Welcomes a New Decade for Sex Equality." A young man and woman sat in a pair of giant scales in equal balance symbolizing feminist aspirations at the local universities.

Still photographs remain a rich source of field data as well as great memory

An Oktoberfest float in La Crosse, Wisconsin, in 1985 bearing the slogan "Oktoberfest Welcomes a New Decade of Sex Equality." Community celebrations like this one have undergone a revival in the upper Midwest since the early 1970s. (Source: S. Smith)

joggers after one has been back home for several months. Photos also generally make much appreciated gifts that can help the researcher establish rapport more quickly. Modern automatic cameras take the guesswork out of shutter speeds, aperture openings (f stops), and focal distance and make photography in the field all but foolproof. A good set of photos is an excellent supplement to field notes.

Portable Computers and Special Software   The most modern of the research tools now used by anthropologists in the field is the laptop computer. With appropriate software, which is easily available, the computer can be used not only to record field data but to perform both qualitative and quantitative (statistical) analysis as well. For some, the laptop computer has become as much of a necessity as a pen or pencil and notebook once were in recording field data. A decade or so ago, the researcher would have to wait to return home in order to use a mainframe computer to analyze statistical data. Today the work can be done in the field. The researcher can now collect new data to answer questions raised by the previous day's field research.

Good Old Pencil (or Pen) and Paper   However, a caution is in order. The wisest course of action is still to have a hard copy of your field notes and your daily journal or diary. If you are relying on a computer to record field notes, print out hard copy after every session. Make several backups of your files. Mail at least one set of disk files and hard copy to a friend or colleague back home as soon as pos-

sible. Computers have been known to crash easily in the field, especially in tropical climates. Losing several weeks' or months' worth of work is not a pleasant experience. Though it may be tedious, handwritten field notes on cards and in
notebooks may still be the most reliable, if not the swiftest, way of preserving
your hard-won findings.

Quality and Quantity

Ethnographic research and writing is largely qualitative. This distinguishes anthropology from other social sciences that rely more heavily on quantitative data.
While cultural anthropologists will use quantitative data when available, they
find ethnography more useful. Why this is so will be obvious to anyone who has
lived in a foreign culture. Quantitative data available are uninterpretable in any
meaningful way if one does not understand the local culture. To do that, the researcher must live among the people he or she studies. Ethnography, for us, is
deep immersion in a culture, to the point where one begins to learn to think like
a native. We have personally only done this for some Latin American cultures
and would not presume to be able to understand African, Asian, or other world
cultures in quite the same sense. For cultures that an anthropologist has not experienced personally, he or she must rely on the accounts of others. While training as a professional anthropologist helps in interpreting the descriptive accounts of others, such as, travelers, missionaries, and government officials, it is
always preferable to experience the culture directly, and second best is to have
available the accounts of other professional anthropologists. The anthropologist
who has become really proficient in understanding another culture can reach
into himself or herself and describe the culture for others.

Most anthropologists go beyond mere description of cultures and societies.
Theories about human behavior require comparative analyses of different societies through the study of many ethnographies. The anthropologist at this level
of the quest is seeking generalizations. Anthropologists do not seek general explanations about human behavior from the study of just one society or one
ethnography. The search for generalizations about human behavior is called *ethnology* and the anthropologist who engages in this quest is called an *ethnologist*. It
is common for a cultural anthropologist to do ethnography in the field during a
part of the year and ethnology during another part of the year while in his or her
office reading and writing. Ethnological research is also called the *comparative
method*.

Most anthropologists tend to focus their research efforts on the intensive
study of one or more communities, or a distinct group of people within a community, more or less within the same world region. For example, our fieldwork
has been almost entirely in Latin America. They will also develop relatively detailed knowledge about the sociocultural systems of one or more continents
from the writings of other anthropologists. In this book we will use examples
from Africa, Asia, and other world regions, relying almost entirely on the works
of our colleagues. (I, PY, have done applied anthropology in Africa.)

Gender and Fieldwork

In the 1930s, Margaret Mead made clear the importance of gender as a variable in data collection and took advantage of her biological sex to do research on women. In the 1970s and 1980s, the issue of feminism attracted many women anthropologists into the study of gender and equality. Women's studies programs became common on campuses throughout the United States with women anthropologists playing a leading role. In Chapter 9, we will have the opportunity to understand the important contributions women make in Sharon E. Hutchinson's study of the Nuer of East Africa. This study, like many other recent works, has added a completely new perspective on the nature of culture that could not be realized when men studied men. Another important example of women expanding the works of male anthropologists is Annette Wiener's restudy of the economy of the Trobriand Islanders. Bronislaw Malinowski originally carried out research among the Trobrianders over seventy years ago. Wiener's work shows the importance of women's roles in the feasts and trade networks, something that Malinowski says little about (Wiener 1988).

Anthropology has become one of the disciplines most sensitive to women and their rights around the world. A complex dialogue has been opened in ethnographies that express women's perspectives and voices. These are written and translated by both men and women anthropologists who let the women of other cultures speak for themselves. One example is the story of Elvia Alvarado, a Honduran woman, who has commented on the "macho" worldview of the males in her culture (Benjamin 1989: 51–52). Two other examples are *The Granddaughters of Ixmucane: Guatemalan Women Speak,* a narrative explaining women's roles in the revolt against the Guatemalan government (Smith–Ayala 1991), and *I, Rigoberta Menchu: an Indian Woman in Guatemala* (edited by Elizabeth Burgos–Debray and translated by Ann Wright (1984). Rigoberta Menchu is a Quiché Mayan woman who won the 1992 Nobel Peace Prize. She has become a spokeswoman for oppressed women in Guatemala, and her work is also presented in Robert M. Carmack, Janine Gasco, and Gary H. Gossen's recent *The Legacy of Mesoamerica* (1996).

Both the work of women anthropologists to rectify male-biased ethnographies of earlier generations and the work by both men and women to let women speak about themselves and their cultures have significantly altered the way we see ourselves and the members of other cultures. This opening to women, created by women and now understood by men, has created a whole new style of scholarship and a dynamic world view lacking in earlier male-dominated works.

Emic, Etic, Ideal, and Real in the Field

Recall the discussion in Chapter 1 where we said that cultural *ideals* are what people think they ought to do, an emic view, and what the ethnographer determines that they actually do is *real,* an etic view. Recall also that we noted that the matter is more complicated. Let us now take a closer look.

First, in addition to cultural ideals, there is another emic view that we may call emically perceived reality. This is what insiders think they and others actually do. It is based on casual observation (not on counting instances); it consists of qualitative statements such as "most (or many, or few) people do that." Such informed observations of insiders can be quite useful in giving the ethnographer clues to how people perceive the degree to which they conform to the rules and beliefs of their own culture, and in giving information on permissible alternatives to ideal behavior and the circumstances under which the alternatives are permissible. (Of course, you have to ask a lot of questions to get all this.) But we must be aware that native statements about actual behavior may in fact not provide an accurate picture of what is really going on. As ethnographers we make our own qualitative observations. This is one kind of etic or outsider view—we could call it the anthropologist's perceived reality. These may coincide with what we are being told, but of course we must exercise caution because our observations may have been influenced by what we have been told. The other possibility is that we may find that people don't appear to be doing—at least not very often, or to the extent reported—what we were told they do. Here again we must exercise caution because our perception of others' behavior may be influenced by our own cultural biases. If we really want to know the extent to which the behavior in a culture conforms to the ideals of that culture, as well as the types and frequency of variation that occur, we must collect a quantitative sample. Such a sample (and its analysis) provides a second type of etic view of reality. For example, if everyone tells you that, corn being the ideal food, half the fields are always planted in corn and all you see after several days' observation is a couple of small corn fields in the midst of a veritable sea of bean fields, then it is clear that something is amiss. Either people's perceptions of what they actually plant is way off the mark, or your observations are. Under these circumstances, you may wish to take a systematic sampling of fields. By collecting all four kinds of data, our ethnography will be enriched; by carefully distinguishing each type of data in our account we make it reliably usable in that other kind of etic analysis that anthropologists engage in, cross-cultural comparison.

Mature adults in many cultures believe that the behavior of young adults does not conform to the cultural ideals they grew up with, and they believe equally strongly that conformity was far greater in their own generation. Among the Ngóbe of Panama in the 1960s most everyone agreed that symmetrical exchange marriage arranged between kin groups—phrased by men as an exchange of *ngwae*, siblings of the opposite sex—was the ideal form of marriage; likewise there was general agreement among members of the older generations that the youngsters of marriageable age were conforming much less to this ideal than had those of their own generation. But was this really the case? Both the conception of what is ideal and the perception of what is real, as described, are views from inside the culture, emic views.

There is another view to consider, an outsider or etic view: that of the ethnographer. It is often to be found in an ethnography along with the insider views. On the basis of observations over a period of time, the ethnographer may develop a sense of what people are doing and make a qualitative judgment about the extent to which her observations coincide with what people say they do. Now, in a case like Ngóbe marriage customs, it is not possible by just observing a man and woman living together to know if their marriage was or was not part of a symmetrical exchange (or for that matter, in some societies, to even know if they are married). In the Ngóbe marriage case, this is what I did (although the sample I obtained was not random in the statistical sense). From a sample of 254 marriages spread over four generations, I found that there had been no significant change in the ratio of exchange to nonexchange marriages in the four generations. The perception of older adults with respect to the marriage behavior of younger adults was faulty, a result perhaps of the "generation gap" phenomenon.

This, then, is quantitative reality—a numerical sample of behaviors that tells us how many people, on average, conform to the cultural ideals and how many do not, and what the variations are. As in the Ngóbe case, the picture provided by quantitative data may differ substantially from what insiders think they do.

Hazards of Field Research

It is easy to get carried away with the romance of anthropology (which is very real) in an introduction to anthropology. But there is a down side of which all students should be aware. Nancy Howell has written a book with the title *Surviving Fieldwork* (1990). She surveyed 204 anthropologists about illness and accidents in the field. In the foreword, Rappaport notes the maxim "anthropologists are otherwise sensible people who don't believe in the germ theory of disease" (quoted in Bernard 1995:157). One hundred percent of anthropologists doing work in South Asia report being exposed to malaria and 41 percent contract the disease. Thirteen percent report having hepatitis A. Accidents kill and injure researchers. Michelle Zimbalist Rosaldo died when she fell from a steep mountain trail in the Philippines in 1981. Thomas Zwickler, a University of Pennsylvania graduate student, was killed by a bus in India in 1985 (Bernard 1995). One of us cannot recall a single instance in his own research when he has not come down with dysentery in the field. The other—he of the cast iron constitution—can only recall two instances of being ill for more than a day or two while in the field, but he was beset by other hazards of the fieldwork enterprise: a broken arm, a cut that required stitches, two unsuccessful *coups d'etat* in two different countries, and a successful one in a third.

Depression is common. One kind of depression is called "culture shock" and comes as the novelty of field work wears off. Depression comes to be mixed with anxiety as the field worker is exposed to some of the negative aspects of field work. Living conditions can be terrible. Smith's worst experience was living on the plantations of the south coast of Guatemala. There violence was endemic and many of the people he worked with lived in squalor. The only way he coped with the situation was a weekly trip to Guatemala City to eat in a Chinese restaurant where the food was always safe. But even when living conditions are delightful (Smith's visit to Jardín), the loneliness of living in a strange culture can bring about intense depression and often a certain amount of paranoia. Often the field worker will pause and wonder if his or her work is worth the psychological pain.

When Young was living with the Ngóbe, he became convinced, after about four months of fieldwork, that his Ngóbe consultants were deliberately lying to him when they said "I don't know" in response to some of his questions. This suspicion turned out to be completely unfounded and a result of people genuinely not knowing some things, the anthropologist asking questions that were not well understood because he did not yet know enough about Ngóbe culture, and the irrational interpretations that people suffering from culture shock often place on events.

Does culture shock cease to be a problem after several field trips? The answer is no, although if one returns repeatedly to work with the same group of people, the condition becomes more benign, and you more quickly recognize the symptoms for what they are. Working in a new culture is likely to produce culture shock as severe as during that first fateful field trip, but the experienced anthropologist will recognize the symptoms more readily and be able to cope more effectively with this endemic fieldwork "disease" than will the novice.

Do tourists get culture shock? Sometimes, yes, if they stay in a place long enough and actually involve themselves in the everyday life of the local culture. But most tourists are usually in a place far too short a time, or are involved only superficially if at all in the local culture, to suffer more than a very mild case of culture shock.

Most anthropologists who conduct long-term field research also experience a phenomenon known as reverse culture shock. Having finally adapted to a foreign culture, the return home can be a trial in reverse. One often grows fond of the strange culture and comfortable in it. Its sights, sounds, smells, and tastes cease to be exotic and become familiar. Living in a remote village with no telephone, no television, unpredictable electricity, gas lanterns, and without the daily demands of modern American culture can be very pleasant, particularly if the researcher has been successfully incorporated into the community. The return home to interstate highways, malls, and the constant bombardment from the electronic media is a shock to the senses and may make the researcher wish he or she were back "home" in the field.

Two other hazards of the field worth mentioning are those of food and drink, and here we are not referring to the potential health hazards of consumption. Rather, we refer to the difficulties of fulfilling cultural expectations and the need to learn how to circumvent them in a culturally appropriate way.

In Ngóbe culture, for example, visitors to a household are always offered food. This is the way hospitality is expressed. To refuse to eat the food is insulting. This is true in many cultures. Sometimes it is only a token amount but often the portion is generous and more than the guest can consume, especially if the guest is an ethnographer who has just eaten at two or three other houses where he was conducting interviews. My (PY) first few attempts at house-to-house data collection were disastrous and ended well before midday. But observation paid off. I noted that there are two culturally acceptable ways to accept food, and then dispose of most of it after a few token mouthfuls without insulting the giver. One is to give most of it to the children in the household. They are always hungry. The other is to make sure you have something with you to wrap it up in and take it home.

In many cultures, offering guests alcoholic beverages is the means of displaying hospitality. Numerous anthropologists have gone through the experience of being offered alcohol in one form or another at every house they visit. One needs to learn quickly the culturally appropriate ways of refusal if one is to remain sober enough to do any research. While claiming to be a teetotaler may seem an easy way out, as Bernard (1995) points out, this may have the undesirable effect of having people mistakenly associate you with missionaries that may be in the area.

Summary

Perspectives on cultures are special ways of looking at some of the features that all cultures have. John Bennett focuses in much of his work on the adaptive or coping strategies of cultures. He views cultures as dynamic systems interacting with their environments and with other cultures. Arensberg and Kimball examine an important unit of all cultures, one that has served as a major basis for the study of cultures: communities. Edward Hall examines in detail the different ways in which cultures organize, regulate, and utilize space and time.

The mechanisms by which our brain processes information are called *cognitive processes*. While all normal humans are endowed with these cognitive processes, distinct cultural patterns come into being and are perpetuated through a general phenomenon known as *enculturation*. We do not fully understand how the mind interacts with its surroundings to produce these patterns. The ability to use human language is biologically based; the ability to communicate in a particular language is learned. Scholars are not in agreement about whether the language capacity is localized and distinct from other cognitive processes or generalized and part of a network of such processes. Language is, however, one of the most important ways in which humans store, process and retrieve information, and communicate with one another. It is one channel through which we learn our culture; other important channels are observation and participation (imitation).

All human languages share several characteristics that are not found together in the known communication systems of any other forms of life. An unsettled issue is the nature of the interaction between language and culture.

Anthropologists gather information about different cultures by conducting field research. The process begins with a search of the existing literature about the society or community to be studied and the region in which it is located. Anthropologists then usually spend several months in the field living with the people, learning their language, participating in and at the same time observing their daily lives and activities and special events. Casual conversation provides general information about the culture and leads that may be followed up using more formal interviewing techniques. While much of the data ethnographers collect is qualitative, survey questionnaires and other means of collecting quantitative data are frequently used as well. Despite the hazards that are often encountered in field research, most ethnographers find the experience very rewarding, and survive to produce an account of the people they studied, an ethnography.

Key Terms

Allophones	**Free Morphemes**
Bound Morphemes	**Infix**
Descriptive Linguistics	**Morphemes**
Enculturation or **Socialization**	**Semantics**
Ethnographer	**Syntax**
Ethnographic Present	**Whorfian Hypothesis**

Anthropological Theories

3

*I*n today's world of rapid change, anthropological studies of cultural change and adaptation are particularly relevant. There are many theories dealing with various types of cultural change and with **human ecology,** itself a form of change, that focus on human environmental adaptation. These range from evolutionary transformation to attempts by self-proclaimed modern societies to impose their economic models on others, to borrowing from other cultures and adaptations to local habitats, to the impact of technological innovation on human society, changes in environments (e.g. the end of the Ice Ages), innovations of **institutions** (changing rules), hegemonic expansion of successful states (which may require all of the above), changes in the importance of ideology, and so on.

How is the study of culture change achieved? Let's turn to **Mesoamerica** for an example of the problems of studying culture through time. If we fly down to modern Mexico we find that there have been dramatic changes in Mesoamerican culture over the past ten thousand years. The same landscape has been treated in very different ways by at least three distinct cultural systems: those that existed prior to 1492, the colonial Hispanic cultures, and modern Mexico. The material culture, the behavior, and the symbols through which humans interpreted their lives during these three periods are as different from each other as we are from the tribal Yanomamo living in the Amazon. How do we conceptualize the changes that have occurred?

Anthropologists face a series of dilemmas in studying culture change, the first of which is the mental categories we are forced to use because of our language, and the second is explaining the mechanisms of change. Archaeologists take horizontal slices out of the ground and try to stack them on top of each other to see what the changes have been in material culture through time. If we go to the region of Puebla, Mexico, we can find the remains of hunter–gatherer **bands** who camped on the shore of Lake Valsequillo ten thousand years ago. A little further south, we enter the Valley of Tehuacán, where maize was domesticated between five thousand and two thousand years ago. We can imagine the bands of hunters and gatherers gradually giving up their nomadic ways and settling down to become **tribes** of horticulturalists (gardeners). If we take a bus to La Venta in southeastern Veracruz, we can find temple tombs that belonged to people who worshipped a jaguarlike being, built cities, and had lordly leaders about seven hundred years B. C. Their organizational level was that of **chiefdoms;** they are known to us as the Olmec, and some scholars believe theirs was the mother culture from which all future pre-Hispanic cultures in Mesoamerica developed (Coe 1962). Northeast of Mexico City we would find ourselves at the gigantic ancient city of Teotihuácan, which dates to the time of Christ and had a **state** level of organization. Further south, in the lowlands of Guatemala and Honduras, we read the monuments at Tikal and Uaxactun, two major Mayan cities. Here we learn that the descendant of the founder of Tikal, Great Jaguar Paw, waged war against Uaxactun and captured that city on January 16, A. D. 378. We know the conquering general's name was Smoking Frog, but at other sites we find no writing, and the relationships among cities are elusive. Later, this region was dominated by Spain, which imposed its colonial models on the whole of Latin America to create a very different set of sociocultural patterns. In modern times, capitalism has brought about yet other transitions and the relationship between modern Mexico and its colonial heritage, let alone its prehistory, is problematic. How do we interpret our slices of time?

One way is to give the names of band, tribe, chiefdom, preindustrial state, and capitalist state to hundreds if not thousands of snapshots we have taken through time using archaeology, historical research, and modern ethnography.

Aerial photo of Tikal, an ancient Mayan city.

Here we are doing what children do when they collect stamps, leaves, or toy cars. They sort them into categories based on similarities and differences they perceive to be salient. Do our categories reflect reality? Not entirely, but they probably do capture some significant differences. If we had a great deal more information, we might choose to use very different categories. More than a century ago Lewis Henry Morgan used the terms *savage, barbarian,* and *civilized* to distinguish among snapshots of time (1877). But our knowledge is vastly different today and so are the terms we use to label our categories.

How do we explain change? Just a decade ago we would have talked about the *evolution* from band to tribe, tribe to chiefdom, and chiefdom to state, and we could have used Leslie White's interpretation that the changes were caused by the invention of new technologies, primarily irrigation systems and changing subsistence techniques (hunting and gathering to rainfall agriculture to irrigated agriculture) (1959). But the detailed knowledge that archaeologists, ethnographers, and historians now have of Mesoamerica and other world regions has forced us to abandon this oversimplified explanation. Now we are examining world systems that emerge as they are successful in trade, war, and managing ecological resources as superior explanations. Later we will discuss Douglas North's concept of transaction costs (1990, 1992) and we will speculate about how bureaucracies might decrease the expense of war and trade, thereby allowing certain societies to become dominant while others remain peripheral. This theory currently seems powerful, but to many people so did White's theory thirty years ago, and thirty years from now we may expect a new **paradigm** (a set of values, facts, and definitions used to interpret raw data). This process of discovery, categorization, interpretation, theorizing, and moving on to new theories about the nature of reality, when new data do not fit the old theories, is what science is all about.

When we apply our scientific methods to the vast body of data about culture change, we must always keep in mind the simple fact that our culture, including our interpretation of what science is, binds us to a certain amount of ethnocentricity in our models. Every generation hopes that its models are closer approximations to reality, but it is always wise to be skeptical. The ultimate reality is not ours to understand. We can only take small steps in that direction. We assume that there *is* an ultimate reality, at least so far as the laws of nature are concerned, of which our perceptions are only approximations. This is an assumption not shared by postmodernists and some relativists. In the following pages, we will give an overview of several different ways in which anthropologists have conceptualized the nature of culture and culture change. One of the great dangers, always, is that while anthropologists strive to achieve an objective (scientific) understanding, they are also members of their own cultures and so their views reflect ideological biases, often without conscious intent. Of course, in this respect, we are no more prone to error than are the scientists who study the nonhuman aspects of nature. We may believe we are free of bias today, but looking back a hundred years from now, our descendants will no doubt make sport of our own cultural naiveté.

The Early History of Anthropological Thought: Unilineal Evolution and Diffusion

Tracing the early roots of anthropology, specifically cultural anthropology, will help us to understand how ideas about culture change have evolved. While cultural anthropology is still in the process of taking shape, the terms *ethnography* and *ethnology* have been around since the middle of the nineteenth century. What is more important, the ideas that came to dominate cultural theory existed in the writings of the luminaries of the Enlightenment. These ideas not only emerged as modern anthropology, they also became economics, sociology, political science, psychology, and historiography. An important point is that, in the history of Western civilization, there have been debates between sets of thinkers, and the debates are the setting for the rise of society as we know it today. Anthropology emerged as a discipline in the middle of the debates and was shaped by them. As noted in Chapter 1, a key characteristic of anthropology, one that distinguishes it from the other social science disciplines, is its holistic perspective toward cultural systems. While anthropology is made up of four subdisciplines, it is a synthesizing discipline of connections and holistically brings ideas from other disciplines under its own mantle.

Because so much of modern anthropology was shaped by the Enlightenment, the discipline has many apparent architects, from John Locke to Descartes, Hume, Turgot, Diderot, and Rousseau. Not only were many of the architects of the Enlightenment very "anthropological" in their perspective, but the list of themes they wrote about is quite long and looks like the index of a text in modern anthropology. Driving most of the theories were questions regarding universal truths derived from Greek philosophy: What does it mean to be human? What is good? What is beautiful? What is order? What is civilization? What is the nature of change? While important schools of theory can be distinguished as early as the mid-nineteenth century, the application of cultural knowledge has been continuous and constant.

The use of cultural knowledge to implement change has apparently been important as far back as the Greek writer Herodotus, according to John Van Willigen, an applied anthropologist. Van Willigen also notes that in the Middle Ages, Pope Gregory used his missionaries to convert animal sacrifices to forms more appropriate for newly converted Catholics (1993). With the expansion of core societies, concern for native populations led to the creation of such organizations as the Aborigines Protection Society, founded in London in 1838. Work with these populations helped develop sets of anthropological theories about the evolution of society. Unfortunately, the evolutionary theories of the nineteenth century were racist and ethnocentric in nature. The concept of evolution was confused with the concept of "progress," which is largely a process whereby a population becomes increasingly more industrialized. There are some today who would question this meaning of *progress*, but in the nineteenth century there was no question but that progress meant the growth of capitalism, and all four words—*evolution, progress, capitalism* and *civilization*—were used interchangeably with each other as though they were synonyms. During this period, anthropologists supported the establishment of direct administrative control over native populations (many would consider this to be an imperialistic role), and anthropologists were called on to provide data for policy-making and problem-solving, although they seldom served as administrators.

At the same time, two major schools of thought sought to explain change: **unilinear evolution** and **diffusionism.** According to Marvin Harris, the earliest schools of evolutionary anthropology and diffusion had one thing in common: Biological and cultural facts were confused (Harris 1968). In the nineteenth century there was no clear idea of the difference between biology and culture, culture and behavior, or behavior and biology. The ideas of civilization, progress, and evolution were also confused. Their science of anthropology was closer to a "folk taxonomy" of societies around the world based on armchair speculation than to ethnographic observation. Loren Eiseley, the noted science writer, calls the nineteenth century the Age of Darwin due to the importance of evolutionary theories (Eiseley 1958).

Diffusion theory, while usually separated from evolutionary theory, was a form of evolutionary theory that stressed space rather than time. There were two schools, a British version associated with G. Elliot Smith and William Perry, and a German version associated with Father Wilhelm Schmidt. British diffusionism speculated that the most important characteristics of modern civilization could be traced back to ancient Egypt. Those cultures that no longer had Egyptian traits were "degenerate," their peoples having forgotten Egyptian culture. The German school argued that there were several early centers for civilization, a point of view that was called **Kulturkreise** (culture circles). It too argued that those cultures that did not have civilized traits had degenerated and put nonwestern cultures outside of the frame of reference. While these extreme forms of diffusionism are rejected by scholars today, diffusion itself, of ideas as well as tangible objects, is recognized as one source of cultural change.

But it is the evolutionary theories that dominated anthropology in the late eighteenth and early nineteenth century as knowledge about the biological evolution of the plant and animal kingdom improved. By 1780, the Frenchman Comte de Buffon had clearly thought out most of the theory that today we attribute to Charles Darwin. Darwin was able to come up with the mechanism of change: variation and natural selection. According to his theory, plants and animals have a tendency to multiply at rates faster than increases in the food supply. The limited food supply forces competition between members of the same species. Variation occurs naturally in biological populations, and some of the variants give their hosts greater opportunity to survive. Those that survive successfully pass their genes on to their descendants.

While theories were being developed about biological evolution, there was also considerable speculation on how humankind had gone from primitive hunting and food-gathering societies to complex agricultural and then industrial states. Most of the theories of the nineteenth century are called "unilineal" theories, because the theorists argued for a series of worldwide developmental stages. Societies were seen as evolving from simple to more complex. The earliest stages were usually identified on the basis of speculative assumptions about what was most primitive. The assumptions were that polygamy (multiple marriage), the worship of nature gods, infanticide (the killing of unwanted children), and the use of primitive tools were indicators of "primitiveness."

Most of the information used by the theorists was drawn from reports of missionaries and travelers who were invariably ethnocentric, passing judgment on others based on the presumption that their own behavior and beliefs were "superior." Today we understand many of the same cultural characteristics as having ecological and economic rationales. The characteristics of societies that were put in between "primitive" and "modern" were also speculative guesses about what could be considered not really modern, but not primitive either.

Both diffusionists and evolutionists viewed cultural change as a process of mental improvement. Those who belonged to "superior" cultures had obviously evolved to a higher level of intelligence (a theory that is repeated today in the "bell curve theory" of Richard Hernstein and Charles Murray (1994). This theory was based on Darwin's principle of survival of the fittest: Evolution came to mean natural selection for people of increasingly higher intelligence. When coupled to the belief in the superiority of certain races, these evolutionary and diffusionist explanations came to be tantamount to a rationalization for racism and imperialism throughout the world, and this was made explicit in the **Social Darwinism** of the British sociologist Herbert Spencer.

One of the most famous theoreticians of the nineteenth century was Lewis Henry Morgan (1818–1881). A lawyer and banker, Morgan worked directly with the Iroquois of New York State. His ethnographic descriptions of the Iroquois are still used by scholars. Although he admired the Iroquois and American Indians in general, his own theory misled him and he placed American Indian culture in an intermediate stage in his evolutionary framework. In his *Ancient Society* (1877), Morgan set out a speculative theory of **cultural evolution.** His research data were not totally based on armchair speculation but on research he did for an earlier work, *Systems of Consanguinity and Affinity in the Human Family* (1870). For that study, he sent questionnaires to people around the world who he thought would report honestly on what they observed: missionaries, businessmen, colonial administrators, and diplomats. Once he received their replies, however, he tended to associate the descriptions with his own evolutionary stages of savagery, barbarism, and civilization. There were many other speculative theories, such as those of Henry Maine and E. B. Tylor. While these theoreticians had some valuable insights about cultural change, their general theories are seen today as being ethnocentric, racist, and contradictory. Both diffusionists and evolutionists misunderstood biological evolution and linked culture and biology. Today, we separate the two and have come to realize that cultural differences are not a measure of biologically inherited intellectual capacity. And cultures, like people, can no longer be considered more or less evolved, more or less better. To do so is to commit the fallacy of thinking that evolution equals progress. Cultures are distinct ways of working out adaptations to complex processes, some of which we will examine in the next several chapters.

The Classic Phase of Anthropological Thought, 1900–1970

During the period from the turn of the century to roughly 1970, most of what we term the classic theories were formulated. While many of the following theories are out of use today, or have been greatly modified, they underlie a great many of the arguments of contemporary anthropology.

Franz Boas and the Reaction to Speculative Evolutionary Theory

Franz Boas, known as the father of the American school of anthropology, is responsible for taking the first important step toward a theory of culture in his careful distinction between culture and biology. Franz Boas was a German, originally trained in geology and physics, who came to the United States and founded modern anthropology at Columbia University at the turn of the century. Boas did not share the evolutionary theories of his contemporaries. His anti-evolutionism was not so much an attack on evolution per se but an attack on theories that were too speculative and had no empirical basis. He was also offended at the racism of cultural evolutionary theories and fought for most of his life to rid anthropology of racism and ethnocentrism.

Marvin Harris, in *The Rise of Anthropological Theory* (1968), shows that much of Boas's perspective in anthropology was based on the theories of the philosopher Emmanuel Kant. While it is not necessary (nor wise) to go into Kantian Idealism at length here, it is necessary to make a short excursion into philosophy to understand the development of Boasian anthropology. Kant's philosophy goes back to Plato who believed that behind all "things" were ideas (shadows in the cave). For Kant, the only "reality" was in the mind, and for Boas the science of anthropology was to find out what is going on in the minds of people being studied. The job of the anthropologist was to find out what the individual had experienced, what was in his/her "mind." The laws behind behavior were to be found in the operation of the mind, not elsewhere. This was the essence of ethnographic science to Boas and his students. This is also the basis of what came to be known as the American school of anthropology. This is close to the contemporary interpretivist perspective of anthropology. Interpretivists argue that the culture of the ethnographer biases his or her writing and that it is important, as far as possible, to get into the mind of the native (see below).

In taking the position he did, Boas clearly separated biological phenomena from mental phenomena. Boas also differed from nineteenth-century writers in abandoning the idea that natural selection works on culture. While natural selection might work on nature, it does not work on ideas. Boas lived among the peoples of the northwest coast of the United States and among the Inuit, and collected an impressive amount of ethnographic data. His detailed descriptions of the cultures of these peoples were what he meant by science.

Boas was the most influential of the anthropologists of the first part of the twentieth century. The list of students whom he influenced and who in turn influenced the discipline grows very long. Among the more important names are those who were his students or his associates: Alfred Kroeber, Robert Lowie, Margaret Mead, and Ruth Benedict.

In 1909, Alfred Kroeber published a famous paper on kinship in which he argued that the laws of culture were largely psychological, an argument that fit the neo-Kantian paradigm of the importance of mind. He also argued that culture was an entity *sui generis,* a thing unto itself, with its own internal laws (1917). Kroeber was never to explain those laws, although he did explain how the lengths of women's dresses rise and fall with economic changes (Kroeber 1948). The search for psychological laws of culture led many anthropologists of the 1930s to try to use the theories of Sigmund Freud to interpret culture, a fad that has now long passed. Alfred Kroeber established a West Coast version of the American school of anthropology at the University of California at Berkeley. Kroeber, like his teacher, Boas, sent students around the world to collect information on the peoples of the world, including some who attempted to study American culture.

British Social Anthropology

Across the Atlantic, in Great Britain, a second nonevolutionary school of anthropology was developing called structural–functionalism, or often simply **functionalism.** It had its roots in the writings of the French sociologists Emile Durkheim and Marcel Mauss. The position of the structural–functionalist was that society (not culture) responded to the laws of sociology, not psychology. The key concept was that of **solidarity,** the social bond between individuals. The theory was that the *structures* (some would call them "institutions") of society (e.g., kinship structures, political structures) could best be explained in terms of their functions and as adding to the solidarity of the society. It is this point of view, shared by sociologists of the mid-twentieth century, of which Wolf (1982) is critical in *Europe and the People Without History.*

British structural–functionalists were not able to take their theoretical explanations very far. The most elaborate theories were those created by A. R. Radcliffe–Brown and Bronislaw Malinowski. Both scholars were more famous for their field studies than for their theories.

The most important achievement of British structural–functionalism was in methodology. Raymond Firth became very well known for his research on economics in Oceania, while Darryl Forde made his reputation studying the relationship between ecology and social systems. Radcliffe–Brown did detailed work on the political and kinship systems of African tribes and chiefdoms. The major achievement of their work was to clarify the different kinds of systems that form cultures or societies: kinship systems, political systems, social systems, religious systems, and so on. Their work, read in the United States, began forcing American anthropologists to examine the "systems" of culture and to get away from the more amorphous problem of defining culture.

Of particular importance was the work of W. Lloyd Warner (1949; Warner and Hunt 1942), who was influenced by Radcliffe–Brown when the latter taught at the University of Chicago. Warner began a series of important studies on American communities that stimulated anthropologists to do similar work elsewhere. Warner influenced a generation of scholars who learned the art of community study, and developed ethnographic field methods that are still used today.

Structural–functionalism and American anthropology of the 1940s were poorly matched. For the Americans, the idea was to get into the mind of a few informants (emic anthropology). The structural–functionalists, in contrast, insisted on much more detailed ethnographies based on interviews and censuses in order to create models of systems (etic anthropology). Detailed analysis of economic, political, and kinship systems became very important.

During this classic phase, American historical anthropology and British structural–functionalism cross-fertilized each other. In the United States, the work of anthropologists improved in quality and relevance, focusing on education, nutrition, culture contact, migration, land tenure, and many other topics of culture change. The New Deal drew a large number of anthropologists into applied work for the federal government. The Applied Anthropology Unit of the Office of Indian Affairs was created by John Collier, who had been appointed Commissioner of Indian Affairs and was responsible for the rapid expansion of federally employed anthropologists.

American government agencies, with the help of anthropologists of both camps, carried out projects relating to economic and resource development on various Indian reservations. The involvement of anthropologists in the study of policy questions in American communities also expanded well into the war years. For example, some anthropologists contributed to the U.S. Department of Agriculture's Rural Life Studies, which provided six community studies that focused on change in rural communities. Walter Goldschmidt's classic *As You Sow: Three Studies in the Social Consequences of Agribusiness* (1978) documented economic exploitation by large corporate landowners and led to his vilification by California's agribusiness (Van Willigen 1993).

One of the most significant projects to come out of this time period was organized by the Committee on Human Relations in Industry at the University of Chicago. Included among the anthropologists were W. Lloyd Warner and Burleigh B. Gardner. This project produced the classic Western Electric or Hawthorn Works study of the relationships between working conditions and productivity that is still used in modern business management texts (Van Willigen 1993). These applied research projects fed back into academic anthropology.

Several anthropologists trained at the University of Chicago, such as John W. Bennett, worked on materials from modern industrial societies, such as Japan (Bennett 1958). Bennett's work on forestry management in postwar Japan was

Agribusinesses are often not ecologically sustainable.

years ahead of its time, showing how Japanese institutions influenced the way that forests were managed.

Leslie White: Universal Cultural Evolution

In the 1950s, a century's worth of research in archaeology was raising questions that had evolutionary implications. Parallels in the apparent cultural evolution of Mesopotamia (the Middle East) and Mesoamerica (Mexico and northern Central America) were becoming clear. How could two regions of the world that were so distant from each other have parallel evolutionary patterns (or so it appeared)? Other questions were being raised by ethnographers as they discovered great similarities in the kinship systems of peoples in very different parts of the world. How could people in places as far apart as Central America and Central Africa have identical named categories for relatives?

Leslie White, who established the Department of Anthropology at the University of Michigan, did his original graduate work in the Southwest on the Pueblo Indians and developed an interest in the relationship between technology and **social structure.** As a young professor of anthropology, he traveled to Russia and came under the influence of Marxist theoreticians. While his own work cannot be judged Marxist, some aspects of it are Marxist enough that he had a great deal of trouble getting his ideas accepted by the scientific community in the United States. This was especially true in the 1950s, when McCarthyism flourished, a time when many evolutionary and ecologically oriented anthropologists got into trouble for their ideas—ideas that looked suspiciously Marxist (and often were).

There are several components of White's work that are worth looking over and were published for the first time in 1959 in *The Evolution of Culture,* one of the landmarks of the age of classical anthropology. A core component in White's thinking was the importance of the First and Second Laws of Thermodynamics. White began with the laws of physics, not psychology (a challenge to the American school of anthropology). For White, culture, like everything else, has to respond to the laws of physics. White's definition of *culture* is similar to the one used in this text, "an extrasomatic, temporal continuum of things and events dependent upon symboling" (White 1959:3).

In short, for White, culture included the symbols in the mind, things made by humans, including social organization, and events (behavior). With this definition White could argue that culture is an energy-using system, and his axiom, C = E (culture equals energy), underlay his argument that the evolution of culture was the result of cultural systems drawing greater and greater amounts of energy from the environment through increasingly more efficient technologies (T).

White's concepts of energy and adaptation are common today in human ecology, which is discussed later. For White, culture is an energy-capturing system whose survival depends on a continuous battle against disorganization. It is this battle to capture energy, to move in the direction of greater organization, that White defined as cultural evolution.

For White, any culture is both a symbolic system and a thermodynamic system. White placed a great deal of emphasis on energy, tools, and their products. Energy meant "the ability to do work," and work and energy were almost interchangeable. Because of this "interchangeability" culture should be measurable in caloric units. White and his followers attempted to measure the relationship between "culture" and "energy" with some degree of success as long as gross differences are used between relatively broad evolutionary stages. Thus, hunting and gathering bands derive much less energy in the form of calories from their environments than do modern societies, about 1/20th of a horsepower per capita, in contrast to modern societies that generate hundreds of horsepower per capita (White 1959:42). For White, energy was the cause of cultural evolution, so energy capture should be directly translatable to distinct evolutionary stages. Thus, a contrast between hunting and gathering societies and our own would show that while we consume hundreds of thousands of calories every day in the form of fossil fuels that drive our machines, less technologically advanced societies would consume much less. A male hunter–gatherer might only consume the amount of energy he personally put out each day, about two thousand calories.

For White, culture had four key components: technology (T), economy (E), society (S), and ideology (I). For him T was the driving mechanism, the component by which humankind derived energy from the environment. Another characteristic of White's theory was that he treated the environment as a neutral system, as having little to do with cultural evolution. He saw culture as a self-driven, self-evolving system. Because of his perspective, White was and is accused of being guilty of "technological determinism." Outside of contemporary anthropology, theoreticians working in "complexity theory" are once again looking at culture as a self-evolving set of systems and subsystems that are part of the universal tendency towards the growth of complexity (see Waldrop 1992, Lewin 1992).

While White's technological determinism is widely in dispute, the thermo-dynamic part of his argument is implicit in this text, but we try to avoid either technological or economic determinism. In another chapter, we argue that cultural change today is dependent on the acquisition of greater and greater amounts of energy from the environment but that we are in danger of destroying world **ecosystems** through an excessive use of energy. In John W. Bennett's work, which is cited later in this chapter, we turn to the idea that what drives change are innovations in how we solve problems through "anticipation" and "coping." Adaptation is a form of decision-making, and that includes the choice of tools and innovations in technology. In addressing our ecological problems, we may turn to new technologies, but we are also likely to turn to new institutions of economic organization, new political systems, or new ideologies. These in turn may bring about new technologies or new technologies may drive changes in these other systems. Modern anthropologists dismiss the notion that culture change is driven by any one force or system. We argue further that culture change cannot be understood as a series of simple cause–effect events. A cultural system is a dynamic system consisting of numerous interacting variables and feedback loops.

Julian Steward:

Parallel or Multilineal Cultural Evolution

The second important evolutionary theoretician is Julian Steward, who was an archaeologist and an ethnologist. He worked in the western Andes on the ancient civilizations of Peru and Ecuador. He also did ethnographic research among the Ute and Paiute of Nevada and Utah, and like White became interested in the relationship of technology and social organization. In the 1940s, he was appointed by the Smithsonian Institute of Washington, D.C. to put together the *Handbook of South American Indians.* This book was made up of studies that ethnographers had carried out on the Indians of South America over the last century as well as descriptions of the ancient Inca made by writers of the sixteenth, seventeenth, and eighteenth centuries. It is quite possible that if he had been asked to do the same kind of editorial work on North American Indians, or Africa, or Southeast Asia, he would not have come up with his organizational format. However, South America is characterized by the coexistence of peoples of different levels of sociopolitical organization within short distances of each other, such as states and tribes. His system of organization is very "natural" given the kind of material he was working with. While the format of the *Handbook* itself is a modified culture area arrangement, in his "South American Cultures: An Interpretive Summary" (1949a), in Volume 5 of the *Handbook,* Steward developed a culture type classification based mainly on sociopolitical and religious organization. This culture type approach is further developed in his "Levels of Sociocultural Integration: An Operational Concept" (1951). We will be using a modified form of Steward's evolutionary taxonomy in this book, one developed by Elman Service (1962). Because many of Steward's assumptions about levels of organization have been brought into question, we will not go into his categories.

Figure 3.1   **Ecological adaptations in Native South and Central America and the Caribbean.**

INDIGENOUS
ADAPTATIONS IN
SOUTH AMERICA

N

0   1000 Mi.

0   1000 km

Slash and burn tropical forest
farming, fishing, wild game (deer,
peccaries, armadillos, monkeys)

Slash and burn farmers

Xerophytic seed collectors

Highland swidden farming,
small scale irrigation

Small scale irrigation
farmers and pastoralists

Intensive irrigation farming

Coastal shellfish gatherers,
and marine hunters

Fishing, wild game hunters

Gallery Forest farmers, wild food
(palm) collectors and farmers

Source: Steward, Julian H. and Louis C. Faron (1959). *Native Peoples of South America*
(p. 45). New York: McGraw-Hill Book Company, Inc.

Steward was critical of White and considered him a unilineal theorist, much
like Morgan, a perspective that is based on White's view that there was only one
world culture to which all other cultures belonged. Steward called his own view
a theory of multilinear evolution. He argued that many distinct cultures have
evolved parallel to each other due to the working of the same scientific laws, and
he made it his life work to find the laws. He was extremely interested in the fact

that in various parts of the world, such as the Middle East, Mesoamerica, and Peru, there appeared to be parallel developments in cultural evolution (see his 1949 paper, "Cultural Causality and Law: A Trial Formulation").

Steward differed most greatly from White in his emphasis on "cultural ecology," on the interrelated processes of human adaptation to the environment. While White was accused of being a technological determinist, Steward and his followers were sometimes accused of being environmental determinists. For Steward, culture was also made up of components, though he used different labels. Steward thought there were two important components to culture: the cultural core and the superstructure. The core was made up of technology and subsistence activities—very close to what Harris means by *infrastructure* (the use of technology to derive food from the environment) while the superstructure was everything else. Interaction between core and environment led to evolution, though Steward was vague about how this occurred. He was unable to come up with a more specific theory of this complex interaction and died without ever having become more specific. Some of his students and followers borrowed a natural selection argument from Darwin, whereby innovations in behavior were selected for by the environment if they gave the society adaptive advantage, and this has become modern "cultural materialism," which is explained in a later section.

Both White's and Steward's theories attributed changes in other aspects of culture to technological change. However, Steward did not see technology as the sole cause of evolutionary change, and he argued that environmental changes as well as changes in nontechnological aspects of culture could also precipitate technological change. The two theories were synthesized by Marshall Sahlins and Elman Service in 1960 for a "synthetic theory of cultural evolution." The concepts of consecutive evolutionary stages of band, tribe, chiefdom, and state were introduced and have been in use ever since, albeit not without criticism. Today, there is growing awareness that cultures may evolve and change due to shifts in religion or ideology, and that government policies can determine the development of technologies. The relationships among environment, technology, economic and political systems, as well as ideologies, are viewed as having much more complex interconnections than they were in White's or Steward's time. Steward and his associates, to their credit, did foresee these complexities, as evidenced in *The Peoples of Puerto Rico* (1956) and *Contemporary Change in Traditional Societies* (1967). And anthropologists do acknowledge that a critical variable in culture change is technology. Only a moment's pause to reflect on the changes in American culture over the last four decades, due to developments in automobiles, road building, communications, aerospace, and computers, will convince the reader of the dramatic role technology plays in culture change.

Homer Barnett: Innovation and Culture Change

Homer Barnett, in his classic study, *Innovation: The Basis of Cultural Change* (1953), takes a psychological approach to understanding change. Where White focuses on technology and energy conversion, and Steward on environment,

Barnett focuses on the human mind as the wellspring of all cultural change. His argument is detailed and sophisticated. He sees individual adaptation as the ultimate source of cultural adaptation. The cognitive processes of the mind are the basis for our perceptions and our sorting, synthesizing, categorizing, ignoring, discarding, and recombining into new configurations all of the information we receive as input. Innovations, whether they are new combinations of ideas or of things resulting from ideas, are entirely the products of mental activity. But mental activity itself is culturally structured and socially defined. As Barnett puts it,

> . . .mental content is socially defined; its substance is, in major part, dictated by tradition. But the manner of treating this content, of grasping it, altering it, and reordering it, is inevitably dictated by the potentialities and the liabilities of the machine which does the manipulating; namely, the individual mind. . . . [The] custom-determined substance [of a thought] will determine just which one of the possible mental reaction patterns it will provoke. Understood in this way, there can be no legitimate distinction between the psychological and the cultural approaches to the problem of cultural change (1953:16).

The last statement makes it plain that Barnett's definition of culture is ideational; that is, it is the stuff in the mind, not what people do or make. These, for Barnett, are products of culture. Barnett is careful to point out that many, if not most, innovations are not conscious and may even go unnoticed by those whose minds produce them. Many successful innovations, which are accepted as standards of material culture in some society, we call inventions.

With the renewed interest among cultural anthropologists in the relationship between cognitive processes and culture, Barnett's ideas, after much neglect, will perhaps receive the careful review they deserve. Much of Barnett's discussion in *Innovation* is relevant to the developing field of cognitive science.

In sum, Barnett sees the human mind as prime mover and ultimate source of all cultural change. And this it undoubtedly is, but we must take care to distinguish between how the human mind innovates in the sense of functions of cognitive processes, and why humans innovate, that is, what motivates people to innovate, to change their ways of doing things. Motivating forces are largely external to the mind. What motivates one mind may not motivate another. What motivates minds in one culture to produce innovations that are accepted and thus produce culture change may leave the minds in other cultures indifferent. And, given that motivation occurs, response in terms of the exact nature of the innovations may also differ. The human mind is indeed a marvelous data-processing mechanism and that it innovates there is no doubt; but innovations are not necessarily correct or adaptive. They may in fact be downright devastating to the culture concerned. And, as Barnett rightly points out, many innovations fall by the wayside; that is, they are not accepted and thus do not result in noticeable cultural change.

Contemporary Theory in Cultural Anthropology

The classic period of American anthropology included several other interesting schools of thought that cannot be gone into here, but which were mentioned in the last chapter or will be mentioned elsewhere in this text (culture and personality, structuralism). But the classic period appears relatively simple in contrast to the many schools of thought debated in contemporary anthropology. We will briefly discuss only those sets of ideas that bear on the problem of culture change. In this regard, we discern three overall directions in theory today. The first of these is **materialism** and is embedded in the theories of Leslie White and Julian Steward and to some degree is derived from the ideas of Karl Marx. This direction underscores the need for a scientific approach to the study of culture change. Its foremost spokesperson is Marvin Harris.

The second, **interpretivism,** is a rejection of the materialist position, emphasizing a more humanistic approach that places importance on symbols and their meaning. Clifford Geertz is the most eloquent spokesperson for this view. A third approach, used in this book, combines ideas from both materialist and interpretivist perspectives as well as insights from human ecology and the political economy approach of Eric Wolf and many economic anthropologists (see Acheson, ed. 1994) in an attempt to understand how and why cultures change; this approach we will call, following a current trend, the **political ecology** approach.

Materialistic Perspectives:
Cultural Materialism and Marxism

In the late 1960s and 1970s, a school of thought developed out of Julian Steward's cultural ecology called **cultural materialism.** The leading proponents of this approach were Marvin Harris, Andrew Vayda, and Roy Rappaport, although Rappaport has recently distanced himself from materialistic anthropology (Rappaport 1979). Materialistic explanations are those that reduce complex cause–effect relationships to physical, mechanical, or bioligical laws (laws of physics, laws of mechanics, laws of genetics, laws of evolution). Cultural materialists excelled at arguing how seemingly nonrational practices—warfare, pig sacrifices, potlatches (redistribution feasts), the ritual sanctification of cows in India, human sacrifice among the Aztecs—have positive (though usually unrecognized) consequences in that they regulate population density, the availability of protein in the diet, the redistribution of food from areas of surplus to areas of shortage, and so forth.

Cultural ecology and cultural materialism make use of **cybernetic theory** with its emphasis on feedback relationships within systems and between various systems. Cybernetic theory is the basis of computer technology and focuses on information processing . While the majority of writers in cultural ecology and human ecology subscribe to the idea of feedback relationships between culture and environment, according to cultural materialism the environment or habitat se-

Fossil fuel–powered machines are part of the agricultural revolution.

lects for "traits," such as pig sacrifice and ancestor worship (the theory is based on population genetics in biology). Parallels can be drawn between this type of "environmental selection" and Darwinian natural selection. Individuals living in a society produce new variants of behavior at the **infrastructural level,** some of which are more effective than others in withstanding environmental selection, and these new variants survive while the less well adapted variants tend to disappear. Infrastructure, within sociocultural systems, consists of those "systems" that are materialistic (physical, mechanical, genetic, biological). The forms of human behavior change, much as a gene pool changes, as adaptation to the environment progresses. In this perspective, an innovative form of human behavior, which originates in certain members of the group, is analogous to a biological mutation. According to Marvin Harris, the foremost proponent of cultural materialism:

> . . .selection processes responsible for the divergent and convergent evolutionary trajectories of sociocultural systems operate mainly on the individual level; individuals follow one rather than another course of action, and as a result the aggregate pattern [of culture] changes (Harris 1979:60).

The cultural materialist explanation, which continues White's emphasis on technology as the driving force at the infrastructural level, is very widely accepted as both a logical model and as one that has received considerable scientific support. The archaeological record appears to support the generalization that changes in technology precede changes in other aspects of human culture. However, we must remember that the archaeological record produces little more than a record of material culture, that is, technology. The cultural materialist position is so all-pervasive that most sociology and history texts present the rise of capitalism as a consequence of the development of certain technologies such as the steam engine, McCormick's reaping machine, the cotton gin, and other familiar technologies.

Nonmaterialists argue that there are two dangers in interpreting the cultural–environmental interface in this manner. First, Social Darwinism is allowed to sneak in the back door under a new cloak of scientific respectability. "Superior traits" are chosen by environmental constraints to produce human sociocultural evolution. Luckily, cultural materialists are sensitive to this issue, do not declare one culture superior to another, and maintain their cultural relativism; but the danger of ethnocentrism is certainly there. Second, when cultural materialists try to distance themselves from pure technological determinism, they risk falling into another determinism: the old trap of environmental determinism. In this view, variant behaviors produced by human beings as members of social groups are selected for by the environment and only some become dominant while others tend to disappear; the cultural system itself is considered to be passive. It cannot change of its own accord, as a result of human decision-making and effort or because of internal processes and strains, but must await the activating forces of environmental necessity. By choosing an approach closely modeled on population biology, anthropologists risk reinstating environmental or other kinds of determinism.

Another problem with cultural materialism is that it is best used for long time periods in human history and on the broadest of cultural changes. It is not very valuable or useful when looking at recent changes or recent problems in human adaptation. It is possible that in the extreme long run, environmental natural selection may make the ultimate difference in the choice between two forms of behavior, but the actual relationships between behavior and environments are so complex that it is purely speculative to predict what will succeed or what will not. As Marshall Sahlins once said, in critique of both the passivity-of-culture and passivity-of-environment positions:

> To adapt. . .is not to do perfectly from some objective standpoint, or even necessarily to improve performance; it is to do as well as possible under the circumstances, which may not turn out very well at all. . . . An adaptive perspective, goes the moral, must not presume that whatever is there is good, rational, useful, or advantageous. Lots of things people do are truly stupid, if understandable, and many cultures have gone to the wall (1977:220–1).

Echoing Karl Marx, Wolf prefers an anthropology that stresses laying bare the laws or regularities surrounding the production of wealth. Marx, one of the last major figures to aim at a holistic human science (Wolf 1982:21), argued that every stage of history was represented by different **modes of production,** a materialistic line of reasoning. For example, as we will read in the next several chapters, hunters and food gatherers are organized into family-based kinship groups of various types, as are tribal agriculturalists. Marxist writers would theorize that social structure was determined by the way in which these societies obtained a living, in other words, by their modes of production. In chiefdoms, the sources of production are organized on the basis of **redistribution:** goods are given to a central figure, a chief, and then redistributed. Social structure reflects the economy with the society often being organized into the shape of a conical **clan** containing ranked **lineages** in which the chief is usually the highest-ranking individual in the highest-ranking lineage. In such a system, everyone believes he or she is descended from the same founding ancestor. Early states had **tributary economies** of peasants who paid tribute to high-class lords, producing more complex hierarchical social structures.

Wolf argues that we should look to the modes of production in order to understand ourselves at different points in time. He shows how different modes of production help to explain the distinct but dynamic adaptations that humans have produced around the globe through time. Many of his ideas will be incorporated in this text on contemporary culture change. However, we argue that to Marx's modes of production must be added the primary forms of human acquisition: property rights, which are intellectual attributes based on ideas. These ideas can change institutions, which are the rules governing adaptation. We use care here: It would be a mistake to propose that property rights are more important than modes of production, or vice versa. Forms of production and property rights are related in such complex ways that it is of little benefit to argue about which came first or about which is most important. But trying to understand societies without the analysis of property rights leads to a one-sided view of culture change as materialistically determined by the forms and sources of production. Property rights and modes of production play equally significant roles. The following are found together: a kinship mode of production with public and then collective ownership rights, a tributary mode of production with state con-

Figure 3.2   **This diagram shows the relationship between human population growth and changes in modes of production.**

trol of property rights (modern socialism fits within this category), and capitalism with private property rights. There is a vivid "connectivity" between production and property rights that comes out in the recent work of Douglas North, the 1993 Nobel Prize winner in economic history. North is opening a new window to anthropological analysis for those who would look. Because so many contemporary socialist and state capitalist societies are going through transitions from state ownership to private ownership of property, it is a mistake to look only at forms of production as the causal factors forming "connectivity" and "process." Yet another force that changes society in complex ways is trade. In today's world, trade has become a transformer of societies, and social scientists are beginning to examine the role of trade in history. It is a particularly important primary feature of globalization.

Culture change, according to Marxist logic, is determined by dialectical forces, forces that are in opposition to each other, such as various forces of history and social classes of elites and masses who have differential access to the sources of production, for example, feudal landlords and peasants or modern capitalists and factory workers. Tensions between forces produce transformations, often through revolution. The new transformations, in turn, have their own internal contradictions that bring about new revolutions. Marxism attempts to explain revolution and rapid culture change as being due to the internal contradictions between the haves and the have-nots. In capitalist societies, change is driven by the interests of those who own the sources of production and those who do not (capital versus labor). Marxism tends to emphasize the internal sources of conflict (Harris 1979:141).

A weakness of Marxist and neo-Marxist models is that it is extremely difficult to analyze the "dialectic." There are so many oppositional forces at any point in history that analysis often gets bogged down or the analyst arbitrarily selects only the most obvious forces. In addition, there are many assumptions about the nature of class relationships that have not turned out to be true. In American society, the working-class and the capitalist class have often had the same conservative interests, and there has been little in the form of revolution. Another weakness of Marxist theory is a tendency to ignore the forces of property ownership and of trade, of ecological adaptation, and of external global forces to which the society must adapt. It is now argued by Marxist theoreticians that the Soviet Union collapsed because it attempted to remain closed and self-sufficient in a world of open trade and competitive markets. It had locked itself into a nonadaptive strategy that prevented it from participating effectively in the world market economy.

While Marxist theory and research strategies can be questioned, Marxist contributions to history and social science are indisputable. Of particular significance was the attention paid to the importance of economic factors in helping to form the social fabric. At a time when all other theories of cultural evolution were based on racial differences, Karl Marx's contribution to science is really remarkable. However, Marx's insistence, and that of his followers, that history (evolution) must move from infrastructure (modes of production) to structure (political institutions) to superstructure (ideology), due to dialectical forces, is the weakest feature of Marxist theory.

Marxism, evolutionary anthropology, and cultural materialism tend to rely on "deterministic" explanations, that is, simple cause–effect models (also called linear–causal models). This approach has weakened their appeal in recent decades. When writers in these schools break out of simple environmental or technological paradigms, their writings can have a great deal of power. Recently, Marvin Harris has revised his earlier version of cultural materialism by including in his "infrastructure" cognitive elements, which are much less materialistic (1994).

Interpretivism: Symbolic Anthropology and Postmodernism

Two recent schools of thought, which are often in opposition to materialistic explanations as well as each other, are postmodernism and symbolic anthropology. Postmodernism is principally a critique of conventional ethnography rather than a theory of culture. Postmodernists contend that the construction of cultural reality is not limited to a member of a culture, but is also true of the ethnographer writing about culture: He or she is bound to interpret that culture according to his or her own experiences as a culture-bearing human being. Postmodernists argue that a scientific and objective ethnography is not possible.

Postmodernism is a movement with origins in architecture and literary criticism that has permeated fields such as philosophy, history, and women's studies, as well as anthropology. Within anthropology, James Clifford, George Marcus, and Michael Fischer (Clifford and Marcus 1986; Marcus and Fischer 1986) argue there is no such thing as scientific ethnography. Marcus argues that postmodernist anthropology should be a "deconstruction" of ethnographic texts (showing how they are biased by the culture of the writer) or "experimentalist ethnography," creating new methodologies of ethnographic writing. One form of experimentalism is a dialogue between ethnographer and informant in which the process of communication becomes the object of study. Postmodernists look at writing about cultures as "text" and not as reality. At best, the postmodernist critique has opened the door to new kinds of ethnography—poetry, for example, and highly inventive writing that resembles novels. When done well and with sensitivity, these explorations open new vistas to understanding other cultures, or that of the ethnographer. But when done poorly and with little regard for scientific standards, postmodern ethnography degenerates into anyperson's commentary on another culture and herself or himself.

However, postmodernism is not really a theory of culture, nor is it a theory about culture change. It a theory about texts and the way that texts are constructed. In and of itself, it contributes little to our understanding of the stresses of globalization, a theme of this book, except for the stress it places on the importance of context. But the importance of context in understanding cultural practices and cultural change has long been accepted by professional ethnographers.

More pertinent to the points of view adopted in this text is **symbolic anthropology.** This is a subdiscipline of anthropology that has been the hallmark of Clifford Geertz and his followers, who defend ethnographic writing against the criticisms of postmodernists. Geertz's approach to ethnography is to emphasize the interpretation of the meaning and values of symbols in a culture. For this reason, his approach is sometimes referred to as **interpretivism.** Symbolic anthropologists argue that they have never thought of their ethnographies as pure science or pure reality, that they have always understood the problem of bias, but that techniques can be used that reduce bias. Clifford Geertz has developed a **thick description** model that attempts a rather Boasian understanding of culture from the point of view of the members of the society. This Geertz does by writing about an ethnographic event, such as a funeral or a dance or a theatrical presentation, in intense detail. These events are interpreted in light of the cultural setting and require an extensive understanding of the subject culture and its history.

   Geertz's writing is particularly rich and has become important to the Indonesian peoples whom he has been studying for many decades. He has been able to show how Indonesians respond to culture change by emphasizing their

Zulu attack on 80th British Regiment, 1879. The history of South Africa is not solely one of European success: The Zulus fought back.

own symbolic world, despite the pressures to abandon traditions. His approach is a continuation of the American school of historical anthropology and, in the right hands, can offer brilliant insights into other cultures. It is, to use a term introduced earlier, a fine example of emic analysis in anthropology.

Postmodernism and symbolic anthropology are both humanistic approaches to ethnography and both are rich in descriptive complexity, but only symbolic anthropology really addresses cultural change through study of how people respond to outside pressures by developing pride in their ethnic heritage. Another set of approaches depends on models—simplifications or abstractions of reality—that seek an understanding of how sociocultural systems work, adapt, and change.

Models of Change and Adaptation in Contemporary Anthropology

The two most important theoretical approaches to emerge over the last decade are the political economy model of cultural change and human ecology, also known as cultural ecology and human systems ecology (Smith & Reeves, eds. 1989). As mentioned earlier, political economy was the dominant approach of the social sciences before they specialized, and modern anthropology is the heir apparent of that approach (Wolf 1982). Culture change theory has its origins in the writings of many political economists, including many of the great writers and thinkers of the eighteenth and nineteenth centuries. Interest continues in the twentieth century, as exemplified particularly in the writings first of Julian Steward, Sol Tax, and Leslie White, and later of John W. Bennett and Eric Wolf. In modern anthropology, the political economy approach makes use of social science theory in the analysis of the creation of wealth, economic development, and disparities between rich and poor. In today's world, entire countries can be categorized into a world social structure of wealthy societies and poor ones. Many of these same writers have been concerned with cultural or human ecology, the examination of the human use of the planet's natural resources.

Political Economy Models How do cultures change? Theories of culture change in modern anthropology have been strongly influenced by models of economic development produced by development sociologists, economists, and economic historians. There are four distinct theories or models that have been important to anthropologists over the last half century: modernization theory, dependency theory, world systems theory, and the new institutional economics. These theories are not mutually exclusive, nor are they "right" or "wrong." The study of cultural change is a complex enterprise, and one in which the same data can often be interpreted in very different ways by distinct theories. Adding to the problems of the analyst, political leaders in developing regions of the world often use the theories described in textbooks, but get results that are at odds with what the theoreticians expect. Political theories that don't work have ways of producing political movements and countermovements, each with its own rhetoric. These four theories have been very important to the literature on cultural change.

Modernization theory held that the differences between the rich and poor countries of the world could be addressed by the introduction of Western technology and institutions. Modernization theory had an important impact on American political decisions made during the Cold War. For example, W. W. Rostow, an important advisor to the Kennedy–Johnson administrations during the war with Vietnam, argued that communist revolutions would occur in poor societies unless Western technologies and Western norms were adopted by them. He argued that if communist revolutions could be staved off and struggling societies could be Westernized, they would grow out of their poverty, and communist ideas would lose their attraction. Modernization theory reinforced American efforts to support the "democratic" governments and subsidize the introduction of advanced technologies and the development of industries that would produce goods once exported from rich countries to poor countries. The problem was that, in an effort to promote capitalist enterprises and fledgling democracies, the United States often overlooked the corruption that later bred violence. Also, many of the attempts to industrialize did not carefully consider the cultural context, and this led to failure. In Vietnam, American policies were first those of modernization, then the introduction of military advisors, and then an expanded role for the American military, none of which addressed the corruption of the Vietnamese elites. The attempt to "modernize" corrupt governments before they fell to communism became a leitmotif in the 1960s and 1970s.

At the same time that the United States was pouring development money into underdeveloped nations, Latin American economists developed an emic view that contradicted the etic view presented by modernization theorists. Responding to labor unrest, inflation, growing poverty, and political repression, they argued that instead of developing they were "underdeveloping" (Frank 1967). According to the United Nations Economic Commission on Latin America (ECLA), led by the Latin American economist, Raul Prebish, the emphasis placed on modernization only made poor countries more "dependent." According to **dependency theory,** as it came to be known, it was impossible to compete internationally with the more efficient firms in the industrialized West because of the monopoly the more efficient economies had over markets and production around the world, and particularly in the lesser developed parts of the world.

As this theory, developed by Latin American economists, was applied to other third world countries, the term *dependency* took on several meanings. However, in essence, the theory postulated a continued state of poverty for underdeveloped nations because these countries could never produce manufactured goods as efficiently as industrialized nations, no matter how they tried to adapt Western technology. Consequently, they were locked in a relationship with the strong countries according to which they had to export low-priced nonindustrial primary goods (minerals, foods) in exchange for high-priced secondary industrially manufactured goods.

At the same time that dependency writers were making their case, scholars in the new economic history were presenting contradictions to dependency theory. Their studies showed either that economic failures in Latin America were indigenous or that the Latin American economies were much more successful than the *dependista* literature showed (Coatsworth 1974, 1979, Duncan and

Rutledge 1977, Holloway 1977, McGreevy 1971, Stone 1977, Hunt 1973, Leff 1969, Dean 1969).

By the early 1970s, it became apparent to dependency theorists that their model was too narrow and did not take into consideration global forces that were transforming the world. In 1974, Immanuel Wallerstein published the first in a series of books and articles expounding world systems theory. **World systems theory** has largely supplanted or incorporated dependency theory. The world system perspective was a means to rethink the issues emerging out of the changing world economy of the 1970s and 1980s. World systems theory came about when a group of radical researchers led by Immanuel Wallerstein found that there were many economic and political relationships in the modern world that dependency theory could not explain. First, dependency theory could not explain the rise of the East Asian economic giants (Japan, Taiwan, South Korea, Hong Kong, and Singapore). Second, socialism, the dependency theorists' answer to dependency, was in a crisis state around the world. Third, there was a crisis in U. S. capitalism as the Vietnam War, Watergate, OPEC, national debt, negative balance of trade, and competition with the East Asian block took its toll (So 1990:170–171).

The new world systems description was not that of the relationship between an imperialistic country and its colony (Spain and Mexico, for example) but of the relationship between rich countries and poor and semi-poor countries, known as "core" and "periphery." The core consists of a network of connections among the countries that control the international capitalist system. The periphery is controlled by the core, and consists of those regions that export primarily nonprocessed commodities (raw materials) from mines, forests, or agriculture. The core grows, according to the Wallersteinian model, by extracting surplus from the periphery through its monopoly on world trade. The relationship of core to periphery thus guarantees the underdevelopment of the periphery.

The semi-periphery consists of regions that are in between core and periphery in their structural relationship to the world capitalist system. Thus, partially industrialized countries like Mexico or Brazil are considered by some to be semi-periphery (and by others are still periphery). The status of semi-periphery appears evolutionary as certain regions may go from periphery to semi-periphery to core with the proper policies (So 1990:184–185), as did Korea, Japan, and Taiwan.

Wallerstein's model allows for the analysis of the exploitative relationships between rich and poor states over the long run, and allows the development of more complex models that include the operation of international banks and lending agencies of rich countries. The monopolistic control and military domination of the periphery and semi-peripheries explain the growth of the core and the semi-periphery and poverty of the periphery. According to Wallerstein, the core "blocked" the periphery from becoming more prosperous and democratic.

To address this inequity, dependency and world systems theorists proposed the nationalization of privately owned industries in the periphery. These industries would then be protected from foreign competition by high tariffs on imports and supported further by government subsidies. Two distinct types of political economies emerged from this reasoning: state socialism and state capitalism. In fact, these two types are hard to distinguish from each other, and tend to be ideal types. State socialist or "command" economies lack true markets and have state ownership of resources. State capitalist systems are very similar but have market economies (Russia is a good example of state socialist and Mexico is a good example of state capitalist). Political leaders in many developing countries adopted these suggestions until the mid-1980s, when these protectionist measures eventually led to inefficient industries and bankrupt governments. Instead of becoming independent, these third world countries had to go back to the core nations to borrow money to stave off economic decline.

The world systems model has had a profound impact on anthropology, but Wallerstein's etic model saw these undeveloped societies as passively "acculturating" to Western norms while being kept poor. Eric Wolf has expanded Wallerstein's model in his book *Europe and the People Without History* (1982) in which he details the counterreaction by the peoples of the periphery to Western influence. His study shows that the cultures of the periphery were, first of all, not isolated societies but influenced by each other that they responded actively to Western core infiltration by selectively adopting certain norms and practices and resisting, often violently, other aspects of Western culture.

In the 1980s, global forces beyond the control of single states brought about the collapse of both state capitalism and state socialism, and brought these theories into question. The most dramatic example, of course, is the former Soviet Union, but other examples are found around the world so that only a handful of societies in the 1990s continue to operate according to either dependency or world systems theories. While many theoreticians continue to support the old models, the larger question of what happened to state capitalist and state socialist systems to cause them to collapse is drawing the attention of writers of economic history. New changes in the world's global economy are producing new models of economic change. One of these is the "new institutional economics" of Douglas North (a political economy approach). North, in *Structure and Change in Economic History* (1981), examined how trade, warfare, private property rights, politics, and the changing landscape of western Europe gave rise to capitalism in the sixteenth century. Instead of examining world systems, he examines the internal institutions of the core countries. He argues that the most important changes to countries are institutional, and that institutions matter and are forces in their own right. For example, if a country like Mexico cannot protect the property rights of peasants, how can it protect them against powerful ranchers or plantation owners? And if peasants are poor because they have few rights, is it not going to be difficult to pay industrial workers a high wage if they will be competing with poor rural people for jobs? The beginning point is securing the rights of the rural poor, and these rights cannot be secured without a basic change to Mexico's institutions, a subject discussed in another chapter.

North's recent work (1990) has shown how private property rights and the institutions of early capitalism influenced each other. Much of his work is being avidly read by economists in former socialist societies as they try to adapt their institutions to world trade. Jean Ensminger (1992) and James Acheson (1994) are leaders in promoting the ideas of the new institutional economics in anthropology, albeit not without criticism from dependency and world systems theorists. Ensminger's work with the Galole Orma of Kenya has shown how the Islamic religion has functioned to reduce transaction costs, improved the performance of trade, and led to greater centralization and "connectivity" of these nomadic peoples with other African societies. Acheson, who has been a long-time advocate of the study of property rights, entrepreneurship, markets, and efficiency (1986), has introduced Douglas North's theoretical perspective to modern cultural anthropology (1994). In a series of studies of furniture makers and fisherfolk in rural Mexico, he has shown how to study the relationships between transaction costs and institutions to explain how poor people overcome exploitation to survive in modern Mexico (Acheson 1995, 1996; Acheson and Wilson 1996). While world systems models and the new institutional economics appear to be opposed, we would like to argue that they are not. We hold that it is necessary to understand both the connections between rich and poor countries, (dependency and world systems theories) as well as how the institutions within rich and poor countries work (the new institutional economics).

In summary, three earlier models of economic history are now being called into question. Modernization theory was too naive in arguing that capitalism could be grafted on to the institutions of developing countries. Dependency and world systems theory, on the other hand, were equally guilty of assuming that developing countries could evolve in a capitalist world without capitalism. These three models do not explain what happened to the economies of the world over the last fifty years or since World War II, but what theoreticians thought happened. The new institutional economics argues that transaction costs (the expense of an economic transaction) must be lowered through reductions in corruption (which forces up the costs of transactions) in order to have prosperity. As will be examined in some detail in the regional chapters (9–12), the new institutional economics is very amenable to an economic anthropology approach, with anthropologists placing greater emphasis than economists on threats to values (ideology) and world view as significant transaction costs. We will argue that the success of the most recent model depends on some form of democracy. The evidence of institutional change in the direction of greater human freedom is apparent, but the negative impact of capitalist growth on ecosystems has not been removed. New problems are emerging in the forms of ideology and nation-building that were largely invisible during the cold war, when the only debate was the evils of socialism or capitalism. We now examine the issue of human adaptation to physical habitats.

Human Ecology and Political Ecology   According to Moreno–Black and Young (1992), human or cultural ecology models are meant to gain an understanding of habitat use by humans. The models test hypotheses through the use of systems concepts. These models constitute conceptual frameworks and vary from narrow models addressing specific situations to very broad models, but even the narrowest model is very complex and does not admit of linear causal reasoning (in a linear model, *a* causes *b, b* causes *c, c* causes *d,* and so on). The particular approach used is referred to as the **ecosystem approach** (Moreno–Black & Young 1992), and it suggests that culture and human biology grow out of concrete problems that people must solve in their everyday life (citing Moran 1982, 1990).

The ecosystem approach directs attention to biological, physical, and behavioral–cultural factors. However, most of the ecosystem models developed over the last half-century have not addressed the question of how human institutions, that is, human decision-making, is important to the process of human adaptation. The majority of anthropologists writing as "cultural ecologists" tended to focus on "human behavior" or "human culture" very broadly defined. But, as we learned in the last section on models of political economy, there are human constraints on behavior, and these constraints are due to the rules societies follow.

Currently, the study of political economy is having an impact on the study of human ecology. As outlined above, human ecology and cultural materialism both grew out of the pioneering work of Julian Steward on human/environment relationships. The paradigm that examines how systems interact through feedback loops has led to an interest in how institutions (decision-making) influence those feedback connections. A conference in 1985 attempted to distinguish the new interest in institutions by modifying the term *human ecology* to *human systems ecology*. The papers of that meeting were published in the volume *Human Systems Ecology* in 1989, and the ideas of that volume led to the book *World in Disorder: An Anthropological and Interdisciplinary Approach to Global Issues* (Smith 1995).

The approach of human systems ecology depended on the work of John W. Bennett, one of the few human ecology specialists to examine how such institutions as state bureaucracies, local political organizations, marketing, and the use of ecosystems interacted in a series of studies carried out in southern Saskatchewan. Bennett's work has had a dramatic impact on human ecology. Bennett argued that the interactions among ecosystems, cultural institutions, and human behavior play such a fundamental role in culture change and adaptation that they cannot be taken apart but can only be understood as analytically distinct systems that have complex feedback connections to one another. He holds that cultures and environments together form **socionatural systems** (Bennett 1976, 1993). This view differs from cultural materialism in its consideration of the institutional arrangements that mediate between human beings and the natural environment. Bennett's approach further diverges from the cultural materialists in that he conceptualizes humans as adapting to local ecosystems through human decision-making, not through natural selection. Bennett refers to this process as "minding," "anticipation," and "coping" (Bennett 1993). In Bennett's approach, local ecosystems become part of institutional change at the local level. For example, the Upper Middle West of North America has been transformed by American farming, and has transformed the original frontier cultures to such an extent that it is quite impossible to separate nature from culture. Finally, Bennett's human ecology does not accept either a materialist or symbolic anthropology point of view but combines both.

In Bennett's work, the macrosystems of the world interact at the local level through what he refers to as the "micro–macro nexus," the interaction of ecologies and institutions at the local level influenced by macro forces such as international trade (Bennett 1985). Bennett's work on the human systems ecology of modern southern Saskatchewan, Canada, shows how the people of the town of Jasper—farmers, ranchers, Cree Indians, and Mennonites—all respond to each other and to national, international, and local ecological pressures in a continuous process of adaptation and change (Bennett 1969). Bennett's work looks at the intersection of the forces of cultural change and human ecology.

In a series of papers dependent on Bennett's approach, scholars described a series of complex models that included regional ecosystems, hierarchical market and administrative forces, pressure groups, and other forms of quasi-organized social and political interests, that is, institutions (Smith and Reeves, eds. 1989). A major achievement of Bennett's ecological perspective is that it combines a concern for studying complex socioeconomic processes with a flexibility of analysis that takes into account micro- and macro-level decision-making as well as institutional pressures and facilities (Smith and Reeves 1989, Stonich 1993, Moreno-Black and Young 1992).

Human systems ecology models study the complex interrelationships among ecosystems, institutions, and world forces at the local level, thus complementing the more global models of cultural change. However, very recently the term *human systems ecology* has been replaced by **political ecology** in order to emphasize the importance of the political in the adaptive process (Stonich 1993: 25), and we are going to use that term here. Bennett's approach is clearly political ecology, but it is interdisciplinary, not just an anthropological approach, for it also belongs to geography and political science. Most of this text relies on a political ecology appoach. According to Susan Stonich, *Political Ecology = human ecology + political economy*. She argues that approaches of political economy models are not adequate by themselves to understand human adaptation at the local level, nor is a human ecology approach by itself. She argues for a more inclusive framework that "integrates political economic and human ecological analysis" (Stonich 1993:25):

> The political–economic analysis examines the interacting roles that social institutions (international, national, regional, and local) play in providing constraints and possibilities that affect human decisions that in turn affect those institutions as well as the natural environment. Human ecological analysis allows the consideration of crucial demographic factors, environmental concerns, and issues related to human health and nutrition. It expands the perspective of political economy to include a systematic examination of the distribution and use of resources and the dynamic contradictions between society and natural resources).

Understanding the Interaction of Changing Cultural Systems: Political Ecology

A political ecology approach unites the political economy model (focusing on institutions) with the human/environment interaction model (an approach that does not usually consider institutions). The political ecology model is truly interdisciplinary and it spells out many complex relationships among institutions and behaviors, political and economic development, demographics, and human resource management and exploitation.

The political ecology approach is very productive, particularly right now. In this time of rapid social change, we must look at not only relationships between institutions, but also how the transitions in one system influence transitions in the others. Most significantly, the tide of global capitalism, and the ineffectiveness of socialist command economies or protective state socialist economies are forcing transitions in political–economy institutions from "closed" systems to "open" systems. This can be called the economic transition. The economic transition is having a significant effect on the political systems in the countries making the transition to capitalism. In the process of privatizing property and businesses, the previous totalitarian, authoritarian, or communist systems are forced to relinquish some power and control. At the same time, the privatized companies, the individuals who control capital, and who now have global markets in which to participate, are gaining more power. They can demand increased representation in the political institutions. The interest groups representing new market forces must be balanced through the participation in the political arena of all previously disenfranchised groups. Otherwise, public support for market reforms will dwindle and disappear. This initiates a process of democratization we can call the political transition. Thus, we see that the economic transition forces a more democratic, or at least a more representative, form of government in several (but not all) nation states. But many Asiatic countries, such as Singapore, Malaysia, and Indonesia have not gone through the political transition. What political ecology tells the researcher to do is to open his/her eyes to institutions, but not to expect some unilinear causal connections as in earlier macrotheories of human cultural evolution.

There are many examples of the linkages between these two systems (economic and political) found throughout this text. A critical example is Russia, where Boris Yeltsin has been trying to force his country through the economic and political transitions while the political transition so far has only been from communism to authoritarianism (see Chapter 7). Another example is modern Mexico where three successive presidents, Miguel de La Madrid, Carlos Salinas de Gortari, and Ernesto Zedillo, have been attempting a very similar operation, introducing free markets into a one-party state controlled by a corrupt government (Chapter 12). Capitalism is thriving in Mexico, but Mexico is having a great deal of trouble making the transition to democracy. While capitalism opens the possibility to democratic reform it does not insure that the process will succeed.

Capitalism, in its global form, is often subject to outside pressures from the World Bank or the International Monetary Fund, outside investors, or various interest groups (international institutions) to force state capitalist and socialist systems to open their societies to outside investment and democratic reform. There are many examples. Outside pressures forced the current experiment with democracy in South Africa (Chapter 9), and it brought about the shift to democracy in Chile, Argentina, and Brazil (Chapter 12). Very recently internationalist pressures towards capitalist and democratic reform have weakened the power of the Congress Party in India, the single party that has ruled India since the 1950s.

The final expression of the political transition may be representative democracy, such as is found in the United States, or a more controlled, one-party state (Liberal Democratic Party) such as Japan or even more socialist style democracies such as Sweden, Norway, or Denmark. In some cases, the transition to capitalism does not lead to change in the political system. For example, Indonesia and Malaysia are capitalist societies with nondemocratic governments (Chapter 11). They may stay authoritarian for a long time, but the evidence from other Asian countries, such as Thailand and Korea, suggests that prosperity produces democratic forces. There is a long-standing debate between scholars who support the democratic transition process and those who do not, particularly supporters of the authoritarian governments of Singapore and other Asian states that have instituted Confucianist policies to reduce corruption (the topic of Confucian philosophy is covered in Chapter 11). According to these writers, Asian countries do not need democracy because they have self-disciplined governments that put the interests of people first.

Whatever the final outcome is, it will depend on the interaction of these two systems, political and economic, as well as the cultural values and ideology of the country. Sweden, for example, values equality, and Swedes are willing to distribute their wealth in the creation of a welfare state that minimizes the extremes between the wealthy and not-so-wealthy. While Americans supposedly believe in equality, there is also a very strong emphasis on unfettered capitalism, individualism, the work ethic, and the idea that anyone who tries hard can become prosperous. These values, however, have produced extremes of wealth and poverty.

The third system that is intricately related to the political and economic systems is the ecological system. The human concern with the environment is paramount in societies that live close to the land, such as most hunting–gathering and pastoral societies. With the advent of agriculture, humans began to shape the land to satisfy human needs, and populations swelled, putting more and more demands on the land. With industrialization, the link between humans and the land became even more tenuous and, for decades, our environment was abused and our natural resources depleted. During this time period, economic and political systems became disarticulated from each other, and human societies became disarticulated from their ecological systems, and we are now facing the consequences.

J. W. Bennett has called this process the ecological transition. His original meaning was quite different from ours, more pessimistic, with the transition from sustained yield societies (societies that live off nature's bounty) to modern societies characterized by nonsustainable growth (Bennett 1976). Nonsustainable growth is economic expansion that consumes the very resources needed for survival. But before discussing how we might approach a more optimistic model of the ecological transition, we need to understand a fourth transition to which it is intimately linked, called the demographic transition.

The demographic transition was first described in 1957 by H. Leibenstein in *Economic Backwardness and Economic Growth*. Leibenstein provided the first consistent theoretical framework explaining why families were getting smaller in prosperous societies. Previous theories had worked primarily on the basis of ethnocentric and naive, if not outright racist, assumptions about the nature of human sexual behavior. "Malthusianists" quoted Thomas A. Malthus and tended to believe in the natural sexuality of humans that cannot be controlled without state-imposed policy. According to Malthus, populations grow by geometric progression while agricultural production only grows arithmetically. Thus, according to Malthusianists, the world is doomed unless states pass laws preventing population growth.

"Natalists" on the other hand, tended to believe that growing populations develop the incentive to increase their economic production to keep ahead of population. Thus, population growth produces wealth (Overbeek 1974). Both the Malthusian and Natalist positions are myths.

Leibenstein's perspective is more enlightened. He views humans as having different values in terms of family size at different points in what is called the "demographic transition," which is basically the transition from poverty to prosperity, from agricultural to industrialized societies. He assumes that parents are able and willing to make a rough calculation of the costs and benefits of procreation; they are not blindly driven to reproduce. Parents will stop having children when the utility or satisfaction of the added child just matches the disutility or negative satisfaction of an added child (Leibenstein 1964, cited in Bennett 1976).

Leibenstein distinguished between three types of utility children yield to their parents. First, for most parents, children are a source of pleasure and can be considered like consumption goods. Second, children have value as productive agents, especially in more traditional and rural situations. And, third, children can provide insurance for old age or illness. The costs of the added child include the direct costs of food and shelter. Opportunity costs, or opportunities foregone, are the indirect costs. An example would be income that could have been earned by a woman had she not had to take care of a child, or a vacation trip that was foregone to pay for college tuition.

Leibenstein drew attention to what happens with prosperity and modernization: There is a higher survival rate for children and new occupational environments characterized by greater specialization and increased mobility. There is an increased need for expensive educations. Even with rising incomes per head, the cost of an added child goes up but his/her contribution to family income goes down because he/she must support his/her own family in modern societies. It becomes rational to have fewer children, and this is what happens.

This is the ideal model. But what has happened in the periphery? We should take a closer look at the demographic transition. John Bennett points out that the demographic transition has three stages:

1. The first stage is defined as the typical stage of affairs for most human beings: high birthrates balanced by high death rates with a slowly growing or fluctuating population. This describes India, China, and most of the countries of Latin America and Africa until recently, when modernizing institutions altered the picture.
2. The second stage, considered to be the true transition, occurs when improved nutrition and medical care, associated with early stages of industrialization and modernization, result in a lowered death rate while birthrates remain high; this

results in rapid population growth. Europe and North America went through this stage from about 1860 to 1950. This process has been operating to a greater or lesser degree in non-Western countries for the past century.

3. The third stage is associated with low birth and death rates, and a low rate of population increase. This comes about as levels of living rise, education spreads, and people begin to "trade off" fewer children for a better way of life (Bennett 1976:113).

It is the second stage that is a problem in the periphery. For various reasons, the transition from the second to the third stage is "blocked." Population growth is interwoven with other feedback cycles. For example, the drop in mortality rates in the periphery is due largely to improved disease control, which has been introduced quickly and cheaply, and has greatly outpaced significant economic change. The resulting population increases tend to cancel out small increases in wealth and goods due to economic growth. Given current high population growth rates and low economic growth rates in most countries of the periphery, the issue is whether these countries will ever reach the theoretical point of economic prosperity at which people opt for small families.

Having discussed the demographic transition, we would like to propose a three-stage ecological transition beginning with (1) the transition from hunting and food-gathering (food extraction) to food production, (2) a shift from pre-industrial to industrial production that is highly damaging to natural ecosystems, and (3) a shift that is occurring now from societies that are totally committed to industrial production to societies that are committed to sustainable resource management. This last phase is not to be regarded as a shift back to phase one in any sense, but is an outgrowth of the contemporary interest in trying to protect natural resources and wild habitats. Sustainable resource management is a commitment towards managing nature's resources (primarily extractive components of the economy: forests, seas, grazing lands, farms, mines) to do the least possible destruction to ecosystems. The control of policies that govern ecosystem misuse is usually in the hands of local, state, and federal governments. These attempt to minimize the impact of privately owned businesses, but in democratic societies there is a balance that has to be worked out between those who wish to preserve ecosystems and those who wish to expand the economy.

Now notice the links between the transitions. It appears that an economic transition leads to a political transition, and this leads to a demographic transition, which in turn leads to an ecological transition. That there are links between these four systems is clear, but why and how they are linked is not clear. In many instances, the process begins quite the other way, with a cultural and value shift in the direction of an ecological transition. In the United States, the value shift towards an ecological transition began in the 1960s. Modern Mexico, even with its blocked political transition, is trying to bring about an ecological transition, and this is true in many poor countries. One must be careful here because this is only an apparent link between "systems" without the study of institutional choice. Societies must make choices through their (changing) institutions as to how they are going to choose which of these transitions will be followed and how far. A democratic society may not choose to protect its habitats, but may choose to emphasize employment instead. This was true until quite recently of fairly democratic communities on the northwest coast of the United States that chose to cut down forests in order to give loggers jobs. Of course, the lumber corporations had much to gain from this choice and put pressure on communities to choose in an anti-environmental direction. Finally, the federal government, with pressure from other American communities, forced the protection of habitats, and many logging communities felt that their interests and democratic rights were being overridden by a powerful government.

The connections between the transitions, then, are mediated by institutions that are part of the transition process. There is nothing mechanical or really predictable about the connections between "systems." We return here to the link between a postulated ecological transition and an economic transition. It may be easier to protect habitats when societies are wealthy. Again, to many this will sound like a complete contradiction: Doesn't the creation of wealth destroy ecosystems? Yes. The evidence around the world for the last three hundred years is very clear, but the odd contradiction is that once societies have become economically prosperous, an ecological transition is possible and it is necessary. Why? Because one must invest wealth to protect habitats, and it takes wealthy societies to insure the protection of nature. More: We have no choice; We have to protect the planet we live on.

It is not possible in this text to articulate all the interactions between the systems and to show the adjustments that have been and are being made in the transitional periods of rapid change. Instead, we only wish to point in the direction of institutional analysis. One cannot study only how humans adapt directly to their habitats, but we must also examine how instiutions intervene in making choices. And before getting caught up in overly optimistic predictions, we should end here by pointing out that transitions can be blocked. Blocked transitions may be more common in our experience of the last century than positive passage.

A blocked transition is the lack of ability to pass through one of the four transitions because of a failure along one or more of the other transitions. As an example, the ecological transition is blocked in China because its authoritarian central government has chosen to support short-term economic development over habitats. Plans to build the Three Gorges Dam on the Yangtze River is opposed by every ecological group in China, but to little avail (see box in Chapter 11). The lack of democratic process blocks the possibility of people making choices that would facilitate an ecological transition. In India, a huge and growing population acts as a block on both the economic and political transition, and these blocked transitions act, in turn, to block either a demographic or ecological transition. Another example, given in the final chapter, of how a lack of movement in one transition can act to block movements in other transitions, comes from modern Mexico. There attempts to protect habitats are blocked by poor people whose values are locked into day-to-day survival (Chapter 13).

In the following chapters, students will have the opportunity to understand how these various transitions and blocked transitions operate without our (the writers) trying to explain every link, a task that would be monotonous to read and write. The study of the linkages between transitions appears to us to be the greatest challenge facing anthropologists in the rapidly approaching twenty-first century.

S ummary

Nineteenth-century ideas about cultural change were unilineal evolutionary theories postulating that all cultures progress inexorably from simple to complex. One of the most famous of these theories was that of Lewis Henry Morgan, who argued that cultures progress from a state of savagery to barbarism to civilization. Another set of theories to explain culture change and differences were those of the British and German diffusionists who believed that the development of civilization occurred in only one or a few centers and differentially diffused outward from these centers.

During the classic phase of anthropological thought, from 1900 to 1970, which began with a reaction against the speculative evolutionary theories of the nineteenth century, historical particularism as a school of thought was developed by Franz Boas and his students in the United States. Structural–functionalism (also known as British social anthropology) developed in Great Britain with two different emphases, those of Radcliffe–Brown and Malinowski. Both were to influence American anthropology in the 1940s and 1950s.

Three prominent theoreticians of the 1950s, Leslie White, Julian Steward, and Homer Barnett, held different ideas about culture change and evolution. White resurrected some of Morgan's ideas and postulated a form of unilinear or universal cultural evolution, based on human control and use of different forms of energy. Steward focused on the relationship between cultures and their environments and argued for a theory of multilinear or parallel evolution. In Steward's view, cultures that began as very similar would evolve in different directions if subjected to different forces, and those that began looking very different would end up looking very much the same if subjected to the same forces. Steward is considered to be the father of cultural ecology. Barnett, with his theory of innovation, located the source of all culture change in the human mind.

Contemporary theory in cultural anthropology is divided among four views, each with its variations: materialism, Marxism, interpretivism, and postmodernism. Cultural materialism is an outgrowth of both Steward's emphasis on environmental factors and White's heavy stress on technology as the basis of cultural evolution. Marxist explanations also emphasize the role of technology but tend to ignore environmental factors. Interpretivism, a continuation of historical particularism, focuses on the symbolic side of culture, looking to understand the meanings and values of symbols through the eyes of a culture's members. Postmodernism has its origins in literary criticism and is more a critique of ethnography than a theory of anything. Postmodernists argue that ethnography is a type of fiction constructed by the ethnographer.

Two currently important models of culture change are those of political economy and human ecology. In anthropology, political economy models examine a variety of economic and political factors as central to the process of cultural change.

Recent theories include modernization, dependency, world systems, and globalization. Human ecology models are an outgrowth of cultural ecology and cybernetics or systems theory. These models assume that humans and their cultures are simply one part of ecosystems that are always in a state of dynamic change. John Bennett says cultures and environments cannot be separated from one another.

Political ecology has become the more current designation for human systems ecology. Political ecology combines the interests of political economy in the links between productive activity and the distribution of power with the interests of human or cultural ecology in the interactions between humans and their biophysical environments. It is the perspective of political ecology that will be found throughout this book.

In the following chapter, we will look through anthropological eyes at some aspects of a complex culture of the core—the United States of America. In Chapters 5, 6, and 7, we will look at the progression of cultural complexity, beginning with cultures of the remote periphery (bands and tribes) in Chapter 5, examining chiefdoms and premodern states in Chapter 6, and providing an overview of the rise of capitalism and modern world systems in Chapter 7. These chapters are followed by four chapters covering major regions of the world and by a final chapter that summarizes current global issues.

Key Terms

Bands	**Mesoamerica**
Chiefdoms	**Modernization Theory**
Clan	**Modes of Production**
Cultural Evolution	**Paradigm**
Cultural Materialism	**Political Ecology**
Cybernetic Theory	**Redistribution**
Dependency Theory	**Social Darwinism**
Diffusionism	**Socionatural Systems**
Ecosystem	**Solidarity**
Ecosystem Approach	**States**
Functionalism	**Symbolic Anthropology**
Human Ecology	**Thick Description**
Infrastructural Level	**Tribes**
Institutions	**Tributary Economy**
Interpretivism	**Unilinear Evolution**
Kulturkreise	**World Systems Theory**
Lineage	

Culture in America

4

*I*n this chapter, we look at some ideas about how what we call American culture originated and some of the more important changes that its institutions have undergone during three hundred years. We are using *American* in the narrow sense of "United States of America." American culture has gone through several economic and political transitions. These transitions have involved different forms of democratic capitalism and distinct forms of decision-making that have changed through time. Many economic historians would argue that both democracy and capitalism have been important institutions in American culture from its very beginning, but the models for decision-making of two centuries ago are not those of today. Today, many argue, globalization is threatening American institutions and culture. Others argue that the threats are imaginary. But people act on the basis of what they believe is true. If Americans believe American culture is not what they expect or want it to be, then such perceptions are acted on politically through the decision-making process and new adaptations are worked out. But there is no sure way of knowing in advance how those decisions will affect the adaptive process. Will we be able to protect our natural habitats as we make decisions to adapt to the newly emerging "environment" of trade? How do we know? In making decisions about the future, the past can provide important guidelines.

It is important that American students have some sense of their own culture history and of the changes in America since the time of *Leave It to Beaver* in the 1950s (see the case study, page 122), a period in which the distance was great between lived reality and the media portrayals of it. In other words, the period was mythologized. But myth or not, much has changed, and it is important to understand the impact of those changes on American communities. The current macroprocess of globalization may threaten our democratic political culture or it may reinforce it. We are currently on the cusp of political change and it is difficult to judge which way we will go, but looking at the history of American society it is apparent that democracy as an institution has been an important feature of our culture since its early beginnings.

Institutions, wrote Bronislaw Malinowski (1960), are the charters of the culture, the basic codes or rules of living. Every culture has its basic rules, whether set down in religion and mythology or in an abstract written document such as the American Constitution.

Capitalism and Democratic Politics

The key facet of American adaptation, to both the natural habitat and to "world systems," has been capitalism. Capitalism informs the nature of minding, community organization, the use of time and space, psychology, and cognition. Capitalism is the institutional structure that dominates American culture. Another feature of American culture is democracy, a characteristic that is also a feature of Great Britain, but limited to the period since 1870. The histories of the two cultures are closely entwined. Great Britain and America have often been portrayed as the cultures that express democratic capitalism in its purist form. This generalization may or may not be true, but there is historical reason to believe that the British and Americans led in the innovations on how to balance democracy and capitalism. In Chapter 7, we will examine how capitalism, in its most open free market form, **laissez faire,** was highly damaging to the working classes of both cultures, an argument voiced by Karl Marx and other political economists.

Periodically, in British and American history, uncontrolled capitalism produced class stratification and the impoverishment of the working classes graphically described in the works of Charles Dickens. When this happened, the democratic forces in Great Britain and the United States imposed controls over the free market systems in attempts to protect the laboring classes. Social movements would move "to the left," in support of labor. While the reforms were often successful, they inevitably slowed economic growth because of the financial investments made in security nets for workers (Polanyi 1962). As the engines of growth slowed, the democratic alliances between workers and the middle classes would shift in the direction of capital interest groups, and the protective laws benefiting the working classes would be lifted. Social movements would move "to the right" in support of business. There would then be another cycle of rapid growth, class stratification, exploitation of the working class—and the rich got richer as the poor got poorer. Then the engines would reverse the process again. Karl Polanyi, examining democratic capitalism in Great Britain on the eve of World War II, greatly feared that democratic control of capitalism would be lost during the war. Many conservative scholars would argue that the opposite appears to have happened, although they share Polanyi's view that capitalism and democracy reinforce each other. Liberal theoreticians produce the opposite message, that capitalism is a threat to democracy due to its impact on the working class. Both positions have been defended with equal alacrity, for the evidence is always ambiguous.

The role of democracy in the United States has not remained stable. In the late nineteenth century, democracy contracted as industrial capitalism expanded. As the working classes were threatened by the same forces operating in

Great Britain, support for democratic government emerged, particularly during the presidency of Theodore Roosevelt. The collapse of the world economy in 1929 brought many antidemocratic movements into existence in the United States, but these largely vanished with the success of Franklin D. Roosevelt's programs, the impact of World War II, and later American political success during the Cold War. With the end of the Cold War, new political movements are once again emerging. Many are democratic but some appear to threaten our democratic institutions.

The United States has gone through cycles of political economy very similar to those described by Polanyi for Great Britain, usually at about the same time, hinting that there are worldwide cycles to capitalist expansion and contraction, an idea central to Immanuel Wallerstein's modern world system model. Two forces, expansion of capitalist production on the one hand versus protecting those who are least able to protect themselves on the other, drive American life (right versus left, capital versus labor). In general, since the turn of the century, conservatives tend to argue in favor of the first force and liberals in favor of the second. Since the beginning of the Great Depression, when the Democratic Party captured the White House up until the 1980s, the United States has been controlled by liberal political forces. Many conservative scholars argue that the country is currently going through one of the great generational changes in the direction of increasing economic growth by cutting back on liberal legislation protecting the working classes and the environment. Liberal scholars argue, on the other hand, that it is not a cyclical change but just a minor shift in voting patterns and that the new conservative direction in voting patterns will not last long. Regardless of who is right or wrong, the ability of Americans to change the direction of their economy is directly tied to a democratic government, which is a talisman of American culture.

The Origins of Democratic Capitalism (Community)

Americans are proud of being citizens of the most powerful democratic country in the world. Yet few know the origins of their own belief system, which arose in the American Enlightenment and is basic to understanding "American community." In the early 1960s, many college students were expected to read Alexis de Tocqueville's *Democracy in America,* a book originally published in the 1840s for the citizens of France. Its author wanted to explain what impact the ideology of democracy might have on culture and community, particularly what democracy might mean to the future of France, an objective he accomplished by studying American culture for two years (1831–1832) much as an anthropologist would. His book reads like an ethnography of America in the 1830s.

De Tocqueville's message was not particularly optimistic, for he speculated that there would be a steady deterioration in moral values if American culture was fully democratized. This warning is prescient of debates that are currently occurring. Think, for example, of the current conflict between those who favor the right-to-life and those who favor the right-to-choose. Is this an example of moral deterioration or is it the case that in a society as complex as that of America there is no single set of agreed-on moral values? Does democracy necessarily lead to the deterioration of moral values? Who determines acceptable moral values? De Tocqueville's underlying message is that Americans need to fully understand their own democratic heritage and its dynamic. It is a lesson we need to relearn.

During the past two decades there has been a reduction in the emphasis on Euro-American history and culture, as educators caught up in the multiculturalism movement argued the importance of giving equal time in the classroom to non-white, nonmajority cultures. This is an important message, and cultural anthropologists would generally agree. However, the framework of the society we live in is formed by the cultural values generated in the American Enlightenment, by its cultural ideals, particularly the core concept of tolerance. While American society has had its experiences with intolerance, particularly white intolerance of African Americans and Native Americans, the other cultures of this planet are rarely designed around the idea of tolerance. American students need to learn about American culture in order not to operate in a vacuum as to the origin and rationale for their own cultural values. However, we should bear in mind that all versions of history contain cultural biases, ours included. It is reasonable to suggest that the only way to really understand American culture is to learn about its multiple origins. It is thus valuable and important to introduce students to other culture histories, as it is also important to teach students about American culture. In this chapter we will not attempt this enormous task; rather we will provide an introductory overview to American political economy. This is not a history of America but an account of changes that have occurred to its key institutions, and to the relationship between democracy and capitalism.

New England Origins

American culture can be traced back to the Puritan and Pilgrim settlers of New England whose roots lie in the manorial villages of Champion country of East Anglia in England. The East Anglia community was a local specialization of the open-field village of the North European plain. It was brought to the fenlands of England by the Angles and Saxons from the mouth of the Elb River. The New England communities set up by the Puritans were highly democratic and egalitarian and were planned and organized well in advance of their construction and conformed to Yankee ideology (Arensberg and Kimball 1972: 103). The New England town was a political statement of equality.

The New England community consisted of a town built around a commons or "green." Next to the green were a church and town hall where the community's membership congregated to make political decisions and to worship. Democratic ideology determined democratic behavior. The territory of the community stretched over fields and woods used by farmers while artisans and shopkeepers clustered around the green. All were equal members of the community and had a right to speak and vote at town hall meetings. Unlike England, there were no aristocrats, and democracy was total. This is the culture that formed the basis for American political organization after the Revolutionary War, and it is the culture that de Tocqueville experienced and about which he wrote. It is also the ideal culture that Americans look back on, and it is the model on which American civilization was designed. Note, however, that equality extended only to the members of the community so conceived and did not include the Native Americans who were displaced from their lands—often killed—to make way for these democratic communities.

The nucleated settlement pattern meant that neighbors were fellow-townsmen. Neighborliness meant friendship and mutual help relationships (e.g., threshing rings). Communities were egalitarian and unstratified. They tended to support nuclear families that hived off easily to start new communities. The towns were ruled by householders who hired and fired their own clergy. They also

> . . . determined their own orthodoxy, enforced conformity and morality, easily mistaking their own common one class customs, under Calvinist Protestantism freed of hierarchical and external control, for exclusive religious truth, through the whole gamut of customs from belief to sumptuary law and Sabbath meeting (Arensberg and Kimball 1972: 104).

De Tocqueville wrote that this egalitarian culture was the most law-abiding on earth. There was a rule of law, and it needed but a very small number of law enforcers, not because laws were not broken but because everyone participated in enforcing the law so that it was difficult for a lawbreaker to escape.

In early America, the Village Green combined democratic politics and religion in the same church/city hall.

This egalitarian, no-nonsense democracy did not last out the colonial period, and social stratification occurred as the successful farmers and businessmen put distance between themselves and their common neighbors during the industrial revolution. The new nonegalitarian social order was that of the mill town and factory city.

Mill Town and Factory City

After the Revolutionary War, following the writing of the *U. S. Constitution,* with its acceptance of democracy as a spiritually sanctioned characteristic of the American people, a new type of political culture evolved in the United States: the mill town and factory city. These grew up in response to changes in material culture. The development of steel and railroads transformed the rural community in both the North and the South, as well as in Middle America. This new cultural model destroyed the democratic culture of old American society. The mill towns and factory cities were adaptations to the industrial revolution and were first imported from Great Britain in the early part of the nineteenth century. The cultural use of space was quite distinct from what came before. Mill towns had a stratified use of space, with the rich on the hill, the middle classes in the center of town, and the poor on the periphery and in slums (Arensberg and Kimball 1972: 113).

Factory and mill towns were developed in New England, Middle America, and the Deep South to create a new uniformity. They were constructed in a series of zones (Park, Burgess, and McKenzie 1925). In the center of town were the middle-class shops clustered around the main city park, often with a band shelter in the middle. Around the park were the monuments of the town: city hall, the county seat, the police department, the library, and the dominant church. The lower-class factory workers and immigrants lived on the outskirts of town, in the most blighted regions near the mills.

Economic historians, Robert W. Fogel (1964) and Albert Fishlow (1965), have shown how the material culture of the railroads transformed the American landscape due to increased efficiencies of transportation. In the middle of the nineteenth century, as railroads were introduced, stations were placed downtown, and hotels grew around them. From the train station and the downtown a grid pattern of streets grew, creating geometric towns and cities. Material culture transformed community organization, and was transformed by it. The railroads allowed the creation of suburbs where many of the middle elites of the mills and factories moved to live. The pattern of graded and successive zones of better or worse neighborhoods "mirrors perfectly the scaler stratification of incomes, of power, and of prestige in zonal succession as one moves inward from withdrawn garden suburb to blighted tenement district" (Arensberg and Kimball 1972: 113).

The use of time in the new towns of the industrializing nineteenth century differed from that of earlier rural communities, for now the factory whistle rather than the sun determined human activities. It was no longer the seasons that determined work effort, but the supply and demand schedules of industrial society with which we are so familiar today. Here, again, is an example of how symbolic culture was transformed by material culture. However, this "Victorian" style community, symbolized by the manager looking at his pocket watch, is now rapidly passing out of existence. The age we live in is the logical working out of the invention of the automobile, the branch factory, the proliferation of "peer groups," the growth of huge suburban communities, the interstate, and the mall (Arensberg and Kimball 1972: 114). The automobile, the mall, and the interstate, all examples of material culture, continue to funnel American community organization in directions that appear unstoppable. Cheap goods coupled with efficient and rapid transportation crunch old community patterns of life, and ways of behaving that are hundreds of years old give way to new patterns as part of an adaptive process, without people being fully aware of the changes themselves or the potential magnitude of their consequences.

But lest we get caught up in too deterministic an explanation of culture change (cultural materialism), we have to realize that we, as members of our communities, agreed to buy cars, and made choices that have in turn transformed our lives. In many regions of Europe (e.g., Belgium), laws have been created outlawing malls. In England there are regions of "high roads" that battle the coming of the malls, but the price paid for their goods is much higher than ours. Before material culture can transform community, behavior, and ideology, institutions have to change to accommodate the new inventions.

One approach in anthropology to describing national changes in a complex nation state is to focus on a single community. The case study beginning on page 116 is of the once village, once town, and now city of La Crosse, Wisconsin (50,000). Like most communities in the United States, La Crosse both reflects cultural change at the national level but has its own individual peculiarities not so shared, which set it aside as its own culture with its own identity.

The Modern American State: Mass Democracy and Pluralist Society

We have detailed cultural changes at the community level for La Crosse, Wisconsin from the frontier period (1840s) to the modern period. At the national level, the nation state of the United States went through a parallel series of transitions. The modern capitalist and democratic United States is, in terms of world history, a relatively novel phenomenon that is now disappearing. Many of its features were considered ideal by leading American and European intellectuals of the Enlightenment such as René Descartes, Denis Diderot, John Stuart Mill, David Ricardo, Adam Smith, Thomas Jefferson, and Benjamin Franklin. Their visions presented an outline of what the culture of modern capitalist democracies should look like. Distinct writers stressed different parts of the model. Some stressed capitalism (Adam Smith), others democracy (Rousseau), or private property rights (David Ricardo), or human rights (Diderot), and a few discussed the productive balance among the four (Jefferson and Franklin). Jefferson and Franklin appear to have been fascinated by the relationship between capitalism and democracy.

The United States went through three phases between 1865 and 1970. The first phase saw industrial elites controlling the masses through hand-picked politicians. Democracy was threatened. This phase coincides with the beginnings of corporate capitalism and lasted roughly from the end of the Civil War until just before World War I. The second phase is that of "mass democratic capitalism," which required the political integration of the nation state to the point where it could compete with other like societies for core status in the modern world system. It begins with Teddy Roosevelt's attack on monopoly capitalism. The key to this phase is the capitulation of capitalist elites to the political needs of the middle classes and working classes whose support was needed in order to gain control of the international economy. It was a phase of extreme nationalism as the political integration of the nation–state demanded patriotism. Two world wars were fought during this phase, and they proved the patriotism of the various ethnic groups and social classes of the United States.

The period between the wars and directly after, particularly the 1950s, has become the touchstone of our image of family life. This is the period when the transition from the rural to urban social structures had been completed, and largely European ethnic groups had assimilated to American culture. Large families of five or more children had been replaced with the smaller "American nuclear family," with a father, mother, and two or three children. The symbolic culture of the time just before and after World War II idealized the successful family as one in which the father faced the outside world of the community and the mother dealt with the family's day-in, day-out struggle. The male head of family and the female had two separate spheres of influence, community (male) and family (female), but these distinctions have never been firm. The television series, *Leave It to Beaver*, of the 1950s and 1960s, captures the intricacies of these relationships, for the father often had to explain the morality tale for the story in question (inside the family) and the mother often participated in community life, where she also had her own domain with other women. In the period since the 1950s, the male role as authority figure in the family has faded to a co-partner role, and the role of women outside of the family has grown in ways that are hard to measure. The symbolic culture of the time just before World War II and directly after had set expectations of the ideals of American culture: equality and the resolution of life's problems through technology. These images of American life were caught in the early years of television and now have become nostalgic set pieces as we realize how much more complex the institutions of the family are, and that the impact of technology is often disorienting and destructive.

The third phase, that of "**pluralist democracy,**" begins after World War II. In the earlier phase of mass democracy, the dominant ethnic white population was in control and paid scant attention to the needs or rights of minorities. In the third phase, the development of a rule of law forced the dominant white, Protestant, Anglo-Saxon culture to share power. One reason for this shift is clear: the need for the political support of all ethnic and minority populations by the state. In modern, industrial societies, the infrastructures of transportation and indus-

Case Study: Culture Change in La Crosse, Wisconsin

La Crosse is a community of 50,000 people located in Western Wisconsin on the Upper Mississippi River. Although a very scenic part of the United States, it suffers intensely cold winters and often hot muggy summers. The history of La Crosse is fairly representative of the New England–Upper Midwest pattern (the New England model was exported to the Upper Midwest). The main sources for this case study are Berthrong (1948), Miller (1959), and Sanford and Hersheimer (1951).

The Frontier Years As is true for most Midwest communities, the original community plan was brought in by Yankee settlers in the early nineteenth century. This plan was mildly modified by German settlers who escaped the aftermath of the German Revolution of 1848. The original highly democratic Yankee pattern became more stratified with the introduction of Germanic culture, but the underlying political system remained. La Crosse was and is a river town, with a highly developed commercial culture and behavior. The community was transformed into a mill–factory town in the late nineteenth century that more or less corresponded to the introduction of Germanic culture.

The frontier phase of Prairie La Crosse had a plural set of cultural characteristics found in most river towns. The material and symbolic culture of river towns differs drastically from "inland" farm towns. La Crosse was a river town, with steamships trading cargo from Minneapolis and St. Paul to the north to St. Louis and New Orleans to the south. There was also the important trade across the river to and from points west. Front Street, on the Mississippi, was a tolerant mixture of lumberjacks, traders, rivermen, hunters, and businessmen. One temporary resident was Buffalo Bill (Cody), whose long-haired friend James (White Beaver) Powell ran a local pharmacy (and some say he was a patent medicine doctor). The city developed a distinctive "live and let live" attitude that was quite distinct from inland farming cities with their sober-sided, church-going ways. The inland towns were formed by less heterogenous ethnic groups: Lutheran Norwegians or Protestant (or Catholic) Germans, who farmed and complained of the wild ways of the river folk. Later, when a college was established, the party town reputation of the city became a permanent label, and the inlanders continued to view the city of La Crosse as a wild and woolly place. In recent years, Oktoberfest, a regional festival, has continued the symbolic statement with a focus on beer drinking and polkas, often much to the dismay of those who wish the city to have a quieter image.

Another American cultural characteristic of the city was its polyethnic culture. La Crosse, like most American cities, is multicultural and always has been. Sawmills and logging attracted Scandinavians, while trapping and trading drew the French (giving French Island its name). As the city became a mill town, other ethnic populations were attracted: Greeks, Syrians, and Germans. In recent times the city has absorbed Hmong, Vietnamese, and Cuban refugees.

The Winnebago Indians, who today refer to themselves as the Ho Chunk Nation (People of the Original Speech), deserve special mention because of their complex relationship to the city and region. The Ho Chunk people, whom archaeologists trace to the Oneoto cultures of the Upper Mississippian (an archaeo-

In the 19th century, the economy of the Upper Mississippi River depended on colorful paddle wheelers.

logical phase), are a Siouan people who migrated from the region of Green Bay in the seventeenth and eighteenth centuries. Estimates are that a village of 600 lived in the La Crosse region before the Anglo village of La Crosse was built in the 1840s. These people suffered the indignities typical of American Indians, in addition to which they were under a government mandate from the 1840s to move from western Wisconsin to the Turkey River in northeast Iowa. They were reluctant to leave and were forced out at gunpoint, but many filtered back to small villages on the outskirts of the growing city of La Crosse. About one-half of the tribe finally moved west to Iowa, Montana, the Dakotas, and Nebraska. Never a reservation people, they were forced to move from the region, but always trickled back. Between forty to fifty families became a part of the city, and participated in the city's growth,

but other Ho Chunk, called the Non-Treaty faction or "Wandering Winnebago," maintained an identity apart. In very recent years, many of these Wisconsin families have used their federally recognized status to develop casinos that have financed improvements in their lives.

La Crosse has gone through several cycles of ecological and cultural change. Beginning as an agricultural town based on the lumber industry, lumber was transported primarily by river steamer, which helped to develop a river-oriented commercial culture. In the 1870s, the lumber industry grew, dramatically transforming the village into a mill town with many industries specializing in wood products.

While the workers in the forests and lumberyards were primarily Scandinavian, the owners of the mills were New England Yankees. Class stratification at the turn of the century had the Yankees and Germans on the top of the pyramid. Scandinavians, Greeks, and Syrians were on the bottom. There were few blacks, Hispanics, or other non-Europeans.

The first public buildings in the new city were churches, the first of which was Baptist (1852), followed in immediate succession by Congregationalists (New England), and Methodists. Several German Jewish families escaping the Revolution of 1848 founded the Hebrew Indigent, Sick, and Burial Society, which came to be a prominent organization. A synagogue followed quickly. Typical for nineteenth-century American communities, there was a tremendous flurry of organizational activity right after the community was founded. This organizational facility of young America was a fact that struck the young de Tocqueville as one of the prominent features of American culture. He was accustomed to his native France where most people expected government to do everything. The idea of people building their own schools, hospitals, or libraries was astonishing to de Tocqueville. One of the first successful endeavors was founding a public library in the 1850s, along with public schools. The city was organized in 1851 (with a population of 1,636 Americans and 304 foreign born), and the first school was built only four years later in 1855.

The Middle Years The first settlers built along the Mississippi River, and the first streets followed its curves. But by the 1860s, the residents of La Crosse tried to impose the New England model on the landscape with a grid form of street organization. Another organizational feature that appeared at this time was a dual division between the city's north and south sides. The wealthy upper and middle classes of Yankee and German extraction built their homes on the south side while Scandinavian, Polish, Greek and other ethnic groups organized neighborhoods on the north side of town. The railroad split the town in half. The north side became the home of the railway workers and other working-class populations. The southern part of the North side became the ethnically diverse "Goosetown," which later became a part of the present University of Wisconsin–La Crosse when it expanded in the 1960s. (When the University expanded in the 1960s, it bought out the people living in Goosetown. In the late 1980s, when multiculturalism became popular, the area in question was given a special entranceway, and Goosetown was ceremoniously symbolized as a part of the campus. No one seems to know why the area came to be called Goosetown in the first place.)

During its Middle Years (1870–1929), the city became highly diversified in commerce and manufacturing but lost much of its democratic ethos. The list of enterprises is long and ranges from boat-building to the construction of doors, church decorations, plows, automobile gauges, and the production of beer. Many of the German immigrants founded micro breweries with associated beer halls. By the mid-1880s, La Crosse was one of the Midwest's major trade and jobbing centers.

One consequence of the city's economic diversity was great stability and the lack of a clear division between social classes. Despite the north–south division mentioned above, the status grades of the city blended into each other, and this is reflected in the city's architecture. There are wealthy homes but there are no wealthy neighborhoods, and almost all working-class neighborhoods have a scattered number of substantial or expensive homes. This democratic pattern is mirrored in the graveyards, which reflect the city's architecture: Even in death there is no clear stratification. Thus, in the material culture seen in the architecture and graveyards, the symbolism of democracy was maintained despite the autocratic norms of the elites in the late nineteenth and early twentieth centuries.

After the lumber industry collapsed *circa* 1910, the city's newspapers predicted the collapse of the regional economy. But the La Crosse Board of Trade and the La Crosse Manufacturers and Jobbers Union developed a policy of hiring jobless workers. The result was economic stability. Few recessions or depressions have affected the city as badly as in other parts of the country. Most businessmen were conservative and tended not to overbuild, so when economic difficulties struck they were able to ride them out and actually hired workers from other closed plants.

In the late nineteenth century, there was a concentration of power in the hands of a few families who controlled city hall. Democratic La Crosse of 1850 had been replaced by the turn of the century with class stratification. Family dynasties grew and intermarried. For example, Franz Bartel founded Bartel Brewery and was president of his own corporation. His brother was vice-president, another brother was secretary–treasurer. Franz was alderman for the eleventh ward and later president of the common council. The economic elite and the political elite were the same group of wealthy industrialists. This feature of American life has disappeared in many places. Today in small towns and cities the economic elite seldom serve in political offices. But at the turn of the century, the city's political economy was monopolized by a few intermarried families. A reading of the organizational charts of the city's dominant enterprises at the turn of the century shows members of elite families sitting on each other's boards of directors, and their names appear as mayors and aldermen. The same individuals dominated almost all of the city's major civic and service clubs, churches, and business organizations. This feature of American life was common across the country at the turn of the century. A small clique of wealthy businessmen ran the city, and most of the citizens admired this rather narrow nobility.

While the commercial elite of the city controlled political life, most people had little to do with city politics. At the turn of the century the needs of the people were met through voluntary associations put together on the basis of common interest. Many of these were ethnic organizations, such as the German Deutcher Verein and Turnverein, the Norwegian Sons of Norway, and Irish Ancient Order of Hiberians. Most other ethnic groups, such as Czechs, Poles, Austrians, and Swedes, centered their activities in their churches. During this time period, while the Winnebago and other American Indians of the region were ignored or discriminated against, the paintings of Indians playing the game of La Crosse became common in public government and educational buildings.

The Modern Period   The Modern Period began in 1929 and continues, although since the late 1980s La Crosse has been affected by globalization, so historians of the future may distinguish the post-1985 period. It is characterized by the decreasing political activity of the local elites and the increasing influence of state and federal governments. It is also marked by the disappearance of ethnic voluntary associations and the specialization or disappearance of many other voluntary groups.

New political movements once again introduced democratic reforms. Many of the reforms were initiated by the populist president Teddy Roosevelt at the national level. In Wisconsin, the reforms were introduced by the Progressive Party. Next door in Minnesota, political changes were introduced by the Farm Labor Party. These became most noticeable during the 1930s when Franklin D. Roosevelt became president. The major complaint at the turn of the century was that when the Democrats took over city hall they were usually Catholic and would turn the Republican Lutherans out of office. The "spoils" system of patronage dominated municipal government. Political "bosses" rewarded their followers with jobs. After 1910, the Progressive Movement, led by "Fighting Bob La Follette," ended the spoils system. A merit system was introduced to determine who was hired for city departments. These democratic features became common in other communities of the United States as well during this time period (although Chicago and Kansas City continued to be run by bosses until the 1960s).

In part this transformation is the consequence of the changing political structure of the United States. Political reforms during the Progressive Era (coinciding with the presidency of Theodore Roosevelt) led to greater democracy as more people were allowed to vote. However, while more people voted, they voted against the leadership of the old elites. By the 1920s, the elite families ceased to participate directly in the political system but continued to exercise considerable control behind the scenes.

The Crash of 1929 and the following Depression was economically devastating for the United States. Characteristically, the city of La Crosse got off lightly, thanks to the large number of small, distinct kinds of industries and commercial activities. World War II took the city out of the Depression with the rest of the country.

During the 1950s and 1960s, the city began to lose its political autonomy. In the late 1980s and 1990s, it lost its economic identity due to globalization. As is true for all American communities, state and federal laws began to regulate the environment, schools, social security, business enterprises, and human rights. The city's elites retired even from behind-the-scenes politics, and in many instances sold their companies to national corporations. While many small businesses continued to be locally owned, the larger enterprises either became nationally known corporations (such as the Heileman's Brewery and Trane Air Conditioning) or they were purchased by national corporations. In the last decade, the two largest employers, Heileman's Brewery and Trane Air Conditioning, entered the age of globalization when the companies were purchased by transnational interest groups, had their assets manipulated, faced bankruptcy, downsized by firing workers, were streamlined and modernized. Trane, now known as Altec, Inc., which was begun by a local entrepreneur, is now controlled by transnational interests and no longer is identified as a local company. Many working-class residents feel they no longer have a sense of identity with these or other companies as regional loyalties and identities are globalized.

The community of La Crosse is a microcosm of socioeconomic trends throughout the United States. Urban crime, gangs, drugs, and increasing insecurity for the working class, all once considered the characteristics of Chicago or Milwaukee, are now reported in the local *La Crosse Tribune*, which underscores in its reporting the intimate nature of the threats of globalization.

---

try are sensitive to attack by any group. Electrical grids, telecommunications, and road systems are easily damaged, in contrast to earlier centuries. The more sophisticated the technology becomes, the more sensitive it is to damage. Thus, in the modern age it is dangerous for the state to antagonize its ethnic and minority populations because they may attack the structures of the state through sabotage of the technology it depends on.

There is a second reason for this transformation, and this is the spread of the American ideology of the rule of law described by de Tocqueville. According to the philosophy of the rule of law, I cannot expect others to obey the law if I break it (or, put another way, don't expect me to obey the law unless you do the same, de Tocqueville 1957). In the middle of the twentieth century, the working classes and ethnic and minority groups threatened the White middle class and elites with warfare and with the disruption of the society if they did not develop and obey laws protecting all. This doctrine of equity is critical in the modern age, when the weakest group can do immense damage to private property and to the state if not given equal treatment. A modern technologically advanced society needs the talents of all segments of its population. It cannot compete with other countries if part of its own population is held back or held down.

Individualism in American Society

While many of the values that characterized Beaver's generation, such as a positive attitude towards work and effort, a belief in moral absolutes, and a powerful sense of American destiny, have either disappeared or have been reduced in importance, individualism has not. Visitors to the United States are still impressed by the great importance placed on individualism, self-reliance and freedom. Many visitors have a hard time understanding the expression of individual rights, such as the lack of gun control, and the stress placed on self-reliance. Children are often perceived as overly assertive, and Americans are often stereotyped as "abrasive, chaotic, and impulsive," particularly by Asians (Harris and Moran 1987: 342). The Chinese American anthropologist, Francis Hsu, noted the importance of self-reliance, an expression of individualism, in his studies of school systems in the United States over forty years ago. He wrote that self-reliance was a "militant ideal" parents inculcated in their children, a concept that was diametrically the opposite of the Asian ideal of collective responsibility. For Hsu, the American writer and philosopher Ralph Waldo Emerson idealized individualism and self-reliance in his writings.

The political philosopher, Harold Lasky, believed that the American tradition of individualism was reflected in the suspicion of the state, which was derived from the frontier experience. The job of Americans on the frontier was to build a house, sow crops, and put physical effort into survival, which gave self-reliance and individualism special sanctity as virtues. Jeffersonian democracy was a political expression of this ethos and pragmatism was its philosophy: the priority of action over theory (Lasky 1948).

In their popular book, *Habits of the Heart*, sociologist Robert Bellah and his colleagues found that individualism was still the heart of American culture, but that in the almost half-century since Lasky's book, Americans have lost their sense of community and responsibility (1985). Bellah did not locate individualism on the American frontier, as in Lasky's interpretation, but in the seventeenth-century English radical philosophical defense of individual rights. These rights come from "nature" and precede society (they precede the "social contract" forming society), a concept derived from the writings of John Locke. Bellah and his colleagues view individualism as coexisting with "classical repub-

■ *Case Study: Leave It to Beaver: The Mythologizing of Corporate America*

*L*eave It to Beaver set down for white Americans the ideals of their own culture, but the picture was stereotypical and more mythological than real. We are instructed in what the American "ideal" culture was a half-century ago by studying *Leave It to Beaver*. Theodore "Beaver" Cleaver, seven years old, his father Ward, mother June, and twelve-year-old brother live in an average American neighborhood in an average American town. Ward Cleaver goes to work every day at a job that is not identified. However, by clothing and language, one assumes he has an occupation working for a bank or corporation. June Cleaver stays home and keeps "the Beav" out of trouble.

This sitcom is perhaps the most enduring example of the American middle-class landscape. The first run of the series lasted six years, but in 1982 it was still being shown daily in thirty-five of the largest U. S. cities, as well as in Japan and Africa (Himmelstein 1984). Himmelstein describes the early sitcom as follows:

> . . . suburban-middle-class landscape television comedy was a comedy of reassurance. Beneath its funny situations . . . was a very narrowly uniform world view . . . the "urban outlook" [framing] a world in which principles of fair play prevailed; judges were sober; lawyers were intelligent and honest; police were calm, understanding, brave, and, above all, incorruptible; everyone had a right to freedom of speech; everyone

An icon of "Middle America": The Cleaver family.

was entitled to the best possible education; the able hard-working person would, with a bit of luck, do well financially . . . . (1984:88–89).

Leave It to Beaver is really a series of morality stories explaining white American ideology to viewers. It supplies the viewer with an explicit commentary on American values in the 1950s, and, as mythology, it poses a strong contrast to contemporary American culture with all of its self-doubt and violence. Unlike the modern family, husband and wife constitute the basic kinship unit, the nuclear family. There is brother Wally, Beaver, father Ward, and mother June. The Cleavers are "average" and middle-class. One assumes that Ward has an average income; he drives an average car and lives in an average house. Like most Americans, Ward, and June have just two children (average). Divorce was not common in the culture displayed, and one assumed that Ward and wife would one day move into an average retirement home.

Arthur Niehoff and Conrad Arensberg refer to one common American characteristic that Beaver learns as *twofold* judgments. Typical of 1950s America was the tendency to make judgments by assigning an event to low or high value: moral–immoral, legal–illegal, right–wrong, success–failure, clean–dirty, modern–outmoded, civilized–primitive, developed–underdeveloped, practical–impractical, introvert–extrovert, secular–religious, Christian–pagan (Niehoff and Arensberg 1963). Beaver is taught that there is a right and a wrong, truth and falsity, and grows up in a secure world where the players all know which is which.

The Beaver is taught to *equate work with time,* using the least amount of time to produce the greatest work—the American idea of efficiency. He is taught that people are paid for sustained effort, but that they must budget and plan the hours "spent." The tyranny of time appears in the clock over the kitchen counter to which everyone in the family ties their day.

But, *effort is a good unto itself,* and Beaver learns this lesson. With every effort one can expect success. The high value placed on effort and activity pass to the principle that: "It is better to do something than to sit back and do nothing" (Niehoff & Arensberg 1963: 124). The national linking of effort to activity and the notion that these are linked to success are particularly American, a lesson for the Beaver, and reflect a severe moral code. Those who were not active, and thus not successful, were not moral, not acceptable.

Effort and success in turn were linked to *a belief in progress* and a positive view of the future that is always in the process of becoming. The accent is on youth, success, progress. No one grows old in Beaver's white world, and no one fails. Does the Beaver have grandparents? In the TV series, there are no old people in retirement homes in the 1950s, and there are no street people.

A disappearing feature of American culture depicted in the series is the importance of voluntary associations. In the series, Beaver's father and mother are constantly attending parent–teacher meetings, Rotary, Elks, church and other adult groups, while Beaver and his brother train for future participation in voluntary associations by joining Cub and Boy Scouts. Many worry today about the reduction in American participation in voluntary associations. De Tocqueville saw these as the heart of democratic American culture. With reduced participation in civil activities and politics, and increasing volatility associated with differences in moral perspectives, will Americans turn increasingly to authoritarian ideologies that will tell them what to do?

Finally, Beaver and Wally learn two other important principles that Americans value today: equality and humanitarianism. Social equality is an ideal to strive for. Our legal and institutional heritage prescribes equal rights and condemns privilege. Everyone should have an equal opportunity. But in Beaver's world such violent incidents in American history as Selma, Alabama, are ignored, nor is there any reference to Martin Luther King and racism.

With egalitarianism goes the American trait of humanitarianism, which the Beaver extends to cats and dogs. Americans respond liberally to calls for help and give all they can to others during a disaster. He learns that this is a heritage of his pioneer ancestors, and he applies it in many of the morality tales.

The values that the Beaver learned in his idealized and mythological world were broadcast throughout America, and it was widely accepted that this was the way America was, despite considerable easily observable evidence to the contrary. This model, which never accurately reflected reality, has fragmented, shattered. Many Americans now stand looking back at this media-constructed, mythological world of the 1950s and 1960s, and contrast it, rather than the realities of that time period, to their postmodern present.

licanism" and "biblical religion," both of which have faded and been replaced by a more "therapeutic" ethos devoted to replacing "community" with special arrangements to maximize the individualistic longing of Americans. They cite de Tocqueville's classic *Democracy in America*, which described both individualism and the high rate of participation by Americans in community organizations. They argue that special schools and therapy groups such as "parents without partners" have replaced Rotary Club, Lion's Club, Kiwanis, Chamber of Commerce, and the Knights of Columbus. Americans are, more than ever, members of a "lonely crowd," the title of David Riesman's sociological best seller in 1950.

While Bellah's book may overstate the loss of community organizations, recent reports show a dramatic decrease in participation by Americans in community organizations. The recent trend towards anti-state politics and attacks on the federal government fit both earlier and recent interpretations of American individualism and self-reliance philosophies. Globalization, which is seen as threatening both family and community, also plays a significant role. What is globalization?

$\mathcal{G}$lobalization and Our Postmodern Society

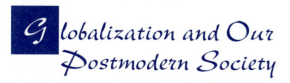

Globalization has radically restructured American community organization and culture, often in ways we are discovering we do not like. *Globalization* is the term used to describe the linkage of finance to robotics and high-powered computers around the world as well as the linking of households to each other through electronic media. We are living in the age of a revolution in information technology, one in which the largest growing sector of the economy is the software industry. Jobs in the steel industry are vanishing as countries like the modern Philippines or Indonesia build steel plants using cheap labor. The United States and other former industrial countries are being pressured to "push the envelope" in the development of ever more advanced information technologies. The "transaction cost" of communication is dropping almost to zero, and in reality it costs very little more to call someone in London than in the United States. The cutting edge of the economy is no longer automobile manufacturing, but internet communications with thousands of new jobs produced that could not even have been thought of a generation ago. This process began in the 1970s and information technology has largely replaced "modern" or industrial technology. This means that we are into a new world system distinct from the "modern world" system in which Beaver grew up. The term "postmodern" is sometimes used to describe societies that are based on information processing rather than industry.

The changes in the world system depend on the export of computer/robot-based technologies to the countries of the periphery and semi-periphery (including former socialist societies). As information processing becomes more critical to the "old core" and new jobs are created that require a knowledge of computer technology, the old industrial occupations are being transferred to the old "periphery" and "semi-periphery." The high-wage industrial jobs created by the determined efforts of labor unions between World War II and 1980 are evaporating. Governments, such as Thailand and the Philippines, offer transnational corporations tax breaks to develop industries in order to escape age-old poverty. The consequence is that industrial occupations are being lost by the core to the countries of the periphery and semi-periphery. As jobs are lost, the standard of living of the "average" American slips and members of the middle class fall into the lower class. Beaver's world has vanished and his values are questioned (the same process is occurring in Europe with similar political consequences).

The collapse of portions of the middle class into the lower class is having ripple effects throughout the American political landscape. Everywhere politicians are blamed for processes of change that are beyond their control. In the United States, the consequence was the loss of the 1992 election by Republican George Bush to Democrat Bill Clinton, and more recently the take-over of the Senate, the Congress, and many statehouses by conservative Republicans.

A new social-class system is developing in the United States. Highly educated people are likely to find good jobs and will be able to take advantage of new occupational opportunities. Those who are not well educated face a future of shrinking opportunities and poverty (and we are seeing the creation of an underclass). The most affluent 20 percent of American households average twelve times the income of the poorest fifth, and that poorest fifth is more often than not minority and inner city. The promises that the extension of civil rights offered in the 1960s and 1970s crumble beneath a stark economic reality in which jobs do not exist for those who are not highly educated and cannot take advantage of high technology occupations.

In a postmodern society, that which is central to successful adaptation lies in the worlds of finance, information processing, and telecommunications (what were once relatively unimportant sectors of the economy). These are now the drivers of the modern world's economy. They are the core of the new sociocultural system. Industrial production is still important and will remain so, but it is no longer the driving force. As traditional industries become increasingly robot and computer controlled, many jobs requiring complex skills are displaced by computers and fewer skilled workers are needed to assemble industrially made products. Behavior is changing to fit the demands of the new technology. Industries can be constructed anywhere in the world to take advantage of cheap labor. Thus, automobile plants can be built in Sri Lanka or Paraguay as easily as Pennsylvania or Maryland, but labor costs are much lower in the periphery. Workers in such plants in the core will see their wages fall because of the lowered need for the highly specialized knowledge that gave their parents high incomes. In addition, fewer people are needed to run the new robot plants, putting many out of work permanently unless new technologies are developed to create new occupations. Workers lose jobs for one of two reasons: (1) it is cheaper to use capital equipment (computers) or (2) cheaper labor is found elsewhere. In instances where neither (1) nor (2) operate, then skilled workers will keep their jobs at regular wage rates.

The only way that Americans can maintain or gain status and prosperity is to push the envelope of technological innovation at the edges of science and to replace the old industrial plants with new ones based on skills requiring high levels of education. But this presents a real threat to those without good educations. They become angry at their lot in life and often act out their emotions through violence. American society is experiencing one of the most violent periods in its history.

Competition in the new global system is going to require changes in the way that Americans think about their institutions. This is particularly true for the family, community, education, government, and industry and their relationships to each other. Ideologies will change as globalism transforms the society. But, we are not alone. The ills that befall Americans are found throughout the countries of the old core. However, American problems have become exacerbated over the last decade due to the growth of the national debt, which has made it next to impossible to temporarily "fix" many of the things that are "broken," such as the inner cities, education, the environment, health care, and the homeless poor. The traditional right to own guns has contributed to increasing violence. Murder rates in cities such as Los Angeles and Detroit are among the highest in the world. American expectations about individual privileges and rights have led to a large drug culture that has become intricately interrelated with violence.

In Beaver's time, American society pioneered modernization and American institutions were among the most advanced in the world. In the modernization process, institutions must be constantly changing to adapt to technological shifts and world trade patterns. But in a society as powerful, rich, and successful as the United States, complaints that American institutions were becoming outdated fell on deaf ears until recently. Most of the critiques of American society that are becoming part of modern populist political movements have been voiced for decades (Reich 1991, Thurow 1992, Lodge 1990, Etzioni 1993). An overwhelming focus on the Cold War and international relations prevented American political leaders from being sensitive to the deterioration of their own society due to a reduction in community and family values in favor of the individual. It was not until the end of the Cold War that Americans began to look more closely at their own society and became disillusioned.

Anthropology, Ethnography, and Research on American Social Issues

Many anthropologists, including Roy Rappaport (1994), think that American institutions are out of adjustment due to the revolution in information technology that has created behavioral problems. He argues that anthropologists should turn from research on "the other" (bands, tribes, chiefdoms, peasants) and concentrate their efforts on how the institutions of American culture have deteriorated. He argues that anthropologists should help solve some of the problems that occur in the transition from industrially based societies to societies based on information technology. Several recent ethnographies address public policy issues objectively, but the in-depth approach of ethnography makes it apparent that there are no simple solutions.

The Inner Cities: Racism and Ethnographies of the Dispossessed

As we have learned, over the last three decades high technology industries have moved out of the inner cities and into the suburbs, taking high-paying jobs with them. White flight to the suburbs coincided with the collapse of many of the low-skill industries, which moved abroad, particularly in steel and automobile manufacturing. These labor-intensive industries no longer exist or are vastly reduced. The consequence is a lack of jobs for the inner-city poor. Earlier in the century racism created towns with white centers and outlying pockets of poor, predominantly African American neighborhoods. Now the centers are made up of minority populations (mostly African American and Hispanic) and the outlying districts are predominantly (but not entirely) prosperous white. African Americans, Hispanics, and other inner-city minority groups feel that they are victims of racism (Wilson 1987, 1991).

William Julius Wilson, an African American sociologist at Harvard University, has recently presented a critique of government policies in the inner cities. In *When Work Disappears* (1996) Wilson argues that it is not poverty but joblessness that is producing violent social pathologies in the inner cities. Joblessness leads to men not marrying. Without the civilizing influence of women, some men turn violent. Mass unemployment destroys the institutions that create and enforce social behavior: small businesses, voluntary associations, informal friendship networks, but most importantly, the family. For men, he argues, employment is strongly linked to marriage and fatherhood. Men who cannot support families do not form them. Among African Americans of inner-city Chicago whom he studied, almost 60 percent of those between the ages of eighteen and

Los Angeles is a multicultural experience.

forty-four have never been married. African American men who were born in the early 1940s were more than twice as likely to marry than those born in the late 1950s, when blue-collar occupations were disappearing. It has been an ancient argument in anthropology that women teach men (and boys) to be nonviolent; so it is easy to understand that when men do not marry, social pathologies emerge in the form of violence and aggression.

When violent behavior is combined with drugs and guns, then life turns cheap. These trends are producing populations with social pathologies that have recently been described by ethnographers of the inner cities. Philippe Bourgois, an anthropologist at San Francisco State University, has summarized his experiences working with Puerto Ricans in New York City (1996). His description begins with an exhortation to fellow ethnographers for detailed studies of the type he has tried to carry out because of his conviction that such studies could raise critical debates. His ethnography of Puerto Ricans in New York fleshes out Wilson's sociological description for African Americans of Chicago, but it does not lead to neat policy suggestions. His studies raise questions about public policies that he does not pretend to answer.

Most telling is the portrait of the creation of violent personalities through the very agencies meant to save the youth of the inner city. Bourgois reaches out to describe inner-city gang members and crack dealers, but is repelled by their extreme violence. His analysis shows how Caesar, brutalized by his own family, turns to lord it over those weaker than he. He describes Caesar's "gratuitous violence," which put him into a "special education" category in junior high school. Once in special education, Caesar could claim Supplemental Security Income and laugh at the entire system. Bourgois's ethnography neither minces words nor editorializes, but it does underscore the point made in Wilson's work: Unemployment, not poverty, leads to the disintegration of the family and the appearance of the violent male, one who has little to lose through antisocial behavior, and whom society both fears and admires (for shunning "the system").

Migration, Ethnicity, and Ethnic Conflict

A related topic of research is that of migration and cultural conflict in the United States. The Immigration Act of 1965 opened the doors of the United States to immigrants from all over the world, but over the last several years there have been political questions in the state of California and elsewhere about a continued open-door policy. Many African American supporters of the Democratic Party (including the late Congresswoman Barbara Jordan) have begun to question support for immigrants who compete for jobs in the inner city. Interest groups supporting immigrants, which also have ties to the Democratic party, favor continued support for open migration policies.

There have been conflicts between minority groups of the inner city and new immigrants captured in the ethnographic research of Kyeoung Park of the University of California–Los Angeles. As with Bourgois's work on inner city Puerto Ricans in New York, Park's work on ethnic Koreans in Los Angeles does not suggest policy, but it does explain the nature of conflict between Koreans and African Americans in Los Angeles. Park begins by focusing on the shooting death of Latasha Harlins, a black teenager killed by a Korean grocer, Soon Ja Du, in a dispute over a $1.79 bottle of orange juice. A Superior Court Judge fined Du $500.00 and ordered her to perform 400 hours of community service. The judge did not feel that Du was a menace to society. The light sentence angered the African American community: "You shoot a dog and you go to jail. You shoot a black kid and you get probation" (Park 1996: 492).

Park carried out an ethnographic study of the conflict between the two groups. He argues that the situation is not just a dyadic opposition between African Americans and Koreans, but a triadic one based on white racism, an assertion which is difficult to prove. His analysis shows that the minority community of inner-city Los Angeles has been increasingly isolated and marginalized, losing 70,000 high-wage, stable jobs between 1978 and 1982. Major companies such as General Motors, Goodyear, Firestone, and Bethlehem Steel closed plants in and around South Central Los Angeles so that by 1990, only 59 percent of adults worked. This is the time period when Korean immigrant merchants entered urban neighborhoods where the cost of starting or purchasing a business was relatively low. Koreans relied on traditional means of capital accumulation, such as the *kye*, a rotating credit association that allowed members to contribute capital to a central pool to be used to start a business, which was then paid back for use by others in the association. The small businesses used few or no employees, but depended for labor on family members. The Korean ventures were comparatively successful; for example, 70 percent of the area's gas stations are now owned by Koreans (Park 1996: 493).

Conflict between African Americans and Koreans is rooted in the diminishing resource base of South Central Los Angeles, but it is exacerbated by cultural differences. For example, Koreans believe themselves to be more civilized than "any other people except the Chinese" (Park 1996: 494), but in the United States they are forced to occupy a subordinate position in the U. S. system of ethnic stratification, and, having experienced discrimination, some turn around and apply the treatment they have received to other minorities. Korean merchants attribute the main causes of incidents between the two groups to differences in culture (some arguing that Koreans have more culture than African Americans, others arguing that White oppression towards the African American community explains its members' behavior). Both groups, African Americans and Koreans, argue that the media exacerbates cultural differences and makes situations appear worse than they are (Park 1996).

Like Bourgois, Park has shed light on the dynamics of race and ethnicity through ethnographic description. Both writers stop short of suggesting changes of public policy, and leave the reader more sensitive to the plight of minority groups of the inner city. This type of scientific research, while it raises more questions than it answers, is extremely valuable.

Ethnography and Globalization in Rural America

The notion of globalization tends to be applied to urban and suburban regions, but it applies to the rural heartland of America as well. Ethnographic and ethnohistoric research by Shaunna L. Scott on Harlan County, Kentucky, shows how pervasive the impact of globalization has been (1995). Harlan County has been of interest to social science since the 1930s due to labor union activities against the domineering mining industry.

Appalachian coal miner kisses grandson.

In the 1930s, Harlan County became known as "Bloody Harlan," a familiar story of Appalachian ethnic culture facing outside interest groups with solidarity and tight union cohesion, but by the 1990s, Harlan County residents have fallen away from union solidarity. Scott shows how the increased mechanization of mining, the growing prosperity of a workforce no longer involved in mining, and the increased employment of women replacing men in the mines has led to decreased union identification and activity. Despite obvious antagonisms, the mining community has diminished resources on which to mobilize union activity, a common feature of globalization in American culture where labor unions have only a third the strength they did a generation ago.

The Family, Sex, and Gender in Modern Societies

What is the family? Is the family a father, mother, married children, and their children as we find in modernizing China? Is the family a woman with several children and no resident husband–father, as often occurs in American society? Do two coresident lesbians and a child form a family? And, what is marriage? Is marriage the legal union of a man and woman to legitimate their children? Does a couple who simply live together differ from a couple who are legally married? These questions illustrate the paradoxes of trying to define marriage and the family. They also touch on some contemporary social debates with legal implications in American society today.

Here is an early anthropological definition of marriage:

> Marriage is a union between a man and woman such that the children born to the woman are recognized as legitimate offspring of both partners (Royal Anthropological Institute 1951).

Clearly this definition would not work well in modern American society, nor does it work well with the varied marriage and family structures studied by anthropologists around the world. One recent definition suggested by sociologists to incorporate all the different family forms defines marriage as **sexual bonding** and the variation of family systems is defined through the use of the phrase **family realm.** This suggests that the family is a cross-generational set of relationships that includes a concern for members, caregiving, and altruistic but intense emotionality (Eschleman 1994: 3). However, these very broad definitions would not satisfy the narrower ideas of family held by members of different cultures around the world. Other more specific definitions would be what the German intellectual Max Weber would refer to as **ideal types.** Ideal types are abstractions and do not reflect reality (Weber 1949). The ideal for the American middle class is the **nuclear family,** composed of a married pair who are husband and wife, and the children of the marriage. In this ideal type, marriage legitimates the children of a sexual union between husband and wife. In Beaver's time, the majority of marriages in the United States led to nuclear families with **neolocal** residence, according to which husband and wife set up housekeeping without reference to the families of the bride or the groom.

Arland Thornton has documented many changes to the family since Beaver's time. There has been a weakening of the ideal of marrying young, having children, restricting intimate relations just to the marriage bed, and maintaining separate roles for men and women (Thornton 1989). Many sociologists and anthropologists believe that the changes to the family are the consequence of a loss of functions. As early as the 1930s, William Ogburn argued that the family would disappear if it continued to lose its key functions, which he listed: economic, prestige and status, education, protection, religion, recreation, and affection and procreation (Ogburn 1938). He believed that as the nuclear family lost these functions it would disappear. Modern conservatives argue that the reason for the disintegration of the family is a self-fulfilling prophecy: The family has changed from nuclear family to the blended family because of the American ideology of freedom. Religious conservatives argue that selfish values have changed policy and the family has fallen apart not because of a loss of functions but due to policy changes on the part of government that reflect the selfish world view of the middle class.

The first position, which is a traditional social science argument, begins with the point of view that American society in the nineteenth century was patriarchal with its roots in religion, and as religion became less important, the patriarchal family was transformed into the nuclear family. With further losses in functions, the nuclear family fell apart. The patriarchal family is the one described by the Apostle Paul:

> Wives submit yourselves unto your husbands, for the husband is the head of the wife. . . . Therefore as the church is subject unto Christ so let the wives be their own husbands in everything (quoted in Eschleman 1994).

Sociologists and anthropologists like to argue that, as Americans lost their religious beliefs, the patriarchal family disintegrated and that by the late twentieth century it had lost its functions and disappeared. In patriarchal American society, the wife was caring, submissive, slender, and erotic while the husband was self-reliant, strong, aggressive, and dominant (Eschleman 1994: 13). Sociologists argue that as the functions of the family disappeared, men and women became more equal and challenged the notion of male supremacy, changing relations between the sexes, and with that, inventing new forms of family structure. The commonly held belief is that blended and matrifocal families are America's unique answers to achieving equality. The real picture shows that new forms of family life may not be as adaptive as social scientists once hoped.

A 1994 study by the U. S. Census Bureau found that, indeed, the nuclear family is disappearing. In 1991, 50.8% of all children still lived in such families. But that means that nearly half lived in some other arrangement: with single parents, stepparents, half siblings, and so on. In 1970, 66 percent of all families were nuclear.

When broken down by ethnic groupings, the statistics are even more dramatic. Fifty-seven percent of White Americans live in nuclear families, 38 percent of Hispanic Americans, and 25 percent of African Americans. In 1991, of 7.5 million African American families in the United States, 3.43 million or 45.9 percent were headed by single women. Anthropologists refer to these families as **matrifocal.** The figure for white Americans is 13.2 percent. Of those matrifocal families with children under the age of eighteen, about one-fifth of the mothers were divorced, and nearly three of five were single. In other words, most matrifocal households among African Americans never had a husband present but were created by births to single women.

The phenomenon of teen-age pregnancy has become a political issue, with conservatives arguing that the best way to deal with the issue is to stop supporting teen-age mothers through welfare. Research among teen-age mothers reveals several other issues that also promise to heat up the debate. One thousand teenage mothers interviewed reported that their sexual liaisons were predominantly with older men, not for children but for love. These young mothers reported that it was their own poor self-image that drove them into the arms of older lovers who had no intention of marrying them. The report further states that all of these children with children had no fathers.

Liberals argue that the reason for the matrifocal structure of African American communities is poverty. In 1991, 51.1 percent of all African American families and 28.4 percent of all white families below the poverty datum line were female-headed. Does the family structure explain poverty or does poverty explain family structure? Probably each contributes to the other, but what policies would begin to shift the two around? Robert Staples shows that the proliferation of matrifocal families has been the most significant change in the African American family in the last thirty years (Staples 1985). William J. Wilson argues that a fundamental cause for these changes is globalization, the erosion of America's industrial base. The lack of jobs for many less-educated African Americans has severely damaged their ability to provide for their families and to maintain traditional male roles. Wilson argues that it is the lack of jobs, not welfare dependence, that is responsible for the increase in African American matricentric families (Wilson 1987). But given our current welfare policies, a resident male with a job will likely make a mother ineligible for Aid to Dependent Children. If the male doesn't make enough to support the family without aid, the absence of the male can be seen as a strategic adaptation.

Sexuality in American Life

An important element in the arguments and assumptions of academic writers regarding human sexuality was and is the need to increase human rights to match the natural human sexual response. Several decades ago, William H. Masters and Virginia E. Johnson's book *Human Sexual Response* (1966) put forth statistics regarding American sexuality that led to changes in American attitudes towards marriage and sexuality. Their report showed that both men and women had sexual affairs before and after marriage at higher rates than usually assumed or accepted. Most social scientists assume that sexuality has steadily increased since their book was first published, and the American mass media reflects these assumptions, particularly in movies. However, a recent and surprising study by researchers at the University of Chicago's National Opinion Research Center (Michael, Gagnon, Laumann, and Kolata 1994) gives a very different picture.

According to this study, extramarital affairs are actually rare. About 94 percent of American couples living together are married. Most stay faithful to each other and, on the average, have sex with each other once a week. In any one year, only three to four percent of married people have affairs. Another startling and anti-Masters statistic shows that only 15 percent of all couples have sex with someone other than their spouse at any time during their marriage. Homosexuality is rarer than commonly thought: only 2.2 percent of men have had sex with another man in the past year.

The other statistics fall into more familiar patterns. The biggest change from fifty years ago is sex before marriage. Women are catching up to men. Girls are becoming sexually active at an earlier age. In 1960 the average age was 19; in 1990 the figure was 17. Women are also marrying later. The net result is that there are longer periods of sex before marriage (on average 7.5 years for women and 10.4 for men). Americans are still having lots of unprotected sex with many different partners, but with marriage, both partners stick to one another.

The impact of this study has yet to be assessed. What it is saying is that while people experience sex early, overall they tend to be more dedicated to each other over a lifetime and less apt to be involved in relations with persons other than their lover or spouse than is popularly assumed. One could interpret these results to mean that increased premarital sex coupled with marriage at a later age leads to greater faithfulness (less cheating) and more stable marriages.

The Structure of the Family in Modernizing Societies

In American and Western European society, the social transition has been from patriarchal, large families to small, more egalitarian families. Women's struggles for equal rights have not been met by mass resistance, although there are political movements that challenge the growth in women's rights. But women still fall far short of true equality. How are family structures and gender rights changing in other societies? We will take up these issues in other chapters touching on other world regions. Here we summarize a few of the assumptions of Western social scientists and make some very general comments about modernizing societies. It is difficult to generalize to all developing regions because there is tremendous variation from, say, Iran with its Islamic fundamentalism, to South Korea with its imitation of Western popular culture and respect for traditional Confucian and Buddhist values.

In Chapters 5 and 6, we examine kinship among bands, tribes, chiefdoms, and premodern states. All human societies are characterized by complex webs of kinship that tie together family groups and regulate sexuality, childbearing, and the relationships of kinsmen to one another. Earlier Western-based theories in sociology and anthropology assumed that the transitions would be from clans, lineages, and large families to small but stable nuclear family units such as once characterized the countries of the core. The kinship systems of peoples of the old cores and peripheries were viewed as strange and anthropologists traveled around the world to describe unusual systems of kinship and marriage, such as societies where women married one another, or where men and women married but then immediately obtained divorces and took on lovers, or where homosexual men (called Berdaches among the Cheyenne) were considered normal and allowed to live as female men, or where women bore children out of wedlock and the children were raised by the child's grandmother until the mother found a husband. Today, American systems of kinship and marriage contain these and many other customs of marriage that were once considered "pagan" or "uncivilized."

At one time it was theorized that non-Western kinship and family organization would one day take on Western characteristics. But, while families are, indeed, getting smaller following the demographic transition, they are not changing in the direction of isolated nuclear families, nor is the family breaking up, American-style, in all modernizing cultures. One of the reasons for the lack of "Westernization" is that the violence in American society and its "throw-away" consumer-oriented culture are often pointed to by editorial writers and politicians in developing countries, such as Mexico and Guatemala, but also Shanghai and Taiwan, as not healthy and the consequence of the breakdown of the family. Many social critics tend to point to traditional cultural and family values as a means of escaping the trends in American society. Whether this means that, in the long run, the family in these cultures can escape the social forces at work in American society, or if in fact those forces are self-fulfilling prophesies, is difficult to gauge. Both arguments can be made to work with the facts. We should also note that in America, the cost of care for the elderly continues to climb, and more and more American families are caring for elderly parents in their homes, thus creating an extended family arrangement as an adaptive strategy. While societies may influence one another's forms of kinship, marriage, and family organization, what stabilizes as a predominant pattern for any significant length of time will represent a strategic adaptation to existing context and circumstances.

In Asiatic countries like India or China, while families are getting smaller, people still continue to trace descent back through clans and lineages to ancient times. In India and China (which we will look at more closely later), males are so important to the succession of the family that women abort female fetuses in favor of males. In other Asian cultures, such as South Korea, Taiwan, and Hong Kong, family social structure is used to maintain business enterprises. This is particularly true among the elite social classes, and is less true among rural laborers who move to the urban regions of Asia. Nonetheless, anthropologists are aware that the simplistic and mechanistic explanation that modernization causes the breakdown of the family does not apply in many instances (So 1990). It is becoming more and more evident that marriage and kinship are not just influenced by technology and economic change, but that they are greatly influenced by ideology: by what people believe is good or bad. And what people believe is good is usually what people believe will be a successful strategy—even if, in the long run, it turns out not to be.

Social movements with ideologies of female equality have influenced human relationships rather dramatically since the 1960s in Western cultures. **Feminism** has become a powerful movement towards equality on college campuses and few lack a department of women's studies today. In Latin American countries, the argument in favor of women's rights is quite often countered by arguments in favor of the family and of religion. Women's rights movements are often viewed as threats to society in general, but many of the trends found in the United States, such as the sexual abuse of women by men, the trend towards single-family households headed by women, and the disruption of male occupations, are evident in Latin America. Latin American clerics and conservative social critics tend to blame American values, particularly feminism, for these trends. Liberal journalists and many academics argue that both the United States and Latin America are responding to the same forces and that women need to be granted greater rights and protection.

Whatever the differences between American and modernizing societies, one of the difficulties young women face around the world is the great pressure to work outside of the home and at the same time to marry, bear children, and take care of the family. While men increasingly share in household chores, most studies show that they fall short and women do most of the household work everywhere. It is also a relatively universal fact that women earn less than men, in many instances far less.

Summary

American culture, and the other cultures of the core, are going through very similar changes. While this chapter has focused on American culture, were one to study Great Britain, France, Germany, or Italy, the same features of culture change would appear. Globalization has reduced peoples' trust in their political systems. There has been a general trend towards borrowing so that all national debts are relatively large, and all governments in the core are going through the identical and painful processes of "downsizing." As governments trim down, people feel less supported by their governments and are less supportive of them. Ethnic intolerance has become more common throughout Western Europe, although not yet in the violent form found in Yugoslavia, a topic covered elsewhere. The lack of trust in central governments has politicians worried. In the United States, the bombing of the federal building in Oklahoma City is an extreme example of the sudden lack of trust by some Americans in their own government. The Freemen movement is another example.

Women in rich countries are demanding greater rights, and to some extent achieving them. Their sisters in poorer countries often work outside of the home and support families without the political rights and powers women in rich countries are beginning to take for granted.

There is a general movement throughout all core countries, including such social welfare experiments as Sweden and Norway, toward a reduction in the extent of state control. Parallel changes are occurring in the countries of the periphery and semi-periphery, but perhaps for very different reasons, such as the growing importance of democracy in poor countries. With the growing conservatism, however, there is an increased awareness of the importance of habitat, of ecosystems and their preservation. When political conservatives began making threats against environmental laws in the United States, voters soon made it obvious that their anger against the state was not to be confused with a lack of interest in protecting the environment.

This chapter has focused on American society and its increasingly out of balance institutions. Part of the change that is occurring worldwide is that the core is losing control of world trade and the countries of the periphery and semi-periphery are suddenly shifting in their allegiances to core countries and in their institutional arrangements. Their successes and challenges will be examined in the chapters on world regions.

Key Terms

Family Realm	**Matrifocal**
Feminism	**Neolocal Residence**
Globalization	**Nuclear Family**
Ideal Type	**Pluralist Democracy**
Laissez Faire	**Sexual Bonding**

Bands and Tribes: Remote Peripheries

As we begin this discussion of bands and tribes, we must note that modern bands and tribes do not necessarily bear much resemblance to their paleolithic and neolithic ancestors. Only to a limited degree can we understand the bands and tribes of the distant past through the study of historic survivals on the peripheries of modern civilizations. A combination of archaeological evidence, historical accounts, and ethnographic descriptions allows us to make inferences about the economy, sociopolitical organization, and material culture of bands and tribes that existed prior to the development of chiefdoms and states. But we should remember, in doing so, two important points: First, that the classification we use (band, tribe, chiefdom, state) is itself an arbitrary categorization of a continuum of culture types; second, that all of our historic and ethnographic, and much of our archaeological, data come from cultures that are the products of complex cultural evolutionary processes, not pristine paleolithic and neolithic forms.

Bands of hunters and gatherers and tribes with a variety of different subsistence techniques exist or coexist on the periphery of the modern world system. In the past, they were present on the peripheries of archaic empires. They generally lack forms of hierarchy. All other things being equal, which they never are, it is the remoteness from archaic or modern cores that best explains the lack of hierarchy in bands and tribes. The closer they are to trade routes, the more likely they are to develop hierarchical forms of organization.

Hunter-Gatherer Bands: Existing Outside of Civilization

Hunting and food-gathering bands are the most remote societies both in time and space. Almost every region of the world still supports a handful of these societies and they are extremely important to modern anthropology because they can teach us something about how societies once "lived lightly on the land." They also teach us that hunters and food-gatherers are radically different from ourselves in ways we would not expect. While they hunt animals, they are generally peaceable. The relationships between men and women tend toward egalitarian, and while they worship nature, their attitudes toward day-to-day events are pragmatic and optimistic. (Tribal societies, on the other hand, whether pastoral or agricultural, tend to be warlike, and the treatment of women is highly variable.)

The family level of sociocultural integration, which is the only enduring level of organization, typifies band societies. The family is the unit of production, consumption, and decision-making par excellence. Forms of organization beyond the family level exist but are temporary and flexible in membership.

For most of human history, hunters and food-gatherers, as well as tribal people, have gone about their lives largely unaware of civilizations, and when aware, unflinchingly unimpressed with what civilizations had or have to offer. One writer has described the economies of tribes and hunters and food-gatherers as *anti-civilization.* Their economies are based on **reciprocity** or gift-giving, rejecting the profit-based maxim of modern society. One develops the impression that hunters and food-gatherers are not to be pitied, but admired. And so it has been for thousands of years.

At the moment before the European discovery of the Western Hemisphere in 1492, there were ancient civilizations around the globe that controlled regional trade empires. We know of their presence in Mesoamerica, the Andes, along the Great Silk Road of North Africa and Asia, south into the Rift Valley of Africa, the Asiatic civilizations of China and India, and minor theater states in Southeast Asia. In Western Europe, small feudal states fought wars with each other to gain control over long-distance trade.

More remote from these centralized and bureaucratic states were chiefdoms, societies too far away to be brought under central control, but participating directly in long-distance trade. These will be examined in the following chapter. Examples are the chiefdoms of the Hawaiian Islands, the Northwest Coast, the Mississippi Valley, the eastern slopes of the Andes, possibly along the Amazon, in the southern parts of the Rift Valley of Africa, and in the mountainous regions of Asia away from the central valleys. Yet more remote were tribal societies too numerous to summarize here, and most remote were hunting and gathering bands. But while they were remote, research by anthropologists over the last several decades challenges our immediate notions of what the lives of hunters–food-gatherers were like.

From earliest times, we find that humans organized themselves within a variety of biomes into hunting and food-gathering societies that anthropologists call **bands.** Bands are highly homogenous despite considerable differences in environments. More than 30,000 years ago, during the **Late Paleolithic,** hunting and gathering societies achieved levels of technological sophistication in the art of hunting and food-gathering only superseded, perhaps, by the traditional Inuit (Eskimo). In many parts of the world where agriculture and other ecological adaptations are impossible, hunting and food-gathering continues today in forms similar to that of the past except that the encroachments of modern "civilization" have made traditional survival difficult.

Ten thousand years ago, all societies were hunters and food-gatherers, although some of these may have achieved tribal levels of organization in parts of Southwest Asia where agriculture was developed. The same may have occurred a few thousand years later in the Western Hemisphere hearths of agriculture in Mesoamerica and South America. By the time of Christ, only half of the societies of the world were hunters and food-gatherers. When the Western Hemisphere was visited by Europeans, hunters and food-gatherers occupied only 15 percent of the earth's land surface (Murdock 1967:13–14).

The older literature in anthropology tended to suggest that "the specter of starvation" stalked the hunter and food-gatherer. Marshall Sahlins argues that this was far from the case, and that hunting bands were the "original affluent" societies (Sahlins 1972). Sahlins asserts that the perception of hunters and food-gatherers as societies of scarcity is an ethnocentric bias of peoples living in civilizations. Hunters and food-gatherers had no one to compare themselves to and did not feel deprived. Richard Lee's work among the Dobe !Kung of the Kalahari desert in southern Africa describes an example of modern hunter–gatherers who survived comfortably on their traditional resources. Elman Service (1962) points out that, during a good season, a single hunter may not work more than three to four hours a day. Studies show that hunters tend to be healthier, on an average, than modern industrial populations. Slowly we have learned that hunters and food-gatherers suffer few of the diseases and pressures of modern society, are healthy, and, as we will see in the case study on pages 148–149, eat very well.

Only a few isolated pockets of hunter–gatherer folk survive today. Among them are 45,000 Bushmen of southwest Africa. Most are attached to the Tswana tribe as serfs, but 5,000 of them pursue their aboriginal nomadic mode of life. One of these populations, the !Kung, has been studied extensively by the ethnologist Richard Lee. His studies give a sense of the "ethnographic present" of band society (see case study beginning on page 148). The Koroca of southwestern Angola appear to resemble the Bushmen in culture and physique. About 170,000 Pygmies still live in the tropical forests of central Africa. Many of these are partially agricultural. In the Ituri forest of the Congo basin, however, the Aka, Efe, and Mbuti still preserve an aboriginal way of life. In East Africa, the Dorobo and the Hadza have been recently studied. There are half a dozen groups of hunters in central Ethiopia. In India there are a number of hunting societies but these are dependent on agricultural villages and are often treated as specialized castes. Australia still has havens of a few hunter and gatherer Aborigines. Many Inuit in North America still carry on their hunting–fishing way of life (Murdock 1966:13–20). In South America there are still some small groups who depend heavily on hunting or fishing, and gathering, but the nonagricultural groups of far southern South America such as the Yámana (Yahgan) and Selk'nam (Ona) of Tierra del Fuego, and the Alacaluf of the Chilean archipelago have disappeared in this century.

There are many other hunter–gatherer populations that no longer practice their traditional economies but who have been of great importance in anthropological research. Among these are the Shoshones and Yumans of the Great Basin, the Paiute of Nevada, the Apache of the Southwest, and the Siriono of

Figure 5.1

Calvin and Hobbes   **by Bill Watterson**

Calvin and Hobbes © Watterson. Dist. by Universal Press Syndicate. Reprinted with permission. All rights reserved.

eastern Bolivia. The societies of the Great Basin are thought to be very similar to the hunting and gathering societies of preagricultural Mesoamerica, which we will be examining in a later chapter.

Generally speaking, there are broad similarities between hunting and gathering bands despite drastic differences in environments. However, even those remaining groups listed above have changed and become increasingly dependent on the outside world economy, often to the point that it is not clear whether they are still hunters and food-gatherers. Many have been placed in settlements that are much like reservations. Sadly, many live in a state of welfare dependency; and alcoholism and suicide are common. The observations made in this chapter are based on studies carried out on those just mentioned and other now extinct groups in the nineteenth and early twentieth centuries.

When making comparisons between ancient and modern hunters and gatherers, one must exercise extreme care, as we noted at the beginning of this chapter. Modern forms of adaptation are comparable only in the most general of terms. There is little doubt, for example, that hunting and food-gathering during the Late Paleolithic was a much richer form of adaptation than it is today. On the other hand, today many hunters and gatherers have access to high-powered rifles and sophisticated traps that make the job of hunting somewhat less onerous than it once was—but can also rapidly deplete resources. Resource depletion and the destruction of local ecosystems often leads hunters to become dependent on the resources of powerful and modern nation states such as Canada and the United States. The remaining native populations of the Arctic are particularly dependent on the resources of advanced industrial societies, and are increasingly vulnerable due to habitat loss from logging and oil exploitation. However, if we keep our perspective, recent and modern hunters and food-gatherers can tell us much about the past and about how they adapted to their environments.

Demography, Technology, and Subsistence

The remote societies referred to here as hunters and food-gatherers, like other societies in this text, should not be understood as a primitive stage or as "the first stage in cultural evolution." We should look at them as dynamic forms of adaptation to either geographic or historical necessity. Hunters and food-gatherers exist in areas quite remote from the trade routes of powerful civilizations. Once brought into those trade routes, as Aleutian Islanders were brought into the trade networks of the powerful Russian state of the nineteenth century, their ways of life tend to be destroyed and they end up on the bottom of the state hierarchy.

Hunters and food-gatherers are not really "primitive," although that may be one's first impression because they live by strategies of adaptation that depend almost entirely on human energy. The variations in strategies show us how social organization can be used to make effective use of energy systems. The technologies of people like the Inuit are remarkably advanced in both their sophistication and complexity as were those of the hunters of the Upper Paleolithic. On the other hand, the tools of some agriculturalists, the simple digging stick combined with fire to burn down trees, may be considered "primitive," but it was a highly efficient way to farm. To assume that there is an evolutionary progression from simple to complex in sociocultural organization caused by technological change is simplistic.

While technology is most certainly important to adaptation, we usually find that human technologies tend to be as complex as the jobs that need to be done, given the environment and sociocultural level of adaptation that the society has achieved. In the Arctic, survival requires complicated and sophisticated tools that probably represent thousands of years of experimentation. Take, for example, the method the Inuit use to dispose of wolves. They take a sliver of sharp bone and soak it in urine until it is soft. Then they bend it into a semicircle and shove it into a piece of blubber, which they then throw out on the snow, where it dries and freezes. A wolf will usually swallow the blubber whole because it is hard to chew in a frozen condition. The blubber thaws in the wolf's stomach, the sliver of bone springs open, and the wolf is stabbed from the inside, hemorrhages, and dies. Ingenious, though hard on the wolf (Spencer 1959: 268).

On the other hand, life in a tropical forest does not require complex tools and sophisticated clothing (actually, the less the better), but it does require an appreciable knowledge of the environment. The same is, of course, true of the Arctic. Here we see that one of the biggest problems with generalizations about hunting and food-gathering bands is technological determinism. It is easy to assume that the simplicity of band social structure is the result of simple low-energy technologies. However, knowledge of the environment may require much greater sophistication than the knowledge of tools. And tool systems, as among the Inuit, may in fact be extremely complex. It will become apparent that hunter–gatherer social organization is not an adaptation to tools but to environments.

The Shoshone of the Basin-Plateau area of the United States are an example of a technologically simple society. A quantitative analysis of their technology showed that, if one breaks down their culture into details such as basket weaves and shapes, religious beliefs, social practice, and other details, the total includes 3,000 items. In contrast, the U. S. forces landing at Casa Blanca in World War II unloaded 500,000 items of material equipment alone (Steward 1968:69).

One concomitant of a hunting and gathering existence is the need to follow after migratory animals. A nomadic existence in turn places limitations on material culture. Generally, weapons and utensils must be kept at a minimum. An exception is the Inuit. They have harpoons with detachable heads, compound bows, stone blubber lamps, the igloo, kayaks (men's boats), umiaks (women's boats), and dog sleds, to mention just a few of their items of material culture. However, it is also true that the Inuit are not all that nomadic. They focus their attention on sea-going mammals and place their hunting sites on the migration routes of a variety of animals. The greatest change occurs between summer and winter when they move inland away from the coast to hunt caribou and other land mammals.

The single greatest problem for the hunter is the storage of food because, with the exception of the Arctic where food can be frozen, meat simply does not last long; there is no way to store it. This means that it is foolish to spend more than a certain minimum of time hunting. A surplus of meat is wasted meat. And,

Figure 5.2   **Locations of the major hunting and gathering societies of the world.**

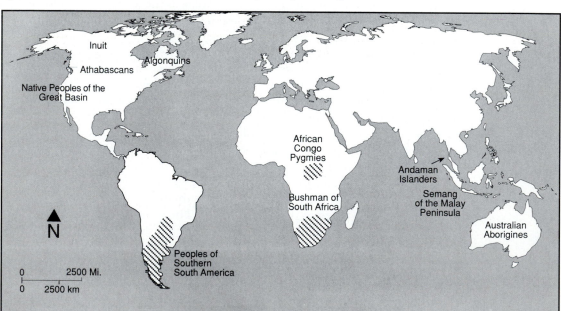

because of this basic fact, meat is usually shared with all members of the band through **reciprocity**. Reciprocity is a type of economic relationship between individuals (not groups) in which transactions are based on the idea of gift-giving. If I have been lucky enough to kill an animal, I give the surplus meat to my close relatives as gifts, expecting gifts in return when they have equal luck. This type of sharing and return sharing is the *sine qua non* of a hunter's existence. It is not to be confused with barter, which will happen between groups. One is expected to be generous within the band; between bands one can negotiate an advantage.

One of the most persistent stereotypes of the subsistence techniques of hunters and food-gatherers that has been overcome in recent studies is the role played by the animals hunted. Recent research shows that plant (and sometimes marine) resources are often much more important than animals in the diet. As Richard Lee (1984) points out, the hunter–gatherer subsistence base is surprisingly dependent on plant foods.

While the technologies of hunters and food-gatherers are highly variable, some (e.g., the Inuit) being as complicated as those of peasant agriculturalists, the ecosystems yield roughly the same calories per individual. Population densities are kept down through a variety of means, including abortion, infanticide, and reduced sexual activity due to taboos. Also, women who depend on high-protein diets will tend to have lower fertility rates than those with diets high in carbohydrates.

These variables tend to support a cultural materialist interpretation of life in hunting and gathering societies. Limited calories means limited population densities, and limited population densities determine or influence the other "systems."

Gender Roles in Band Society

Among hunting and gathering peoples, there is little division of labor except by age and sex. All men are hunters, produce their own tools, build their own shelters (with considerable help from their female friends), and so on. It is usually reported in ethnographies that the men do the hunting and the women do the gathering but that may be partially a result of the way that male ethnographers have collected their data. If one examines ethnographies about hunter–gatherer societies, if a woman picks up the eggs from a bird's nest, that is called "gathering"; if a man does it, it is called "hunting." If a man gathers crawfish, that is fishing; if the woman does, that is gathering. Such a built-in bias may have affected the way that we see the division of labor between men and women in hunting and food-gathering societies. In the final analysis, we will probably find that, while men do most of the hunting and women do most of the gathering, the boundary between these two activities is less than clear.

The relationship between men and women in band societies tends to be fairly equal. However the degree of equality in a marriage is directly tied to the economic productivity of the women. As a general rule, the more women contribute to the "public economy" the greater equality exists between the sexes and the less tenuous is the contract between men and women in marriage. The public economy is the visible economy, that which contributes to subsistence—gathering food. In a hunting and gathering society, as is shown in the case study on the !Kung (see pages 148–149), women contribute very obviously to the food quest. This dynamic of gender equality is similar to that in the contemporary United States where there tends to be more equality in marriages when both men and women are wage earners. The more a woman earns, the more power she has in the relationship. The consequence, in both the United States and among the !Kung, is that women can abandon the marriage and survive on their own if the male becomes oppressive, and it often appears as though the male needs the economic talents of the female more than she needs him. These observations about the !Kung were made twenty years ago when Richard Lee made his first studies and are changing today as !Kung society becomes based less on hunting and gathering and increasingly on the ability of the male to market his skills (though the overall picture is very ambiguous; the tradition of female equality is powerful).

Social Structure: Family, Macroband, and Microband

While band economies are extremely different from our own, kinship relations in band societies show some remarkable parallels at the family level to the kinship relations of modern industrial societies, at least for certain hunting–gathering populations (both the Inuit and the !Kung). Hunter–gatherer and modern industrial societies have **bilateral networks**, informal kinship systems in which kinship is traced out from a man or woman to relatives on both sides of the family. The kinship relations diminish in importance as the relations become more distant. Social structure consists of the rules by which social organization is de-

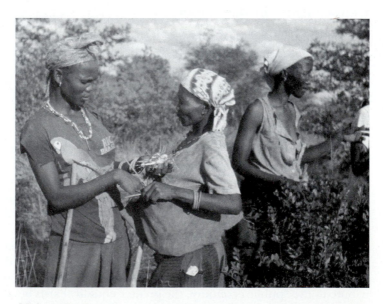

Modern !Kung women.

termined. In societies with bilateral networks, social structure ensures flexible social relations of kinsmen. One of the basic determinants of social structure in both band societies and modern industrial societies is the need for economic and ecological flexibility. Economic reciprocity (transactions) is tied to egalitarian networks. Bands must take advantage of changing and not always predictable resources scattered over large territories. Likewise, working families in modern corporate societies have to move several times during a lifetime to take advantage of different job opportunities. As with the band, the modern family cannot develop an extensive and centralized organization of kinsmen, such as lineages, clans, or other large and stable networks of kinsmen. In both kinds of societies the nuclear family and a close network of kinsmen are the major building blocks of social organization. However, there is an important difference in that the family in hunting–gathering societies cannot survive without the help of other families, while it is not at all uncommon for families to survive today without cooperation from other families (but not without the help of the state or corporate entities).

Band population densities may only be one person per square mile or less and a band's territory may include several hundred square miles. This is true whether one is examining the Inuit of the Arctic, the Athapaskans of subarctic interior Canada, the Australian aborigines, or the Mbuti or Hazda of Africa. Such low densities are a response to resource distribution and availability. Hunting and gathering bands do not have highly structured memberships. They tend to grow into macrobands or break up into small microbands according to the availability and concentration of resources. A microband may consist of one to a few families while a macroband may contain up to a hundred or more individuals. The microband–macroband social structure reflects the availability of resources (the micro-environment) and the attempt to control resources. Interestingly, similar features are found in modern industrial societies with elites that have resources, often using their extended kin (macroband) relationships to control wealth, although living in single-family dwellings (microband), while in the poorest social classes many families (microbands) may attempt to pool their economic resources and live in the same apartment structure (macroband).

Vanstone has described the shift from micro- to macroband in his study of the Athapaskan Indians of western Canada, while Richard Lee has documented the same for the Dobe !Kung. The smallest unit would consist of a few families depending on restricted resources. With increased food supplies, the number of people would increase to 200 or so. But formal leadership was minimal, if it existed at all. Band size depended on resources, and many of the populations in the interior of Canada and southeast Africa, where resources were limited, tended to stay in microbands unless something unusual happened, such as a large kill from a herd of migrating caribou (Athapaskan) or the occurrence of a large number of mongongo nuts (!Kung). The populations along the major rivers (Canada) or around waterholes (Africa), where resources were (are) richer, tended to form macrobands and to stay relatively large unless resources dropped, and then the macroband would break up into microbands. It was only when macrobands formed that ceremony became important.

Case Study: Subsistence and Division of Labor among the !Kung

Lee wanted to know how much of an effort was involved in hunting and food-gathering, and how much the women contributed to the public economy. He carried out a series of experiments ranging from driving some !Kung to a place where food was easily available, to following them on the food quest. What he discovered was surprising to those who had assumed that the majority of a hunter–gatherer's time would be put into the food quest or that male hunting would be the dominant economic activity. The following describes Lee's first experience after he drove some !Kung men and women to gather mongongo nuts, their major food.

> Without ceremony, the women fanned out and started to pick. Grabbing my camera, stopwatch, and notebook, I hastened to follow them. They bent from the waist with a smooth and effortless motion and picked 5 or 6 nuts each time and popped them in their *karosses*, one-piece garments-*cum* carrying bags. Every ten minutes or so, each would return to the truck to spill out her load on the spot she had picked out. The individual piles began to accumulate rapidly. The men were collecting too, using smaller bags than those of the women. I sampled how rapidly the women were able to pick. They were gathering at a rate of 40 to 60 nuts per minute, or 2,000 to 3,000 nuts per hour. By two o'clock everyone was finished;

they dumped their final few onto the piles, which looked enormous to me (Lee 1984:35).

Lee calculated that each woman had gathered enough food to feed a person for ten days and each man enough for five days.

Lee's studies revealed that the !Kung enjoy a good diet and that they do not work very hard to get it. He determined that this was partly attributable to the fact that they depend primarily on vegetable food that was gathered by women. Meat brought in by the men contributed only 30 percent of the calories. In addition to the mongongo nuts, the !Kung have an inventory of over 100 edible plants and the availability of plant foods made it possible for them to subsist on less than twenty hours a week of work. Not bad when one considers that the average industrial worker in this country puts in forty hours a week or more!

The tools of !Kung women are relatively simple, consisting primarily of the digging stick and the kaross, which serves not only to carry vegetable foods in, but as a blanket as well. It is primarily their vast knowledge of the growth, ripeness, and location of local plants on which they depend for survival. However, they are selective of the foods they eat, just as we are, depending on the mongongo nut as a primary food. Lee evaluated their "food hierarchy" and found that they tended to eat their way out of a camp, first eating the foods they desired, and walking further and further out, later eating foods that were less desirable but closer to camp.

Despite the lesser contribution to the overall nutrition of the !Kung, Lee points out that meat has a great social value. When a large animal is killed, great cauldrons are used to cook and people gather to celebrate. The distribution of meat is done with great care, according to traditional sets of rules; for example, the wife's mother always gets the superior cut of meat. Successful distributions are remembered with pleasure, while improper distributions cause wrangling for weeks (Lee 1984:45).

Hunting depends on the bow and poison tip arrow, the knife, a springhare hook, and rope snares. Guns are almost entirely absent. While the !Kung hunt by tracking and killing, most of the successful hunting is done with dogs or by following burrowing animals underground or by snaring. The !Kung are superb trackers and can make accurate deductions from the faintest marks in the sand. They can identify an individual person merely by the sight of a footprint in the sand. They can deduce species, sex, age, speed, and physical condition from an animal's tracks. They can also deduce the number of hours or minutes elapsed since an animal passed by.

Once a man has successfully killed an animal, he does not receive the kinds of social rewards we would expect. Instead, the hunter's game is insulted during a ritual that Lee calls "insulting the meat." The successful hunter must be modest; here is a quote from the hunter Guago:

Say that a man has been hunting. He must not come home and announce like a braggart, "I have killed a big one in the bush!" He must first sit down in silence until I or someone else comes up to his fire and asks, "What did you see today?" He replies quietly, "Ah, I am no good for hunting. I saw nothing at all. . .maybe just a tiny one." Then I smile to myself because I know he has killed something big (Lee 1984:49).

The hunter who has killed "something big" can expect the following razzing from fellow hunters who go out to help him butcher the animal:

You mean you have dragged us all the way out here to make us cart home your pile of bones? Oh, if I had only known it was this thin I wouldn't have come. People, to think I gave up a nice day in the shade for this. At home we may be hungry, but at least we have cool water to drink (Lee 1984:49).

The proper response to the insult is:

You're right, this one is not worth the effort; let's just cook the liver for strength and leave the rest for the hyenas. It's not too late to hunt today, and even a duiker or a steenbok would be better than this mess (Lee 1984:49).

Insulting the meat, as Lee points out, is a means of maintaining equality in the group. Even Lee was not free from insults, as he found out one Christmas when he had an ox butchered for the group among whom he had lived and had to endure the teasing and insults that all hunters had coming to them.

By the time the ice had broken up and the river was clear and high, the Peel River Kutchin were gathered at three or four fishing camps along the lower river. This was a time of year when games and ceremonies were held and when raiding and warfare with the neighboring Mackenzie Eskimos took place. In summer, following a season of fishing and leisurely life, the larger groups in the fish camps would break up and return once more to the mountainous areas of the upper river (Vanstone 1974:41).

Writers describing hunting and gathering societies stress the lack of centralized authority and political structure. Vanstone describes the Athapaskan bands as composed of close kinsmen who regularly changed membership. Any particular band might be in existence only one or two generations. Even so cooperative working groups were important as were religious **sodalities** in ceremonial performances on ritual occasions (a sodality is a unit of social organization that crosscuts the band, but is not based on kinship). The shift from microband to macroband was an important occasion for the exchange of women in marriage, which was always associated with the exchange of ceremonial gifts. The exchange of gifts for women between micro- or macrobands was a critical economic and ceremonial event, possibly related to the origins of trade.

Marriage in Band Societies

Marriage is a form of recruitment of persons to band societies, and marriage was one of the key rituals of the life cycle, along with birth and death. Generally, women left the microbands into which they were born and married men of other microbands (but usually within the macroband). This allowed bands to form alliances with each other, which of course helps expand the kinship network. In band societies, women usually married out of their **families of orienta-**

Ingalik Indian and fish trap.

tion (the families into which they were born), but their **families of procreation** were often formed with men of their own macrobands. It was and is important that the husbands were not close kinsmen (a practice called **exogamy**). Studies of modern hunters and gatherers show that the emphasis on women leaving their own macroband has been overstated. That is, residence after marriage was not always **patrilocal**. Men might move out of their bands in search of a mate or might be attracted to a woman in a band where resources were richer. This practice is called **matrilocal** postmarital residence. In band societies, much depends on resource availability and much less on ideal rules. This flexibility diminishes among tribal societies in which postmarital residence is usually more structured.

In hunting and gathering societies, as in our own today, marriage is often a matter of individual choice, although parental advice is not uncommon. Unlike our own society, however, marriage is more of a matter of economic necessity than a romantic event. A man without a wife or a woman without a husband is often miserable. The average man and the average woman cannot survive well without a mate. Steward says of the Shoshone:

> The irreducible minimum of Shoshonean society was the nuclear or biological family. Isolated individuals could not well survive in this cultural-environmental or ecological situation, and unmarried or widowed persons generally attached themselves to a nuclear family. This family was able to carry out most activities necessary to existence, for husband and wife complemented each other in food-getting and together they procreated, reared, and socialized their children. Women gathered vegetable foods, made baskets needed for this purpose, and prepared all food. Men devoted most of their time to hunting, which, though not very rewarding, was extremely important and time consuming (Steward 1968:78).

Steward's observations about the Shoshone can be extended to the Hazda, the !Kung, the Athapaskans, and the Inuit. In all of these societies many events might break up a marriage in addition to the death of a spouse. Either mate might become attracted to someone else or one of the two spouses might not be a good provider. Whatever the reason, marriage was not very stable and most men and women married at least twice during their lifetimes. This does not mean that marriage was taken lightly or casually. Jealousies tend to be just as serious as in our society and often result in homicide or suicide.

Religion in Band Societies: Existential Ideologies

Religion and ritual refer to those organized social relationships, practices, and beliefs that mediate the relationship of the members of a group to the deity or deities associated with that group (Rappaport 1979). The mediation ultimately connects humans to nature, and in hunting–gathering societies in which religion is integral to all aspects of life, religion helps to maintain a balance between humans and the resources of the habitat.

Elman Service writes that the religions of hunters and food-gatherers are "existential ideologies" and tend to reflect adaptations to their environments. They tend to be "naturalistic" rather than "supernaturalistic." That is, their worlds tend to be populated by forces and powers that are derived from the forces of nature rather than something that goes beyond nature. Often, the world is thought to be pervaded by a power, not too unlike George Lucas's *Star Wars* concept of "The Force." Anthropologists call this nonhuman "force" by the Polynesian word **mana.** Mana has been likened to an electrical force field. Humans and animals can gain access to mana through proper observation of certain rituals. As an example, among the Washo of California, a sorcerer, who controlled mana, might "shoot" a foreign body into a victim because he/she had violated some taboo, such as mistreating wildlife. A cure would be carried out by inviting a shaman, also with mana, who would pray, smoke tobacco, and sing special songs. These rituals would pull out the evil influence from the victim (Downs 1971:188). Both the sorcerer and the shaman used "mana" but in directly opposite ways, one for bad magic and one for good magic. The curing rituals themselves usually have something to do with fertility or hunting magic. The man or woman of power is one who has learned how to handle mana and often, if he or she is very successful at the manipulation of mana, he or she may become a shaman. While anyone can acquire some mana, and most persons know some of the rituals involved in being a shaman, the job implies danger and is avoided by many. This is because mana is often thought to "backfire" on the person using it (sometimes turning the user into a sorcerer). Mana is treated with healthy respect, and not all believe in their abilities to control it.

Mana pervades the forces of hunting and gathering societies, many of which have clear animal origins. The wind, rain, stars, and other forces of nature are also often personified. Animals are often "changelings," like the werewolf, and can and do change into human form; by the same token, humans can often transform themselves into animals.

The ties of the members of the band to the land is often reinforced by the personification of outstanding features of the landscape such as huge rocks, caves, tall trees, and water holes. These may be conceived as the abodes of the ancestors or other spirits. Territoriality blends into religion. One might say that the hunting band often worships its habitat.

Humans and animals are perceived to have souls, although hunters and gatherers' ideas of "soul" differ considerably from our own. Instead of just one soul, a person may have several, some of which have an animal basis. Illness is often thought to be based on soul loss when one of the souls, or a part of a soul, may fly away or is captured by an evil shaman. Good Inuit shamans are famous for the trances they go into, during which their own souls fly out of their bodies and recapture someone's lost soul.

A variety of taboos on the hunting of certain species or overhunting a given habitat are obviously connected to the preservation of habitat. Other taboos, such as taboos on sex before the hunt and ritual occasions, may act to lower the birth rate, but other practices such as infanticide and the purposeful limitation of children may have a more significant adaptive impact. An example of a taboo that may have an ecological impact is the Inuit belief in Sedna, the goddess of the deep. Sedna protected animals from overhunting by setting out very specific totemic laws. An Inuit could not hunt more than three male red foxes in any one day. He had to place his knife on the body of any fox trapped so that its soul could take the soul of the knife back to the village of fox souls. If the hunter disobeyed these edicts, Sedna would sneak up and tip over his kayak, drowning him in freezing Arctic waters (Spencer 1959: 255–330).

Art and dance tend to reflect the naturalistic religions of hunters and food gatherers. Artistic expression, while differing in terms of style, is usually an expression of hunting and fertility magic. Drawings that depict humans and animals involved in the hunt may be designed to magically encourage fertility. Dances are often tied to rituals of fertility and the hunt, with men and women dancing in imitation of the animals they have hunted or personifying the wind and the rain.

A **deity** is omnipresent and a source of ultimate power. A deity can be a force of nature or a force that is beyond nature (supernatural). Both magic and religious actions or thoughts involve supernatural phenomena. They differ in that religion assumes supernatural intervention for human benefit (or harm) while magic assumes cause and effect relationships that humans attempt to manipulate directly—for good or evil. Both religion and magic help explain that which cannot otherwise be understood. People at a distance from ideologically driven states (e.g., China, the Mexica, the Inca) are attracted to religions that explain events as due to magical or nature-based forces. Particularly in hunting and gathering societies, those activities touching on life-threatening experiences, such as birth, illness, and death, tend to be the center of shamanic rituals based on nature and nature's forces. **Shamans** are persons who have access to power that appears to come from nature, such as a spirit helper in the form of a bear or wolf who intercedes on behalf of humans to protect them. The closer a society is to one of the ideologically driven states, the greater the mix will be between naturalistic beliefs and those based on supernatural forms and forces. As an example, hunting and gathering societies in Southeast Asia tend always to have elements of Buddhist or Hindu religion mixed in with the natural religions, while those on the periphery of the ancient Mexica states had elements of sun worship.

We have noted that in hunting and food-gathering societies, every person is politically and legally autonomous. It is also true that in such societies, every person is his or her own religious functionary. No third party is designated to act permanently as minister or priest and to mediate with the deities. Religious roles are just as undifferentiated as the others we have looked at. Some people do take on the role of shaman but this is a part-time, and sometimes temporary, occupation.

Tribes of the Periphery

Tribal societies were generally closer geographically to archaic core states than bands, but they were far enough away that trade and warfare seldom resulted in hierarchical structures. And they were too far from the core states for those states to dominate them. For example, the Inca empire of the highland Andes often attempted to dominate the tribes of the eastern Andean piedmont, but the distances were so great that the cost in food alone made warfare and domination too expensive. In addition, many tribal societies fiercely resisted and states paid great prices trying to subdue them. It was usually cheaper to leave tribes alone. This is no longer true, and in the modern age many tribal societies that maintained their independence from the pre-European states of the Americas have been subjugated by modern core states such as Argentina and Chile.

At the most, tribal societies may be stratified in two tiers, a nobility and a commoner class, but more usually there are no strong class differences. Individuals may be ranked on the basis of kinship for some purposes but most social interaction is egalitarian. Prestige is usually achieved through personal ability rather than ascribed at birth. For example, among the eighteenth-century Cherokee, a young man would join his first war party in his teenage years and between twenty-five to thirty would receive a war rank based on his success as a warrior. Between fifty to sixty, he would cease being a warrior and would become a "beloved man." Young men were expected to defer to the judgments of beloved men (Gearing 1971:154). Tribal societies have more highly structured social systems than do hunter–gatherer societies, but at times it is difficult to make the distinction between the two. In reality, all societies form a continuum from simple to complex with respect to social structure, technology, and other features. The difficulty of distinguishing between tribes and hunter–gatherer bands is often the result of our arbitrary scheme of classification. This does not mean that the classification is not useful for analytic purposes. It does mean that some societies in terms of social structure and level of technology, for example, straddle the boundary between band and tribe or between tribe and chiefdom.

The Shift to Food Production and Animal Domestication

One general distinction between hunting–gathering societies and tribal societies is that tribal societies produce food, either growing it as crops or as domesticated animals. There are, however, tribes that depend on wild food plants, such the Indians of California, and many who practice hunting, such as the buffalo hunters of the American Great Plains, whose resources are great enough to support large populations and a tribal social structure, but who do not rely on domesticated plants or animals.

There were at least four major regions in which food production independently originated: the hilly flanks of Mesopotamia, the Tehuacán Valley of Mesoamerica, the northern part of the Amazon–Orinoco basin in South America, and Southeast Asia. In Mesopotamia, the beginnings of food production occur directly after the last stages of the Upper Paleolithic. During the Lower and Middle Paleolithic, hunters ate whatever they could find. In the Upper **Paleolithic** (Stone Age), beginning about 18,000 years ago, they were able to concentrate on a single species of animal, cattle (Redman 1978:58). Cattle, which are large and travel in herds, would have best been hunted by organized bands. Tools were carefully worked blades like those found in western Europe during what is known as the Aurignacian. As time went by, the blades became more specialized and smaller, and are referred to as **microblades.** These are considered diagnostic of the shift from the Paleolithic to **Mesolithic** (Middle Stone Age), a term given to the period when humans made the shift from hunting and food-gathering to food production. Some of the microblades were used to cut wild grasses, the ancestors of modern wheat and barley. Other important discoveries are mortars and pestles used to grind grains. In the area just north of the Tigris and Euphrates Rivers, in the foothills of the Tauros and Zagros mountains, it is clear that hunters and food-gatherers began to rely on domesticated grains and cattle, and that they began to settle in villages. Charles Redman, the archaeologist, has argued that at the site of Malaha in the Upper Jordan Rift Valley, people had become tribal between 11,000 and 9,000 B.C., living in a large village (fifty houses) of semi-subterranean structures with floors of flagstones (Redman 1978:73).

A similar model can be applied to the shift from hunting and food-gathering in the Western Hemisphere. This happened in the Tehuacán Valley of the southern part of the state of Puebla, Mexico. But it happened later in time than in Europe and Asia (between 7000 and 2000 B.C.), and there were no domesticated animals involved. The early domesticates were maize (corn), beans, squash, and chili peppers. The first three became known as the triadic staff of life for the peoples of Mesoamerica, but the chili pepper was also important as an appetite stimulus and for the vitamins and minerals it provided. Settled villages, implying tribal social structure, can be traced to 2000 B.C. for the highlands of Mexico (Kehoe 1981).

Marshall Sahlins points out that in western California, southern Alaska, the American Northwest, parts of New Guinea, and other world regions (eastern Australia and the hilly flanks of the Tauros–Zagros mountains of Iran in prehistoric times), there were exceptionally abundant food resources and high population densities and no need for the production of domesticated plants or animals. In the Northwest it was salmon, in California it was acorns, and in New Guinea it was sago (Sahlins 1968:39). Sahlins refers to these seasonally available resources as a "natural agriculture." Important skills were developed to deal with the poisons in acorns, the storing of salmon, the processing of sago. The California populations had both matrilineal and patrilineal descent, and despite the lack of domestic agriculture, were tribal in social structure.

Technology and Subsistence Practices

There are many different types of subsistence practices associated with tribal society. The following is a summary of a few of the most important ones. The variations of subsistence practices produce a great number of variations in the types of sociocultural adaptations found in tribal societies.

Forest Agriculturalists   Most tribes of the modern world are forest-dwelling agricultural societies distinguished by slash-and-burn cultivation, also known as **ladang, milpa,** or **swidden** horticulture. Once practiced in temperate as well as tropical zones, the spread of intensive agriculture has eliminated slash-and-burn horticulture from temperate zone countries, along with most of the tribes that formerly practiced it. A 1957 United Nations Food and Agriculture Organization report estimated that some 14 million square miles of the tropics are inhabited by 200 million slash-and-burn cultivators (not all of whom are tribal peoples) (cited in Conklin 1961:27). Today it is likely that even more swidden cultivators occupy even less land area.

In swidden horticulture, the trees in a small plot of forest land are cut down, as is the undergrowth. Very large trees may be "slashed," meaning that a strip of bark is cut away from the tree exposing the cambium layer and effectively killing the tree. Toward the end of the dry season, using care to prevent forest fires, the cut-over area is burned. The plot is planted for from two to four years at the end of which time it is abandoned (except for the tree crops) and another plot is opened. While plot abandonment after just a few years has been regularly attributed in the literature to declining soil fertility, Robert Carneiro long ago presented evidence to show that this conclusion is in most cases unwarranted. The rapid growth of weeds appears to be the main reason for abandonment of swidden plots (Carneiro 1973). It used to be thought that swidden horticulture was detrimental to the fertility of tropical soils. However, Betty Meggers has shown that planters of swidden plots imitate the layered structure of the forest itself by planting tree crops, such as bananas, plantains, and certain palms, interspersed with a large variety of different root and seed crops. Tropical forests tend to be made up of thousands of different species of plants and trees. According to Meggers, garden trees and forest trees have the function of breaking up the force of tropical rains so that soils are not irreparably damaged (Meggers 1971). Having many species of plants within a small area also reduces the possibilities of crop destruction due to disease and insect pests. Most important, by moving their subsistence plots every few years, the cultivator and his family allow the tropical forest to regenerate.

Slash-and-burn horticulture, depending on soils and climates, can often support fairly dense populations with complex tribal and even chiefdom social structures. In the Southeastern United States, in pre-Columbian times, slash-and-burn horticulture supported large and dense tribal societies, such as the Creek and Natchez nations. The Natchez, who had a matrilineal descent system, may have been at the chiefdom or incipient state level. The Natchez are thought today to have been responsible for the development of chiefdom or state-level societies in the Southeastern part of the United States and as far up the Mississippi river as St. Louis, Missouri. One of the most spectacular archaeological sites along the Mississippi is Cahokia, with its giant Monk's Mound complex, located in East St. Louis, Illinois. Monk's mound, the central temple, is 100 feet, high, covers sixteen acres, and may have taken 200 years to build. Archaeologists have compared Cahokia and other southeast temple complexes favorably with structures of the politically sophisticated societies of Mesoamerica. The Maya groups of the lowlands of Central America, most with patrilineal descent, were organized sociopolitically at different times in structures that ranged from tribes to chiefdoms to city states with attached peasant populations.

Equestrian Hunters   A highly specialized type of tribal society developed on the American Plains during the frontier phase of American history. This is the period when land-owning eastern woodland Indians who had moved onto the plains and Indians from the dry southwest adopted the horse and the gun to hunt buffalo on the high plains. The Indians migrating from woodland to plains abandoned their agricultural way of life. A similar kind of culture appears to have emerged in southern Argentina and Chile and the Gran Chaco of Paraguay due to similar circumstances: the availability of the horse, the rifle, and herds of large game animals. The animals were the rhea (an ostrichlike flightless bird) and the guanaco, an American cameloid like the more familiar llama, although, unlike the llama, never domesticated. Descendants of some of these populations became the gauchos of the plains of Argentina. Among the more famous of these equestrian hunters, noted for their resistance to subjugation and incessant raids on Spanish settlements, were the Abipón and the Mbayá.

The stereotypical image of the American Indian is that of the Plains tribes: the Sioux, Cheyenne, Comanche, and Arapaho are better known than the Creek or Chippewa, woodland Indians of the eastern United States. However, Plains culture was an extremely brief episode that lasted only about 300 years after horses were introduced into Florida and migrated into the Plains region in the sixteenth century. The tribal culture of the Plains Indians may have been fading towards a band-type social structure as they shifted away from woodland agriculture to the hunting of buffalo (Oliver 1962).

Pastoral Nomads   Another major form of adaptation of tribal societies is pastoral nomadism. Pastoral nomads tend to be highly independent and warlike. Their importance historically in trade has been underrated by anthropologists. It is very likely that at least some pastoral nomads had reached the chiefdom level of organization in ancient times. Pastoral nomadism is the ecological converse of forest agriculture with a commitment to animal husbandry rather than growing crops in a tropical rainforest (Sahlins 1968:33). Pastoral nomadism is thought to be as old as agriculture (Redman 1978:135–140). Pastoral nomads traded milk, meat, and hides to agriculturalists in exchange for grain and manufactured goods after the domestication of the horse and camel made pastoral nomadism possible, which may have been six thousand years ago (Sahlins 1968:33).

The classic region for nomadism is the dry belt that crosses the Sahara desert and East Africa, runs up through the Persian plateau and inner Asia, through Manchuria, Mongolia, Tibet, and into China (Sahlins 1968:33, Wolf 1982). The most famous pastoral nomads are the "Noble Bedouin" of Arabia and the "Turkic" hordes of Inner Asia. Pastoral nomadism is also found in attenuated form in the north Eurasian forests and tundra, practiced by Sami (Laplanders) and various groups of reindeer herders of the Kamchatka Peninsula. In Africa, there is a great arc of grassland north, east, and south of the forested Congo where are found the Fulani of West Africa, the Turkana and Masai of East Africa, and the Hottentot and Herrero in southwestern Africa (Sahlins 1968:33). These are all societies that rely heavily, if not exclusively on pastoralism.

Case Study: The Natchez

That slash-and-burn horticulture can support fairly sizable populations with complex social structures is supported by the case of the Natchez. The social system of the Natchez was particularly complex, with a dual division and aristocratic classes. The Natchez, who lived near Natchez, Mississippi, and were described by early Spanish explorers, may have been responsible for large temple complexes found throughout the Southeastern United States. The Natchez people were sun worshippers, much like the Aztecs to the south in Mexico. They built pyramids to the sun, usually one at each end of a large plaza. On each mound was the dwelling of a priest chief, the Sun of Suns, brother of the celestial sun. He greeted his illustrious relative before the Sun temple while a perpetual sacred fire was tended in another temple.

The Natchez, typical of the Southeast Woodland peoples, were divided into **moieties** or dual divisions. Each village or town was organized into two groups that exchanged wives with one another. But the Natchez had an unusual marriage rule. There was a moiety of commoners and a moiety of aristocrats; the aristocratic moiety was divided into Suns, Nobles, and Honored People. The commoner or lower-class moiety was referred to as Stinkers. The Natchez were matrilineal, with status traced through women. The unusual rule was that Aristocrats had to marry Stinkers, which elevated the children of male Stinkers to the status of their aristocratic mothers who could be Suns, Nobles, or Honored People. But the children of male Aristocrats who married Stinker women dropped in status. Anthropologists have questioned how such a social system could survive, because the children of male Aristocrats would be Stinkers, and in every generation, children of the successful male members of the ruling class would drop in status. But the emerging archaeology of the Southeast now shows that these horticultural people were hegemonic, conquering the surrounding peoples. Stinker warriors took wives from conquered towns, so there was a continued inflow of tribute in the form of women who would receive Stinker status.

Tribal Social Structure

Social organization in tribes is usually based on corporate descent group membership and not solely on the loosely structured bilateral networks commonly found in bands. However, there are tribal groups whose social structure is so lacking in hierarchy as to be very similar to bands, and some tribal groups are so hierarchical as to be confused with chiefdoms (and may be chiefdoms). Tribes occur on the peripheries of states or chiefdoms. They had much more varied kinship systems than hunters and food-gatherers, and we will only be able to sample a few here. While social structure is influenced by subsistence practices, it is also influenced by nearby chiefdoms and states. Any attempt to find a one-to-one relationship between subsistence practices and social structure has foundered except at the most general level. In general, tribes are less hierarchical than chiefdoms and their social structures tend to be more direct expressions of

A drawing made by DuPratz for his 1758 account of the "Great Sun" of the Natchez being carried in a litter to the harvest festival. Such recognition and special treatment of persons of high status makes its appearance at the chiefdom level of social organization.

adaptation to local ecosystems. Those tribes directly involved in trade tend to have greater hierarchy than those that do not, and often are considered chiefdoms. For example, the peoples of the Trobriand islands tend to be classified as tribes by some writers and chiefdoms by others.

Bilateral Kinship   Strictly speaking, **bilateral kinship** is not a means of reckoning descent from an ancestor; it is a means of acknowledging who your relatives are by tracing links from yourself through your mother and father. Because bilateral kinship is traced from an individual (known as Ego in the anthropological literature), the networks of kinspersons thus recognized will be the same only for full siblings. These bilateral kin networks do not form corporate groups, although the kin relationships themselves may be socially important. Such networks may be the only basis of social relations in band societies. They can, and often do, exist alongside groups based on principles of descent in tribal and chiefdom level societies. In a bilateral kinship network, the entitlements and the responsibilities of an individual are established directly and only by links to others through one's parents and not by virtue of descent from some ancestor. Bilateral kinship networks are also called personal kindreds.

Types of Descent Systems

Tribal societies tend to be of two basic types. In those with **cognatic descent,** there is little gender inequality and little hierarchy. In societies with **unilineal descent,** gender inequality and hierarchy are usually more pronounced. We will examine here cognatic descent and the two common types of unilineal descent, matrilineal descent and patrilineal descent.

Cognatic Descent   The important difference between a bilateral kinship network and a cognatic descent group is that the latter is ancestor-oriented rather than ego-centered. In other words, membership in a cognatic descent group is determined by virtue of being able to trace one's ancestry back to the group founder. The most important feature of cognatic descent, and the one that makes it most confusing to those of us who do not use it as a form of organization, is that ancestry may be traced back to the group founder *through any combination of male and female links.* Tracing descent in this way has two important consequences for the individual. First it means that he or she can potentially belong to any of several cognatic descent groups—often eight because the group founder is rarely more distant than a great-grandparent. Second, societies with cognatic descent systems normally have rules about activation of membership and this means that individuals will have to make some strategic choices during their life. In other words, choosing to be a member of one or two cognatic descent groups may preclude membership in others. Among the Ngóbe of Panama, for example, cognatic descent groups own land and individual members have use rights. A man or a woman may claim membership in a group and farm land belonging to that group if either a parent or grandparent has exercised such rights. If neither a parent nor a grandparent has used the land, then an individual can no longer claim use rights, even though the individuals who do use the land are considered to be relatives through bilateral kinship reckoning. Availability of land is a major factor in the choices made by the Ngóbe.

The strategic or adaptive advantages of cognatic descent are flexibility and choice (although not as much flexibility as provided by bilateral kinship networks). Among many of the tribes of the Great Plains, cognatic descent provided the flexibility needed to balance populations and resources. Cognatic descent groups are also found among Amazonian peoples such as the Kalapalo and the Xinguana, and among many of the peoples of the Pacific islands.

An important feature of most tribes with cognatic descent is that they generally have low population densities and live in remote regions. Their trade connections appear to be undeveloped and they tend to be more self-sufficient than other tribal societies. Men and women tend to regard each other with a fair degree of equality, but men control public leadership posts, as they do in tribal societies with unilineal descent systems.

Unilineal Descent   The other major type of tribal social structure is unilineal descent. In unilineal descent systems, membership in a descent group is determined by birth and an individual belongs to only one group, that to which his mother or his father belongs. If descent is traced back to a founding female ancestor through a line of females, the group of living members is called a **matrilineal descent** group. If descent is traced back to a common founding male ancestor, the living members constitute a **patrilineal descent** group. Descent groups that collectively own land or other property are considered to be corporate groups. Such groups are usually referred to as **matrilineages** if membership is determined through a line of females and **patrilineages** if descent is determined through a line of males. Unilocal postmarital residence rules are common in societies with unilineal descent. If a man must live with his wife's relatives, this is called matrilocal residence. If a woman must go to live with her husband's relatives after marriage, this is called patrilocal residence.

Lineages may in some societies be associated in larger groups know as **clans.** Lineage members can usually trace descent back to a genealogically known common ancestor; clan members also believe themselves to be affiliated by descent from a common ancestor but this ancestor is often a mythical being or a heroic figure of the distant past to whom precise genealogical links cannot be traced. Usually lineages have many functions in both everyday life and ritual. Clans, on the other hand, rarely have other than ritual functions, although they at times have served as the basis for units of warfare as among the ancient Scots. However, it is more common for warrior groups to be organized as sodalities that crosscut unilineal descent groups. Such warrior associations were found among the Plains Indians and in many African tribes such as the Masai.

Clans may be **dispersed** or **territorial.** Dispersed clans have members in many communities throughout a tribal area. This results from a rule of clan **exogamy,** that is, a rule that says that a person must marry someone who is not a member of his or her own clan, combined with a rule of either patrilocal or matrilocal residence. Dispersed clans are common among the indigenous peoples of Southeast Asia, such as the Hmong, who live in the highlands of Laos, Cambodia, and Vietnam. **Territorial clans** are found in places like the densely populated highlands of New Guinea, among some groups in the Amazon basin, and were found among the ancient Scots. While not all of the members of a territorial clan live in a particular village or territory, the majority do and they dominate politically the few members of other clans that may reside in the area. Territorial clans may result from a rule of clan **endogamy,** a rule that specifies that a person must marry a member of his or her own clan. Territorial clans seem, by and large, to have more strongly developed trade connections with other clans, tribes, chiefdoms, and states. In territorial clans, patrilineal descent tends to predominate, although there are exceptions. Marriage to women of other clans is a means by which alliances can be developed with neighboring clans. The clan claims and defends a territory that is the core of the clan's land.

Clans themselves may affiliate into larger groupings, usually on the basis of descent from a putative common ancestor. If the clans of a society divide themselves into only two such groups, the groups are called **moieties** and the society is said to have a moiety system. In societies where such a dual division occurs, a concept of dualism is usually manifest in many other aspects of social organization and symbolic thought. Dualism is a pervasive concept in the traditional organization of the Gê-speaking peoples of Brazil such as the Sherente, Shavante, and Bororo. Sometimes clans will form higher level groups but there will be more than two such groups in the society. Such groups are called phratries (sing. **phratry**). Unilineal descent groups, whether lineages, clans, moieties, or phratries, are bound together not by the living but by the ancestors.

When tribes became chiefdoms and then states, as occurred in the Valley of Mexico, the underlying tribal structure was sometimes retained. The Aztecs of Tenochtitlán were organized into four major hue-calpullis or phratries (multiclan forms of social structure) that quartered the city. These, in turn, were divided into calpullis or clans, which consisted of land-owning corporate lineages. The same was true with ancient Rome, which preserved its tribal social structure until quite late (many of the technical terms used by anthropologists to describe kinship were derived from Roman social organization).

Brian Schwimmer, an anthropologist at the University of Manitoba in Canada, has developed a World Wide Web site with an excellent set of tutorials covering the principles of kinship, descent, marriage, and postmarital residence. These tutorials contain quizzes at the end of each unit. Any student who is feeling even slightly confused by any of the above discussion should visit this site. The address (URL) is *http://www.umanitoba.ca/anthropology/kintitle.html*.

Functions of Descent Systems

Descent systems appear to have had several distinct regulatory functions. These are regulation of food production and distribution, property rights, and warfare, population and trade.

Anthropologists generally agree that food production allows tribal societies to maintain larger and denser populations than bands, but disagree as to why larger populations would pressure the development of corporate descent groups. Ecological and evolutionary explanations favor the idea that food production leads to population increase, and *larger populations need greater regulation* than hunter–gatherers. Larger aggregates of people need more formal means of social control. This means law must be more formalized, and there must be those who enforce the laws. This leads to increase in hierarchy and stratification, although most social control mechanisms remain informal. The most formal procedures emerge when there is conflict between groups, such as lineages or clans, that must be resolved by an intermediary.

It is also theorized that *cooperation among groups* larger than the family is needed to produce the food to feed larger population. Lineage and clan groupings emerge in order to handle the more complex tasks of planting and weeding, and in the manufacture of household goods. The distribution end of the economy, it is thought, may have brought about the development of a "big man," a central figure who could gather surplus production from families and redistribute it within clans or villages, *particularly if the families are producing different kinds of foods and other goods due to ecological variation* in the tribe's habitat. It has also been argued that as food production and distribution become more complex, it is possible for authority figures to gain access to power and to use their positions to expand authority and control beyond what is needed by the local group. But all these theories are problematic: The difficulty of measuring the relationship among such variables as power, technology, population, calorie production, social structure, climate, and resource scarcity makes it difficult for any theory on the origins of tribal social structure to gain prominence.

To explain tribal organization as a simple function of plant or animal domestication and food production would ignore the many subsistence-based food-producing societies that do not have lineages and clans and closely resemble hunters and food-gatherers in organizational simplicity. It would also not account for hunters and gatherers and fisherfolk, such as those of the Northwest Coast of North America, who have highly developed corporate lineages and are clearly tribal, if not chiefly, in their level of organization. The key does not appear to be agriculture by itself, but pressures on resources. If population densities are low, it would not be economically worthwhile to spend a lot of time and energy on the maintenance of descent systems. People practicing agriculture in regions with relatively low population densities tend not to have unilineal descent systems. Instead, they have cognatic descent groups or simple bilateral kinship networks. Both provide options in terms of group affiliation. Unilineal descent systems, in theory, do not, although it should be pointed out that, in reality, *ad hoc* adjustments are common in unilineal descent systems to take account of such things as demographic fluctuations in relation to land availability.

In hunting and food-gathering societies it does not make much sense for a band of people, whatever their internal organization, to own territory, whether they hunt land or sea animals. What would be wiser is to have an agreement (a verbal treaty) between people living in a region that everyone has equal access to all resources, as long as no one overexploits them. This is **public ownership** of resources, and differs significantly from **corporate ownership** typical of tribes. As we saw, the Dobe !Kung dole out permission to use the resources around their various waterholes freely, which is a form of generalized reciprocity or public access, as long as no one abuses the privilege. Hunting societies, then, would tend toward bilateral kinship networks because these are the most elementary of all systems and require the least amount of organizational effort and there is no ownership of natural resources. This would also be true for food-producing societies in which the pressure on resources is so low as to not make the ownership of resources important. In societies with low resource pressure, whether hunter–gatherers or food-producers, the ownership of resources would be public.

With increasing population pressure, resources become more scarce and control becomes more important for survival. Thus, a shift from public ownership of resources to corporate ownership by tribal lineages or clans is to be expected. The "bounded" quality of tribal units of social structure is then easily explained by the corporate ownership of resources by lineages and clans within which rights are collectively defined by birth. Such rights are **ascribed**, that is, they accrue to an individual by virtue of birth into a given lineage or clan.

It would seem that once intensive use of resources begins to produce scarcity, open access is no longer advisable. Now labor investments intensify and it makes sense to restrict the sharing of the land and other resources to the group that is putting in the effort. *Ownership of resources now matters.* There are legal and cognitive reasons for the increasingly corporate or collective nature of resource ownership. It is necessary to find a very simple mechanism by which to determine rights. Because these are not societies with complex courts and legal systems like our own, the simplest way to structure rights is by birth. A child is born and his/her rights are determined by whether the society wishes the rights to run from mother to child (matrilineal descent) or father to child (patrilineal descent).

At the tribal level of organization, land, pastures, crops, and animals are usually held by descent groups, not by individuals. Families have use rights to property because of their membership in these larger corporate groups. That is, the individuals have the right to use land and other property through their family, and that family has a right to use land through the lineage, and the lineage has ownership by virtue of the relationship of its members to a common ancestor. Unlike modern capitalistic societies, every person has an inalienable guarantee of a livelihood. No household can be excluded from direct access to the means of its own survival.

One popular theory developed by cultural materialists and human ecologists, particularly Marvin Harris and William Divale (1976), was that tribal social structure, religion, and warfare were means of controlling population, and that types of descent were the products of different forms of warfare. This theory is illustrated in the following case study.

Patrilineal descent tends to be associated with patrilocal postmarital residence (the woman goes to live with her husband) and matrilineal descent with matrilocal postmarital residence (the man goes to live with his wife). Residency in turn appears to be determined by a complex of variables. According to Marvin Harris and his associate William Divale, patrilocal societies, which are statistically dominant in tribal societies, occur when it is advantageous for the society to be patrilocal, and this would occur whenever men are dominant in the food quest and when *warfare is local.* On the other hand, when women are dominant in the food quest and *warfare or trade are long-distance*, it is advantageous for the society to organize itself around women because the men are gone much of the time. Matrilocality structures the family around a core of mothers, daughters and sisters, but it does not produce peace. In such societies, groups of men from neighboring villages go on long-distance trade or warfare quests. The example given of matrilineal–matrilocal societies practicing long-distance warfare and trade is the Iroquois of New York, who preyed upon the Huron, and vice versa. Other examples are the Nayar, a soldier caste in the state of Malabar (India), which specialized in long-distance warfare, and the Mundurucu of the Amazon (Divale and Harris 1976).

Warfare, whether local or long-distance, is found among both matrilineal and patrilineal tribes. It is a universal characteristic of tribes (but not of hunter–gatherers). Harris and Divale argue that warfare can be interpreted as a means of population control, but not through the death of men. They argue that

Case Study: Yanomamo Descent and the Male War Complex

*I*n 1968, Napoleon A. Chagnon published a description of his initial contact with the tribal Yanomamo. The Yanomamo, who occupy the border country between Venezuela and Brazil, have subsequently come to represent the violence of men in tribal societies. Chagnon described how the men blow green powder up each other's noses through hollow tubes, which then causes a green mucus to flow from their nostrils. After ingesting the drug, the men sit half-naked and shout at and pound each other, first with fists and then with their clubs. The patrilineal Yanomamo engage in local warfare. Sneak raids on their neighbors account for thirty-three percent of all deaths (Chagnon, 1968, 1974). Similar levels of violence are reported for other patrilineal tribal peoples around the world, including the Dani and Tsembega Maring of New Guinea. This led anthropologists to the initial idea that patrilocal residence, patrilineal descent, and warfare might be tied to each other as a means of reducing population. However, Marvin Harris pointed out that, first, the deaths of the men did not reduce population increases because women bear the children, not men, and second, matrilineal societies are equally warlike. Marvin Harris expanded the theory into what he called "the male war complex" and it explains not only warfare but descent.

Yanomamo warriors lining up at dawn prior to departing for a raid on an enemy village. They paint their faces as well as their legs and chests black with masticated charcoal.

the male war complex tends to give males high status and females low status among both matrilineal and patrilineal societies, leading to the practice of **female infanticide**, the practice of putting female children to death. Harris and Divale show that, statistically, tribal warfare leads to a lowering of fertility rates among tribal peoples by lowering the number of women who survive each generation.

Harris and Divale's theory about the relationship among descent, warfare, and population control is controversial, but it does suggest why bilateral hunters–food-gatherers and food-producers with low population densities have very low levels of warfare, and why tribes with high population densities have unilineal descent (both matrilineal and patrilineal), and high levels of warfare. The kind of warfare found among tribes is what we would call a type of feuding. It is sporadic and small-scale and, in the view of the new institutional economics, it produces high transaction costs, that is, it makes trade very expensive.

The Political Economies of Tribes: The Impact of Trade

Fredrik Barth, a student of Persian nomads (Iran) has described how pastoral nomads achieve "fictive chiefdoms." Their conical clans have a chief or chiefs at the top that makes them appear like true chiefdoms. They are almost always patrilineal with descent traced through the male line from a founding ancestor, usually the mythical founder of a clan, down to the present day "chief" (Barth 1961). However, as Barth's close analysis of the Basseri nomads shows, the chief is really first among equals. He can only initiate an activity after the other adult males of the clan agree to his decision. According to Barth, the reason for the apparent but not real political centralization is the need for there to be a leader who can "appear" to make complex decisions about which way the herd of animals should go. This is so in order that outsiders are given the impression of great consolidation of power in the hands of one man. A second reason for the fictive chief is the need to have one individual represent the tribe when dealing with city dwellers who are accustomed to the idea of centralized authority. But, back on the desert, the exigencies of a nomadic existence make every family an independent decision-making unit in most things.

The nomadic societies described by Barth were adapted not only to their arid environments but also to trade relations with other like tribes and to settled town and city dwellers. They operated within and between evolved states and they had done so for literally thousands of years. The ancestors of people like the Basseri nomads appear to have operated in chiefdoms that were components of ancient states, such as the Persian Empire (226–641 A.D.), which dominated trade routes for several centuries in the Middle East.

Instead of "fictive chiefdoms," at least some pastoral nomads may have been, and others today certainly are, true chiefdom social systems in which the ranking of relations between clans and settled "khans" represents hierarchical connections determining complex trade relationships. A settled Khan, who may be linked by marriage to members of a state, cannot be considered as "first among equals" or as a fictional chief, but as a **paramount chief** who acts to negotiate trade relationships with settled villagers and trade brokers. This brings us to the topic of the impact of trade on tribal societies, and the relationship of trade to social structure.

Trade is more important to tribal societies than traditionally thought, and trade relationships helped produce corporate property ownership and redistribution economies. This model is derived from Eric Wolf's *Europeans and the People Without History* (1982). Wolf suggests that before the rise of the European–American world system, elaborate trade routes existed around the world. He describes several of these trade routes, including those of Mesoamerica, the Andes, Africa, Central Asia, Southeast Asia, and Europe. He goes on to describe how these trade systems were displaced and destroyed by the trade systems put into place by European civilizations in the centuries after 1600 (Wolf 1982).

The model presented here is also reminiscent of an earlier ethnographic model presented by Edmund Leach in *Political Systems of Highland Burma* (1954). Leach conducted research among the Kachin of Burma as best he could while serving in the British military during World War II. The region of Rangoon, a port of trade, was organized into an Asiatic-style state. Further upriver, which was the path of trade, existed Shan chiefdoms. These were intermediate nodes on the way to the "periphery." The periphery, the region of the Kachin, was tribal, but not an isolated sphere of human activity. Rather, it was integrated into the economy of the whole of Burma, and even today, under a socialist dictatorship, the "hill tribes" maintain much of their tribal independence and trade opium for Western goods.

It is possible to make the following generalizations about the relationship of tribal societies to distant states.

1. Ethnographically described tribes are not the self-sufficient, autonomous representatives of an earlier evolutionary stage they were once thought to be. They are, rather, the remains of societies that, while peripheral to states and chiefdoms, were none the less connected to them, and to other tribes, through trade.

2. Tribes, prior to the rise of Western Civilization, had goods worthy of state attention but not usually of sufficient importance or quantity to energize the state into conquest.

3. The relationship of state to tribe also was mediated by geography—the remoteness of the tribe. Distance makes the transportation of goods expensive (it raises transaction costs). Thus it is not economically efficient to conquer distant tribes because of the costs not just of conquest but of maintaining control; but such tribes can be integrated into the trade network of the state. Distant tribes remained for thousands of years, warlike and nonhierarchical at the edges, but increasing in hierarchy where trade was of increased importance.

4. The principal unit of production in a tribe is the household. Kinship is the chief means of organizing the economy, but goods may be amassed

by a big man, traded, and the returns redistributed in the more hierarchically organized tribes.

5. Corporate ownership of resources prevents individuals from trading away the group's resources.

Interestingly, hunting and gathering bands of Canada and New England were transformed into tribes and from tribes into chiefdoms when English and French traders offered money and guns for furs. Warfare between previously peaceful bands of hunters escalated overnight and internal hierarchy and ranking became common. Similar processes occurred when the slave trade in Africa transformed bands into tribes and tribes into chiefdoms or statelets (Wolf 1982).

Tribal social structure, that is, the kinship and descent system, is a response to a number of factors including two features of political ecology. First, there is a need to control local resources for the production of goods for trade (as well as consumption). This would intensify the need for collective ownership of resources by the group. Second, there is a need to respond to the complexity of trade. As the number of people and the number of goods increases, trade relations become more complex. It is one thing for two to twenty persons to exchange a few goods with each other, but quite another when several hundred exchanges of many different types of goods takes place. The complexity of transactions increases exponentially as the number of people and goods involved goes up. As the complexity of trade increases, it becomes more efficient to select representatives to act as traders, thus creating hierarchy (here the role of big men as intermediaries and traders becomes clear). At this point, the logic of tribal society fades, and the rationale for chiefdoms becomes clear. The complex interaction of resource control and trade produces hierarchy. Thus, tribes with minimal hierarchy are those with the least developed trade connections and mechanisms of resource control.

Embedded Economies

Neoclassical economists tend to look at an economy as an institutional component of society that can be treated as a unique and separate system, distinct from other societal institutions and operating according to its own laws. Many anthropologists argue to the contrary, that in tribal societies economies are "embedded" in the social matrix.

Karl Polanyi, an economic historian, argued that an economic exchange is no more than a temporary episode in a continuous series of social transactions. In tribal society, the value of a good is determined not by anything intrinsic to the good but by the relationship of the two persons exchanging the good. That is, social relationships take primacy over economic ones. In tribal societies, those things that an economist would not consider "economic," such as kinship and politics, are the very heart of the economy. Tribal economic systems resemble, yet are quite different from, the band systems of hunters and food-gatherers.

Like band systems, economic relations are familial and the foci of economic exchanges are extended families. Production, for the most part, is a domestic function, as is consumption. According to current theory, production is geared to family needs, not to the demands of "consumers." But, unlike band societies, household production is not self-sufficient and there must be exchanges between extended families, villages, or tribes.

There is a tension between the tendency towards hierarchy brought on by trade, and the tendency towards egalitarian values based on the equal access to resources. When trade gets the upper hand, the tribe becomes increasingly hierarchical, with certain families gaining monopolistic control over trade. These families often act like petty aristocrats. If this process continues far enough, the egalitarian tribal structure is transformed into a chiefdom with hierarchical structure and status distinctions—and later, class distinctions (such as we found with the Natchez). The process of hierarchy creation helps to explain the big man complex and its transformation into the chiefdom. The collapse of trade networks can reverse this process; thus, the nondirectionality of adaptive evolutionary change.

The Big Man Complex: Redistribution or Trade?

Tribal societies tend to be characterized by what Sahlins has referred to as the "big man complex." A variety of this complex called the **potlatch** is found among the indigenous groups of the American Northwest Coast. It is a widespread institution and many attempts have been made to explain it. Sahlins sees the big man as the center of an egalitarian redistribution system that assures equality and surplus (Sahlins 1968). At the heart of the potlatch is the "big man" who acquires privileges and ritual recognition for himself and his group through his generosity. One ecological explanation is that the big man acquires vast quantities of wealth, usually in the form of food, in order to give it away during feasts, thereby overcoming short-term and local food shortages. A competing interpretation, we propose, is that the big man complex is not an egalitarian giveaway at all, but a means of distributing trade goods within a regional trade network.

The big man complex, like other economic aspects of tribal society, tends to fit snugly into the social structure. In tribes with little hierarchy, feasts tend to be local and include only close kinsmen. As we examine more hierarchical tribes, the big man complex increasingly resembles a pyramid. When we cross the fuzzy line from a tribe to a chiefdom, we find that feasting tends to be focused on a single chief, who is the center of a large political and ceremonial system, such as is found in Hawaii. In a chiefdom, as Sahlins puts it, the political order is underwritten by a centralized circulation of goods, flowing toward the top of the social pyramid and down again instead of laterally. And, in a chiefdom, each presentation implies a relationship of rank. This pyramid is a redistribution system and, as we will see later, with some modification, it becomes the basis for early state-type societies.

Potlach ceremony among Indians of Northwest Coast.

Trade and Ritual in Tribal Society

Why would tribes trade? One good reason would be to overcome ecological differences in resource availability. According to modern ethnographic studies, tribal societies had elaborate sets of trade networks that developed both within a geographically widespread tribe and between tribal groups that were adapted to distinct ecological zones. For example, there was a large trade center at the Dalles in eastern Oregon situated between two different tribal groups, the Chinook Indians of the lower Columbia River and the Umatilla Indians of the upper Columbia River. The two Indian tribes were adapted to different ecological conditions; west of the Dalles is rain forest country and east of the Dalles is grassland desert. The two tribes met at the Dalles and traded goods from the two distinct ecological zones. The Chinook traded dried salmon upriver and the Umatilla traded deer meat downriver. Lewis and Clark, who visited the trade center, described it as controlled by aristocratic families, as were the trade routes. Trade was carried on further west down the coast of Oregon by other trade partners of the Chinook.

Because some of these tribes were hostile toward each other, certain individuals had ritual relationships with specific members of other tribes with whom they were "blood brothers." Blood brothers were sworn to protect each other and were supposed to avenge attacks on trade partners by members of their own tribes. Such ritual networks crisscrossed North America far back in time so that archaeological artifacts from as far south as Florida are found in the Midwest along with goods from the Northwest. There is much evidence of prehistoric trade between Mesoamerica and the southwestern, southeastern, and midwestern regions of the United States as well. Archaeological evidence also hints at extensive trade networks throughout South and Central America and between Mesoamerica and the Andean region.

Summary

In this chapter, we have examined two levels of sociocultural integration: bands and tribes. Hunting and gathering bands currently exist only on the remotest peripheries of modern states and they have become dependent to varying degrees on the economies of state systems. Prior to the domestication of plants and animals, hunting and gathering was the only game in town, in habitats resource rich and resource poor. We cannot know exactly what these early hunting and gathering societies might have been like, although we can be sure there was variety in their adaptations. The family was, and is, the only enduring unit of social organization within the band. Larger units were flexible and temporary. Beyond a less than rigid division of labor based on sex and age, egalitarianism carried the day in band societies. Generalized reciprocity (gift-giving) serves as the principal—sometimes the only—means of resource distribution. We base our inferences about the life and times of ancient hunters and gatherers on archaeological evidence, historical accounts, and ethnographic descriptions, as we do for the tribes of old.

Modern tribes exist on the peripheries of states and are partially dependent on them. In tribal societies egalitarianism still predominates, and the family is still an important decision-making body as well as a primary unit of production and consumption. But larger and denser populations intensify resource use and result in the need to develop controls over resources. Trade brings access to a wider range of resources but, in the process, exacerbates the need for resource control. Collective ownership of property vested in corporate descent groups with use rights available to individual members and families is a common tribal solution to the problem of control over resources and trade. In the tribal level of organization we see the beginnings of unequal access to resources, of rank and hierarchy, preconditions for the development of full-blown systems of social stratification at the chiefdom level.

Key Terms

Achieved Status	Mana
Ascribed Status	Matrilineal Descent
Bands	Mesolithic
Bilateral Networks	Microblade
Bilateral Kinship	Milpa
Cognatic Descent	Moiety
Corporate Ownership	Patrilineal Descent
Deity	Phratry
Dispersed Clan	Potlatch
Endogamy	Public Ownership
Exogamy	Reciprocity
Family of Orientation	Shaman
Family of Procreation	Social Structure
Female Infanticide	Sodality
Incest Taboo	Swidden
Ladang	Territorial Clan
Late or Upper Paleolithic	Unilineal Descent

Chiefdoms and Pre-Modern States: Core-Periphery Relations

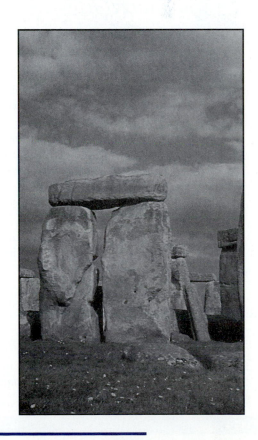

Pre-modern states occupied the cores in the continuum from core to periphery, and did so since very early times. Chiefdoms, in many regards, resemble states, and may have been an evolutionary stage between tribes and states. Here we treat them not as an evolutionary stage, but as societies with greater centralized authority than tribes that operate on the margins of true states, but are not themselves true states.

Characteristics of Chiefdoms and States

States, in all times, have been the central cores of hegemony. In precapitalist times, before the origin of a "world system," each region of the world had one or several such state cores. Out from the cores were chiefdoms, usually separate and independent of states. While they are organized like miniature states, chiefdoms do not have the capacity to control territories the size of states. Both states and chiefdoms are hierarchical, but in states the division between the rulers and ruled is sharp, while in chiefdoms such a division is less clear-cut.

Chiefdoms

There are many ethnographically recent chiefdoms that give us some idea of what the ancient chiefdoms may have been like. The populations of chiefdoms are larger than tribes, ranging from 5 to 50 thousand depending on the carrying capacity of the habitat. However, while all chiefdoms have large populations, their adaptations were quite varied. Knowledge of European chiefdoms is extremely limited, so our model relies on nonwestern societies studied by anthropologists.

Chiefdoms have varying types of social structures. Some societies evolved into chiefdoms with matrilineal descent (Northwest Coast), others with patrilineal descent (Mesoamerica), and others with cognatic descent (Polynesia). Europeans appear to have evolved patridominant, extended family systems, possibly at the clan level. Certainly local ecosystemic adaptations (technology, subsistence) contributed to the transformations in certain regions, but recent theory suggests that outside pressures (other societies, trade, war) were also key factors in the shift from tribal organization to chiefdoms, and from chiefdoms to states (Wallerstein 1974, Wolf 1982).

The chiefdoms of the Northwest Coast (Kwakiutl, Haida, Tlingit, Tsimshian, Bella Coola) were hunters and food-gatherers depending on the rich coastal fisheries of salmon and trout, sea mammals such as porpoises, sea lions and whales, and land animals such as bear, deer, duck, and geese, which occurred in profusion. There were also riches in berries, roots, and other plants, and the forests supplied cedar and fir for their long houses. The traders and warriors of the Northwest Coast plied the waters between Alaska and northern California.

The chiefdoms of Africa, the Kpelle of Liberia, the Bemba of Zambia, the Lozi of Zimbabwe, the Ngoni of Tanzania, and the Zulu of South Africa, to name a few, practiced intensive hoe cultivation (with very little irrigation) of sorghum, millet, maize, and cassava, sometimes combined with cattle herding.

The chiefdoms of the Pacific such as Samoa, Tahiti, Tonga, and Hawaii, like the peoples of the Northwest Coast, depended on the bounty of the Pacific, but also grew taro, coconut palms, and breadfruit using irrigation, hoes, and hillside terraces. In the middle and lower Mississippi valley were found several chiefdoms (some possibly states), the most famous of which built the temple mounds at Cahokia (near East Saint Louis) and had an economy extremely similar to the earlier chiefdoms of Mesoamerica: pot irrigation of maize, beans, and squash and the hunting of deer and turkey.

Earlier evolutionary/ecological theory on the emergence of chiefdoms argued that chiefdoms overcame ecological specialization through the use of redistribution mechanisms, such as ritual feasts. The classic example was the high islands of Hawaii where, it was theorized, villages and kinship units had specialized in the production of different goods found in distinct ecological zones on the large islands. However, ethnohistorical research by Timothy Earle now shows that neither villages nor kinship units specialized in the exploitation of distinct ecosystems. Earle found that kinship units tended to generalize their adaptations by including production in many separate ecological zones (Earle 1987). Recent research on state organized societies in the Andes, such as the Inca and their predecessors, shows that they too did not specialize in production by ecological zones, but, as in Hawaii, families tended to organize their kinship units to exploit many distinct ecosystems (Moseley 1992, Van Buren 1996). Because trade was an extremely common feature of Polynesian society, with giant canoes plying their wares between the high islands, redistribution may have been a way of exchanging goods between different chiefdoms in order to facilitate trade. The genesis of chiefdoms, then, lies not in overcoming ecological specialization and uncertainty but in the monopolization of trade by powerful chiefdoms. Trade is also a key feature of chiefdoms in the Andes, and in other regions of the world. Evidence for trade is particularly well demonstrated for the early chiefdoms of Mesoamerica, such as the Olmec of La Venta.

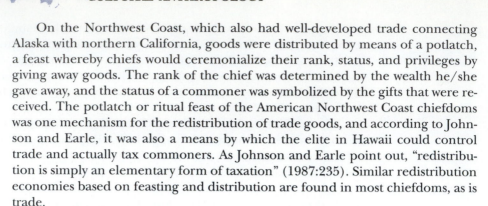

On the Northwest Coast, which also had well-developed trade connecting Alaska with northern California, goods were distributed by means of a potlatch, a feast whereby chiefs would ceremonialize their rank, status, and privileges by giving away goods. The rank of the chief was determined by the wealth he/she gave away, and the status of a commoner was symbolized by the gifts that were received. The potlatch or ritual feast of the American Northwest Coast chiefdoms was one mechanism for the redistribution of trade goods, and according to Johnson and Earle, it was also a means by which the elite in Hawaii could control trade and actually tax commoners. As Johnson and Earle point out, "redistribution is simply an elementary form of taxation" (1987:235). Similar redistribution economies based on feasting and distribution are found in most chiefdoms, as is trade.

Chiefdoms were ranked and stratified societies with a single **paramount chief** at the top of a pyramidal hierarchy. Unlike states, everyone in a chiefdom believed that they were descended from a single founding ancestor. A myth of common descent unified all. In fact, the elites were usually endogamously separate from commoners (endogamy occurs when members of a group or class marry one another, as opposed to exogamy in which members marry out of a group or class). The male elites were usually free to take women from commoner ranks as wives or concubines, but the reverse was never true. Chiefdoms were stratified into at least two classes: nobles and commoners. Sometimes a third class of slaves occurred at the bottom. And sometimes a class of warriors or artisans was present and intermediate between nobles and commoners.

The paramount chief was considered sacred, like a god. His close relatives formed the elite bureaucracy and were supported by taxes and tribute (in part derived from the control of trade). The tribute payers were commoners, sometimes other chiefdoms, and nearby tribes that had been subjugated by the chiefdom. The aristocracy manipulated trade and warfare, and, not incidentally, religion, the three major sources of power within these societies.

States

In states the central authority figure (king, emperor) can initiate a political act while in chiefdoms the central political figure does not have the authority to act without the support of his/her direct kinsmen and subsidiary chiefs whose authority ramifies down through lower levels of hierarchy (subchiefs or clan heads). This distinction between chiefdoms and states depends on the idea that in a true state, the authority of the people to act is vested in a central leader. Here the state is an abstraction, a contract between the ruler and the ruled, usually mediated by religion. The king may represent a god or he/she may be god; this is not true of a chief.

States are **stratified** into one or more social classes. The very upper class, the aristocracy, was endogamous, but did not pretend to be related to the commoner class. In fact, the elites usually ritually separated themselves from commoners on special occasions and in their dress. Rules, called **sumptuary laws,** were often passed preventing commoners from dressing or behaving like the aristocrats. The elites might also be stratified according to kinship connections to the ruler. The clearest line of separation was between the elites and commoners. The commoner class could also subdivide into other class divisions. One common distinction was between urban dwellers and the peasants living on the land. In addition, there was often a final distinction between all of the above and a caste of slaves, or of people with no rights, such as the **untouchable** caste of India. The more powerful the state, the greater the levels of hierarchy that tended to occur between the king and his close kinsmen and the bottom caste. The distinction between **class** and **caste** is that members of different classes can marry each other but members of distinct castes cannot. Thus, in the above, the aristocrats, commoners, and slave groups were often organized into distinct castes, while inside the commoner caste there might be many levels of social class.

One of the most difficult problems in analyzing the differences between states and chiefdoms is that chiefdoms were sometimes incorporated into states when states had the resources to become highly centralized, but then might become independent chiefdoms when the state contracted, a feature very common to Asiatic states and chiefdoms.

Early states resemble chiefdoms in that their economies were also based on redistribution, but the act of distribution by the state had the political function of securing the support of the commoner class, particularly of those specializing in military activities and household manufacturing. Commoner classes specializing in the manufacture of goods (potters, weavers) depended on the largesse of the state to feed them, and the state depended on specialists for the ceremonial goods it needed to set itself apart. Peasants, who grew food for the state, were usually outside of this "welfare" redistribution system.

Another feature setting states and chiefdoms apart from tribes, and from each other, is warfare. One of the characteristics of chiefdoms which sets them apart from tribes is *the occurrence of ritualized warfare*. Among the peoples of Mesoamerica at the chiefdom level, warfare was part of a ritual complex in which warriors were captured for sacrifice (something like an elaborate football game between chiefdoms). Warfare in tribes was initiated by warriors to gain personal status, while warfare in chiefdoms was controlled by the chief. In both chiefdoms and states, warfare was not local, but long-distance, and it was part of the process of gaining tribute from other societies. Chiefdoms and states, with their long-distance warfare, *reduced the costs of trade transactions* by preventing local warfare. In both states and chiefdoms, peace was usually sanctified by the development of a ceremonial center, often the focus of pilgrimage. While pilgrimages were found in state level societies, peace was maintained not by sanctuaries but *by the force of the state through the use of armies*. These were trained for the purpose of imposing rule throughout a large territory. In exchange, soldiers were supported by the state, a characteristic not found in chiefdoms in which the warriors were never full time but were the kinsmen and retinue of the chief.

Case Study: The Olmec Chiefdom of La Venta

In the 1950s and 1960s, the island site of La Venta in eastern Mexico was thought to be a temple–pyramid center dating to about 1100 B. C. with no antecedent settlement and with no surrounding homes or farms. It was thought to be a temple complex where slash-and-burn farmers came from afar to worship local gods. Trade and warfare were not considered important. Archaeologists assumed the Olmec were a peaceable people who spent their time worshipping stars and numbers. The site was re-excavated in 1986 by Robert Sharer and William Rust (Rust and Sharer 1988). Rust and Sharer discovered that there were several antecedent settlements and that the site of La Venta at 1500 B. C. was already a temple complex surrounded by a large village or town. They also discovered that warfare and trade were important elements to Olmec society. The site was much older than originally thought. One hundred seven occupation sites were located, mostly along a river levee (Rust and Sharer:1988).

The site was destroyed by a flood and then, between 1750 and 1150 B.C., it was reoccupied. Pottery was more elaborate and was an object of trade. There was more of it and it was better made. Grinding stones were discovered along with obsidian, which had to have been imported, indicating long-distance trade. Marine species decreased and fresh water species increased and a mangrove swamp disappeared. This implies that the region was being drained through the construction of drainage–irrigation systems, and that agriculture was much more complicated than slash-and-burn (possibly the Olmecs had irrigation agriculture). Research showed that the river was silting up, and the Atlantic was becoming more distant. The irrigation works imply organized human labor, and that implies hierarchy.

Figure 6.1 **Diagram of La Venta from Coe, Snow, & Benson, *Atlas of Ancient Americas*, p. 98.**

La Venta

Between 1150–800 B.C., an elaborate pyramid in the shape of a volcano was constructed. There was an increase in pottery and it was more elaborate. Forests were being cleared, polished green stone celts were manufactured or traded in. Social stratification increased and the site may have been the center of a chiefdom or simple state. La Venta is a spectacular site. A large pyramid, which has never been fully excavated, was flanked by a plaza. Special precincts and platforms were surrounded by large basalt columns. Excavations uncovered tombs and "offerings" of serpentine and jade celts, ceramics, and jade beads were buried along a line running through the center of the plaza. Underlying the plaza floor and small platforms were mosaic pavements and massive offerings of serpentine (Grove 1981:378–379). By 900 B. C., La Venta was abandoned and its monuments ritually shattered.

Nearby San Lorenzo and Tres Zapotes show similar if not more elaborate constructions. The pattern of trade and the emergence of chiefdoms is found in highland Oaxaca, Morelos, and in the Valley of Mexico. Similar sites occur throughout Mesoamerica at about the same time period, and archaeologists have noted the connections between chiefdom social structure and trade (Flannery and Marcus 1983).

Jade cache from La Venta.

The Rise of Chiefdoms and States

Several theories have been proposed to explain the appearance of chiefdoms and their transformations into states. Particularly important have been ecological and evolutionary explanations. Some of the factors that are thought to have been important in the transformation of tribes to chiefdoms and chiefdoms to states were: increasing energy consumption; changes in technology; increasing population densities; irrigation agriculture; and "ecological circumscription" (White 1959, Sahlins & Service 1960, Steward 1955, Harris 1979). More recently, trade has become a very important factor in explaining the transitions. However, none of these theories is adequate by itself, and some regions require explanations that place a greater weight on ecology and other regions on trade.

Ecological Explanations

The most common explanation for the shift from tribes to chiefdoms and then to states is an ecological one based on **ecological circumscription.** This ecological theory, developed by Robert Carneiro (1970), begins with the introduction of simple irrigation technology within a tribal setting. As irrigation technology improves, the population grows until it reaches the boundaries of its ecological setting (usually rich alluvial soils set in arid habitats or bounded by mountains). Populations ramify into different ecological zones and expand in numbers at the same time, introducing needs for social control, redistribution, and further improvements to irrigation technology. These three features—social control, redistribution, and irrigation agriculture—it was theorized, interacted to transform tribes into chiefdoms, and chiefdoms into states.

While the theory of ecological circumscription works for regions with alluvial valleys and arid habitats (Mesopotamia) or mountains (the Andean states), it does not work at all well for regions like the Hawaiian Islands or the Northwest Coast of North America. In both cases, chiefdoms developed, but they either had no agriculture at all (Northwest Coast) or had very little irrigation (Hawaii). Similar problems emerge with states described in this text arising in East Africa with pastoral nomadism (and no irrigation) or many states in Mesoamerica that lacked complex irrigation systems, or at least systems that could only be built by states. There is also the problem that some peoples with complex irrigation agriculture, such as the Ifugao of the Philippines, remained tribal.

Trade Factors

As early as 1974, a special seminar brought together archaeologists and economic anthropologists who emphasized the importance of trade in the emergence of complex societies. K. C. Chang, Robert McAdams, Jeremy Sabloff, and

David Friedel in Sabloff and Lambag-Karlovsky (1975) and others suggested that involvement in trade can bring rapid, massive changes in the structure and technology of society, as well as in patterns of motivation, mobility, and leadership.

The recognition that trade was a factor in these sociopolitical changes altered the traditional view of bands, tribes, chiefdoms, and states as independent evolving social units. A new perspective, which places states in the center of trade networks with chiefdoms, tribes, and bands progressively more peripheral, owes much to Eric Wolf's book *Europe and the People Without History* (1982). Wolf argued that anthropologists should stop trying to understand bands, tribes, chiefdoms, and states as autonomous and isolated social systems evolving toward some equilibrium endpoint justified by local resources. More recently, Richard Blanton and Gary Feinman (1984) have been studying the rise and fall of the civilizations of Mesoamerica (Mexico and northern Central America) in terms of interacting networks of trade rather than a series of independently evolving "empires" or "states" that replaced each other through time. Other anthropologists are responding to Feinman's theory by describing other regions of the world as "world systems," such as Darrell E. La Lone's study of "An Andean World System" (La Lone 1994), but the phrase "world system" is a problem because Immanuel Wallerstein used the term "*modern* world system" to describe the world's economy since its emergence in the sixteenth century (1974). What we are looking at is not "modern," and it is not capitalist in the sense defined in the next chapter. Wallerstein described the modern world system as composed of a core of wealthy and capitalist states in Western Europe, a periphery made up of societies that contributed wealth to the core and became poor, and a semi-periphery of societies that emerged in the twentieth century that were intermediate between core and periphery (e.g., Mexico and Brazil).

While Wallerstein's terms are useful, they should be modified for a premodern world. The term **tributary empire** is used here to refer to those "world systems" that existed prior to 1492. Within these, **hegemonic cores** dominated **tributary states.** Tributary states supplied tribute to the cores (the centers of empire). Outside of the empires, chiefdoms, tribes, and hunting and gathering bands were in contact with each other, warred and traded with each other. Sometimes the chiefdoms were turned into tributary states when the empire spread, and at other times they were independent of the core. This expanding and contracting model characterizes many of the regions of the world, such as the Valley of Mexico or the Tigris and Euphrates river valley. The periphery would be the regions of bands and tribes. The semi-periphery would correspond to chiefdoms.

Chiefdoms of the semi-periphery were found in places that were less able to monopolize trade than hegemonic cores but where resources would support large populations (such as the high islands of Hawaii or the Northwest Coast of North America). Tribes of the periphery were more remote still. From time to time tribes responded to trade and warfare by transforming into chiefdoms, and chiefdoms into states as happened in Central Asia with the Mongols under the leadership of Genghis Khan.

If the forces producing hierarchy were not maintained, the states or chiefdoms would collapse back into tribes. This happened to many empires in Asia, and it also appears to have happened in Central America and Colombia after the Conquest by Spain. Hunters and gatherers continued to occupy places that would not sustain large populations. In this new perspective, trade and warfare are viewed as dynamic components of political ecology, not as independent economic or cultural variables, and not really "causes."

The transaction cost model of Douglas North can be applied to the origins of chiefdoms and ancient states. North uses the concept of "transaction costs" to explain how trade affects human institutions. There are two types of transaction costs: the cost of transportation and the cost of gathering information to make trade predictable. The first type of cost is easily understood: It takes energy to move goods over a landscape, and that energy is the cost of transportation. Transportation costs can be lowered by making transportation easier (inventing the wheel, carrying goods by horse, using a boat). The second meaning is not as clear, but is easily understood. Any economic transaction, whether between individuals or groups, requires information. The following are examples of information needed: What is the distance to be traveled? How many men and women will it take to carry the goods or how many pack animals? How many boats? What are the dangers involved? Who will have to be paid off (toll booths, regional warlords)? What will the trader receive for his/her goods? How many battles will have to be fought, and how much will it cost to pay your protectors? It takes work to find the answers to these questions, and that work (also energy) is the information costs of a transaction. If a way can be found to reduce information costs, trade (or war) becomes more efficient. Those societies that can lower the costs of trade (or war) are more efficient, and all other things being equal, will have the greater opportunity to survive. We have seen that there are other variables probably at work, so trade and its costs do not provide a full explanation for the origins of chiefdoms and states, but they are important factors.

If this sounds too abstract, think for a moment what happens when you go shopping. The work put into shopping is a transaction cost. You lower the cost of transaction by studying newspaper advertisements. For example, think of buying a used car. You would never think of driving all over a large city to check the costs of a used car because the transaction costs (gasoline, time) would be very high. By reading a newspaper, you drop your transaction costs, and your "trade" relations become more efficient. Think of a city with no newspapers, where every good has to be checked on by every buyer each time there is a transaction. This is an example of high transaction costs. Introduce newspapers and other types of advertising and transaction costs drop, making economic transactions more efficient. This is an example of reduced transaction costs.

Hegemonic empires, cores and tributary states, have been described by Carla Sinopoli in her studies of the Vijayanagara Empire of India, and the model applied to precapitalist states (1994a, 1994b). Applying North's idea of transaction costs, we can connect hierarchy to trade and warfare through the idea of transaction costs. Hierarchy, in the form of bureaucracy, is one way to reduce transaction costs; it is a means of organizing complex events to make a transaction more efficient. Bureaucracies can aid in improving transportation by directing the building of roads and their maintenance, developing armies to protect the roads, but they are also a means of reducing information costs by collecting information on future transactions (spying?). But at the same time, bureaucracies can be expensive because it takes work and specialists (who have to be fed) to staff them. A bureaucracy or hierarchy will expand as long as it increases the efficiency of a growing political system, but may collapse if it overextends itself and becomes unprofitable (as appears to have happened over and over in human history).

In societies in which the ownership of resources is in collectives (clans), transaction costs can be reduced by centralizing decision-making into a chiefdom. In such societies, traders benefit because the demands of kinsmen from clans and lineages are reduced, and they are better able to cooperate with the evolving authority system in the development of monopolies of trade (and may themselves be a part of the evolving or independent state). Additional centralization into states can reduce transaction costs further. The ownership of resources will shift from collective ownership in clans and lineages to the ownership of major resources by the state. It makes no sense to develop hierarchy and bureaucracy when there are no gains (profits) to be made, so only those societies that are in the paths of trade will benefit by greater hierarchy. Shifts in trade routes can bring about the development of chiefdoms and states, but can also bring about their collapse.

The emergence of ritual warfare may be connected to decreasing transaction costs. Among the first patterns that appear with chiefdoms is the ritualization of warfare. The classic feuding style of warfare found among tribes, which makes violence against the traveler unpredictable, was transformed into ritual war. Ritual war is predictable, almost like a weekly football game between two cities, and can reduce the costs of transactions (allowing trade) when societies

The Vijayanagara Empire of India was, in part, a response to overland trade.

wish to exchange goods, because the center of violence can be avoided. Among the Olmec of Mesoamerica, we find evidence for ritual warfare in the form of capturing warriors of other chiefdoms for human sacrifice. This appears to have been a well-organized, ritual event, and from time to time took *the form of a ritual ball game* played in ball courts. The losers of either wars or ball games were sacrificed.

Another feature that appears in chiefdoms and states is the religious pilgrimage. Pilgrimages resulted in a substantial number of travelers going to a sacred ceremonial center where they not only worshipped their gods, but exchanged goods. The evidence for pilgrimages occurs in the archaeology of La Venta, but also for most of the early chiefdom sites in Mesoamerica such as San Jose Mogote and Chalcatzingo in the Central Mexican highlands. Similar types of developments have been mentioned for the Shan chiefdoms of Burma, and a few archaeologists have argued that the cores of the first chiefdoms were pilgrimage centers (Flannery and Marcus 1983, Drennan 1976). The pilgrimage–trade connection is still common in the Andes today among the Aymara and Quechua, who organize pilgrimages to carry the images of Christ and the Virgin Mary to Catholic cathedrals, where markets are established and goods are bought and sold. It is suggested that sacred pilgrimages were one way of reducing transaction costs by producing a safe zone where economic transactions could occur without fear of war. Both institutions, ritual warfare and pilgrimages, reduce transaction costs by making trade predictable and possible.

The type of trade that occurred between chiefdoms was primarily stimulated by differential access to resources between neighboring societies (not differences within societies). This is particularly evident in Mesoamerica where highland–lowland trade appears to have stimulated the development of La Venta, San Lorenzo, and Tres Zapotes in the lowlands of Mexico and Chalcatzingo, San Jose Mogote, and Cuicuilco in the highlands. The peoples of the lowlands traded such goods as feathers, shells, stingray spines, and other products from the Pacific littoral for such highland products as obsidian, jade, mica, and other minerals.

The essential difference between trade between tribes and trade between chiefdoms is that in chiefdoms trade is organized by a central authority (the paramount chief), while in tribes it is not (and transaction costs are very high in trade between tribes. . .a lot of work is involved because trade is between individuals). The centralization and the control of production in chiefdoms for purposes of trade and redistribution would have increased efficiency. The same is true for ritual warfare. Both long-distance trade and long-distance ritual warfare benefit through increased levels of hierarchy.

Chiefdoms evolved as populations increased, as resources were worked more intensively to support them, and as trade increased in volume and distance. The institutions of chiefdoms became those of states. Ritual warfare became tributary warfare as it intensified, increasing the need for hierarchy, and improving the efficiencies of organization, which in turn expanded the success of both trade and warfare. In tributary warfare, states are subjugated to the power of a core and forced to pay tribute in food or other forms of wealth. It is no longer enough to "count coup" by touching another warrior with a stick or sacrificing him during a ceremony; now it pays to demand tribute from the defeated warriors. While the Olmec had ritual warfare, by the time of the Aztecs, war was for tribute. The Aztec state gathered tribute from hundreds of other cities, towns, and villages throughout the highlands of Mexico that were in subsidiary ritual relationship to it; this was also true of other imperial states. The wars were similar to those of the chiefdom level and were formalized, but the losers now became a part of empires and paid tribute in many forms, including women, quills filled with gold, mantles, fine feathers, jade, and gold (Gasco and Voorhies 1989).

Gradually, local alliances or warfare allowed a few chiefdoms to gain access and control over the resources of the surrounding tribes, incorporating them into the core chiefdom. Over time, these systems became hegemonic empires. Societies that were too far away, too warlike, or whose resources were poor would be left alone and retained their tribal social structures. An important point to remember is that a hierarchical bureaucracy is costly to maintain, and is itself a type of transaction cost. It will not survive unless there are strong incentives. When the expense of maintaining hierarchy becomes too great, hierarchies collapse (North 1990).

Successful incorporation of other chiefdoms led to the transformation of land ownership from the independent clan or lineage of the tribe to the paramount chief. When this process continued, chiefdoms were converted into states. Where the process could not continue, chiefdoms retained their structure for hundreds of years, until the emergence of the modern world system after 1492 caused their collapse.

Why did not all chiefdoms evolve into states? There was a limit on the expansion of certain chiefdoms where resources were limited, such as Polynesia or the Northwest Coast. Trade and warfare are expensive, and are associated with growing tax and tributary rates. As chiefdoms grew larger, their armies and traders had to go further afield. The demand for greater taxes from commoners and tributary fiefs had their limits and alienated the commoner class. Societies located in a region where trade could not be monopolized could not transform themselves into states. Such would occur in oceanic situations where chiefdoms could not monopolize sea trade or where there are few natural boundaries, such as mountains, forcing trade through narrow river valleys.

The Dynamics of Archaic States and Empires

The picture usually drawn for the evolution of the state is that it was a slow, incremental process during which people passed from a relatively egalitarian tribe–chiefdom social system to a bureaucratically organized and hierarchical state. The changes are explained technologically through the introduction of intensive irrigation-based agriculture, over which the elites first gained control, and then used to control commoners, peasants, and slaves. So much time passed in the process that when the state came into existence, the average commoner had no memory of the garden of tribal or chiefdom Eden. But this picture is inaccurate. In the two regions of the world where good data are available, Mesopotamia and Mesoamerica, the shift from chiefdoms to states was dramatic and very rapid. In Mesopotamia, the shift from multi-village desert chiefdoms to the state of Uruk took only a few hundred years, and the population going through the transition must have been aware of what was happening and participated in the transition. In Mesoamerica, the shift from the chiefdom of Teotihuacán (pop. 35,000) to the state of Teotihuacán (pop. 150,000) happened with the same speed and drama, literally overnight. There is no evidence of force being used to coerce commoners to accept the authority of the emerging state.

As noted earlier, societies do not evolve independently within an ecological setting that limits their final stage of sociocultural organization; rather, societies are interconnected in networks extending over natural regions, and it is the interconnections that facilitate change. In Mesopotamia, between 4500 and 4000 B. C., several Ubaidian desert chiefdoms were transformed into the Mesopotamian state system of Uruk (Algaze 1993). In Mesoamerica, chiefdoms at Teotihuacán, Cholula, and Monte Alban in the highlands and Tikal, Bonampok, and Palenque shifted from chiefdom to state status between 1100 and 700 B. C. Between the same years, there emerged an Andean hegemonic system in South America, the core of which was ultimately dominated by the Inca state in the fifteenth century A.D. before it fell to the Spanish invaders.

The model that emerges at the state level is the same as the one described for chiefdoms, but bigger and, paradoxically, less complex at the level of decision-making. And while chiefdoms are similar to each other, the institutions

Aerial view of Ur with Ziggurat of Umannu.

of core states at the center of hegemonic systems share even greater similarity. Philip Curtin, a historian, argues that after a certain point the institutions promoting cross-cultural trade become the same, even though they operate inside very different cultures. Why this is so brings us back to the relationship among trade, tributary warfare, and hierarchy. Distance and volume of trade or war makes these activities expensive and complicated. To lower expenses societies become increasingly hierarchical and bureaucratic. The ownership of resources is taken over by the state (the king), and large bureaucracies are created, managed by aristocrats who can show kinship connections to the king or who pledge unwavering allegiance. The bureaucracies take over the decision-making process; fewer people make more of the decisions for the society, and in a sense complexity has been resolved through simplicity (there are fewer people running the show; commoners obey elites, and do not make their own decisions). The paradox: complexity creates simplicity.

States, Elizabeth Brumfiel writes,

> are powerful, complex, institutionalized hierarchies of public decision-making and control. They are created to implement the relations of production in stratified societies and to mediate conflict between diverse economic interest groups (1994:1).

Let us look briefly at some of the preindustrial state systems (or empires) that existed prior to the development of the "modern" world system.

The Early Mesopotamian Empires

The prehistory of Mesopotamia is exceedingly complex. City-states and empires rose and fell. Beginning about 6000 B. C. or much earlier, widespread trade came into existence and was extensive throughout the area and beyond. Economic and political allegiances shifted and changed, and cross-cultural communications were probably extensive. Despite considerable archaeological research, the record is still lacking in detail and precision. Below we provide only a brief account.

Core temple communities implying a chiefdom level of organization begin to appear as early as five to six thousand B. C. in Southwest Asia. In the Levant, which is located just on the margin of the eastern Mediterranean, fairly substantial agricultural chiefdoms existed at 6000 B. C. Jericho was a town with a high wall and several thousand people, and has the features we expect of chiefdoms. Further east, on the "hilly flanks" of the Taros and Zagros mountains, economies based on herding sheep, goats, pigs, and cattle and growing wheat and barley were well developed. Agriculture began its spread from this region into Europe and transformed hunting and gathering societies into tribal agriculturalists over the following millennia (Renfrew 1987).

Some of the upland villages grew large and had well-designed temples, implying chiefdom social structures. One of the most remarkable was Çatal Hüyük in south central Turkey that was thirty-two acres in size at 6000 B. C. Further east in the highlands of Iran and Iraq were other similar temple communities such as Jarmo, Sawwan, and Choga Mami. The temple centers apparently also served as storage centers for surplus foods that were needed by the tributary villages during periods of drought (Frankfort 1956).

The chief of the core community would probably have been first on a line of descent from an originator god or an earlier chief (Krader 1968:56–57). Like chiefs in many chiefdom societies, he would have been also a reservoir of religious knowledge; and he would have been able to control the community because he was the conduit of communication—the crucial link—between the people and their deities. Since one of the primary threats to the community in Southwest Asia would have been drought, there is good reason to think he would have also been a "water wizard." That is, there may have been a strong belief that the chief's relationship to supernatural forces was responsible for bringing water. (We find a similar belief in Mesoamerica.) Few would be tempted to challenge such power because the result might be a dry spell brought on by angry gods through the medium of an angry chief. There is evidence from one chiefdom, Eridu, that the temple community worshiped Enlil, a water god represented by a fish (Eridu is one of the many sites classified as "Ubaidian," discussed below).

At about 3400 B. C. in Southwest Asia, and somewhat later in Egypt and China, we find the chiefdom-structured temple community with its probable collective ownership of property under a single chief shifting in social structure to become the city-state, the core of an archaic empire. Growing populations, increasingly more complex water works, trade relations with other growing states, and, probably of greatest importance, the subjugation of weaker peripheral chiefdoms and tribal societies to the status of tribute-paying members of the core state are the significant factors that brought the city-state into existence. Thus, Uruk, the first of a series of city states in this region, came into being.

This change occurred not in the fertile hilly flanks region, but south on the dry Mesopotamian plain. For most of its length, the Mesopotamian plain of the Tigris and Euphrates rivers is less than 200 miles wide. It is arid, a rain shadow region of the Pontic mountains to the west, and was originally best suited to pastoral nomadism. Anthropologists once theorized that the development of irrigation agriculture stimulated state development, but it is now clear that trade down the two river systems was the stimulus (Algaze 1993). The first known city-state was Uruk. Emerging out of the Ubaid chiefdom-level cultures, it became the core of the first hegemonic empire (4000–3100 B. C.).

The Ubaidian cultures, and those of Uruk that followed, belong to the region of Sumerian language and culture. Uruk first became a core city-state dominating outlying villages and towns, and then spread into the highlands to control trade and tribute over a vast region. The shift from the latest Ubaid phase (known as Ubaid 4) to the city of Uruk was dramatic. First there were just a few villages, then during the Early Uruk phase the population suddenly tripled in size, going from 800 to 2,400 people, and the population of the region jumped from 6,000 in sixteen villages to 20,000 in forty-five villages (Johnson 1973). Many of the sites contained workshops where artisans produced high-quality ceramics that were traded throughout a vast region. Within a few hundred years accounting devices were produced that used styluses to mark soft clay tablets. These were fired in ovens. The tablets indicate that bureaucrats in the core were concerned with production, trade, tribute, and control over a periphery of lesser states and chiefdoms. Often a chiefdom would become transformed into a hegemonic state, only to become the tributary state of another core. As an example, one of the first cores was at Kish, an early kingdom. But its ruler came into conflict with the then-ruler of Warka, Gilgamesh. Gilgamesh conquered Kish and turned it into a tributary state of Warka. During this early period, it was common for the core of power to shift from one city-state to another.

The city continued to expand in the Middle Uruk period during which time monumental architecture appeared, suggesting the increasing importance of state and religious activities. Elite government administrators were appointed to the outlying peripheral states as ambassadors or consuls and kept track of tribute owed and paid by using small clay counting devices kept in hollow clay balls. Early theories held that these urban systems came into existence because of irrigation agriculture, but the Uruk irrigation systems were not large enough to feed the city dwellers. Much food was probably received as tribute from the periphery (as was the case for the city of Tenochtitlan in highland Mexico, and probably for the earlier Teotihuacan').

In the following millennium, from 3000 to 2000 B. C., the Uruk core acquired the characteristics of true urban society with 70 to 80 percent of the population living in urban centers of 1000 people or more. The city of Uruk grew to 40,000 people or more. Each city belonged to a founding god drawn from the complex Sumerian pantheon to whom a large temple was dedicated. These temples, called *ziggurats*, were giant stepped pyramids made of clay bricks. A temple bureaucracy controlled the urban centers.

Uruk collapsed when it was unable to sustain control over Mesopotamia. It was followed by Ur at 2800 B. C., which grew to be even larger than Uruk. Archaeologists believe that Ur had larger armies and more efficient bureaucracies than Uruk. The bureaucracies were a means of decreasing transaction costs, but were themselves an expense. The bureaucracies were also involved in the development of waterworks, particularly irrigation systems, the building of roads, and the protection of cities. The economies were centralized and goods were distributed to the various social classes according to status. During the development of Ur, true writing evolved out of the record-keeping clay tablets and this may explain how it became more efficient and able to control a larger area. Writing, bureaucracies, and trade were all linked. As trade expanded in volume and distance, writing became more efficient and the state more bureaucratic. With the growth of the state, the power of the ruler grew. In death, the ruler of Ur and other royalty were accompanied by sacrificed soldiers and retainers, which were entombed along with wagons and oxen. One tomb of the later core city of Ur contained seventy-four people, of which sixty-four were women of the court in ceremonial dress. Human sacrifice is common in the period of early states both in the Old World and the New World. Human sacrifice is a means of symbolizing the power of the state and the sacred quality of the king; it not only conferred power on the king but may have been a means of social control as well.

The core–periphery set of relationships in Southwest Asia changed through time for reasons that are very poorly understood. Later, new core states would emerge and in turn collapse as they abused their ecosystems or lost their efficiencies of war and/or trade and became corrupt. Today, the floor of the Tigris and Euphrates has many examples, including that of Ur, that collapsed because of salinization, the process in which irrigation cannot clear away the accumulation of salts or poor planning led to waterlogged fields, problems that still plague this region today and make irrigation an important feature of state planning (Spooner 1982). Babylon followed Ur and, in turn, was followed by the Assyrian and Persian empires in Southwest Asia. All of these "inland empires" were based on the monopoly of long-distance trade, redistribution economies (markets are very rare), and the construction of massive cities with gigantic architecture symbolizing the power of the state and its rulers and absolutist religions. It is easy to argue that the religions of these inland empires were personality cults based on the power of the king and his queen. The massive quality of these early inland states, the control of trade by the state, and the absolutist qualities of religion continued through the time of the Persian Empire, and then gradually ceased as economic and political power shifted to the empires of the inland sea.

After the seventh century A.D., the rise of Islam led ultimately to the rise of the Ottoman Empire in Turkey. World War I, and the monopolization of trade by Western Europe and North America, transformed the Mesopotamian hegemonic system into a periphery of the modern world system. Its primary function became that of supplying oil to the Western industrial core. In recent years, Iran and Iraq have warred with each other to reclaim control of the region where ancient civilizations once flourished. The Persian Gulf War can be understood as the attempt by Saddam Hussein to give birth to a new and powerful Mesopotamian civilization (potentially dangerous from the viewpoint of the Western nations).

Empires of the Inland Sea: The Mediterranean

The empires of Mesopotamia were primarily based on overland trade following river systems. Overland trade made these empires rich as long as they could monopolize the regional economies. Irrigation supported large populations, but to it were added the taxes paid by tributary states upriver and downriver. Boats were used where possible, but trade relied heavily on wheeled vehicles pulled by draft animals (horses, asses, and oxen). Transaction costs were high in these geographically massive inland empires. West of Mesopotamia, a very different series of tributary states evolved based on waterborne trade, which pushed down transaction costs. Here were found Hissarlike (Troy in western Turkey) and Kultepe, whose building styles were the basis for those of the later Greek and Roman empires of the Mediterranean.

Troy was a port city on the Aegean Sea. The rich royal tombs of Troy, excavated by Heinrich Schliemann in the late nineteenth century, contained the bodies of men and their wives accompanied by fine ornaments made of copper and gold. Troy and other city-states of the Aegean and eastern Mediterranean were involved in long-distance trade, which slowly turned to the use of small sailing ships that were able to sail further and further from shore. Contact with Mesopotamia increased and trading centers called *karums* emerged with marketplaces. The karums were neutral entrepots or commercial centers where prices were regulated by the authorities of the cities, but it appears that the giant trade monopolies of the inland empires were not characteristic of the city-states of the inland sea.

Mainland Greece had been inhabited as far back as 6500 B. C. The people first lived in stone and mud houses connected by courtyards and passages (Fagan 1985). Similar villages are found on the island of Crete as far back as 5500 B. C. After 3500 B.C., southern Greece developed the cultivation of olives and grapevines interspersed with cereal crops. There was a tremendous increase in village crafts as well as the manufacturing of painted pottery, marble vessels, and magnificent stone axes. Copper and bronze were introduced and were tied to the rapid increase of trade throughout the Aegean (Renfrew and Wagstaff 1982).

According to Brian Fagan, the Aegean is well endowed with comfortable ports that allowed waterborne trade and easy communication among the various islands. Sailing vessels are depicted on Cretan seals as early as 2000 B. C. Trade in olive oil, wine, metal tools and ores, marble vessels, and pottery flourished. With the shift from overland to sea-based trade, transaction costs plummeted, and there began an inexorable shift away from massive, theocratic states with the architectural emblems of empire to trade empires that depended less on complete hegemony for survival. Could it be that giant pyramids were killed by ships? The building styles that emerge in the Aegean are much less massive than what preceded them in Mesopotamia or Egypt. (Egypt is covered in the chapter on the Middle East.) Might it not be that the shift from overland trade to sea trade was tied to a shift in energy used from monument-building to building ships? This is an interesting but speculative idea. However, as Leslie White argued almost fifty years ago, societies at any given time have access to only limited amounts of energy and must make choices about how to use it.

The Minoans   The Minoans were famous shipbuilders, and while their palaces at Knossos on the island of Crete are fascinating, the monuments are nothing like the massive constructions of Mesopotamia and Egypt. On the other hand their ships were huge and magnificent, transporting gold, silver, ivory, wine, and olive oil, in exchange for ornaments from Central Europe, the Aegean, and the Near East. Even ostrich eggs from North Africa were traded.

At least nine periods of Minoan civilization have been uncovered. Greece and the mainland of Italy had Minoan colonies, and formed the periphery of the sea-based civilization. Even in the earliest periods, trade occurred with ancient Egypt. At 3730 B. C. signs of long-distance trading increase. In 1700 B. C. an earthquake leveled the palaces, and building began anew. The palace at Knossos reached its greatest size between 1700 and 1450 B.C. (The palace at Knossos has been replicated in a fine restaurant found on the wharf in Tarpon Springs, Florida.) These buildings, made of limestone blocks and wood columns, are noted for the fine artwork on the walls that tells us a lot about life on Crete. The buildings themselves are not spectacular. Among the scenes depicted are acrobats leaping across the backs of bulls and aristocratic courts.

The Cretans were renowned mariners, and paintings of their sea exploits are found on the walls of the palaces at Knossos. Their religion included human sac-

Palace at Knossos.

rifice and the worship of Zeus as a bull, and an Earth Mother complex. The exact nature of their social and political structures is not well understood because their writing system, called Linear B, also used by the mainland culture of Mycenae, has not yet been completely decoded. However, the gods of the people of Minoa are very similar to those of the Greeks who follow. One tantalizing piece of the jigsaw puzzle was the story of the Minotaur, a mythological creature who was quartered in a "labyrinth" under the central palace of Knossos. The story of Ariadne, who used a string to find her way in and out of the labyrinth, was told by the Greeks a thousand years later, but the meaning of the legend is puzzling. Was the Minotaur evidence for a fertility cult? Did it have something to do with the cult of bull acrobatics in which young men and women grabbed the horns of onrushing bulls and leapt over their backs? These legends and the archaeology of the palace yield thin clues, and there is much guesswork. It is fairly obvious that the power of the Minoan elite differs significantly from Egyptian or Mesopotamian kings. Religion is not a personality cult, and it is difficult to identify specific kings and their queens. Religion has shifted, possibly in the direction of Greece with its mysteries and oracles, from a centralized and totalistic religion linked to a massive bureaucracy, to something very different, in which the "gods" have more human dimensions. In 1473 B.C., a volcanic explosion destroyed Minoan Crete, and the core of power shifted in the direction of the Aegean mainland.

Ancient Greece   European civilization traces its roots back to Greece, which itself was preceded by Mycenaean civilization. Mycenaean kings ruled over walled fortresses and were buried in spectacular shaft graves. The lives of the kings were immortalized in the epics of the poet Homer. The Mycenaeans refined a writing system originally developed by the Minoans. Mycenae dominated Mediterranean trade until it was destroyed by northern barbarians. After the fall of Mycenae in 1200 B.C., small-town merchants on the Greek mainland continued to trade. By the seventh and eighth centuries, B. C., small colonies of Greek settlers lived on the northern and western shores of the Black Sea and along the north coast of Anatolia.

In Greece many fertile agricultural areas are separated by ranges of mountains. Traders formed networks of small city-states that competed with each other for trade and political power. Athens, one of the larger and more prosperous states, was rivaled by Sparta. Greek city-states only unified in times of political stress, such as when the Persian King Xerxes tried to dominate Greece. His defeat at Marathon (490 B.C.), and again ten years later in a naval battle at Salamis, brought the Greek city-states together and produced the age of Classical Greek civilization (Fagan 1985).

Athens was the foremost of the Greek city-states and became the head of a league of maritime cities, which were transformed into an empire. Athens attracted wealthy immigrants, built the Parthenon, and produced philosophers and playwrights whose works come down to us today: Plato, Socrates, Sophocles, Aeschylus, and many others. Classical Greek civilization only flourished for fifty years, yet during this brief time produced the idea of a democratic civilization.

The lowered transaction costs of sea trade made a thriving economy possible without theocratic bureaucracies. Athens produced a democratic civilization with a religion that was much less totalistic than anything that came before. Reading Greek mythology, one has the feeling that the gods and goddesses were much less frightening beings than those that preceded them. They demanded much less of people, and acted a lot more like humans than powerful gods. Even the Minoans practiced human sacrifice, but with the Greeks that ritual ended. Is there a relationship between reduced transaction costs, democracy, and a flourishing maritime economy? This is an interesting question that cannot be answered with the limited data. But the relationships are provocative and worth mentioning.

Athenian supremacy was not to last, however. Bickering with Sparta never abated, and there were deep animosities between the two cities. Sparta's government was based on military discipline and a rigid class structure, while Athens was more mobile and democratic. Rivalries led to the disastrous Peloponnesian War (431–404 B.C.), which left Sparta dominant but Greece in disarray. Greece soon fell under the control of Philip of Macedonia, who ruled between 359 and 336 B.C. His son, Alexander the Great, then created an empire that embraced the entire eastern Mediterranean as far as Mesopotamia, uniting the entire ancient world. But his empire too was not to last and fell apart within a generation.

One other state worth mentioning arose where Lebanon is today. Known as the Phoenician empire, it resembled the Greek city-states but was less of an empire than a network of trading cities with their anchor in Lebanon. The Phoenicians set up cities throughout North Africa, the most famous of which was Carthage, which was to challenge the power of the Roman Empire.

The Roman Empire   None of the civilizations that we have examined in the Mediterranean dominated the surrounding region as totally as the ancient societies that preceded them. This is not true of Rome, which developed into a massive trade-based empire. The Roman empire developed out of earlier small

Etruscan democratic city-states, not unlike those of the Greeks. Some of the Etruscan buildings were substantial and the architecture and art evolved into Roman building and art styles.

The Etruscans were the first people to fortify the famous seven hills of Rome. In 509 B.C., the last Etruscan king was expelled by native Romans, who began to develop their own city-state. Influenced by Classical Greek civilization, the Romans created their own distinctive culture. By 295 B.C., Rome dominated the whole of central Italy, and by 280 B.C. the entire Italian Peninsula (Freeman 1993). At this time, Rome was democratic, governed by a delicate balance of aristocratic and popular authority (Fagan 1995:457). After two hard-fought wars with Carthage, the Romans achieved mastery over the western Mediterranean by 200 B.C. By 133 B. C., much of Asia Minor was under Roman domination. As Rome expanded, civil strife led to autocratic rule, first under the dictator Julius Caesar, who was followed by his great-nephew and heir, Octavian (also called Augustus) (Freeman 1993). Under Caesar, the Mediterranean and much of Europe was brought under Roman rule. Roman legions campaigned in Egypt, Mesopotamia, India, and as far as western Europe and Britain.

The Emperor Augustus reorganized the civil service and established the Pax Romana over a vast region. There followed a period of great material prosperity and peace, but in the second and third centuries Roman rule began to founder. Shortage of land for farming and increasing disrespect for Rome led Germanic tribes at the periphery of the Roman core to challenge Rome's hegemony. In A. D. 395, when Emperor Theodosius died, the Roman Empire split into a western and eastern division. Tribal- and chiefdom-organized societies to the north continued to attack, and finally sacked Rome itself. The European provinces were overrun by warrior chiefdoms, and Rome collapsed.

What were these warrior chiefdoms? The Romans themselves have left descriptions of the Celtic and Germanic tribes and chiefdoms, and they are essentially like the tribes and chiefdoms we have discussed: They were organized into matrilineal (Celtic) or patrilineal (Germanic) clans, under chiefs who had control of mana, and who relied on magicians for their power (think of Merlin the magician in the court of King Arthur). Roman rule was never able to completely dominate the chiefdoms of the northern fringe, and descriptions of these people come down to us in Roman writing and European mythology. Among the best known are the Celtic tribes of what are today Scotland, Wales, and Ireland. These, and their Germanic neighbors to the east, constantly challenged Roman authority. Roman towns were found in the lowland valleys along rivers, but Roman rule did not control the tribes and chiefdoms of the periphery, fitting the model we have described (core–periphery). Rome overextended itself, and it is not that the "barbarians" of the periphery became stronger than Rome, but that Rome itself lost its capacity to control its bureaucracy and army. For example, the Roman government sent "consuls" to rule the provinces, often granting them land. The representatives from Rome often married into the local chiefly aristocracy, and their children lost their loyalty to the central core. Later, when the Roman armies tried to subject rebellious chiefs on the fringe of their empire, they faced fighters trained in Roman techniques of war.

After the collapse of Rome, the tribes and chiefdoms of the periphery over time became the European states, particularly as they assimilated the new Christian religion which spread from Rome as it disintegrated. In the next section we will discuss these peoples, particularly in western Europe where the manorial system, established by the Romans originally, became coupled to medieval Christianity and emerged as feudalism.

Brian Fagan points out that Rome left an impressive legacy:

> Its material legacy can be seen in the road system, which still provides a basis for many of Europe's and the Near East's communications, and in the towns, like London, which are still flourishing modern cities. In cultural terms, its principal legacy was the legal system, which lies at the core of most Western law codes. Roman literature and art dominated European culture for centuries after the Renaissance (1995:458).

The collapse of the Roman Empire created a vacuum in the Mediterranean that was filled by the development of the north African Islamic empires. These sat on the Great Silk road, and made inroads as far as central France and most of Spain, controlling all trade for centuries. These new cores, mostly city-states, monopolized the overland trade routes east to China and the sea routes of the Mediterranean. The lack of access to trade was one of the most important factors pushing the European states into the "Dark Ages," from which they were not to emerge until after the Spanish drove the Moors out of Spain, united under the Catholic monarchs, Ferdinand of Aragon and Isabella of Castile, and sponsored the voyages to the Western Hemisphere, opening new trade routes west over the Atlantic Ocean, and later across the Pacific.

The Origin of Feudalism in Ancient Europe

Until 1985, the world was dominated by the modern world system made up of a Euro-American core with peripheries in Africa, Asia, and Latin America. Today the modern world system is being transformed into a global system in which the core is fragmenting and segments of the periphery are taking on core characteristics (open markets, capitalism, private property rights, democratic reform), in ways that are very surprising to traditional anthropology. The origins of the modern world system are inauspicious and lie in cultural adaptations of west European states. In order to understand their origins, we have to delve into their prehistories.

While chiefdoms emerged in Western Europe quite early, there was a lack of stimulus for their transformation into states until very late. Explanations for this supposed backwardness range from primitive technologies to mythic religions. However, Western Europe simply did not lend itself to the development of irrigation-style civilizations with large populations, such as are found in other parts of the world, and trade was not a major stimulus to development. There are two reasons for this. First, fertile regions are not circumscribed by mountains and deserts in Europe. Western Europe, for the most part, is a region of vast plains and woodlands. The populations of the region used a form of slash-and-burn agriculture from about 5000 B. C. to about 1500 B. C. when the Bell Beaker people (named for the shape of a pottery bowl) introduced the iron-tipped plow and oxen. But even the introduction of this new technology did not give rise to any dramatic changes. The lack of circumscribed environments meant that people were free to migrate to new locations whenever population densities began to produce unacceptable social and economic pressures. There was little to tie people to specific regions. As late as the fourteenth and fifteenth centuries there was a lot of unoccupied land, particularly in northern Europe. Population pressures resulted in migration, not hierarchy. While trade was important, it remained local and limited in scope. Trade was limited because first Greece and then Rome dominated trade in the Mediterranean. Later, Islamic empires were to control the same trade routes. It was not until Europe spread to monopolize those routes that trade stimulated the rise of states in Western Europe.

A second factor is the prevalence of rainfed agriculture. Irrigation agriculture is both a means of sustaining large populations and a means of controlling them. Irrigation systems were not needed in Western Europe. Rainfall was adequate for productive agriculture. Without irrigation or trade there was little stimulus to restrict settlement to river valleys, develop large communities, or develop the management complexes needed by early irrigation-based societies (such as the Chinese mandarins). The introduction of agriculture does not seem to have had the same impact on the region of Western Europe as it did in other world regions where civilizations evolved. Even after the spread of Bronze Age cultures through the Central Aegean (Crete, Greece) into parts of Southeastern Europe between 4,000 B. C. and 500 B. C., little dramatic change in level of sociocultural integration occurred in western Europe.

Colin Renfrew, one of the foremost archaeologists working on European prehistory, thinks that most of Western Europe was occupied by clan-based chiefdoms (Renfrew 1979) until the period of Roman domination. These chiefdoms would never number more than a few thousand people. They would be tied to local nature gods, to whom the people would make sacrifices. Very little of this ancient time comes down to us. We do know that the people spoke various Celtic dialects, some of which became Scots, Irish, Welsh, and Cornish in later history. Like other chiefdoms, they were warlike, with the men painting their naked bodies blue before going into war, which they fought in the nude. Their religions we can only speculate about. The religious celebrations centered on burial vaults where the great chiefs and ancestors were buried. These burial vaults are scattered throughout most of Western Europe as massive standing rocks called **menghirs, dolmens,** and **passage graves.** What mythology we have of the time period implies some form of matrilineal descent (for Celtic peoples), which was also practiced on the other side of the ocean, in eastern North America, until the European Conquest. We also know very little about trade during the prehistoric period. Agricultural states were relatively late on the scene in Western European history, coming into existence only in the seventh century A. D. These European states differed from other archaic world systems in that they were highly decentralized and comparatively weak. The story of the development of city-states and peasant societies in Western Europe begins and, then, for a while, ends with the rise and fall of the Roman Empire. The chiefdom societies that existed in pre-Roman Western Europe are poorly understood today, despite extensive archaeological remains. The remains range from such impressive structures as Stonehenge on the Salisbury Plain in southern England to burial shafts known as dolmens, which are found as far north as Denmark and as far south as Spain.

The Impact of Roman Rule

The imposition of Roman rule changed the chiefdom social structures significantly in some regions, but not in others. The strongest changes were in West Central Europe where Germany and France are today. Portions of eastern Great Britain were also substantially changed, and many Roman ruins are found there today. However, the regions of Wales, Ireland, Cornwall, and Scotland retained much of their ancient forms of organization, continuing to operate in decentralized chiefdom social structures until after the Middle Ages. The major organizational shift in all of these regions was the development of the Roman administrative town, strategically placed in important military and trade locations. These towns were primarily garrison towns, but they also had important trade and tribute functions as Rome traded its manufactured goods and wines up into the northerly provinces of its empire in exchange for grains and timber. Soldiers, garrisoned in the towns, protected traders against thieves and bandits. Certain of these towns, such as London and Paris, achieved the status of city-states, although it is doubtful that they controlled much of the countryside or developed a peasantry until the seventh or eighth centuries A. D.

The relationship of the town to the rural countryside is fuzzy. It does not appear that the rulers of the garrison towns and city-states originally had direct control over the rural peasantry. Rather, it appears that while the towns were ruled over by "consuls" appointed by Rome, often from the regions where they lived, the country people were still organized into clans under the rule of chiefs,

A chiefdom from pre-Roman England: Stonehenge.

who in turn paid homage to the towns and city-states and were responsible for the actions of their kinsmen. The Romans looked down on the country people and referred to them as "barbarians" (Cunliffe 1974).

It is extremely difficult to pinpoint when this social structure began to shift. However, with Roman rule, which lasted almost 500 years, population densities began to climb. Land became increasingly scarce and it would appear that the rural chiefdoms were slowly converted into fortified manors as the competition for land intensified. By 700 A.D., which marks the end of Roman rule and the beginning of the Middle Ages, the social structures of Europe were made up of key towns, usually established on the banks of major rivers, most of which survive today, and a rural countryside made up of fortified manorial estates. The manors were originally occupied by representatives of the Roman state, and may have been the origin of the "manorial system" we will describe later. The manors fed the towns and were administratively tied to them, and were not part of the distant chiefdoms. The riverain towns monopolized trade along the river valleys. When Roman rule ended, the administrative power of the towns waned, and a class of manorial lords found themselves in control of a rural countryside, but then lost control to rural chiefs. The disintegration of Roman rule resulted in a period of extensive, although not always intensive, conflict, as manorial lords vied with one another to expand their rural holdings. In many instances, the local chiefs replaced the manorial lords, but in many other instances the manorial lords shifted their allegiances to the chiefs and became part of the manorial system (the exact series of events is not clear).

While 700 A.D. more or less marks the end of Roman rule in Western Europe, it also marks the beginnings of the spread of Christianity, trade, and the growth of tributary states. At the heart of the newly emerging economy was the manor and the river-based town. The manors were agricultural, while the towns depended on trade. Christianity differed from the traditional nature religions of the ancient Celts and Germans in being "universalistic"; that is, Christianity was a religion that could appeal to anyone, not just a person from a specific locale. The lords of the manors adopted the new religion as missionary priests migrated from Rome into northern Europe. The new religion served the political function of uniting people within the **manorial system.**

The manorial system, as a distinct rural economy, emerges after the seventh century from the rule of Rome. It is based on agriculture. The manor is an estate, the patron of which is a chief who controls many manors. The occupant of the manor has the right to use the estate in exchange for tribute paid to the chief, but does not really own the land. As in chiefdom systems, the chief controls the land, and in traditional society, before the introduction of Roman rule, was magically identified with it. The introduction of Christianity reduced the connection between religion, a specific chief, and a specific territory controlled by a single clan (the leader of which was the chief). Religion and trade produced greater centralization, and small manors were brought under the control of more powerful chiefs. War and the centralization of authority continued in a familiar pattern. In England, the invasion by William the Conqueror in 1066 brought about the further centralization of rule and the appearance of the state. The new Anglo-Saxon state was never to be at peace with itself, and the familiar conflict between the ruler and his chiefly supporters became one of the themes of English history. With William the Conquerer, feudalism had emerged.

The economy of the rural manorial system is called **feudalism,** a word derived from fee, an estate in land. It was based on tenancy, not ownership, of land (manorial system and feudalism amount to the same concept). The king was the owner, and from him the tenants "in-chief" held their estates in return for military service. At the bottom of the scale was the serf or **villein** who paid the rent to his "lord," who occupied a middle position between serf and king (Halliday 1989:40). The power of the king was dependent on the Christian church, whereas much as the power of the chief had been dependent on magical religions.

The Christian church, in effect, replaced Roman rule. It also had profound influence on the next thousand years in the organization of the manorial states and the weak city-states. These arose along the river systems of Western Europe where trade moved on rowboats, sailboats, and rafts. In the following, we will pay some attention to the organization of the feudal societies of Europe from which capitalism sprang. It is important to keep in mind that, while our stereotype of the Middle or Feudal Ages is that of authoritarian and despotic regimes, the political systems of Western Europe were extremely weak, in contrast to many other despotic systems, such as India or imperial China. Trade was very local in Europe during the Middle Ages. Fairs were held within trade towns, tying in several manors and their lords. Trade flowed through the rivers of Western Europe, but the manorial lords, who placed barriers in the path of trade by demanding taxes of traders, increased the costs so that trade could not expand until the states expanded in size. In the tenth century, a manorial estate was the size of a small county, and became the base of that political unit in British history. Blocking any further development of trade, however, was the monopoly over trade by North African states along the Mediterranean and Mongol states in Inner Asia.

European Feudal Society

Most agrarian states throughout the history of the world have had feudalistic social structures, but there is considerable variation in these structures. Scholars who generalize from European historical models outward to Asiatic systems, such as those found in India and China, make a grave error. And the reverse is also true. There are also places in today's "Third World" countries which, because of similarities of the human experience (poverty, despotism), scholars describe as feudalistic. One of these world regions is Latin America, but the similarities are superficial and Latin American countries are not feudal, but centrist. During the colonial period they were elements in a highly centralized state bureaucracy run by Spain and Portugal.

European feudal systems never achieved the level of integration of China or, for that matter, the level of any other major pre-modern imperial state. Europe, for a long time, was made up of a series of small, regional, manorial systems that paid tribute to a central but relatively weak authority. Such principalities might, in turn, pay tribute to a yet more central authority, such as a king or queen of a relatively large territory, such as France. But the authority of that final level depended on the cooperation of the middle-level tribute givers and takers. These were weak feudal systems in which the rights to prop-erty, people (labor), their inventions, and productivity rested primarily in the hands of the barons in the middle range and only secondarily in the hands of the members of the highest "ruling" level. Kings and Queens ruled only at the mercy of the middle level. This appears to have been particularly true of Eng-land, somewhat less true in Spain or France. These two countries became highly centralized in the period from the tenth to the fifteenth centuries. The reason England had the least centralized of the feudal estates may lie in the di-minished influence of Rome on the far-off English domains, particularly the "western fringe," Wales, Scotland, Cornwall, and Ireland. But it is also true that the western fringe was a trade periphery. This would change radically with the development of shipping technology during the sixteenth century when new worldwide trade routes opened up.

It is the lack of some overall integrating force that sets apart the European states between A.D. 700 and A.D. 1700 from other regions. It also helps to ex-plain the rise of capitalism in the West instead of the East. No one would have predicted the vast growth in the wealth and power of England and the Nether-lands and the failure of China to keep up with the West had he or she compared England and China in the tenth or eleventh centuries.

It is argued that capitalism emerged first in Western Europe precisely be-cause of the weak feudal social structure. France and Spain were much more centralized and resisted the capitalist transformation that England went through. Once England was transformed, it came to dominate the world through its much more efficient forms of political and economic organization, which insured (for a time) its domination of the seas and thus the major routes of oceanic trade.

The chief landowner during the Middle Ages was the Roman Catholic Church. It was the repository of learning, and its top-heavy bureaucracy amassed wealth in the form of land in exchange for salvation. In the Middle Ages, when a man or a woman died, their place in heaven would be secured if they turned over their estates to the Church. In many respects, the Church had the trappings of a state (North 1981:125). Western Europe is the region where classic Euro-pean feudalism emerged.

In tenth-century western Europe, law and order existed only within settled regions where the manorial system dominated and where the Catholic faith pulled cultures together. Beyond these settled regions banditry interfered with trade and commerce, raising transaction costs so that trade was minimal. It cost more to move goods than to move labor and so we say that goods had a higher "transaction" cost. On the other hand, there was a lot of surplus land available, so laborers were brought to the manor where they could farm the land and re-ceive protection from the lord of the manor. Manors appear to have had limits in size. There were economies of scale in production; that is, the larger the manor was, the more it could produce—up to a point. As the number of inhab-itants protected by the lord of the manor grew and the distance of farmed lands from the castle increased, the costs of protection went up and the efficiency of the manor dropped. This means there were limits placed on the efficient size of a manor, which in turn limited political centralization.

The local castle and the knights of the manor were the protection that was needed for the manor to function. The local lord was in turn linked to overlords; a series of linkages that ran up to a king. Between the king and the local lords there might be several intermediate levels. At each level the lord provided knight service for his superiors (North 1981:127).

Property rights in the feudal states of Western Europe were grants of tenure in return for military service, but a feudal lord could flout the demand of his king for that service. However, the lord of the manor did not own his land; the land belonged to the king. The lord and his knights were both a warrior class and a ruling class whose survival depended on militarism. Douglas North, the economic historian, writes:

> The ideological gloss overlying this class was chivalry, a term that brings to mind King Arthur, the Round Table, knight service, and courtly love, but in practice was more a rationale for a class that lived by violence (North 1981:127).

Property rights of peasants and freeholders were conditional grants of tenure in exchange for services, goods, and rent. The social structure established on the economic base of a tributary peasantry and a manorial elite has been described for England by George Homans, a sociologist (1968), a description we will summarize here.

In most villages there were two social classes. The more substantial villagers were called the *husbonds*. They had houses instead of cottages. Poorer farmers were called *cotters* or *cotmen* and they lived in cottages; the husbonds were substantial farmers and it is from this social class that we get the word *husbandry* (and *husband*). The local two-class system appears to have been common throughout Europe. The husbonds had control of units of land called *yards* or *yardlands* (in northern England they were called *oxgangs*), usually about thirty acres in size (Homans 1968:339). The smaller fields, usually about five acres in size, were called the cotlands and were held by the cotters, or cotmen. Oxgangs and yardlands were fixed parts of larger units called plowlands in the north and hides in the south; both were about 120 acres in size. Homans thought the most important circumstance explaining size was that 120 acres was the amount of land that one plow team could manage in one year's work (Homans 1968:340). It was a unit for assessment of taxes and other charges. The farmers who worked these tracts usually combined their efforts, working collectively for the lord of the manor. The exact size of plowlands and hides, of course, actually differed, depending on environmental and climatic conditions, and so the number of individuals working the land would also tend to differ from region to region.

Homans described one English manor of the thirteenth century that he argues was not necessarily typical, but was well described. His analysis gives us insights into the social structure of Medieval Europe.

According to Homans, in 1279, Angareta de Beauchamp held the manor of Spelsbury as her dower of the inheritance of the Earl of Warenne and Surrey and, at her death, the manor reverted to the earl. *She did not own the manor*. As was typical at the time, she had a right to tribute from those who worked the

Figure 6.2   **Thirteenth-century manor.**

land, but the land itself belonged, ultimately, to the king. The Earl of Warenne and Surrey's lands were in turn held by the Bishop of Worcester, who was over the earl, and the bishop, in turn, "held of the king" (Homans 1968:344).

Three plowlands of the manor were in *demesne*, which means they were tilled under the management of the officers of the manor; the rest of the land was in the hands of her tenants. There were three kinds of tenants: freeholders, *villeins* (serfs or peasants), and cotters. There were six freeholders (a freeholder did not have to work, but paid rent, and had a higher rank than a villein), the wealthiest rented a mill and six acres of land that freed him from almost all services. Thirty-three villeins held one yardland each in villeinage; but too poor to pay rent, they were required to till and harvest the lady's plowlands. The villeins also had to collect nuts in the lady's wood and to give her wheat from their own plot of land. In addition, once a year, she took whatever portion she pleased of the money and goods of her villeins (Homans 1968:344).

The poorest class was that of the cotters, of whom there were six, three men and three women. They also tilled the lady's land, but did fewer hours of work and got less land. The differences in status of the three groups were class-based, and reflected rank, often determined by military service to the lord of the manor. Of the structure of the manor, Homans writes:

> There were two parts of the manor, a greater part, which was in the hands of tenants, and a lesser part, the demesne, which was managed by officers of the lady of the manor and tilled by her servants and her villeins. On this demesne there was probably a manor house and court, with farm buildings, and in the hall of the manor house the hallmotes [meetings] would be held. According to the amounts of land they held and the rents and services they rendered in return for their land, the tenants were divided into classes, which were also called by special names. Among the tenants also were men who held particular positions in the economy of the manor: the miller, the smith, the reeve [overseer], the bedell [messenger and arranger of events]. Lastly, besides having her rents and services from her tenants, the lady exercised certain other rights over them, especially the right of holding a manorial court. They had to attend it, and she took the profits of its justice (Homans 1968:345).

Such was the structure of the English manor in the thirteenth century. The relationship of the lord of the manor to the tenants was permanent. As long as he lived, the lord would have the same families of tenants and vice versa. The two were perpetually bound together in a patron–client relationship, but the relationship was seldom face-to-face; many lords held many manors. However, while the relationship between the lord and tenants was based on tradition and appears rigid, the lord could only make so many demands on the tenants, and the king could make only so many demands on his vassals. If the lord became too exacting, the tenant would run away and find another lord. If the king made too many demands on his vassals, they might revolt. Here we see a definite limit to oppression, and there is also a limit on hierarchy and centralization. While the tenant had good reason to stay in the lord's good graces, there was much mutual loyalty and understanding (Homans 1968:347).

The Catholic Religion

Integrating feudal social structure was religion. The Catholic religion dominated Europe until the Protestant Reformation in the sixteenth century. The universe was organized hierarchically based on the six days of creation. Lower ordered things were farther down the hierarchy and were created within the first days of creation. Man was conceived as standing on top of the pyramid because he was created last. Woman was perceived as having lower status than man because she was created out of man. Woman was the vessel for the "seed" of the man, his children. The hierarchy of creation had several mirror hierarchies that explained to people the nature of the social, ecclesiastical, and supernatural universe. The religious universe was a projection of this world's social structure.

In the social model of the feudal world, the king represented God on earth and ruled by divine right. Beneath him came his direct relatives, who formed the nobility. Beneath the nobility was an aristocracy that was also ranked according to the relationship of the individual to members of the nobility, their wealth, and military ability. The aristocracy basically formed the manorial elite. Beneath the landed aristocracy were the peasants, who were also arranged according to rank.

The ecclesiastical model of the world was composed of a semi-divine Pope on top and a hierarchy of cardinals, archbishops, bishops, and priests. There were also a large number of monasteries and nunneries inhabited by members of the aristocracy, who ruled, and peasants, who toiled. Most families, from the peasant classes on up, won recognition for giving at least one son or daughter to the mother Church. Behind the ecclesiastical model there was the supernatural model composed of God the Father, his Son, and the Holy Ghost, forming a triumvirate. In addition, and often equal in importance, was the Virgin Mary. Joseph, her husband, was also prayed to and perceived as a god who could intervene on behalf of humans. There was also a vast pantheon of saints, both men and women, who were ranked according to their importance to humans. While Christians like to state that Christianity is monotheistic, in fact, from a non-Christian viewpoint, it looks quite polytheistic. Villages and individuals were named for saints and the saints were treated as lesser gods.

Individuals were born into this world as a component of one or several of the social pyramids. Their status, like that of the Chinese or Indian peasant, was fixed at birth and was not questioned. Fate determined all. State religions imposed on peasants generally explain reality in terms of the acceptance of one's fate and role in life.

While the religious beliefs and social structures of the peasants in the early feudal period were relatively stable, the social structures of the European chiefdomlike states were weak in contrast to those of the conquest states that emerged in Mesopotamia, the Mediterranean, and elsewhere. There was lack of a stimulus to bring about the early development of such tributary empires in Europe.

 ummary

On the eve of the discovery of the New World, there were a set of empires around the world based on agriculture and the control of trade over vast regions:

an Asiatic empire centered in China and India, a north African–Southwest Asian empire connected to China along the Great Silk Road, made up of Islamic states that shifted in core status, an Andean empire with the Inca at its core, and a Mesoamerican empire controlled by the Aztecs. While productive agriculture was a general characteristic of chiefdoms and states, control of trade best explains the status of the cores of these hegemonic systems. Several of the most powerful early Muslim states, which based their cores in desert regions such as Saudi Arabia, had no agriculture to speak of but depended on tribute for food. The core states of these systems rose and fell and shifted depending on success in trade and warfare. Other lesser states were either tribute payers to the cores or stood as semi-independent societies, in either case collecting tribute (or booty) in turn from the smaller societies that they dominated. Examples are the Tarascans of western Mexico and the Tlaxcalans of central Mexico who were never completely dominated by the core states of the central valley. On the peripheries of the core were many chiefdoms. A short list of chiefdoms would include the American Northwest Coast, Polynesia, the lower Mississippi valley, the Great Rift Valley of Africa, and the Western Isles of Europe. Several of these regions became states, but several, such as Polynesia and the Northwest Coast, did not. More peripheral yet were tribes, and bands of hunters and food-gatherers. All of these systems operated in symbiotic relationship with each other, connected through trade and warfare. These regional economic systems were semi-autonomous, on their margins trading with each other. Processes of expansion and contraction were continuous in these empires.

In this chapter, we have focused on the emergence of chiefdoms, city-states, and empires and we have argued that population increase and demand for additional resources provided the stimulus in some core areas for the intensification of patterns of trade and warfare. In the process, tribal forms of organization were transformed into chiefdoms and some of these, perhaps due to a combination of technological, political, and economic innovations, came to dominate their neighbors. These became the early city-states and archaic trade and tribute empires.

We have sketched a trade–tribute–redistribution model of chiefdom expansion and we have shown how this model presaged the development of early states and empires. We have drawn on data from ancient Mesopotamia and the Mediterranean to illustrate the process of early state formation. Finally, we have sketched a picture of feudal Europe and examined some ideas about why state formation in this region occurred so much later than in other regions and why, for a long time, European states remained weak and decentralized. When a trade empire finally begins to emerge in Europe at the end of the sixteenth century, its worldwide impact goes far beyond anything we have examined so far. It is out of Western European feudal societies that the modern world system emerges.

In 1492, with Columbus's arrival in the Western Hemisphere, all of the world's regional trade systems were rapidly connected to each other. A new core in Western Europe, which was in the form of chiefdoms in the seventh century A. D., by the fifteenth century had become the states of Spain and Portugal; these then monopolized all the trade networks of the world and transformed the archaic empires into a single world system, the one Wallerstein calls the "modern world system." By the early seventeenth century, Spain and Portugal gave up their "core status" to England and Holland, and later the other Western European countries became members of the core of the modern world system. The modern world system survived until 1985. All this will be described in the next chapter. We are currently in the throes of another transformation into a "global world system" with postindustrial societies rapidly taking the place of industrial societies. This development will be covered in later chapters.

Key Terms

Caste	**Paramount Chief**
Class	**Stratified**
Ecological Circumscription	**Sumptuary Laws**
Feudalism	**Tributary States**
Hegemonic Cores	**Tributary Empires**
Manorial System	**Untouchable**
Menghirs, Dolmens, and Passage Graves	**Villein**

The Modern World: Capitalism, World Systems, and Globalization

7

*I*n the year 1492, and for the next decade, Western European civilization made exploratory connections with the other hegemonic empires of the world. The Americas were claimed, Africa explored, and Asia opened to trade. China's core and peripheries were already well known due to the travels two centuries before by Niccolo Polo and his son Marco. These merchants from Venice represented the newly developing commercial viewpoint of Western European societies. These societies, as you learned in the last chapter, were predominantly feudal and agricultural. But changes were occurring in Venice and northern Italy. Here the new viewpoint of mercantilism was evolving, a philosophy that forced Europeans to look beyond the limited structures of feudalism, and to world trade. Venice, and other northern Italian city states, represented the high point of the **Renaissance**, marking the transition from the medieval to the modern world. The Renaissance, or rebirth, was the consequence of the increased importance of the older Roman and Greek ideas of science and philosophy over the predominantly religious ideas of the Middle Ages. England was still mired in feudal philosophies and legal structures. Its day in the sun was yet centuries in the future, and the Venetian adventurers of the waning fifteenth century would be surprised to find how the world would be structured three hundred years later in 1792. For these adventurers, the world was a closed place that they were helping to open. In the year that Columbus set sail to the Americas, China and India dominated and controlled trade and power in the Orient. The Mediterranean was still in the hands of the followers of Muhammad in Egypt and Damascus, Syria. These Islamic states had a trade monopoly. Later, the Islamic core would be moved to Turkey as the center of the new Ottoman Empire. The Europeans began nibbling at the control of the Islamic states in North Africa. Spain, in the same year of 1492, drove the "Moors" (Arabs) out of Spain and the western Mediterranean. Japan, at this time, like England, was an island wrapped in feudal duties and social structures.

To the north of Italy, inland along the rivers of the Rus, Volga, and Dniepper, Slavic chiefdoms accepted Christianity and were transformed into a state with its core at Kiev in modern Ukraine (Krader 1968). The new state was influenced by the Eastern Orthodox religion with roots in the Byzantine Empire. Not unlike peoples of Great Britain, the Russian state began with a weak feudal system, but in the centuries that followed, Russia took a distinct turn toward a highly centralized state. In the eighteenth century, the new Russian empire would be dominated by Peter the Great, who would expand its borders to the east, a topic to which we will return at the end of this chapter.

The Mercantilist Roots of Capitalism

The ideas of modern capitalism would have appeared absurd to people in 1492, and the centuries immediately to follow. Modern capitalism is founded, in part, on the idea that trade leads to wealth, and that wealth itself can be unlimited. In the fifteenth century, the dominant philosophy of political economy was **mercantilism**. Mercantilism rested on the basic and simple assumption that all wealth was limited. One nation's gain was another nation's loss. One nation could only become wealthy if another country became poor. This philosophy underlay the expansion of the countries of Western Europe, and explains their constant wars (Boorstin 1983:653). Besides being large, a country had to balance its trade relations by constantly increasing its source of gold and silver. Monopolies were granted to special government authorized companies to search for and control wealth. Many private adventurers sought riches in the lands found by the explorers searching for trade routes.

Spain and Portugal were very successful at expanding their empire states, but there were threats of war over how to divide the lands found by Christopher Columbus. A rivalry between King John of Portugal and King Ferdinand of Spain was settled by the Pope, who, at the Treaty of Tordesillas, divided the world in two, the line splitting the two running north and south 1,200 nautical miles west from the Cape Verde Islands. Lands west of the line belonged to Spain and those east of the line belonged to Portugal (Boorstin 1983:174).

The new empires were based on mercantilism. However, in imposing their theory of mercantilism, the adventurers, traders, and representatives of Spain and Portugal destroyed the old hegemonic empires and created peripheries of destitute societies everywhere their policies prevailed. The Aztec and Inca empires, as well as the societies of the West Indies (Caribbean) and the East Indies (Indian Ocean), were soon poverty-stricken backwaters as internal trade was destroyed or monopolized by Spain and Portugal, and later by other European states.

The Age of Exploration

The search for wealth, the competition for colonies, and the constant need for expansion coincided with the Age of Exploration. The Portuguese crossed over to North Africa in 1415 and captured Cuenta, reaching Madeira in 1419 and the Canary islands shortly after. The Azores were colonized between 1439–1453. The Portuguese worked their way down the west coast of Africa. In 1488,

Bartholomeu Diaz rounded the Cape of Good Hope, putting the Portuguese in East Africa, the Persian Gulf, Indian Ocean, China, and the islands beyond. In 1493, Columbus returned to Spain to describe his discoveries in the western hemisphere. Vasco da Gama, under the flag of Portugal, reached India in 1498. Ferdinand Magellan, a Portuguese, discovered the Philippines, where he died in 1521. In 1528 de Soto landed in Florida, discovered the Mississippi River and traveled as far north as Kansas (Hughes 1987:8).

The knowledge we have of the events of this period and the consequences for the peoples of the periphery has dimmed the halos of heros of exploration. An example is Vasco Nuñez de Balboa. An adventurer born of obscure parents, he discovered the Pacific in 1513 in western Panama. Originally, he was more interested in the discovery of gold than unknown seas, an interest for which he was criticized by the son of a Panamanian chief (*cacique*):

> What is the matter, you Christian men, that you so greatly esteeme so little portion of gold more than your own quietnesse . . . If your hunger of gold, bee so insatiable, that onely for the desire you have . . . I will shewe you a region flowing with golde, where you may satisfy your ravening appetites (Boorstin 1983:257).

The son of the cacique went on to describe how to find a sea where they would discover ships carrying gold. While searching for gold and accidentally discovering the Pacific, Balboa encountered the village of the Quarequa, whose

Figure 7.1   **The voyages of discovery were the first phase of "globalization."**

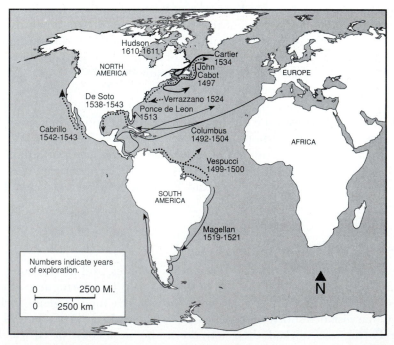

customs so incensed the Spaniards that they set their hunting dogs to tear these people apart. Six hundred people were slain. Similar incidents can be reported for most of the explorers. However, it is much too easy to pass judgment on their accomplishments. Any student of the histories of this age knows that the explorers and conquerors were both heroic and antiheroic. Columbus did have the will to keep his crews together, as most students have read. But he was responsible for acts of genocide against the Indians of the Antilles. The explorers were not working to expand the knowledge of Europe, as children have been taught for centuries, but to gain access to new lands, and to dominate trade with those lands. Heroism and exploitation went hand in hand. There is the incredible heroism of Hernando Cortez in his fight to save his men from ritual sacrifice by the Aztecs, but then there is his role as the conqueror of the peoples of Mexico, for which he received royal titles, land, and the free labor of the people he enslaved.

The events of discovery are difficult to tie to the events that followed discovery. The descriptions of adventure are usually not coupled to the spread of disease and population collapse, but there were connections. Diseases were introduced by the explorers, and the other Europeans who followed them. Also, the impact of mercantilist trade philosophy was devastating to the people of the non-European regions of the world. The collapse of regional trade led to the wholesale collapse of economies, and, often, the incentive to live.

The Impact of Spain and Portugal on Latin America

The colonial period in Latin America begins in the early sixteenth century with the conquest of the Aztec in Mexico by Hernando Cortez in 1521 and of the Inca empire, centered in the Peruvian Andes, by Pizarro in 1533. The Spanish explorers and the *conquistadores* followed the philosophy of mercantilism to the letter. The conquistadores discovered wealth in the form of silver in Mexico and gold in Peru and Bolivia. Very quickly, they established a new economy in their colonies based on mining and large *haciendas* (large and self-sufficient farms). Labor was given by the Indians in the form of *encomiendas*, tributary obligations to the new nobility (discussed in Chapter 12). New cities, built with Indian labor, were the administrative centers of the mining economies: Mexico City, Guadalajara, Guatemala City, and on down to the tip of remote Chile, where Santiago was built to administer the domains of the southern Andes.

Within the next four decades, all of the major cities of Latin America were built with cheap Indian labor. The cities of Latin America had a very different institutional structure from those of Puritan New England, and preceded them by a century. The cities of the Americas, both Portuguese and Spanish, were administrative cities with large and expensive bureaucracies whose function it was to supervise the extraction of wealth from the landscape, not the production of wealth (Portes and Walton 1976). Economic theory had no place for investment and economic development. Trade was a form of plunder. Wealth poured into Spain and Portugal. The myth of El Dorado (the gilded one) drove such explorers as de Soto to discover even more wealth, but the consequences were not those predicted. Instead of wealth, Spain and Portugal suffered from inflation; prices for bread and shoes quadrupled during a great inflationary spiral that lasted throughout the last part of the sixteenth century. This period is referred to as the "crisis of the sixteenth century," and Immanuel Wallerstein identifies it as one of the major causes for the movements of people out of western Europe (and into the periphery) due to growing poverty. This spiral was not limited to Spain and Portugal, but spread throughout Europe producing economic panics, which in turn spurred more exploration and further expansionism, and more inflation (Boorstin 1983:653). While Europe suffered economic deprivation due to massive inflation, the Americas suffered from population collapse.

During the period 1560 to 1580, much of the Indian population of the Americas collapsed in "the great dying" (Wolf 1982). The population collapse was the consequence of diseases and brutal treatment at the hands of the Spanish and Portuguese. After the collapse, which has been estimated to have taken between 60 and 90 percent of the entire population, vast lands were left wide open. The children of Indian and Spanish unions, the *mestizos,* as well as many Spaniards, took over the lands and transformed them into haciendas (Wolf and Mintz 1957). By 1700, the economies of the Americas were composed of large cities run by extensive but inefficient bureaucracies, giant haciendas, and gold and silver mines. These three institutions, taken together, accounted for up to 80 percent of the productive wealth of Latin American societies. The bureaucrats, mostly from Spain, formed the upper levels of aristocracy, both secular and religious. Beneath them came a lesser nobility of locally born Creole elites, many of them the owners of extensive hacienda lands. Beneath these, in turn, were mestizos. Some of the mestizos had come into control of large haciendas and had considerable status, but not as much as the Spanish and Creole aristocrats who controlled the offices of the bureaucracies. Beneath the mestizo landowners came poorer mestizos, Indians, and black slaves.

The impact of Spain and Portugal on the Americas is usually described in terms of the benefits of new European technologies. But the collapse of regional trade networks and the monopoly of trade by the new elites brought famine and population collapse, not economic development. It was not until four centuries later that the population began to make a comeback, but the region has continued to be troubled by the institutions of mercantilism and its philosophies.

The Impact of Western Europe on Africa

The story for Africa mirrors that of Latin America: When the populations of the Americas collapsed, slaves were taken from Africa to do the work of the settlers of the new territories, which robbed Africa of its young. While silver, gold, and sugar were the wealth that was taken out of Latin America, in Africa the exploited commodity was "black ivory"—human beings captured and then sold into slavery (Wolf 1982:195).

The demand for slaves came initially from South and Central America after the collapse of Indian populations in the sixteenth century. Slaves were imported to work sugar, coffee, and cotton plantations. Later, the growth of cotton

Figure 7.2 . . . **but early global economies were based on the slave trade.**

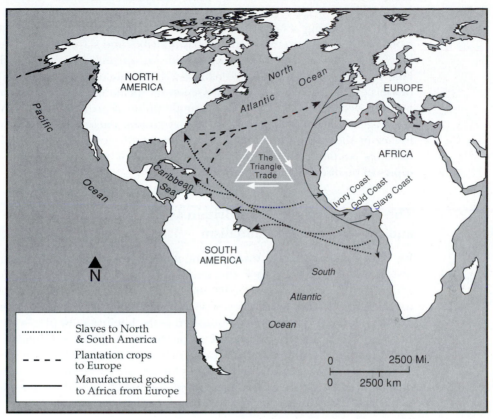

and tobacco plantations in the southern United States added to the demand (Wolf 1982:197–198). Europeans radically transformed African societies when they brought in metal, hardware, firearms, gunpowder, textiles, rum, and tobacco to exchange for slaves. Generally, Europeans did not hunt for slaves but created politically powerful elites to obtain slaves for them. Many of the slave hunter societies became centralized states with kings, courts, and bureaucracies. Shillington writes about the extent of the slave trade:

> With the rapid expansion of slave exports in the eighteenth century virtually every part of the Atlantic coastline from Senegal to southern Angola became involved in the human traffic. The greatest concentration of European trading forts was along the so called "Gold Coast," the coastline of the modern state of Ghana (Shillington 1989:174).

The slave trade increased the level of warfare along the western interior of Africa and it caused a serious loss to the productive potential of the region. All regions of west Africa were seriously affected by a loss of manpower. The incalculable suffering of the slaves is probably impossible to understand. The impact on African society was immense because the slave trade went on for over 300 years.

African slaving states rose and fell as they received support or lost support from European slavers. Slave tribute-paying tribes and slave-taking states came to hate each other, and as their relations with Europeans changed, so did their relations with each other (Wolf 1982:228–229). Many of these hatreds remain in modern tribal societies in Africa. Generally speaking, in the post-colonial or modern period, one of the greatest single political problems facing Africans is these age-old tribal feuds based on the slave trade. These hatreds were especially fueled in the late nineteenth and early twentieth centuries when colonial authorities administratively grouped together ethnic groups that were enemies, topics to be discussed in Chapter 8.

The Emergence of Great Britain as a Trade Empire and the Collapse of Feudalism

We have examined world history from, roughly, ten thousand years ago, to the historic date of 1492. Since the development of the first hegemonic states, roughly in the time between 4000 and 3000 B. C., the long view of human history has been a story of unrelieved poverty for the masses of peasants and urban dwellers. It is only in the last two hundred years that just a few places in the world have enjoyed prosperity: Western Europe, the United States, Canada, Australia, and Japan. In the nineteenth century, it became apparent that the members of these societies were eating better, living longer, and were more secure than the peoples who had lived in the hegemonic empires discussed earlier (Rosenberg & Birdzell 1986).

Slaves were transported under inhuman conditions.

Between the sixteenth and nineteenth centuries, this prosperous industrial core emerged with a dependent periphery, the former hegemonic empires discussed in the last chapter. There has been a great deal of research carried out attempting to explain the "rise of the West." The explanations range from outright racist theories on the superiority of Western European societies (which do not explain Japan), to Marxist theories that explain prosperity in the core as a consequence of the poverty of the periphery, to ideas about the impact of the Protestant religion on Western European economic ideology. More recently, a theory is emerging that explains the origins of capitalism as the consequence decreasing transaction costs for trade on the part of Great Britain, a point of view consistent with the changes in social structures in traditional social systems examined in the last two chapters. Here, we wish to explain other theories first, and then to discuss how trade theory applies to social structure.

Two theoreticians who attempted to explain the rise of capitalism were Karl Marx, in *Capital,* and Max Weber in *The Protestant Ethic and the Spirit of Capitalism* (1958). For Karl Marx, the explanation for the rise of capitalism was largely materialistic. To put his argument simply, the invention of new technologies brought about new relationships between human beings as workers and as producers. The new relationships of production changed class structures. For him, capitalism was largely the same as the emergence of a profit-making class of people, the capitalists, the producers who dominate society. Marx explained the rise of wealthy social classes as a consequence of the exploitation of laboring populations in Western Europe. Immanuel Wallerstein (1974) has taken Marx's analysis and made it the basis for a description of "the modern world system." According to Wallerstein's more global perspective, the wealth of the core is due to the plundering of the poor societies of the periphery. Marx and Wallerstein's positions are distinctly materialistic, and rest on the origins of the new technologies of the West as the means for exploiting cheap labor.

Max Weber, while not denying the materialistic base of capitalism, saw the impetus for change as coming from a new *geist,* a new spirit, which was to be found in a new attitude toward productivity based on the Protestant Religion, an ethic of competition. But Weber's thesis does not explain the rise of Japan in the nineteenth century, nor does it explain the impact of globalism in our age.

A third position examines the changing institutions of British society to explain why Great Britain became the core of the new world system, and not some other society. The economic historian, Douglas North, has shown that there were crucial changes to British economic institutions, particularly private property rights and the organization of trade, that help explain the rise of capitalism (1981). We have examined in the last chapter how, in precapitalist societies, property belonged to the state, particularly the most productive property: land. North's perspective is that the state in Great Britain abandoned the control of land, and that a landed elite emerged whose point of view was "entrepreneurial," who sought to make profits by investing in land, and that these changes led to the rise of industrial entrepreneurs in the major urban areas of Great Britain. Only when these changes were in place could Great Britain shoulder aside the mercantilist states of Western Europe, for its institutions had become more efficient and able to dominate world trade.

Douglas North's explanation of capitalism does not begin with Great Britain as a core dominating a periphery, but with the question of how Great Britain's institutions became more efficient than those of Portugal and Spain. The transformation of British institutions occurred at the time that Spain and Portugal dominated the world, in the sixteenth and seventeen centuries. By the eighteenth century, Great Britain had replaced Portugal and Spain as the new core of the modern world system. How did that happen? While the answer is not simple, we will attempt to summarize it.

North argues that the manorial system in England led, very gradually, to an expansion of population, a process that happened all over Western Europe in the thirteenth and fourteenth centuries. The consequence of population growth was overpopulation. The Black Plague in the second half of the fourteenth century, a biological disaster of immense proportions, resulted in the death of between one-half to three-quarters of Europe's population. Land became cheap, and labor dear, giving peasants economic leverage in demanding higher wages. In Great Britain, the change in labor value occurred just as new merchant towns were growing, and the peasants were able to bargain for higher wages, threatening the structure of feudalism.

The challenges to feudalism were met throughout Europe through the assertion of authority by centralizing states. The kings and courts of Great Britain, realizing the threats to national survival by the other states of Europe (France, Spain), followed the flow of the challenge to feudalism by *abandoning land tenure based on tribute,* turning over the ownership of property to the aristocratic classes. The state ceased to own the land, and invested more heavily in trade, supporting the construction of ships and port cities. It is important to emphasize here that the feudal system of Great Britain was never strong. It was better to give up feudalism for a distinct type of political economy, one based on trade and the private ownership of property, rather than attempt to emulate the more centralized and bureaucratic economies of, for example, France and Spain.

With the innovation of private property rights, and a growing emphasis on trade, new trade towns evolved in Great Britain. The development of trade towns in Great Britain produced new wealth and it became possible for kings to hire mercenaries instead of relying on a knight's tribute of forty days of service per year, further eroding the tributary system. The size of a king's army no longer depended on tributary relationships to the lower nobility but on the size of his purse, which expanded as taxes were paid on private property. This was another factor in the shift from tributary rights to private property rights, as the king sought to base his power on the taxation of private property and trade, not on tribute. North argues that the demand by the newly landed elites that they have some control over the taxes they paid to the king led to the founding of the British Parliament. While early parliamentary politics can hardly be called democratic, here was the origin of democracy as we know it today. It began with private property rights, the need to protect those rights against a hungry state, and the slow increases of prosperity to the entire population, a process that took the better part of three centuries.

The story of politics in Great Britain is basically the struggle between a monarch wanting to increase his/her hegemony over world trade through a powerful military, particularly a navy, against the interests of an aristocracy whose growing wealth depended on investments in land and industry. Over time, a new social class emerged as former feudal peasants moved from the countryside to the city, became factory workers, and then formed the ranks of an urban-based middle class whose interests lay in directions opposite to those of the king and the aristocracy. These middle-class entrepreneurs used their growing wealth and numbers to support either the king or the aristocracy as they tried to increase their own powers.

The emergence of private property, the growth in the expense of the military, and the success of trade towns led to the destruction of feudalism and the development of capitalism. In Chapter 4 we examined the development of democratic capitalism in North America. At this point, remember that, while Great Britain was going through the changes described in these pages, America was developing a powerful trade society that did not have to worry about the conflicts between a king and his aristocracy, and therefore was able to build a society based on lower transaction costs for trade.

The Industrial Revolution and the Rise of Capitalism

According to Eric Wolf (1982), the major engine of the transition to capitalism was the development of the textile industry in eighteenth century England. Karl Marx would agree with his analysis, and would put an emphasis on human greed, the new capitalists, and exploitation of an urban **proletariat** (a social class without property). Max Weber, on the other hand, would explain the development of capitalism as due to the "rationalist" values of Protestantism. According to Weber, this new religion taught the idea that success in this world rested on good works, and good works depended on entrepreneurial investment and competition in this world, not the next.

The alternative argument, presented by Douglas North (1981), points out that before any of these changes occurred, new legal relationships to land and property had evolved and were stimulating productivity. North points out that economic relationships were being reorganized from peasant-based tributary agriculture to a society based on private property rights, and that it was changes in those rights that kicked off the industrial revolution. He believes that capitalism has less to do with making profits than in changing property rights. Changes in land ownership stimulated the production of food, which became cheaper. At the same time, the idea of private property rights was extended to the ownership of rights in ideas. The protection of ideas led to new inventions, and these led to the industrial revolution. North argues that the real basis of the industrial revolution was in the innovation in law, in developing a state that protected people's ideas. Innovations in sea trade occurred at the same time: The invention of clocks, **astrolabes** (optical instruments used to navigate by the stars at sea), and other innovations made British ships highly competitive.

These three theories (changes in the forms of production, new competitive values, and changing private property rights) are often presented as opposing each other, but they are all different parts of the same story. A growing supply of agricultural goods in the countryside and the development of industrial technology in the urban sectors led to a stimulus–response relationship between urban and rural areas. Technological innovation in industry led to a demand for labor in urban areas, while the same technological change had the opposite effect in the countryside. These were the consequences of new institutions, but did lead to human exploitation as well as a transition to capitalism. England became the core of an economic system based on a new type of economy. Mercantilism was being replaced with capitalism; peasant tributary economies were disappearing in favor of urban workers in factories.

Capitalism differs from mercantilism in several respects. First, it defines wealth as unlimited; new forms of production and trade lead to new levels of prosperity. Second, the ownership of resources is not by the state but in the form of private property. Third, production is no longer in agriculture, but in urban industry. The new industries were not organized by feudal ties, but by **corporations**, which are legal fictions giving groups of men and women the rights of individuals (private property rights are extended to corporations and protected by the state).

The earliest changes toward modern capitalism were carried out in their most extensive forms in Great Britain and in its North American colonies. These two economies, with the Netherlands, abandoned mercantilism. The other countries of Western Europe soon began to modify their economies in the direction of capitalism, a procedure that is called **economic liberalization.** Most Western European countries, by the middle of the eighteenth century, were complex mixes of capitalism and mercantilism. Economic liberalization was a threat as much as it was a promise, and had the potential of destroying aristocratic classes where these did not have the economic resources to take advantage of the changes.

Two examples of societies that were slow to liberalize are France and Russia. Both had state dominated economies, powerful aristocracies that benefited from tributary economies, and the domination of old mercantilist ideas, not entrepreneurial capitalism. Despite these generalizations, both countries possessed economic interests that were able to imitate the industrial technologies of England, and quickly developed urban working classes. In both countries, the urban and rural poor often allied with each other, and in the end destroyed the aristocracies of both countries, first in 1789 with the French Revolution, and then in 1917 with the Russian Revolution. Peter the Great (Czar of Russia from 1682–1725) was to utilize the philosophy of mercantilism to expand Russia's colonial base from the west to the east, and the expansions continued under Catherine the Great (1762–1796), and her dynastic offspring until the abdication and execution of Nicholas Romanov in 1917. Eric Wolf has shown how the feudal social structures of both France and Russia led to these two most famous revolutions (Wolf 1969). The remarkable lack of similar class revolutions in Great Britain (though there were civil wars, such as the war leading to the beheading of King Charles I in 1649) underlines the point that, while capitalism exploited the working classes, in Great Britain innovations stayed ahead of radical demands for the redistribution of wealth, while the opposite happened in those societies that had failed to liberalize their economies. The lack of epic class struggles in Great Britain was due to the slow and incremental shifts in human rights policies that benefited the urban working class.

Industrialization and Political Change in England

The development of industry, and the slow gains on behalf of the working classes, have been well documented for England. It is always obvious that the wealthy benefited at the cost of the poor under capitalism, but it is also fair to observe that the working classes were not without their own political talents and were able to demand and receive a share of the growing prosperity.

In the 1780s, Thomas Coke of Norfolk began scientific farming on his estates, and in 1784 published his new techniques in his *Annals of Agriculture*. This period is a classic demonstration of capitalism and the demand for efficiency. Coke's improved efficiencies led to far greater yields, but they also led to the enclosure of estates as wealthy landowners bought out smallholders and deprived cottagers of their pasture rights on the commons. The enclosure of lands led to higher rates of wool production, and these were the consequences of greater efficiencies of land use, but the cost to the rural cottagers was enormous. It meant that wealthy landowners were able to buy out small landholders, who had previously been protected by the tributary economies that gave them rights in land. Peasants were reduced to becoming landless laborers, and many were forced to migrate to the growing urban centers (Halliday 1989:154).

Mechanical innovations transformed the cotton and wool industries, pulling the landless poor to the cities, while at the same time destroying cottage industries. A spinning machine, an invention that led to the growth of textile factories in Lancashire and Yorkshire, developed in 1769 could do the work of a dozen women. Edmund Cartwright invented a power loom in 1785, though it was not perfected for thirty years, forcing weavers, their wives, and children to become factory employees. James Watt developed the steam engine in 1769, leading to further efficiencies of scale in industry and a revolution in transportation. After 1780, large-scale production of food and manufactured goods began to supersede small-scale farming (Halliday 1989:154–156).

The publication of Adam Smith's *Wealth of Nations* led to a *laissez-faire* (French for "leave it be," or "leave it alone") philosophy of political economy. While the wealth of the few was multiplied, poverty and misery became common among the masses who were not protected by the state. Peasants and former textile producers were driven into the slums and forced to work long hours for appallingly low wages. England became split into a country of rich and poor. Political movements appeared and were repressed. The Habeas Corpus Act was suspended, allowing people to be imprisoned without trial. Many were shipped to Australia as convicts. But fears grew among the ruling classes as similar pressures in France led to the French Revolution in 1789 and the rise of the French Republic. This same period coincided with a series of wars with France that lasted until 1815, the year that Napoleon was defeated by the Duke of Wellington at Waterloo.

The defeat of France was followed by a period of extreme repression on the European continent and in England. Technological change continued apace and in 1830, Stephenson's train "Rocket" achieved a speed of thirty-five miles an hour. Further technological innovations were introduced to the factory system, but new revolutions brewed in Europe, and fear grew among the British elite that they might lose everything. There was great distress in England, with strikes in towns and riots in the countryside. In 1833, Parliament passed a series of measures to help the poor. The first Factory Act was passed prohibiting the use of children below the age of nine in cotton factories. The state assumed greater responsibilities for the poor, and the Poor Act of 1834 offered some relief, but was still essentially harsh. Charles Dickens's novels describing the inhumanity of the Poor Law made their appearance. A People's Charter was drawn up demanding universal suffrage; its rejection was followed by riots. But the conditions of the working class continued to deteriorate. The repeal of the Corn Laws, which had prevented the importation of cheap food from abroad, led to an improvement of living conditions, but it was not until the 1870s that reforms finally improved the lives of the British working class, particularly the Education Act of 1870, which established primary schools. In the 1880s, new reforms made employers responsible for accidents in the workplace, children had to go to school, wives could keep property separate from their husbands, and the third Reform Act gave the vote to agricultural laborers.

But England's economic success in the nineteenth century was the consequence, to a great extent, of other countries' failures. While Europe and the United States had suffered from war and revolution, England had remained politically stable. A free trade policy, inaugurated in the 1840s, allowed the importation of raw materials cheaply, and the foreign policy and merchant fleet carried goods around the world. The slow growth of wealth in England, and the improvement in the lives of the working class was directly linked to Britain's markets around the world for its inexpensive goods. In turn, these successes were the consequence of Great Britains being the center of a near monopoly on world trade—the core of the modern world system—whose growth and success held the promise, not yet fully realized, of solving many of the problems of the poor.

The period from the middle of the nineteenth century to World War I was one of nationalism, competition for control of world trade, and the creation of colonies in the peripheries (Great Britain, France, Italy, Germany, and the Netherlands were the dominant countries of the core). The United States was not greatly involved in competition except in its own backyard of Latin America. Great Britain maintained its dominance throughout this period, but each core country developed its own trade periphery, often loaning money, as Great Britain did to Argentina, to develop railroads, mines, and farm systems.

Britain's efficiencies of trade were due to continuous internal changes in the institutions of political economy, reducing the frictions between social classes, and keeping transaction costs low. All the Western European countries in these years went through significant internal change, as they vied for external advantage, but they were not as successful, overall, as was Great Britain, which became the model of liberal political economy. The success of internal change led to greater nationalist sentiments, external competition for world markets, and friction, leading finally to World War I.

Colonialism: The British in North America

According to Immanuel Wallerstein, the modern world system began to form in Western Europe in the sixteenth century. The core consisted of those countries that controlled trade and production (So 1990:186–187, Wallerstein 1988). As England gained control of the world system, its economy shifted in the direction of capitalism, as described above.

Wallerstein and other world system theorists have worked out a pattern of "waves" of colonialism, some of which date back to precapitalist times. The waves were connected to the economies of the core. The world system expanded in a series of waves beginning in the sixteenth century. Wallerstein's explanation for the waves is that they were responses by the world system to economic events in the core. We have described the "crisis of the sixteenth century." For Wallerstein, that period of inflation was the primary reason for the expansion of European colonialism to the periphery. Two facts are clear for the sixteenth century: (1) inflation created a class of paupers who sought to improve their lives by migrating, and (2) capitalists in Western Europe tried to soften the impact of inflation by investing in the periphery (Wallerstein 1979).

Population growth, indeed, explains a great deal about the cycles of colonization. We have said that population growth in Europe was cyclical. From the middle of the tenth century to the early fourteenth, there was strong growth with great economic investments in such structures as the Gothic cathedrals of the time. This episode of growth ended with the Black Death of 1347–1348, when from one-third to one-half of the population may have perished. Recovery took generations; estimates of the English population show a total of 3.7 million in 1348, followed by a loss of 600,000 by 1350, with only 2.25 million remaining by 1374. As we have mentioned, recovery from that catastrophe occurred as Britain was evolving new institutions, and may be a partial cause of cultural change. By 1545, Britain had a population of 3.2 million, but rural depopulation had already begun as the economy shifted from feudalism to early forms of capitalism (Hughes 1987:8).

English colonial expansion in North America, Australia, and New Zealand had its origins in the nation-building process in Great Britain. The Spanish and Portuguese had split the world between them. The other European countries were soon in competition either to find other unknown lands, or to take lands away from the Spanish and Portuguese. In 1496, Henry VII issued letters of patent to the Genoese adventurer Giovanni Caboto (John Cabot) to find new lands, and on the 24th of June, 1497, he reached Cape Breton (Nova Scotia), which he claimed for Henry VII. His discovery, and those made by his sons, established the English claim to North America. The first permanent English settlement was made in Virginia in 1607 with a charter from James I. The Pilgrims (English dissenters) landed in 1620 at Plymouth, and the British began to expand into other possessions in North America, followed quickly by expansion into Australia and New Zealand (Hughes 1987).

The English immigrants brought a form of adaptation that differed considerably from the originating model of sixteenth and seventeenth century England. In 1606, the Virginia Company was chartered to launch a colonization venture at Plymouth (where it was known as the Massachusetts Bay Colony), organized through joint stock companies. Shares had been sold to individual investors, and many of these became colonists of the Pilgrim religion. Each family participated equally in running the townships. The cost of government was very low. In addition, every citizen in the new colonies was expected to read the Bible, producing a 100 percent literate society, very different from what had been left behind in England. Out of this early New England culture a new political economy, democratic capitalism, emerged in the nineteenth and early twentieth centuries.

While the British had to support the cost of royalty and aristocracy, and a large and expensive bureaucracy as well, a leaner, more efficient, model emerged in the United States. For example, as late as Theodore Roosevelt's presidency (1901–1908), the American government only absorbed 7 percent of the gross national product. That figure did not change significantly until the New Deal (1933–1938) under Franklin D. Roosevelt when it jumped to just over thirty percent. The transaction costs of European governments have always been higher. The consequence was the rise of a new and very prosperous form of democratic capitalism.

The Capitalist Legacy: Destruction of Indigenous Worlds

Europeans monopolized the trade of the various hegemonic cores: Egypt, China, India, Mexico, and Peru. The internal trade networks maintaining these empires collapsed, as well as those maintaining chiefdoms. European traders and explorers did not reach most of the chiefdoms until the seventeenth and eighteenth centuries. By that time the vast regional trade networks had vanished, but the remains of temples and towns in Hawaii, Mesoamerica, Mesopotamia, China, India, and the Andes bore mute testimony to these vanished systems. European imperialism further destroyed the natural adaptations that the peoples of these regions had worked out over thousands of years. In their place Europeans introduced strange practices that were poorly adapted to the habitats and further eroded human adaptive responses until fairly recent times, when populations began to make a comeback. While the decline of native populations in the New World ceased in the late eighteenth century and began to recover at the beginning of the nineteenth century, increase was very slow until the early twentieth century, when many native populations in Latin America, for example, began to increase at rates comparable to those of the general population in the nations where they lived.

Capitalism has been a continual threat to the indigenous peoples of the world. Some, such as the various Native American groups and the Maori of New Zealand, survive today. Others, such as the Puelche of Argentina, the Yahgan of

BOX 7.1

■ Case Study: Triangles of Trade in the Caribbean

The British, in competition with Spanish, Dutch, and French interests, initiated plantation agriculture in the Caribbean in the sixteenth century. Many of the islands changed hands several times. The British colonial model in the Caribbean is very different from those of North America, but formed a part of a larger economic system in the form of "triangles of trade," which included North America. Thus developed one of the most inhumane forms of trade based on three resources: (1) rum produced in New England was shipped to Africa for use in the slave trade (rum was used to pay for slaves); (2) slaves were sold to the Caribbean to be used on sugar plantations; and (3) sugar was shipped to New England to produce rum. All the Caribbean islands began as properties of Spain, but by the eighteenth century Trinidad, the Bahamas, and Jamaica were in British hands, and Haiti and Martinique were in French hands. Most of the other islands remained in Spanish hands (Mintz 1985).

The social structures of the Caribbean islands, whether British, Dutch, French, or Spanish, were based on racial stratification: Social structure depended on the ownership of land and the color of skin. Blacks were poor and powerless; whites were rich and powerful. Cuba, Puerto Rico, Haiti, Jamaica, Trinidad, the Bahamas, Curaçao, and parts of coastal Central America came to be a part of the Caribbean plantation system, and part of the triangle of trade. Not until well after World War II did the British and other countries begin to abandon plantation economies, but the heritage of sugar wealth, racism, and power politics based on trade still dominates the region.

the island of Tierra del Fuego in Chile, and the natives of the island of Tasmania did not. The people of the peripheries have suffered many adverse experiences at the hands of the colonizers. Some were placed on reservations. Many suffered genocide (biological destruction) or ethnocide (destruction of their cultures). Those who survived the onslaught of Western civilization have managed to adapt to the modern world without completely giving up their cultural heritage and ecological adaptations. Many are trying to live in both our world and in theirs, an extremely difficult task.

John Bodley has described the phase of migration of people from the evolving core into the tribal periphery as "the uncontrolled frontier." Governments around the world allowed their citizens into tribal regions but did not protect the tribal populations from the inevitable attacks by "civilized" people on "uncivilized barbarians." The pattern of tribal destruction in Latin America is remarkably similar to that described for the United States. In the 1820s, most of

Despite attempts to destroy their culture, the Maori celebrate a traditional dance.

central Chile and the Argentine pampas were occupied by the Mapuche (Araucanians) and Tehuelche, who held back the encroachment of Western civilization. Settlers moved on to their lands, and, inevitably, attacked the natives, who counterattacked. The military was called in, and by 1883 they were finally defeated and vast regions of rich agricultural land were opened for white settlers (Bodley 1982:50).

Originally used as penal colonies, Australia, New Zealand, and the island of Tasmania were opened for migration from Great Britain in the late eighteenth and nineteenth centuries. The large British-owned islands were used to reduce prison populations in Great Britain and specialized in sheep production; the wool was shipped to England. As with North America, these Pacific regions were used to relieve the pressures of a growing population. The native populations of the island of Tasmania were decimated by the middle of the nineteenth century as their island was taken over for sheepherding. A similar story is told for the Australian Aborigines, although many more survived than in Tasmania because the interior of Australia was not very inviting, and it continued to support hunters and food gatherers well into the early part of the twentieth century.

The Maori of New Zealand fared a little better, perhaps because they were able to counter European aggression with some of their own. Immigrants from the British islands settled New Zealand and by 1840 thousands of settlers, traders, and missionaries shared the island with about 100,000 Maori, who tolerated and even aided foreigners. By 1858, due to the usual frontier pattern of white exploitation and disease, the Maori population had fallen to 56,000 and the white population had risen to 40,000. The government pursued a vigorous policy of land alienation. The colonists demanded the best lands, drawing the resentment of the Maori. They began to resist, and in 1858 elected their own "king" and organized troops. Social revitalization movements arose and the Maori returned to their customs, such as tattooing. A war broke out that lasted twelve years and killed thousands on both sides. Today, as in the United States with the Native Americans, the Maori and the European New Zealanders are trying to come to terms with a painful past.

A similar but not as well-known story occurred on the Pampas of Argentina. As Europeans developed refrigerated shipping, the grasslands of Argentina became specialized in growing beef on lands once occupied by Puelche and Tehuelche Indians. Where these native populations did not die off, they were integrated into rural Argentine life as *gauchos,* South American cowboys. The gauchos became a rural lower class dominated by the light-skinned masters in Buenos Aires, distinctions that are yet today reflected in rural folk songs in which the rural cousin mocks his rich relatives from Buenos Aires and their "civilized ways."

In other parts of the world, such as highland Bolivia and Peru, colonizers encountered mostly peasant farmers who were already the subjects of state systems, not independent tribal peoples. We have examined the colonial systems imposed on the peoples of Latin America, and will examine them more closely again in Chapter 12. While initial contact brought high death rates due to the introduction of diseases and the collapse of trade, most of these populations today have been incorporated into modern nation states, and have been politically very active in protesting their own abuse for the last half-century.

North American Indians: The Effects of the Fur Trade

Eric Wolf links the genocidal attack on the Native peoples of North America to the fur trade. Until the British conquest of Canada, the Dutch West Indies Company (also active in the Caribbean) controlled the international fur trade and Amsterdam received a large percentage of furs obtained in North America. The earliest target of the fur trade was beaver, and after its biological collapse due to overtrapping, it was replaced with sea otter. Beaver and otter furs were primarily used for hats as European taste shifted from wool to fur. Only in the nineteenth century did furs go out of favor to be replaced with hats made of silk and other materials. As early as 1608, the British established a trading post at Jamestown, Virginia, followed by posts at Fort Nassau at Albany in 1614, New Amsterdam in 1624, New Plymouth in 1620, and Massachusetts Bay in 1630 (Wolf 1982:163).

Each post, which soon became a fortress town, was located on a major trade route to the inland riches of the fur country. The French controlled the trade on the St. Lawrence River, which led to the Great Lakes, allowing them to monopolize northern trade in furs, while the English controlled the southern access to trade along the Hudson River. The fur trade disrupted customary Native adaptations. Traders demanded fur from one group after another, paying them with European artifacts and forcing Native American groups to compete for new hunting grounds, thus intensifying warfare. Entire populations were decimated. Frenchmen and Englishmen supported different tribes and supplied them with guns and powder to attack each other. European diseases further decimated the same populations. Disease and warfare combined brought on population collapse. For example, the Eastern Abenaki of the Maine coast had a population of

10,000 in 1600, but by 1611 only 3,000 survived. The survivors gave up their traditions of coastal fishing and hunting water fowl and established small family hunting territories inland, causing larger kin groups to lose their social integrity.

The Wendar (Huron), a confederation of between 20,000 to 30,000 people committed to horticulture, entered into the fur trade in the early seventeenth century. They and the Iroquois developed a warring relationship with each other. The English supported the Iroquois and the French supported the Wendar. The Iroquois, a confederacy of six tribes—Mohawk, Oneida, Onondaga, Cayuga, Seneca, and Tuscarora—did not have many beaver in their territory. According to Seneca traditions, the League of Five Nations—Mohawk, Oneida, Onondaga, Cayuga, and Seneca—was in existence by about A.D. 200. The Tuscarora became a part of the league in the early eighteenth century. In 1648, the Iroquois destroyed the Wendar for their beaver lands. In 1656 they destroyed the Erie and the Neutral Nation, and opened war on the Illinois in 1680. Iroquois success was aided by the superior firepower of their English allies.

The fur trade and warfare fed on one another and changed the ecological adaptations of the northeastern tribes. Agriculture was abandoned by the men for warfare and trade. Women continued to grow crops, and it is possible the new ecological relationship reinforced already existing patterns of matrilineal descent. Continuous warfare forced many tribes to migrate west. Thus, the Potawatomi, Sauk, Fox, Kickapoo, Mascouten, and Illinois were driven west from lower Michigan and Ohio. Many tribes combined to form new groupings as populations declined. Fusion and alliance led to the loss of old rituals and the development of new ones.

For example, the collective Feast of the Dead practiced among Huron and Iroquoian speakers was replaced by the Midewiwin. The Feast of the Dead, as Eric Wolf explains, was a celebration of local villages that, once every ten to twelve years, would bring together the bones of the dead in a central location. All of the bones would be mixed together symbolizing the solidarity of the entire tribe (say the Huron "nation"). While the Feast of the Dead celebrated local group identity and the succession of local leadership, the Midewiwin was directed towards the individual and his integration into a "hierarchical association that transcended both locality and descent group" (Wolf 1982:172). The association was translocal, integrating local tribes into the fur trade through identification with a Mide lodge, an association of warriors. Entry and advancement into the higher grades of the Mide lodge required wealth, and the fur trade was a source of that wealth. Each member of a Mide lodge owned a "medicine" bag of religious artifacts, including a shell. The new member was "shot" with "rays" from the shell, and was then reborn as a member of the lodge (the influence of Christianity was strong). In this way, local descent groups yielded to the development of a translocal "church," connecting local groups to outside forces, including traders, government officials, and missionaries (Wolf 1982:172).

In 1830, President Andrew Jackson pushed the Indian Removal Act through the U. S. Congress. The act called for the removal of all eastern tribes to reservations in the Great American Desert west of the Mississippi. U. S. government policies, competition, and warfare drove tribes west. Many adapted to horse nomadism on the Great Plains and became buffalo hunters. Traders established trading posts to purchase buffalo hides, and the competition was renewed until the buffalo were practically destroyed. By 1840, a frontier had been organized beyond which the Native Americans were supposed to live and a string of forts was established running from Texas to Canada (Bodley 1982:87). But when Texas, Oregon country, and the Southwest passed into American control in the 1840s, settlers began to stream across the plains and conflict was inevitable. Coercion was used to dispossess the Indians of their western lands. In 1890, Native Americans owned over 137 million acres of land. By 1934, those holdings had been reduced to just 56 million acres. Most of the lands were not suitable for agriculture. Reservations grew smaller and their resource bases were insufficient to support their populations. Native Americans revolted constantly against the system that was destroying them. In the end, many Native cultures were destroyed. Alcoholism, depression, and suicide became a common part of reservation life, with few exceptions.

The Rise of Modern Democratic Capitalism

The story of the peripheries of the world, however, is not the story of the core countries; these have experienced a very different world, which we will try to describe in the next section. The political economies that emerged in Great Britain and North America are called **democratic capitalism.** These were novel systems that emerged between 1700 and 1850 out of mercantilism. The capitalist system, as a distinct "system," was only described for the first time by Adam Smith in *The Wealth of Nations* in 1776. At the outset, it is important to point out that not all capitalist societies are democratic, but all democratic societies are capitalistic. The relationship between democracy and capitalism is an important attribute of this type of political economy, but why the two work well together has never been clearly spelled out, and the topic is controversial. Since the middle of the 1980s, a number of Latin American countries have attempted to democratize, going from authoritarian states to democratic states, and the Soviet Union has attempted to introduce both free markets and democracy. China has also attempted to adopt capitalism, but without democracy. Other regions in Eastern Europe, Asia, Africa, and the Middle East have experimented with various mixes of capitalism and democracy, but all these regions are troubled because it is very hard to keep the two transitions (the transition to democracy and the transition to capitalism) in balance with one another. Recent consequences have been an upsurge in ethnic nationalism and regional violence instead of peace and prosperity.

It is important to understand that capitalism is a powerful machine that can do much damage to people and environments unless carefully monitored by democratically elected officials. Joseph Schumpeter, one of the twentieth century's chief economists, was an extreme pessimist about the potential survival of democratic capitalism during the 1930s because of the Great Depression and the looming war in Europe. Karl Marx made similar predictions in the nineteenth century about the demise of capitalism. Both predicted the replacement of democratic capitalism with totalitarian dictatorships of the right, called **state capitalism** (Schumpeter 1967) or the left, called **state socialism** (Marx). The histories of the political economies of the core since World War II have been very different from what was predicted for them. At the end of the twentieth century, the majority of state capitalist and state socialist governments are moving in the direction of democratic capitalism, even with all of its ups and downs. For example, since 1985, every Latin American country, except Cuba, has had democratic elections. Many would question just how democratic many of these countries really are, particularly in Central America, but the direction of change is clear.

The differences between state capitalism, state socialism, and democratic capitalism are not always clear, often shading into each other. State capitalism is a type of political economy that operates according to market forces but lacks democracy, in which state intervention in the economy benefits those who already have wealth (and who control the state). Mexico and most other Latin American republics have used the rhetoric of socialism or capitalism to gain the support of the working or capitalist classes, but have been predominantly state capitalist since the 1940s. The introduction of reforms to sell off state-run industries and introduce democracy over the last decade has been rocky at best. State socialism lacks true markets, and should operate as a redistribution economy benefiting the working classes. Such were the ideal goals of the Soviet Union, China, and many African republics. Instead the state grew extremely rigid and bureaucratic, and was unable to compete in world trade, and in each region has gradually collapsed. Attempts to introduce democratic capitalism in all these regions have had very mixed results, the consequence of **structural power** (the tendency for the old elites to retain control of the political economy). We will deal with the problems of how the various regions of the world react to the twin transitions to capitalism and democracy after providing a basic definition of democratic capitalism.

Characteristics of Democratic Capitalism

The chief attributes of modern capitalism (not democracy) are: entrepreneurialism; competition; the search for profits; the operation of land, labor, and capital in "free" markets; and cycles of expansion and recession along with continuous technological innovation.

Entrepreneurialism   Schumpeter (1967) described entrepreneurialism as one of the chief features of modern capitalism. Entrepreneurs are individuals who can recognize a market for a good and can organize capital, land, and labor to produce that good. Schumpeter recognized that there is a pattern to entrepreneurial activity. First, there is the success of the single entrepreneur, say Henry Ford, who invents either a new good or a new way to produce a good. This is followed by the second characteristic of capitalism.

Competition   The entrepreneur's success is followed by a *swarm* of competitors, which causes prices to drop and demand for a good to increase. But sooner or later, all of the competition floods the market, and the demand for a good goes down. The activities of the swarm more or less describe a business cycle that begins with expansion and ends with contraction. It is the business cycle that is the most dangerous feature of capitalism because the cycle can be either moderate (soft-landing in a recession) or extreme (such as the Great Depression). Extreme cycles can produce powerful social movements, such as fascism or socialism, that threaten the institutions of democratic capitalism.

The Search for Profits   Driving the activities of the entrepreneur is the search for profits. In order to increase personal profits and those of shareholders, the entrepreneur constantly searches for ways to decrease costs. This can be done in two ways: increase efficiency or decrease labor costs. Increases in efficiency are possible only by investing more capital in improving technology, which may also reduce the amount of labor required for a task. The reduction of labor costs puts the working class and entrepreneurs in conflict with one another. As noted for Great Britain, a continual drop in wages brings political violence on the part of the working class. Under favorable circumstances, democratic reforms are the result.

Free Markets for Land, Labor, and Capital   One of the most controversial characteristics of capitalist societies is the free market for land, labor, and capital

Entrepreneurship has ancient roots in North America.

(one reason why wages fall). The histories of the core countries describe the rise and fall of governments that come into existence to protect one of the three components of capitalist markets, particularly labor. The conflicts between the entrepreneurs and the politicians protecting land, labor, and capital have been continuous. As long as countries were more or less autonomous and could survive on the sale of goods within national markets, competition between countries for markets had little effect on labor and labor unions. In the last two decades, globalization has had a particularly severe impact on labor in the core. Investments by transnationals in the former periphery are causing radical job losses that, in turn, are causing changes in American social structure and decreases in the power of labor unions. Part of the lower middle class has dropped into the working class and part of the working class has dropped below the poverty line, which is the amount of income the U. S. government has decided one must earn to support a family without undue hardship (about $15,500 in 1995 for a family of two adults and two children).

The drop in the demand for labor and the increase in capital investments have produced third world conditions within the core. It has become common today for people to be without homes and jobs, social and economic characteristics that were once only found in places like Mexico or Tanzania. Families are suffering from these changes, and so are the relationships between men and women, which we discuss in another chapter. Tensions between different ethnic groups have intensified significantly. Core and peripheries are merging to look more like each other with problems in common. As an example, the kind of urban poverty that was once found in squatter settlements around Mexico and other Latin American cities is beginning to characterize the inner cities of the countries of the core. On the other hand, the suburbs of Mexico City look increasingly like the suburbs of American cities across the border in the United States. Automobiles, air pollution, long drives between the central city and the suburbs are no longer only American prerogatives.

Expansion, Contraction, and Technological Change   Important features of democratic capitalism, which grow out of the first four characteristics, are continuous technological change and the expansion and contraction of the economy (our business cycles: recession and depression). Entrepreneurs come up with new goods (for example, computers and software) that require workers to learn new tasks. The new goods cause changes in the culture (you may be able to work at home on a computer instead of driving to a job). Competition, expansion, and contraction of the economy cause a great deal of pain (you may not be able to find any job).

This kind of constant innovation, expansion, contraction, and the push for continuous change has now been a characteristic of the core countries since World War I, if not before. International competition, beginning in the 1970s, has reached the point where no region of the world is safe from the demands of capitalism. While all cultures undergo more or less continuous change, the changes are often so slow in nonindustrial societies as to be almost imperceptible. It is the *rate* of change that is so remarkable in industrial (and postindustrial) societies today. For example, from the turn of the century until the 1950s, the two cities of Puebla, Mexico, and Medellín, Columbia, were relatively small, with little in the form of modern technology. In the 1960s, their populations expanded to half a million, and today are well over two million. Although they were once predominantly rural, urban sprawl spreads from both cities and the countryside is rapidly disappearing as it is industrialized.

This has been a century of incredible change within the core countries. Many writers attribute the growth in the wealth of the core countries to the theft of the wealth of the periphery. In the early period of modernization, in the sixteenth and seventeenth centuries, there is reason for the argument because the wealth of Mexico, Egypt, and India ended up in the coffers of British capitalists (Hobsbawm 1962). The wealth of the United States is explained by continuous investment in poor countries, and the removal of profits from those countries. However, most of the recent wealth of the core has been due to investments by core countries in core countries. About 96 percent of all economic investment is by core countries in core countries. Only about 4 percent of all Wall Street investments go to the periphery, which is part of the reason for the poverty found there. Core investment in the periphery was somehow thought to produce dependency and poverty by robbing these regions of their natural wealth. But recent increases in investment are accompanied by increasing prosperity. The percentage of people in absolute poverty in Chile, for example, has dropped from 36 to 26 percent in the last five years. Even so, patterns of exploitation of periphery by core still exist, but are shifting from raw materials to cheap labor.

Writing in the 1960s, modernization theorists, such as Marion Levy (1966), viewed **modernization** in a positive way (modernization was the idea that the introduction of modern technologies would lead to the transformation of traditional institutions to democratic capitalism). But challenging their writings were those who feared that capitalism would not work in the periphery. Dependency theorists argued that instead of improving the lot of the average worker, capitalism had the opposite effect, causing increasing disparities between rich and poor. The answer proposed was state intervention in the economy to protect people and natural resources. In the middle of the 1980s, the debate became confused as the Soviet Union began its transition to capitalism and democracy. In the United States, economic theoreticians nervously eyed the apparent growth in the power of international capital interests and the lack of ability of the American political system to control capital flow. By the late 1980s, the impact of what is now known as "globalization" began to threaten the political economies of the Western European countries due to the loss of jobs to the countries of the periphery. The job loss led to many in the middle class dropping into the working class, while the working classes suffered a steady erosion in earning power. These economic shifts gradually led, in the 1990s, to a general lack of support for elected governments. This phenomenon is growing in the United States in the form of anti-government political movements, such as private militias in the Western states, that threaten a once reasonably stable political economy. To the extent that governments can no longer insure the economic well-being of their citizens, they are increasingly viewed with suspicion.

Blocked Transitions to Capitalism: Articulation, Disarticulation, and Structural Power

Since 1985, many countries that introduced socialist or state capitalist economies earlier in the century began to attempt the transitions to capitalism and democracy. Countries that go through the economic transition to capitalism successfully are said to have **articulated** economies, those that do not are **disarticulated.** In articulated economies, the characteristics of capitalism described above lead to an increasingly more efficient work force, which is rewarded by higher wages. In short, the working class is more or less integrated into the capitalist economic sector, usually because of the growing importance of democracy. Examples would be South Korea or Taiwan; both countries were state capitalist and antidemocratic until very recently.

In disarticulated economies, which are much more common, wages and productivity are not linked, a historical problem in the countries of the periphery. *Disarticulation* is a term meant to describe the *disconnection between the increasing efficiencies of the work force, as more efficient technologies are introduced, and the rewards to workers.* Nation states that are predominantly nondemocratic tend to have great difficulties in overcoming disarticulation. Both Mexico and Russia are examples. In addition, if the economies are based on international trade, with the cost of labor being determined by forces outside the control of a nation state, disarticulation will be hard to overcome. Thus, when international economic forces cause capitalists to lower wages in order to compete, then disarticulation occurs. The United States has gone from having a highly articulated economy to one which is increasingly disarticulated. The economies of the peripheral countries, in certain instances, may be moving in just the opposite direction: from disarticulated to articulated. However, successful articulation requires democratic

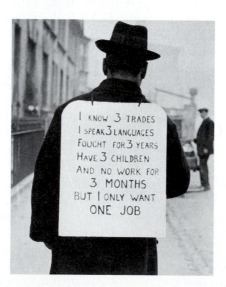

Capitalism's other face: recession and depression.

reform so that growth in the economic sector is distributed more or less evenly among social classes and government corruption is avoided.

The transition to capitalism, without democratic reform, will founder due to disarticulation. But the transition to democracy is difficult in formerly authoritarian and totalitarian countries. In early sixteenth century England, property rights came first, followed by political rights to a very limited aristocratic class. To a great extent, what we call representative democracy in the United States is the consequence of the extension and recognition of political rights to the individual by the state after first protecting property rights. In early English society, the transition came from the top down with the British aristocracy being granted property rights by the Crown in the sixteenth century, and later political rights (North 1981). Several centuries went by before those rights were extended to the mass of the population. In the United States, similar rights were extended first to white, male property holders and then only slowly to the rest of the population.

The anthropologist Eric Wolf (1994) argues that the organizational possibilities for democracy are limited by **structural power.** Structural power refers to political forces created by state capitalism and state socialism that continue to dominate after the collapse of these political economies. As an example, the "dinosaurs" of Mexico's archaic state capitalist system are holding back democratic reform through the assassinations of reformers. Similarly, in Russia, the old Communist politicians try to hold back President Yeltsin's reforms. Structures of power block the transitions to democracy. State capitalist and state socialist societies bog down because of authoritarian and totalitarian forms of structural power, old elites who refuse to give up. Attempts by countries to democratize as they go through the economic transition to capitalism are often blocked by the very models of economic organization they are trying to overcome.

Since World War II, **authoritarian** governments have associated with state capitalism and totalitarian one-party states with state socialism. The two political systems mirror the economies they manage. Authoritarian systems are composed of the various economic elites of the countries in question. Thus, in Central America, where plantation economies dominate, the elites tend to be planters and military men. In Argentina, Brazil, and Chile, which have more complex economies, they tend to be industrialists, planters, bureaucrats, and military men. Authoritarian political systems often have multiparty forms of organization, but no one can mistake them for true democracies. For the most part, authoritarian systems are anti-labor and function to reduce the wages of the working class, which leads to economic disarticulation (de Janvry 1981).

Anti-Capitalist Revolutions

The second part of the great transformation, from colonialism to independence (the first part was from feudalism to capitalism, mentioned earlier), was accompanied by peasant revolutions in those societies outside of Great Britain but in the core. In traditional societies, peasants may have been exploited by elites but certain minimal rights were also protected. With the introduction of private property rights and the disappearance of tributary rights, exploitation of the peasants increased. A wave of revolutions occurred in the nineteenth century in Western and Eastern Europe. Most of these early revolutions have been called "peasant revolutions" (Wolf 1969, 1982). Two major examples are the French Revolution of 1789 and the German Revolution of 1848 (Hobsbawm 1961, Wolf 1969).

Karl Marx's theory of capitalism was explained earlier. It was meant to explain the revolutionary violence in the Western European countries in the nineteenth century, not violent social movements in the periphery. Nonetheless, in the middle of the twentieth century, and in the decades to follow, his theory on the exploitative tendencies of capitalism was applied to violent political movements outside of Europe by such writers as Peter Worsley (1968), A. G. Frank (1969, 1979), and Immanuel Wallerstein (1974). Basically, the predominant view was that the development of prosperity in the core produced poverty in the periphery, and that violent social movements were the natural results of exploitation. These theories, culminating in Wallerstein's world system theory, were attempts to explain a second wave of violent peasant social movements in the countries of the periphery. While capitalism and democracy were the key driving forces behind the transformation of the core, these were blocked by the core in the periphery through such mechanisms as protecting corrupt dictators and preventing the redistribution of wealth.

Applying Marxist theory to the periphery, the anger of the peasant classes led to violent revolutionary transformations. In general, socialism and state capitalism were viewed as means of redistributing wealth, and challenging the capitalism of the core. According to Wallenstein (1979), these "peasant wars" were anti-system revolts. In the twentieth century, anti-system revolutions occurred in Mexico in 1910, in Guatemala from 1946 to 1954, in El Salvador from 1946 to 1949, in Nicaragua from 1979 to 1990, and in Bolivia from 1937 to 1940. With the sole exceptions of Cuba and Nicaragua, socialism did not succeed, but state capitalism did. State capitalism, seen most clearly in Mexico, depends on **corporatism,** a form of political economy in which the state owns and controls most of the factors of production, but does so with theoretically open markets (i.e., markets that respond perfectly to supply and demand). Corporatism envisions the state as a giant corporation protecting the rights of the various classes and preventing them from exploiting each other. Unfortunately, the long-run experience of state capitalism in Latin America has been largely negative, as we will examine in Chapter 12, with industrial elites developing who use the power of the state to advance their own ends.

In the same years that Mexico went through its radical revolution against industrial capitalism, roughly from 1910 to 1917, the country of Russia went through similar crises, but the resolution was socialism, not state capitalism. Communism, or "socialism" (the two terms are usually interchangeable), where introduced, abandoned the use of open markets in favor of a centrally organized state that made private property illegal (unlike state capitalism in Latin America). Many of the countries that emerged in Asia, such as India and Pakistan, never went so far and more resemble state capitalist models, but used the term "socialist," all of which is confusing. Common features of state capitalist, state so-cialist, and communist models are *a lack of trust in private property and a high level of optimism that the state will solve economic and political problems.*

The Soviet Union was created by the Russian Revolution of 1918, and a communist state was brought into being in China in 1949. The American war in Vietnam ended in 1975, with that country becoming socialist, along with its neighbors, Laos and Cambodia. In the 1960s, "anti-capitalist" transformations also occurred in much of Africa, leaving it with a majority of socialist governments by the 1980s. The same is true for much of the Middle East and Asia. Former colonies of core capitalist nations chose socialist or state capitalist political economies, at least initially.

The Soviet Experience: Revolution, Reform, and Blocked Transitions

The last decade of the twentieth century is experiencing a dramatic series of transformations, primarily in formerly socialist states in Asia and Africa, but also in state capitalist societies such as those found predominantly in Latin America. These movements are largely nonviolent, but the transition from either socialism or state capitalism is turning out to be more difficult than many anticipated, primarily because of the resistant structures of power. Russia's difficulties underline the problems of transition to open markets and democratic politics. One of the primary problems, in addition to the structure of power, is disarticulation.

Before Russia became the Soviet Union, it had brought much of the region east of Russia itself under its control. Russia at the turn of the twentieth century was a curious amalgam of imperialism, capitalism, and feudalism. It was a semi-peripheral and medieval society with an advanced capitalist urban economy coupled to a feudal rural society controlled by an authoritarian Czar (Goldman 1992:5). During World War I, much of the military and the peasants began to rebel against a war which seemed to have the primary aim of adding to the status of a French-speaking aristocracy, and little to do with the interests of the working classes that fought the war.

On November 17, 1917, the Bolsheviks seized control of the key centers of administration and communication and the Czarist government collapsed. According to the historian Paul Johnson, Vladimir Lenin, the architect of the future Soviet Union, had no real power base in Russia and never sought to create one. He concentrated exclusively on building up a small organization of "intellectual and sub-intellectual desperados" that he could completely dominate (Johnson 1992:59). Lenin's Bolshevik elite had little support from peasants or workers; skilled workers tended to support the opposition Menshevik camp.

While the Russian revolution was fought by industrial workers, peasants, and soldiers, it was Lenin who had the final say in the reconstruction of Russian society. In early 1917, the first All-Russian Congress of Soviets (worker unions) met with 822 delegates, which Lenin attempted to dominate, but instead alienated. He was forced to escape to Finland, but returned to challenge the provisional Kerensky government and, on the 25th of October of 1917, seized the city of Petrograd, and in the following months imposed Soviet rule on Russia. In the initial stages of his takeover, Lenin depended entirely on armed bands (Johnson 1992:65). Thus began the great terror that Joseph Stalin would continue after Lenin's death.

Under Stalin, state terrorism came to be the common modality of rule. Both Lenin and Stalin carried out purges of the Communist Party and genocide against those ethnic populations of the Soviet Union that resisted the demands of the new socialist state. There is no accurate figure on the number of people who died, but estimates are that 30 million people may have been sacrificed to this experiment in socialism, which ultimately failed (Goldman 1992:11).

Marvin Harris, a leading American anthropologist, attributes the collapse of the Soviet Union to the "structural incompatibilities" of Soviet institutions (Harris 1992). A prime source of infrastructure malfunctioning derived from the inherent limitations of the bureaucratically top-heavy, centrally planned and administered command economy. At the enterprise level, managers were watched by bureau chiefs in order to assure conformity with a massive list of rules and regulations that had various unintended consequences. Money for incentive bonuses was determined by the number of workers an enterprise employed and this led to the hiring of large numbers of unneeded workers. Crude quantitative quotas resulted in the production of inferior goods and invited falsification. "Since salaries, bonuses and promotions depend on achieving the plan, the temptation, indeed the pressure of the centrally planned system is to fake output" (Armstrong 1989:24, cited in Harris 1992).

When there is no connection between worker productivity and reward to the worker, the incentive to be productive is lost. This is a form of disarticulation common in socialist economies. Perhaps the true genius of Mikhail Gorbachev was his ability to see through the myth of socialism as a means of saving Russia from the outside imperialist powers and to realize the extent to which it was producing economic disarticulation. Gorbachev realized that it was no longer possible to close Russia off from participation in the evolving global economic enterprise. For Russia to survive, it had to link with international capitalism, and link worker productivity with economic incentives.

Gorbachev's attempt to do this began with a reform plan called *perestroika,* or restructuring, which was introduced in 1986. This plan loosened state control over the economy and attempted to stimulate individual initiative. *Glasnost,* or openness and candor, introduced in the political sector, relaxed the political environment. Perestroika also had a large impact on foreign policy, changing the Soviet Union's relationship to the core. This was only the beginning of a five-year period of turmoil that resulted in Gorbachev's replacement by Boris Yeltsin in 1991.

Boris Yeltsin became responsible for taking a much reduced Russian state through the transitions to open markets and democracy. Two fundamental institutional reforms are critical to achieving a capitalist market economy. Russia had to release price controls and privatize the economy. When Yeltsin tried to get political support from the parliament (the Duma), he was blocked by members of the old power structure. In order to force the Duma to his will, he had to order the army to attack the Russian Parliament building. On October 3, 1993, tanks under his control pounded the parliament into a blackened shell. This act made Yeltsin appear to be "antidemocratic," and many accused him of acting like one of the old Czars. Thus, the very process of attempting reform of the socialist economy forced Yeltsin into nondemocratic methods.

Yeltsin's next move was to abandon the old parliamentary leaders and to call for a new election, which ratified a new constitution giving him greater powers. In the election of December 12, 1993, Russians ratified a new constitution, but they also elected both the upper and lower houses of a "new parliament." In the election, many of the old communist leaders were reelected along with antidemocratic nationalists. Within two hours of the opening of the State Duma, a debate about procedure turned into a shouting match and the communists and nationalists were soon at each other's throats.

Yeltsin attempted to bypass the parliament by ruling by decree, appointing free market reform advocates to his cabinet. But the blocked political system prevented the new laws from having much effect, except in the central urban areas such as Moscow and St. Petersburg. Yeltsin was given advice by Jeffrey Sachs of Harvard University, who urged him to push through a rapid reform package in order to escape disarticulation, but his message failed. There is a lesson here about the connections between the economic and political transitions. Jeffrey Sachs may have been correct about the need for immediate and radical economic reform back in 1991–1992, but his advice to Yeltsin may not have been realistic. This underscores Eric Wolf's warning about structures of power. By pursuing reforms that were too dramatic and not understood by the Russian people, Yeltsin lost the very support he needed for reform. Now having slowed down the

Russian President Boris Yeltsin's attack on the "White House," or Duma (the Russian Parliament) in 1993.

pace of reform, he is able to gain greater political support, and so can pursue a somewhat more conservative direction of reform, but reform nonetheless. But democratic reforms were to be blocked on another front as well.

In 1995, Boris Yeltsin was forced to deal with the breakaway republic of Chechenya, an ethnic republic of Chechen speakers who have long sought independence. The Russian army invaded Chechnya and bombarded its capital, Grozny. Russian women tried to get their young men back from the front, embarrassing Boris Yeltsin on television with an image of a less than effective military. Close scrutiny of the military led to allegations of corruption and further undermined Yeltsin's regime.

In the election of December, 1995, the Peasant Party and Communist Party made strong inroads against reform-minded parties. Yeltsin scrapped his pro-Western foreign minister in favor of one who is not as strongly Western. But, by 1995, he had pushed reforms to the point where real markets began to emerge. In 1991, most forms of private business were illegal. Russia now has about 2,500 licensed commercial banks, 600 investment funds, and 40 million shareholders. Prices have been set free since 1992, and over 16,000 medium and large state firms have been privatized so that now 62 percent of the economy is privatized. Russia's state-owned sector is now smaller than Italy's (*The Economist* 5/20/95).

There were many fears that the new market economy was going to produce such deprivation that the communists and nationalists would win the election of 1996. Yeltsin, in fact, began weakly against challenges from former communist and nationalist blocks. However, in the last days of the campaign, Russian voters appeared to realize that they did not want to return to a socialist system, and Yeltsin won a closely contested election. But he is a physically weakened person and suffers from a heart condition. In the meantime, many argue that the free market has created a new wealthy class in the central cities while those working for state enterprises and living in rural areas remain poor, and so are potential sources of support for the socialists and nationalists.

The difficulty of keeping the transitions to open markets and democracy on an even keel is dramatically spelled out in the recent history of Russia. However, many other countries have also experienced the difficulties of balancing the two processes, including most of the countries of Eastern Europe and Latin America, and a few countries in Africa and Asia. While the details differ from region to region, the difficulties of moving from closed to open economies and reforming the political process towards democracy are among the most complex problems of the end of the twentieth century and the beginning of the twenty-first century.

The Globalization of the World System

The recent elections in Russia in the summer of 1996 began with an initial success by the left-of-center parties sympathetic with the restoration of the old Soviet Union. But as "structures of power" began to win the election, support increased for Boris Yeltsin, leading to his reelection. The 1996 Russian elections tend to support the argument that the transitions to democracy and capitalism are still attractive to Russians, despite all of the pain. Similar arguments can be mustered for most world regions: Despite the pains of reform, few regions are willing to return to either socialism or state capitalism if voters have a choice.

Globalization is forcing many countries into reforms supported by the International Monetary Fund and the World Bank, and by the countries of the core. But the final consequences of change are impossible to measure at this time. Immanuel Wallerstein (1988), looking at the crises of the 1980s, predicted that core nations would look for cheaper labor rates. This is happening, but what was not predicted was the opening of markets, the abandonment of socialist-style closed economies, and the innovation of new forms of participatory democracy. These new models, such as those found in Russia and Eastern Europe, may not be the familiar ones of North American–style political economies, but they are a far cry from the old anti-system answers of the middle of the twentieth century. In addition, many economists are currently arguing that the attraction of cheap labor rates is more than offset by the lack of education in formerly third world countries. Initial investments tend not to lead to profits, but to poorly made goods. These discoveries are affirming the need to improve education in the United States and other core countries in order to compete in the international trade arena. In the 1996 U.S. election, economic nationalism in the form of protected trade was beaten back and nonisolationist views prevailed.

We are now witnessing the emergence of a new world system called the "postmodern" or "global" world system. The final phase of the *modern world system* lasted from the end of World War II until approximately 1985. The world is currently going through a process of economic reorganization due to a shift in the core countries from economies dominated by the industrial sector to those dominated by the service sector and by investment capital rather than industrial capital (Nash 1994:11). Investment capital is capital that is invested in projects strictly for profits, not for social welfare or national needs. Industrial capital is capital that is used to generate an industrial sector in a modernizing society. The motivation on the part of state officials and investors is to create a stable society by expanding the industrial sector creating jobs. For example, in the period from World War I until the early 1970s, Detroit's automobile manufacturing was central to American productivity, and was a key industry producing jobs. In the 1980s, automobile manufacturing became highly computerized, and jobs were lost. In the 1990s, the key sector of economy is in the software industry, in jobs that are no longer central to the industrial economy, particularly in such "service" occupations as communications and finance. The modern world system was characterized by an industrial core and a largely agricultural periphery and semi-periphery to which the core exported finished industrial products. The institutional policies of the states of the core supported the growth and development of privately owned transnational corporations and large military complexes. These two systems were intricately tied together into "military–industrial complexes." The policies of the core countries were designed to make the military–industrial complexes successful, if not always efficient. The success of the private sector and the military was thought necessary to compete with the state

BOX 7.2

■ Case Study: Soviet Socialism and Environmental Destruction

The collapse of socialism in the former Soviet Union and Eastern Europe has brought to light environmental destruction due to socialist industrial development beyond the worst nightmares or fears of environmentalists. It also underlines the desperate need for market connections to the global economy at the international level to succeed while at the same time democratic reform at the national level gives people power to protect their habitats: Both of these must be accomplished in order to pass through the ecological transition to sustained development.

Documenting the damage alone is a monumental task. Boris Yeltsin ordered the Geography Institute of the USSR Academy of Science to collect statistical data and to map the dimensions of the Soviet Union's environmental mess. Much of the following is derived from that study (Sneider 1992).

As an example, a gigantic steelworks known as the Magnitogrosk Works was a showcase for socialist progress. Begun by Stalin in 1929, it grew to a sprawling combination of ten gigantic blast furnaces, thirty-four open-hearth ovens, and dozens of rolling and finishing mills. The Institute reported that the Works produced 800,000 tons of waste a year that were pumped into the air. Nearby, another steel center pumped an additional 350,000 tons of waste into the air. Soil samples twenty-four kilometers away (fifteen miles) found concentrations of metal five to ten times the natural rate. More than a third of the adult population and two-thirds of the children suffer from respiratory diseases in the city of Chelyabinsk (Sneider 1992).

The region of Chelyabinsk is also the site of several once-secret nuclear facilities, including Chelyabinsk–65, the largest secret nuclear waste reprocessing site in the former Soviet Union. Several major accidents beginning in the late 1940s spread nuclear radiation over the area. Huge amounts of unprocessed nuclear waste are stored there with seepage going into ground water and Siberian rivers (Sneider 1992).

Other statistics about environmental damage to the landscape of the former Soviet Union are numbing. To compensate for agricultural inefficiencies of the collectives, the Soviets used massive and uncontrolled amounts of pesticides and chemical fertilizers. As a consequence, 30 percent of all produce is contaminated and should not be eaten; 42 percent of all baby food has unacceptable levels of nitrates and other pesticides (Sneider 1992). Industrial growth has put 70 million out of 190 million people living in 103 cities in danger of respiratory and other diseases from air that has five times the U. S. allowed limits of pollutants. Almost three-quarters of the surface water is polluted and one-fourth is completely untreated. Wastes are killing many important bodies of water including the Aral Sea, the Sea of Azoz, the Black Sea, and Lake Baykal, the deepest lake in the world (Sneider 1992).

A radiation map, never released to the Russian public but made available to *U.S. News and World Report,* pinpoints more than 130 nuclear explosions, mostly in European Russia and conducted for geophysical research, to create underground pressure in oil and gas fields, or simply to move earth for dams. No one has any idea how much they have contaminated land, water, people, and wildlife. The map has red triangles marking spots near the large island of Novaya Zemlya where nuclear reactors and other radioactive wastes were dumped into the sea. A nuclear submarine reportedly sank there (Goldman 1992:224).

The once pristine region of Siberia is no longer pristine. Some 920,000 barrels of oil are spilled every day in Russian Siberia, the equivalent of one Exxon Valdez spill every six hours. One pool of spilled oil in Siberia is six feet deep, four miles wide, and seven miles long (Goldman 1992:224). Thousands of gas flares in Siberia create the largest pool of light in the Eurasian land mass. Sulphur dioxide from the flares has created acid rain that has destroyed 1,500 miles of timber, a region half the size of Rhode Island. The forests of Siberia are being cut down at the rate of 5 million acres a year, posing a bigger threat than the destruction of the Brazilian rainforest (Goldman 1992:224).

Much of the damage surveyed above just touches on the ecological disasters of the Soviet Union. These disasters were the consequence of a "growth-at-any-cost mentality" and reflect the Soviet Union's obsession with gigantism

Chernobyl: a twentieth- century ecological catastrophe.

and its ability to twist science into a tool of politics. Everyone has heard of Chernobyl because it happened at a time when the Soviet Union had initiated glasnost. But another disaster was not reported until recently: In 1957, a nuclear storage facility near Chelyabinsk exploded, sending eighty tons of radioactive waste into the air and forcing the evacuation of ten thousand people (Goldman 1992:225). The extent of deaths and destruction is unknown.

Stewardship of the environment appears to have been remote from the minds of the central planners of the Soviet Union. We will close the topic of the environment with a short survey of the impact of Soviet thinking on the Aral Sea, one of the largest inland lakes in the world. Water use is one form of energy consumption and world use of water for irrigation grows every year. China plans to build the largest dam in the world to control its river systems in central China. It might pay close attention to what the Soviet Union did to its ecosystems with similar plans.

In the 1930s, economic planners decided to construct extensive irrigation canals in order to create cotton farms in the drylands of Soviet Central Asia. The irrigation ditches fed off two rivers, the Amu Daria and the Syr Daria. These flow into the Aral Sea, a body of water about the size of Lake Huron. By 1989, the sea received only one-eighth the level of water it had in 1960. Its water level had fallen forty-seven feet, more than a quarter, and its volume had shrunk by two-thirds. Its total area diminished by 44 percent (Sneider 1992).

Fishing villages lost their livelihoods as the shoreline moved ten miles. A new desert was created on the open beaches of the old sea, creating vast dust storms. In addition, the central planners saturated the cotton fields with fertilizers, insecticides, and pesticides, contaminating all water resources. The populations of the region were deprived of clean drinking water and their soils were poisoned. Diseases and child mortality shot up.

The problems of the Aral Sea have been dumped into the laps of the new rulers of the five Soviet Central Asian states that form the Aral Sea's water basin. In the meantime, the people of the region feel as though they had been exploited by imperialists. Their lands have been destroyed while the lone cotton crop was the only thing the bureaucrats in Moscow wanted (Sneider 1992).

---

socialist block as it gained allies in the countries of the periphery and semi-periphery. From 1950 to 1985, the capitalist core and the socialist block competed around the world during the Cold War. With the collapse of the Soviet Union, there has been a shift from industrial to investment capital strategies. One consequence is that industrial occupations, the mainstay of core workers, moved to the periphery and semi-periphery. Educated and efficient workers have become street people. (There is the perception that "jobs are being lost" to poorer countries.) The developing countries may be the beneficiaries of "postmodernism," as the period of globalization is called by American academics. Finance capital is responding by "fleeing" to where the profits are highest, and that often means where labor costs are relatively low.

Many economists argue that multinational corporations and international financial institutions have accumulated such vast power and influence at the expense of national capitalism and state agencies that, by the end of the 1990s, multinationals will control more than 50 percent of the world's economic production. Alvin Wolfe, an anthropologist, has long theorized that supranational organizations are stronger than nation states (Wolfe 1977).

But there is another view. Several recent surveys of the world economy published in *The Economist* show that there has indeed been a dramatic change in the world's economy between 1979 and 1995, but not one favoring the rich transnationals. The boundaries between national financial markets have dissolved and a truly global financial market has emerged along with a tremendous increase in international trade, the growth of multinational businesses, and a rise in international joint ventures. However, the strength and importance of specific multinational corporations have diminished since the 1970s when between two to three hundred transnational corporations dominated the world economy. Today there are more than 35,000 transnationals competing for the same limited capital. These companies do not have the same capacity to control economic events as their predecessors, and many have had to decrease in size or break up into separate companies (IBM recently broke up into thirteen different companies).

Instead of Wolfe's nation state being at the mercy of transnational corporations, *both transnationals and nation states have limited control over the flow of international capital.* Who, then, controls the flow of capital? According to *The Economist:*

> It is run by outlandishly well paid specialists, back room technicians and rows of computer screens. It deals in meaninglessly large sums of money. It seems to have little connection with the 'real' world of factories and fast-food restaurants. Yet at times such as October 1987, when all over the world stock markets crashed, it seems to hold the fate of economies in its grasp. The capital market is a mystery and thus a threat (*The Economist* 10/19/92).

The integration of this vast economic powerhouse is not due to a conspiracy by a few wealthy transnational capitalists, but is the by-product of the decision-making of hundreds of thousands of investors who use their computers and instant electronic information superhighways to assess the profitability of an investment. Financial investments are now being made by individuals whose computers give them access to world markets, and choices are being made in the transfer of capital entirely on the basis of profitability rather than the development of nation states, or the creation of jobs, or the survival of specific transnational corporations. In short, the state, corporations, and labor unions have all lost the ability to regulate investments in favor of their own interests. While this transformation was occurring in core countries, in developing regions the same forces brought about the collapse of state capitalism and socialism, for roughly the same reason. It became impossible for states to control the movement of capital. One consequence of this worldwide economic transformation is that efficiency and performance of corporations have become the definitions of success. Poor efficiency leads to reductions in employment both in labor and management. Job loss is no longer a threat only to the lowly employee, but to middle- and high-level managers as well. This means that if someone can organize an efficient plant in Mexico or Indonesia, capital will flow to it.

How can these changes be measured? One measure is the increase in the rate of capital flow around the world. The international business of banks in 1965 was $55 billion. By 1980, the stock of "international" bank lending was $324 billion. By 1991, the figure had risen to $7.5 trillion. In the meantime, Japan and the countries of the Pacific Rim became a part of the core at a time when the Soviet socialist experiment began to founder. In 1985, Mikhail Gorbachev came to power in the Soviet Union. First, he attempted to reform the Soviet Union under the twin banners of *glasnost* (the idea of political openness, opening to democratic reform) and *perestroika* (restructuring: privatizing state-run industries and introducing open markets). But, by 1990, it was apparent that the new openness had led to such political instability that the Soviet Union was dissolving. In 1991, it dissolved itself and the Cold War officially came to an end. The end of the Cold War radically changed the relationship of the United States to Latin America, the Middle East, Africa, and Asia, as well as the Newly Independent States (NIS) of the former U.S.S.R. Basically, the United States reduced its interest in the politics of developing countries, and these then began to move in directions that were ideologically the opposite of what they had been during the Cold War (ideologically, they were generally anti-American).

The emerging postmodern or global world system is characterized by a new core that consists of the United States, Western Europe, Japan, and the "Asian Tigers." The socialist "counter-core" has evaporated. Certain countries of the semi-periphery, such as Mexico and South Korea, are beginning to resemble the core in the high-rise buildings of their central cities. On the other hand, the inner cities of the United States are beginning to resemble the crumbling old mega-cities of the periphery, and many former socialist societies are slipping into the poverty of the periphery. June Nash, an anthropologist who specializes in the study of southern Mexico and Guatemala, argues that there is a global crisis in the making as capital flees the core and is invested in the periphery (Nash 1994). Entire industries that once belonged to the core are migrating to the semi-periphery and periphery. Jobs are being lost in the core, which is also experiencing homelessness and illiteracy. She argues that capital invested in the periphery is creating ecological wastelands due to the abuse of environments (Nash 1994), an issue we will explore further in later chapters. There is an economic transition under way in the countries of the periphery towards capitalism. The transformation is more or less universal, but many argue that this transition is also marked by an increasing gap between the rich and the poor, and greater absolute poverty among the lowest classes.

Summary

This chapter has covered the emergence of modern capitalism, the modern world system, the expansion of both, and the destruction of tribal societies. We have also examined the problems of economic disarticulation and the difficulties of the transition to capitalism and democracy. We looked closely at Russia to see just how difficult it is to introduce both market reform and democracy under pressures from a globalizing economy. One of the biggest questions is whether countries trying to reform themselves can do so, or if the burden of moving from economic disarticulation to economic articulation is too difficult to achieve within a democratic form of government.

In the following chapters, we will examine globalization more closely. Globalization depends on new economies that depend on the control of information and its dissemination. Globalization holds new promises, particularly to the countries of the former periphery, many of whom are finding themselves released from their dependent relationships on the core. But it remains to be seen if the processes of globalization can successfully address the interrelated challenges of reducing poverty and managing resources sustainably.

Key Terms

Articulation	Gaucho
Astrolabe	*Haciendas*
Authoritarian	Mercantilism
Conquistadores	Modernization
Corporations	Proletariat
Corporatism	Renaissance
Democratic Capitalism	State Capitalism
Disarticulation	State Socialism
Economic Liberalization	Structural Power
Encomiendas	Totalitarian

lobalism led to the collapse of socialism and state capitalism in the former Soviet Union, in Eastern Europe, in Africa, and Asia, and has destabilized working-class groups in countries with democratic capitalism. These changes have produced new social environments that, in turn, have produced new social movements. Social movements are a fact of history and have ranged from peaceful political and religious reforms to violent revolutions. But now, in the latter part of the twentieth century, these social movements are more explicitly based on ethnicity and are surfacing in a myriad of forms ranging from **civil rights movements** in countries practicing democratic capitalism, to **ethnonationalism** in formerly socialist countries, to movements aimed at protecting the rights of indigenous peoples around the world in all types of countries. Some of the movements are peaceful, attempting to work within the system to gain equal recognition before the law (civil rights movements). Other movements are violent and seek to change the system, with one group vying for power and political control over other groups (ethnonationalism). Yet other movements are of people who simply want to be able to retain their own traditions, who want to leave others alone, and want to be left alone (indigenous movements). To understand these movements that have so much to do with ethnicity and ethnic identity, we must first explore the concept of ethnicity.

We begin this chapter with the topic of ethnicity: What is it? We then examine how ethnic societies are changed through assimilation and acculturation around the world, and then focus specifically on American society. We consider social movements in the twentieth century, some of which have been ethnic movements, but many of which have not. We study five types of movements: transformative, reformative, redemptive, alterative, and ethnonationalist. We examine the reformative movements towards multiculturalism and indigenous rights movements, radical ethnonationalist movements, revolutionary transformative peasant revolutions, and we end with a discussion of the current reformative trends around the world towards capitalism.

Ethnicity and Ethnic Identity

What is **ethnicity?** Technically, it can be defined as regional or national identity based on language, religion, or heritage. But what does that mean exactly? Is the label *American* an ethnic or multiethnic concept? The same question can be applied to German identity, to French identity, or Lithuanian identity. Each of these countries is also made up of people with distinct regional identities, which are sometimes more important to them than their national identity; also, these countries were in turn cobbled together from smaller entities, many of which have "ethnic" identities today. For example, many Parisians, from the city of Paris, do not like to be confused or identified with people from the region of Lorraine because of its proximity to Germany. Germans, too, often think of themselves more in terms of the urban region they come from (thus John F. Kennedy's famous statement, "Ich bin ein Berliner," by which he intended to say "I am a Berliner," but which means "I am a jelly doughnut," in a speech in Berlin), rather than having a German identity. However, when either of these countries has been at war with each other, the regional distinctions evaporate, and the national identities suddenly appear to be exceptionally important.

David Maybury-Lewis, one of the creators of Cultural Survival, Inc., has commented that "ethnicity is one of the obscurest issues of all" (Maybury-Lewis 1997):

German family at picnic in La Crosse, Wisconsin, in the 1890s.

In spite of the fact that there is much talk nowadays about ethnicity and ethnic groups, it is not always clear exactly what that means or why ethnicity should have such a powerful hold on human imagination and behavior. Ethnic conflict has supplanted communism as the specter that is haunting the world. Writers, commentators and newspapers are currently telling us that people are everywhere giving in to the primordial urge to band together with others like themselves and to harass or kill those who are different (Maybury-Lewis 1997:ix).

Social scientists have tried to define ethnicity by establishing categories of behavior, identity, and symbols called ethnic "markers," but such ambitious research projects have usually resulted in more confusion than clarity. The reason is that ethnicity really means the same thing as social or group identity, and such identity can be remarkably vague and difficult to define. Ethnicity is the identity individuals ascribe to themselves that is generally accepted by others. Ethnic "markers," then, can be religious, regional, matters of national origins, or language-based, and usually depend on how individuals view themselves. Often the view changes with time. I (SS) am of Spanish American (my mother) and Scot-Irish (my father) ancestry, but I grew up in Bolivia, Colombia, and Mexico, so while I look Anglo (blonde, blue-eyed, ruddy complexion), I feel Latin American, and I speak a Colombian dialect of Spanish. I am really Spanish-Scot-Irish American, but my background is too complicated to explain, so I usually call myself American. When making out the census form, I check the category for "white," but I often wonder why I don't check that for "Hispanic." These categories are very arbitrary. Affirmative action programs have probably prompted many to mark an "ethnic" or "minority" category in order to gain some advantage. I must admit at times to having thought of adding my mother's Spanish surname to my own as Sheldon Smith-Montez because of my pride in my Spanish heritage and curiosity to see what would happen, but I have grown children and changing my last name now would become too complex, so I stick to my "American" heritage. How many of us can change our "ethnic" identity more or less at will? Also, when I lived in Latin America and when I travel there I tend to think of myself as an American, but when I am in the United States my ethnic identity tends to shift in the direction of Latin American, particularly when I am around people from Latin America. My ethnic identity, as is true for many people, is not completely static.

Societies tend to simplify reality, and the fact that I mark myself as white is because I have been taught to think of myself that way. My actual background, like most other human beings, is far too complex to categorize by any one ethnic marker. Much depends on the situation. Is a particular identity important? When looking at all my choices (markers), I realize ethnicity is a way of simplifying reality and gaining an identity as a member of a group, most of the members of which share enough features in common to give themselves a common identity. But the groups I've belonged to have changed over my lifetime. We usually shop around for the most obvious means of giving ourselves an identity (and an advantage). Usually, people tend to accept these differences in each other, bond within a larger definition of national identity, and get along. But it is apparent that such a bonding pattern is not the case in some parts of the world, such as the Israelis and Palestinians in the Middle East, or the Guatemalan Ladinos and Maya, the Muslims, Croats, and Serbs in Bosnia, the Irish and British in Northern Ireland, the Basques and Spaniards in Spain, and so on. How do we approach an explanation of why ethnic violence has surfaced at the end of the twentieth century? Many scholars are currently arguing that the reason for ethnic violence is the disintegration of the modern state due to globalism. Others are offering the argument that ethnicity has always been important, but that social science theories on the development of states prevented ethnicity from being a subject of study. When ethnicity is studied, it turns out that when societies discriminate against ethnic groups those groups tend to become antagonistic in the preservation of identity.

Why has ethnicity received so little attention until recently? According to Manning Nash, an anthropologist at the University of Chicago, the modern nation–state was supposed to replace ethnicity "as the most potent, maximal, and perduring form of social and political organization," so social scientists paid little attention to the category (Nash 1989:1). The modern nation–state was founded on the idea of citizenship that "has overtones of voluntary allegiance, loyalty, and of exclusivity," while "ethnicity was viewed sometimes in romantic terms like a 'volk,' a vestigial, colorful remnant of earlier times, soon to be swamped by the inexorable tide of the nation–state, that most rational, efficient, modern, and natural form of social and cultural being." The old assumption of the importance of the modern nation–state and the disappearance of ethnic identity was tied to a drive to create an all-encompassing social science theory (functionalism, discussed in Chapter 3), which drove out the category of ethnicity altogether. But, as Nash points out, a universal theory of social science never came about, and we are forced to try to grasp ethnicity not as an arcane feature of preindustrial society, but as a feature of modern life. Today, however, something else is happening. It now appears that far from being unimportant, perhaps ethnicity has always been with us and always will be (Nash 1989:2). The question remains, why have some ethnic groups suddenly become violent?

Samuel Huntington, a political scientist, argues that ethnic wars are cultural wars and that these are inevitable in the next century (Huntington 1996). He argues that ethnonationalist wars, such as that in Bosnia, are the form of conflict in the future. Because of globalism, the state is threatened everywhere and ethnic groups that were previously separated are now brought directly into confrontation with each other: China, Russia, India, and Muslim cultures will be in conflict. In short, for Huntington, the disappearance of the state is tied to the appearance of ethnic conflict, which is pretty much the opposite idea of the appearance of the modern state bringing about the disappearance of ethnicity altogether.

It is argued in this chapter that ethnic conflict is not the consequence of the collapse of the state, but that a peculiar kind of state is collapsing, the socialist state organized around ethnic identity. While all societies appear to experience ethnic conflict, few experience "cultural wars." The lack of attention to ethnicity due to the idea of the emergence of the modern state is surprising when examining the various nation–states of the world. It is not possible to drive through any country without running into ethnic variations that range from mild to dramatic. A drive through any large American city will show dramatic differences, but so would a similar drive through European, African, Asian, Middle Eastern, or Latin American countries. Such variations are often not apparent to the tourist. For example, in Mexico, there are language and value differences between those from northern Mexico and southern Mexico sufficient that locals often refer to other Mexicans from elsewhere as "gringos." Poblanos from the highland city of Puebla distinguish themselves from the coastal natives of Veracruz. Very similar distinctions are made between those from the region of Antioquia, Colombia, the state in which Medellín is located, who are called "paisa," and those who come from the northern coastal cities of Cartegena and Baranquilla. Paisas will often hold themselves aloof as speakers of pure "Castilian" (*Castellano*), and will mock lowlanders for their dialect of coastal Creole. Most of these differences are pointed to in fun, but recently the paisas have warned of creating a separate state of Antioquia in order to maintain their "ethnic" purity.

A drive inland from Lagos, Nigeria, astonishes the traveler with the range of ethnic variation in just in a short distance: One sees Ibos, Hausa, and Fulani, all dressed in their own "tribal" outfits. A similar tour of Addis Ababa in Ethiopia or Tehran in Iran, or of the Chinese or Russian countryside reveals extensive ethnic and regional variations. These differences are rarely, if ever, commented on. People live with differences. For the most part people of different ethnic identity are left to their own devices; they manage their languages, their religions, and go about their tasks while participating in a national culture that may require them to speak a second language (Nigerian English, Ethiopian Italian, Farsi, Chinese, or Russian). But in many regions of the world, ethnic identity and heritage were outlawed by politically dominant groups, and where this has been true, ethnicity stands out as extremely important, as something to be achieved and expressed.

Several regions of the world, including the United States, have attempted **ethnocide,** the destruction of the ethnic identities of subordinate cultures. There are many examples, including American Indian groups that have largely lost their identity because their languages and customs were made illegal, much as has been true for southern Mexico for a variety of ethnic groups. In recent years, many Mexican Indian populations, particularly the Maya, are retrieving their ancient identities, as the case study on the following page demonstrates.

Assimilation, Acculturation, and Multiculturalism

As is well known, many cultures in American history have been forced to submit to domination by the ethnically dominant white groups but have been kept apart and have retained separate cultures: American Indians, African Americans, and Hispanic Americans. But, the histories of most ethnic groups in North America have not been stories of segregation but **assimilation.** Many groups were assimilated to American culture, at least in the early history of the Republic, because that was the only alternative. The Anglo- Saxon elite expected new-

BOX 8.1

Case Study: Sna Jtz'ibajom, the House of the Writer

Ethnologists have been working for several decades among the Maya of the Mexican state of Chiapas and across the border in Guatemala. The Maya of Chiapas have been at odds with the Mexican state for several hundred years. The Maya are among the many minority peoples around the world who have been persecuted. The persecution is not just in the form of economic exploitation, it is also cultural. For example, the Mexican Balet Folklorico, held at many Mexican universities, is a series of ethnic dances from throughout Mexico, all but one of which portray Mexican regional and ethnic groups as heroic and proud. The dance of the Maya occurs last and mocks the Indian who is portrayed in a drunken and debauched state, barely able to stand, making lewd gestures to his mate. This racist dance has nothing to do with traditional Maya but it does show how many Mexicans think of the Maya Indian.

The dynamic culture of the Maya is thousands of years old. In the last decade, much like Indonesian theater made famous by Clifford Geertz, a rebirth of native pride is bringing native Maya back to an appreciation of their own cultures. Robert M. Laughton, an ethnologist with the Smithsonian Institute of Washington, D. C., has recently described the role that anthropologists played in a cultural renaissance of the Maya (Laughton 1994).

Up until the 1950s, Maya Indians of Chiapas were held in debt peonage (a form of slavery) on coffee *fincas* (farms, ranches, and haciendas). The Mexican government introduced the National Indian Institute (INI) to San Cristobal las Casas, the major city of Chiapas, with the mission to "civilize" and assimilate the Indian. Originally, the program was designed to give anthropologists knowledge about the Maya of Chiapas, but, in 1982, representatives of the Maya told Robert Laughton:

> You have published many studies, but always in other countries where we never see the results. Our people are now literate in Spanish but they don't know a quarter of what their fathers or grandfathers know about our culture. When the elders go to the grave they take their knowledge with them. We would like, at least, to put on paper our

comers to adopt their customs and values. John Quincy Adams expressed it this way:

> To one thing they [immigrants to the United States] must make up their minds, or they will be disappointed in every expectation of happiness as Americans. They must cast off the European skin, never to resume it. They must look forward to their posterity rather than backward to their ancestors; they must be sure that

customs for the sake of our children and grandchildren (1994:13).

Cultural Survival was organized in 1973 by David Maybury-Lewis to help preserve threatened peoples and cultures around the world. Laughton approached Cultural Survival and received seed money to help the Maya achieve their goals. So was born Sna Jtz'ibajom, the House of the Writer.

INI provided office space, and Maya Tzeltal speakers, with the help of linguistically trained ethnologists, organized to preserve their heritage. The Mexican government published their bilingual (Spanish and Tzeltal) booklets. The new booklets gave the Tzeltal the earliest Spanish descriptions of their encounters with the ancestors of the modern Maya. They recorded folk tales and described customs that are now of the past. However, these books were only taught in local schools using the Spanish version because the instructors did not know how to teach any of the Mayan dialects.

In 1988, Laughton and his associates tackled this problem by training the Maya to read and write their own dialects. They offered a six-month course to be taught in Mayan homes. To their surprise, men, women, and children lined up for the classes. In three-and-a-half years, 1500 diplomas were awarded. Laughton writes of the school that "every one of its teachers wants to teach and every one of its students wants to learn" (Laughton 1994:14).

In 1992, twenty teachers in the federal school system of Chamula asked for the same training. It has been a major breakthrough to have teachers admit that they are not doing a good job teaching; half of the instructors received diplomas. Literacy in the native dialect has stimulated confidence and ability to learn Spanish.

The success of Sna Jtz'ibajom has moved beyond the classroom. The Bread and Butter Puppet Theater was invited to help the Maya learn how to put on skits using their texts. Thus was created the Teatro Lo'il Maxil, Monkey Business Theater. There followed the rebirth of Maya theater in Chiapas:

> Their latest play, *The Jaguar Dynasty*, closes the circle. For the first time in a thousand years the Mayans are witnessing on the stage the lives of the forgotten kings of Yaxchilan and their royal wives (Laughton 1994).

The theater of the Maya has gained much prestige and has traveled to Mexico City, Guatemala, Honduras, Canada, and the United States. Mayan culture is recovering its centrality, and Mexicans are picking up an image of the Maya very different from that of the drunken dancer and his mate.

whatever their own feelings may be, those of their children will cling to the prejudices of this country (quoted in Calhoun et al. 1994:250).

Early immigrants were expected to surrender their ethnic identities and adopt American culture, and the American public school system was created in order to insure the enculturation of non-Americans. The assimilationist model was clearly the one that dominated American life prior to the middle of this century. School books were written to enculturate children to the "norms" of American culture. But the United States was not alone in this model. It was typical for countries like Mexico, Chile, Brazil, and Argentina that, before the turn of the century, opened their doors to immigration from Western Europe with the expectation that the new immigrants would assimilate to the national characteristics of these countries. It is not at all unusual to meet blue-eyed, blond, European-looking individuals in cities like Puebla, Mexico, who speak and act totally Mexican, and whose parents have only dim memories of German or Polish ancestors.

Assimilation is an asymmetrical form of social interaction: The dominant group expects the subordinate group to adapt to its standards, or else it cannot progress economically. Despite the socialization tools of the public schools, by the early twentieth century it became apparent that some cultures would not assimilate, but they would adopt some of the values of the dominant culture. When one culture adapts to the culture of another society, the process is *acculturation.* Acculturation includes:

> those phenomena which result when groups of individuals come into continuous first-hand contact, with subsequent changes in the original cultural patterns of either or both groups (Redfield, Linton, and Herskovits 1936:149).

Why have some groups been totally assimilated to American culture while others remain only partially acculturated? Probably the simplest explanation is that some of the immigrants to the United States (or to Brazil, Chile, Argentina, and so on) came in large colonies of several thousand and managed to retain some of the markers of their ethnic identities, while others came in small groups of only a few hundred and were culturally swamped by the dominant culture. An example of the second type is my mother's Spanish community of La Farma, a settlement in Moundsville, West Virginia, at the turn of the century. The first generation spoke Spanish and practiced the Catholic faith, but by the second generation, the language had been forgotten and the Spanish community had dispersed. An example of the first type is the town of Westby near La Crosse, Wisconsin, which was settled by Norwegians in the mid-nineteenth century but still actively retains its traditional Norwegian values. Westby was settled by several thousand Norwegians, not by a few hundred. The size of the community, then, has a lot of influence on whether an ethnic group is assimilated or acculturated.

Assimilation is obviously a political tool in the hands of elites to impose cultural control on others. Acculturation is a more neutral, less political process that will occur in any cultural group moving into a new culture. I (SS) had the experience of being a member of very small American communities throughout Latin America because my father was a Foreign Service officer, and it was far easier to learn Spanish and adapt to Latin American culture than to expect others to speak my language or understand my ways. But there was little pressure placed on me to assimilate; instead I chose to live in two cultures, and have done so most of my adult life.

One explanation behind the survival of ethnic identity was developed by

Fredrik Barth in 1969. He proposed that ethnicity is tied to ecological adaptation when people occupy a distinct niche (Barth 1969:19). We will see many examples of the way in which ecology reinforces ethnicity in the chapters to come; for example, the distinctions between pastoral nomadism and farming have always been of primary importance in establishing ethnic distinctions in the Middle East and parts of Africa. However, as shown in the case study of the Greek community in Tarpon Springs, Florida, starting on page 260, such a relationship is far from one-to-one.

A third political model, **multiculturalism,** has appeared in the latter part of the twentieth century in the United States, Canada, and Western Europe. This model is based on the increased political power of various ethnic groups. Multiculturalism is really a social movement and will be discussed later in this chapter. It is a movement that demands a certain degree of cultural autonomy and recognition.

While multiculturalism has gained prominence in American society, the rights of a group to maintain its customs often run into the demands by other groups that they change behavior. There are several examples here, one from Muslim and one from Hmong immigrants, both of which have cultural practices that allow men to control women. An extreme version of male dominance is expressed among a very limited number of Muslims who practice clitoridectomy, a form of genital mutilation of young girls that Americans find repugnant and that has been made illegal in many communities. Among the Hmong, there is the practice of the future husband kidnapping a future bride who is often only ten or eleven years old. Several Hmong men in the Minneapolis–St. Paul region have been arrested and jailed on kidnapping and rape charges, often with pressure from feminist groups to impose harsh punishments on the perpetrators. Judges, who are sensitive to both multiculturalism and women's rights, have been torn between the demands of the two groups.

Ethnicity in the United States

Many minority ethnic groups in the United States believe that our society, like others, is plagued by ethnic strife. Populist writers often argue that ethnic differences lead to conflict. Others argue that ethnic conflict is the consequence of discrimination and American society has a long way to go to achieve promises to the poor and minorities, but that conflict can be erased. Attempts to address discrimination has resulted in affirmative action programs and multiculturalism since the 1960s, not just in the United States but in Western Europe as well. In Chapter 4 we examined several cases of ethnic conflict in the United States. The growing anti-minority and anti-ethnic rights sentiments of extreme right-wing movements in the United States, Great Britain, France, and Germany have left social scientists puzzled. A few support the idea that it is people's differences that produce conflict. Others explain the current and ominous conflict between ethnic groups as the consequence of economic deprivation. They argue that globalization, with its impact on jobs in the countries of the core, is why skinhead and neo-Nazi groups are attracted to extreme nationalist movements. Recent attacks against Turkish immigrants in Germany are blamed on young people whose jobs

A century later, in the 1990s, Hmong girls graduate from La Crosse's Central High School.

are being threatened by immigrants. Similar problems were described for African Americans and Koreans in Los Angeles in Chapter 4.

The civil rights movement in the United States can be traced to the abolitionist movement that grew in the period directly before the American Civil War. In 1970, Nathan Glazer and Daniel Patrick Moynihan (now a Liberal Democratic senior senator from New York, then an eminent sociologist), published a book called *Beyond the Melting Pot*. Until their book was published, it was commonly assumed that all ethnic groups in the United States were in a melting pot and ethnic cultural values were disappearing due to the dominant American culture. Melting pot theory assumed that schools, which had been organized to force children to forget their traditional languages and ethnic values, had succeeded. Glazer and Moynihan surprised American society by showing that, in fact, ethnic groups were not disappearing but were a part of American life. They summarized statistics on the survival of ethnic groups and ethnicity for New York City that are surprising. As of 1970, New York had 859,000 Italians, 564,000 Russian Jews, 389,000 Poles, 312,000 Irish, 220,000 Austrians, 175,000 British, 100,000 Hungarians, 50,000 Greeks, Czechs, and Rumanians, 50,000 Yugoslavians, 5,000 Mexicans, and over 1,000,000 African Americans. The statistics have changed since then. Today there are many more Mexicans and, in addition, there are thousands of Vietnamese and Hmong.

Five years after their 1970 book, Glazer and Moynihan published a theoretical text, *Ethnicity: Theory and Experience* (1975), in which they tried to explain why ethnic populations survived in American society. One explanation was that

the development of the welfare state promoted the interest of ethnic groups, and, secondly, that inequality prevents ethnic groups from being assimilated. But this is only part of the picture. In the early 1970s, the radio storyteller, Garrison Keillor, invented the community of Lake Wobegone, Minnesota, made up of Norwegian Lutherans and German Catholics. This community has become a mainstay of his popular *Prairie Home Companion* broadcast Saturday nights by National Public Radio. There are Scot folk in Virginia who stay home Saturday nights to learn about events in Lake Wobegon with its war memorial to the "Lost Norwegian" (the community "which time has not forgot nor can the decades improve. . .where all the women are strong, the men good-looking, and the children above average"). While Lake Wobegone may be Keillor's invention, the town is not really very different from the Norwegian community of Westby, Wisconsin, just thirty miles from La Crosse. The Norwegian spoken in Westby is "purer" than that spoken in Norway, and Norwegian linguists have been known to visit the region in order to study the earlier versions of their language, which is no longer spoken in Norway.

Keillor's ethnic Germans and Norwegians were not products of welfare economics and they certainly cannot be regarded as members of unequal castes or classes, not in Minnesota and not in Wisconsin. The answer seems to lie in a quite different direction: Ethnic groups currently survive in the United States because no one tries to make them illegal. American society is multicultural because that is the way it now defines itself. Most studies of modern ethnic groups focus on minority populations and discrimination against them. It is not very difficult to understand that those groups that are discriminated against will tend to persist because they are not accepted into the larger American community. But Glazer and Moynihan's discoveries remind us that there are many ethnic groups that survive and persist despite the fact that they are not currently discriminated against.

In 1981, the conservative historian and writer, Thomas Sowell, who is also an African American, wrote a book that also details the ethnic variations in American society: Irish, Germans, Jews, Italians, Chinese, Japanese, blacks, Puerto Ricans, and Mexicans form the American "mosaic," as Sowell calls American society. He makes an interesting point: The mosaic of American society cannot be discussed as minority versus majority because there is no majority. The largest single strain that can be ethnically distinguished is people of British ancestry, and they make up only fifteen percent of the American population (Sowell 1981:4). Sowell also points out that no ethnic group has been wholly unique, and no two are completely alike. Each one has a different history, its own geographic distribution, and they even have distinct age differences reflecting distinct fertility patterns. Incomes, occupations, and unemployment rates differ significantly, and there is no simple explanation for all of the variations. Discrimination has influenced the prosperity of distinct groups, particularly those with dark skin pigmentation, but some have succeeded despite extreme discrimination, such as the Chinese communities on the West Coast. In Chapter 4, we examined several ethnic groups, all of which have been discriminated against, which appears to be a common thread in Sowell's descriptions of the histories of ethnic communities. But interethnic violence, of the kind emerging around the world, is extremely rare, and it cannot be explained solely by examining American ethnic history. For explanations, we have to step outside of the United States, because our own definition of American ethnicity is multicultural and multiethnic.

Contemporary Social Movements

The collapse of the Soviet Union has led to the sudden explosion of ethnic revolutions and regional wars throughout the old socialist periphery of Eastern Europe, where terrorism and genocide are common. In the 1980s and 1990s, there have been many ethnically based wars raging in both capitalist and socialist countries. Examples are Azerbaijan, Iraq, Guatemala, Peru, Ethiopia, Angola, South Africa, Sri Lanka, and Mozambique. The Philippines is involved in a twenty-year war with communists and Muslim insurgents. Looking around the world, it is hard to avoid the impression that almost every other country outside the core is either ruled by extremists or just barely able to maintain a democratic government.

Explaining Social Movements

There have been several attempts to explain the explosion of ethnic violence around the world. An example is Samuel Huntington's new book (1996), which argues that these are cultural wars and that they are an inevitable response to globalism. He argues that the process of globalism is bringing together cultures of very different types that were previously separate, and which respond to each other with violence,: Hebrews, Palestinians, Chinese, Tibetans, Russians, Croats, and Serbs are at each others' throats and the communist menace has been replaced with the menace of cultural wars. Huntington's point of view represents the view of many who believe that the state as in a process of free fall, and that with its disappearance, ethnic groups will go at each others' throats. Civilization will disappear. But there is an alternative explanation, which is that ethnonationalist conflicts are social movements produced by relative deprivation, a theory of history, and have limited scope and world impact. Other less violent social movements are movements toward indigenous rights, civil rights, and multicultural movements. Social movement analysis depends on two major variables: theories of history and the theory of relative deprivation. An analysis of ethnonationalism and other ethnic rights movements, given these two variables, produces the image of a less explosive world, but it is still not a pretty one.

Theories of History　　There have been many attempts to explain moderate social movements, revolutionary violence, terrorism, and genocide. Earlier theories explaining social movements tended to look at the relationship between imperialism and social movements. It was relatively easy to understand that the Mexican Revolution, which began in 1910, was a revolt against the dictator Porfirio Diaz, who had attempted to modernize Mexico by allowing foreign capitalists to gain an economic stranglehold over much of the Mexican landscape. The same is true for the revolt of Fidel Castro against the dictator Juan Batista in

Cuba in 1959 or the revolt of the Sandinistas in Nicaragua against the dictator Somoza in 1979. But how do we begin to explain current ethnic genocide in former Yugoslavia and other East European countries, or the terrorist activities of Palestinian Arabs and Iranians? Or how do we come to grips with the often extremely complex play of events in socialistic and mixed capitalist–socialist countries in Africa, such as Uganda? Or, how do we come to understand the grassroots Muslim fundamentalist movements in Iran and Algeria? As we move into the latter part of the twentieth century, explanations that seemed sufficient at midcentury no longer pertain. That is, the argument, so popular for the last thirty years, that capitalism and modernization are the root of all violence no longer works. Theories of history, that is, explanations about why history operates as it does, are a feature of all analytical approaches to social movements.

Theories of history are generally teleological: That is, the ends of the social movement are viewed as somehow destined (Aberle 1991:318). The goals of the leaders of the movements can be explained as willed by God (Muslim fundamentalists) or the product of secular forces such as cultural evolution (cultural materialism), dialectical processes (Marxism), the long course of history (political economy), the destiny of the ethnic group (ethnic nationalism), or the destiny of a particular minority group (liberation of American minority groups). As Manning Nash (1989) has noted, the theory of history that dominated social science until the early 1980s was the inevitability of the nation–state, and the consequent disappearance of ethnic identity. Now we find ourselves working towards a more realistic assessment of the relationship between states and ethnic groups.

The spokespersons for social movements are usually charismatic, and regard themselves or are regarded as being in touch with superior forces, or as having superior knowledge about the forces of destiny (this generalization would also apply to the "theorists of history," such as Max Weber, Karl Marx, Talcott Parsons, C. Wright Mills, and so on). The charismatic leader is a prophet who explains to his/her followers what is about to happen. An example of a recent American prophet involved in our moderate civil rights movement would be Martin Luther King. An example of a prophet of radical revolution would be Cuban leader Fidel Castro. An example of a prophet of ethnonationalist change would be the Ayatollah Khomeini of Iran. The three prophets cannot be separated from their messages, which are three very different readings of history.

Theories of history serve to mediate, channel, and constrain the actions of individuals and groups, and the above three prophets were successful in channeling new forms of behavior. King structured his message within the ideology of American political economy: reformist messages of change. Fidel Castro structured his within a Marxist theory of history: His was a radical message advocating the destruction of capitalist social structures. The Ayatollah Khomeini offered a vision of Islamic fundamentalism: God would replace the satanic capitalist state. When politicians and other power brokers attempt to mobilize (manipulate the behavior of) the masses, they often combine raw emotions with racist theories of history. An example would be Serbian President Slobodan Milosovic's vision of history based on the myth of Serbian greatness coupled to socialist ideology, which drove many of his followers to commit genocide in the Bosnian civil war. Certainly another example would be Hitler's theory about the

BOX 8.2

Case Study: The Greek Community of Tarpon Springs, Florida

An example of one ethnic group surviving in a multicultural society is the Greek community of Tarpon Springs, Florida. This quite large community has adopted many of the characteristics of American culture while holding on to many of its own, a very common process in acculturation. One of the reasons the original community never let go of its Greek ethnic identity is the size of the original population. Like many other ethnic groups, the Greeks of Tarpon Springs were first discriminated against for their dark skins and foreign language. But they managed to find niches for their economic specialization, sponge-diving, fishing, and, today, tourism, that brought them up the economic ladder. The occupations the Greeks tended to adopt also allowed Greek men to express *philotimo,* a sense of manliness, which was very attractive in the early part of the twentieth century to other Americans in South Florida. A tour of Tarpon Springs in the mid-1990s shows that the acculturated Greeks are proud of both their American and their Greek identities, but an older anthropological theory, one that dismissed the importance of ethnic culture and heritage, predicted the demise of this and other ethnic communities.

In 1966, anthropologist Edwin Buxbaum, who had made a study of the Greek community of Tarpon Springs, Florida, declared that it would disappear in twenty years. He theorized that it had lost its specialized occupation of sponge-diving and could not survive another two decades. In 1996, articles continue to appear in newspapers about the Greeks of Tarpon, Springs and their sponge-diving culture. In

1979, the city planner of Tarpon Springs told me (SS) that "the Greeks are stronger than ever." She argued that rather than disappearing, the Greeks of Tarpon Springs have given the city its particular political identity such that the city is continuously asserting its autonomy, authority, and independence against the county within which it is located and against its sister cities.

Buxbaum, working with 1960s social science models of community, had predicted the demise of Greek culture because he viewed the community of Tarpon Springs as a closed "organic" model in which various institutional features were functionally adapted to each other (structural-functionalism). He argued that when one or more such feature disappeared (sponge-diving), so would the community. The current theory about the growing importance of ethnicity in a secularizing world helps explain the continued survival of Greek ethnicity. The role of political identity and the need to maintain identity against the hegemony of outside forces does a lot to explain why, a century after their arrival, the Greeks of Tarpon Springs continue to survive.

Tarpon Springs was originally established as a "spa" for wealthy Philadelphians and, between 1882 and 1885, catered to wealthy Northerners. In 1899, John K. Cheyney, a wealthy banker from Philadelphia, had his yacht in the area and learned about the large sponge beds of the Gulf of Mexico. He used his influence to interest sponge merchants in New York City, most of them of Greek and Jewish background, to initiate sponge-diving in the area outside the harbor of Tarpon Springs. In the following decades, the Greeks of Tarpon

Springs effectively organized themselves into a political community within which Greek symbols are used with great rhetorical power against other groups.

Between 1891 and 1900, there was a large migration of sponge-divers to Tarpon Springs led by John Cocoris and his brothers (Buxbaum 1967). The early Greeks of Tarpon Springs are much as described by Joseph Campbell, an anthropologist, in his study of Greeks on mainland Greece (1964). They were highly individualistic, characterized by *philotimo* (spiritually strong), *kumbaros* (the godfather of a child), and a highly democratic civic culture. Immigration to Tarpon Springs was mostly from the island of Halki, north of Rhodes. By 1905, there were 500 sponge-divers, and by 1940, over a thousand. Typically, males would live alone for several years and then return to Greece to obtain a Greek wife. The sponge-diving industry brought its own support system: Greek boat builders, ship chandlers, provisioners, marine mechanics, financiers, and wholesalers, called "packers," who sold the sponges up north. In 1907, the Greek community constructed an impressive Greek Orthodox Church with a gold dome, which later became a shrine for Greeks throughout the United States. The church was organized through "The Community," a fourteen-member council representing the various islands, as well as several Greek–American associations, were active in the community.

Between 1900 and 1948, the sponge industry grew dramatically along with the Greek community of Tarpon Springs. The spa culture of Philadelphia died out due to the Depression and in reaction to the success of the Greek community. The Greeks were very industrious and acquired real estate and material goods, becoming middle-class "Greco-Americans." They were described as highly aggressive; some gravitated into banking and politics. The Greeks came to be represented in the city's political system. Several became mayors, police chiefs, and fire chiefs, commissioners, and so on. However, while their combined population was greater than any other group, internal competition and contentiousness prevented stronger alliances. As Buxbaum put it, "Where there are three Greeks, there are five parties" (Buxbaum 1967:42).

In 1947, at the height of the sponge-diving industry, a "red tide" struck, eliminating sponges along the Gulf of Mexico (the red tide is a bacterium that attacks sponges and other sea life). Panic hit the Greek community of Tarpon Springs and many predicted the end of the community. In 1946 there were 400 sponge boats operating out of the port. In 1967, there were only seven, and by 1979 there were three. A few remain today for tourists. In addition to the red tide, in the late 1940s, the Dupont Company introduced synthetic sponges, which were much cheaper than organic sponges. The boat crews dispersed and the skills were lost. Many of the younger men left the community and went to work in the steel mills of Youngstown, Ohio, and Gary Indiana, where new Greek communities were formed. Many predicted that with the disappearance of sponge-diving, which was considered the Greeks' ecological niche, the Greek community would disappear.

There were acculturative changes. Patriarchal family structure has practically disappeared and the status of women reflects changes in American society. Arranged marriages have completely disappeared, as has *philotimo* and *kumbaros*. The animosities of the early settlers towards each other no longer exist, but the Community is still strong, though few children learn Greek. The most important and significant event lasts three days, the Epiphany Celebration, beginning January 6th when the Archbishop of the Greek Orthodox Church of North and South America throws a gold cross into the bayou. Boys from the Greek community dive into the bayou to retrieve the cross, an event that is reported in the *Tarpon*

Springs Leader. The newspaper always prints the names of all the boys who have ever found the cross, back as far as the 1920s. The paper congratulates the Greek community for its celebration and all of the industries and commercial enterprises of the region print large ads congratulating the Greek community.

A close study of the history of the Greek community in Tarpon Springs shows that it has survived because it had the political skills to do so. But it also continued to exist because it is a relatively large community of Greeks. Smaller communities have not survived as well, as Greeks find mates who are of different ethnic backgrounds. But it is also important to note that American political theory has built into it the idea of equality. Such is not the case, surprisingly, for the former Soviet Union and the former socialist societies of Eastern Europe, which we turn to later in this chapter.

Germans as a master race, which led to the genocide of European Jewry. These theories combine the manipulation of emotions (patriotism) with the creation of a scapegoat (Jews, Muslims), which is used to explain why the hero (Germans, Serbs) has not succeeded.

The existing institutions of a society constrain the extent to which the message changes society, producing relative deprivation (explained next). If conflict itself is a part of the theory of history, then deprivation may produce a strong likelihood of periodic violence (Cuba, Iran). To the extent violence is not a part of the theory of history, it will play a lesser role, but given extreme deprivation, it is always a possibility (United States).

Relative Deprivation   One explanation for social movements is based on the assumption that **relative deprivation** provides the motivation for action. According to the theory of relative deprivation, all people consider themselves deprived of something—status, wealth, power, or acceptance. Obviously, and objectively, some people are more deprived than others. However, some people don't feel deprived, while others do. Social movements develop when a large number of people feel deprived and are frustrated at their inability to overcome their deprivations and achieve status, prosperity, power, or acceptance by others. Many different types of movements arise as a result of this frustration: Some are violent and some are nonviolent; some demand total change and immediate gratification; others demand only partial change and moderate improvement in lifestyle.

Social movements in this and other centuries were and are movements by people who organize themselves to effect change in the face of resistance (Aberle 1991). In this century, the single most constant factor producing social movements has been the desire of certain groups to improve their economic and political well-being. Movements early in this century were largely secular, while more recent movements are spurred by religious and ethnic beliefs. One interpretation is that the demands by people early in this century were basically economic and political, but that social changes did not add meaning to life, and that ethnic and religious movements appeal as much to inner feelings of self-worth and well-being as to economic and political desires.

In the histories of the nineteenth and twentieth centuries, core countries have largely stayed ahead of feelings of relative deprivation and have experienced a largely peaceful existence. While the prosperity of elite classes grew, so did the prosperity of the middle classes and the working classes. Working-class occupations in the first two-thirds of the twentieth century grew to the point that it has become difficult to distinguish middle and working classes. However, in the 1980s, the living wage of working-class and many middle-class groups fell in the United States. This has produced a spiritual malaise and has led to relatively peaceful multicultural movements and also a rise of fundamentalism.

Resource Mobilization   But deprivation cannot by itself explain social movements because it is too universal a characteristic; some discontent can always be found, but social movements are infrequent. One suggestion is to examine **resource mobilization,** that is, how a group is able to mobilize resources on its behalf. Without sufficient resources, which include the ability to organize, even the most angry cannot launch a social movement. What are the resources needed to produce a social movement? They are tangible assets, such as money, channels of communication (such as leaflets, newspapers, radio, and television), and human skills such as leadership, organizational talents, personal prestige, and knowledge of the people and institutions the movement hopes to change. Also critical are the time to devote to the movement and the commitment of followers to their cause (Calhoun, Light, and Keller 1994:555).

Patterns of peaceful accommodation have not been followed in the countries of the periphery. While total wealth has increased, the rate of increase for elites has been extremely high. The standard of living of the rural classes has actually decreased in a great many countries over the last thirty years. Many of the rural poor have fled to the cities and become the urban poor. The middle classes have generally expanded and enjoyed some of the wealth—at the expense of the working class, some would argue. As the distinction between rich and poor grew early in the century, there were increasing numbers of social revolutions, particularly as the poor gained access to modern forms of communication (resource mobilization). Today, where socialist models have not worked, people are turning to ethnonationalist and religious movements to address their feelings of deprivation.

In addition to resources, the social environment must be conducive to change (structural power, explained earlier, is a factor in allowing change; totalitarian or authoritarian governments will not allow change). Thus, the general prosperity and the open political system of the United States in the 1950s and 1960s were factors behind the rise of various social movements, including the civil rights, women's, and environmental movements. There must also be *cognitive liberation,* that is, the belief that one can succeed against superior forces and powers. Cognitive liberation is usually tied to a theory of history that stimulates a group to act because it believes it can succeed; examples are the peasant revolutions examined at the end of this chapter (Calhoun, Light, and Keller 1994:556).

Types of Social Movements

Among the more sophisticated studies of social movements is David F. Aberle's study of Navajo reaction to their deprivations. Aberle showed that many Navajo turned to a *nativistic* religion (this means to return to the traditions of one's ancestors), the worship of Peyote, as a means of coping with poverty and powerlessness on their reservation (1991). Today, Muslim populations in the Middle East are turning to fundamentalism for much the same reason, and in Eastern Europe and the former Soviet Union people are turning to ethnic identity, as well as religion.

According to Aberle, a **social movement** is an organized effort by a group of human beings to achieve goals in the face of resistance by other human beings. Social movements are organized and differ from individual acts, such as that of a mugger knocking down an elderly woman and stealing her purse or a psychopath who randomly kills people in a McDonald's restaurant. Such pathologically aberrant persons are not to be confused with revolutionaries or terrorists, although they are at times recruited to such movements.

Aberle points out that social movements are always associated with some notion of distress due to deprivation, dysphoria, or discontent with the current state of affairs. The concept of relative deprivation requires the existence of a **reference group,** (that is, a group with whom one can contrast the status, power, success, and worth of one's own group) such as people living in the same vicinity who have higher degrees of wealth and/or power. The spread of television to almost all areas of the world, even the most isolated village in the Amazon rainforest, has suddenly provided an immediate and wealthy reference group, the people and cultures of the core. People around the world who are not in the core respond to the blocked transitions to prosperity and democracy with frustration and anger, which often translates into social movements. Aberle classifies social movements into four types, the first four discussed below. The fifth was not in evidence when Aberle wrote.

Transformative Movements
Transformative movements aim at total change in the social order. The Mexican, Russian, and Chinese Revolutions, Marxist revolts in Africa and Asia, as well as activities by the Palestinian Liberation Organization and modern, Marxist revolutionary movements, and the Black Power Movement (which had a violent and transformative ideology distinct from the reformative civil rights movement) of the 1960s are a few examples. These are true revolutions. Such movements usually have secular theories of history (that is, they are rarely religious). In the first half of this century, most major revolutionary movements were predominantly secular, but not democratic. Many were decisively antireligious, such as the Mexican Revolution and the Russian Revolution, both of which outlawed religions (Mexico outlawed the Catholic religion, particularly in the 1930s, but then legalized it once more in the 1950s). These movements are always violent and have the aim of overthrowing the ruling class, which by definition will require violence. Certain movements that were once transformative have themselves changed through time, as Aberle points out. For example, the African National Congress (ANC) began as a transformative social movement in

South Africa, but with the release of Nelson Mandela and democratic changes in the social environment, it became a reformative movement moving away from a radical ideology. Some movements begin as reformative but become transformative or redemptive when they do not succeed.

Reformative Movements   **Reformative movements** target certain aspects of society for change. Examples are the many civil rights movements on behalf of racial and ethnic minorities, women, homosexuals, and so on. Today we can see two examples of these movements that will be discussed later: multiculturalism in the United States and indigenous rights movements, predominantly in Latin America and Africa. In former socialist countries, such as Russia and in many developing countries such as Mexico and Brazil, current reformative social movements favor capitalism and democracy. Like transformative movements, these movements also tend to be secular. But these movements are reformative rather than transformative because the illusion that society can be transformed overnight has vanished. The people in these societies are not like their predecessors, who rejected their own societies and tried to dramatically transform them. The reformers accept the social order as basically okay. They have come to realize that the millenarian dream is not to be achieved, and now it is acknowledged that the only path open is one of slow reform, the attempt to pass through the political and the economic transitions, both of which have to be carefully balanced. That is, the aim is not to throw out the social system but to insure that it distributes benefits fairly and democratically.

While these movements are reformative, they can be quite violent. The Zapatista revolt in Chiapas has claimed several hundred lives, but its aims are relatively moderate, mostly the demand that the Maya participate in the political process, not that the world be changed to a Marxist dream state. Recent violent

Revolutionary or glorified bandit? Pancho Villa and his Army of the North. The Mexican Revolution was a transformative movement.

In the 1960s, Americans of all ethnic backgrounds strove to improve civil rights: Martin Luther King and followers. The civil rights movement is a reformative movement.

protests in Bulgaria are shaking up the capital city of Sofia, and next door the Serbs are serving President Slobodan Milosevic his walking papers.

Democratic reform movements appear, by their nature, to occur whenever modernizing societies attempt to introduce free market reforms. This is because free market systems tend to exacerbate the worst features of corrupt, nondemocratic governments making the rich richer, and the poor poorer. Democracy is viewed as a means of combating corruption and allowing everyone to participate in the developing capitalist economies.

One of the most difficult problems today in achieving the transition from totalitarian or authoritarian governments, whether these are state capitalist or state socialist governments, is the danger of opening the door to ethnonationalist movements. These movements, as will be described, are both transformative and redemptive, but they are also violent and nondemocratic.

Redemptive Movements   **Redemptive movements** attempt to change individuals, but not society. According to Aberle, the defining characteristic of redemptive movements is the search for a new inner state of grace. Changes in behavior are sought to achieve that state of grace. Virtually all such movements reject at least some aspects of current society. They find the world to be evil and they aim to help the individual expel evil from his own soul. **Sectarian** (religious) movements, such as the "born again" Christian movement and the "Moonies" are American examples. The Peyote religion, the Ghost Dance of the Plains, and the millenarian movements (cargo cults) of indigenous peoples in Oceania are examples.

The Peyote religion is a movement occurring on American Indian reservations. Peyote was originally used by Mescalero and Lipan Apaches in the 1770s, and then diffused to the Plains tribes where it was adopted, and then spread to Canada. The use of peyote was organized into the Native American Church. Aberle's classic study showed how the Navajo Indians of the American Southwest, who had suffered economic deprivations, such as the loss of sheep (wealth) when the U.S. government decided to cut the herds, turned to curing ceremonies within the Native American Church. At first legalized, the movement has been recently made illegal, and it has gone underground. Another very famous redemptive movement is the Ghost Dance religion of the Plains Indians.

The upsurge of Muslim fundamentalism in the Near East is a contemporary example of a redemptive movement that has global implications because of its impact on national political systems, such as in Iran, but also in Algeria, Egypt, Turkey, and other cultures of the Middle East discussed in Chapter 10.

Alterative Movements   **Alterative movements,** which call for a partial change in the individual, are quite familiar to all of us. Birth control movements, movements aimed at teaching sex education and movements aimed both for and against abortion (family planning versus right to life), antismoking groups, and "just say no" are examples (we will not be dealing with alterative movements here). These movements vary; some are secular and some deeply religious.

Aberle differs from many social scientists who use relative deprivation theory by pointing out the importance of the directing ideology and program of the movement. He also points out that many movements succeed and become the establishment. A group that once aimed at revolutionary change may turn to trying to maintain its own existence as a successful revolutionary elite instead of proceeding to deliver on its original promises, such as in present-day Cuba. It is also not unusual for an organized movement, once having gained success, to largely disband and join the establishment. Such is largely what happened to the antiwar movement of the 1960s, and it is also true for the civil rights movements. Success often leads to disintegration of a movement as the ideology of the group becomes difficult to support in light of the disappearance of the reference group (the young become older, have children, and the reference group of the "older establishment" disappears, and with it an antiestablishment ideology). In addition to the four types of movements described above, we now see a fifth type emerging that combines the characteristics of transformative and redemptive movements.

Ethnonationalist Movements   **Ethnonationalism,** with the goals of achieving ethnic and religious separation from the larger social system, of the kind we see in former socialist and developing regions, combines the characteristics of transformative and redemptive movements. It tends to be antidemocratic, volatile,

BOX 8.3

Case Study: The Ghost Dance of the Plains

In 1869, a Paiute prophet named Wodziwob had religious visions that foretold the end of the existing world, the ousting of whites, the return of dead relatives, and the restoration of Indian lands and integrity. These doctrines spread rapidly among Plains tribes whose way of life had disintegrated under white pressure and the extermination of the buffalo. Though attempts at military resistance generated by cult doctrines were smashed, the cult spread widely and diversified into local versions. Then in 1890, a second Ghost Dance cult, inspired by another Paiute prophet, Wovoka, spread eastward across the Plains and even to some Eastern Woodlands tribes. Again the cult stressed return to the traditional ways of life that had broken down. If the patterns of traditional culture were purified and restored, the vanishing buffalo would return, the dead ancestors would come back, and the Indians could drive out the whites with magical protection against the power of bullets (from Keesing 1981:407–408).

and violent. An example is the Iranian Revolution of 1979, which brought to power the charismatic Ayatollah Khomeini and established a Muslim theocracy (discussed in Chapter 10). Other examples are the attempt to establish a separate Sikh state in India (described in Chapter 11), and the various Muslim fundamentalist movements in the Middle East (described in Chapter 10). In such a context, to the extent that cultural differences, ethnic identities, and religious affiliations crosscut one another to produce myriad diverse combinations, the likelihood of violence will increase, particularly if a motivating factor is a belief in the superiority of one group over another, or a history of subjugation by one group over another. Likewise, if a region contains several groups with distinct cultural or ethnic identities who are accustomed to an autonomous or semiautonomous existence, then any attempt by a territorial state to deprive these groups of their autonomy and their identities, to homogenize them, to insist that a national democratic identity take precedence over ethnic or religious based identities, is likely to produce resistance, possibly in the form of violence, against the state. In Russia, ethnonationalists such as Vladimir Zhirinovski promise a return to the glory days of the Soviet Union, including the recapturing of Alaska. In Algeria (North Africa), a former socialist government is attempting to introduce democracy, but is destabilized by Muslim fundamentalist movements. We will, in this chapter, closely examine the case of Bosnia in the former country of Yugoslavia.

There are many other examples of ethnonationalism discussed in the chapters to come, but not all of them have clear goals. For example, there are the con-

BOX 8.4

Case Study: The Vailala Madness

Other millenerian movements were the cargo cults of Melanesia. These were similar to the Ghost Dance religion in the importance ascribed to the ancestors, for whom the native populations marched hoping for the delivery of cargos. Early in the movement, the ancestors would deliver the cargos in sailing ships, but after World War II, expectations were high that the deliveries would occur in Flying Boxcars.

As of 1919, the Elema of coastal New Guinea had experienced waves of European influence: missionary teachings, early experience as plantation laborers, introduction of the few items of European hardware the Elema could afford, and pacification.

In that year, a movement broke out among the Elema that for a time set whole villages into collective "head he go round," a psychophysical state reminiscent of the dancing mania of plague-ridden medieval Europe. People lost control of their limbs, reeled drunkenly, and eventually lost consciousness. Who formulated the ideology is not clear. Central in it was a belief that the dead would return, bringing with them a fabulous cargo of European material—knives, cloth, canned goods, axes, and so on. Sacred bull-roarers and other ritual objects were destroyed in a wave of iconoclasm, in communities in which dramatic rituals and spectacular men's houses had been focal points of life. The Elema abandoned normal gardening projects and devoted their efforts to elaborate preparations for the return of the dead (from Keesing 1981:409).

flicts in the African countries of Rwanda and Burundi between Tutsi and Hutu (Chapter 9) and in Bosnia between Serbs, Croats, and Muslims (this chapter), and other ethnic groups in the former country of Yugoslavia. The savage attacks, ethnic cleansing, and mass rape occur between people who have lived as neighbors for generations, most of whom suffer from the same economic deprivations. And from most points of view, these ethnic groups are not really competing for the same jobs. Why, at this point, are ethnic conflicts so common, particularly in former socialist states? To the argument of economic deprivation must be added the point that ethnic groups in these regions are trying to gain control of the levers of newly emerging states.

The nineteenth and twentieth centuries have experienced great change, and in the process of world modernization many people have suffered at the hands of others. Reference fields are constantly changing for many peoples throughout the world, for modern communications brings the world to people in once isolated towns and villages. As Aberle points out, the changes that result in alterations in relationships are multifarious. For example, Mexicans can follow events in Poland on national television as that government goes through the political and economic transitions. Guatemalans are highly aware of changes in modernizing Russia, and so on.

In the following, we wish to examine several modern social movements, all of which have very different characteristics. We begin with the largely reformative civil rights and multiculturalist movements in the United States, movements that have secular reformist ideologies. Then we look at indigenous rights movements, ethnonationalist movements, peasant wars of the twentieth century, and finally, at current reform movements towards democracy and capitalism.

This chapter is followed by four chapters on distinct regions of the world: Africa, the Middle East, Asia, and Latin America. Each chapter details the secular transformational movements (peasant wars) of the early and middle twentieth century, discusses the democratic reform movements, and then touches on a few of the ethnonationalist movements that occur in each region. This chapter is intended as a theoretical overview of these movements to provide a context for understanding.

Multiculturalism and Indigenous Rights: The Legacy of The Civil Rights Movement

The development of human rights movements around the world dates back to the period directly after World War I, a period when idealistic political movements arose to insure that ethnic strife would not block the transitions to democratic reform around the world. The goals were achieved, largely, in the core but failed in the periphery. In Latin America, a movement called *Indigenismo* developed in the countries of the Andes, particularly Peru, Ecuador, and Bolivia, sponsored by Raul Haya de La Torre, the creator of the Peruvian political party APRA. APRA, which began as a radical and transformative movement, lost its force when its leaders were incorporated into state capitalism, a political movement described in Chapter 12. Very similar movements developed in Mexico and Central America. The Indian rights movement ran into grave problems in Guatemala and Central America, resurfacing as a violent transformative movement in the 1970s and 1980s. The Shining Path Movement and Tupac Amaru are two violent transformative movements that rose out of the failure of the largely reformative indigenous rights movements in Peru.

Many human rights movements in Africa were transformed into anticolonial transformative movements in the 1960s, and we will discuss what happened to them in Chapter 9. In South Africa, the African National Congress began as a reformative movement, and then changed to radical transformative in the 1960s, 1970s, and 1980s when it appeared that a peaceful approach would not work, but then recently converted back to its original reformist ideals.

Human rights movements in Asia in the 1930s, largely due to a lack of success, became radically transformative in the 1940s, although Ghandi's reformist approach to the rights of the Indian people succeeded. But in China, human rights and civil rights movements became radically transformative in the creation of the Chinese Communist state, and similar changes occurred in Burma, Vietnam, and Cambodia, topics covered in Chapter 11. Today, these radically transformative movements have shifted to a reformative mode, attempting the transitions to capitalism and democracy.

In the United States, the cross-fertilization of anticolonial movements in the periphery combined with minority rights movements on behalf of African Americans during the Depression years. But, in the period after World War II, these movements were, in turn, transformed into reformative movements towards granting equal rights to women, as well as gays and other groups. Included in these movements were environmental and animal rights movements that strove to grant nature its rights.

What began as the movements to grant former slaves equal rights in the United States blossomed into multicultural movements to preserve the ethnic identity and civil rights of many other ethnic groups as well, many of which did not fit into the label of minority. Many "liberation" for minorities concepts were broadly expanded, as mentioned above, to include women, gays, and recent immigrants. The rights of humans were also extended to the rights of nature (Nash 1989), resulting in environmental movements.

Multicultural Movements in the United States

Multiculturalism in the United States has its parallels in other prosperous countries, including most of Western Europe. An example is Switzerland, where people of German, French, Italian, and Romansch heritage preserve their distinctive cultures in integrated communities. Switzerland is currently studied as an ideal model for multiculturalism because it has long used open markets and an extremely open democratic style with a federated political economy that permits a great deal of flexibility in allowing ethnic identity to be a major factor in community political organization. The Swiss model is one that should be closely examined by people in other countries suffering ethnic conflict, such as Canada with its French minorities or Spain with its Basque minorities. Those countries that have tried to impose rigid centralized political states are the ones that are suffering from ethnic conflict.

Multiculturalism is a matter of policy in countries like Switzerland and the Netherlands, but in the United States it has become a reformative political movement that has attempted to use affirmative action programs as a tool to distribute jobs and power more equitably to a variety of groups. As members of various ethnic groups have expanded their ability to mobilize resources, they have attempted to use affirmative action programs to insure themselves government funding for academic positions, training, and special consideration in minority hiring in small businesses. The use of affirmative action is an excellent example of resource mobilization because American culture was open to the demands for equality at the same time that the groups demanding reform were achieving some degree of control over the political process.

While in the period of the 1960s, 1970s and 1980s, Americans accepted the argument that ethnic and minority groups that were not politically represented should be given special help through "affirmative action" programs, such a theory of history is losing support. Affirmative action programs were meant to provide jobs to members of minority groups and the disadvantaged, but globalization, which now threatens the jobs of many middle-class voters who once supported these programs, has brought a shift in national ideology. It is difficult to predict at this point whether affirmative action will be kept in its original form. Referendum 209 in the state of California recently sought to end race- or gender-based preferences in state and local government hiring, contracts and education. Just over 54 percent of the voters supported the measure, while 46 percent opposed it; the measure was blocked by a federal judge as unconstitutional.

The history of the American civil rights movement is a study in changes in the theory of history that drives social movements in the United States. Beginning with a strongly reformist movement in the 1960s that attempted to aid groups through affirmative action and other programs, globalization has decreased the strength of the movement. The current change in theory appears to argue that it is more important for the American economy to create jobs for all rather than to selectively help those who are disadvantaged by discrimination.

Indigenous Rights Movements

Here we come to another type of social movement that is becoming more common throughout the world. It is a type of civil rights movement common in the countries of the periphery. It is the plea by the people who first occupied many world regions that they be allowed to protect their lands and dignity. The term **ethnic** has been used here to refer primarily to populations in modern and modernizing countries who view themselves as having a common heritage, often including language and religion, who believe they are distinct from other similar groups. But whether they are minorities or majorities, they have been living in modern nation–states of one type or another for several generations. The term *indigenous* is a special category used for ethnic groups who are not accustomed to being members of modern states, but who have primary claims on lands that have been taken from them, or their cultures are threatened by members of the evolving states in which they live. This may be a little confusing. Are ethnic groups different from indigenous groups? Yes and no. In terms of cultural configurations, there may not be a great deal of difference in the phenomenon called culture. But indigenous peoples are those who were the original inhabitants of a territory and whose claims to the ownership of the land are based on the lands having belonged to them before anyone else. It is this particular claim, and its denial by those who control the state, that makes it important to add the term *indigenous* to our list of concepts.

According to Maybury-Lewis, indigenous peoples "were there first and are still there and so have rights of prior occupancy to their lands" (Maybury-Lewis

1997:7). These criteria work well in the Americas to distinguish Native Americans from those who came after 1492. There is also little trouble in distinguishing the Aborigines of Australia or the Maoris of New Zealand as "indigenous" from European settlers who came later (Maybury-Lewis 1997:8). On the other hand, in Europe, Asia, or Africa, the distinction between "indigenous" and "ethnic" groupings falls apart. In these regions mosaics of different peoples who have lived next to each other for thousands of years make the labels *ethnic* and *indigenous* difficult to apply, and the distinction is probably not important in such cases.

Another important characteristic distinguishing indigenous peoples as a distinct type of ethnic grouping is their marginalization or subordination to others, usually members of nation–states. Indigenous group have usually been:

> . . . conquered by peoples racially, ethnically, or culturally different from themselves. They have thus been subordinated by or incorporated in alien states which treat them as outsiders and, usually, inferiors. Isolated or marginal groups that have not yet been conquered by a state are also considered indigenous, because it is only a matter of time before they are subordinated (Maybury-Lewis 1997:8).

Ethnonationalist Movements

Just seven years ago, writers like ourselves (see Smith 1994), were optimistic that "the democratic transition" and "the capitalist transition" would be passed through relatively quickly. But at the same time that democratic reforms were beginning, new antidemocratic movements appeared. Unlike the reformative movements we have just examined, many of the new movements were neither peaceful nor reformative, but were and are violently transformative and redemptive. They are given the name ethnonationalist. Ethnonationalist movements, unlike the transformative peasant wars such as the Mexican, Russian, or Cuban revolutions, are not secular movements; rather, the participants wish to impose their religions and ethnic values on others, or to carve out separate nation–states for themselves. These movements are largely based on terrorism, genocide, and a very different theory of history than the theories that drove peasant revolutions, or the civil rights movements in the United States, or the current democratic reform movements discussed below and in the chapters to follow. Examples of these movements are found in the following chapters: in the chapter on Africa, the genocide in Rwanda and Burundi; in the chapter on the Middle East, the rise of Iran, the Muslim fundamentalist movements in Turkey, and the Israeli–Palestinian controversy; and in the chapter on Asia, the conflict between Sikhs and Indians. In this section, we will examine the conflict in Bosnia, a state of the former country of Yugoslavia.

One explanation for modern ethnonationalism is that as authoritarian countries begin to democratize, ethnic groups that were never allowed self-expression find a new possibility of grabbing control of the state. Deprivation of ethnic identity, due to its suppression by the state, emerges in the form of ethnonationalism. That is, when old authoritarian or totalitarian states attempt to

BOX 8.5

Case Study: Maya Land Tenure in Guatemala and Mexico

The loss of land and the reestablishment of traditional forms of land tenure have been central themes in indigenous movements, particularly in southern Mexico, Central America, and the Andes of South America. The Maya, and other Indian groups, lost much of their land to large ranchers and coffee growers during the period of the 1880s. Most of the revolutions in southern Mexico and Central America were produced by the relative deprivation of the loss of land, which was and is the only economic source of survival. While many groups have used revolutionary violence, there has also been a long-term legal movement by Indian and poor rural peasants to reclaim their land rights by legal petition in Mexico and Guatemala (Smith 1982). Often groups fight off the encroachment of large plantations, such as occur in the state of Escuintla on the coast of Guatemala, by hiring lawyers who have worked with the government to create cadastral maps that show exactly who owns what. But these attempts have largely failed.

In countries like Mexico, Guatemala, Peru, Ecuador, and Bolivia, and much of the periphery, the state provides little protection of private property rights for any social classes. Property is defended with power. The elites in southern Mexico, Central America, and the Andes hire small armies to protect their rights, and the poor fight back, producing civil war. But, even when the dust finally clears and groups reduce their violence, property rights are unclear. Often after conflict has ended, it begins again because of the lack of clarity of rights. As one Peruvian economist put it, peo-

ple cannot be prosperous without owning property, and as long as states cannot guarantee property rights, conflict continues. An excellent example of the problem with property rights and conflict is found with the Maya of southern Mexico in the state of Chiapas.

Land Ownership Why don't states create private property rights? In part because wealthy elites find it against their interests, but so do indigenous groups. The problem is that indigenous peoples face a dilemma when it comes to land ownership that is classically portrayed by the Maya. If indigenous peoples have economies that are traditionally based on collective rights so that basic economic forms such as reciprocity and redistribution are based on those rights, and these rights underlie collective identities and collective social structures, what happens when governments argue in favor of private property rights and various groups sue to develop those rights? Should the traditional forms of land ownership continue or should they be replaced by private property rights ?

In many instances around the world indigenous peoples have lost their land rights to others more powerful than themselves. When development anthropologists work with newly democratizing governments on behalf of indigenous peoples to reclaim stolen lands, collective forms of property are hard to protect. This is because of the lack of title to specific plots of land by individuals. When a village, a clan, or lineage collectively owns land, it is difficult to protect that land with laws designed for individual ownership. When large tracts of land in remote regions are involved, it is doubly difficult for governments to intercede on behalf of someone whose lands are being used by others. For example, a tribal group in Malaysia may petition a government to protect its lands against lumber cutters, but by the time action is taken, the trees have been cut and removed, and the loggers are long gone.

Land Tenure and the Zapatista Revolution
The complexity of this issue has been brought to light recently in the Zapatista Revolution in the state of Chiapas in modern Mexico. On January 1, 1994, several thousand Maya Indians attacked the provincial capital of San Cristobal Las Casas, calling themselves *Zapatistas* after the revolutionaries who were active in the period from 1910 to 1923 to the north in the states of Puebla and Morelos. The Mexican army counterattacked and forced the Zapatistas back into the lowland jungles. Their spokesman, the enigmatic, pipe-smoking Sub-

Comandante Marcos, declared that the attack was a response by the Mayan people to the North American Free Trade Agreement (NAFTA) and to attempts by the Mexican government to privatize their collective plots of land, which are called *ejidos*. American academics sympathetic to the Maya promptly appeared on American television to describe how the treaty and privatization would destroy the collective lands of the Maya Indians. They argued that NAFTA would lower tariffs between Mexico and the United States, allowing American farmers to flood Mexican markets with cheap food. The anthropologists further argued that government privatization would lead to the *ejido* land of the Indians being taken over by local ranchers. But several anthropologists, in reports published in *Cultural Survival Quarterly*, presented a somewhat different picture, one that is much more complex than at first understood, but that underscored the complexity of politics and collective land tenure.

A Zapatista band in lowland Chiapas, Mexico, 1994.

The Zapatista movement was first assumed to be a radical, Marxist, transformative movement. But very quickly, comments from Sub-Comandante Marcos made it obvious that Zapatista interests were reformative, not transformative. What the Zapatistas wanted was fair democratic representation in a region that had long put power into the hands of old elites, both ranchers who owned their lands as private property and Mayan coffee farmers who owned their lands in collectives, both of whom supported the Institutional Revolutionary Party of Mexico.

George Collier, Professor and Chair of the Department of Anthropology at Stanford University, who has been studying agrarian politics in Chiapas since the 1960s, argued that the aim of the Zapatistas was not to overthrow Mexico, or the state of Chiapas, but to reform the corrupt political system that had controlled Mexico since 1926, and that has abandoned the Maya in Chiapas. Collier points out that the PRI redistribution of lands in Chiapas in the 1930s had favored those peasants who could be co-opted by the state. Instead of freely giving lands to landless Mayan peasants, the PRI helped to create an elite of coffee-growing Indian communities in highland Chiapas, particularly in the community of Chamula.

A closer examination revealed other complexities. The Zapatistas came from the eastern part of lowland Chiapas where poor migrants from the overpopulated western highlands had moved, following trails blazed by loggers in the 1950s. These people were originally Mayan Catholics, like their brethren in the collective coffee lands of the highlands. But in the 1980s, these people abandoned Catholicism in favor of evangelical Protestantism. According to Collier, the Maya of the eastern lowlands "shucked ethnic origin for more generic peasant identities" (Collier 1994:15). The reason for converting to Protestantism was to escape the demands of the cargo system, described in Chapter 12. Basically, this traditional Catholic ceremonial system puts enormous pressures on Mayan peasants to expend large amounts of money and other wealth on folk Catholic religious celebrations. This practice shores up the collective identity of the Mayan towns, but at the cost of investment in land. The new "evangelicals," as they are called by the Catholics, also became opposed to the PRI, and the PRI responded by dismantling subsidies for the farmers of eastern Chiapas. These populations did, indeed, feel threatened by the opening of markets that were forcing the peasants to compete against falling international prices for their agricultural goods. Maya Indians in the traditional highlands continued to support the PRI, and continued to receive subsidies, while in eastern Chiapas, the PRI used harsh tactics to keep peasants in line. "Protestants" were expelled from highland villages. According to Collier, the government accepted the expulsions as consistent with the rights of natives to prescribe customs in their communities, but he believes this was a justification for supporting "henchmen who wanted to rid themselves of opposition at the local level" (Collier 1994:17).

Gary Gossen, Director of the Institute for Mesoamerican Studies at the State University of New York at Albany, adds further detail. He points out that Chiapas is not ethnically homo-

become democratic, ethnic and religious groups that have been suppressed try to gain control over state policies. This point of view is diametrically the opposite of what social science theory of history originally predicted in theories of "modernization" (Esman and Rabinovich 1988:11). Modernization theorists anticipated that democratic reform would lead to secularization, and the demise geneous and that the Maya are many different Maya. Of particular importance in recent years has been the conversion of Maya Indians from the town of San Juan Chamula to Protestantism. Converts were driven out at gunpoint in the 1970s: "for Chamula's highly centralized, cacique-controlled municipal government correctly perceived them to be a threat to its authority" (Gossen 1994:19). Gossen argues:

> The rebels are indeed Maya in origin, ethnicity and language, yet they are, in a sense, twice-cursed and (perhaps twice politicized), for most of them are both Indians and displaced persons—individuals who have been obliged to seek their destiny as de facto refugees from their Indian communities of origin (Gossen 1994:19).

Gossen agrees with Collier that it is NAFTA's threat to small farmers that prompted these Maya to revolt, but that it was not the Indians of the collectively owned lands who were in the Zapatista army. It was unhappiness on the part of Protestant Maya with the authoritarian structure of the predominantly Indian *municipios* that really prompted the attack against highland towns.

> It is ostensibly for this reason that thousands of Maya Protestant converts have lost their landholdings in certain Indian communities since 1965. They have been forcibly expelled as disruptive "non-traditional" cultural influences. In fact the Protestant converts have been the most likely to challenge traditional cacique authority, and the caciques have hidden behind state protection of traditional

religion to get rid of threats to their political monopoly (Gossen 1994:20).

Gossen's and other studies show that there has already been a great deal of change in the direction of open markets and that many peasants are no longer real peasants. What is most surprising is that the cargo system and the elders, which have been positively described by many writers, turn out to be linked to the PRI and the source of the alienation of Protestant Maya who form the core of the revolt.

This brings us back to the issue of land tenure among the Maya and other indigenous groups. The issue of land tenure is a complex one that has no simple resolution. In the 1930s, collective *ejidos* were created in part to gain support for the PRI, but a close examination of the factors leading to the Zapatista Revolution shows that a simple "return to the *ejido*" is not quite the benevolent option many assume will reinforce Mayan values. Neither does the privatization of older *ejidos* appear to produce anything other than more conflict.

The complexity of this problem cannot be solved by the simple choice between supporting collective or private property rights. The assumption that the Zapatistas were protesting only threats against the collective ownership of land is not accurate. What is the case is that the Zapatistas were protesting the lack of democratic alternatives between their exploitation at the hands of the ranchers or their alienation from the old collective lands. Their protest underscores the value of the transition to democracy in regions of the world that have been dominated by one-party states.

of ethno-religious identity entirely, not its reemergence. Thus, early in this century and until recently, the assumption made by social scientists was that democracy leads to secular societies. Social scientists tended to pay scant attention to ethnicity or religion except as background or history to their antiethnic theories.

But democracy and secularism appear to have parted company in certain world regions. The abandonment of socialism has produced violent ethnic and nationalist movements in Eastern Europe and in the Republics of the former Soviet Union. The best known conflicts are between Armenians and Azerbaijanis in the southwestern part of the Commonwealth of Independent States and between Croats, Muslims, and Serbians in Yugoslavia (particularly in Bosnia). However, these are just two of many nationalist/ethnic conflicts that are occurring throughout Eastern Europe and the Commonwealth. Among the other ethnonationalist conflicts are those of Bashkirs, Chechen-Ingush, Gagauz, Abkhazians, South Ossetians, Meskhetians, Tatars, Georgians, and Moldovans. The Serb/Croat conflicts will be examined in some detail. The others will not because: (a) they are too historically complex to be dealt with in this text, and (b) the conflicts are similar to each other.

There are several interpretations for the root causes of ethnic violence and genocide that are popular right now. One argument that is made about ethnonationalism and conflict in Eastern Europe and the former Soviet Union is that it is very old, in some cases dating back hundreds of years. A second explanation is that ethnic conflict is usually rooted in religious differences, particularly Muslims versus Christians, but also Catholics versus Protestants, and Christians versus Jews. A third point of view is that the two world wars have exacerbated ethnic hatreds as various ethnic populations systematically practiced genocide against one another. Yet another point of view is that the ethnic groups in question identify with specific territories and are fighting for ancient lands.

These arguments, on the surface, make sense. Most of the ethnic conflicts at the present time are, in fact, territorial. Ethnic groups are either trying to gain back control over old lands or they are trying to expand the lands they control. Religious differences, age-old animosities, conflict over language usage, and cultural differences are all ammunition for nationalist fighters. At the present time there appears to be little that outsiders can do to bring peace. It is as though first there must be a sacrifice of thousands of innocent human beings and a general destruction of the economies of these regions before the fighters will come to their senses. But these pessimistic views of history may already be challenged by events in regions of the world that are predicted to collapse in paroxysms of ethnic violence.

David Maybury-Lewis argues that such theories about the future of ethnic warfare are too extreme. He argues that ethnic violence depends on the social environment, that it is a response to the policies of states:

> A closer look at ethnicity shows that is not an innate attribute of human behavior, but rather a potential which all of us have and which may or may not be activated. Nor do feelings of ethnic solidarity inevitably lead to conflict when they are activated. It all depends on the context.

He goes on to argue that it is the state "which has to decide whether to recognize their distinctiveness, if so how to accommodate it, and if not how to suppress it" (Maybury-Lewis 1997:xi).

Stanley J. Tambiah of Harvard follows the direction expressed by Maybury-Lewis. He theorizes that these ethnonationalist movements are due to political deprivation imposed on ethnic populations by former socialist states. According to Tambiah, ethnic conflict is the consequence of the perceived political deprivation of certain ethnic groups that have been deprived of power, wealth, or status by other ethnic groups. The Russian anthropologist, Valery A. Tishkov, gives a similar and interesting interpretation to ethnicity arguing that the real culprit is a theory of history that produced ethnonationalist policies in socialist states. This theory of history argues that socialist states were organized according to ethnic identity, not democratic equality. Socialist states thus set ethnic groups against ethnic groups. Today, as democratic reforms open these societies, those ethnic groups that had a monopoly on regional control or were discriminated against by socialist states attempt to capture state control, and ethnonationalist war ensues.

Soviet Policies and Ethnonationalism   Tishkov, who is Director of the Institute of Ethnography and Anthropology of the Russian Academy of Sciences and former Minister of Nationalities in Boris Yeltsin's government, argues that Soviet and East European policies created ethnonationalism. He explains that most East European and Soviet scholars tend to view ethnicity as heavily "primordialistic," based on an academic theory of "ethnos" that overlaps with Marxist–Leninist theory. In Eastern Europe and in the Soviet Union, where most of the ethnic conflict is occurring:

> Anthropological and historical writings provide dominant groups in particular regions with their own cultural heroes, roots (reaching back even into upper Paleolithic times), and sense of pride as "indigenous nations" (Tishkov 1994:444).

This view of ethnicity was tied to the Marxist–Leninist ideology of ethnonationalism that dominated the Soviet state, a state in which ethnic groups legitimated their borders and statuses by forming administrative units or republics:

> The scholarly taxonomic classification of "types of ethnic entities" (tribe, *narodnost,* and nation)—involving such conceptual categories as 'ESO' (ethno-social organization) and "ETHNIKOS" (people of the same nationality living outside of their "own" state territories)—justified the administrative statehood granted to what I call titular nationalities (i.e., those which gave titles to republics) (Tishkov 1994:444).

Ethnonationalism, rather than being a remote and unimportant category of identity, in Eastern Europe and the former Soviet Union was legitimated by Soviet academic studies, which produced policies that shaped the definitions and arguments "of politicians, intellectuals, and the common man" regarding ethnicity. Even recently, Soviet specialists continue to argue in support of ethnic rights, elaborating lists of grievances against others, justifying territorial, political, and cultural rights, and finding people and cultures to blame. The scholars "explain events in terms of materialistic, economic, and social class analyses; a simplistic, culturally based, 'we-they' dichotomy" (Tishkov 1994: 445). In short, scholars in the former Soviet Union and Eastern Europe, by using socialist theories of ethnic identity, may be part of the problem rather than the solution.

Tishkov goes on to explain that ethnonationalism was extremely popular among European social democrats in the nineteenth and early twentieth century, and was used to form a new political map of Eastern Europe after World War I. During and after the Revolution of 1917, Lenin and the Bolsheviks used the slogan of ethnic self-determination to win non-Russians to their side, and ethnonationalism became the basis on which socialist federalism was based. All Soviet constitutions embodied the principle of a right to self-determination for ethnonations:

> But it should be stressed that this 'brave' social experiment arose within the context of one-party, totalitarian rule and strict centralization enforced from Moscow (Tishkov 1994:447).

But the principle of ethno-nationhood was not equally applied, and in each territory one ethnic group or another was recognized as having superior rights, often given the power to be the governing group. In other words, the socialism of the Soviet Union and Eastern Europe was not egalitarian socialism, with all persons having equality before the state, but the purposeful creation of ethnic republics ruled by dominant ethnic groups within a socialist national framework, in turn ruled by Russians. Relative deprivation was the inevitable consequence of such discrimination, and ethnonationalist warfare is the current consequence.

Tishkov believes that such a social system has made it extremely difficult to create even the most rudimentary civil institutions in Eastern Europe and in the former Soviet Union:

> Ethno-nationalism became prominent as an alternative to a strong, centralized state with ineffective representation at the local level. It called on romantic, emotional images for a new form of solidarity without necessarily resolving the problems of democratic representation at the local level. If and how these are to be resolved under ethnonationalism remains to be seen. . . . After decades of literary and practical nation-building, ethno-nationalism has become entwined in a wide spectrum of public ideologies and political mentalities. It has won considerable social support. And peristroika greatly facilitated the process (Tishkov 1994:448).

David Maybury-Lewis presents a similar argument. He points out that after the Russian revolution, Lenin wrote a constitution in which Russians would be one of a number of equal peoples within the Soviet state. After Lenin's death, Stalin went on to organize the Soviet Union along ethnic lines, but not in any egalitarian sense. Instead, he organized Soviet states in administrative hierarchies. At the apex were the Soviet Socialist Republics, each conceptualized as the domain of a particular ethnic group. In addition, there were Autonomous Republics and Autonomous Districts and National Regions, each also defined in terms of an ethnic nationality. Stalin, and Lenin before him, assumed that ethnicity and nationalism would fade as socialism became dominant. But in practice, certain ethnic groups always gained greater rights than others, and Russians formed the upper echelon of government everywhere. People who were given special rights could use their own language, publish their own books, and maintain their religions. At the same time other groups did not receive state recognition and were denied their cultural heritage. Thus, from the beginning of Soviet rule, certain ethnic groups were relatively deprived as opposed to others (Maybury-Lewis 1997).

This same model was used in Yugoslavia and in other East European socialist states. The dissolution of socialism brought about the collapse of the Soviet Union, but it also brought about the collapse or near collapse of other socialist countries, such as Yugoslavia. Ethnic conflict in "socialist" ethnostates had been suppressed by powerful armies for the better part of this century. With the collapse of socialism, various ethnic populations have demanded the right to rule themselves and to create their own countries, no matter how tiny.

From Anti-Capitalist to Pro-Capitalist Movements

Theories of history have championed distinct kinds of movements throughout this century. Radical transformative movements of a largely secular, socialist type drove movements around the world outside of the core countries until very recently. These movements, largely tied to the disintegration of colonialism around the world, will be examined in the chapters that follow. The revolutionary movements described were, for the most part, anti-systemic (anti-capitalist), but they were not based on ethnicity. They were anti-capitalist and nondemocratic, although they may have had the patina of democracy. They were anti-systemic because the "system," global capitalism, was viewed as a danger that would destroy weak systems. Today, the anti-system systems, socialism and state capitalism, are being abandoned because they have not worked. Recently, peaceful pro-capitalist movements have emerged.

Peasant Wars

Eric Wolf has shown that modernization had the initial impact of disturbing age-old ecological adaptations of peasants to their environments and their tributary relationship to governing elites (Wolf 1969, 1982). In traditional societies, peasants may be exploited by elites but certain minimal rights are also protected. With the introduction of colonial capitalism and the disappearance of tributary

BOX 8.6

Case Study: Ethnonationalist Movements in Bosnia

Particularly troubling right now are the civil wars in the disintegrating country of Yugoslavia, particularly in Bosnia, a state of Yugoslavia. The civil wars, which started in the summer of 1991 with federal military action to suppress separatist movements in the Yugoslavian states of Slovenia, Croatia, and, in the spring of 1992, Bosnia–Herzegovina, have killed more than 200,000 soldiers and civilians, wrecked the economy of central Yugoslavia, and created a half-million refugees. For all intents and purposes, Yugoslavia no longer exists.

The Communist order that held Yugoslavia together began to disintegrate as early as 1986, and entered a crisis in December of 1989, which the international community failed to recognize (Burg 1993:363). Yugoslavia was a federation of the south Slavic peoples created in 1918. Yugoslavia united the unstable ethnic enclaves of Slovenia, Croatia, Bosnia–Herzegovina, Serbia, Montenegro, and Macedonia (from north to south). Yugoslavia was invaded and occupied by German and Italian forces in World War II. The Germans allied themselves

Figure 8.1   **A map of Yugoslavia before it fell apart in 1991–1992 showing the constituent "ethnic" republics.**

with various ethnic groups with whom they had historical connections, such as Slovenes and Croats, and used these peoples to subjugate the region, committing genocide, particularly against Serbs. When the war was over, the Yugoslav Communists (mostly Serbs), led by the Croatian Joseph Broz Tito, were militarily dominant. Yugoslavia became a communist republic in 1946.

Conflict between all of these groups was continuous throughout history, though it subsided under Tito. But in the 1980s, ethnic conflict emerged again due to economic differences (Goldman 1992:171). Under Tito, each state of Yugoslavia was dominated by a single ethnic group. Serbia was under Serb control, and other ethnic groups had few rights. Croatia was under Croat control, and so on. As the Yugoslav state began to disintegrate, and democratic options opened up, and as the world stood back waiting for a new democracy to emerge, instead the various distinct ethnic groups attempted to wrest the control of each emerging state for themselves.

The ethnic conflict began when Albanians living in Kosovo province in southern Yugoslavia, which was under Serb control, attacked Serbs and Montenegrans. Albanians tried to terrorize the Serbs (Goldman 1992: 171). Serb resentment of Albanians mounted and they looked for help in state and Serb party authorities, particularly Slobadan Milosevic, who became the President of Serbia and encouraged pro-Serb, anti-Albanian rallies throughout the republic. He attempted to establish Serb control of the political system by taking over the police, courts, and civil defense in southern Yugoslavia.

Serb nationalists gained control of the Yugoslavian military, particularly the air force, while Yugoslavia began to disintegrate into its constituent territories (Slovenia, Croatia, Bosnia–Herzegovina, Montenegro, and Macedonia). As Yugoslavia disintegrated, Serbs in Serbia and those living as ethnic enclaves in the other emerging states tried to increase the size of Serbia or tried to take control of the regions they lived in, causing civil war.

Of the former states of Yugoslavia, it is Bosnia–Herzogovina that came to suffer the most. Bosnia–Herzogovina is a multiethnic state composed of ethnic Muslims (44 percent), Serbs (31 percent), and Croats (17 percent); Yugoslavs form only 6 percent of the population. The three ethnic groups are separated not so much by ethnic differences, but by their histories and religious beliefs. The Bosnian election of 1990 produced a polarized political situation between Croats, Serbs, and Muslims. This was resolved with a coalition government composed of representatives of the three ethnic groups. However, Croats and Serbs in Bosnia wanted to join a "greater Serbia" and "greater Croatia" and civil war ensued. The United Nations and NATO agreed to prevent the Muslims from arming themselves, and the civil war soon turned to a genocidal attack with Serbs and Croats carrying out "ethnic cleansing" of Muslims in their ethnic regions, and both tried to expand their territories.

Until recently, Serbs were fighting Muslims and Croatians. These two ethnic groups fought each other and the Serbs. Muslim women were forced into "rape camps." The city of Sarajevo (where World War I began with the assassination of Archduke Ferdinand, the heir to the throne of Austria and Hungary) was subject to continuous bombardment by Serb forces in the surrounding hills. The problem from hell was born. United Nations peacekeeping forces from time to time had brought cease-fires to the fighting and opened the airport at Sarajevo so humanitarian supplies could get in to the population, but the fighting continued until 1995, with the Dayton Accords, when the United States and the United Nations forced

Concentration camp victims in Bosnia in 1994.

peace on the three groups. This was followed by an imposition of peace when the United Nations, with a contingent of American forces, brought the fighting to an end by using the threat of force in Bosnia–Herzegovina.

The ethnonationalist theories of Croatian and Serb leaders produced civil war, and they led to an invasion by NATO as well as an economic boycott by the United Nations, NATO, the United States, and Western Europe. Ultimately, the boycott led to economic suffering. In addition, a new type of relative deprivation evolved in the early months of 1997. Many had not supported the ethnonationalist ideas of Slobodan Milosovic and suffered the images of themselves as racists. In early 1997, these groups began massive protests that may lead to the collapse of the Serbian government. This new movement in Serbia resembles the democratic reform movements that brought an end to socialism in Poland, Hungary, and the rest of Eastern Europe. It is too early right now to predict events in Serbia, but this is the first sign that perhaps the future will not be one of ethnonationalist uprising and the end of civilization as we know it.

rights, peasants were exploited more than they had been before the introduction of capitalism (Wolf 1982). The new transformation set off violent revolutions in various core countries. The first wave of revolutions occurred in the nineteenth century in Western and Eastern Europe. Most of these early revolutions have been called "peasant revolutions" (Wolf 1969, 1982). Two major examples are the French Revolution of 1789 and the German Revolution of 1848 (Hobsbawm 1962, Wolf 1969).

A second wave of violent socialist movements began outside of the core in the periphery in the twentieth century as the destructive characteristics of capitalism spread through colonialism. Why was democratic capitalism successful in the core, but destructive in the peripheries? While capitalism and democracy were the key driving forces behind reformist movements in the core, the democratic component was blocked by the core and local elites in the periphery. This is because the elites in the periphery were put into power by the elites of the core, they were antidemocratic, and they wanted to retain power. The revolts were the consequence of relative deprivation, oppression by local elites, and blockages to modernization. Most of the revolts were radical, anti-core, revolutions with theories of history that were anti-capitalist. The consequence was the development of a series of radical, secular, communist–socialist societies, many of which were also antidemocratic, and were often also against religion (Wolf 1969, 1982, Huntington 1993). A short list provided by Eric Wolf in his study of peasant revolutions in the twentieth century includes Mexico (1910–1917), Russia (1918–1921), Algeria (1958–1961), China (1946–1949), and Vietnam (1963–1975) (Wolf 1969). Indirect spin-offs from these major revolutions occurred throughout Central America and South America, Africa, and Asia. All of these movements turned out to be against religion because religion was viewed as part of the old traditional social system that exploited the peasant classes.

Pro-Capitalist Reformative Movements

Each of the next four chapters ends by examining the emergence of new reformist movements. These largely democratic social movements began in the 1980s and are occurring now (Huntington 1993, 1996). Samuel Huntington refers to these movements as the "third wave" (the first wave was the nineteenth-century European revolutions, the second was the transformative revolutions just discussed). This third wave appears to be tied to the process of globalization, explained in Chapter 7. The most recent social movements are difficult to classify because many of the movements have yet to consolidate into identifiable political forms. Most of these are reformist movements; they are largely antisocialist, favor free market systems and multi-party democracies.

These movements have so far not been violent (an exception is the Zapatista revolt in southern Mexico); they do not seek to overthrow the state. Instead they are seeking to reform their institutions so they will provide incentives to escape poverty and create prosperity. However, and inevitably, as open market reforms begin to take effect, the reforms create distortions between haves and have-nots; that is, those with wealth and power gain more wealth and power, and those without get less, producing relative deprivation and explosive political tensions (and an example here is the Zapatista Revolution). The only way to resolve these tensions is through democratic reform, the demands for which often follow directly after the introduction of capitalism making it difficult to separate the two transitions anywhere. These pro-capitalist, pro-democratic reform movements are occurring throughout Eastern Europe and in parts of the Soviet Union, but are also occurring in Africa, Latin America, and other regions of the periphery, and we will examine these movements in the chapters to come. These reformist movements are not transformative peasant revolts as were the earlier ones, but are largely made up of urban and industrial peoples who have become disillusioned with the promises of socialism and communism (Huntington 1993). The movements can best be classified as reformative because they are gradualist, moving a step at a time to dismantle communism and socialism. While a few movements began as transformative, such as Russia in 1991, by 1996–1997, they have slowed down to move a step at a time because of the complexity of reform. The movements are also reformative rather than transformative because they are not utopian or millenarian; that is, the leaders do not believe that society can be magically transformed overnight, as did the revolutionary leaders of the early twentieth century.

Summary

While the end of the Cold War was greeted with relief and the hope for the end of hostilities around the world, such has not happened. Hostilities have actually increased dramatically. While in the United States civil rights movements are losing their ideological vigor, ethnonationalism in former socialist countries threatens the regional stability of Eastern Europe and the Middle East. The capacity of the United States to bring about peace in the former Yugoslavia is being tested by the complexity of the issue, and the same is true in the Middle East. At the same time, new democratic movements are occurring in formerly authoritarian and totalitarian parts of the world. As part of these budding new democracies, indigenous groups are developing strategies to reclaim ancient lands and revitalize cultural heritages.

There are many complex transitions we have to examine globally that have to do with the creation of a new world, one that could not have been imagined just half a century ago. It does not rest on socialism, the promise of the past, but on the very democratic capitalism that was once thought such a threat. But the transitions to capitalism and democracy are not easy; they may undermine traditional ways of life, and we will spend time in the next four chapters trying to grasp these complex issues. Anthropology has a claim to explanations regarding these complex issues, and in the following chapters we will gain a better understanding of the future role of this extraordinary discipline.

Key Terms

Alterative Movement	*Municipio*
Assimilation	**Redemptive Movement**
Civil Rights Movement	**Reference Group**
Ethnicity	**Reformative Movement**
Ethnocide	**Relative Deprivation**
Ethnonationalism	**Resource Mobilization**
Indigenismo	**Sectarian**
Indigenous	**Social Movement**
Multiculturalism	**Transformative Movement**

Africa: Overcoming a Colonial Legacy

9

*M*odern Africa is a troubled land. Europeans substantially altered Africa's history through the dramatic expansion of slavery in West Africa and mineral exploitation in East and South Africa. In the late nineteenth century, Africa south of the Sahara was divided among European states, and then in the middle of this century began a slow emergence into independent, but troubled African states. Hunger, disease, and ethnic violence have replaced the once utopian hopes of social planners in the 1950s and 1960s. Africa enjoys geographic and geological riches that should be more than adequate to insure prosperity. However, Africa is a continent of great diversity, containing vast deserts and rain forest. The problems of living in these extremes contribute to low population densities. The harsh nature of the environment makes transaction costs very high and has contributed to slow economic development, so that even the best of intentions are blocked. Deserts and rain forests make the construction of roads and railroads in certain regions extremely expensive. In West Africa, an inhospitable climate supports dangerous endemic diseases such as malaria, river blindness (onchocerciasis), and African sleeping sickness (trypanosomiasis), borne by the tsetse fly and dangerous to both humans and cattle. Cholera is reemerging as a ravaging disease in regions where it has not been seen for decades. Both cholera and the tsetse fly have had a devastating effect on the transitions to political and economic development. AIDS is also reducing the capacity of certain African countries to modernize, particularly Uganda and Zaire (Weeks 1992).

Drought along the Sahel region south of the Sahara has caused the deterioration of ecological conditions to the point at which populations can no longer survive. In vast regions, certain problems of adaptation may be the consequence of ecological mismanagement, such as the misuse of water and the mismanagement of range land. European colonial intervention helps to explain some, but not all, of modern Africa's problems. Drought and brush fires in Ghana, Cote d'Ivoire, Togo, and Benin have transformed forests into deserts. These same forests are natural resources that could sustain logging, but often uncontrolled cutting has led to deforestation and then to desertification (Sullivan 1989:59). The *harmattan*, a dry wind that blows out of the Sahara in January and February, has exacerbated drought and helped the spread of desertification (Sullivan 1989:15).

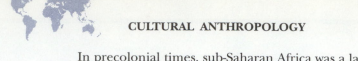

In precolonial times, sub-Saharan Africa was a land that spawned numerous chiefdoms and tributary states that were involved in trade networks extending across the continent, linking with the trade routes of North Africa and the Mediterranean. This picture contradicts the one presented by the first anthropologists to venture into Africa, which portrayed precolonial Africa as a continent of isolated, autonomous tribes. A more balanced perspective on Africa's past and present may be gained by examining the human ecology and political economy of precolonial Africa.

Africa and Anthropology in the Twentieth Century

Africa has played a special role in the development of anthropology as a discipline, and has acted as a giant mirror reflecting the excesses of anthropological theorizing (Moore 1994). The first theories showed Africa to be what European intellectuals wanted it to be: a land of primitive tribes remote from European civilization, a precapitalist cultural Eden that could show scholars what very ancient Europe must have looked like during the Stone Age.

In the 1930s, anthropologists turned away from evolutionary speculations and tried to move in two other directions. The first was to search modern Africa for its prehistoric "tribal" roots, a search for how premodern societies were func-

Figure 9.1   **Map of Africa showing trade routes ca. 1000 B.C.**

tionally integrated into "systems" of social production, economy, clanship, and religion. This approach was called "structural-functionalism" as expressed in the writings of Bronislaw Malinowski, who had first written about tribal society in Melanesia, and whose theoretical perspective profoundly influenced African scholars when he was appointed the first chair in anthropology at the University of London (London School of Economics). "Modernization" was viewed as the destroyer of African tribal society.

During this period of anthropological research, roughly from the turn of the century to the 1960s, Africa was under the control of European colonists. Europeans had monopolized long-distance trade, particularly in East Africa, for well over a century. The Europeans had also pacified African societies, imposing European administrators and their courts on traditional African society. Tribal societies, it appeared, had little to no trade and were functionally integrated into small egalitarian communities. The anthropologists were often philosophically opposed to European rule, but only the very few dared to challenge colonial authorities. Overall, there was the unquestioning acceptance that a "tribal" Africa had preceded the colonial period, and that their job was either to find out what that tribal society was really like before the introduction of colonial rule, or to describe the impact of "modernization." The idea that precontact societies might have resembled European or Asiatic empires was not seriously considered. The anthropologists were searching for the exotic, the traditional, the "pre-modern." Exotic tribes were needed to substantiate the thesis of a precolonial tribal existence.

The structural-functionalism of Malinowski and Radcliffe-Brown and their students and colleagues resulted in numerous classic ethnographies containing detailed studies of kinship, social organization, economic organization, and religion and magic. Underlying most of these studies were two orienting assumptions: (1) all aspects of culture were believed to be interrelated; and (2) the societies themselves were considered to be highly static, essentially unchanging, and always tending toward, if not actually being in, a state of equilibrium. Characteristic of the African ethnographies of this period was a strong emphasis on cultural ideals often to the virtual exclusion of descriptions of real behavior that deviated from the ideals.

To researchers, Africa had become a place of "urban" moderns (those who had accepted Western ways) versus rural "tribes" (those who had not become Western). Those who worked on these two subjects (modern and tribal) had a tendency to keep the two topics separate, and a reader of their studies today would have the impression that urban African and tribal Africans lived in two different worlds.

In the 1950s and 1960s, Africans began to throw off the yoke of colonialism. African writers in the newly independent African states became critical of the theories of anthropologists. Africans felt that they had been pigeonholed as "tribal others" that really had little to do with their own histories or experiences. At the same time, the structural-functional equation came to be replaced by a multiplicity of interests in archaeology, kinship, gender, economic development, political change, art, religion, and many other topics. The idea that societies were structurally bound into "systems" began to fade as the complexity of Africa replaced an assumed tribal simplicity.

In the past few decades, archaeologists have unearthed ancient civilizations in sub-Saharan Africa that have characteristics similar to other ancient states we have examined. These characteristics include trade, war, empire-building, the importance of hierarchy in the central place, and the existence of nonhierarchical societies at the peripheries. The notion of African society as "tribal society" has been replaced with that of an Africa that is no more "traditional" than any other world region. Many writers are resolving the distinction between the urban modern and the tribal "other" by doing away with these simplistic and contrived distinctions. Does the term *tribal* still have meaning? Only if one realizes that tribe is not an evolutionary stage but an adaptive level of sociopolitical integration that frequently occurs at the peripheries of core states. As to anthropology's early tendency to overtheorize, Sally Falk Moore writes:

> Anthropology is older and wiser now. It is clear that in all societies there are newly "invented" elements that are given legitimacy and prestige by being labeled traditional [tribal]. Local assertions of what is traditional are just that—assertions. They do not necessarily constitute an account of actual happenings in the historic past (Moore 1994:128).

The Geography and Ethnography of Africa

When talking about Africa, what is most striking is the diversity of the cultures that exist on this continent, as well as the diversity of the environments in which they live. To begin, Africa is immense. It is fifty-two hundred miles from Tangier in North Africa to Capetown in the far south, and it is forty-six hundred miles from Dakar in the far west to Cape Guardafui, the easternmost point of the African horn (Bohannen and Curtin 1995). For the most part, this chapter focuses on the peoples south of the Sahara, primarily because the "Middle East" includes much of North Africa, which is discussed in the chapter to follow. However, the distinctions between geographic regions are Eurocentric, and no assessment of Africa can exclude ancient Egypt, which will be included in this chapter.

Despite the distinction of Middle East and Africa, the Arabian peninsula is part of the African continent. The Rift Valley, which cuts through Africa, begins in northern Turkey, forms the Jordan Valley and the Dead Sea, the Red Sea, and cuts a vertical swath down to Lake Rudolf. The Rift divides and spreads around Lake Victoria, joining again at the head of Lake Nyasa, and then runs south to the Shire and Zambezi river valleys. The Rift forms some of the deepest lakes on earth and is part of one of the most ancient trade routes (Bohannen and Curtin 1995:19). Along the Nile, the Rift Valley to the south, and into southern Africa were found chiefdoms and kingdoms prior to the colonial period.

Some of the prominent rivers, such as the Niger, the Nile, the Volta, the Zambezi, and the Congo, end in basins that empty into the sea. However, most rivers fall off steep escarpments into the sea, limiting navigation from the sea for most of the continent. Not only is navigation difficult, but the environment seriously constrains the development of agriculture. While the northern and southern ends of Africa enjoy a Mediterranean-like climate and vegetation, just inland vast deserts and arid plains cover thousands of square miles. Humid forests straddle the equator, producing gallery forests along major streams. These tropical forest zones have little topsoil and do not lend themselves easily to permanent field agriculture. Going south and north are found true deserts, the Kalahari and Sahara. Between the humid forests and deserts are extensive savannas that occupy the greatest number of square miles in Africa. The savanna is made of stretches of tall grass, intermittent bush, and scattered trees, and it is this habitat that played the greatest role in the development of the human ecology of Africa in precolonial times. Of particular importance was the development of a combination of **settled farming** and **transhumance herding.** Settled farming tended to occur in those regions where rainfall resources or irrigation from rivers would support settled villages. An example would be the Nile River Valley, which has supported settled villages for well over four thousand years. Often viewed as an opposite form of adaptation, in fact the herding of cattle, sheep, goats, or camels was often combined with settled villages. For example, the settled village and town populations along the Nile and elsewhere often also supported herders who had to find grasses to forage at some distance from home. Other peoples practiced true transhumance herding, going back and forth over the landscape as though it were a giant carpet, using the settled towns and villages for trade purposes. Often members of their families would settle in the villages and act as intermediaries between settled agriculturalists and transhumance herders. These should not be thought of as opposite poles of adaptation, but as options or alternatives ranging from settled villages to transhumance herders with all combinations in between.

Political Ecology, Trade, and Empire-Building

One of the first observations that comes from the study of Africa is that empires and states are not new, but have an ancient history based on trade and human adaptations to natural habitats, and that transhumance herding has been of great importance. The political ecology of Africa, before the period of European colonial domination, can be explained, at least in part, as hegemonic empire-building to reduce the transaction costs of trade following a tremendous arc running from Egypt in the north to the Zambezi River Valley in the south.

The cores of empires shifted through time, primarily due to changes in the importance of trade routes and the rise of imperial states outside of Africa (Rome, Byzantium), but with the colonial period, the collapse of trade and the imposition of European rule led to the destruction of indigenous institutions, particularly along the trade route running south of Egypt, through the Rift Valley, and down to what is now called the "Lake Country" of Central Africa (Ensminger 1992). In the modern period, attempts to create new institutional structures have been met with many frustrations, which will be described in this chapter.

Village Agriculture

The evolution into a "food-producing" way of life occurred between 7000–8000 B.C. in Africa and the Middle East. There is more known about this transition in the Middle East than in Africa, particularly in the hilly flanks region just north of the Tigris and Euphrates rivers (discussed in Chapter 5).

The evidence for a neolithic way of life is, however, strong in the Nile River Valley, particularly in the dry Fayum Depression just south of Sakkara and Memphis. The Fayum Depression was the site of a lake fed by the Nile River that supplied villagers with water for crops and herding. Houses were small, semisubterranean oval houses with mud walls.

In both Southwest Asia and northeastern Africa, the first movement towards crop cultivation began with the gathering of wild grain. There were natural concentrations of heavy-yielding "grasses" known as "cereals." While wheat and barley were domesticated in Southwest Asia, certain strains of wild barley were cultivated by the people of Egypt and Nubia (south of Egypt's first cataract), perhaps as far back as 10,000 B. C. Sorghum and millet originated in Northeast Africa, and were harvested in the Khartoum region of the upper Nile by 6000 B. C. People decreased their reliance on hunting and increased their dependence on domesticated plants, but also animals. With the development of farming, people began to settle down in permanent settlements, and populations increased in size. Women could bear more children and care for them, and more children meant more labor. These early communities, however, did not become completely dependent on agriculture for some time, continuing a partially hunting and gathering existence. The climate was wetter then, and provided some vegetation west and east of the Nile. Gradually, the climate dried out to the point at which there was no rainfall and the desert encroached on the banks of the Nile. Between 5000 and 4000 B. C., permanent settlements of full-time farmers became established in the Nile, their farming techniques adapted to the river's annual flooding. By 3500 those north of the first cataract had combined to form the kingdoms of Upper and Lower Egypt.

Crop cultivation based on barley and wheat spread along the Mediterranean margins of North Africa. The region south of the Sahara was far wetter between 8000 and 4000 years ago than it is today. A belt of rivers and lakes stretched across the continent from the upper Niger delta in the west through Lake Chad to the upper Nile. Large settlements of fishing communities developed, but turned to farming as the region became drier after 4000 B. C. The Sahara desert spread, rivers declined, and lakes disappeared. Between 3000 and 1000 B. C., neolithic farming spread throughout this growing savanna belt (Shillington 1989:30–31).

The new farming way of life spread to the tropical zones of West Africa, and new crops were domesticated for a distinct forested ecological zone. Considerable evidence from the Cameroons in West Africa depicts a way of life dependent on palm nuts, yams, fruits, and goats by 1000 B. C. Most people south of the equator remained hunters and food-gatherers until iron was introduced two thousand years ago, at which time tropical agriculture spread south and eastward through the forest zones, finally reaching the region of southern Zaire and northern Angola (Shillington 1989:31).

Gold was mined and traded throughout West Africa, and was an important factor in state evolution. Several trade empires flourished in West Africa before the colonial period. Islamic trade states also emerged, such as the Songhay empire, the state of Kanem and Borno near Lake Chad, and the Hausa and Yoruba of Nigeria.

Divine Kings, Trade States, and African Art   These precolonial states shared certain characteristics. At the center was a divine king whose well-being and the well-being of his people were combined. If the divine king was healthy, so were his people. If he became sick, his people suffered. Towns were unusually large, urbanization was tied to trade, and each region had its own "king," usually a patrilineal kinsman of the divine king, whose powers were similar. These states were "commercial emporiums" (Smith 1988:6). The divine king usually had a monopoly over all trade and the most important single trade article was cloth. West African states offered security along the trade routes combined with specialization in agriculture and crafts. Markets occurred here on a larger scale than anywhere else in Africa, and men and women had highly developed artistic skills for the production of objects made out of wood, stone, ivory, terracotta, or cast out of bronze, brass and iron. Many of these objects are venerated by modern collectors of art around the world. One of the modern ethnic groups of West Africa with a reputation for the production of African art is the Yoruba, whose ancestors once formed the kingdom of Yoruba, a state-level society.

Figure 9.2   **West African States, 1000 A.D.**

BOX 9.1

■ Case Study: The Yoruba

Settled village agriculture reached state levels of organization about a thousand years after the introduction of agriculture to West Africa. The Yoruba of modern Nigeria are the descendants of one of the many precolonial states of West Africa, and are typical of the tropical agricultural societies of the region. The homeland of the Yoruba is ecologically variable, stretching from swamps and lagoons of the coast across rain forests, and rising towards the oil palm bush and woodland savanna at the bend of the Niger. It is a fertile region, watered by many rivers and streams. The Yoruba kingdom depended on a form of food production common to West Africa, mixed crop agriculture, which included the common yam, the cocoyam, plantain, its close relative the banana, kola trees, and oil palm. In the sixteenth century, cassava and maize were introduced from South America (Smith 1988:4).

While there was one major king, the Alafin, the society was organized into twenty or more kingdoms, some, but not all, ruled by members of the same patrilineage, often known as "obas." In the extreme north was found the great capital city of Oyo, where lived the Alafin, or sacred king, while a hundred miles to the south was Ile Ife, the spiritual center of the Yoruba people. The kingdom of the Yoruba at one time occupied a region as large as England. Today the Yoruba form one of the largest ethnic groups in Africa's most populous country, Nigeria. Many of the modern chiefs are descended from the obas, and have the same title and sacred qualities. They often find themselves in conflict with the modern state of Nigeria. Because the formation of modern states is based on former colonial divisions that were seldom congruent with the territories of ethnic groups, modern Yoruba are also found in the neighboring republics of Benin and Togo. When the Portuguese arrived in the fifteenth century, the Yoruba had been organized into major and minor states for several hundred years.

Yoruba traditional religious ideas, with origins in the state and body of the divine king, were incorporated into the Islamic faith after the tenth century. Of particular importance to Yoruba religion was the idea of the journey, particularly of the human spirit, through birth, death, and reincarnation. Yoruba men and women, as slaves, brought their religion to the Americas, where it became Candomble in Brazil, and Santeria in Cuba and modern Miami and New York. Ritual parties occur in New York City led by priests of the Yoruba deity Obatala (Drewal 1992). In Brazil, Santa Barbara of the Thunder, a Catholic deity, is the reincarnation of Oba, the Yoruba goddess of the river Oba, and the third wife of the god Xango; market vendor priests are "obas," the ministers of Xango.

Pastoralism: The Cattle Keepers

Cattle were a source of wealth, prestige, and social status for many pastoralists in East Africa, and led to divisions between rich and poor and a domination of women by men. The importance of cattle has led writers to name this economy "the cattle complex." Men were the keepers of the cattle, women grew food and processed it. The wealth of a man depended on the number of wives he had, and their children. Cattle were traded for women, and alliances formed between elite cattle herders were based on the exchange of women for cattle (cattle "cemented" the marital union). As men grew older, they ceased to care for the cattle and became the managers of the work of women and of young cattle herders, their male children. The man who was successful in marriage, who expanded the size of his herd, whose male children married successfully, and who was successful in giving his daughters in marriage to other successful men became regarded as a "chief."

Shillington, the African historian, points out that, through a process of natural increase, a herd of fewer than twenty cattle could multiply to several thousand in one human generation, allowing men to accumulate wealth that their male offspring inherited. Cattle were used as bridewealth, and men with large herds could thus acquire several wives. Women were the main cultivators of the land, and **polygyny** (the marriage of a man to more than one woman) increased a man's ability to feed a large family and added to his wealth. Cattle could also be used in trade. Men with no cattle became dependent on the wealthy, and those with many head of cattle owned the material basis for the status of chief (Shillington 1989:147). When cattle herders were able to monopolize trade and owned very large herds of cattle, they became an upper class, in some cases a kind of aristocracy. Those who failed as cattle keepers became tillers of the land or herded the cattle of others, forming a lower class. Alternatively, cattle herders dominated foreign groups of subsistence agriculturalists. However, under normal circumstances, the constant movement of cattle kept the social structure fluid, and the rise to power of chiefs and the development of states was relatively rare.

Cattle were important in economic transactions and were used almost like money. They also had tremendous symbolic value. There was a whole system of beliefs surrounding cattle that prevented their regular slaughter for food. (However, there is also evidence that the prevalence of ritual occasions gave cattle subsistence value.) Thomas Barfield underlines the importance of cattle:

> The symbolic value of cattle among East African pastoralists was so high and their use in social transactions so critical that they literally defined the cultural order. . . . Raiding for cattle, lending them to friends, exchanging them in marriages, sacrificing them in rituals, decorating their bodies and singing their praises was an end in itself: pleasing to the mind and giving life a purpose (Barfield 1993:36–37).

When successful and in the center of trade, these pastoral populations expanded and transformed into states ruled by kings whose control was reinforced by developed or borrowed myths that gave them divine status as god–kings.

When Europeans began to dominate the region, they often allowed the upper-class aristocrats to continue ruling (as was true in Uganda, Rwanda, and Burundi).

In Chapter 5, we briefly examined pastoral nomadism as an ecological adaptation. The pastoral region of Africa lies south of the Sahara, running west to east in the Sahel across the whole of Africa, and north to south in the savanna grasslands of East Africa, following the line of the Great Rift Valley (Barfield 1993:4–7). There are no true "nomadic" pastoralists in sub-Saharan Africa; most combine cattle with agriculture (Middleton 1995).

The maintenance of large mammals, particularly cattle, sheep, and goats, in some areas precedes agriculture. Sites in the north African states of modern Algeria and Libya show very early pastoral societies, dating as far back as 7000 B. C. The most important animals were sheep and goats, with cattle becoming most important after 4000 B. C. Cave paintings show every aspect of domestic life: huge herds of long-horned cattle are cared for by people of Mediterranean and Negroid types who wear woven cloth, had elaborate ornaments and hairstyles, and used round pots to store milk and cattle blood. The presence of grinding stones suggests that they harvested grain, and were part-time agriculturalists, not unlike the modern Masai of Kenya. It is thought that cattle displaced other nomadic mammals, and that overgrazing may have led to rapid and final desiccation of the Sahara after 2500 B. C.

Pastoralists south of the Sahel and throughout East Africa have very similar social structures. Patrilineal descent is combined with age set associations or sodalities. The age set determines the status of distinct generations, as well as the privileges and responsibilities of a male through a lifetime. Herding is young men's work; they go off during the day, returning to the compounds, called cattle kraals, in the late afternoon or evening. These populations had a common adaptation, but had distinct ethnic identities (which would include language and religion). They were migratory pastoralists who managed livestock through "communal" land tenure of pastures. This was combined with the ownership and management of the herds by individuals (Bennett 1993:293). That is, cattle or other forms of livestock were not owned collectively by tribes or clans. Producers moved with the herds, or they settled in villages. They combined semipermanent residence with transhumance in order to maximize the use of pasture. Pasture was seasonally variable. Since the herds moved at intervals, it was impossible to assign "permanent" ownership of land. Instead, a complex legal code evolved regarding use rights to land and water. A cattle owner's rights to graze his stock were derived from his membership in a grazing group, which was usually a tribal subsection holding customary rights in different regions.

Herd owners worked out mutual arrangements to prevent a "tragedy of the commons" from occurring. Negotiations, pushing and shoving, armed resistance, and raiding were part of the adaptive response to pastoralism. Low-intensity ethnic conflict was a common adaptation. According to Bennett, these and other techniques were reasonably effective in a region of low fertility and low-density populations. However, with population expansion and the imposition of colonial and then modern states, changes in tenure and increases in population have fueled ethnic conflict in an arc that roughly corresponds to the traditional territories of pastoral populations.

The Camel Nomads of North Africa

The Middle East and North Africa were characterized by a human ecology of camel nomadism. The term *Arab* used to be applied to those people who were desert dwellers and lived in black tents, but over the past century, this term has been turned into an ethnic label for all Arabic-speaking peoples of the Middle East and North Africa. The term *Bedouin* is now used to set aside "desert dwellers" from sedentary townspeople. The Bedouin produced many of the ruling dynasties that conquered sedentary kingdoms and formed the core of armies that spread Islam, transforming the desert from a barrier to an overland highway (Barfield 1993:58).

Wild camels became extinct long ago, but two domesticated species survived: one-humped camels (dromedaries) that evolved in southern Arabia between 3000 and 2500 B. C., and two-humped camels (bactrian), which were domesticated in Central Asia between 2500 and 2000 B.C. (Barfield 1993:58). It is the dromedaries that are the most numerous type of camel today and form the basis of human ecology in North Africa and the Middle East. They are well adapted to hot and dry lands; using them, the Bedouins were able to exploit vast arid zones. These truly remarkable animals store fat (not water) in their hump, and can go for long time periods without water. When they do drink, camels can consume up to 100 to 120 liters at a single watering.

Camels provide both transportation and food, carrying loads of up to 200 kilograms and supplying milk (they are rarely slaughtered for meat; only on rit-

Bedouin man on camel.

BOX 9.2

Case Study: The Nuer

One of anthropology's most celebrated people, the Nuer, are an excellent example of a pastoral nomadic people. The name *Nuer* is well established in the literature and we will use it here. However, as with numerous groups of people throughout the world, the Nuer have their own name for themselves, *Naath*, which means "human beings." In the last two decades they have been caught up in a violent civil war in the southern Sudan (discussed later in this chapter). These people were described in the important ethnography by Sir Edward E. Evans–Pritchard (1902–73). Evans–Pritchard's ethnographic study of the Nuer (1940) is considered to be one of the great classics of anthropology, ranking with Bronislaw Malinowski's studies of the Trobriand Islanders. These two peoples have been the subject of countless lectures, papers, dissertations, and books. The Nuer, as lovingly described by Evans–Pritchard, appear outside of time, a relentlessly democratic pastoral people who love their cattle and have little interest in trade or the outside world, and who use controlled feuding as a form of social regulation.

In the early 1980s and 1990s, a young woman ethnographer, Sharon E. Hutchinson, tried to understand the forces that had transformed Nuer society since 1940, when the first Nuer study appeared in print. The picture Professor Hutchinson presents does not have the solid lines of Evans–Pritchard's classic study, and she was struck by the fluidity and violence of Nuer society fifty years after the classic picture was laid down. Evans–Pritchard's studies were based on the theories of British structural-functionalists, who dominated African studies in the middle of the twentieth century. These viewed all components of society as mutually

and structurally connected with "unity," "equilibrium," or "order" as the explanations for the institutions of a society. The ethnographer's job was to explain how the various components reinforced and explained each other. The following sets out the logic of Evans–Pritchard's theory about the Nuer, which was extended to include most of the pastoralists of East Africa.

Polity: The Segmentary Lineage Evans–Pritchard and other structuralists were convinced that trade was essentially nonexistent among the Nuer and other tribal societies of East Africa. They devised a powerful model to describe Nuer social structure based strictly on pastoralism. This model, as pointed out previously, became the model that anthropologists applied to African society in general, producing the impression that African societies lacked trade (or at least that it was singularly unimportant) and were egalitarian, politically and economically autonomous tribes. Evans–Pritchard, who estimated the Nuer to range between 250,000 to 300,000 people, viewed them as an isolated people who were tied morally to each other by a religion that valued cattle. In their isolation, they had no need for permanent chiefs or leaders, and so had devised an **acephalous** political system that lacked political office (*acephalous* means "headless"; the clans lacked chiefs at the very top and tended to depend on democratic alliances among family heads). Clans and lineages were neatly organized by means of descent through the male line (patrilineal descent). In his streamlined model, the maximum unit of organization was the patrilineal clan, which subdivided into maximal, major, minor, and minimal lineages. These sociological constructs were expressed on ritual occasions when people sacrificed cattle to their male ancestors. Minimal lineages would celebrate the deaths of immediate ancestors (they were the equivalent of extended families); minor lineages would include these and other heads of the minor lineage; major clans would celebrate major clan heads, and so on to the top. But this formal model appears only to have been a representation of ideal culture. Reality was much more flexible (Hutchinson 1996).

Rituals of Adulthood: Entrance to the Age Sets   Evans–Pritchard documented the initiation rites of young men and women. All male Nuer were initiated by a severe operation called *gar,* in a ceremony performed between the ages of fourteen and eighteen. Their foreheads were cut to the bone with a small knife in six long cuts. The ritual gave them membership in an age set. Nuer age sets are generational sodalities of warriors that crosscut (and thereby linked) the Nuer clans. The function of the ritual was to define the relationship of every male Nuer to every other male Nuer (Evans–Pritchard 1940:257). The ritual of gar symbolized the passage from adolescence to manhood. Similar rituals are commonly found among all the Nilotic peoples of the Rift Valley. No ritual marks the passage to adulthood for Nuer girls. Rather, a girl was considered to be a woman after she had given birth to her first child (Hutchinson 1996:190).

Complementary Opposition   In the 1960s, Marshall Sahlins suggested that the Nuer were not at all isolated, and that what Evans–Pritchard had described could best be understood as form of "predatory expansion," the key feature of which was complementary opposition or the "massing effect" (Sahlins 1961, 1968). Individuals in low-level units of social structure (minimal lineages) would come into conflict with each other over women, cattle, and bride-wealth, but they would combine to face higher-level opposition. Thus individuals within minimal lineages would fight each other over local slights, but would collaborate to oppose the interests of men at the level of minor lineages, and these would combine to oppose major and maximal levels. At the very top, the Nuer people, as a whole, would unite against the neighboring Dinka. This model fit neatly into the raiding/feuding facts of life reported on the ground, and helped to explain how a people relentlessly feuding with each other could, at the same time, cohere as an ethnic group.

How could the Nuer prevent intra-ethnic conflict from tearing their society apart? There were two answers, one was the *Leopard-skin chief* and the other was *ritual pollution*. The leopard-skin chief, also known as the earth priest, prevented conflict within Nuer society from getting out of hand through the use of mediation. Homicide was one of many ways of polluting society, or "putting matter out of place" (Douglas 1966). The sacrifice of cattle could restore order, and the function of the earth priest was to force men from different social units to sacrifice their precious cattle to restore order. Disorder or a lack of harmony with Kwoth, the overarching god of the Nuer, could also be brought about through incest, through nonpayment of bridewealth, and by not fulfilling the obligations of widow remarriage (also known as ghost marriage). Thus, feuding, cattle ownership, and obligations to Kwoth were drawn into marriage and kinship. This description was applied to the Nuer, and by extension, most pastoral nomads until recent times. We will return to an evaluation of the changes they are suffering through later in the chapter.

While the Nuer may have been tribal, and probably never had a centralized political system, other pastoral populations achieved chiefdom and state levels of hierarchy. This primarily appears to have occurred in ecological settings where rainfall determined a pastoral way of life, but trade opened the options leading to hierarchy: Herders created complex states. The history of North Africa and Southwest Asia is one of shifting dominance between these two modes of adaptation, settled villagers and herders, sometimes as tribes, sometimes as chiefdoms, and sometimes as states.

Transhumance pastoralism of cattle is particularly characteristic of the region of Eastern Africa, and today includes the countries of Sudan, Ethiopia, Somalia, Kenya, and Tanzania (Bennett 1993). Complex institutions, such as the belief in divine kings, evolved around pas-toralism, and these have been studied extensively by anthropologists. But these were not isolated, marginal, tribal peoples. Trade, not subsistence, was the powerful force impelling the transformation of tribal societies into chiefdoms and states, which have been common in East Africa since ancient Egypt. When trade was cut, as it was during the period of European domination and control, these societies did not disappear but shifted back to their primary adaptations, and continued to survive in another form as dependent peasants or warlike tribes on the periphery or margins of other trade states (Ensminger 1992).

ual occasions). Camels became particularly important with the development of trade in incense from southern Arabia. Incense was used in the temples of the ancient world, and camels became the indispensable transporters over the desert highways. The nomads who raised them were politically unimportant until they found a way to fight from atop one-humped camels without falling. Before this time, it was not possible to use swords and lances because of the insecure seating. The breakthrough took the form of a special camel saddle, a wooden frame placed around the hump. While camels could never compete with horses in war, horses could not survive where camels could. For this reason, control of the desert caravans fell to the desert Bedouins, particularly after the development of Islam, a topic we discuss in the following chapter.

The Development of Trade along the Nile

The region of the Bedouin, North Africa and Southwest Asia, became the Islamic empires after the eighth century A. D., and are not dealt with here. Those empires unified the peoples of what is today known as the Near East or Middle East. Before that time, Rome and or the Byzantine Empire controlled North Africa, including Egypt. Prior to the rise of Rome, the core of trade and control was Egypt. Egypt integrated trade throughout the Mediterranean for several thousand years, and its history is critical to understanding the rest of Africa.

Egypt   The civilizations of Southwest Asia overlap those of Egypt, and both were based on peasant agriculturalists, who had developed irrigation-based villages and towns. Archaeologists first find evidence for tribal societies along the Nile about 5000 B. C., which are referred to as the **Badarian.** People lived in small mud huts, and paid a great deal of attention to the burial of the dead. The next phase was a continuation of a tribal type of society, but with increasing signs of stratification and trade called the **Amratian.** Burials were placed on top of Badarian burials, suggesting cultural continuity. Fine monochrome pottery was manufactured with geometric and naturalistic designs. Egyptians decorated themselves with green or gray eye makeup, and used maces in warfare. At 4,000 B. C., new institutions emerged that reduced the transaction costs of trade, and theocratic chiefdoms appeared during the **Gerzean.** Gerzean craftsmen were highly accomplished, manufacturing beautiful pottery, stone bowls, stone maceheads, and jewelry, which shows the existence of a vast trading network. By late Gerzean times, the agricultural economy was highly developed and supported a class of wealthy people, many of whom were buried in *mastabas,* stone tombs that were to become the giant pyramids of the Old Kingdom (Redman 1978:282–283).

There is evidence of trade connections between Mesopotamia and Egypt as far back as 3500 B.C. (Fagan 1995). Trade may have run from as far north as Turkey through overland routes to Egypt, and then far to the south, transforming tribes into chiefdom type societies. Egypt, in North Africa, became ultimately transformed into one of the most powerful prehistoric states, its influence extending far to the south.

Of particular importance to traders were metals: first copper, and then bronze, and of course gold. One of the earliest known sites for the mining of copper was Sinai, the small piece of land in northeastern Egypt that links Egypt to the Middle East. Early copper-working in this region is thought to date as far back as 4000 B. C.; copper and bronze were widely used in both ancient Egypt and in Southwestern Asia.

Evidence for Egyptian religion is found in the early chiefdoms. Grave goods depict the peculiarly Egyptian preoccupation with death and the afterlife, which became the foundation for Egyptian ideology. It is clear that the religion of the Egyptians was based on tribal and chiefdom nature worship transformed into a state ideology. The pharaohs claimed to be earthly incarnations as gods, much as chiefs and kings of other African chiefdoms and states did. The rulers of early farming communities are thought to have been religious leaders and "rainmakers" who controlled the floods of the Nile. As their power and authority grew, they came to claim direct descent from the gods themselves. The early animal gods were transfigured into beings with human bodies and the faces of hawks, cats, dogs, and crocodiles. These were to be found in the formation of the stars, thus producing a complex cosmogony that connected the earth with the sky. Anubis was the jackal-headed god who collected the soul on death, Osiris was the god behind the pharaoh, Isis the lion-headed mother goddess, while Set, the evil god who opposed Osiris, had a human head and the body of a serpent.

By 3250 B. C., regional chiefs had been subjugated by kings, one ruling Upper Egypt (southern Egypt) and the other Lower Egypt (northern Egypt). The trend toward centralized power and social organization continued with King Narmer, Egypt's first pharaoh, who conquered Lower Egypt and built the first Egyptian city at Memphis. He made himself into a divine god, the head of a theocratic state. However, while Egypt had its famous temples and pyramids, it was not as urban as Mesopotamia, with most of the peasantry living in rural villages. Occupying the temple complexes were priests and the bureaucrats who ran the state. While the symbols of kinghood were different, based on a distinct culture with distinct gods, the singular statement of power very much resembled that of

Ur, but was also quite different (see Chapter 6 for a discussion of Ur). For example, the religion of Ur was based primarily on fertility and the fear of flooding, and angry or authoritarian gods (elements of Sumerian religion were incorporated into the Old Testament), while Egypt, which had control over floods through its fine irrigation system, had a religion based on a pleasant afterlife. There were few human sacrifices in Egyptian early history, unlike Ur. Hieroglyphic writing on papyrus was also developed and, as with the clay tablet writing of early Sumeria, was a form of temple accounting for an evolving state. The peaceable theocratic state gave way to a conquest state with river-based cities vying for power to control trade up and down the Nile.

At 3100 B. C., Egypt established a central government, initiating the First Dynasty, and became a historical entity. Inscriptions and monuments of the rulers of the early dynasties have been discovered and identified. The First Dynasty is dated to the same time period as the Early Dynastic for Mesopotamia. By the beginning of the Second Dynasty, the capital was established at Memphis, a strategic location unifying Upper and Lower Egypt. Intermarriage and warfare were used to stabilize the Egyptian state, with kings from the south taking their brides from the north. These rulers fostered international trade. Wood and rare stones were brought in from the Levant (modern Lebanon), metal ore from Nubia, and ivory from farther south in Africa. The administration of long-distance trade and irrigation was controlled by a bureaucracy at Memphis, and characterized Egypt for 3,000 years. A festival of royal power took place regularly, and a cult evolved centered on the person of the god-king whose death was ceremonialized by his burial in a giant pyramid. Writing and science flourished, and hieroglyphic writing became common.

A modern symbol of ancient Egypt is the pyramid, the first of which was built at Saqqara and is dated to 2700 B. C. This first structure is a step pyramid. The giant pyramid at Giza, a true pyramid, was built in 2600 B. C. for King Khufu

The signs of complex bureaucracy: Tomb of high officials of Ramese's Court.

(Cheops). Thirty dynasties would follow, with pyramids characterizing the early periods, but giant statues and burial temples, such as the rock tombs of the Valley of Kings (1500 B. C.), typical of the later dynasties. The final years of Egypt were dominated by Greece, and later Rome. One of the final dramatic episodes was the love affair between the Roman aristocrat Anthony and the Egyptian ruler Cleopatra. Their suicide deaths and the incorporation of Egypt within the Roman empire by Emperor Octavian is accepted as the end of the Egyptian Empire (30 B. C.), but its power really continued into modern history.

Meroe   As far back as Old Kingdom times Ancient Egypt had conducted trade with the Nubian region to the south. An elaborate chiefdom or kingdom known as the "island of Meroe" emerged near the fourth cataract, just to the north of where the Blue and White Nile rivers come together. This region lent itself to rain-fed agriculture, cattle, and other forms of livestock. With the help of iron tools, the people of **Meroe** developed a mixed economy that combined agriculture with cattle. This pattern became typical in the savanna regions of tropical Africa, and where agriculture was marginal pastoralism dominated.

Meroe was able to control trade into the Nile Valley, and it could and did develop trade to the east to ports on the Red Sea. When relations with Egypt became strained, or when Egypt was under the control of Greeks or Romans, Meroe developed state-level institutions and monopolized local trade. Trade connections extended far to the east to India and Indonesia. Meroe exported its traditional products of ivory, leopard skins, ostrich feathers, ebony, and gold. The cattle herders and peasant cultivators were spread over a wide area and were ultimately under the control of a king and court. But Meroe was much less centralized than the Egyptian state, and most families were ruled by minor chiefs and heads of family clans. In a similar fashion, the people of Meroe moved over a wide arc to the east and west, and retained a great deal of political autonomy from Egypt and other empires.

Anthropologists a generation ago assumed that states evolved due to the development of irrigation agriculture and large populations. But it is apparent that Meroe did not have irrigation or large populations. Complex chiefdoms and states arose as strategic adaptations to control trade and trade relations with surrounding populations. Other kingdoms, many based on pastoral nomadism, rose and fell in an arc just south of Egypt, until the Roman empire challenged their hegemony and trade and empire-building shifted elsewhere.

The Development of Gold Trade

Trans-Saharan trade, connecting East and West Africa with North Africa, stimulated the rise of other kingdoms, such as Great Zimbabwe, the Nok of Nigeria, the ancient empire of Mali, located where modern Ghana is, and the more recent Kongo empire based in Zaire. The period after a thousand years ago is generally called the **Later Iron Age,** and it was once thought new peoples had come into East Africa and displaced people of the Early Iron Age, for it was an age of great economic, social, and political development. It is now evident, however, that there were no great population migrations but that local people had been stimulated to develop chiefdoms and states as a consequence of the external demand for African gold, copper, slaves, and ivory, which was especially important in India for bridal ornaments.

Indian Ocean Trade Centers   The east African coast was known to Greek and Roman traders, who referred to the region as "Azania," and there are references from 100 A.D. to coastal market towns. The people of Azania were experienced fishermen and were very knowledgeable in the use of small coastal boats made of wooden planks that were knotted together with lengths of coconut fiber (Shillington 1989:124).

Trade in the Indian Ocean was given a great boost by the spread of Islam in the seventh and eighth centuries. The region came to be called "the Land of Zenj." Arab sailing ships, known as dhows, were able to take advantage of the monsoon winds, which blow towards east Africa between November and March, and towards India and the Persian Gulf between April and October. As the demand for African ivory and gold rose, Muslim settled along the coast, developing trade towns speaking Swahili, a trade language based on Bantu grammar with many Arab words. The Swahili-speaking towns, with their camel caravans, in turn stimulated the rise of chiefdoms and states in the East African interior (Shillington 1989:128). In addition, other camel caravans from Islamic states in

Figure 9.3   **East African trade routes in eighth and ninth centuries A.D.**

North Africa crossed the Sahara and further added economic stimulation, which brought about new states in West Africa in Senegal, Mali, and Niger at about the same time.

Gold Trade in East and West Africa   One of the East African states that holds great fascination for modern archaeologists is Great Zimbabwe. Between 1200 and 1450 A. D., this great city-state developed with a subsistence base of nomadic pastoralism. However, its wealth was based on trade in gold. The region to the west, known as Leopard's Kopje, was rich in gold-bearing rock and was made into a tributary of Great Zimbabwe. The modern country of Zimbabwe (once known as Rhodesia) is named for this ancient empire, the center or capital of the larger Shona state. Elaborate stone walls, probably not built for defensive purposes, encircled clay dwellings. The enclosures were built to enhance the power, mystery, and prestige of the Shona kings. The kings and their courts lived in luxury, surrounded by gold and copper ornaments, and ate off imported plates made in Persia and China. Craftsmen made fine gold and copper implements, which were traded east.

As was true for the other peoples described, cattle were very important, but so was big game hunting, particularly elephants for their ivory. Shillington (1989) points out, however, that the most important factor governing Zimbabwe's power and wealth was the capital's strategic position on a trade route. The remains of the Great Zimbabwe capital are at the head of the Sabi river, an ideal location from which to control trade to and from the goldfields of the western plateau and the Arab–Swahili town of Kilwa on the coast. Fage (1995:133) agrees that trade was important but suggests that the location of Great Zimbabwe was actually less than ideal with respect to both major goldfields and major trade routes. However, overpopulation and competition from the Zambezi Valley came to influence survival. By 1400, the city had as many as 11,000 people and by 1450, the region could no longer support them as trade shifted in favor of the Zambezi Valley. Another Shona state, that of the Mutapa, used military domination to gain control of trade, and Great Zimbabwe collapsed. By this time the Portuguese were beginning to control sea trade off the east coast of Africa, and soon Mutapa also collapsed. At this time the chiefdoms and states of Africa were being threatened by the Portuguese monopoly over sea trade. As the coastal cities were brought under alien control, the chiefdoms and states of the interior began to crumble. Five hundred years later, archaeologists ponder how they came into being in the first place.

The search by anthropologists for the essence of tribalism in Africa prevented scholars from examining the links between trade, the development of chiefdoms and states, and the relationship of these to less centralized tribal societies on the peripheries or margins. The model that emerges today for many world regions is not of an evolutionary set of successive stages (band, tribe, chiefdom, state), but rather a dynamic and replicated center–periphery model. (We use this classification with the specific meaning of levels of sociocultural [including political] integration. While over the long term there were bands before tribes, tribes preceded chiefdoms, and chiefdoms came before states, once all levels were in existence a dynamic relationship came to exist among co-existing groups at different levels of integration. In addition, the level of integration of any given group could and did vary through time, depending on such major factors as population size, political economy, trade, property rights, and relations with neighboring groups.) This is the model that emerges from a careful look at the precolonial history and prehistory of sub-Saharan Africa. The center, either a true state or a chiefdom, responded to the need to reduce transaction costs by developing hierarchical social structures. In true states, a king could initiate a political action, but in a chiefdom his (or her) actions were limited by a need for support from close kinsmen and the leaders of supporting clans. The distinction between states and chiefdoms is probably impossible to really ascertain, and, from our perspective, not particularly helpful. It is fairly apparent that the greater the importance of trade, the more important the state and its hierarchical structure.

The Emergence of Slave Trade Societies in the West

New and powerful states emerged in the period after the sixteenth century associated with the European slave trade, such as Oyo, Dahomey, and Asante (located where Ghana is today). Slavery had existed in Africa well before the colonial period, and as an institution had ancient roots. Slaves were used as wealth and for trade, but much depended on the nature of the political economy of the society. In tribes, slaves, for the most part, had the status of household workers. In chiefdoms and states, they formed a special category of labor, and were used in exchange for goods. But slaves could buy themselves out of slavery, or marry and join households. The demand for slaves by industrializing European societies, particularly as plantation workers, escalated and transformed the slave trade in West Africa as some African rulers decided to trade one of their most precious resources—labor—for European trade goods.

Portuguese sailing ships first reached the West African coast in the 1470s in a search for gold, but slaves soon became more important than gold. We have seen in the last chapter how the demand for slaves in the Americas had a severe impact on African social structure, robbing it of its young. Some 293,000 slaves were landed in the Americas and Europe between 1451 and 1600; in the seventeenth century, slave exports quintupled to 1,494,000 in response to the growth of sugar plantations. In the eighteenth century, over six million people were exported from Africa and, although Britain abolished the slave trade in 1807, two million more slaves were transported from Africa to the Americas between 1810 and 1870 (Fage 1995:254–255; Wolf 1982:197–198).

Europeans radically transformed West African societies when they brought in harder metals, hardware, firearms, gunpowder, textiles, rum, and tobacco to exchange for slaves. Portuguese slavers stirred up war between the Kingdoms of Kongo and Ndongo, which collapsed. The Ashanti state came into being as a slave state under the support of European slavers. Generally, Europeans did not hunt for slaves but relied on politically powerful African elites and merchants to obtain slaves for them. Many of these slave hunter societies became centralized states with kings, courts, and bureaucracies based on the West African model of divine kings, but with much greater importance granted to warfare. Tribute-paying societies remained at a tribal level dependent on agriculture. But both the slave states and tributary tribes had very similar kinship systems, for the most part based on patrilineal clans. Shillington writes about the extent of the slave trade:

> With the rapid expansion of slave exports in the eighteenth century virtually every part of the Atlantic coastline from Senegal to southern Angola became involved in the human traffic. The greatest concentration of European trading forts was along the so-called "Gold Coast," the coastline of the modern state of Ghana (1989:174).

The main source of slaves was warfare and the supply of captives at the coast was the result of local wars being fought in the interior. According to some, the prime motive of the wars was the formation and expansion of states based on the slave trade. Shillington argues that the slave trade was the prime motivation for warfare, leading to the total destruction of weaker societies by the stronger slave states (Shillington 1989:176).

However, it seems unlikely that the African kingdoms would destroy the resource that was central to their own economic well-being. Fage (1995:265–266) offers an alternative perspective, namely, that African rulers engaged in the slave trade with full regard for their own well-being, balancing labor needs against their desire for European trade goods, and in fact controlling the export of slaves.

Slave tribute-paying tribes and slave-taking states came to hate each other, and as their relations with Europeans changed, so did their relations with each other (Wolf 1982:228–229). Many of these hatreds remain in modern societies in Africa, and form at least a part of the basis for ethnic conflict in countries such as modern Nigeria and Ghana. As an example, the Yoruba state collapsed and was followed by the slaving states of Oyo and Dahomey, and Asanti, which had very similar religions and social structures, but greater access to slaves. The Asanti were particularly known for the symbol of Asanti kingship, the Gold Stool. These three states preyed on the people of the interior, who became slave-givers, while Oyo, Dahomey, and Asanti became slave-takers.

The Heritage of Colonialism

In the late nineteenth and early twentieth centuries, particularly in the period beginning in 1884–85 with the Congress of Berlin to the period just before World War II, Europeans carved up Africa into colonies. One of the many contributing causes of World War II was the assumption by Europeans that they needed colonies to supplement their own diminishing resources. Europeans did not physically colonize West Africa, primarily due to climatic conditions. They did colonize East and South Africa, to a degree because of mineral riches and a healthier climate. But in all of Africa south of the Sahara, boundaries were imposed by European politicians and diplomats who were primarily concerned with gaining control over natural resources and who paid scant attention to the needs of native populations (Carter and O'Meara 1986) or ethnic group boundaries.

In many instances, previous slave-raiding populations were organized within "countries" containing the tribes they had previously raided. During the colonial period, European administrators tended to favor certain tribes over others to administrate the new countries (such as the Ibo in Nigeria). Sometimes these "ruling" tribes were previous slave-raiders or slave tribute-givers creating intractable tensions between rulers and ruled. The new governments of Africa have inherited geographic boundaries that are arbitrary and contain populations that sometimes are intensely antagonistic to each other. A major problem is uniting the various groups so that they function as one nation. This problem is compounded when ethnic distinctions and antagonisms are used by modern authoritarian regimes to maintain power.

The history of southern Africa needs special mention because it does not fit the overall history of Africa discussed so far. Southern Africa had been settled by cattle herding peoples from Late Iron Age times. The societies were mostly self-sufficient tribes and chiefdoms, such as the Sotho–Tswana of Namibia, the Nguni of the region east of the Drakensberg Mountains, and the Xhosa and Khoisian speakers of the south. During the sixteenth century, European sailing ships, especially Dutch and English, began using the southwestern Cape as port of call in their long voyages around Africa. Europeans wanted cheap meat from cattle, and the natives were not always willing to sell at low prices. Europeans would seize the animals and sail off, causing the natives to attack traders.

The Dutch set up the Dutch East India Company to solve these problems, forming a permanent settlement at Table Bay in 1652. The Dutch hoped to monopolize the regional economy and control trade in food. Khoisian pastoralists managed to unite in opposition against the Dutch in 1659 but were decimated. The Dutch declared a "right of conquest" and took over the Cape Peninsula establishing the Cape Colony. The Dutch are today known as the Boer or Afrikaners, and continued to immigrate into the region forming a Dutch colony. The Afrikaners expanded the colony and came into conflict with other tribal and chiefdom societies, pushing them into what later, in the modern state of South Africa, would become their regional "homelands" or Bantustans, a topic we will return to later.

Adaptation to the State and Development

Traditional African societies did not passively accept the Europeans, and they responded politically to the expansion of European interests. In West Africa, a variety of distinct crops became the focus of European exploitation. Palm oil replaced slaves as slavery became illegal in Europe and America. Palm oil was important in soap-making and as a lubricant. Eric Wolf explains that warrior elites and state organizations geared to the slave trade found it difficult to adapt to the new palm oil trade. The elites responded by using slaves on palm oil plantations. But middlemen on the coast and small peasant cultivators undercut the elites and soon European wholesalers began to deal directly with the new producers. Former slaves, educated in European religious missions, became the new commercial elites. The spread of European all-purpose money replaced iron, copper, and cowrie currencies, further undermining the old economies (Wolf 1982:330–332). The West African economies expanded and then contracted with the economic depressions of capitalist societies, particularly the Great Depression of 1873. Europeans and Africans struggled to control local supplies and to drive down prices, particularly the price of labor.

Conflict ensued and Europeans called for law and order. Having abolished slavery in their own countries, Europeans used its continuance in Africa to justify wars with the old elites and the establishment of colonial rule (Fage 1995:267). The kingdoms of Asanti, Dahomey, Oyo, Benin, and Aro were conquered and European control was imposed on West Africa.

The Tide of Liberation

The exploitation of Africa was not received passively, and by the end of World War II, African leaders had strong popular support in their efforts to return Africa to African rule. The ideas of independence were not new in Africa, and were inspired by the same documents that led to democratic changes in Western Europe in the late nineteenth century. As would be true in wars of liberation fought in Asia, the new leaders of Africa used the same arguments about human dignity and worth put out in the founding documents of Western Civilization: the French Rights of Man and the Bill of Rights in the United States Constitution. African scholars, such as Arnold Temu and Bonaventure Swai, searched and found arguments regarding ideas of freedom originating in African history (1981). Many of these ideas were incorporated into the political positions taken by the African National Congress and made more explicit in the election of Nelson Mandela as President of South Africa.

New political ideas were highly diverse, ranging from Islamic concepts about the equality of the faithful to American ideals of liberal democracy. In Eastern Africa, the Kikuyu of Kenya, whose fertile lands had been enclosed by European farmers, had begun their protests as early as 1921, when the Young Kikuyu Association was formed. By 1929, many independent African churches claimed "Africa for the Africans," and after World War II the forces for liberation accelerated. The war itself had created great demand for African goods, and rural peoples were attracted to the cities, which doubled and tripled in size. Explosive political movements began to transform African society. In 1945, a gathering in Manchester, England, of the sixth Pan-African Congress, brought together the new revolutionary leadership. Many leaders were the future presidents of free African states: Kwame Nkrumah of Ghana, Jomo Kenyatta of Kenya, and Nnamdi Azikiwe of Nigeria.

Sally Falk Moore, writing about the role of anthropology during this period, sketches how African leaders came to question the way that European and Amer-

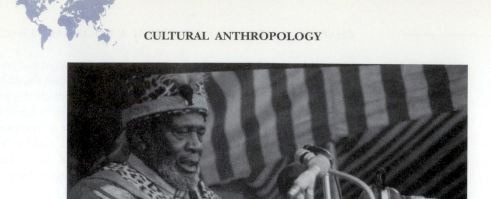

Jomo Kenyatta of Kenya.

ican scholars had appropriated African history. Anthropologists "found themselves in an uncomfortable state of political self-consciousness" (1994:76). They became critical of their own theories and substituted world system and dependency theories for their outworn evolutionary models (Moore 1994:77). Many embraced Marxist interpretations of history, as did African leaders. In the 1990s, anthropologists, other African scholars, and African politicians are all searching for new models that are neither capitalist nor Marxist.

The Rise of Socialism

In the 1960s, anthropologists and African intellectuals were optimistic about Africa's future. In the 1990s, the optimism has been replaced with anxiety. Very few of the newly independent countries of Africa managed to develop democratically elected governments or to achieve economic stability. Within a decade of independence, colonial capitalism had given way to the rejection of democratic–capitalist norms and the adoption of blends of Marxist–Leninist–Maoist revolutionary thought in a majority of the developing countries of Africa (Sklar 1986:13). But it was not only the experiences of African leaders that led them to choose socialism. Many leading western intellectuals, anthropologists, other social scientists, and historians vigorously supported socialism as the means to overcome dependency. Several influential writers thought socialism was a natural form of political organization for African tribal societies.

Western "Marxism" was integrated into African political theory by Western thinkers to produce "Negritude," a new ideology of African socialism that was supposed to break the bonds of slavery, capitalism, and imperialism, particularly in formerly French colonial countries. Revolutionary leaders in Africa adopted anti-Western, anticore ideologies based on Marxism, and used the language of socialism to develop one-party mass political movements. Often these political structures were Marxist in name only. A common theme developed, proposing that the countries of Africa, more so than any other developing region, should use socialism to achieve economic development because the premodern societies of Africa were socialist in nature due to their dependence on the collective ownership of resources. The confusion between collective ownership of property in tribal societies and centralized socialist governments has led to problems no one intended or predicted.

Conflict between ethnic and tribal groups played an important role in the selection of socialism, because many African leaders did not believe democracy was possible in societies where interethnic strife was high (Sullivan 1989:4). To maintain order, many Africans chose military states with socialist style governments, such as Nigeria. Others attempted state capitalism, such as Liberia. But both approaches depended on heavy-handed rulers. Financial policies emphasized economic investment in urban regions and disinvestment in rural regions, which often alienated rural ethnic groups, reinforcing urban–rural splits. Where resources allowed, the political leaders borrowed money from international banks, and distributed the largesse among their followers, leading to increasing political conflict. In the 1980s, international banks began calling back their debts due to internal economic pressures in capitalist countries, intensifying the demands for political change in Africa. Many of the once hopeful socialist governments were faced with rural violence, and tried to meet violence with violence, adding to the spiral of ethnic and regional warfare. Examining the region of East Africa will help to illustrate how human ecology and ethnic nationalism have fueled violence, often in the form of genocide.

Regional War and Ethnic Conflict

One of the most serious problems facing the African republics is the animosity between different ethnic groups. Some locate the source of modern ethnic conflict in rivalries that existed in precolonial times, while others see such conflict as largely a product of colonialism. There is some truth in both of these views. There is also evidence that modern African elites in some countries have used ethnic differences as a political tool. Warfare and feuding were clearly widespread in the precolonial societies of Africa, particularly among pastoral groups. Even though most intergroup violence ceased during the colonial period, the memories of what one group did to another centuries before became part of the ideology of conflict between modern peoples. Many of the regional conflicts in Africa appear to have their origin in ideological disagreements, such as Marxism versus capitalism, but on closer scrutiny it turns out that ancient animosities underlie the modern rhetoric. The breakdown of order and the extensive feuding that destroyed Somalia from 1990–1992 is a case in point.

Figure 9.4   Contemporary map of African States, with areas of conflict highlighted

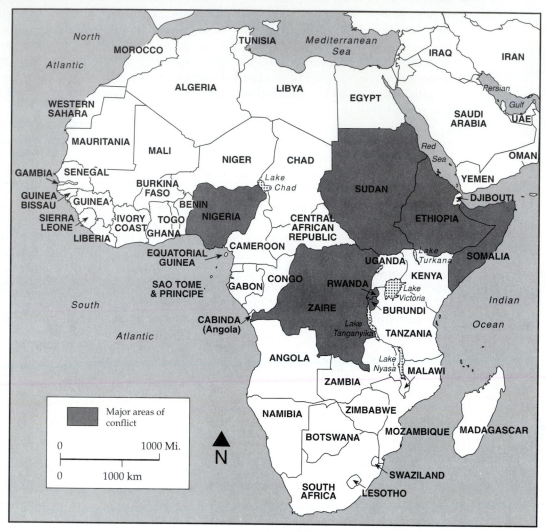

Among the many "ethnic" distinctions found in East Africa, of particular importance is the one between "cattle-owners" and "tillers of the soil." This is more an ideological than pragmatic distinction, as no group is purely pastoral. Lucy Mair, writing in 1974, points out that these two groups go by different "ethnic" or "tribal" names in different regions. In Rwanda and Burundi they are Tutsi and Hutu. In southern Uganda (Bunyoro) they are Huma and Iru. In the former kingdom of Ankole (also in Uganda), they are known as Hima and Iru (Mair 1974:166–192). While in modern communities the distinction between cattle owners and farmers seldom applies (many have other occupations), the aristocratic bias of these distinctions continues, and, as we shall see in the section on

Rwanda and Burundi, may be used as an excuse for genocide (though this is obviously not the only or even dominant basis of genocide). In the 1970s, Idi Amin and Dr. Milton Obote fought a war to determine which "tribe" would control the state, a war that decimated Uganda and made outsiders aware of the horrors of genocide.

Adding to the political volatility in East Africa is feuding, both within and between pastoral societies. Traditional feuds between clans and tribes have escalated with the introduction of modern weapons. Alex de Waal, an anthropologist who has worked on human rights issues in Sudan, makes the point that guns have exacerbated what was originally a controlled form of feuding, to the point that, among some groups, "people adorn themselves with images of firearms and use cartridges as jewelry" (de Waal 1996:242).

Ethnic and tribal conflicts in Africa have often erupted into complex regional wars. Refugees, soldiers, and revolutionaries from several poor African states spill across each other's borders, at times attracting international attention and interference. These ethnic–regional conflicts are found throughout Africa, and have become more intense over the past decade. As a consequence, Africa contains the world's largest number of refugees.

While modern populations of the states of the region are primarily sedentary, relatively significant proportions of the populations of Kenya (12 percent), Somalia (70 percent), and Sudan (22 percent) (Bennett 1993:297) continue to follow this age-old adaptation to fragile arid and semiarid lands. J. W. Bennett argues, in a recent overview of migratory pastoralism, that, while the slave trade and colonial repression were major forces affecting indigenous peoples, many of the disturbances of the region today—regional wars, genocide, and hunger—are the consequence of the collapse of a "man controlled ecological system" (1993:303). Here, we focus on migratory pastoralism as a socionatural adaptation in order to emphasize the close interrelationships among adaptation, ethnicity, identity, and conflict.

The ethnic groups that are to be found in the arc from Ethiopia to South Africa are tribal and chiefdom societies, but many became true states, and have distinct political heritages despite similar human ecologies. They include peoples of Christian, Animist, and Islamic religions. They speak many languages, and include the Karamojong of northeastern Uganda and northern Kenya and the Masai of central Kenya and northern Tanzania. Farther south along the east African coast, town-dwelling, Swahili-speaking Arabs were interspersed with cattle raisers of the same ethnic background; and far to the south, Tswana, Nguni, and Sotho peoples had expanded below the Drakensberg Mountains into modern South Africa by 1400 A.D.

In the following, we will examine some of the regional conflicts in East Africa, once a region of predominantly pastoral peoples. Over the last two decades revolutionary conflicts have overwhelmed East Africa, particularly in the countries of Ethiopia, Somalia, Sudan, and most recently the twin countries of Rwanda and Burundi. The conflicts are impossible to contain in the countries where they begin. Ethnic groups who are in conflict with each other often live in more than one country, and warfare crosses borders, producing regional conflicts. Many of these people are migratory pastoralists for whom national borders mean little. Adding to ethnic tensions in the region is the migration of refugees across the borders of the countries they live in to other countries where they can be cared for in refugee centers or where they can find protection living with members of their own ethnic groups. For example, during the war in Uganda, many Ugandans took up residence with relatives in the Sudan, and during the Sudanese civil war of 1955–1972, many southerners crossed into Uganda, Zaire, and the Central African Republic to live with relatives there (personal communication of PY with Zande in and around Yambio, southern Sudan in 1982).

Ethiopia: Failure of Cheap Food Policies

The Ethiopian Empire, headed by an aristocratic king, Haile Selassie, collapsed in 1974. The Soviet Union supported the new pseudo-socialist state, which nationalized foreign companies and the lands of the aristocracy. Political rivalries resulted in mass executions and disappearances. In 1978, Mengistu Heile Mariam came to power as the head of a Marxist one-party state allied to the Soviet Union (the party was named the Workers Party of Ethiopia).

Heile Mariam introduced policies that favored the urban working class, thereby alienating a number of ethnic groups, including peasant farmers and pastoralists of the rural regions. Farmers and cattle herders were paid low prices for their produce in order to keep food cheap for urban workers. Liberation movements in Eritrea, Tigray, and Welo provinces led Heile Mariam to use scarce funds to support his military rather than for rural economic development. Policies to keep food cheap for the urban population, coupled with excessive investment in the military, had the consequence of blocking economic development and virtually destroyed the economies of the three revolutionary provinces. Lack of significant investment in the economy and two civil wars led to widespread hunger and starvation, which received worldwide attention. In part, hunger was the consequence of cheap food policies that induced peasant farmers to abandon the land, and pastoralists to convert cattle to grain. And, in part, hunger was the consequence of the several revolutions. The government refused to allow food to be transported by international relief agencies to Tigray and Welo provinces because of the belief that the food would be used to support the rebels.

The recent transformations in Russia and Eastern Europe, the general questioning of socialism as a means of escaping underdevelopment, and the abandonment of one-party states caused Heile Mariam to introduce reforms, including the reintroduction of market mechanisms. However, he was too late because the Eritrean People's Liberation Front defeated his army in Eritrea and declared their independence, while a second revolutionary army from Tigray province defeated what was left of his army in Ethiopia.

Ethiopia's new president (since 1991) is Meles Zenawi, the leader of the victorious Tigray guerrilla movement (Tigray is still a province of Ethiopia). He and his supporters have redrawn the country's borders along ethnic lines, arguing that they have learned from their communist predecessors not to force peoples of widely different ethnic backgrounds to conform to the same federal rules and regulations. The new Council of Representatives has agreed to let the regions have as much say as possible in their own governance, with their own representative assemblies, judiciaries, and police forces. The central government will control defense and foreign affairs. This has caused some to fear "regionalism run rampant," but the advocates of division along ethnic lines believe that the new democracy they are creating will ameliorate any resentments that might exist among ethnic populations (Smith 1995). Independent Eritrea's president, Issaias Afwerki, is cooperating with Zenawi as they attempt to put both houses in order.

Somalia: The Breakdown of Clan-Based Social Controls

Somalia sits on the eastern horn of Africa. An Islamic society, it acts as a link between Africa and Arabia. It is an arid to semiarid country the size of Texas and has a population of 8 million, mostly pastoralists. During the colonial period, the north was controlled by Great Britain while the south and east were controlled by Italy. The country became independent in 1960, but secessionist movements gave way to civil war in 1987 and 1988 (Sullivan 1989:110–111).

Until recently, Somalia was ruled by the Revolutionary Socialist Party. The RSP first allied itself with the Soviet Union until 1977. At that time, its head of state, Major Mohammed Siad Barre, felt threatened by Ethiopia's new socialist direction and its ties to the Soviet Union and allied himself with the United States (Bohannen and Curtin 1995:266). He granted the United States naval facilities at the capital of Mogadishu and at Berbera. These bases have been used as staging areas for the U.S. Rapid Deployment Force. Somalia has also participated in U.S.-organized war games and has received substantial economic aid. Despite a Marxist-style dictatorship, the mismanagement of food aid, and a poor human rights record, the United States continued to support Barre until the civil war when his violent attacks on civilian populations forced suspension of U.S. aid (Sullivan 1989:110–111).

Before Barre imposed a socialist one-party state government on Somalia, subclans used Sharia law (the Islamic legal code derived from the Koran) in organized village courts. Each village had a subclan chief and village elders who maintained social control. Usually family heads were expected to maintain social control over the young, and punishment was family- or subclan-based. Once a dispute occurred between subclans, the elders would mediate the dispute, as is common among pastoral peoples. Each village and town was controlled by the clan elders of the most powerful subclan. Barre imposed local governments controlled by young socialists who introduced secular law and challenged the rule of the elders. The power of the state alienated the traditional clan leaders.

Exiles formed rebel armies in the country and overthrew Barre in 1990, but then clan-based factions began fighting with one another, primarily led by the young socialists, not the clan elders. The country was awash with weapons provided by the United States and the Soviet Union. Two warlords split the country into warring subclans. While Somalis should be less divided than many other African people because they share the same language, and all belong to the Sunni branch of Islam, in fact they are split into warring clans and subclans. Mr. Barre suppressed clan warfare for twenty-one years. But, with no central government and with the elders having been pushed aside, lawlessness reigned and heavily armed gangs representing different clans, often of the same tribe, killed each other in the countryside and in the streets of Mogadishu. However, they usually kill more innocent bystanders than each other (Smith 1995).

The major battle was between two warlords of the same clan, General Muhammed Farrah Aideed and Mr. Ali Mahdi Muhammad. General Aideed was angered when clan leaders gave the presidency to Ali Mahdi. The resulting fight between the two killed 4,000 people. In December of 1992, the United States sent a 35,000-man army to back United Nations forces in pacifying the country. General Aideed and Ali Mahdi shook hands and agreed to put an end to violence. They also agreed to take their "technicals," heavily armed trucks, out of the major cities and to store them until agreement could be reached on the first step towards the political reconstruction of Somalia, but, in the process of searching for peace, the United States forces lost several men. Due to public pressure, the United States was forced to remove its forces as Americans became critical of the United Nations, and later the United Nations also left before any real peace had been achieved. General Aideed was killed on August 1, 1996. His Mogadishu-based rivals, Osman Ali Atto and Ali Madhi Muhammad, called a cease-fire. Aideed's son and successor, Hussein Muhammad Aideed, did not cooperate. He renewed attacks, vowing to exterminate his father's enemies (*The Economist*, August 31, 1996, 7).

A young American soldier in "downtown Mogadishu."

Rwanda and Burundi: The Politics of Ethnic Violence

Rwanda and Burundi are two small, densely populated countries with overlapping histories. They are located just north of Lake Tanganyika and northwest of Tanzania. In both countries in precolonial times a majority of agricultural peasants, called *Hutu,* (89 percent of the population in Rwanda and 85 percent in Burundi) were dominated by a smaller minority of pastoralists, called *Tutsi.* The Tutsi, in both countries, were organized into aristocratic clans with kings and queens in control of the two distinct lands (there was a Tutsi king and queen for Rwanda and a Tutsi king and queen for Burundi). The kings controlled trade and extracted tribute from the Hutu, often in the form of labor. Tutsi dominance of Hutu in precolonial times does not appear to have involved any large-scale or systematic violence in either Rwanda or Burundi (Prunier 1995; Lemarchand 1994).

Lucy Mair, in her ethnohistory of the region, argues that the Tutsi established domination over the Hutu several centuries ago, creating a kingdom with petty states. Secrets of ritual and taboo were kept by a body of hereditary experts, who used a secret code and esoteric language to keep their faith secret from the Hutu. This council formed the advisors to the kings, and were responsible for naming and installing successors, as well as distributing land and cattle to Tutsi overlords. Rwanda and Burundi kings appointed territorial subordinates, who acted as chiefs. Below the aristocratic cattle herders, the Hutu had their own chiefs, who were subordinate to the Tutsi. The Hutu could herd cattle for their owners, and did most of the work for them, but could not own cattle and, thus, could not acquire wealth (Mair 1974:174).

Alex de Waal does not agree with Mair's interpretation and says that in Rwanda the Hutu, Tutsi, and Twa (a small minority group) were "three different strata of the same group, differentiated by occupational and political status" (1994:1). He likens the relationship to that of a caste system but says that individuals could, with difficulty, change categories. While he does not dispute Tutsi dominance in precolonial times, de Waal points out that Hutu and Tutsi shared the same language, culture, and religion and lived in the same communities.

Lemarchand presents a similar view of the precolonial Hutu–Tutsi relationship in Burundi. He argues that the concept of "tribe" is "patently inappropriate to describe communities that speak the same language (Kirundi), that share much the same type of social organization, and whose members lived peacefully side by side for centuries" (1994:4). He further notes that the term *hutu* has the meaning of "social subordinate," as well as being an ethnic identity label (1994:10).

During the late nineteenth century the two regions were a part of German East Africa. After World War I, Belgium became the protector of the two new countries of Rwanda and Burundi. After World War II, the two countries became United Nations mandated territories, and colonial authorities continued to rule through the Tutsi aristocracy. Scholars agree that the colonial governments enhanced Tutsi dominance. In both countries, Belgian authorities simplified the government bureaucracy and granted the Tutsi higher-level posts and special privileges. The Tutsi came to look at their power and privileges as natural rights (Des Forges 1994).

In both countries, independence has brought a sharpening of ethnic distinctions, with both Tutsi and Hutu politicians and intellectuals developing distinct versions of history to support their views of themselves and the other (Lemarchand 1994; Prunier 1995). While cattle have lost their importance in modern times, the Tutsi view themselves as the descendants of the true cattle-owning elite, and believe that only they have connections to the true gods who originated the region. They identify with their herds of cattle, and believe farming is lower-class work. The Hutu view the Tutsi as exploiters, a lazy, and pretentious people of violence who use their status to exploit the poor Hutu. The Hutu view themselves as victims of Tutsi exploitation, as hard workers, as peasants who understand and identify with the land, and as Catholics.

After the French and Belgian authorities turned Rwanda and Burundi back to their own peoples, both Tutsi and Hutu began to form political parties based on ethnic identity. Each had its own militant wing. In 1959, in Rwanda, a band of young Tutsi killed one of the few Hutu subchiefs, leading to a Hutu attack on Tutsis, when many died. Chiefs on both sides organized attacks and counterattacks. In 1963, Hutu authorities executed all those Tutsi in positions of power, killing ten to fifteen thousand Tutsis. There followed a Tutsi massacre of Hutus.

The popular press has taken a primordialist view in its reportage of the conflicts in Rwanda and Burundi (and, for that matter, elsewhere). In this view, cultural or ethnic identities are believed to have an essentialist character; that is, they have ancient, enduring features. An opposing view, one favored by many scholars, is that political processes play a fundamental role in the formation and consolidation of ethnic identities. This is called the instrumentalist view. The ethnic violence in both Rwanda and Burundi in the late twentieth century seems best explained not by ancient antagonisms from a bygone precolonial era, not by primordialism, but by deliberate manipulation on the part of radical politicians and military officers, by instrumentalism (Lemarchand 1994). De Waal points out that the coup in Burundi in 1993 received immediate international condemnation, which prevented extremists from holding on to power. He goes on to note that the genocide in Rwanda in 1994 did not receive the same swift international condemnation because the killers succeeded in convincing the United Nations and the press that it was spontaneous ethnic violence (1994:2). A small group of elites, both Tutsi and Hutu, have been responsible for mythologizing history, exaggerating ethnic differences into perceived hatred, and engineering genocide for their own political ends. Yet the question remains, how can a small number of extremists convince a large number of people that they should carry out massive killing, mostly of their neighbors? Perhaps Mary Gore provided one answer when, at the Cairo World Population Conference in September, 1994, she said: "Rwanda is a tragedy and a warning. It is a warning about the way in which extremists can manipulate the fears of a population threatened by its own numbers and by its massive poverty" (quoted in Prunier 1995:353).

Sudan: A Clash of Cultures

The Republic of Sudan is one of the largest countries in Africa. With its rich agricultural and pasture lands and its trade potential, it could also be one of the most prosperous. Instead, it has had a history of famine, revolution, and regional war. The famine is partly the consequence of desertification, but it is also the consequence of the regional wars that have been consuming East Africa for the last decade. According to John W. Bennett, the Sahel has suffered desiccation due to overgrazing because pastoralists are being forced into smaller regions, the opening of marginal lands to cultivation, and drought cycles (Bennett 1993:258-259). Spooner (1982) blames aridity on the increased number of tub wells, which attract more cattle than a region can absorb. The cattle crop the grasses, and turn grassland to desert. The Nuer, an important pastoral group, live in the central Sudan (considered a part of the south), and presently form a part of the southern revolutionary army, the Sudanese Peoples Liberation Army (SPLA).

The region was under the rule of Egypt and Turkey in the nineteenth century until an Islamic revolt established an Islamic theocracy in 1881. The theocratic state of Sudan was overthrown by Great Britain and made into a British colony until 1956, when the country was granted independence. Until 1956, the British ruled the Arabic-speaking Muslim peoples of the north and the black African Christian and pagan south as separate territories. The Muslim north was based on agriculture, cattle raising, and trade centered in the ancient city of Khartoum, at the confluence of the Blue and White Niles, and Port Sudan on the Red Sea. Here, Muslim culture dominated. The southern region, with the city of Juba as its capital and hub of trade, was populated by transhumance herders, such as the Nuer and Dinka, and village agriculturalists such as the Zande (of anthropological fame) who had once been a part of the Zande tributary state, which encompassed parts of the southern Sudan, Zaire, and the Central African Republic. The southern groups were either pagan animists or had adopted Christianity. Both the Muslims and the Animists had histories of feud and war. The Nuer were on the margin of the ancient Islamic state in the north. After independence, northern and southern Sudan were merged into one country, an action many social scientists consider to have been a grave error (Shillington 1989:385). Unlike the situation in Rwanda and Burundi, the cultural differences between northern and southern Sudan are striking.

The non-Muslim southerners considered rule by the Muslim northerners as no more acceptable than rule by the British. Civil war tore the country apart between 1955 and 1972. In 1969, socialist Jaafar Nimeiri came to power, and in 1972 the southern regions were granted semiautonomy, southern military officers were integrated into the higher ranks of the military, and the fighting ceased, but southern discontent did not disappear. The Nimeiri government sought to rebuild and modernize the war-torn country with aid from numerous international donors, including USAID and the United Nations Development Program (UNDP). However, the National Islamic Front, under the leadership of Dr. Hassan al Turabi, became increasingly influential and began to receive help from radical Iran after 1979.

In 1983, responding to the National Islamic Front, Nimeiri instituted Muslim Shari'a law to replace the penal code and he purged the southern officers from his military. Southerners reacted by renewing armed civil conflict. Colonel John Garang led the southern-based Sudanese People's Liberation Army (SPLA) against the central government. His army was predominantly made up of Dinka and Nuer warriors who replaced their traditional spears with automatic weapons. The region around the southern city of Juba and the city of Wau in central Sudan became rallying points for SPLA forces. The fighting disrupted cattle herding and, combined with drought, drove people into the cities (which are held by the government). Both the rebels and the government have prevented food aid from reaching civilians (Sullivan 1989:112–114).

Nemeiri was overthrown in 1985, and in the election that followed in 1986, Sadiq Al-Mahdi, the great grandson of the Mahdi, the leader of the theocratic state of the Sudan in the 1880s, was elected prime minister. While the new prime minister wished to reduce the role of Shari'a law, Muslim fundamentalists in his regime prevented a return to secular law and attempted to make Shari'a even more extreme (Sullivan 1989:112–114).

In June of 1990, the Revolutionary Command Council for National Salvation, under the leadership of Lieutenant-General Omar al-Beshir, deposed Sadiq-Al-Mahdi in a military coup. The coup was masterminded by Dr. Hassan al-Turabi. The new military junta, headed by the Islamic Front, is racing to become the first regime in Africa to impose Shari'a law on a nation that is almost one-third Christian and Animist.

We examined the traditional Nuer in Box 9.2. By 1983, the Nuer were caught in the complex civil war that tore the Sudan apart, as the northern Sudan attempted to impose Shari'a law on the southern Sudan. But the Nuer were also caught up in the ethnic wars in Ethiopia, and they tried to find refuge there, as well as in the ancient city of Khartoum, where Sharon Hutchinson was able to interview them in refugee camps. Many were no longer rural people, but urban migrants trying to establish a foothold in a rapidly changing world, one that they understood quite well.

Most dramatic, in this society in which cattle defined life, cattle, the repository of wealth in the age of their parents and grandparents, were replaced by guns, the bigger the better. The use of guns entered into the definition of women and bridewealth, as well as the power of families, chiefs, and courts. The new warrior association was a subsection of the SPLA led by John Garang, which often fought other warrior associations of the SPLA, and other Nuer families. The influx of guns from the outside world caused inflation in the cost of cattle and thereby in the bridewealth given for women. The world has been turned upside down, as recalled in the words of a fifty-year-old refugee:

> This is not the first time I have seen terrible destruction. I am old and the first [civil] war [1955–72] was there as well. This one began in 1983. Everything horrible you can imagine was done. Bentiu town was full of gun-toters. The Arabs lacked nothing: whatever they wanted from the people, they seized. They would beat you, steal your cattle, and then [try to] marry your daughter with cattle stolen from you! If you refused, they would just take her! So, we left with nothing because the soldiers took by force. If your son had a wife, they would just fall on her [and rape her] without a word—even in her husband's presence! Living conditions grew worse and worse until 1985. That's when our young men became strong and went to the bush to unite with the SPLA. They were fed up with being beaten! (Hutchinson 1996:18).

Nuer boys with guns.

Nigeria: The Dismal Tunnel

On November 10, 1995, Ken Saro-Wiwa and eight of his followers from the Movement for the Survival of the Ogoni People (an Ibo subgroup), an environmental movement attempting to preserve Nigeria's peoples and lands from the worst excesses of oil exploitation and military rule, were executed by the military government of General Sani Abacha. They were guilty of protesting attacks against the Ogoni people and environmental destruction from the vast oil industry. In 1993, the political situation was promising: An open election appeared to put Moshood Abiola, a wealthy businessman, into the presidency and would have put Nigeria in the center of democratic reform in Africa. Instead he was jailed, and in June of 1996, his wife was shot dead in her car. Many label Nigeria as the most corrupt country in the world; it should be among the most wealthy.

Like many countries in Africa, Nigeria is an historical product of the colonial era. It was created by Lord Frederick Lugard, a British colonial governor–general, and named after the Niger River. Nigeria brought together three huge and highly developed ethnic groups: the Muslim Hausa and Fulani in the north, and the Yoruba in the west (discussed earlier in this chapter). In addition, to the east were the tribal Ibo (also called Igbo), an egalitarian people who were famed for their works in bronze (Harden 1990). In the 1960s, these four ethnic peoples created political parties based on ethnic identity, and then proceeded to slaughter each other in a genocidal civil war. The war ended with the defeat of the Ibo people, whose mineral-rich "country" of Biafra was brought back within the boundaries of the Nigerian state. The end of the war also ended the ethnic conflict, but it did not bring democracy.

General Yakubu Gowon, the winner of the war, was overthrown in a palace coup in 1975. Since then Nigeria has suffered through a series of civilian or military dictatorships. Richard Joseph argues that Nigerians are caught in a "dismal tunnel" syndrome, a consequence of a theory of state called **prebendalism.** According to this theory, state offices are regarded as prebends (stipends, or political entitlements) that can be appropriated by officeholders for themselves to be used to generate material benefits for themselves, their constituents, and their ethnic and kin groups (Joseph 1996). The present Abaja regime has put the theory into practice to an extreme, having created more millionaires than any predecessor government. Politically and economically, Nigeria is in disarray and continues to function only because of its wealth in oil. The international community considers it a rogue state but continues to buy its oil. However, Nigeria is not representative of Africa. African countries, such as South Africa, Tanzania, Zambia, and many others, are experiencing transitions to democracy.

The Democratic Transition South Africa

Autocratic governments have given way to democratically elected ones in South Africa, Zambia, Cape Verde, Sao Tome, Benin, Madagascar, Lesotho, Niger, Mali, the Central African Republic, and, it is hoped, soon in Zaire (renamed Congo). Many would argue that the movements are not indigenous and that the leaders are puppets of the Europeans and Americans, but a close analysis of the recent history of Africa's transitions to democracy and capitalism show otherwise.

Nowhere has the transition to democracy been more unexpected or more sudden than in South Africa. Also, no other country better demonstrates the interconnectedness of politics and markets and the force of globalization in transforming a society. But many doubt the significance of the democratic transitions of the late twentieth century. John Comaroff, Professor and Chair of the Department of Anthropology at the University of Chicago, quotes Gerlta Riviero, the ex-Hungarian ex-wife of the hero of Malcolm Bradbury's *Doctor Criminale,* a futuristic novel:

> "Democracy, the free market," she asks, "do you really think they can save us?. . . Marxism [was] a great idea, democracy just a small idea. It promises hope, and it gives you Kentucky Fried Chicken" (Comaroff 1994:34).

Until 1994, South Africa was rigidly segregated by race according to the laws of apartheid. Apartheid, a formal system of segregation of the races, was adopted by South Africa in 1948, although racism dates back to the origins of the Afrikaner colony in the seventeenth century. Apartheid was a legal code according to which every citizen was typed on the basis of skin color and ancestry:

white, colored, Asian, and Bantu. Government policy regarding political rights, housing, education, and welfare in general were determined by the Apartheid code (Sullivan 1989). Many believe that capitalism underlay apartheid, but South Africa has hardly been capitalist. Like many Latin American countries, it was state capitalist; capitalism was compromised by the state for the rich people. These rich people now realize that their own prosperity depends on promises of prosperity for everyone (Camaroff 1994:35).

Under apartheid, about 17 percent of the population is white and had full rights and access to resources. Every black person was a citizen of a tribal homeland, called a *bantustan,* but had no citizenship rights in the country of South Africa. A bantustan is like a country inside of South Africa, such as Siskei and Transkei. These are not to be confused with the black townships surrounding the industrial cities of South Africa. However, many of the workers in the townships have citizenship in the bantustans, which is one reason the government of South Africa claims that people living in the townships cannot also have South African citizenship. However, about a quarter of the black African population of South Africa lives in or near one of the industrial cities in black townships. Until 1986, blacks had to carry passes on which were stamped their work permits. Attempts to protest the lack of rights led to a series of attacks by the government on black townships, including the Sharpeville massacre of 1960 during which more than sixty persons were killed. The Black Consciousness Movement during the early 1970s was led by Steve Biko, who was arrested after an uprising in the Johannesburg suburb of Soweto and beaten to death in jail (Sullivan 1989). Sanctions were imposed on South Africa by the United States, and by many members of the United Nations. By 1987, the pressure began to take its toll.

On September 6, 1989, white South Africa's reactionary approach to the race issue came to a sudden end with the election of a Nationalist leader from Transvaal Province, Frederik de Klerk. On December 13, within months of taking office, de Klerk broke with tradition by meeting with the leader of the ANC., Nelson Mandela, who had been in jail for twenty-seven years. In a surprising move, de Klerk lifted a thirty-year ban on the ANC on Feburary 2, 1990, and on Feburary 11, he released Mandela from jail. Mandela described de Klerk as "a man of integrity." While Mandela initially supported a Marxist state, soon after his release from jail and before the election, he abandoned Marxism and embraced the free market. But supporters of **Inkatha,** the conservative political movement led by Zulu Chief Mongosutho Buthelezi (Shubane 1992), attempted to block the election, as did white right-wingers, both of whom wanted to have their own "homeland."

On March 28, 1994, Inkatha supporters marched into Johannesburg to protest at the ANC headquarters. ANC and Inkatha gunmen shot at each other and into the crowd, killing several dozen, leading some to fear that the April 27, 1994, election would be derailed. Further meetings were held, and Buthelezi and Zwelethini were given assurance by the ANC to important roles in the new government, no matter what the election results were. The final election was a stunning success for Mandela and the ANC. Camaroff captures the symbolism of the election:

BOX 9.3

Ecological Maladaptation: Famine in Africa

Much world attention has focused on the problems of hunger in Africa. In the 1980s, famine was widespread in twenty-two African nations. The Food and Agricultural Organization (FAO) estimated that 70 percent of all Africans did not have enough to eat (Sullivan 1989:2). While food supplies have improved slightly in some African nations in the 1990s, this has been due largely to international food relief. Africa's population growth continues to outpace growth in agricultural production. In the 1990s, the FAO listed six sub-Saharan African countries with critical food security problems and sixteen with marginal food security. Although drought is frequently cited as the main factor, one cannot ignore the impact of misguided state agricultural policies of former colonial and modern African governments on food security. These policies have favored the transformation of peasant-based food production for local consumption to an industrially based agriculture favoring the production of exports. The consequence has been a steady decrease in food grown for human consumption and an increase in hunger.

During the seventy or more years of domination by Europeans, the economies of the African colonies were organized to benefit the colonists. Cash crops, such as cocoa, coffee, groundnuts (peanuts), cotton, and rubber were substituted for food crops and exported to international markets (Sullivan 1989:3). While some peasant farmers benefited, in many regions large plantations were established and run by foreigners. Migrant labor was encouraged, leading to the decline of food production in the home villages of the laborers. Mining was also developed by European companies using migrant African labor, further reducing the number of farmers in the countryside.

After independence was achieved, many of the plantations and mines continued to function as foreign "enclaves" within Africa or they were nationalized. But even when they were nationalized they maintained their export orientation. Through this process, large masses of land were taken out of the production of food for local consumption and turned towards the production of export commodities.

By the late 1960s, with large plantations specializing in growing export commodities,

1:15 p.m., Monday 2 May, a warm winter day in Cape Town. The Grand Parade, an old square redolent with the icons and echoes, the buildings and barricades, of South African colonial history. Nelson Mandela, formally elected President in Parliament just an hour earlier, is due to speak to an assembled mass—and the nation at large—from the balcony of City Hall. It is the same place where he gave his famous speech, in February 1990, after being released from prison. Perhaps two hundred thousand people clog the square, many of them holding aloft banners; an most local food production depended on small peasant plots of land owned by households. With the introduction of modern farm practices in the late 1950s, small peasant and tribal farmers stayed ahead of the demand for food. But with decolonialization and the movement towards socialist governments, new policies were initiated that had unintended consequences. Socialist governments, trying to get the support of urban workers, held down local food prices by forcing farmers to accept artificially low payments for the food they grew. On the other hand, artificially high prices were placed on export commodities to stimulate export agriculture, which generated foreign currency, needed to pay off foreign debts (Reeves 1989; McCorkle 1989).

The consequence of these two policies has been devastating. Most rural populations are subsistence-oriented and grow enough to feed themselves and their neighbors. They also grow a small surplus to sell at market to buy clothes, seed, fuel, and other amenities that families cannot produce. This small surplus has fed most of the urban populations for decades. By motivating farmers to grow only export commodities and by lowering their motivation to grow food for local consumption, there has been a continuous lowering of agricultural productivity in Africa (Reeves 1989).

At the same time that food production has been dropping, the population of Africa has increased dramatically. The evidence that is available points overwhelmingly in the direction of a serious and deepening agricultural crisis in Africa south of the Sahara. The most visible symptom of this malaise is declining per capita food production. Sub-Saharan Africa is the only region of the world where per capita food production declined over the last two decades. With a population growth rate of 3 percent per year, Africa managed only a 2 percent annual increase in food production during the 1960s, 1970s, and 1980s. By the end of the 1970s, per capita food production was only 80 percent of its 1961 level. Famine has rapidly become the most common symbol of African life at a time when Asia and Latin America managed to achieve per capita increases in food production (Lofchie 1986:161).

In the mid-1980s, food riots in cities and starvation in the countryside, collapsing economic conditions, the disintegration of social services, increasing urban violence, and reluctance on the part of international lending agencies to loan more money caused many Africans to question the totalitarian political economies that had evolved over the last three decades. Many African countries have begun to abandon socialist-type governments and to move in the direction of democratization and privatization (Knight 1992).

airplane, advertising a local radio station and trailing the sign "God Bless President Mandela," flies overhead. Hundreds of brightly colored new South African flags are draped all over City Hall. Alongside is an old Victorian commercial building. It too has flags flying from poles on its front balcony; eight in all, each one about three times the size of the national flag. These, however, are white and plain. They bear the visage of another old man; he is white. In large letters beneath his image are inscribed three words: KENTUCKY FRIED CHICKEN (Camaroff 1994:38).

President Nelson Mandela, a new world leader.

The election of April 26 had to be extended for two more days due to the huge throng of voters and the inexperience of the government in organizing the elections. Thousands of people stood in the sun in long lines and with great patience for the opportunity they never thought they would have: to vote. Black South Africans, who had been waiting for the vote since the birth of modern South Africa eighty-four years ago did not seem to mind the long wait. Violence did not take a holiday; bombs went off in Kwa Zulu Natal killing several dozen. But voters would not be deterred; some even suggested they would be glad to die to have the opportunity to vote.

Not surprisingly, the ANC won 63 percent of the vote, and the National Party came in second. Nelson Mandela took the oath of office on May 10, while Frederik de Klerk was made Second Deputy President. The First Deputy President was Thabo Mbeki, a loyal supporter of President Mandela. Camoroff observes that the election in South Africa in 1994 was more than electoral process, it was a social movement, democracy with a large D: "It is striking how frequently the battle was described as a millennial, sacred gesture; how hardened atheists, alumni of the struggle, spoke of spilling tears in the polling booths" (Comaroff 1994:37).

Mandela faces tremendous challenges in pushing through the political transition. He is a revolutionary used to giving commands, but now he must act democratically. One of his first actions was to invite Chief Buthelezi into his cabinet. The ANC now dominates the new government, and has made many promises to black South Africans to redistribute wealth (Cramer 1994:208–211). At the same time, Mandela dare not decapitalize the economy in meeting his promises. Blacks lack electricity, jobs, and education. Whether they have the patience to achieve these slowly, and not to alienate the whites who dominate the economy, is an open question. An equally important question is whether whites will realize that they have to pull in their belts for a number of years to accept responsibility for imposing a heritage of apartheid on the blacks of South Africa.

The question boils down to the blocked transitions. Population growth among blacks in South Africa is high; poverty is high. Environmental destruction has been high. Prosperity has to be achieved through the close balance between the political and economic transitions: Jobs and education must be created. Yet, the ANC dare not implement the Marxist rhetoric of its revolutionary past if it is to create a democratic South Africa. To the north, there are many Marxist–socialist governments that have collapsed, many of which were based on black one-party states based on rule by a single tribe. From Angola to Mozambique, from Somalia to Sudan, from Liberia to Rwanda and Burundi, the message is to proceed cautiously along the twin transitions to democracy and open markets and not to alienate any one of the various ethnic/minority groups in the new South Africa.

Summary

Africa and its peoples have suffered tragically at the hands of European colonial governments. They are suffering again under the totalitarian regimes of their own leaders. Africans are becoming aware that simple European models of capitalism or Marxist socialism are not going lead them out of ethnic conflict and regional war, nor help them achieve economic stability and sustained development. Awareness is growing that the answers may lie in the introduction of democracy, open market systems, a reduction in the growth of the population, and balancing African economic demands with the demands of the natural environment and human health. But there is also a growing awareness of Africa's ancient heritages, of its many successes, its gifts to a world that once was.

The most critical understanding of all is that competing in the modern world trade system is not a matter of choice, but a need that can only be met with peace and democratic reform. Many countries have begun the hard work, and in a later chapter we will spend time examining some of the most surprising changes to have taken place in Africa, particularly the election of Nelson Mandela in South Africa.

Key Terms

Acephalous	**Late Iron Age**
Amratian	*Mastabas*
Arabs	**Meroe**
Badarian	**Polygyny**
Bedouin	**Prebendalism**
Complementary Opposition	**Settled Farming**
Gerzean	**Transhumance Herding**
Inkatha	

The Middle East: 10
Ethnicity, Oil,
and Conflict

*T*his chapter describes the changing political ecology of the Middle East. The Middle East is a region difficult to define, because the term has been used in so many ways to include many different groups of countries. Today, "Middle East" refers to the region that includes northern Africa and southwestern Asia, including Turkey, once the heart of the great Ottoman Empire, which spread well into Eastern Europe. Going across the face of Africa from west to east, the following countries are currently considered to be a part of the Middle East: Morocco, Algeria, Tunisia, Libya, Egypt, Israel, Lebanon, Turkey, Syria, Jordan, Iraq, Iran, Saudi Arabia, Kuwait, Bahrain, Qatar, the United Arab Emirates, Oman, and Yemen. Today the peoples of this region use the terms *Middle East* and *Middle Eastern* to refer to their region and to themselves (Rassam 1995:xxxv). In the past, a distinction was made by some scholars between North Africa and the Middle East, with the latter including Egypt and all the rest of the non-African countries listed above. French scholars use the term *Near East* to refer to Egypt plus the non-African Arab countries.

In this region Mesopotamia and Egypt were the first cores of civilization; here are found the earliest dates for the first cities of the world. It is one of the cradles of civilization, and it is the region in which Judaism, Christianity, and Islam evolved. These three religions are based on the first mythic religions of the first states, of Ur, Sumer, Babylon, and ancient Persia. Egypt lent its early influence to the creation of these religions as well, and later Greece and Rome added their imprints. The interplay among ecological, political, and economic forces, many of which are from outside of the region, are not easy to sort out, nor can one discuss this region without some mention of the great passions involved.

The region is culturally complex and diverse. In addition to the three religions of Judaism, Christianity, and Islam, it contains four major cultural complexes, three ancient and one recent. The old culture complexes of this region are Arab, Iranian, and Turkish; the recent one Israeli.

The tendency in the popular press is to stress the conflict between the religious differences of Jews in Israel and Palestinian Arabs living on the West Bank, or what is left of Palestine. But there are many other conflicts due to distinctions of Islamic identity whose nature is impossible to understand without knowledge of the culture history of the Middle East. Conflicts are also fueled by differences between radical (socialist) revolutionaries who espouse state control of resources, such as factions in the governments of Libya, Iraq, and Syria, and Sunni fundamentalists who wish a return to nonsocialist, religiously based governments. The Sunnis, in turn, struggle with the Shiite factions, who also wish for theocratic states and who are supported by the Shiite government of Iran. Within Israel, there are factions that want to create a Jewish ethnic state and there are factions that want a modern and secular society.

The Middle East is a passionate place, one in which political ecology, the emotions of ethnic diversity, and the stages of history are so intricately combined as to not be separable. In the following, we combine these into a single story, which will then lead into the current conflicts and controversies of the Middle East.

Political Ecology and Cultural Diversity: An Historical Overview

Because the Middle East spills across North Africa, Southwest Asia, and parts of southern Europe, geography tends to be highly diverse. As with Africa, land tends to lend itself to either settled village agriculture (grain agriculture or tree and vine crops) or pastoral nomadism. Because of the destruction of land over the centuries, in regions where there is no irrigation, the lack of land for agriculture is a serious problem. Most of the forests have been cut down. A few areas, particularly around the Persian Gulf, have vast petroleum reserves, but only a few countries have access to the oil, creating wealth in Saudi Arabia, Iran, Kuwait, Iraq, and the United Arab Emirates, but making other countries poor cousins. But oil did not become important to the region until after 1945. Before then, control over trade in a variety of goods (over many of the caravan routes of antiquity) tended to determine wealth. As discussed in the last chapter, trade was a constant feature of North Africa, tying together ancient city-states and civilizations all the way up into Afghanistan.

Mountainous regions in eastern Turkey, northern Iraq, and southern Iran have considerable rainfall but altitude and cold winters make them ill-suited to extensive agriculture; these regions are used to raise sheep and goats. There is considerable work being done to capture the highland water and pipe it into lowland regions, but this may cause conflict between different states whose water may be taken by others (e.g., Iraq and Syria are angry that Turkey is damming up the waters from the Tigris and Euphrates for its own use).

Transportation has always been a problem because of deserts and mountains, but, as Bernard Lewis, a noted historian of the region, puts it, the sands of the deserts were major transportation links for pastoral nomads; the camel was like a ship adapted to sand. Trade formed the "connectivities" of the Great Silk Road on through the Sinai, up into present-day Lebanon, Syria, through Turkey, Iran, and Afghanistan, then on to China. The goods that were exchanged are familiar: gold, silver, slaves, ivory, dates, palm oil, wine, pottery, spices, and the creations of nomadic pastoralists, woven carpets (Wolf 1982). Most cities that were the cores of imperial states were located at junctures between bodies of water and overland trade routes through dry lands. Colonialism between 1830 and 1950, and ethnic warfare over the last thirty years, seriously disrupted transportation and trade, impoverishing the urban populations who once depended on trade and manufacturing for a livelihood. During the colonial period and to modern times, transaction costs were raised by interethnic violence. In earlier ages, transaction costs were reduced by those states that could control the violence between the members of distinct ethnic groupings.

The history of the Middle East has been one of conflict between local ethnic groups and powerful states that imposed peace and attempted to monopolize trade. Often the ideology of the challenging ethnic groups was a type of populist egalitarianism based on pastoral nomadism. The story behind the conflict is the mythology of Cain and Abel: Cain, the agricultural townsman, slays Abel, the rural pastoral nomad, a conflict presented in all three major religions. This fa-

Figure 10.1 **Physiographic map of Middle East**

Figure 10.2   **Map of trade routes or Great Silk Road**

ble encapsulates the often repeated conflict through the ages, the small sect of true believers versus the state that binds all to a creed of toleration.

An early example is Manicheism, the creed of Mani, a blend of Christian and Zoroastrian beliefs that opposed the pagan Roman state. A second example was the "heresy of Mazdak." Mazdak, who flourished during the early sixth century in Iran, espoused religious communism, which underlies the modern Shiite ideology found in Iran and among Hizbollah radicals (the party of God). Another example is the Maccabees, a volatile Jewish sect that led resistance against the Syrians and then the Romans. The Roman state practiced a polytheistic form of religion centering on Zeus. The Maccabees refused to sacrifice animals to Zeus, but were finally crushed in 70 A.D. after almost two centuries of guerrilla tactics against the state (Gilbert 1990:36–37, Lewis 1995:31).

The dialogue between advocates of populist egalitarianism and imperial authoritarianism has been continuous since ancient times. Peace and trade were never achieved without the smoldering resentment of Christian, Hebraic, or Islamic sects, each of which saw itself as the true follower of an egalitarian, but not democratic, faith. Today, religious and ethnic tensions continue between authoritarian states imposing order and radical movements demanding populist forms of governance.

Much of the conflict and tension through time can be understood in terms of control of trade and competition for resources in a region of relative scarcity. The Middle East has always been a region of diverse ecological zones: deserts, foothills, mountains, plateaus, plains, river systems, and forests. Into these ecosystems distinct ethnic villages with their varied cultures and religions evolved over thousands of years, sometimes drawn into the control of states and sometimes remaining on the tribal margins of great civilizations. The earliest evidence for trade and the imposition of chiefdom social control about 7000 B.C. at the site of Jericho. Jericho, at a crossing point on the Jordan River, was on a major trade route and may have been the first chiefdom or mini-state in ancient Mesopotamia. Its people lived in round, brick houses, had irrigation agriculture, and reared livestock. They also had a spectacular stone wall 1.6 meters thick and over 2 meters high, surrounded by a ditch 8.5 meters wide. On the interior of the wall was a stone tower over 8.5 meters high; both the wall and tower were probably defensive works. Trade during this early period was in salt, bitumen, and sulfur from the Dead Sea area, turquoise from the Sinai region, cowrie shells from the Red Sea, and obsidian and greenstones from Anatolia (Redman 1978:78).

Brian Fagan makes the point that ecological differences would have produced distinct trade goods, and that states would draw otherwise antagonistic peoples into peaceful trade relations (Fagan 1995). Trade routes of camel-herding nomads crisscrossed the region, bringing in the goods the region lacked, such as fine woods and metals, for which grain and local goods were exchanged. Trade moved up and down the Tigris and Euphrates by boat and camel caravan to the highlands of Iran (Persia) and into the deserts of Pharaonic Egypt. As trade expanded, city-states grew, competition for goods intensified, and city-states fought for dominance. Distinct states had their day in the sun and then vanished as trade routes shifted, climates changed, or regimes fell apart. When they were successful, states became powerful and highly stratified. But stratification based on ruthless administrators and increasing demands for tribute from diverse peoples produced poorly integrated, volatile empires. Nonetheless, the archaeology of the region, including a recent discovery of Bronze Age shipwrecks, shows that the Middle East has always been the crossroads of Europe and Asia, lying athwart the water route from the southern Ukraine to the Mediterranean via the Black Sea, the Bosporous, the Sea of Marmora, the Dardanelles, and the Aegean Sea. One-hump camels traversed the deserts of sand as far back as 3000 B.C., while boats and rafts navigated rivers and seas (Goldschmidt 1983:9).

Human Ecology

The human ecology of the Middle East parallels much written in the previous chapter, in part because North Africa is considered part of the Middle East. Southwest Asia, as discussed in Chapter 6, is the birthplace of agriculture and pastoral nomadism. Nature did not endow the Middle East lavishly; there are no grassy plains, and nine-tenths of the forests have been cut down. Water is scarce and precious, and while minerals have been mined since ancient times, they do not amount to much, except for oil. In addition to trade, the two other major adaptations have been irrigation agriculture (the oasis) and pastoral nomadism (which, of course, was an aspect of trade).

Irrigation Agriculture   From the earliest settled towns and villages, irrigation agriculture has been an important facet of human ecology in the Middle East.

The dates for the first irrigation in Southwest Asia are very close to those for Ancient Egypt. Simple family-based irrigation probably dates at least as far back as the site of Çatal Hüyük in ancient Anatolia, dated to 6,000 B.C. (Redman 1978:185). These early systems are still used today and are called *qanats,* and can be used whenever water-table elevations under a hillside are higher than the land surface in an adjacent valley. Vertical wells on the hillside are combined with horizontal wells to channel water fanwise into fields (Bennett 1993:207). Another similar technology is the *kerese,* a shallow well combined with tunnels and manholes. Both of these technologies could easily be worked by a single clan and did not require great organization. These systems can be found in tribal and chiefdom villages throughout the modern Middle East.

Grander but more brittle were **perennial irrigation** works controlled by states, the oldest of which dates back to three to four thousand B.C. These required massive inputs of human labor and a great deal of knowledge of hydraulics. While these systems had the advantage of operating throughout the year, they had the disadvantage of flooding or losing fertility due to **salinization,** the accumulation of salts. The qanats and kerese were ecologically sustainable, but the perennial irrigation systems on which the great civilizations of the Middle East were dependent were not. Unlike Egypt, with its predictable hydraulics, the water systems of Southwest Asia (especially the Tigris and Euphrates) were apt to be influenced by sudden rainfall in the nearby Tauros and Zagros mountain chains, producing floods in the valleys (Spooner 1982). These unpredictable floods may explain the early needs for "water wizards," shamans who could control rainfall, and are a part of the mythology of the three major religions, particularly the story of Noah and the Flood.

Pastoral Nomadism   The last chapter presented a description of camel nomads, which are also found in the desert lowlands of Southwest Asia. In addition

Pastoral tribes in Afghanistan share the road with trucks.

BOX 10.1.

Ecological Maladaptation:
Desertification in the Middle East

Desertification, the process of desert expansion as a result of human degradation of fragile semiarid environments, is a worldwide process. There are few regions that escape the problem, but it is particularly serious in the Middle East. With a high proportion of these marginal lands, the Middle East must support one of the highest populations living in this type of environment (Spooner 1982:15). To make matters worse, the population is growing rapidly, encouraged by Islamic state policies. Iraq, for example, has an annual population growth rate of 3.53 percent, a rate that will double the population every twenty years. Iraq's population in 1975 was 11 million; today it is 19 million.

According to Brian Spooner, a key researcher of Middle East problems, desertification constitutes a serious threat to food production (1982). Desertification occurs at two ends of an adaptive continuum in the Middle East and Africa: (1) irrigation agriculture, and (2) pastoral nomadism. For centuries, these adaptations functioned effectively until economically oriented development efforts upset the delicate ecological balance in this fragile environment. These two forms of adaptation were components of interrelated food production systems. For thousands of years, nomads traded meat and animal products to agriculturalists for cereal grains, fruits, and vegetables.

Although irrigation can make an arid region productive, it can also destroy the soil if the process is mismanaged. Unfortunately, this seems to have been the case throughout the Middle East, according to Spooner. Huge development schemes have been intent on increasing the amount of water introduced into the soil, but have ignored the importance of the soil–water balance. Just as too little water can render a soil unproductive, so can too much water. Spooner estimates that almost half of the irrigated land of the region is no longer productive, due to salinization, waterlogging, and leaching, all attributable to inadequately regulated irrigation. Salinization is the

to camels, various distinct ethnic groups also herded sheep and goats on horseback, muleback, or by foot in the mountains and valleys of Iran and Anatolia. Sheep and goat economies were highly flexible and allowed tribal populations great independence from the states of the region.

Thomas Barfield shows how sheep and goat herders follow the concept of *il rah*, the tribal road: synchronized migrations by different tribes over the lands they exploited (1993:93–104). Fredrick Barth has commented that it is as though the tribes were following gigantic carpets over the landscape. The **khans** or chiefs of these tribes controlled the maps of movements, often living in towns, offering their allegiance to the state. Or, if times were bad, they led tribes in attacks on the same towns and states, demonstrating the two sides of the **trade/raid nexus.** When in his trade mode, the tribesman on horse, mule, or foot connected up accumulation of salts in the soil, which are toxic to most plants, caused by inadequate drainage and rapid evaporation. Poor drainage can also cause waterlogging, a condition in which water-soaked soils become highly acidic and oxygen-deprived. Leaching dissolves the nutrients in the topsoil and carries them down into the lower soil levels, thereby depleting the topsoil.

Irrigation mismanagement is found along the Nile in Egypt, the Tigris and Euphrates in Iraq, the Oxus and smaller rivers of Soviet Central Asia, and the Helmand of Afghanistan (Spooner 1982:41). Engineering skills and hydraulic theory have been transferred to these regions, but institutions needed to manage massive irrigation systems in an environmentally sound manner are lacking.

The second major cause of desertification is the settling of pastoral nomads. The pastoral adaptation evolved in an environment that could not support intensive farming, and functioned effectively for thousands of years. However, encouraged by state-sponsored development schemes, scores of nomadic groups have either abandoned their herding to farm this arid land or have increased the size of their herds in order to be able to export meat, hides, and other animal products. Those who maintain their pastoral lifestyle are restricted to much smaller grazing areas, which results in overgrazing. This has caused long-term deterioration of vegetation and soil erosion. Unfortunately, intensive use of these marginal lands is turning them into true deserts, which can support neither agriculture nor herding economies and is causing starvation among previously well-adapted peoples.

According to Spooner, misguided policies have done very serious damage to formerly productive land, where desertification has affected almost 300 million of 410 million acres in Iran, 135 million out of 161 million acres in Afghanistan, and only a slightly smaller proportion in Pakistan. These vast areas have been so poorly managed that they can no longer be used efficiently for any kind of food production.

Clearly these development policies have failed the people and abused a fragile ecological system. Spooner argues that development specialists should help transhumance herders to more effectively develop the traditional talents and techniques they already have and not to introduce nonadaptive forms of economic behavior. The technology of pastoralists has been generally assumed by development planners to be uncomplicated. The fact is that it is a fairly complex, highly effective, and ecologically sensitive adaptation that should be studied by planners, not dismissed as primitive and inefficient.

with the townsman and formed linkages in the trade routes running east and west across the Middle East. When at war, the links broke down, the tribesman vindicated his honor, but suffered poverty. Whether a herder of camels, goats, or sheep, the tribal nomad could be the raider or trader. The cycle of the peaceful pastoralist versus the warlike nomad is connected with the Cain/Abel analogy offered earlier, and the cycle is also a part of the rise and fall of religious sects and states, which in turn connects to the political economy of the three religions of the Middle East: Judaism, Christianity, and Islam (the People of the Book).

Political Economy and Religion

The histories of ancient empires in the region of the Middle East go back, of course, to Mesopotamia and Egypt, and overlap many cores and peripheries, religions, state ideologies, political movements, and conflicts. There is no simple cakelike "layering of history," with historic levels cutting from Gibraltar to Damascus. Instead, the closest analogy is conglomerate, the geological formation made of a complex mix of gravel, large stones, boulders, and a matrix of cement (time). States, with their religions, spread, encompassed ethnic groups, converted them, encouraged peace, imposed bureaucracies, then gave way to new states and became their peripheries. New state religions rapidly became ancient legacies, and these in turn became incorporated within new states with new conversions. Every belief system in the Middle East has ancient roots, dating back to pre-Islamic empires, and combining nature worship, ancestor worship, and **monotheism** (the belief in one God). The modern peoples of the Middle East are the descendants of ancient empires, and their beliefs correspond to one of three books: the Christian Bible, the Jewish Torah, or the Islamic Quran (Koran). But still today on the peripheries are tribal peoples with beliefs some of which probably go back to Pharaonic Egypt and Ur.

The "pagan" religions that precede and are partly incorporated in Judaism, Christianity, and Islam, were **polytheistic,** worshiping many gods, and they were **cosmic**; that is, they had to do with the natural powers of the cosmos. They grew out of tribal and chiefdom religions, which they resemble; the animal-headed gods of the Egyptians and the great interest in the connections of the gods to the stars is a good example of a polytheistic and cosmic religion. Judaism, Christianity, and Islam differed from pagan religions in that (1) they are **a-cosmic,** they search for principles that go beyond the visible powers of our cosmos, and (2) they are monotheistic, believing in one God. The powers that they seek to explain are not natural, but are **supernatural.** Scholars of religion have suggested that the origin of the three religions may be found in the monotheistic religion created by the Egyptian Pharaoh Amenhotep IV, also known as Akhnaton or Ikhnaton. Akhnaton developed a religious sect that ousted all of the gods of the Egyptian pantheon except one: Ra, symbolized by the Aton or sun disk. The Jewish historian Martin Gilbert finds the link between Judaism and Akhnaton's sun worship in the Hebrew word *Adon,* which means "Lord" (Gilbert 1993:13). In a remarkable paper written in 1948, the anthropologist Leslie White wrote:

> In Egypt in the fourteenth century before the Christian era some remarkable events took place. Monotheism came to the fore and waged war on the old polytheism. All gods were abolished save one, and he was made Lord of all . . . What caused this upheaval that shook Egypt to its foundation and extended its influence even to us today? One of the answers has been: Ikhnaton (White 1949:235).

However, White rejects the idea that one man changed history so profoundly, and instead presents the position that the monotheism of Akhnaton was a long-term trend in Egyptian history that Akhnaton exploited to gain power for himself, his supporters, and his deity, Ra, against the priesthoods of all the other gods. Akhnaton was discredited by his successor Rameses II, who came to the throne in 1292 B.C. Martin Gilbert believes Rameses II was the pharaoh mentioned in the Bible who enslaved the Jews. But it is also thought that Moses and the captured Hebrews already had the concept of monotheism before they were brought to Rameses II's court. However one looks at it, it is the religion that Moses inspires that becomes Judaism, and it is this religion that underlies both Christianity and Islam. The Jewish faith is more than a religion. In addition to faith in a single deity, it embraces a set of ethical and moral principles covering every aspect of life, from hygiene and behavior to justice and equality before God and the law.

From Ur to Babylon: The Roots of Judaism   Many aspects of Hebrew culture bear traces of the influence of Babylonian culture. The story of the Flood, the sacrifice of a loved one (Isaac), and the finding of a child in the bulrushes who is really a prince are all Mesopotamian in origin (Gilbert 1990:3). Abraham, the father of the Jews, is said to have come from Ur of the Babylonians, mentioned in earlier chapters. Abraham was of a Semitic tribe that became powerful in Babylon around 4000 B.C., after migrating from the Syrian desert into the Mesopotamian delta, perhaps as traders. Semites controlled Ur until it was conquered by the Sumerians, a non-Semite population possibly from central Asia. Sumer flowered, and the seeds of monotheism took root, originating as a reaction against polytheistic cosmic religions. Abraham and his followers, about 2000 B.C., wandered westward with their flocks of sheep, perhaps to Canaan (modern Palestine), where Abraham died. His followers continued on and crossed the Sinai into Egypt, where they settled about 1800 B.C. This is about the time that the Hyksos, an Asiatic people, conquered Egypt and dominated it for the next two hundred years. The Hebrews, or Haibiru, appear to have formed a special social class with various functions and roles, of both low and high rank, within and outside the law in the Hyksos-dominated society. As a tribe of sheepherders, they may have been looked down on by the urban Egyptians, and may even have been sacrificed to the Egyptian gods (a Biblical theme).

In about 1550 B.C., the Egyptians revolted against the Hyksos, and it has been suggested that it is at this time that the Hebrews were enslaved by the Egyptians. Egyptian life was strictly ordered by its priestly class, and it is during the apotheosis of Akhnaton that monotheism becomes a challenge to that class, appearing again with Moses a hundred years later. Moses, it has been theorized, was an Egyptian prince who converted to the religion of the "untouchable" Haibiru. Others believe that Moses was a Hebrew who was "adopted" by a royal princess and raised as an aristocrat. Whether the Hebrews were expelled from Egypt or they left of their own accord is a matter of conjecture. The fact is that Moses led his people from Egypt back to the land of his "father," Abraham, in present-day Palestine–Israel. There is much debate whether his followers were many or just a few, thousands or hundreds. Once in the land of Abraham, they linked up with a loose federation of nomadic tribes of Semitic origin, converted these to Judaism, and established the small state of Israel. But it remained a federation of tribes for decades.

It is possibly during this time that the Jews developed their standards of hygiene. Records show that, whenever ethnic groups have been forced to live in adverse conditions, it is the Jewish community that stays healthiest. Israel survived under a series of unstable dynasties until the death of Solomon in 930 B.C., and then divided into two kingdoms, a northern kingdom called Israel and a southern kingdom called Judah, which held on to the temple of Jerusalem. Judah had the advantage of the sacred shrine and it had the better rulers. In 722 B.C., Israel fell to the Assyrians, who were in turn conquered by Babylon in 612 B. C. In 597 B.C., the king of Babylon, Nebuchadnezzar, captured the holy city of Jerusalem, and the kingdom of Judah was destroyed and its people sent into exile. The Hebrews survived their exile by returning to their nomadic existence, called the **diaspora.** They dispersed, carrying their religion with them in the form of three books that contained their laws and ethical codes. The new religion emphasized the importance of life in a region in which many of the cults focused on death: the Roman and pagan religions. The new code stressed that humans had to choose between good or evil. It was during the diaspora that the laws were codified and written down. The Biblical code of the Jews was not the first written law. The code of Hammurabi was much earlier and established the legal bases for such matters as sale, purchase, inheritance, theft, and manslaughter. But Jewish law was the first set of laws based on an understanding of moral principles. The books of the Bible were also important in that they stressed the special relationship between religion and ethnicity: Judaism and the Hebrews. Judaism is the only one of the world religions to have this characteristic. It has been theorized that it was this exclusive connection between religion and ethnicity that led to the more inclusive religion of Christianity, which is not based on ethnic identity. The Jews have remained a separate people who refuse to assimilate to the religious belief of their conquerors. They have also always been among the primary traders and commercial people in any region of the world where they settle.

One of the most remarkable characteristics of the Jews, which goes back to their earliest origins and remains true today, is that the emphasis on reading and interpreting the Old Testament has meant that each man, and most women, are literate. This has meant that the Jews, in their wanderings, were often the chief scribes, the bureaucrats, the traders, the bankers, and have always been commercially successful. In a sense, they traveled as a group through the cradles of civilization, and were always among the most sophisticated, often becoming the major advisors to kings. The Greeks referred to them as "philosophers of race." It was not only the Jewish people that inspired others, but their religion awed the peoples of these ancient civilizations, and the ideas of the Jews underlay the major philosophies of others. Even at the high point of the Middle Ages, when Jews were relegated to the lowliest of occupations, that of moneylenders, they succeeded and became the focus of jealousies that come down to the present age.

This brings us up to about two thousand years ago, when the region that we call the Middle East was divided between two powerful and contentious empires: Rome and Persia. The western half, including the countries of the eastern Mediterranean from Bosnia to southern Egypt, was part of the Roman Empire. The eastern half belonged to Persia, which had incorporated Babylon. The cultures and languages of these two empires were very different from today, and while Egyptian culture was yet distinctive, it had been incorporated into the Roman Empire.

The Persian Empire was composed of the remnants of the earlier empires of Sumer, Akkadia, Assyria, and Babylonia. Cyrus the Mede, the founder of the

Persian empire, overthrew Babylon in 539 B.C. Recognizing some commonality between the religion of the Jews and his own Zoroastrianism, a religion that also stressed the belief in a single god, and distinguished between good and evil, Cyrus released the Jews from captivity and ordered the rebuilding of the Temple at Jerusalem. The Hebraic religion came to be influenced by several Zoroastrian ideas, among them the cosmic struggle between the forces of good and evil, between God and the Devil, judgment after death with reward or damnation, and the coming of a savior (Lewis 1995:28). The Jews rose to prominence under Persian rule, even though they had the option of returning to Israel, which many did.

The Persian Empire fell to Alexander the Great (336–23 B.C.), and the Jews adopted Greek dress and lifestyle. They also became familiar with the writings of Greek philosophers, but they did not adopt the pagan religion of the Greeks. Many Jews migrated west along the north coast of Africa, into Eastern Europe, and as far north as modern Russia. They were usually traders, developing firm reputations as experts in commerce.

The Jews were tolerated under the rule of the heirs of Alexander (Ptolemy I and Ptolemy II) but not under the Seleucids. The Seleucids, descended from Seleucus, one of Alexander's Macedonian generals, conquered Judea in 198 B.C. One of the Seleucid rulers, Antiochos IV, attempted to impose Hellenism, the Roman religion based on the worship of Zeus, on all his subjects, including the Jews. In 167 B.C., an altar to Zeus was erected inside of the Temple at Jerusalem. Underground resistance movements were organized against the Seleucid state. One band, the Maccabees, named after their leader Judas Maccabeus, began to win skirmishes against Seleucid forces, finally marching into Jerusalem in December of 164 B.C. to cleanse and purify the temple. Roman rule expanded into Judea, displacing the Seleucids, and at first allowing the Jews to continue their religious practices. However, like the Seleucids, the Romans came to expect that citizens would adopt the Hellenic religion. But Roman religious persecution was no more acceptable than that of the Seleucids, and the Jews soon developed many distinct anti-Roman **messianic** movements (movements of revival and transformation that emphasize faith in the appearance of a messiah; Lanternari 1963:19). One of these messianic movements became Christianity.

The Birth of Christianity and the Rise of the Byzantine Empire   Bernard Lewis (1995) argues that during this age, in the Middle East and elsewhere, the universal custom was for human groups to draw a firm line between themselves and others, insiders and outsiders. Insiders were defined by kinship and ethnicity, and outsiders were the Other, the barbarians. The Jews and the Greeks introduced a new twist: One could become an "insider" by abandoning the religion and identity of Other, and accepting a Judaic God or a Greek pantheon. The Romans expanded the ideas of the Greeks to create a Roman state that incorporated all of its peoples within the Roman empire, but insisted that the Hellenic state religion be adopted by the newly incorporated "folk." Judaism continued to preach that it was the religion of ethnic Hebrews. Christianity arose as one of several Jewish movements, but one with the "Roman twist" of accepting the state, *but not its religion.* The other Jewish movements ranged from the Pharisees, who fought bitter civil wars against the Romans, to the Essenes, who practiced the monastic worship of a future Messiah, and retreated into the desert.

The actual origins of Christianity are both lost in time and are points of serious theological disagreement. One popular perspective is that the Christian sect was one of several Jewish Messianic movements, but one that preached the acceptance of the Roman state, and a live and let live relationship between Caesar (the state) and God (the supernatural). Here is the fusion of the tolerant Hellenic philosophies of the Romans and Greeks, with their fascination in final cause and ultimate principles and the a-cosmic, monotheistic, supernaturalistic religion of the Jews, and the simple idea that religion should not be based on ethnic identity. Christianity, unlike Judaism, did not deny the Roman state, but argued that Christianity was not of this world. The new religion appealed to the lower classes of the Roman state. At first persecuted, it spread quickly and, within 300 years after the death of Jesus Christ, became the state religion of Rome and the Byzantine Empire.

Constantine I (306–337 A. D.), the first Christian emperor of the Roman Empire, established a second, eastern capital at Constantinople. At the end of the reign of Emperor Theodosius (379–395 A.D.), the Roman Empire was permanently split into a western part ruled from Rome and an eastern part ruled from Constantinople. The eastern part became known as the Byzantine Empire. The western empire was soon destroyed by "barbarian invasions." The eastern empire survived for another thousand years, with Greek as the state language and Christianity as the state religion. The Byzantine empire was controlled by a "command economy," driven and planned by state authorities. This continued a tradition that can be traced back to Egypt: The Byzantine rulers tightly controlled the economy. The state intervened in industry, trade, manufacture, and in agriculture (Lewis 1995). Brian Fagan writes:

> What had begun as an adaptation to the realities of living in an arid, but fertile floodplain environment had developed into a web of economic and political interdependency that was far larger than anything the world had seen before—the remote forerunner of the vast global economic system of today (Fagan 1995:201).

The Birth of Islam and the Rise and Fall of the Ottoman Empire   To the east, a new dynastic line, the Sasanids, came to power in the Persian Empire in 226 A.D., with its core in Iran to the north of the Tigris and Euphrates River. Zoroastrianism was restored and became the state religion; Persian (Farsi) remained the state language. The Persian and Roman empires had fought endless wars with each other based on competition for territory and control over the trade routes between East and West. The Sasanids were able to monopolize trade to the east because the most direct trade route ran through Persia. However, the southern part of the trade route ran through the lands of the Arabs of Yemen, but neither Sasanids, Byzantines, nor Romans showed much interest in dominating these people on the periphery, who were described as warlike and savage. The costs of conquering these remote people would have been too great. Arabia, at 100 A.D., was free of any sort of authority, but was surrounded by small states and was made up of peoples who made their living from the trade routes that crossed through Arabia to Yemen, and then by sea to Africa and India (Lewis 1995:41). This region would become the heart of the first Islamic state.

The Ka'bah, Rock of Islam.

Muhammad, also called The Prophet, in 613 A.D., was an undistinguished native of Mecca, a ritual center and trade city in southern Saudi Arabia, who began to denounce the pagan polytheism of his fellow tribesmen. Mecca was an Arab town that held its power from trade, but it was and is important as the site of the Ka'bah, a cube-shaped structure of unknown antiquity that originally housed the idols (360) of the various gods and goddesses venerated by Arab tribesmen (Goldschmidt 1983:25). Travelers and scholars have long pondered why so many ritual centers of Judaism, Christianity, and Islam all occur in such proximity. One working hypothesis is that pilgrimage centers have always been important in regions where trade is a critical economic feature of state development, and that all of these ancient holy sites are on trade routes where tribal war was common.

Three years before, when Muhammad was forty years old, he had experienced a series of revelations from the angel Gabriel. These were later written and became the Quran, Islam's holy book. Within just two decades, Muhammad united nearly all of Arabia into a new religious and political community. Within twenty years after his death in 632 A.D., the followers of Muhammad had seized the Byzantine empire and overwhelmed the Sasanian state, transforming both into an Islamic state. The speed and magnitude of conquest by a religious leader and his followers was unprecedented. Muhammad's utterances and personal example became the model for the behavior of millions, and a new organizational framework was established in the form of the Islamic state (McNiell 1963:421).

The Islamic religion began with the teachings of Muhammad, who is believed to be the last of the prophets referred to in the Bible. Muslims, as well as Christians and Jews, believe that their traditions date back to Abraham, the first prophet. A basic difference between Christian and Muslim belief is that for Christians Christ was the son of (and an incarnation of) God, whereas for Muslims he was just another prophet like Muhammad. Muslims, however, believe that God revealed the text of the Quran or Koran to Muhammad and it is the

Koran and its teachings that set the Islamic religions apart from Christianity or Judaism (Goldschmidt 1983).

At the heart of Islamic belief are the **five pillars.** These are: (1) the declarations of faith; the term *Islam* itself means submission to the will of God (there is no other god but God); (2) the five daily ritual prayers (recited facing Mecca); (3) almsgiving; (4) fasting (during Ramadan); (5) the pilgrimage to Mecca (to the Ka'bah) at least once in a lifetime. Each of the pillars has its own series of rationalizing and validating stories. The *Quran* is the revealed word of God, through Muhammad, the last of his prophets. The Quran cannot be a direct guide to human conduct; it must be interpreted, and it is the interpretations that produce the many Islams. Two sects emerged after the death of Muhammad in 632 A.D.: the Sunnis and Shi'a. The Sunni sect and the Shi'a sect are similar in most respects but they differ primarily in the Shi'a belief that the Islamic community should be led by an imam (priest) who is a direct descendant of Muhammad through his daughter, Fatima, and her husband, Ali. Sunni leaders are drawn from descendants of Muhammad's father-in-law, Abu Bakr. These disagreements have led to major conflicts. The Shi'a have a major religious celebration commemorating the massacre of Ali's son, Husayn, by Sunni warriors. Today, the Shi'a form the poorer classes of the Middle East except in Iran where they are numerically dominant. The distinctions and animosities between the two sects have played an important role in the rise of conflict. Differences in wealth have been a source of relative deprivation for the Shi'a and are a root cause of many fundamentalist Islamic social movements.

The radical transformation of North Africa and Southwest Asia during and after the death of Muhammad has been partially explained by the benefits the new religion gave to the varying ethnic groups of the region, mostly Arab speakers, through the lowering of transaction costs in long-distance trade. Abner Cohen has argued that "[Islam is a] blueprint of a political-economic organization which has overcome the many basic technical problems of the trade" (1971, quoted in Ensminger 1992:59). Ensminger, an anthropologist, points to the well-researched connection between long-distance trade the world over and conversions to Islam. It was the long-distance traders who did much of the converting, and Islam tended to follow major land and sea trade routes. Of particular importance in trade were spices from the east. Islam offered commercial advantages that reduced transaction costs. Conversion to Islam provided a ready-made way to turn outsiders, with whom one might be in conflict, to insiders who shared a world view on the importance of honoring business contracts and other ethical obligations. True believers had a nonmaterial interest in holding to the terms of a contract. The new converts would be subject to commonly held sanctions for default on agreements. Beyond its religious appeal, Islam enhanced trade relationships by facilitating predictability in exchange and lowering transaction costs. That is, inter- and intra-societal feuding were reduced by a common religion, making trade less expensive. But when the religion was highly successful, bureaucracies and centralized authorities were not far behind, dooming many of the egalitarian ideas of Muhammad and his followers, and setting up the cycles of conflict between established states and true believers. These generalizations do not apply to Christianity, which cannot be connected as directly to trade, but, as we noted in Chapter six, was of particular significance in helping to integrate the states of Western Europe in the Middle Ages.

Conflict between Islamic Sects. The simple message of the Prophet, Muhammad, became the basis for a new religion and the ideology for a series of new empires. The new religion accepted Jesus Christ, but as a prophet, not as the son of God. Muhammad was the last prophet and did not aspire to sacred status. The first statement of doctrine had its beginning at Medina and at the ancient sanctuaries of Mecca and the Ka'aba. This first, **charismatic phase,** can be identified with the personality of Muhammad, and included most of the present-day countries of the Arabian Peninsula (primarily Saudi Arabia, but also modern Yemen, Kuwait, and Oman). The charismatic phase was one of theological simplicity that built on existing traditions of both polytheistic religions and the monotheism of Christians, Jews, and Zoroastrians. Muhammad viewed the other religions as having tendencies toward corruption, stemming from the multiple schools of theological debate and interpretation, and he insisted on a very strong monotheism with but one law, that given to him by the angel Gabriel. An essential quality of Islam was and is the argument that it needs no interpretation, for it is the word of God and should be read directly. However, much like the New Testament of the Christians, the Koran, written a generation after the death of Muhammad, gave rise to different schisms that not only gave their own interpretations to the Koran but questioned the legitimacy of the traditions of other interpreters, laying the groundwork for the continuous conflict of the Islamic world.

The charismatic phase ends with Muhammad's death in 632 A.D., and is followed immediately by the development of several distinct traditions of interpretation, many leading to the development of powerful states that extended outside of the Arabian peninsula. Muhammad had succeeded in bringing the Arab tribes (those who spoke Arabic) together but the union was shaky and threatened to dissolve. Muhammad's core followers chose Abu Bakr, his father-in-law and one of his earliest followers, as their new leader. Bakr became the first *caliph* (derived from *khalifa*, an ambiguous Arab word that combines the meaning of "successor" and 'deputy') or successor, but the legitimacy of his rule was immediately challenged by dissident tribal groups. Abu Bakr fought a series of wars to bring back the dissidents and reunite the confederation of tribes established on the basis of this new faith (Lapidus 1988). A small, but disciplined, core brought back the rebellious tribes until Arabia was once again unified at the death of Abu Bakr (634 A.D.).

There followed a brief period of turmoil and political unrest until the Ummayad dynasty assimilated the previous Sasasnid empire and ruled until 750 A.D. During the rule of the Ummayads, the Islamic faith spread as far as Spain in the west and India in the east. This new empire was ruled primarily by Arab followers of Muhammad who maintained tightly knit garrisons of Islamic believers. The Islamic faith was not imposed on the distinct ethnic groups under Islamic rule under the Ummayads.

Paralleling the expansion of the Islamic empire was the codification of the religion. The Quran was composed of the sayings of the Prophet, usually by length, added to the Old Testament of the Christians and Jews. Memories of the sayings and deeds of the Prophet were studied along with the Quran. These *ha-*

diths (authenticated accounts of Muhammad's sayings and actions), as they were called, were kept alive in oral tradition until the ninth century when they were compiled into an official codified version that is recognized as Muslim scripture along with the Quran. Similarly, from the seventh century on, Muslim judges and scholars began to reform existing tribal laws to conform to the moral and ethical standards of Islam. This became *Shari'a,* the sacred law of Islam, not, strictly speaking, the word of God, but considered to be divinely inspired. Shari'a was interpreted by a body of legal specialists, the **ulema** (men learned in Islamic doctrine, but not priests or judges). Under Ummayad rule, other ethnic groups were controlled by their own laws, codes, and judges (Lapidus 1988). The Sunnis accepted the interpretations of the ulema, but the Shi'ites only accepted the ulema interpretations when led by the imam, the true descendant of Muhammad.

While the Caliphs of the Ummayad Dynasty directed the Arab community, they were not considered sacred by the Shi'a sect, who believed that only the ulema had sacred qualities. The Shi'a believed in an *imam* (sacred leader). According to Shi'a principles, there has been a succession of twelve *imams* in Islamic history. Each, except the twelfth, was deprived of worldly rank and murdered by caliphs. The twelfth was divinely hidden by God and is the "Hidden Imam," who has not been seen since 941 A.D., but who will one day return as "the one guided by God" (Pinault 1992). In the absence of the Hidden Imam, worldly authority devolves on the ulema, who are ranked according to knowledge of the Quran and have true authority, even over the caliph. On the other hand, the dominant Sunni sect accepted the rule of the caliph in combination with the ulema (one way to view the distinction is the Sunnis were willing to cooperate with the state and the ulema as controlled by the caliph, whereas the Shi'ites were not). Early conflict between the two groups has lasted to the present.

In 744 A.D., a split between several factions led to the overthrow of the Ummayads and the rise of a new clan from Mecca, the Abbasids, whose empire was much more centralized and bureaucratized. The Muslim capital was moved to Baghdad, at an intersection of trade routes on the Tigris. The Abbasid Empire was distinct from that of the Ummayad in that the role of government became more important, and the office of the caliph was elevated, sanctified, and removed from public view. Instead of sitting with the ulema in the open, the caliph was housed in a royal palace. The new rulers chose consensus and continuity, rather than the rights of the religious warriors. The caliph was no longer one among equals ruling with consent, but an autocrat ruling a vast bureaucracy. With the move to Baghdad, Iranian warriors displaced Arab warriors and the distinction between Arab and other ethnic groups became less and less important as Islam was made a state religion by the Abbasid leadership. Arab ethnicity and the Islamic religion were no longer one and the same. The Arab monopoly of power had ended, and Iranian Moslems became part of the ruling elite. Stress was placed on Islamic rather than Arab identity. One interpretation of events is that the Abbasids represented the reemergence of the Persian empire, with the resurgence of Persian ethnicity over Arab ethnicity. Others argue that the new dynasty represents a political movement away from domination by an aristocracy of Arabs, but that the new dynasty was not specifically Persian (Goldschmidt 1983:68).

Under the Abbasid Empire, the *ulema* became the legal court of all Islamic followers, and not just the court of the Arab faithful. The ulema sat in the marketplace and expounded sacred law, and applied it, and became the true heirs of the prophet. But the caliph and his court also acquired "sacred" qualities to go with their new powers, a characteristic that was antithetical to early Islamic traditions, and added to the divergence between the Sunni and Shi'a sects.

Disputes between Sunni, Shi'ites, and other religious and secular groups led to the weakening of the Abbasid state, which was seized by Persian (945 A.D.) and then Turkish (1055 A.D.) adventurers (McNiell 1963). Before the year 1000, the breakdown of the Abbasid state was complete. In the eleventh and twelfth centuries, the forces of Christendom advanced in Spain and Sicily, Bedouin Arabs swept through Libya and Tunisia, and, from the Asian steppes, Turkish invaders came who were to create a new capital at Istanbul (Constantinople). In the fifteenth century, the Ottoman Empire of Turkey gained control over what was left of the Muslim Middle East and developed a new imperial order. Power shifted from Baghdad, Egypt, and Medina to Istanbul, and the powers of the state were controlled by a hegemonic bureaucracy, which was highly centralized and was ruled by a sultan. The sultan controlled the extensive Ottoman bureaucracy through the ulema, which in turn became a bureaucracy of religious officials (Hourani 1991).

Jewish and Christian communities suffered persecution at the hands of these Islamic states, but no more so than any other ethnic groups. Judaism and Christianity were viewed as monotheistic religions, like Islam, and unless they challenged the Islamic state, were left to their own devices in their own neighborhoods, towns, and villages.

European Expansion, Ethnic Conflict, and the Fall of the Ottoman Empire. Increasing control of world trade by the European core slowly brought about the decline of the Ottoman Empire. European attempts to stop the Muslim armies date back to the eighth century when the Franks (in what is now France) stopped the Muslim expansion at the battle of Tours in 732 A.D. In the eleventh century, European leaders initiated the **Crusades** to beat back the Muslim armies and to return the Holy Land to Christian rule (McNiell 1963). The first crusades ended in the recapture of Jerusalem and the massacre of both Jewish and Muslim communities. The Christian crusaders were also interested in gaining control over the trade routes of the Middle East. By the sixteenth century, the Portuguese had taken control of port cities in the Middle East and into the Pacific as far as Malaysia, displacing Islamic rulers, and in turn being displaced by the Dutch and English (Wolf 1982).

Europeans slowly gained control over the Mediterranean and the Indian Ocean, and while the Ottoman emperor in earlier times could choose when and where to attack Christian Europe, his armies were at the mercy of Europeans, particularly the stronger forces of the Austrian Hapsburgs and the tsars of Russia. In 1699, the Ottomans signed the Treaty of Karlowitz, ceding Hungary to the Hapsburgs and the Aegean coast to the Venetians. In 1774 they lost the Crimea and allowed Russia to speak on behalf of Orthodox Christians. In 1798, Napoleon Bonaparte occupied Egypt and marched into Palestine. Other Muslim dynasties in India, Iran, and Morocco were also losing against the rising might of Europe in the eighteenth century (Goldschmidt 1983:136).

Imperialist advances by the West tend to overshadow the internal problems of the Islamic states, particularly the Ottoman Empire. During the first thousand years of the struggle between the two world systems, the Muslims had the upper hand. Their state monopolies allowed trade to flow, and manufacturing was successful. The only serious advantage of the West was in military equipment, which was imported by the Ottomans. Though Muslim, the rulers of the Ottoman empire originally allowed Byzantine Christians to continue to be governed by the Patriarch of Constantinople. In the sixteenth century, Jewish and Christian communities had lived in special quarters of the Muslim lands and were exempt from paying local taxes or obeying local laws and regulations. There were many other ethnic groups that were also semiautonomous, such as the Kurds of Turkey, the Christians of Armenia, and the Greeks of the Greek mainland, which was under Ottoman rule. With the defeat of the armies of Sulayman the Magnificent at Vienna in 1529, Ottoman leaders recognized that their highly centralized political economy was not as efficient as the less centralized European states. Reforms were initiated, but it was too late.

In general, the Ottoman Empire allowed a great deal of ethnic autonomy, but when threatened could be extremely repressive. Rebellions in the provinces of the Ottoman Empire were met with extreme violence. It is reported that parts of Greece and Anatolia were depopulated during the period from 1623–1640 when sultan Murad IV used extremely brutal means to impose order. Periods of repression continued well into the nineteenth century, and we read today about how the poet, Lord Byron, joined the revolutionary Greeks in their fight against the Turks (Ottomans). By the nineteenth century, the Ottoman Empire was much reduced in territory, mostly to what is today known as the Middle East, including the modern regions of Palestine, Egypt, Turkey, Iraq, and western Saudi Arabia. It soon lost Egypt to France.

During World War I, the Ottoman Empire joined the Austro-Hungarian Empire and Germany against England, France, and the United States, and was defeated. Great Britain led the Egyptian Expeditionary Force that conquered Palestine and coastal Syria in 1917–1918. The winning European powers split up what was left of the Ottoman Empire, but not before its infamous attack on the Christians of Armenia, who were almost destroyed as a people. The genocide of the Armenian people was the beginning of many of the horror stories of the twentieth century. Turkey also lost a great deal of territory to Russia in the middle of the nineteenth century, particularly in central Asia (Goldschmidt 1983) and, by the turn of the century, was the "sick man of Europe." By 1918, the partitioning of the Ottoman Empire was complete. France gained the countries of Lebanon and Syria, and the British took control of Egypt, Iraq, and Palestine. Eventually, the British and Russians divided Persian Iran, but after World War I, with Russia weakened by its own revolution of 1917, the British took over Persia and imposed their own rulers (Keddie 1981). The British folk hero, Sir Lawrence of Arabia (Colonel T. O. Lawrence), helped Sheikh Faisal, a leader of the Saudi clan, to revolt successfully against the Turks. Later, the Saudis were to feel betrayed as Great Britain and France partitioned the Middle East, and the new country of Saudi Arabia was placed under British control (Lacey 1981).

Prior to World War I, the Ottoman Empire responded to increased European competition by allowing European businessmen free reign, and the local elites lost their control of trade and commerce except where they created alliances with the colonials. These converts to European ways were the **compradors** (commercial elites or upper classes), and their children and grandchildren would become the future elites of the Middle East in the twentieth century.

The Rise of Independent States in the Middle East

During the period before World War II, a series of nationalist movements in the Middle East shook the Western powers. After World War II, beginning in the 1950s, nationalist movements became increasingly more violent. Leaders, such as Gamal Nasser in Egypt, demanded complete independence and the establishment of a single pan-Arab socialist state that would unify the entire Middle East, as it had been unified by the Ottoman Empire. But Egypt, along with Saudi Arabia, was alone among the new states in having a strong sense of ethnic identity: both were Arab and Sunni. Such was not the case with most of the other newly created states that were riven by inner rivalries and hatreds (Lewis 1995:359).

In the period directly before and after World War II, the nation–states of the Middle East were ruled by royal houses that traced descent to Muhammad, but many had become corrupt in the eyes of the young members of the military. General Nasser would overthrow King Faruk in 1952, and his action would become the model for many other military leaders in the newly formed countries of the Middle East.

Nasser and other leaders of the Middle East failed to achieve their pan-Arab dream, but by the 1960s the British and French were pushed out of North Africa and Southwest Asia. Iran, however, continued to be dominated by the British, French, and the United States. In the 1960s, the United States began to play an increasingly greater role in the Middle East as the other powers retreated and as the influence of the Soviet Union grew (Lacey 1981).

One transformative movement became dominant in almost all countries of the Middle East: the Bath'ist Party. Bath'ist philosophy, first announced as a socialist movement in Syria, called for land reform, nationalization of basic industries, complete unification of the Arab world, and militant resistance to Israel and imperialism. The anti-Jewish, anti-imperialist philosophy appealed to many Arabs dismayed by the newly created state of Israel in 1948. A few scholars, such as Samir al-Khalil, have argued that Ba'thism was based on an amalgam of Nazi state socialism and Marxism (1989).

One-party bureaucratic states based on socialism emerged in all of the countries of the Middle East with the exception of the richest oil producers: Iran, Saudi Arabia, Kuwait, and the United Arab Emirates. These were ruled by more traditional kings and their families (who had been put into power by the British). By 1979, two types of political systems dominated the Middle East: (1) secular socialist states, provisionally tied to the Islamic ulema, but with a secular public orientation, and (2) royal-ulema traditional kingdoms largely tied to Islamic ulema and ruled by shaykhs (often written *sheiks* in English). Both types of countries

At the foot of the pyramids, a man's ancient labors go on.

were Islamic, but the socialist secular states tried to reduce the power of the Islamic religion, while the royal kingdoms ruled through the Islamic ulema. Both systems depended on oil exports. Both redistributed wealth by selling oil and then giving the proceeds to the general populace through state bureaucracies in the form of subsidies and services. The old comprador class continued to dominate the new economic systems because of their knowledge of commerce. The only exception was Israel, a democracy that sided with the United States, and that became the only predictable ally in the region. The Soviet Union became an extremely influential ally to the new socialist societies, and an uneasy alliance developed between the United States, Israel, and the old oil kingdoms of Saudi Arabia, Kuwait, and the Arab Emirates against the Soviets and their allies.

In 1979, a Shi'ite revolution in Iran established a third type of authoritarian society, one based on a combination of a fundamentalist interpretation of Islamic shari'a law and the redistribution of oil wealth. Shari'a was interpreted by the ulema and headed by its highest authority, the Ayatollah Khomeini; a theocracy had been born. The new society was supposed to be based on the model of Islamic societies of a thousand years before, and its radical leaders began to use Iran's oil wealth to subvert neighboring socialist states and shaykhdoms by financing Shi'ite fundamentalist movements in Iraq, Saudi Arabia, Egypt, Algeria, Syria, and Jordan. Both socialists and royal houses were considered corrupt by the new Shi'ite elites of Iran.

These three types of state systems, secular socialist (Libya, Syria, Iraq, Yemen), theocratic (Iran), and royal-ulema (Saudi Arabia, Arab Emirates, Kuwait, Oman) are, for the most part, one-party states. Two exceptions are Egypt and Turkey, which are trying hard to borrow the European model of *pluralistic democracy*. Turkey is closest to the European model, having rejected traditional models under the leadership of Kemal Ataturk in the period after 1917, yet it is in deep trouble today. But all societies of the Middle East, with the sole exception of Israel, have large one-party governments. Corruption and inefficiency is common and state control of the economy has led to economies that are unable to compete outside the borders of their own countries. High standards of living are only possible in those countries where the population densities are low and the rates of return from oil revenues are high (Saudi Arabia, Kuwait, Arab Emirates, Oman). It has become common for the secular socialist states, such as Iraq and Syria, to spend fortunes on military armament and to blame royal theocratic states for being stingy in giving them funds for the welfare of the poor. It is not difficult to understand that the secular socialist states tend to repress the political demands of their own peoples, squandering billions on their military and alienating the poor, who are drawn to their Islamic religions in protest. The Nasser-inspired idea of a pan-Arab socialist state no longer has the strength it did thirty years ago, in part because of the misuse of financial resources in squabbles between the leaders of those countries that would have formed the United Arab Republic.

The Oil Trade Countries: Conflict and Community

The topic of oil wealth must be added to those of trade, ethnic and religious conflict, and imperialism. Sixty percent of the world's known oil reserves are found in the Middle East, and oil has revolutionized the twentieth century and made the Middle East central to all energy policies. While the globalization of the world economy due to computers and instant communcation has created new forms of power and wealth not imagined two decades ago, the world still runs on oil.

According to Daniel Yergin, three great themes underlie the story of oil. The first is the rise and development of capitalism and modern business. Oil is still the biggest and most pervasive business, and Standard Oil of the United States was among the largest of all multinational corporations in the middle of the twentieth century. Oil deals underly much of the history of twentieth-century business transactions (Yergin 1991).

The second theme is global politics and power. World Wars I and II were fought to determine who controlled the access to oil. The strategic importance of oil did not begin with the automobile, but with the oil-powered battleship. Winston Churchill, who was the first Lord of the Admirality in the period just before World War I, realized that to beat the German navy, the British had to raze its old coal-fired battleships and build new ones to run on oil. He realized that only oil could produce the great efficiency and speed needed in modern naval war, and Great Britain planned to be the master of the seas.

A third theme is the age of "hydrocarbon man," the transformation of society due to the access to fossil fuels. We are so dependent on oil we rarely stop to think about it, but it is the energy from oil that runs everything from hospitals to sports cars. We are not apt to give up our dependence on oil until a better alternative is available. Just how important oil is can be highlighted by looking back at the 1970s. An oil crisis was created in 1973–1981 when the Organization of Petroleum Producing Countries (OPEC), partly made up of Arab oil states, used an oil embargo to protest against the support by the United States for Israel in a 1973 conflict against several Arab states. By 1980, the price of oil had risen from $2.53 to $41.00 a barrel, fueling a period of worldwide inflation.

A decade later, a coalition of the United States, Russia, Syria, Egypt, Great Britain, and France would fight the Persian Gulf War of 1991 against the dictator of Iraq. The war was fought, in part, due to a fear that Saddam Hussein might dominate Kuwait and Saudi Arabia, allowing him to gain control of over 20 percent of all world oil supplies. Saddam's invasion of Kuwait on August 8, 1990, led to an American declaration of war on January 12, 1991. Within a month the war would be over, with thousands of Iraqi casualties to one hundred American dead.

The strategy Saddam Hussein used, gaining stature in the eyes of other Arabs by facing up to the invading Americans and their allies and causing as much damage to them as possible, was short-circuited by an American land invasion that lasted only a hundred hours and resulted in fewer than a hundred American dead. Saddam Hussein's efforts failed to produce anything other than agony for his own people. The air attacks by United Nations forces destroyed Iraq's economic infrastructure and killed thousands of innocent victims. Hussein blamed the United States and its allies. Then, in the months that followed, he systematically repressed the Kurds in northeast Iraq and Shi'ite minorities in the southern marshes (called Marsh Arabs), who thought they could overthrow him.

However, the Persian Gulf War changed the dynamics of power politics in the Middle East. The new alliances with the United States by several old enemies of Israel, especially Russia and Syria, made it possible to work out a peace treaty between Israel and Palestinian Arabs. One interpretation of events after the Persian Gulf War would be that the generation of prosperity in the Middle East is dependent on an end to conflict between ethnic and religious groups, particularly between Israel and the Palestinian people. Conflict destroys the possibility of trade and trade relationships and produces poverty even among the most oil rich people in the world.

Terrorism and Regional Conflict between Palestinian Arabs and Israel

As control of Palestine shifted from Turkey, to Egypt, back to Turkey again, and then to Great Britain after World War I, the lot of the Palestinian peasants or *fellaheen* declined, producing a series of revolts, the first of which occurred as early as 1834 against Egypt. Originally living in villages controlled by patrilineal collectives that redistributed land to member families, Palestinians were displaced by wealthy Arab families, and after World War I, by Jewish communities (Kimmerling and Migdal 1994:16–17). Kimmerling and Migdal argue that of particular importance was the force of the European market economy which put land in the hands of private landowners, both Arabs and Jews, and took it out of the ownership of the fellaheen. But it is in the period after World War I that the lot of the Palestinians became particularly onerous. Peasants sank deeper and deeper into debt to moneylenders, who increasingly confiscated the land which had been used as collateral (Kimmerling and Migdal 1994:18).

Jewish communities lived in Palestine during Ottoman rule, and were tolerated by the ruling Turks. Many of these communities, called the Yishuv, were supported by wealthy Jewish philanthropists. Tension between local Palestinians and Jews only became significant after World War I. Many Jews migrated out of the newly emerging Soviet Union due to anti-Semitic pogroms. Many also migrated from Romania, Bulgaria, and other East European countries where they lived in extreme poverty, attracted by the socialist ideology of early **Zionism** (Zionism was the movement to create a "national home" for the Jews). One of the most important innovations was the *kibbutz*, a communal form of land tenure that was very successful in turning the desert into a garden.

The rise of anti-Semitism between World War I and World War II led to support for immigration by Jews into Palestine. However, Arab populations had grown as the economy of the region improved, and they had not only become accustomed to a degree of self-rule, but believed Palestine to be their own. During World War I, the British had promised the Emir of Mecca that he would be the monarch of an independent Arab state if he would lead a revolt against Ottoman rule, which he did. Palestine was placed into Arab hands, and Jewish migration was supposed to be restricted, but it was not. In the period just before and during World War II, Nazis financed anti-Semitic Arab movements in Palestine. The ambiguous tenure of the Jewish people, the growing size of Jewish communities, anti-Semitism, and the promises to the Palestinian Arabs led to conflict.

After World War II, the United Nations voted to establish a state of Israel, but the plan was unworkable because one-fourth of the Jewish communities were outside of the lands set aside for the new state. This led to a civil war between Jews and Arabs, culminating in the establishment of the state of Israel in 1948. Approximately a million Palestinians fled to the surrounding states, and a state of conflict ensued between these two peoples despite the 1979 Sadat–Begin peace treaty between Egypt and Israel. A million were left behind to live in what was left of Palestine: the West Bank, administered by Jordan.

The Palestinian Movement   In 1967, volunteers from the West Bank combined with the armies of Egypt, Iraq, Syria, and Jordan to attack Israel. The Arab armies were defeated by a well-organized Israeli Army. This is called the **1967 Six Day War.** As a result many of the non-Jewish Arabs who had been living within the state of Israel were forced into refugee camps on the West Bank, which was taken over by Israel. The image of the Palestinian Arab became that of a displaced person, a downtrodden refugee. About a third of the Palestinian Arabs lived in dismal refugee camps operated by the United Nations. Within a decade, great improvements were made in the lives of the refugees, but not of those left behind on the West Bank, the remaining lands of Palestine. The young refugees quickly made the transition from illiterate rural to literate urban dwellers overnight. Generally, more Palestinian Arab refugees enrolled in higher education than other Arab groups (between 80 and 90 percent compared to 53 percent in the Arab world as a whole (Peretz 1977:32).

Egypt, Jordan, Syria, and Iraq competed in their use of the Palestinians for their own purposes. Each country had its own Palestinian "leaders" that it backed. But these states could not cooperate, until the crisis leading to the June 1967 war built to fever pitch. The Arabs, imagining a smashing success against Israel, were willing to cooperate with each other. Countries that had little interest in the Palestinian problem, such as Morocco, Tunisia, Algeria, Sudan, and the Persian Gulf states, became more involved (Peretz 1977:42–43). Israel's defeat of Egypt, Iraq, Syria, and Jordan in the Six Day War had a traumatic impact on the Arabs of Palestine and on the unity of the Arab states. The Palestinian Arabs were no longer able to believe in the leadership of the pan-Arab cause. Four hundred thousand Palestinians were displaced from their homes, many for the second time. Most of the refugees fled from the West Bank to Jordan. The West Bank was conquered by Israel, and Israelis began settling the region in 1968. Tens of thousands of Palestinian Arab refugees began life over again in tents. Nearly all had the common objectives of asserting Palestinian identity and avenging years of Arab defeat by eliminating Israel and Zionism. While Arab leaders continued to define pan-Arab socialism as their objective, Palestinians created the Palestinian Liberation Organization (PLO) under the leadership of Yasser Arafat, with both right-wing and left-wing factions, to destroy Israel and liberate Palestine.

Created in 1968, the PLO became the formal political organization working for the Palestinian cause. Behind it were several organizations that used international terror: Fatah, al-Sa'iqa "Thunderbolt," Palestinian commandos organized by Syria, and the PFLP, led by George Habash. Fatah was the largest organization that carried out terrorist raids within Israeli occupied territories, while the PLO attempted to negotiate with the international community. Other commando groups engaged in sabotage operations against civilian installations within Israel and abroad. Both Fatah and the other groups drew strength from the deep misery of the Palestinian people and were financed by the oil states of the Middle East. The period of the 1960s catapulted Fatah and Arafat from obscurity to an overall leadership of the Palestinian people (Kimmerling and Migdal 1994:214). Over the decade, a new ideology of Palestinian emergence as a people became dominant.

Attack on Munich Olympics: The terrible logic of terrorism.

In the early 1990s, Arafat and the PLO emerged as the spokesperson and the key organization representing the Palestinian peoples. However, within the local Palestinian community, splits emerged between Fatah, supporting Arafat and the Palestinian Authority (the former PLO), and other more radical and militant organizations, such as Hamas (all mostly Sunni groups) and the even more radical Hizbollah, the Shi'ite Party of God. The PLO continued to gain power and their battle against Israel intensified until the United States, in 1991, directly after the Persian Gulf War, decided to become actively involved in brokering a peace agreement. After three years and delicate negotiations that were almost derailed a number of times, an agreement was signed. On May 5, 1994, delegates from Palestine and Israel signed the documents forging a peace treaty between the two sides. The agreement gives Palestinians in the Gaza Strip and West Bank town of Jericho limited self-rule. The autonomy granted to Gaza and Jericho are due to be extended to the entire West Bank. Residents of the autonomous area will carry their own passports, and Israeli soldiers are being replaced with Palestinian policemen, mostly former Fatah fighters of the PLO.

Figure 10.3   **Map of Israel and West Bank**

There are many complex issues to be ironed out, such as the physical size of the security strips around the settlements, into which Palestinians would not be allowed to go, and the extent to which Palestinians will have the right to navigate the Mediterranean waters off the Gaza coast. These and other details will take considerable time and effort to reconcile, and a true Palestinian state will not come into existence according to the treaty for about five years. The pact fails to address many of the most difficult issues, including the final status of borders, refugees, Israeli settlements on the West Bank, or sovereignty over the Palestinian territories occupied by Israel in 1967. But the peace process itself appears well locked into place.

The most critical problems are maintaining continuity to the economic and political transitions, particularly in the Gaza Strip. The Gaza Strip is a roughly rectangular coastal area on the eastern Mediterranean, approximately 28 miles long and 5 miles wide with a population of 830,000 people. Over half of these still live in refugee camps left over from the 1948 and 1967 wars.

Descriptions of the West Bank are little better. The population of the West Bank is 1.6 million, and projections for the year 2010 put the population at 2.3 million, making it, with the Gaza Strip, one of the fastest growing areas of the world (Muslih 1994:73). How does such a poor and highly populated region go through the economic transition successfully?

Then there is the political transition. For the last twenty years there has been one formal center of power: the Israeli military administration, which is made up of military districts run by military governors. Replacing the Israeli military is the PLO, once terrorist organization, once revolutionary movement. Chairman Yasir Arafat must be able to abandon the style of revolutionary leader and become a political leader who can help his people achieve the transition to democracy. Can he do it? This is the thorniest question, for the intifada has given Palestinian Arabs a sense of democracy lacking in the other countries of the Middle East, and many, including Hamas, are in no mood to be told what to do by another dictator. Yasir Arafat is not used to democratic forms of political organization. As a revolutionary, he expects total loyalty out of his followers. He is not a born democrat, and many Palestinian Arabs are highly critical of his authoritarian ways.

Israeli Identity: Ethnic or Civic? We have examined the origins of Judaism. In the twentieth century, the Jews of Israel wanted to create both an ethnic identity for themselves and a civic definition of a secular state. Joel S. Migdal, professor of international studies at the University of Washington, and co-author (with Kimmerling) of *The Palestinians: The Making of a People* (1994), writes that Israel is a society in flux, trying, like its neighbors, to choose between an ethnic or civic definition of the nation state. He outlines Clifford Geertz's early recognition of the split between these two directions, the first recognizing a "primordial" need for identity, and the second recognizing the need for economic progress, political order, and social justice. These two facets of society pull political groups in different directions, and represent modern Israel. The ethnic factor seeks to collapse the nation–state and ethnic group into one, denying other groups certain

. . . but life goes on, a street scene in Tel Aviv, Israel

rights, while the civic factor does the opposite, arguing for membership and full rights to "all who take on the duties of citizenship" (Migdal 1996:183).

Palestine was a creation of the British Empire, originally intended as a multiethnic state and a homeland for the Jews, which became an historical contradiction. Zionism attempted to open the door to the immigration of Jews, who came from a wide variety of distinct ethnic groupings, and were to receive equal representation at Knesset Israel, the Jewish parliament established in 1926. The question of creating a Jewish–Arab Palestinian society was elusive, and tabled during the 1920s and 1930s. The British intent was the creation of a civil society, but the 1948 War led to the partition of Palestine between three states: Israel, Jordan, and Egypt (which claimed the Gaza Strip). A Jewish state was formed in Israel, with Arabs having only secondary rights. Zionist leaders in the leading Labor party supported secular socialist values, and Israeli state institutions reflected a civic tendency, although there were many contradictions (Migdal 1996:193).

The 1967 Six Day War led to an expansion of the territory of Israel over the West Bank and Gaza, and also to a replacement of the civic concept with the claim of a common Jewish ancestry defending the Israeli state: "Society was not a civic construction of mortals but derived from the rights (especially, territorial rights) of the pre-existing nation, the Jews" (Migdal 1996:195). The civic oriented Labor party lost control of the state in 1977 to Likud, also a Zionist party but representing many of the more religious Jewish communities, supporting the idea that Israel should be a Jewish state (Migdal 1996:195). From 1977 to the present, these two parties have continued to support various forms of the civic–ethnic controversy.

One of the most important recent changes is Israel's recognition of the Palestinian Authority, which forms the beginnings of a new Palestinian state. But the statelet is split between competing factions, as described in the following case study.

BOX 10.2

Case Study: Traditional Marriage and the Dilemma of Feminism in Gaza

The Gaza Strip, one of the segmented territories of the Palestinian Authority, is home to hundreds of thousands of Palestinian Arabs.

The Gaza Strip is an area of extreme, almost impenetrable demographic, economic, social, political, and legal complexity. It has one of the highest population densities in the world; over two-thirds of the people who live there are refugees and nearly half are younger than 14. The economy is weak and underdeveloped . . . The visitor to Gaza is first struck by the dramatic juxtaposition of a serene Mediterranean coastline with teeming poverty and squalor (Roy 1994:67).

Gaza contains many radical groups, such as Hamas and Hizbollah, that have been responsible for car bombings in Israel and attacks on the Palestinian Authority, but it is also a close-knit society, one in which there is a considerable survival of Arab traditions, particularly in respect to the status of women. Despite the secular political views of the majority of men and women, traditional male control of women and expectations for *bint 'amm* marriages continue and are supported by Islamic militants. Bint 'amm is the marriage of a man to his father's brother's daughter, technically known as a patrilateral parallel cousin marriage. Such marriages are usually associated with a bridewealth payment from the groom's family to that of the bride (from the father to the father's brother, which may amount to several thousand dollars). Research by Dale Eickelman (1981) shows that the actual category of father's

brother's daughter is not as narrow as the term implies, because a father's male cousins can substitute for brothers, thus expanding the category of bint 'amm marriage to their daughters as well. But regardless of actual genealogical relationships, arranged marriage with close family members is an expectation, especially among the upper classes in the Middle East. The young adults, however, often have their own ideas.

The expectations of radical leaders (members of Hamas and Hizbollah), who are committed to the traditions of Islamic culture, are often contradicted by how young people interpret the idea of "radical," which often means pro-Western, secular, and socialist. The contradictions between traditional Islamic society and feminist ideas from the West are often left ambiguously open. The young often do what they want, as described by Paul Cossali and Clive Robson in their ethnographic report on Gaza society (1986). To show the contradictions in Gaza society, they describe the experiences of several young Arab women.

Maha, aged 19, is not a radical supporter of any movement. She represents the many poor young women whose Western values clash with those of their parents and Islamic militants. Maha has one sister and ten brothers, and she grew up in a traditional Muslim family. In her description of her attempts to become an independent and modern "Western" woman, she has to fight her own mother, who accepted and practiced the subordination of women, as well as her brothers, who were little help:

This attitude encouraged my brothers to try and prove their manhood by controlling me. It was ridiculous sometimes. When my little brother Ahmed was 6 years old he used to demand that I make him tea. If I asked him why I should do that he used to say "because I'm a boy and you're a girl." He doesn't even like tea! (Cossali & Robson 1986:29).

Maha's mother believed that a woman's place is in the home, especially in the kitchen. She believed that nice girls should not go out. So Maha responded by saying, "I'm not a nice polite girl. I'm rude. Now will you let me go?" When Maha tried to get her brothers to clean up after themselves, the mother would get angry and denounce Maha saying, "I'm here to do these things."

Maha complained that there are only a few women in Gaza who studied medicine or engineering, which are men's fields. Men think a woman's role should be to bear and bring up children, and most women think the same. According to Maha, even in radical Gaza society, nearly all marriages are arranged.

What happens is that women who have sons who want to get married visit families where they know there are young single women. The girls come and offer them something to drink, and all the time they're being sized up and asked questions to see if they're suitable . . . One day, shortly after I'd finished school, my mother came to my room and said, "Maha, get dressed. You must meet some women." (Cossali & Robson 1986:29).

But Maha refused bint 'amm marriage, telling her mother she would never marry anyone from her own family. Maha's negative attitude towards accepting the kitchen as her place followed her decision not to marry a kinsman. She felt that it was important that women work outside of the home because it was a way of being independent of the family. She discovered that it is very difficult to be independent.

There is no social life for women—just visiting friends. Even that's difficult. I have to tell my mother where I'm going and who I'm going to see and exactly when I'll be back. If I'm not back on time, then I'll be forbidden to go out for a week. There are no clubs for women . . . (Cossali & Robson 1986:29).

While Maha is not interested in politics, many women are, such as Nabila, a radical activist supporting a secular state. Nabila makes an even more explicit statement of feminist views.

As a women's activist, I see my role as fighting for social change without which the Palestinian revolution can never achieve victory. Women's role in the revolution is as important as men's, and we must have freedom to move and express ourselves on an equal basis with men. This is difficult in Gaza because our society is much more religious and conservative and so we rely heavily on direction and lead from the outside. We take strength from the successes of Palestinian women in Lebanon where the revolution has brought about dramatic change. My aim is to strengthen women's confidence in their own ability to shape their lives and the future (Cossali & Robson 1986:34).

These women represent the secular direction of Gaza society, found throughout the Middle East, particularly among the socialist and radical young. But their point of view is not shared by Muslim fundamentalists, such as Majda, a second-year student at the Islamic University of Gaza.

I owe a lot of thanks to the Islamic University here in Gaza for making religious books available to me so that I could read about Islam. I read about the proper Islamic dress, for example, and then I looked at my own clothes. I felt that I wasn't fully covered. . . . But we are surrounded by unbelievers. Some women are just ignorant and it's our job as believers to show these women the way, step by step. Some have had ample opportunity to know Islam, Sharia Law and Islamic morals and dress. Yet they still stubbornly follow secularism . . . (Cossali & Robson 1986:40).

Cossali and Robson go on to document the severity of the split between secular and Islamic points of view. Their book, *Stateless in Gaza,* was written well before the emergence of the new Palestinian Authority, Hamas, and Hizbollah, but it illustrates well the dilemmas of Gaza society, the support both for secular and Islamic points of view. This split is found in every country of the Middle East. Thus, one should be cautious in generalizing about women's roles, women's issues, and about broader trends in Middle Eastern societies.

Modernization and Islamic Fundamentalism

Paul Magnarella, an anthropologist at the University of Florida, has documented the contradictions between modernization and Islamic religious movements in Turkey (1993). Turkey's dilemma is found throughout the Middle East, from Algeria and Morocco to Iraq, Egypt, and Syria. It is also found in Jordan, in the newly emerging state of Palestine, and in the kingdoms of Saudi Arabia and Kuwait. The dilemma is near universal in the Islamic world. An example is Algeria. In the 1950s and 1960s, Algerians fought a war against colonial France. They were successfully led by the National Liberation Front, a Marxist revolutionary party. After the war, the NLF organized Algeria as a secular socialist country. In 1989, the Algerian government legalized the Islamic Salvation Front and offered free elections, which took place in December of 1991. The ISF won the first round of the general election. The government, headed by the NLF, canceled the second round, outlawed the ISF, and jailed many of its leaders. The government and its NLF leaders fear an Islamic dominated government, and many ISF leaders in fact call for a totalitarian Iran-style government. Others argue against such a government. The government faces a dilemma because it cannot continue its opposition to democracy, yet leaders of the ISF deny democracy. Should the government allow the ISF to win elections with the hope that the new government will face the same pressures for democracy or should it oppose the ISF, thus opposing democracy? President Mubarik of Egypt faces identical problems.

Magnarella looks at what he calls "humankind's susceptibility to indoctrination by ideologies that present faith worlds and faith acts that cannot be empirically validated" (Magnarella 1993:5). He adopts the psychological theory of political scientist Ted Robert Gurr, a student of civil violence, to explain conflict in the Middle East, particularly in Turkey. He argues that interpretive and informational conditions lead to human discontent, and that a society's inability to correct such "infrastructural deficiencies" as rapid population growth, marked differences in the distribution of wealth, an insecure economic situation, demand for improved educational opportunities, and an inefficient and corrupt government will lead to support for ideologies condemning these conditions. The conditions and the ideologies lead to violent action (Magnarella 1993:119).

Turkey: Resisting the Tide of Islam

Magnarella argues that modernization and secularization eventually produced deprivation, particularly in rural regions of modern Turkey. Mustafa Kemal Ataturk introduced a radical secular state to Turkey a full thirty years before it was attempted elsewhere in the Islamic world. In the 1920s, he eliminated Islamic teaching from the public schools and outlawed the Muslim brotherhoods. He nationalized Islamic foundations, eliminated the formal power of the ulema, and outlawed traditional Muslim headwear for men. He replaced Arab script with the Roman alphabet, and replaced the Islamic calendar with the European.

In the 1930s, Ataturk moved even further, prohibiting religious education and converting many mosques to secular use, many of which were turned into museums. Ataturk's control of the government and the military allowed him to impose secularism on Muslim Turkish society. However, his goals of a secular society were achieved primarily among the urban elite, but not in the countryside where Islamic values were preserved. Devout Muslims attacked secularism. For them Islam was the spiritual necessity of Turkish life. They valued Islam as a counter to atheistic leftist movements and ideologies that gained ground after World War II (Magnarella 1993:89).

Magnarella describes how Ataturk centralized the economy through state corporatism (a political economy very similar to that in Latin America during the same time period). In its pure form, state corporatism is a system in which the ruling elite has organized the society's interest groups into a limited number of singular, compulsory, noncompetitive, hierarchically ordered, and economically differentiated units, each with a monopoly of power in its own area of decision-making.

Ataturk's desire was to create a state that was free of foreign capitalism, and controlled by his associates. He died in 1938, on the eve of World War II. After the war, American and Western European pressure forced the Turkish government to open its political system to opposition parties, but the state maintained control of the economy. Since 1985, Turkey has attempted to democratize itself. Under one recent leader, the government tried to abandon state corporatism in favor of capitalist democracy, but it faces many dilemmas, not the least of which is civil violence and political terrorism. Deprivation is particularly visible in the shanty towns that surround almost every Middle Eastern city. In the 1970s, over half the people of Ankara, Istanbul, and Izmir, the largest cities in Turkey, were shanty town residents.

> The all-pervading bureaucracy has not been able to enforce a minimum of town planning, and the majority of urban Turks live in Jerry-built concrete jungles, without parks or open spaces, with polluted air to breathe—often one large slum punctuated by oases of bearable living, which seem to those outside them, as havens of luxury. Rapid change . . . has produced a social as well as economic crisis. The sheer misery of living . . . has bred radicalism (Mango 1979:130).

The rural populations, such as the Kurds of southeastern Turkey, bordering Iran, have suffered economic deprivation as well. The urban situation led to urban guerrilla warfare, in support of Muslim fundamentalism, while the Kurdish situation has led to a civil war in the countryside for the last decade. In the last five years, a new political movement called the Refah (Welfare) party, has challenged

BOX 10.3

■ Case Study: The Kurds: An Ethnic Nation with No State

Most of the Kurdish population occupies an area of mountains and high plains in the contiguous border areas of Iran, Iraq, Syria, and Turkey and the adjacent border areas of the former USSR states of Georgia, Armenia, and Azerbaijan. The Kurds call their land Kurdistan, an area estimated to be between 500,000 and 520,000 square kilometers, and they have lived there for more than two thousand years. They believe themselves to be descended from the Medes who conquered Nineveh, the capital of the Assyrian empire, in 612 B.C. For a variety of reasons, including their distribution in several nation–states with different census policies, it is difficult to estimate their total popu-

lation. Estimates for the mid-1970s ranged from 13.5 to 21 million total for all countries mentioned. A 1980 estimate puts the total at 17.2 million.

Traditionally, the majority of Kurds were pastoral nomads who resided in groups related by lineage and clan ties. Some were agriculturalists who lived in permanent villages. Today, most live in settled villages but many still derive much of their livelihood from pastoralism, sheep and goats being the principal animals raised. Wheat, barley, and lentils are the main crops in agricultural villages. Pasturelands are generally owned collectively by clans while agricultural lands are family-owned. Kurdish society consists of a small class of aristocrats and a

Embracing traditional ways, Kurdish Beritan tribe.

larger class of commoners. Most aristocratic families today live in the urban centers of the region, as do many landless commoners who have moved to cities in search of wage labor.

Kurdish kin groups consist of patrilineages grouped into clans, several of which in turn form a tribe. Membership in clan and tribal units is fluid, permitting outsiders to attach themselves and become fully incorporated after several generations. Traditionally, marriages are arranged first by the women of the bride's and groom's families, then finalized by the men when the bridewealth is agreed on. The ideal marriage is one in which a man marries his father's brother's daughter (called patrilateral parallel cousin marriage). Interestingly, in the 1960s it was reported that the majority of marriages were of this type. Residence after marriage is patrilocal. Sons inherit equally from their father but daughters do not inherit.

Conversion to Islam took place in the seventh century A.D. Today, most Kurds are Sunni Muslims, but a few groups in southern and southeastern Kurdistan are Shi'ite or members of other lesser known Islamic sects.

Rapid social change and recent events in the states occupied by the Kurds have had a differential, but in all cases profound, impact on all Kurdish groups, but it is difficult to predict what the long-term outcomes might be. The Kurds continue their lengthy battle to gain some form of self-governance in the several states they occupy. Some would be content with autonomy within a state while others struggle for an independent territorial state of Kurdistan. Conflicting goals in this regard, coupled with differences between Sunni and Shi'ite groups, have sometimes been manipulated into intra-Kurd conflict, as happened most recently in Iraq in 1996. During the latter half of the twentieth century, the Kurds have been subjected to massive violence and human rights violations in most of the states in which they live. They have suffered repression and vi-

olence at the hands of both the Pahlavi and the Khomeini governments in Iran. The Iraqi government of Saddam Hussein forced the resettlement of several thousands of Kurds, and later gas-bombed Kurdish communities. In Iraq as well, the Kurds are split between the Kurdistan Democratic Party (KDP) and the Iraqi Patriotic Union of Kurdistan (PUK), which distrust one another (though they share the same political goals) and have sometimes engaged in open conflict. And the Turkish government has long refused to recognize that the Kurds exist as a distinct group, though it has sent military forces against the Kurds in Iraqi Kurdistan and has been waging a civil war against the Kurds in the Turkish countryside for more than a decade. The UN has attempted to protect the Kurds from further aggression as has the United States with its "no fly" zone, but to little avail.

The tactics that the various Kurdish groups have used, which often include violence, in their attempts to achieve some degree of autonomy within the territorial states in which they live, seem better adapted to success in the context of the earlier political systems of this region—the tributary states. Modern territorial states, even in the Middle East with the fairly recent legacy of the **millet** system of the Ottoman Empire (a system that provided some degree of religio-political autonomy to religious minorities), are unlikely to grant any meaningful autonomy to the minority Kurdish populations within their borders, or to any other minority. For, unlike the tributary state, the prime directive of the territorial state is to absorb into one nation all the minority nations within its borders.

In the Middle East, as we have seen, this is an adequate, if oversimplified, description of the situation. Dale Eickelman's perspective (1981) on the geographic spread and historical trajectory of Islam is illustrative. (The information for this case study is derived from Busby [1995] and MacDonald [1989].)

the traditional parties, both the Republican People's Party (RPP), founded by Ataturk and the Democratic left, but also the conservative Motherland Party. Fresh elections in December of 1995 gave the Refah the biggest single share of the vote (21 percent), and make the secular leaders of Turkish societies very nervous. One of the fears is that the military, fearing an Islamist takeover, will once again take over the government. Because Turkey is a member of NATO, the growing power of Islamists makes American and European leaders nervous. The dilemma is that as the United States, NATO, and European leaders pressure Turkey to institute democratic reforms, the Islamist forces, such as Refah, grow in power. Very similar movements are to be found in Algeria and Egypt, where openings to democracy are filled with religious parties supporting Islamic states.

Many Islams

Eickelman (1981) rejects emotional explanations of ethnic violence that depend on fears of Muslim "fundamentalism" and "terrorism." He argues that the heart of conflict in the Middle East is the constant reinvention of Islam itself, and its attempt to come to grips with varied cultural traditions and now with modernization. Eickelman writes that the core of Islam transcends specific cultures, including its culture of origin. At the center of Islam is a set of ideals and expressions of religious truth; these are considered immutable. But these core beliefs are subject to interpretation and reinterpretation, producing sects, schisms, and challenges to belief. Islam is a remarkably varied religion, one that anthropologists once thought could be understood as the difference between Great (literate, urban) and Little (folk, rural, provincial) Traditions, following the ideas of Robert Redfield (1941) for folk Catholicism in Latin America. But Eickelman argues that there is a dynamic to Islam that goes fundamentally beyond contrasting written (Great) and folk (Little) traditions. He summarizes a series of recent anthropological studies of Islam, starting with Clifford Geertz (1968), to show that in virtually every community or locale studied over the years Islam is conceived of as a religion or world view that is fragmented, a language that is differentiated into many statements, not a singular and uniform world view (1981). According to Eickelman, these opposing conceptions of Islam are always co-present and form a dynamic tension with each other.

Eickelman argues that there has been a tendency to view Sunni and Shi'a Islam as though they are the major, if not the only, opposing Islamic doctrines. He points out that neither is homogeneous and goes on to discuss other Islamic groups and religions such as Alevi, Sufism, and Maraboutism. He argues that Westerners tend to read their own very Western tradition into the Islamic religion and into Islamic education. For Eickelman it is a mistake to view Islam as a single religion, or even many different religions, but that it is "more accurate to regard belief and practice as prismatic" (Eickelman 1981:235). Westerners, he thinks, have a lack of understanding of the constant innovative quality of Islam, and they do not understand the nature of Islamic education, which we confuse with our own orthodox priesthoods or universities (with scholars delving into increasingly more boring information as they specialize in their respective disciplines).

Students of Islamic schools, rather than becoming priests, become politicians, soldiers, merchants, ministers of state, bankers, and others who move in

CHAPTER 10   THE MIDDLE EAST: ETHNICITY, OIL, AND CONFLICT   367

the real world. The sense of "religious" versus "secular" knowledge is less fixed than in the West. Islam can incorporate science, medicine, and politics to the degree that such knowledge does not contradict Islamic laws. Islamic education provides a rigorous mental discipline, and much of the Quran is memorized, but without the intent of seeking "explanation" (Eickelman 1981). Poor as well as rich could sit in on lectures, and there was no "faculty" or administration in mosque universities. The relationship between the "learned" and the *umma* (commuity) was and is more porous than in our world of academic and nonacademic. There are no rigorous, organized groups of scholars, administrators, bureaucrats, and other Western "educational" apparatus.

The phrase "Islamic fundamentalism" tends to be used to incorporate the large number of distinct Islamic groups that are considered politically radical, but the term may be meaningless. The very process of state-building in the Middle East appears to be tied to protests against the power of the state and the need to return to the original message of Muhammad. Each of the various sects of Islam (Sunni, Shi'ite, Sufist) has built within itself a protest against corruption and power. The history of the development of states in the Middle East is also the history of Islamic protests against the centralization of authority.

Eickelman's analysis fits the view of this text: that each region of the world has its own dynamic that must be understood on its own terms, and not in terms of a Euroamerican cultural model. The picture of the Middle East is of many Islams. Add to this the diversity of cultures and derived ethnic identities, and one begins to appreciate the complexity of this vast region. Add the history of autonomous or semiautonomous governance under the aegis of tributary states and empires until the advent of territorial states in the region in the late nineteenth and early twentieth centuries. Add the presence of two other major religious traditions, Judaism and Christianity, a recently created state (Israel), and peoples like the Kurds who claim shared identity but occupy parts of different territorial states and have no state of their own, but desire one in the current context. With each addition, the level of recent violence in the Middle East is perhaps more understandable, although hardly acceptable.

Summary

Geographic and cultural diversity are characteristics of the Middle East. Deserts and mountains have created isolated pockets where ancient cultural practices are preserved, while invasions have added layers of cultural diversity. While nine-tenths of the population is today Islamic, Islamic cultures overlie and share space with a great many ancient cultures and religions. A global culture spills over this diversity today, encouraging new forms of political participation, some democratic, some not, but also threatening many groups with a universal culture that has caused sects to turn to fundamental statements of their religious principles. Violence has often been the result. The modern Middle East is a region in transition from totalitarian rulers and populist egalitarians towards democratic tolerance on all sides. But the transition has not been smooth, has often been blocked by crosscutting ethnic and religious conflicts, and remains incomplete. In this chapter we have focused on the origins and substance of various conflicts, and we have tried to emphasize that a democratic balance is necessary in the choices people must have if they are to support their governments through tough economic reforms, but that democracy is no panacea. Under certain circumstances, it may become a dead end leading to totalitarian religious sects dominating the scene.

Key Terms

1967 Six Day War	*Kibbutz*
A-cosmic	**Messianic**
Caliph	**Millet**
Charismatic Phase	**Monotheism**
Compradors	**Perennial Irrigation**
Cosmic	**Polytheistic**
Crusades	*Qanats*
Diaspora	*Quran*
Five pillars	**Salinization**
Hadith	**Supernatural**
II Rah	**Trade/Raid Nexus**
Islam	*Ulema*
Kerese	**Zionism**
Khan	

The vast region of Asia is divided into three subregions: South Asia, consisting of the nations (in alphabetical order) of Bangladesh, Bhutan, India, Maldives, Mauritius, Nepal, Pakistan, and Sri Lanka; Southeast Asia, which includes Brunei, Cambodia, Indonesia, Laos, Malaysia, Myanmar (formerly Burma), the Philippine Republic, Thailand, and Vietnam; and East Asia, which includes China, Japan, Korea, Singapore, and Taiwan. Tibet was formerly a South Asian nation but is currently administered by China. Four major world religions, each with many local variants, are prominent in the region: Buddhism, Christianity, Hinduism, and Islam. In addition, there remain many tribal religions, often called animistic religions because of their inclusion of beliefs in nature spirits. And the religious diversity of Asia is surpassed considerably by its cultural diversity and the diversity of its landforms, climatic zones, and ecosystems. In short, "the East" is a designation of convenience just as is its opposite, "the West." In this chapter, we will devote attention to China, India, Indonesia, Vietnam, and Japan.

Asia has drawn the interest of philosophers, anthropologists, historians and other scholars since the Age of Enlightenment. For Georg Wilhelm Friedrich Hegel, the eighteenth-century German philosopher, Asia is the beginning of "history," and Europe is its end, just as the sun rises in the East and sets in the West. The East is a region of despotism, where political subjects are like children "who obey their parents without will or insight of their own" (Hegel 1956), while the West is where rationality and capitalism emerged in world history. This is clearly a very Eurocentric view of the vast diversity of cultures, nations, and religions that comprise Asia.

Changing Ideas about Asia

The alignment of rationality with European civilization neither began nor ended with Hegel, who was writing at the end of the eighteenth and beginning of the nineteenth centuries. The concept of "rational" choice was attached very early to the creation of European capitalism, while other political economies around the world were generally treated as lacking in rationality. The connections between capitalism, rationality, and the origins of science were elemental to the writings of Max Weber, for whom the protestant religion was the basis for the origin of capi-

Figure 11.1   **Physiographic Map of Asia**

talism, double entry bookkeeping, and even Western classical music (Weber 1958a). Weber, who could read neither Chinese nor Hindi, wrote two treatises on the religions of the Orient: *The Religion of India* (1958b) and *The Religion of China* (1951). His book on China maintained that this region of the world lacked significant external trade relations and was a formidable feudal bureaucracy ideologically organized by Confucianism, with a predominantly agricultural economy. India was more "rational" due to its trade connections to the West, particularly when it was under the control of Islamic (Mughal) leaders. But its rationality lay somewhere between that of China and Europe. Religion, in the early twentieth century, was seen as having a key role in the evolution of society: Asian religions were viewed as "naturalistic," originating in nature worship and supporting totalitarian regimes, while Christianity was "world rejecting," supporting secular democratic states, science, and capitalism (Larson 1995:38).

Cultural materialists reversed the argument. They perceived human ecology to play a deterministic role behind political economy, and religion was merely a means by which the elite controlled the peasants. In the writings of Karl Marx, religion was the opiate that clouded the eyes of peasants and allowed society to be controlled by elites. According to Karl Wittfogel (1957), "Oriental Despotism" rested on the ability of states to control the distribution of water in "hydraulic" empires. These were empires dependent on state-run waterworks, such as dams, large drainage systems, and reservoirs. Hydraulic empires, such as China and India, were located largely in regions that were arid or suffered from aridity on a seasonal basis. Irrigation and population density have remained key factors in modern explanations for the rise of centralized bureaucratic states in Asia.

The opposition between a totalitarian East and a democratic, capitalist West is implicit in much social science and historical theorizing in the twentieth century, including that of world system theorists, who treat India and China as "semi-peripheral" regions of the capitalist core. China and India adopted "anti-system" socialist political regimes to escape the ravages of capitalism (Larson 1995:40). While these theories remain important, a new focus on ideology and strategies of state formation is forcing revisions in the stereotype of Asiatic states. Three new and related propositions are emerging. The first is that trade, along with irrigation agriculture, was always important in state formation in Asia. The second is that religion was a means of reducing transaction costs over large regions, improving the possibilities of trade. These two factors, as we have seen, played a dominant role in the Middle East as well. The third proposition is that the association of modernization with the secularization of society, the disappearance of the family, and the importance of the individual applies in the West but not in the East (another term for Asia).

The third proposition does not mean that family and religion are everywhere unchallenged in Asia, for castes, clans, and extended families do not have the cohesion and social significance they once had, and Westernized young people often are indifferent to the religions of their parents. But, in Asiatic cultures, there is less infatuation with ideas of individual freedom, and the search for individual identity outside the family and community is not as appealing as in many Western cultures. Many of these observations apply as well to Africa, the Middle East, and, in the next chapter, Latin America. While the West wakes up to the importance of the family, these cultures remain family-centric and there is much to learn from them.

In addition, the core-periphery model of the world system theorists is being challenged with the emergence of different parts of Asia as either a new core or new cores (depending on the level of generalization), often challenging one another. Japan has long been an affluent and successful challenger to Western core hegemony. South Korea has joined Japan, usually as a partner, and so has Taiwan. These three nations, often called "the Asian Tigers," have, with varying levels of success, made the transition to democracy. China, on the other hand, is emerging as a commercial giant whose political direction may be a threat to the Asian democracies. Then there are the countries of Southeast Asia—Thailand, Vietnam, Malaysia, Indonesia, and the Philippines—all of which are changing with such speed as to make generalizations impossible. These five nations are currently becoming integrated into the global economy. As they do so, their political systems, for the most part, are becoming increasingly more democratic, or the need for democracy is becoming more obvious to their citizens. The successful combinations of family enterprise, capitalism, and corruption-free governments are becoming models for the other countries of Asia. But the same countries are challenging the Western stereotype of Asians, as a powerful work ethic combined with careful investments are drawing jobs away from Europe and the United States, particularly in the textile industry.

India, the geographic giant of South Asia, is a socialist democracy that is being challenged by religious parties whose basis is Hinduism and Indian ethnic identity (despite the fact that India contains hundreds of self-identified ethnic groups). Will India maintain its traditions of democracy, or will it become a Hindu theocracy? What then of its common border with China? Will these giants threaten each other? And what of volatile Pakistan? North of China and India are the former republics of the Soviet Union, many of them wealthy in natural resources but currently engaged in a shaky transition between authoritarianism and democracy. What role will they come to play?

The need for a balanced transition toward capitalism and democracy is nowhere more apparent than in the poverty-stricken country of Bangladesh (with an average income of $183.00 per year), whose people are struggling to abandon a generation of autocratic rule. Bangladesh has a national average population density of 2,097 persons per square mile (twice that of New York City) and a population growth rate of 2.3 percent. The population doubles every thirty years and is currently 120 million. A quick glance at a map of Asia shows that Bangladesh occupies flat delta lands into which flow rivers from Nepal, Assam, India, and China. These rivers receive rainwater from the Himalayas to the north. Most of the country is flat. Once a year monsoons flood the region. The floods vary in severity. In 1988, 1989, and 1990, the floods were extensive. Those of 1990 killed over 50,000 people (Baxter 1992:135). Much of the flooding of Bangladesh is a consequence of deforestation to the north in the Himalayas, mostly controlled by China. Over the last decade, the Bangladesh government has met the problem by constructing large multistoried concrete towers that people use as shelter from the floodwaters. Nonetheless, there are not enough of these structures to protect everyone, and in bad flood years thousands can be expected to perish.

Human Ecology and Cultural Diversity

The geography of Asia reveals endless variation. Mountain ranges and deserts cross and are crossed by political divisions that have changed through time. Parts of northern Asia, for example, were once regions of the Soviet Union, and are so no longer, but their histories have been influenced by the rise and fall of that empire. The heart of Asia is a huge mountain massif with mile-high passes and radiating ranges lying to the east and west. The mountain ranges bisect Asia into a northern tundra of pastoral nomads and southern and southeastern realms of monsoon rains and peasant agriculture. These last two regions lie within "monsoon Asia," and incorporate the major civilizations of Asia, particularly China and India, but also Vietnam and Thailand. The cultures of the mountain regions surrounding the lowland civilization were culturally influenced by them, and, from time to time, have been incorporated into their empires. Mountain ranges isolate separate ecological and cultural units, and historic changes, migration, and the success and failure of empire-building have produced great human and ecological diversity.

Very important to Asia's human ecology has been the history of its irrigation systems, of which there have been two distinct types. The first is found predominantly in China and is associated with the growing of paddy rice. Rice was first domesticated in the Yangtze valley before 7000 B. C., but paddy rice agriculture did not fully emerge until a thousand years ago. Such systems require the development of an artificial environment, a network of ponds and lakes in which the soil is flooded by irrigation systems. An impermeable soil pan is developed that is insulated from the direct action of rainfall by a layer of water and microorganisms that work without oxygen and contribute to the creation of a rich layer of black soil under water (Wolf 1969:27). Such systems require predictable irrigation systems, which in turn require the harnessing of rivers, lakes, and other water systems by the state. Paddy rice agriculture allowed the support of very large populations and required the investment of large levies of workers, and led to the development of complex states.

The ecological zones outside paddy rice were used for the growing of oil-bearing seeds, cotton, tea, or pepper. Mulberry trees were grown for leaves that fed silkworms and generated a whole industry of silk manufacturing. Oil, cotton, tea, pepper, and silk were all key ingredients in the export trade of China. The mutual reinforcement of state power, trade, and the support of large populations historically led to the highly centralized states that dominated China from the beginning of its history.

Less centralized are the tank irrigation systems of India, Ceylon, and Southeast Asia. These are quite similar to those described in the last chapter on the Middle East. However, tank irrigation systems depend on monsoon rainfall, and not on subterranean water sources. Such tanks date from the earliest Indian states of Harappa and Mohenjo Daro consisting of large reservoirs that were used in the irrigation of a variety of crops: rice, wheat, barley, or millet depending on the local environment. In association with the fabricated pools were high ramparts, platforms for houses, and drainages for villages, towns, and cities that allowed the control of monsoon floods. Scholars, such as E. Leach (1961), have theorized that tank irrigation, because it requires local political centralization but not the integration of rivers and lakes, did not require the coordination of state bureaucracies such as those found in China, but would have contributed to local hierarchies like the caste system found in India. Such systems, called *jaj-*

mani systems, were redistribution economies in which foods and goods were distributed back to the laboring population by a jajman, a landlord of sorts, who dominated the political hierarchy of a valley. Goods were distributed back to people according to their level in the caste system. India, unlike China, consists of a hierarchy of local political elites and not a single imperial authority.

From earliest times, the mountain ranges, with their west-to-east river systems and passes, and the northern steppe, were used as trade routes that crossed Asia ending at port cities on the east coast of Asia. It was in these highland regions that pastoral nomadism formed natural adaptations. Pastoral nomadism was basically the same camel (but of the two-hump or Bactrian type) or sheep-based system described in the last two chapters. A little unusual were the yak breeders of highland Tibet, whose animals are adapted to the cold and arid highlands. All three types of nomads contributed to the trade networks that crisscrossed the Himalayan mountains, and still do so today. The mountainous country of Afghanistan is almost totally dependent on trade, sheep, and goat-herding, as is much of northern Pakistan. Just to the south of these regions, the Indus and Ganges rivers, which connect north to south, carried that trade to the Indian Ocean. Where trade and productive agriculture combined, where food could be grown to support urban populations, there evolved the ancient cores of China and India with their distinct irrigation systems. These trade and production systems are a continuation of that found in North Africa, the Great Silk Road, as it meandered toward the eastern terminus in the port cities of Asia: Shanghai, Macau, Saigon, Bangkok, Rangoon, Calcutta, Madras, Bombay, and Karachi.

Unlike Hegel, Marx, and Weber's theories about the tradeless domination of subsistence agriculture on the histories of Asia, trade, in fact, played a powerful role and was intricately combined with irrigation and pastoral nomadic ecologies. The story of trade in Asia compares favorably with the story told in the chapters on Africa and the Middle East. However, with the domination of Euro-

Dolpo caravaners drive yaks down from summer pasture before the trip north to Tibet.

peans, the trade networks collapsed, and so did the critical nature of the human adaptations described, which then became primarily subsistence-based adaptations. Thus Hegel, Marx, and Weber were examining what was left of Asia after the Europeans had monopolized the trade connections, and most of the port cities were in European hands. Today, the Asians are regaining their status in the ancient game of trade, and the core–periphery distinction is falling away.

China: From Confucianism to Communism

With 400 million people a century-and-a-half ago, and over a billion now, China has long been highly populated. It is a vast nation of 3,691,502 square miles, making it almost 670,000 square miles larger than the United States, with tropics to the south and the subarctic to the north (Cressey 1963). The western half of the country has high inhospitable mountain ranges. But these mountainous regions were important to China because through their passes were the trade connections to the west.

The core of ancient China lies along two great rivers: the Hwang Ho in the north (the Yellow River) and the Yangtze in the south, both regions of low-lying plains with yearly monsoon rains. This core region divides evenly at a line between the two rivers into a northern temperate zone and a southern subtropical zone (Cressey 1963).

The Earliest Chinese: Ecology, Technology, and Trade

The alluvial soils of the fertile flood plains are constantly renewed through flooding and sedimentation and lend themselves to intensive agriculture, which is very old. Neolithic, tribal societies known as the Yang-shao, emerged between 6000 and 5000 B.C. These were dependent on rice, millet, pigs, dogs, chickens, and water buffalo and made stone sickles, mortars, pestles and ceramics (Gernet 1996:37). Early Yang-shao villagers practiced shifting agriculture, cultivating millet as their main crop, but burials already show evidence of status differences, and possibly some form of hierarchical clan organization. By 3000 B.C., the Yang-shao were making very attractive pottery vessels for steaming food, the basis of most contemporary Chinese cooking (Fagan 1995:298). Yang-shao pottery may have been an important trade item. Similar cultures were found along the Yangtze with evidence for weaving. These farming villages were followed by the "Hsia" dynasty between 2207 and 1766 B.C., which showed significant advances in craftsmanship, including elegant jade and ceramic wares. The rammed or beaten earth construction of the Hsia, which was used for the bases of temples, possibly marks the beginning of the first Chinese dynasties (Gernet 1996:38).

The first chiefdom type social structures appeared during the **Lungshan** culture, which emerged between 4000 and 2000 B.C., the organizational parallel of chiefdoms in North Africa and the Middle East. By 3000 B.C., Lungshan farming culture was spread throughout northern China in larger and more permanent villages than those of the Yang-shao people, with irrigation and paddy rice cultivation. This clan-based culture had a religion based on shamanism and ancestor worship. **Divination** by means of animal bones (called **scapulimancy**) was practiced. The scapulae of various animals, which had been painted with special symbols, were heated in a fire. Cracks through the symbols were used to predict the future, particularly of the royal elite. Much later, these symbols became Chinese writing. The Lungshan also had highly sophisticated bronze metallurgy and elaborate fortifications of rammed earth.

The Rise of the Chinese Dynasties

Scholars believe that, between 2000 and 1000 B.C., chiefdom social structures evolved into states with the appearance of the Shang Dynasty, and the center of Chinese civilization shifted further west to the region of modern An-Yang in northeast Honan province. Chinese writing, the chariot, divination, human sacrifice, and bronze manufacturing appeared or continued to evolve, and there was an upsurge in the number of sites of archaic civilizations (Gernet 1996:41). Thirty monarchs ruled during the Shang, and there were six changes of the capital in the area of western Shantung, southern Hopei, western Honan, and northern Anhwei. In 1953, archaeologists uncovered a site in Honan province with a wall of rammed earth sixty feet thick, the remains of dwellings, workshops, furnaces, and molds for bronzes. At An-Yang, a royal cemetery contained the burials of the eleven kings, most of which had been looted. In 1976, the unlooted tomb of the wife of a Shang king was found with riches in bronze, jade, and with sixteen human sacrifices. Whole chariots with horses still in their harnesses were excavated. Another recent discovery revealed an army of 7,000 men made of terra cotta. The implication is that the chariot was used extensively in warfare. The Shang chariot was light and strong, with large wheels of many spokes. These chariots were not unlike chariots found in Syria in the seventeenth century B.C. Warfare was combined with human sacrifice. In several graves, decapitated corpses were found, while in others were heads without bodies. Many of these discoveries suggest the existence of rites requiring the sacrifice of prisoners of war (Gernet 1996:42).

During the Shang, roads, staging posts, and extensive canals were used for trade. Silk weaving and the production of cotton textiles became highly sophisticated, as did the use of fire in the production of fine porcelains and bronzes. The production of cast iron became an important industry. China became a big exporter of luxury products: silks, bronzes, ceramics, cotton goods, tea, mirrors, lacquerware, and furniture. China's traffic in fine trade goods extended to every major port city in the Old World. It was because of the success of Chinese trade throughout the next several thousand years that the maritime nations of Europe were drawn to that part of the world in the sixteenth century (Gernet 1996:29).

Shang political economy rested on the idea of the king as a semidivine being who interceded on behalf of his people with the high god Ti through the use of oracle bones for divination (made out of scapulae or tortoiseshells). The royal

Figure 11.2 **Map in China during the Shang dynasty**

palace was the center of activities for a cult of kings, a theocracy, and of an aristocratic society that was hierarchically organized through patrilineal clans. The heads of family were also the heads of family worship. The theocratic kings of China had religions that were very distinct from those of Egypt and Sumeria, but they were, nonetheless, magical beings: humans with supernatural attributes. The Shang domain extended to the Yangtze plain and beyond. The Shang was followed by the Chou dynasty, which formalized the rule of the king within a philosophical tradition spelled out by K'ung Fu-tzu or Confucius (551–479 B.C.).

Confucianism and Chinese Culture

Confucianism was to serve China until this century, and is still a state legal tradition, as well as a moral philosophy, backing the rule by elites in modern Taiwan and Shanghai. Confucius taught that social order was based on virtue, which came from ritual performance symbolizing **filial piety,** or *hsiao.* Filial piety demanded the subordination of the son to the father, the father to his father, all to the interests of *tsu,* or patrilineal clan, as determined by the gentry. The gentry paid homage to the emperor, and the emperor to Ti. Family harmony was based on the worship of the ancestors and acceptance of the hierarchy of aristocratic society. Ancestor worship helped bind the multilayered tsu into a functional whole under the proscriptions of the ideology of Confucianism.

At the root of Confucian philosophy was the traditional family. The traditional Chinese family structure existed up until 1950, when it was outlawed by the Communist state. The family depended on the tsu. The tsu included all people with a common surname who traced descent from a common ancestor (Eschleman 1994). The tsu might be made up of several thousand people, often entire villages. The upper level of the tsu was the gentry, an intellectual class that received income as landlords. Those gentry who were successful in passing a national exam based on Confucian philosophy became members of the Mandarin bureaucracy, which ruled China. The Mandarin bureaucracy was subdivided into nine status levels, each tied to comprehensive state exams, that formed the elites of the clans. At the lowest level of the tsu were the rural farmers, the peasants, who comprised the bulk of the poverty-stricken population. Poverty contributed to poor medical care, particularly for females (Chao 1977).

The outlines of clan social structure were set out in Confucius's codes of behavior. The traditional clan was important for a variety of functions, most of which have been lost today. The tsu loaned money to the peasant class for traditional if extravagant weddings and funerals. It established schools for clan members, exercised judicial authority, collected taxes for the government, and maintained the ancestral graves (Chao 1977). Confucianism spread from China to most of Southeast Asia during China's various conquests. It became the norm for upper-class behavior in Vietnam, Cambodia, Laos, and in most regions that were not influenced by Islam or by Hinduism.

Males held a favorable position in Chinese society, and the Confucian code subordinated women. In the ideal Confucian family, women were supposed to be submissive and to learn from their husbands how to be pure and faithful. A woman should follow the three submissions: obey her father when a child, her husband when she married, and her oldest son when a widow.

Confucianism is based on Chinese cosmology, which sees the world as composed of two complementary elements: the yin, which is female, passive, dark, and weak, and the yang, which is male, bright, strong, and active. In traditional China, female infanticide was common because boys were preferred to girls. Boys continued the lineage; girls did not. Marriages were not based on love and romance but were arranged. The Chinese practiced exogamy, which meant that the girl had to leave her village (the home of her patrilineal clan members) due to the rule of patriclan (tsu) exogamy; that is, she could not marry anyone with the same surname. She would be completely removed from her own family (known as the family of orientation) and would move in with her husband's family (to form a new family called the family of procreation). In the new family, she had to submit to her husband and to her new mother-in-law. She would only have power in her own right through her own son when he was grown and married, and in her ability to dominate her daughter-in-law.

The traditional Chinese wife's responsibilities were to bear male children and work for her mother-in-law. The failure to bear male heirs gave the husband the right to take a concubine or other wives. One indication of female oppression was **footbinding.** Bound from childhood, women's feet were reduced to three inches in length from toe to heel. This practice was found primarily among the gentry, and was a means of restricting women's movement. Peasant women were not required to go through the procedure.

Chinese Feudalism: Peasants and Ethnic Minorities

The basic pattern of Chinese civilization—multiethnic and expansionistic—was maintained for thousands of years. The ethnic group that has been dominant through time has been the Han Chinese. Other distinct ethnic groups have either retained their language or identity or they have been **sinified** (have adopted the Han Chinese language and Confucian ethic). In the sixteenth century, Chinese Han social structure was feudal. However, Chinese feudalism was unusual in that most land was owned by patrilineal clans, not the state, and lands were rented to clan members by the Mandarin elites. Thus, most Chinese peasants were not landless but had access to land either through inheritance or through a complex set of leases or rents. Landlords and cultivators were linked not through hereditary rights, but through business contracts and a bureaucratic elite (Wolf 1969:106). Behind the throne, the ethic of Confucianism helped the state control its various peoples.

China, with its highly centralized state and the ownership of land through hereditary clans, stands in strong contrast to Western Europe in the sixteenth century. Remember that, in Great Britain, a weak feudal system disintegrated, the king turned over land as private property to the aristocracy, and then tried to keep the aristocracy weak by gaining the support of a developing industrial class. This led to the development of capitalism and the industrial revolution. The dynamics of culture change for China were very different. In China, the highly centralized state would go through cycles. These would begin with the invasion of a corrupt China by "northern barbarians," who would establish a new dynasty. That dynasty would become corrupt, leading to the rise of secret societies, many with charismatic leaders, who attacked the state, weakening it. According to Eric Wolf, secret societies with names like the White Lotus, the Eight Tigrams, the Nien, the Great Knife, the Boxers, and the Society of the Faith were traditional to Chinese society. These challengers, often based on anti-Confucian Buddhist principles of egalitarianism and feminism (explained in the section on India), would fight among themselves, and either they would succeed in establishing a new state, or an invasion would bring "northern barbarians" in to establish a new state.

This was the cycle that began in the seventeenth century when the Ming dynasty became corrupt, weakened, and was attacked by secret societies. The Manchu, sinified (Chinese-speaking) tribesmen from the north, found little difficulty in invading China and establishing a new dynasty, the Ch'ing, in 1644 (Wolf 1969:104). The invaders seized North China without much fight, but this would not be true in South China, where the southern Ming held out against the Manchu armies. The Manchu slowly extended their rule, consolidating their empire into the most extensive empire in the world. By 1759, the Ch'ing empire controlled territories covering 13 million square kilometers. Modern China, by contrast, is only 9,736,000 square kilometers. The Ch'ing empire embraced Outer Mongolia, Taiwan, and regions since occupied by Russia. In addition, most of the Asian countries of Nepal, Burma, Thailand, the Philippines, and Korea recognized Ch'ing sovereignty and were dependent on it. In the eighteenth century, this empire entered a period of great prosperity due to an unprecedented upsurge in agriculture, manufacturing, and trade (Gernet 1996:480–483).

This new dynasty was to survive until 1911, when it, too, became weakened by outsiders, collapsed when attacked by secret societies, and was replaced by a communist political system in 1949, a topic to which we will soon turn. Very often, the Confucian ethic was countered with Buddhist religious values, which tend to be antiaristocratic, have often entered the dynastic cycle at the beginning of conflict, and formed the core beliefs of the secret societies. (Buddhism is discussed more extensively in the section on India.)

During each cycle, the Han Chinese feudal system remained intact, and while it might contract during a period of conflict, the same centralized bureaucracy would emerge with the success of a new dynasty, even though the dynasty might belong to another ethnic group, such as the Mongols of the northland. This system of overarching political and social control, based on Confucian values, incorporated many other distinct ethnic groupings with a fair degree of success.

During the 1950s, the communist government of Mao Zedong studied ethnic groupings in China and discovered that, including the Han, there are fifty-six national minorities in China. Through the millennia of Chinese culture, the dominant trend has been to leave the various ethnic groups alone, but with the underlying expectation that they would become sinified; that is, they would imitate the Han Chinese. In the 1960s, during the Cultural Revolution (to be discussed), the customs of minority peoples were censured or forbidden. People were not allowed to use their own language. Traditional healing practices, art, and literate traditions were outlawed (Maybury–Lewis 1992:83).

Chinese social organization and culture remained relatively unchanged for three thousand years, despite repeated rebellions; periods of disintegration were followed by new periods of consolidation and reintegration. Numerous dynasties rose and fell in this fashion as a successful emperor was followed by less and less effective and more corrupt descendants until there was another revolt and a new dynasty, but the basic Confucian traditions and lifeways remained the same.

The question is often raised: Why did China survive for such a long time while the civilizations of Europe, the Middle East, and Africa rose and fell? There are three answers. First, while invasions did occur from outside China, the invaders viewed Chinese culture as superior, and adopted it as their own once in power. Second, Chinese culture has always been relatively tolerant of ethnic differences within its borders and, third, Chinese culture is flexible and adaptive. Confucianism, the core of Chinese values, is not a supernaturalist religion, and does not lend itself to fanaticism. The Chinese, over their long history, have been more pragmatic than dogmatic. But there have been exceptions, such as the Chinese communist period, which lasted from 1949 to 1975.

Collapse of the Empire and the Rise of Communism

In the nineteenth century, beyond the cyclical pressures that troubled all dynasties, there was added the heavy pressure of foreign influence, which weakened the ability of the Ch'ing dynasty to resist disintegration and made it more difficult to achieve cohesion. Africa and the Middle East had been incorporated as parts of a European colonial empire. China, and its neighbors in Asia, did not fall as easily to the Europeans, putting up great resistance. Under pressure from the Europeans, the Chinese government agreed to open treaty ports, or ports of trade where Europeans were restricted to walled-in compounds and only allowed to trade with officials. The Chinese hoped this technique would allow them to keep the rest of China intact. But these ports of trade made China a satellite of the industrializing world, and they expanded despite the tactics of the Ch'ing to keep China pure against outsiders.

In 1795, a peasant revolution in the northwest and Honan province spelled the beginning of the end. The Ch'ing, like the Ming, had come to suffer from corruption; public finance had been squandered without counting the cost. The court and state had lived beyond their means, and corruption "favored by the centralization of power in the hands of the emperor . . . had known no bounds from 1775 onwards" (Gernet 1996:533). As the central court weakened, European traders were at the doors of the trade cities of the coast.

Once the European traders had their foot in the door, they monopolized trade and then used foreign investment to gain control over Chinese industries near the treaty ports. Slowly, the ports became bastions of foreign interest within China (an example here would be English-controlled Hong Kong). Chinese dynastic power was further weakened by a series of wars carried on by outside powers: the Anglo-French War against China in 1860–1861; the annexation of Vietnam by the French; the Japanese war against China in 1894–1895; and the Russo-Japanese war of 1904–1905, which was fought on Chinese soil. In each of these wars, China lost territory to outside imperialist interests. There were also internal rebellions—the Taiping Rebellion (1850–1865) and the rebellion of the Nien (1852–1868), which foreshadowed the peasant–based Communist revolution of the twentieth century (Wolf 1969:119). These revolutions were led by secret societies, such as those mentioned above. However, the root of Chinese disintegration and the despair of the Ch'ing dynasty was the introduction of opium into Chinese society. The British East India Company had gained a monopoly over the production of opium in India that they exported to China. By 1810, four to five thousand cases of opium were being imported into Canton, and imports were to continue to increase rapidly despite attempts by the Chinese government to end the trade (Gernet 1996:536). A series of "Opium Wars" (especially in 1839–42) were fought by the British to prevent China from closing its doors to this drug. Opium was smuggled into China despite draconian efforts to stop the trade. Silver left China to pay for opium, causing a budget deficit that crippled the Chinese government.

By 1870, the Ch'ing empire had practically disappeared. The fighting between the government, revolutionary forces led by secret societies, and the colonial forces who took various sides led to an enormous loss of material and wealth caused by the bitter fighting. The losses in human lives were unparalleled in human history. Whole rich and densely populated areas in Nanking and Hangchow were ravaged: Between 20 and 30 million people died.

The Warlords   The last Chinese dynasty collapsed in 1911 due to both internal and external pressures, and nationalist rebels took over the diminished government. The collapse of central authority led to the increased power of regional warlords. In the period from 1911 to World War II, China was divided into territories controlled by warlords, each attempting to capture the state with his army. Many warlords were the leaders of anti-Manchu, antimonarchic political movements that supported democratic reform. Many of the leaders, such as Sun Yat-Sen, were intellectuals with connections to Europe and the United States (Sun Yat-Sen founded the Society for the Rebirth of China, which later became the Kuo Min Tang). The military governors or warlords collected taxes, seized loot from opponents, and produced and distributed opium. They also borrowed money from foreign banks to keep their wars alive. They recruited their armies from the impoverished peasantry, some of whom were no better than bandits (Wolf 1969:127).

At the same time, industrial capitalism grew in the urban regions of China, but it did not grow fast enough to incorporate peasants leaving the countryside. Foreign banks funded industries run by Chinese workers and protected by the warlords, who lived off the taxes they imposed on both urban and rural populations. The control of agriculture by banks with international connections led to the increased production of export commodities, such as tobacco and opium, but a decrease in food production. Much of the land came to be controlled by absentee landowners who were protected by warlords, and who used their resources to finance their struggles with each other. The introduction of commercial crops and the commercialization of land led to an increase in the value of land, and rents increased. Prices for land doubled and tripled in some regions in the late nineteenth century (Wolf 1969:130).

The Communist Dictatorship and the Cult of Mao   The struggles between the warlords just prior to World War II were reduced to two powerful leaders in contention to gain control of China: Chiang Kaishek, the heir and brother-in-law of Sun Yat-Sen and creator of the Kuo Min Tang or Nationalist Party, and Mao Zedong, the Communist leader of the Share Production Party. Both parties were founded on Soviet models. These two warlords formed a brief alliance, but, in 1927, Chaing Kaishek attempted to destroy Mao Zedong and his Communist followers. In World War II, Chaing Kaishek made himself an ally of the United States, but was not successful in his battle with the Japanese invaders of China, and instead retreated to western China. Mao Zedong was to prove much more successful fighting the Japanese in northern China and Manchuria. At the end of the war, the two leaders faced each other, but the success that Mao Zedong had against the Japanese drew enormous support from peasants recruited to his Red Army, and in 1949, Chiang Kaishek was forced to flee to Formosa (Taiwan), where he organized a new government and established Nationalist China (the new name of Taiwan).

The Communist Revolution of 1949 restructured mainland China according to a millenarian dream (Wolf 1969:154). The origins of Mao Zedong's communist ideas are not in Karl Marx, but tied to China's ancient past: an anti-Confucian core philosophy of revolutionary, egalitarian, and utopian aspirations. What *communism* came to mean after 1949, however, was Marxist: collective discipline, indoctrination to state ideology, public works of gigantic scope, and a highly cen-

The Great Leap Forward led to an agricultural collapse and starvation for millions

tralized statist form of social structure dominated by the Communist Party. In China, as in the former Soviet Union, state institutions were completely controlled by the Communist Party. The party came to be everywhere and directed everything—government administration at all levels, commercial enterprises, rural communes, factories, hospitals, schools and universities—even when it had no competence to do so. As in the Soviet Union, the leaders were the most elderly members of the Communist Party, and the only criterion for promotion appears to have been devotion to political orthodoxy (Gernet 1996:662). In contrast, the socialism of Africa and the Middle East appears mild, more a matter of state control of basic industries than the thorough control of every organization and social structure.

Beginning in the 1950s, China went through a series of attempts to push economic growth. In 1958, Mao announced the Great Leap Forward to accelerate production. Attempts were made to establish iron and steel foundries in the countryside, to force urban intellectuals to live like peasants, and to forcibly communalize and collectivize all agriculture. Intellectuals, especially those with Western educations, were viewed as threats to the state. The Communist state attempted to outlaw Confucianism, viewing this philosophy as the dead hand of tradition that held back the new state. Ancestor worship was outlawed, and the temples of the ancestors desecrated or destroyed. There was considerable resistance to the attack on ancestral temples and the collectivization of agriculture and 30 million people died or were killed between 1959 and 1962 (Ogden 1991:9).

The most extreme period came between 1966 and the early to mid-1970s when Mao Zedong, his wife, and close followers (the Gang of Four) launched the Great Proletarian Cultural Revolution. This was really the cult of Mao Zedong. Mao and his followers tried to radically restructure society through the Red Guard (not to be confused with the Red Army), an elite force of young radicals. It was during this phase that state terrorism was used on the Chinese people. The "Red Book" of Mao was printed by the millions and distributed free to the masses. It consisted of epigrams supposedly written by "Chairman Mao." The Red Guard went on rampages, breaking into homes, stealing or destroying property, shearing long hair off young women, and attempting to eradicate all signs of European or American culture, including classical music. People with formal degrees, such as educators, doctors, and lawyers, were arrested and imprisoned with no charges made against them. It has been estimated that 10 percent of the population, about 100 million people, were the targets of the Red Guard, and that tens of thousands of those targeted were killed (Ogden 1991:11).

Mao Zedong's theory of economic development consisted of cutting off trade connections to the outside world and attempting to achieve overnight urban development on the back of the rural peasantry. China became economically isolated, even making itself into an enemy of its one ally, the Soviet Union. Instead of urban economic development, the whole of China's economy suffered one economic disaster after the other until after Chairman Mao's death.

The Cultural Revolution was a colossal failure, both in human life and in a lack of economic growth. Industrial and agricultural production dropped dramatically. There was also a cultural loss. The Red Guard not only attacked Western institutions, they also attempted to destroy Chinese traditions. Since Confucianism had been specially targeted, and there was no real alternative except for Mao's little Red Book, by 1976 there was an almost total breakdown in both traditional Chinese morality and in Marxist–Leninist values (Ogden 1991:11).

Economic Reforms without Political Reform under Deng Xiaoping   The end of the Cultural Revolution came with the death of Mao Zedong in September of 1976. He was replaced in 1977 by Deng Xiaoping, who became chairman of the Communist Party. On Mao's death, the Gang of Four was arrested and removed from power. Deng began the deradicalization of Chinese society with the introduction of new free market policies. Deng restructured Chinese society without developing a new cult of personality, and has come to strikingly resemble the successful monarchs of Chinese history whose personal qualities are often a complete mystery to following generations. Deng has become the most enigmatic leader China has had in over a century.

Mao was accused of making serious mistakes. Maoism was rigorously questioned. Because traditional Chinese culture had been practically destroyed by the Red Guard, the new attack on Maoist thought left China without any strong belief system. Western values began to filter back but were viewed as "spiritual pollution." Deng Xiaoping attempted to open the door to Western-style free markets within a communist dictatorship.

Deng established five special economic zones (SEZs), predominantly in southern China, and allowed small businesses to open in the major cities. He also allowed farmers to lease state lands and to utilize market principles in growing and selling crops. The strongest of the economic zones are located in Guangdong province, which is located in south China just to the north of the island city of

Hong Kong. Deng's theory was that free market economies could be developed within a socialist framework and that economic reforms should precede political reforms. Free markets were in but democracy was out for the time being.

The question is how successful can the new market system be without democracy? Economic reforms in China have led to enormous economic improvements, but open markets have led to corruption as bureaucrats sold special favors to successful "capitalist entrepreneurs." Many new capitalists took advantage of the corruption of government to make themselves wealthy. While democratic reform is not attractive to the old oligarchy of China, part of the problem is the fear of the political collapse next door of the former Soviet Union. China is equally multicultural, and there are many ethnic republics in China that would like to have their independence.

There are many analysts who believe China is reluctant to implement Western-style democracy due to a fear of the collapse of the Chinese state. On the other hand, it has become apparent that there are new freedoms in China, and that corruption is being attacked. Local committees, originally organized by the Communist Party to oversee the activities of people in the countryside, are becoming openly critical of Communist Party officials in the political centers. Far from being closed down, the government in Beijing is listening to complaints, much as did the old Confucian Mandarins.

This opens an interesting debate: Can Confucian ethics allow the efficient growth of a capitalist society without corruption? Is the democratic capitalist connection a necessary and sufficient one, or can Asian societies operate ethical governments without democracy? The position taken in this book is that democratic reform is eventually necessary to support successful capitalist development. South Korea's recent turn toward democracy, and more limited shifts in Malaysia and the Philippines, support this view. On the other hand, Singapore's success with a one-party, Confucian-based society is a challenge.

The lack of democratic reform culminated in a protest in Tiananmen Square in Beijing in April of 1989. This protest began as a gathering intended to mourn the death of Hu Yaobang, a party leader supporting democratic and free market reforms. He was idolized by youthful university students. Students gathered at Tiananmen Square in central Beijing to mourn Yaobang's death. Thousands of students streamed into Beijing from across the country. Sympathetic railroad workers let them ride the trains free. The mass memorial soon turned into a student protest and a tent city was set up. Students demanded democracy but were not sure what that meant. When asked what they really wanted, they said that what they wanted was to know what the United States stood for (as reported at the time by Dan Rather of CBS News).

This protest was brutally crushed, with the army killing 400 people and the government destroying prodemocracy movements and blocking the transition to democracy. Moreover, after an unsuccessful attempt by hard-liners to stem the tide of capitalism, China is now one of the fastest growing economies in the world, expanding at a rate of 7 to 10 per cent annually. However, continued rapid economic growth may come at a high price in environmental damage. China's construction of a huge hydroelectric dam on the Yangtze river is a case in point (see Box 11.1).

Women and the Family under Communism   While communism may have failed economically and politically in China, sincere attempts were made to emancipate women from traditional Confucian codes. In 1950, new laws abolished the feudal marriage system, which was based on the supremacy of men over women. A new democratic marriage system was established based on the free choice of partners, monogamy, equal rights for both sexes, and protection of the lawful interests of women and children. The laws further prohibited bigamy, concubinage, child marriage, interference in the remarriage of widows, and the extraction of money or gifts in connection with marriage (Chao 1977). A 1980 law raised the minimum legal marriage age from eighteen to twenty for women and from twenty to twenty-two for men, relaxed restrictions on divorce, and stipulated that both husband and wife are obligated to practice family planning. The new laws faced the reality of China's burgeoning population growth.

The laws have had significant impact. Monogamy has become a reality, free choice is the rule in the cities, young people tend to marry at a later age, family size has been reduced, more women have obtained jobs, and the great inequality between men and women has been reduced. However, while many oppressive traditional norms have been abandoned, inequalities remain. Women's subordinate position is reflected in the preference for sons, in women's double burden of full-time paid employment and major responsibilities for child care and housework, the lack of representativeness in political affairs, and in violence against women in the form of infanticide and wife-battering (Eschleman 1994:144).

Particularly noticeable are the differences between urban and rural cultures. The clan was never as important in the cities as in rural villages. Not only does the clan remain important in rural areas, but many of the traditional values described above remain. In urban regions, major changes have taken place, moving dramatically from the arranged pattern to one of greater freedom and personal choice. **Brideprice** (gifts from the clan of the groom to the clan of the bride) has almost disappeared in urban regions, as has the **dowry.** The dowry, which was common in early European history, included material possessions the bride brought into her marriage, such as clothes, jewelry, and land. This wealth was often appropriated by the groom's clan. However, there is little in the form of a "dating culture" even in the cities, because it is still considered inappropriate for males and females to have contact with each other in public, and the opportunities to get to know each other are limited (Eschleman 1994).

While communism may have emancipated women to some extent, the puritanical nature of Chinese culture survives. In one report, Liu Dalin, a scholarly pioneer in the study of human sexuality in China, reported that women had little knowledge of sexual matters. One in three women reported never having an orgasm and not even knowing what the question meant. Because of the absence of foreplay, many wives found sex bothersome and painful. Only 13 percent of married couples had ever made love naked, and when sex did occur, it was restricted to less than a minute (Eschleman 1994:146).

China, with Cuba, is one of the few nations in the world that have managed to slow down the rate of population growth without the wealth increases that usually accompany the demographic transition to small families. As a result of in-

BOX 11.1

Ecological Maladaptation in Asia:
The Three Gorges Dam in China

The Three Gorges Dam project on the Yangtze river is a source of bitter controversy between the bureaucrats who control China and environmentalists in China and around the world. Scheduled for completion some time in 1997, after seventeen years of construction, at an estimated cost of over $12 billion, it will be the world's largest dam. Environmentalists claim that the Chinese government has all but ignored environmental considerations in creating this colossus.

The region of the Three Gorges has inspired Chinese poets and painters for centuries with its serenity and breathtaking beauty. All this is about to change. The dam will dramatically increase water levels in the three gorges—Qutang, Wu, and Xiling—and inundate 8,000 archaeological sites from China's Warring States period (475–221 B.C.) and many sites of even more ancient cultures. Thirteen cities,

140 towns, and 1,352 villages will be submerged or partially submerged by a reservoir that will be 600 kilometers long (equal in length to Lake Superior) and cover about 1,000 square kilometers (386 square miles). The new lake will rise over 175 meters (574 feet) above current river levels, inundating the narrow canyons and rapids for which the region is famous.

More than the natural beauty of the region is threatened. Once residents have been relocated, logging in the region will greatly expand to supply the Three Gorges project. Much of the land surrounding the project site is susceptible to erosion and landslides, and deforestation on a large scale will exacerbate these problems and contribute to a rapid buildup of sedimentation in the lake. Environmentalists warn that high levels of sedimentation will increase the danger of severe flooding upriver, even though flooding below the dam may be better controlled.

tensive Chinese family planning, the birthrate was reduced from 34 per 1,000 in 1970 to 20.9 in 1981 and 17.5 in 1984. The Chinese government not only tells couples that they must practice birth control, but it also tells them what contraceptive they must use.

A one-child policy has had several unintended consequences. Because of the high value placed on boy children, women routinely use ultrasound devices to test the sex of a fetus, and, if it is female, they abort it. Female infanticide is also reported as routine in the countryside. While the government has special incentives for one-daughter families, the desire for boy children has had the consequence of a distorted population pyramid. In the younger generation, there are fewer women of marriageable age today than there are in the older generations. This is also true in India, for similar reasons. The distortion in the population pyramid means that many grown men can anticipate living their lives out

Changes in water flow may damage the existing downriver dike system because of the serious channel scouring that will be caused by water released from the dam. Several species will be endangered by the dam, including the Yangtze river sturgeon and alligator, the freshwater finless dolphin (whose numbers are already down to about 300), the cloud leopard, and the Siberian white crane. Environmentalists argue that the mentality of old line communism that permeates the bureaucracy leads to reckless exploitation of nature for economic development and an almost total lack of regard for the country's most magnificent scenery.

Paradoxically, the Three Gorges Dam may have some ecological benefits. The dam will produce over 18,000 megawatts of power and thus will ease China's dependence on coal for three-quarters of its electrical power needs. This will reduce the country's greenhouse gas emissions. Currently, China is second only to the United States in the production of greenhouse gases. The dam will protect the middle and lower reaches of the Yangtze from devastating floods. A flood in 1954 left 30,000 people dead and one million homeless. Development experts point out that the dam will provide electricity for China's inland central–southern region, opening a relatively backward area to economic development.

Environmentalists, however, insist that the environmental costs will outweigh the economic benefits. But Chinese environmentalists are silenced by the government. They have been systematically excluded from consultative groups, especially after the Tiananmen Square military crackdown on political dissidents. Their proposals for smaller dams and dike control were never seriously considered in policy deliberations that led to the 1992 approval of the dam. China's grassroots environmental movement has been severely repressed by current political leaders who view such movements as threats to their authority. There is little chance that popular movements will emerge with enough force to stop the massive construction project. China is still gripped by the Great Leap Forward mentality of Mao Zedong, a mindset that inspires support for extravagant and ecologically destructive projects not unlike those that characterized the Soviet Union before its collapse. Soviet projects have left a legacy of ecological devastation from which it will take decades to recover.

(*Source:* Sullivan 1995)

without wives. Some writers speculate that this change may finally alter the way that Chinese and Indians view boys and girls, but in the short run, the low value given women is having a profound impact on the future of the family in China.

People on the Periphery: China's Minorities

While China is passing through the transition from socialism to capitalism, the lack of democratic reform and persistent human rights violations remain major concerns. As China grows economically, what is happening to its ethnic minority populations? The Han Chinese majority makes up about 94 percent of the population of China; the other 6 percent is divided among 55 officially recognized ethnic minority groups (called ethnic nationalities in China) with a total population of some 60 million. Some groups such as the Hani number more than one million while others number only about 1,000.

The 1950s was a period during which minority nationalities were recognized, autonomous regions were established, and democratic and agrarian reforms were instituted. This was followed in the 1960s and 1970s by harsher measures such as collectivization, the People's Commune reorganization, and finally persecutions and human rights violations designed to eliminate cultural and ethnic differences. The 1980s witnessed a return to the autonomous structures for ethnic minorities and the opening of free markets in place of the severe collectivism of the previous decade (Lemoine 1989).

The Chinese government counts the Tibetans as a national minority, arguing that China liberated the Tibetans from harsh feudalism in the 1950s (Fei 1981). The Tibetans view their condition as forced subjugation by China, and the Dalai Lama administers the government-in-exile of Tibet from India (French 1994).

The Hani   The Hani are people of Tibeto-Burman ethnic heritage who live in southern Yunnan province and some of the adjacent northern parts of Vietnam, Myanmar (Burma), Thailand, and Laos. There are over 1.2 million Hani in China alone. Traditionally, the Hani lived in small settlements of thirty to forty households in forested areas and practiced slash-and-burn agriculture in some areas and rice paddy cultivation on narrow terraces in other areas. Rice and maize are their main staples but they do raise several cash crops, including cotton, sugarcane, and ginger. The Hani were organized in patrilineal clans that claimed great genealogical depth. Only men inherited property. Hani religious beliefs consisted of polytheism, animism, and ancestor worship, and neither Buddhist nor later Christian missionaries had much success in converting them (Notar 1994). China's revolution not only profoundly affected China, it also affected people like the Hani, who were accused of "local national chauvinism" because of their religious and cultural practices. Subjected to religious and cultural oppression from the late 1950s through the 1970s, the Hani were allowed, in the 1980s, by the Chinese government to return to some of their ancient traditions. But a more subtle threat to their cultural identity may be the incorporation of younger people into national life through education and government jobs. In other countries, such as neighboring Thailand, the Hani appear to be worse off than in China, suffering poverty, lack of citizenship and land rights, and the deceptive recruitment of their young women into prostitution (Tooker 1993:119).

Tibetans   In 1950, the Chinese army invaded eastern Tibet and claimed sovereignty but left the Dalai Lama, religious and political leader of the Tibetan people, as chief administrator. After several years of negotiations, punctuated by violent encounters, the Dalai Lama fled to India in 1959 and has ruled in exile since then. The Chinese government has, since 1953, brutally attempted to eradicate Tibetan culture and is responsible for the death of about one-fifth of the population. Thousands have been tortured and imprisoned. Although China declared Tibet a Chinese "Autonomous Region" in 1965, its own Han peoples were moved in to displace Tibetans. The population of Lhasa, the capital, is already more than half Chinese.

The influx of Han Chinese (the dominant ethnic group of China) has led to

A Hani woman spinning wool.

a decline in the use of the Tibetan language, and has produced increased pressure on Tibetan resources. Pro-independence activists continue to be imprisoned and tortured, and Buddhist monks and nuns are targets of Chinese abuse.

The environment has suffered as well. A major hydroelectric project on Yamdrok Tso, a sacred lake, has caused major environmental loss to the Tibetan people. Tibetan communities in exile have raised international awareness of human rights violations, including religious persecution, international funding for destructive development projects, and forced abortion and sterilization of Tibetan women (McGranahan 1993:125–126). Although the U.S. government declared the Chinese occupation of Tibet to be illegal, its desire to continue to foster the Chinese free market economic reforms has prevented human rights activists from having any impact on policies favoring trade with China.

Modernizing India: The Response to Colonialism

India, in precolonial times, occupied a much larger territory than it does today, though the exact size expanded and contracted as trade, hegemonic control, and agricultural production waxed or waned. Modern India was carved out of precolonial India by British interests, who controlled the South Asian subcontinent until 1947.

Origins of India

India was and is the core of South Asia, and has dominated the subcontinent for over three thousand years. The cultural area of South Asia is extensive, covering such modern countries as Pakistan, Bangladesh, India, Nepal, Bhutan, and the large island of Sri Lanka to the south of India. The dominant religions have been Hinduism and Islam, and it is the region where Buddhism emerged. Buddhism is an offshoot of Hinduism that has been integrated into most of these regions and became, with Confucianism, a dominant religion of China. Karla Sinopoli has shown how the ideologies and power structures of ancient and comparatively recent Indian Hindu states were determined by such factors as distance from the central core, long-distance trade, and control over the production and the distribution of trade goods (Sinopoli 1994b). When trade was successfully monopolized and tied to tank-style irrigation agriculture, powerful city-states emerged. When either of these was threatened, the civilizations contracted, often becoming the vassals of other powerful Hindu states.

South and central India lie within the tropics, while northern India is influenced by the Himalaya-Kush mountains, which separate India from China, and is more temperate. The major rivers of the Indian subcontinent, the Indus, the Ganges, and the Brahmaputra, have their origins in the Himalayas and have been used for long-distance waterborne trade for thousands of years. These rivers carry alluvial soils down to the plains where Indian society originated. Tropical rain forests in the south, interspersed with arid uplands, were the home of tribal societies that were not integrated into states until modern times.

The earliest city-states in South Asia were Harappa at the northern end of the Indus River Valley and Mohenjo-Daro in the south, both manifestations of what archaeologists call Harappan civilization (and both in what is today Pakistan). Both cities were built according to similar plans and their populations, supported by irrigation agriculture, hovered around 30,000. Each contained a large walled citadel made of bricks and had special buildings with pools for ritual baths and temples that were probably used as storehouses. The two cities were located on a flood plain that lacked any mineral resources, but they produced finely crafted objects made of copper, bronze, and jewels. These objects were used in maintaining extensive trade contacts with China and the region of the Persian Gulf. Like China and other ancient civilizations, trade was one of the factors that stimulated the growth of hierarchical social organization. Ceramic representations of humans and animals may have been forerunners of important Hindu deities, and the still undeciphered writing may be early versions of the *Vedas,* texts on which the Hindu religion is based. Hinduism is one of the two major religions of South Asia; the other is Buddhism.

Harappa and Mohenjo-Daro appear to have collapsed around 1500 B.C. According to one theory, the manufacturing of bricks for the extensive fortifications and temples may have denuded local forests and led to extensive flooding and salinization, of which there is evidence (Fagan 1989). The problems of irrigation, deforestation, and salinization are also modern problems in South Asia.

The Rise of Hinduism and the Caste System

The core of South Asian civilization shifted to the Ganges river valley, but many elements of Harappan civilization, including beliefs, survived and formed an important part of ancient Hindu states. Hindu civilization developed after Indo-European-speaking Aryan nomads from the Iranian plateau spread over much of western South Asia. They brought with them Sanskrit, which is the originating language of European civilizations. Hegemonic control by the invading Aryans, rather than irrigation, brought Hindu society into being. The caste system (a hierarchical social structure based on the Hindu religion, explained below) emerged, and a mythology that rationalized it became formalized as the Hindu religion, much as the Koran formulated the Islamic state in Southwest Asia and North Africa, and Confucianism conceptualized the state to the north in China.

The origins of the Hindu religion are extremely ancient, and underlie much of civilization in South Asia, Southeast Asia, and in the western Pacific in Indonesia, Malaysia, and the Philippines. Hinduism underlies many other religions of these regions, including Buddhism and Islam. Hinduism is associated with three major beliefs and objectives. The first one is that of reincarnation, called *samsara,* which holds that one's soul, or *atman,* is reborn each generation in a new organism, but not necessarily as a human being. Whether one is born again as a higher-order spirit escaping the cycle of life, as a lower or higher human of the caste system, as an animal, or as an insect depends on the second major belief: *karma.* Karma is destiny, which is only partially influenced by one's behavior, but can also be influenced by the often capricious desires of dozens of cosmic gods. These must be worshiped, and their special support petitioned to achieve the third objective: *moksha. Moksha* is the ultimate release from the cycle of birth and rebirth, and it is the ultimate aim of the Hindu religion. The Hindu religion explains much of Indian society, including the caste system and the very high regard given to animals, as the rebirth of the soul into a new being. The creatures into whose bodies the souls are born could be one's unsuccessful relatives who are beginning the life cycle again due to a lifetime of corruption (the cow in the road, or the bug under your shoe may be your aunt or uncle). Thus, life is sacred.

The Hindu model resembles the Chinese Confucian classics in laying out a powerful ethic of rule, showing when power should be used to control the lower castes and when it should not, and providing the moral authority to rationalize the caste system. The Indian state, in its various manifestations, depended on Hinduism for the rationalization of the activities of the rulers.

According to Hindu belief, cities and villages were divided according to the specialized activities of people, and people were expected to marry within their occupational group (called **caste endogamy**). There were four *varnas* or castes, each assigned to specific locations and tasks. Traditionally, the lowest *varna* was that of the cultivators and serfs or **Sudra**. The **Brahmans** were the priests and teachers. The **Kshatriya** were also elites, assigned the role of warriors and rulers, while the **Vaisya** were the landholders and merchants (Basham 1959; Keesing 1976). Below the four *varnas* and outside the class system, according to some Indian authorities, were the so-called "untouchables." Each *varna* came to contain within it numerous subdivisions that designated more specific occupations. It is these subdivisions that came to be known as castes (and subcastes) and whose status within the caste hierarchy shifted from region to region. This basic model has remained stable in Hindu ideology for over 2000 years.

The caste system cannot be separated from the Hindu religion; both appear to have evolved together and reinforced one another. The Hindu religion is based on the twin ideas of hierarchy and purity. The Hindu term *jati* refers to a biologically based kinship group that is culturally ascribed to a hierarchical position according to a theory of purity. Those at the bottom are least pure, and those at the top are the most pure, and purity is designated by the practice of rituals leading to **nirvana,** escape from this world by the upper castes at death. Only those at the top are allowed to practice the highest-rank principles of purity, relegating all others to lower levels.

Virginity is an ideal expectation at marriage. A young woman who has lost her virginity may be stoned to death by her own relatives. Marriages are arranged by families to link individuals by caste level. Infant betrothal and the prohibition of divorce were common, and still are in rural areas, as is *sati,* the custom whereby a wife is supposed to throw herself on her husband's funeral pyre.

The entire Hindu caste system is held together by the **jajmani** *system,* which links local castes in a series of traditionally determined exchanges of goods and services. In these relationships, one party is viewed as the patron or *jajman* and the other as the worker or *kamin,* conforming to pervasive notions of hierarchy. In many parts of village India, jajmani relationships between families were hereditary. Technological change, new jobs in cities, and increased participation in the cash economy have caused the breakdown of the jajmani system in recent years.

Buddhism: The Search for Equality

Another important religion that began in India and spread across the entire mainland of Asia to Korea, and to Japan, is Buddhism. Buddhism was born out of Hinduism, but differs from Hinduism fundamentally in its disregard for hierarchy. The religion of Buddhism is largely ascribed to one person, Siddhartha Gautama, who was born about 563 B.C. in southern Nepal. He was a member of an elite caste, who sought religious enlightenment at age twenty-nine, abandoning his wife and child to become a wandering monk. After wandering throughout northeastern India for six years, imposing self-denial and self-torture on himself, he is said to have sat under a shady bo or *bodhi* tree and experienced enlightenment, hence the name *Buddha* was applied to him.

The Buddha's basic message is called **dharma,** which means "saving truth." The Buddha, like Hindu preachers, taught that existence is a cycle of death and rebirth. However, the Buddha discounted hierarchy, and also self-torture or self-denial, and argued that only by abandoning the attachment to worldly goods could one escape into *nirvana.* During the 200s B.C., Asoka, an Indian emperor, made Buddhism a state religion, and it then spread to China, Nepal, and to the rest of Asia. In the meantime, Buddhism became a minor religion in India.

Four schools of Buddhism developed, all with much in common, beginning with Theravada Buddhism or The Way of the Elders, which is the only one of the early schools to survive, and is found today in Burma, Cambodia, Sri Lanka, Laos, and Thailand. This school emphasizes the life of Buddha and the virtues of the monastic life, a practice common in these countries. The second "way" is Mahayana Buddhism, which stresses the existence of many Buddhas who can save people through grace and compassion. Mahayana Buddhism is found primarily in Japan and in other countries of East Asia. Mantrayana Buddhism, found in Mongolia and Japan, stresses a special relationship between a guru (spiritual leader) and his followers. Finally, Zen Buddhism, practiced in Japan, is much like Mantrayana Buddhism but emphasizes a special state of enlightenment called *satori*, a special flash of insight into oneself and the universe.

Islam and Trade in India

The caste system was a form of labor exploitation, and from time to time it was replaced by trade-oriented Islamic rule when Muslim invaders took over India, such as in the Mughal period just before British rule. The Mughal period begins in the ninth century with the gradual expansion of Islam into the trade-based cities of the west coast of India, and then expanded in the eleventh century when the city states of Bengal and Gujarat were brought under Muslim control. Islam later spread into the Malay straits, and east as far as the Philippines and Indonesia. By the fourteenth century, all of India except the Hindu kingdom of Vijanagar was under Islamic control. The Muslim religion considers its members equal and this appealed to many Hindus, who converted to Islam. As Eric Wolf put it, "Islam and trade thus went hand in hand in the Asian seas" (Wolf 1982:234).

While trade cities were brought under the control of separate Muslim leaders, the Mughal Empire brought the separate states under the control of a single hegemonic state, created by Timurid Turks from Turkestan, whose chief, Babur, became the first Mughal emperor in 1527. The Mughal system was further organized by his grandson, Akbar, who placed the power over the new kingdom in the hands of a military elite, called the *Mansabdars,* most of whom were recruited from Turkestan and Persia, but many of whom were local Muslims and Hindu chieftains. The *Mansabdars* formed a cosmopolitan elite who were rewarded with lifetime grants (not unlike the *ejido* system described in the next chapter for Latin America). Under them came the *Zamindars,* local elites drawn from the upper castes of each region. The *Mansabdars* were opposed by many Hindu leaders, including Nanak, the founder of Sikhism. The *Mansabdars* were at first tolerant of ethnic and religious differences, but later they became increasingly intolerant, giving an opening to British interests, which used the divisions between Hindus and Muslims to gain support for the expansion of the British Empire.

Colonial Rule

The English came to India in search of trade, not conquest, in the seventeenth century. They acquired *entrepots* (trade enclaves) from the *Mansabdar* elites. The British had the right to deal with Indian traders, but the rulers of the cities had control over that trade (determining price, profit, volume traded, and so on).

When the British first established their fort cities along the coasts in the sixteenth century, the Muslim dynasty was declining in power (Stavrianos 1982:274). Slowly, Hindu leaders from the southern provinces challenged the power of the northern Muslim elite. The British supported the Hindu elites in order to undermine the Muslim rulers, and the region came to be controlled by an alliance of local Hindu princes (the *Zamindars*) and British merchants (members of the East India Company who were the traders mentioned above). At the Battle of Plassey in 1757, the Muslim *Mansabdars* were overthrown by English troops who were financially supported by Hindu *Zamindar* merchants (Wolf 1982:244).

Conversion to a Capitalist Economy   By 1818, the British were in total control but preferred to rule through the *Zamindar* elites. This type of indirect rule is characteristic of trade and tribute empires. However, the British converted the tributary economy into a capitalist, private property economy with the Zamindars becoming the owners of the land but required to pass along most of the tribute to the British. According to Eric Wolf:

> In the Permanent Settlement that the English introduced in Bengal in 1793, however, the *Zamindars* were turned into outright property owners, required to turn over to the British administration nine-tenths of the tribute received from their peasants, and retaining one-tenth for their own personal use. The English thus created, at one stroke, a class of 3,000 Indian landlords who held the same property rights as English landlords including the right to sell, mortgage, and inherit land (1982:247).

Thus, English rule converted a diffuse tributary system into a centralized tax system based on rights to private property by an upper caste. These changes occurred after private property rights had been established in Great Britain, but their impact in India was quite different. The average peasant was stripped of all his or her traditional rights and was placed into a forced contractual relationship with the new owners of the land, who were now only interested in cheap labor, not with tribute and rights (Wolf 1982:247–248). The lands of previous tributary tribes and states were made the private property of the old elites of India. The British created a new political system in which the old regional elites were transformed into national elites who owned almost all of the resources of their region.

Many of the local populations were clearly disturbed by increased British control and by the transfer of resources to old elites. The Indian military rebelled against British garrisons in the Great Mutiny of 1857. The British put down the mutiny at a great cost of life and imposed a more direct form of British rule that lasted until independence in 1947. For close to one hundred years, British rule favored policies supporting the landowning Zamindars and exports of agricultural products, particularly opium, which was exported to China. The Zamindars forced the peasants to grow poppies (for opium), tea, and cotton for export instead of their traditional foods. The development of Indian industry was discouraged, and so India "underdeveloped" in contrast to the core (Stavrianos 1982:277). The new land laws were to have the long-term effect of reinforcing the Indian caste system, and the Hindu religion, instead of weakening them (capitalism is thought to have weakened traditional institutions in Western Europe, which did not really happen in India).

Liberation and the Rise of State Socialism Mohandas Gandhi led India to its liberation from British rule, and the subcontinent of India was divided into Hindu India and Muslim Pakistan in 1947. (In 1971, what had been East Pakistan became the independent nation of Bangladesh.) After 1948, India came to be controlled by the Congress Party. While there were other parties, a monopoly of power was held in the hands of elite members of the Congress Party, most of whom were members of the landowning classes.

Thus, the British created a hybrid political system. The new system, which dominated the Indian subcontinent after partition, can also be found in other regions under British control, such as Burma (Myanmar) and Egypt. The British colonial system united traditional tributary hierarchical bureaucracies with a private property capitalist model. After British abandonment of colonial control, former British colonies in Asia remained under the control of those elites who owed their dominant positions to British policies. In most cases, the bureaucracies created prior to British abandonment of the colonial system survived to the present time (an exception is Burma, which went through a socialist revolution in 1961).

India chose to move in the direction of state socialism, modeling its economy on a blend of British democracy and an Indian form of state capitalism and socialism. The private sector was not outlawed. The economic system of India constrained the growth of the private sector by allowing it to expand only with government permission. Heavy industry was reserved for the public sector and was stunted by quotas and high tariffs. Controls were placed on land use, on trade in farm products, and on the price of agricultural commodities. In the 1980s, India tried to expand the economy by borrowing and produced large-scale debt. On the political side, the Congress Party, while arguing it was democratic, controlled India much as the Institutional Revolutionary Party (PRI) controls Mexico. Corruption and economic development went hand in hand.

Ethnic Politics: Sikh Struggles for Independence

The Congress Party reserved the most important political and commercial positions for party members, the members of the upper economic classes. Other ethnic and religious groups, such as the Sikhs of Punjab and lower-ranked Hindus and Muslims felt discriminated against. The government and the Congress Party strove to create a secular, socialist state, and came into conflict with various Hindu and Muslim communities. Attacks on the government and counterattacks on ethnic and religious groups grew through the 1980s and 1990s.

Sikh ethnic identity dates to the fifteenth century. Guru Nanak, born to a Punjabi Hindu family in 1469, developed the Sikh religion and distinct way of life. Sikhism is not, strictly speaking, an ethnic identity, but is a way of life based on a religion that is similar to Hinduism, out of which it grew, and differs primarily in rejecting caste and rank (McLeod 1989). Many writers believe Sikhism

Modernizing India. The famous second Five Year Plan of the Indian government began in 1955. The goal was to swiftly create state-owned heavy industry. The plan included construction of steel mills (to join the existing private steel mill at Jamshedpur, shown in picture), dams, power stations, and heavy engineering plants. Costs, especially of needed imports, and the failure of the agricultural sector to expand quickly enough, prevented full implementation of the plan.

is a variation on the Hindu religion in much the same way that Protestantism is a variant of Christianity.

Sikhs distinguish themselves from Hindus by abjuring polytheism and the caste system. Sikhs believe in one god, Akal Purakh, who reveals himself through *sat*, both truth and reality. According to Guru Nanak, man's duty is to meditate on the revelation of *sat* (Kapur 1986). Nine gurus followed Guru Nanak, teaching an egalitarian anticaste ethic that put the new religion into conflict with Hindus and the ruling Mughal dynasties (which were Muslim). The Sikhs of Punjab constructed the Golden Temple of Amritsar, a large palatial structure, to serve as both a religious and political center (Kapur 1986).

Attacks by the Mughal elites on the Sikh religion, including the assassination of one guru, led to the development of specialized militancy by Sikh males. After the conquest of India by the British, Sikh political power in the state of Punjab was shattered. However, Sikh men were recruited to the army, in which they earned a special reputation as fighters. Sikhs were extremely successful economically in Punjab, primarily as farmers of wheat and barley. Throughout the nineteenth and early twentieth centuries, Sikhs demanded the return of control over what they believed to be their province, though they did not represent more than one-third of the population of Punjab. Their demands were based on financial and other contributions to India.

After India won its independence from Great Britain, the debate continued between Sikhs and the Congress Party, which gained control over India. Sikhs wanted to control that region of the Punjab where they were numerically dominant. The Congress Party responded by imposing controls on Sikh religious temples, particularly the Golden Temple of Amritsar. Sikh temples are very wealthy. The Sikhs demanded autonomy for their temples, but the Indian state continued to impose its control, taxing the temples.

In October of 1984, Prime Minister Indira Gandhi was assassinated by her handpicked Sikh bodyguards. This extraordinary and violent act was the Sikh's response to the Indian army's storming of the Golden Temple at Amritsar in the state of Punjab. In 1984, debate over temple control exploded as militant Sikh radicals took over the Golden Temple and used it as a base for terrorist activities against Hindus. The Indian military invaded the sacred temple in an attempt to remove Sikh terrorists, and several hundred Sikhs were killed, including a militant fundamentalist Sikh preacher, Jarnail Singh Bhindranwale (Kapur 1986:226; Hardgrave 1992:106).

For some time, Sikh terrorists have been killing Hindus in the state of Punjab while Sikhs living outside Punjab have been the targets of reprisals by Hindu terrorists. Killings and reprisals have been a part of ethnic animosities for centuries. In 1991 alone more than 5,000 people were killed in the Punjab due to terrorist and counterterrorist activities (Hardgrave 1992:112).

The demands by Sikhs for an independent state, to be called Kalistan, must be put into perspective by mention of similar demands and violence by Muslims in Kashmir state and by tribal groups in Assam and other regions. One tribal group, the Nagas, was promised an independent state at the time of partition, but instead was split between three new Indian states (Assam, Arunachal, and Manipur). The Nagas demand a new state of Nagaland, and are becoming increasingly embittered by Indian repression and human rights abuse (Maybury–Lewis 1997:42). In addition, there are other ethnic and religious movements toward separatism in Bilhar, Uttar Pradesh, and Tamil Nadu.

How can ethnic violence be explained in India and elsewhere? Let's go back to the models presented in Chapters 8 and 10: primordialism, instrumentalism, and relative deprivation. At first glance, ethnic violence in India appears to be the consequence of the first model. India is described by many as an ideal democratic society based on the philosophy of Mohandas Gandhi and his protests against British colonial policy. India appears to have adopted the British system of secular democracy with a prime minister and two houses of parliament. With such a democratic social system, only a primordialist model makes sense because political differences should be settled democratically. However, a deeper reading of Indian history reveals a very different picture. Selig S. Harrison shows India to be a highly centralized and socialistic society, one in which the elite Hindu castes have long controlled the economy to their advantage and discriminated against other castes and ethnic groups (Harrison 1992). This being the case, the point to be made here is that ethnic violence in India is the consequence of ethnic repression by the institutions of the state, not some kind of primordialist urge, and thus is better explained by the instrumentalist model and the deprivation resulting from domination by elites.

The problem of ethnic conflict is widespread in Asia, and, as we have learned, in Africa, the Middle East, and in Eastern Europe. It has become particularly destructive in the island nation of Sri Lanka, just to the south of India, where the Tamil Tigers, terrorists from Hindu communities, are attacking Buddhist communities in a country that is dominated by the Buddhist religion, much as India is dominated by the Hindu religion. One general lesson to be learned from these conflicts is that, in our globalizing world, there may be a great need for decentralized or federal states (such as is being experimented with in Ethiopia). But territorial states feel they must remain highly integrated to fight against economic competition from other states, presenting a real dilemma in the management of national institutions.

Indonesia: An Emerging Tiger

Indonesia, a country in Southeast Asia that consists of more than 13,600 islands, is also ethnically very complex, and its political system is far from democratic. It includes the large islands of Borneo and Java, half of the island of New Guinea, and the newly incorporated island of East Timor. It is a region that, while experiencing considerable ethnic conflict, has also had successful and rapid eco-

For a Balinese woman, perfect balance is a cultural expectation.

nomic growth. In the sixteenth century, the islands of Indonesia belonged to independent Islamic principalities, and before that, most of the urban centers were Hindu. When the Dutch imposed their rule on Indonesia in the seventeenth century, it was a complex mix of religions, peasants, and tribes of many ethnic backgrounds.

The Dutch imposed their own political system on the varied peoples of Indonesia. The anthropologist, Clifford Geertz, described the Dutch colonial pattern of paddy rice agriculture in Indonesia as a form of "agricultural involution" (Geertz 1963). What he meant is that, instead of evolving into a more complex and prosperous economy, Dutch export policies had the consequence of forcing the economy to grow in on itself, becoming ever more complex as the population grew, but producing poverty for the peasants because most of the rice they grew was exported, not eaten (Geertz 1963).

Geertz lived in the Indonesian town of Pare, which is on the island of Java, studying the relationship between Islam and social structure. He was there during a violent anti-Dutch revolution under President Sukarno, who attempted to bring about a socialist-style government, and a counterrevolution in 1965 led by President Suharto. During Sukarno's revolution and Suharto's counterrevolution over 500,000 Communists were slaughtered. When President Suharto overthrew Sukarno, the people of Indonesia were among the poorest in the world with an average income of about $100 a year. Today the population has expanded to nearly 200 million, making it the world's fourth most populous country as well as the world's largest Islamic country, and the economy is no longer "involuting." Indonesia has become one of the Asian Tigers, growing at a rate of 6 percent per year with an average income of almost $1,000 a year, making it the largest Southeast Asian economy.

Geertz, who lived through the bloodbath of the Sukarno–Suharto revolutions, recently reflected on his return to Pare after the killings, in 1971:

> . . . the killing fields had come and gone, the national regime had changed from civilian to military, and what politics existed was dominated by a semi-official umbrella party promoting a semi-official civil religion. Pare was still physically about what it had been. With a net outflow of population nearly matching natural increase, it was not even much larger. The same people, the same groups (though there were no Communists and fewer Sukarnoists), the same bureaus, were still in charge, and most of them operated with the same formal and status ridden ideas of right and propriety. Daily life, except for the fact that the ideologues were quiet or silenced, was not much different . . . what was different, or anyway seemed different to me, was mood, humor, the color of experience. It was a chastened place (Geertz 1996:5).

Clifford Geertz also worked on the nearby island of Bali, which is not Islamic but Hindu, to describe the culture of its people. Balinese dances had been studied two decades before by Margaret Mead and Gregory Bateson. Mead and Bateson's photographic study of the Hindu folk dances caught the importance of status and style, of balance and intricate customs such as the complex *legong,* a girls' dance about ancient longings of love and of battle, and the *bjauk,* which uses masked dancers. These theatrical, courtly and formal dances are usually accompanied with bands called *gamelans* of cymbals, drums, and keyed instruments. The Dutch colonial government did not intervene in the economy of the Balinese, but it did impose its political organization, bringing about the deaths of many of the ritual kings who ruled Bali at the beginning of the twentieth century. The culture of Bali had been left alone by the first Islamic dynasties of Indonesia, and was largely allowed to continue practicing its Hindu culture by the Dutch. Mead, Bateson, and Geertz all studied the relationship between the Hindu religion and the theatrical expression of Balinese culture, which has largely survived today. Hindu culture in Bali is extremely intricate, ornate, and attracts the attention of many visitors.

Because of its protected position, Bali did not suffer the agricultural involution described by Geertz for the other islands. Today, "eco-tour" guides take European, Japanese, and American tourists to view the dances with the same intricate paddy fields in the background once photographed by Mead and Bateson back in the 1930s. Many travel guides are from mainland Java, and the Balinese do not particularly care for the attention they receive, continuing to grow and export rice and fine cloth.

But Indonesia in the 1990s is not the Indonesia of the 1940s. The tourist to Bali, if he or she can read Indonesian, may pick up the local newspaper and read accounts about the battles in East Timor or Iran Jaya (Western New Guinea), where a now aging President Suharto is trying to suppress revolutionaries and is critiqued by Amnesty International for human rights violations. The reports read strangely like Dutch newspaper accounts of the uprising in far-off colonies of Indonesia in the 1940s, prompting the reader to wonder about colonialism in the modern age in which the colonist is the one once colonized.

Changing Vietnam: Another Tiger Emerging

Vietnam has struggled for two thousand years to maintain its independence. For most of its history it has been China that dominated Vietnam, either directly or through puppet emperors. The Khmer Empire, a hydraulic civilization based on paddy rice agriculture and long-distance trade, arose along the Mekong river in modern Cambodia, and gave rise to the distinct cultures of southeast Asia combining Hinduism, Buddhism, and Confucianism. Most northern Vietnamese were ethnically Chinese, but over the years have created a separate identity (Collingwood 1991:93).

North Vietnam was conquered by China as early as 214 B.C., and again in 111 B.C., when Han Chinese established firm control. The Chinese dominated the region of North Vietnam (known as Tonkin) for a thousand years (*viet* means 'people,' *nam* is Chinese for 'south'), and Chinese culture, particularly Confucian values, dominated. The southern part of Vietnam was ruled as a separate

Two decades after a devastating war, the young people of Saigon are on the move.

kingdom by a people known as Champa. Both the north and south were brought under the control of a separate ethnic group known as Annamese in the sixteenth century. By 1700, two distinct Vietnamese dynasties founded by Annamese gained control and separately ruled North and South Vietnam.

In 1787, Nguyen-Anh, a general, signed a military aid treaty with France, which was interested in opening trade along the Red and Mekong rivers (Collingwood 1991:93). France soon dominated Vietnam, and also the neighboring countries of Cambodia and Laos. France called these three countries Indochina. France was to have a difficult time ruling this rich region. Not only is it geographically very rugged, with mountains, rivers, and marshlands, but it also has a highly diversified mixture of ethnic Chinese, Indonesian, Malaysian, Thai, Vietnamese, Laotians, and Khmers, who were traditional enemies long before the French arrived (Collingwood 1991:93).

France became the authoritarian ruler of Vietnam. Its policies toward the Vietnamese people were to have important ramifications in the twentieth century. French policy, over half a century, created extreme forms of deprivation throughout Vietnamese society: peasants, middle classes, and elites all suffered at French hands. The result was a classic peasant revolution whose origins were misinterpreted by American foreign policy makers. That misinterpretation resulted in what is perhaps the most disastrous foreign policy decision of all time for the United States.

The imposition of French rule on Vietnam did not produce an easy union. There were continuous uprisings, which led the French sociologist Paul Mus to warn the French against the "convenient notion" that Vietnamese peasants were "a passive mass, only interested in their daily bowl of rice, and terrorized into

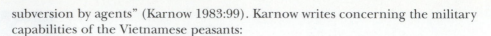

subversion by agents" (Karnow 1983:99). Karnow writes concerning the military capabilities of the Vietnamese peasants:

> Their country's frequent wars also infused in the Vietnamese a readiness to defend themselves, so that they evolved into a breed of warriors (Karnow 1983:98–99).

The French turned rice into an export commodity. Exports in 1860 were 57,000 tons; by 1937, exports had risen to 1,548,000 tons. To make this increase possible, the French supported the development of a class of large landowners:

> The result was that in Tonkin 500 large landowners—both French and Vietnamese—came to own 20 percent of the land; another 17,000 owned a further 20 percent. The remaining small holders, about one million in strength, divided the rest among themselves; the average holding amounted to less than half a hectare per family (Wolf 1969:166).

Land was also drained and irrigated by the French in the Vietnamese South and then sold at low prices in an attempt to recover costs. By 1938, half of the South's arable land was planted in rice, and about 50 percent of this was owned by only 2.5 percent of the landowners. More than half of the southern population of about 700,000 families were landless (Wolf 1969:166).

Deprivation ran high among peasants and middle-class Vietnamese alike and provided fuel for nationalist social movements. Vietnamese intellectuals found weapons for their battle in Western teaching. Children who went to school in France and returned to Vietnam soon found themselves taking increasingly more radical political positions, often based on theories and ideologies they had learned abroad. One of these young people, Ho Chi Minh (Nguyen ai Quoc), trained in China by Maoist leaders, organized the League for the Independence of Vietnam (or Viet Minh) in 1941 to fight the Japanese invaders. On their defeat in 1945, he and his followers assumed they would take over the government. Instead, a civil war ensued, eventually involving the United States.

The war in Vietnam can now be looked back on with the hindsight of history. It was an anticore nationalist revolution much like those fought in Russia and China. The Marxism of the new Vietnamese state did not bring it prosperity, but it did bring the people a sense of dignity. Now Vietnamese leaders are introducing some democratic policies and new open market systems. The Vietnamese refer to the new policy as *doi moi,* a term that has the same meaning as the Russian word *peristroika,* that is, "restructuring." In many ways paralleling events in China, the Vietnamese economy has begun to improve dramatically, but the Communist government insists on maintaining control, much to the anger of the younger Vietnamese who do not remember the war. The government of Vietnam is attempting to attract foreign investment, but foreigners are reluctant to invest in a country that is controlled by an authoritarian government. As in China, the pressure for democratic reform by outsiders and by the young is intense, but the old Communists are afraid to let go control of the country for fear it will dissolve into its constituent ethnic and religious regions.

Vietnam's economy is still among the poorest of Southeast Asia, but the model for the future has shifted from China to neighboring Thailand, whose economy is booming. The United States maintained an economic boycott of Vietnam until December of 1992, when President Bush decided to lift it as a gift to the Vietnamese leaders who had produced extensive new information on MIAs (Americans missing in action between 1960 and 1975) and POWs (former prisoners of war).

The Vietnamese revolution and the war with the United States had the effect of destabilizing all Southeast Asia, particularly neighboring Kampuchea (Cambodia) and Laos, both of which went through violent revolutions and are still seeking to return to a normal existence. Had the United States, in its policy decisions, taken more account of the culture history of Vietnam and less of the chimera of communism, it is likely that much senseless conflict could have been avoided. One of the lessons history provides is that China, the assumed ally of North Vietnam, was as greatly feared as France or the United States by the Vietnamese people. China, in turn, was much too involved with its own internal disputes to overrun the whole of Asia and to transform it into a giant communist state.

Japan: The Leading Asian Tiger

Americans are increasingly concerned with competition from Japan and with Japanese investment in the economy of the United States, including the purchase of baseball franchises and urban real estate. While Americans focus on the success of Japan, the larger story is that the core-periphery set of relationships of the last century-and-a-half is being tilted in a new direction as the countries of the Pacific Rim begin to coparticipate in the development of a new core with two or three centers, Japan being the most powerful of them.

Japan is one of only three major Asian countries to escape domination and colonization by the West (China and Thailand are the other two), although none completely escaped Western influence. Like China, Japan deliberately isolated itself economically and politically from the West in the early eighteenth century. But by the late nineteenth century, Japanese leaders realized that China's strategy was not working and that China was being partitioned by European powers. When Japan was forced to open its doors by Commodore Matthew Perry in 1853, the Samurai elite decided to abandon the feudal system and to introduce capitalism, which transformed Japan after the Meiji Restoration of 1868–1911.

Traditional Japanese Culture

Japan has the oldest constitutional monarchy in the world, dating back to Foundation Day, February 11, 660, when Jimmu was enthroned as the first emperor.

The Japanese language developed out of an ancient Chinese dialect. Japanese culture combined rice cultivation, Confucianism and Buddhism on top of an earlier nature-worshiping religion called Shintoism. These continue today as the core of Japanese culture.

During World War II, Japanese culture became of central interest to American anthropologists, particularly Ruth Benedict, whose book, *The Chrysanthemum and the Sword* (1946), attempted to explain the nature of Japanese institutions. Her book became highly controversial because of its psychoanalytic approach, but much of what she described showed how anthropologists could study the institutions of modernizing societies. Benedict, and many more recent writers, have showed how Japanese culture developed as a type of decentralized feudalism, which differed from the highly centralized state of China. The emperor was basically a figurehead, and the royal family was a symbol of Japanese unity rather than the real rulers. Symbols of power and ritual became very important in Japan, many based on traditional religion. Power was held by feudal lords, who developed a culture based on hierarchy, regard for the family, and ancestor worship within a framework of Shinto, Buddhist, and Confucian values. Feudal rule was sustained by a class of warriors, the **Samurai** (derived from the Japanese word for servant). In 1192, the leader of one of the feudal clans seized control of the country and declared himself the supreme military leader, or **shogun.** Japan evolved a militaristic culture within which Zen, a special version of Buddhism, placed a unique emphasis on self-discipline, a Japanese value that has remained to the present. Anthropologists and historians largely agree that the most important Japanese value became **bushido,** or the way of the warrior, a concept obligating the warrior to carry out his lord's wishes or commit **seppeku,** or ritual suicide.

The Westernization of Japan

Commodore Perry's opening of Japan made the feudal elite realize that the decentralized power structure would not work in a modern world. Japan centralized its political system during the Meiji Restoration, beginning with the abandonment of the samurai feudal system, and the restoration of the Emperor of Japan. Japan sent students and researchers to study in Western universities and it hired foreign engineers and intellectuals to help design a new Japan. Japanese leaders tried to model the country's new institutions on the most successful institutions of the core. For example, it borrowed its financial institutions from Germany and its educational institutions from France (Reischauer 1988).

While Japan imported Western capitalism, it only imported a few democratic ideas. Japanese leaders in the 1880s felt that it would be several decades before the people of Japan would be ready to understand democratic institutions. The British concept of a parliament was turned into a Japanese institution (the Diet) with 1 percent of the population having the right to vote and the prime minister being selected by special advisors to the emperor. Western ideas, such as the separation of government from business enterprises and the development of labor unions to protect workers, were foreign. The Japanese cultural ideal was the *ie,* or "house" (the opposite of the American emphasis on the individual and his or her success):

Simply put, this is the Japanese socio-psychological tendency which emphasizes (in the sense of protecting, cherishing, finding needs for, or functioning best in) "us" against "them" (Yamamura 1987:133).

In Japan, a close working relationship evolved between the most powerful commercial families, called the *zaibatsu* (combines that organized finance, business, and industry), and the government. Government made investments in the private sector subsidizing such powerful families as the Mitsubishi clan in the development of industry. Employees hired to work for the powerful family-owned corporations became like members of the family and their jobs were secure for life. Labor unions were disdained, both by the industrialists and by the workers, who considered themselves to have quasi-kinship connections to the business houses that employed them.

At the turn of the century, Japan had caught up to the West in the use of many industrial technologies. In 1905, Japan and Russia fought a naval battle that proved the superior technology of Japanese battleships (Reischauer 1988). But Japan lacked natural resources to support its growing industry and Japanese leaders decided they should develop colonies on mainland Asia. In the 1930s, Japan gained hegemony over many of its neighbors, particularly Korea, Taiwan, and China. Japan also forced economic dominance on much of East Asia. Japanese expansionist tendencies, particularly in Manchuria, made it a feared nation and brought threats to it from the core countries. In the late 1930s, the Japanese military gained control of the government. Threats, counterthreats, and cultural misunderstandings on both sides brought Japan into World War II on the side of the Axis powers against the United States and its allies.

From a technological point of view, the War in the Pacific was close. Japanese air and sea technology took the United States by surprise. Many have argued that Japan lost the war, not because of inferior technology, but because of poor strategies at several battles, such as the battle of Midway, that were based on Japanese assumptions about the poor fighting capacity of the American military.

The occupation of Japan led to new political and economic innovations imposed on Japan by the American military. One of these was the introduction of American-style democracy (Cohen 1987). General Douglas MacArthur rewrote the Japanese constitution to reflect his own vision of an Americanized Japan. A new British-style "Diet" (parliament) was developed with a separation of powers among the three branches of government: legislative, executive, and judicial. Attempts were made to break up the *zaibatsu* and destroy the power of the old entrepreneurial families.

However, the fear of communism in Asia led the United States to support the rapid reindustrialization of Japan. Reforms to government and industry were soft-pedaled so that, while the political system was reformed to allow greater democratic participation, the bureaucracies were left alone, and the old *zaibatsu* were allowed to reconstitute themselves in the early 1950s into informal *keiretsu* (networks of affiliated companies) (Reischauer 1988:306–307). Of particular importance was the continued evolution of a financial relationship between government and industry that was and is radically different from that which exists in the United States. In Japan, newly developing business enterprises have been systematically supported by the government until they are able to stand on their own feet. Businesses in crisis are often met with financial help from the government. Furthermore, politicians, government bureaucrats, and those in business help each other in ways that Americans would label "corrupt" but which Japanese perceive as "doing business."

The *keiretsu* are central to Japan's postwar growth and success. Western scholars tend to confuse the *keiretsu* with the more familiar conglomerates of the Western core that attempt to monopolize a single industry (such as AT&T's attempt to monopolize the communication industry of the United States prior to 1984). But the *keiretsu* are peculiarly Japanese. *Keiretsu* consist of sets of firms which specialize in different economic tasks such as banking, manufacturing, energy production, export–import marketing, and so on, in cooperation with each other. One can think of these different business enterprises as distinct rooms within a single house. *Keiretsu* attempt to set up firms in every important segment of the economy. Such organizations in the United States would be subject to antitrust laws. Antitrust laws have little importance in Japan. The existence of *keiretsu* allows Japanese firms to integrate the latest developments on matters related to financing, technological development, personnel, purchasing, marketing, and planning in the most efficient and cooperative style possible (Yamamura 1987). Competition between firms in the United States drives up the cost of innovations and their use. The Japanese *keiretsu*, as an inter-firm organization, makes Japanese production less expensive than in old core countries.

In addition to the *keiretsu*, the Japanese have developed new techniques of personnel management that are also highly efficient. American social science research during the Depression years of the 1930s produced many studies suggesting ways to improve corporate decision-making (particularly the Western Electric studies in Chicago) that were never implemented in the United States. Several of these studies were utilized by Japanese corporate managers to redesign manufacturing techniques in Japan after World War II. The most important innovation was the concept of "quality circles," which brought managers and workers into cooperative relationships with each other in manufacturing. Instead of vertical relationships between management and labor, the quality circle approach put managers and workers together on the same level to solve problems in manufacturing. This approach is currently being reintroduced to the United States.

Japan also created one of the most efficient educational systems in the world. Unlike the American educational system, which is highly decentralized and controlled by local school boards, the Japanese educational system is run by the Ministry of Education, which sets all standards and policies. The cost of education in Japan is comparatively lower than in the United States but more children receive a better education (Tasker 1987).

Japan has succeeded as a capitalist member of the world system since World War II because of the close financial relationships between business and government, the *keiretsu,* the quality circle management strategies, and its educational system. Part of Japan's success is due to a general agreement on the part of the Japanese people that they must cooperate if they are to successfully compete in the modern world, an "us" versus "them" point of view largely lacking in the Western core countries.

*S*ummary

In many parts of Asia the development of agriculture in the neolithic before 6000 B.C. gave rise first to settled tribal communities, and later, between 4000 and 2000 B.C., to chiefdom political organizations. Sometime between 2000 and 1000 B.C. state level organizations supported by intensive agriculture and extensive trade began to appear. These early states quickly developed complex systems of class differentiation, highly developed craft specialization, trade networks reaching far to the west into Europe, and great religious traditions such as Hinduism, Buddhism, and Islam, which were intimately connected to the state bureaucracies.

The great civilizations of Asia were subjected to waves of Western capitalist expansion and colonization, beginning in the sixteenth century, that transformed their societies and economies. Europeans colonized many of the Asian nations, and even the few that were spared direct colonization were greatly influenced by European contact. Market economies spread to the furthest reaches of the rural hinterlands. Numerous independence and nationalist movements arose that attempted to throw off the yoke of colonialism and domination. Under the able leadership of such well-known figures as Mohandas Gandhi in India, Ho Chi Minh in Vietnam, and Mao Zedong in China, many Asian nations had achieved political independence by the 1950s, but they remained economically peripheral to the Western core nations. Some, such as China and Vietnam, experimented with forms of socialism in an attempt to develop outside what had already become a global economic system. These experiments were unsuccessful and, as the twentieth century drew to a close, all of the nations of Asia were involved (but to varying degrees) in the world capitalist economy. Several nations, Japan and Thailand among them, have come to be known as the Asian Tigers because of their rapid rise as world-class economic powers. It appears that Indonesia is an emerging tiger and Vietnam may very well be another.

Like much of the rest of the world, many of the nations of Asia are struggling with internal problems of ethnic and religious conflict that have resulted in numerous instances of violence. In India, major confrontations have occurred between Hindus and Sikhs. China, too, confronts problems with its ethnic minorities while struggling to enter the capitalist economy on its own terms. China continues to receive criticism from international human rights organizations and Western governments for its invasion and occupation of Tibet more than forty years ago, while paradoxically continuing to receive "most favored nation" trade status from the United States.

Key Terms

Atman	*Mansabdars*
Bjauk	**Mantrayana Buddhism**
Brahmans	*Moksha*
Brideprice	*Nirvana*
Caste Endogamy	**Peasant**
Caste System	*Samsara*
Chou	*Samurai*
Dharma	*Satori*
Divination (scapulamancy)	*Seppeku*
Doi Moi	*Shogun Bushido*
Dowry	**Sinified**
Entrepots	*Sudra*
Filial Piety (*hsaio*)	**Theocracy**
Footbinding	**Theravada Buddhism**
Gamelans	*Ti*
Gentry	**Treaty Ports**
Guru	*Tsu*
Jajmani	*Vaisya*
Karma	*Varnas*
Kshatriya	*Vedas*
Legong	*Yang-shao*
Lungshan	*Zamindars*
Mahayana Buddhism	**Zen Buddhism**
Mandarin	

Latin America: Political Bosses, Dependency, and Democratic Reform

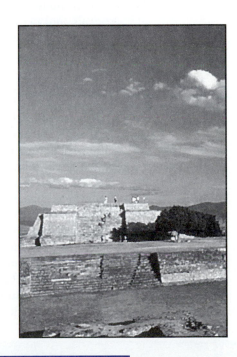

*L*atin America stretches from the Rio Grande in the north, forming the United States–Mexico border, to Tierra del Fuego, a large island that is the southernmost part of Chile. Mexico's topography may be compared to a large funnel with the western and eastern mountain ranges of the Sierra Madre Occidental and Sierra Madre Oriental converging just south of Mexico City, forcing all north–south trade into a narrow region where the great core centers of Mesoamerican history emerged: Teotihuacán, Tenochtitlán, and colonial and modern Mexico City. South of Mexico City, mountainous basins occur regularly to Guatemala, and each of these was occupied by a city state in pre-Columbian times. Lowland civilizations were linked to the highland civilizations, following overland trade routes through lowland Mexico to the central Yucatán.

Central America links the Western Hemisphere's two continental ecosystems, acting as a land bridge between North and South America. It is a thin strip of extremely heterogeneous climates, soils, land forms, vegetation, animal species, and peoples. South of Panama, the Andes mountains contain a series of highland basins running south to north, where most populations are concentrated, while the great Amazon basin to the east forms a lightly inhabited tropical region of threatened indigenous peoples and resources.

We can divide the history of Latin America into five distinct time periods, each characterized by significantly different political and economic institutions: (1) the prehistoric period, characterized by indigenous economies and polities ranging from subsistence-based tribal agriculturalists to city-states and tributary empires such as those of the Maya, Aztec, and Inca; (2) the colonial period, which began with the conquest of Tenochtitlán in 1521 and ended with the beginning of the wars of independence against Spain in 1810, and during which the institutions of Latin America were determined by Iberian models from Spain and Portugal; (3) the period of the *caudillos* (political bosses), which lasted roughly from the end of the wars of independence (1810–1820) to the 1930s, during which time Latin America developed its own internal forms of political organization, primarily based on the colonial *haciendas*, but with economic and political control being exercised by regional caudillos rather than peninsular Spanish administrators; (4) the period of state capitalism or state corporatism from 1930 to 1986, during which the state further developed and protected its

Figure 12.1   **Physiographic Map of Latin America**

industrial base through closure of the Latin American economies; and (5) the period of neoliberal reform beginning in 1986. During the later phase of the caudillo period, from 1870 to 1930, there was considerable industrialization in the most progressive Latin American countries that became the wealthiest (Mexico, Colombia, Venezuela, Argentina, Brazil, and Chile). The rural sector was affected by the tendency toward privatization of Indian *ejidos* (communally held land), and the decimation and sometimes destruction of the Indian communities in Mexico, Guatemala, El Salvador, Bolivia, Peru, and Ecuador, the countries with the largest Indian populations. The period of neoliberal reform is characterized by the North American Free Trade Agreement (NAFTA) among Canada, the United States, and Mexico, and the General Agreement on Tariffs and Trade (GATT), and by open economies and moves toward privatization of formerly government controlled enterprises.

The European invasion caused much suffering and death among the native populations of Latin America and disrupted on a massive scale indigenous polities, economies, and social and family life. Yet, despite this devastating initial impact, and despite over 500 years of domination by a succession of colonial and state governments, Latin America remains a region with numerous indigenous cultures, perhaps more than any other world region, many of which have displayed renewed vitality in the latter half of the twentieth century.

From Tribes to States in Mesoamerica

The transition from a hunting and gathering way of life to one based on agriculture, a transition from simple food extraction to food production and from band to tribal organization, began in the arid highlands of Mexico some time before 5000 B.C. By about 3400 B.C. the plants that would later form the agricultural base of Mesoamerican civilization had already been domesticated: maize, beans, squash, and chili peppers—all seed crops. Several other plants of lesser importance were also domesticated. The transition from heavy reliance on food extraction to overwhelming dependence on food production was gradual. By 2300 B.C., the peoples of the Tehuacan valley in Mexico still relied on hunting and gathering for 70 percent of their food. But by 1500 B.C. the balance had shifted and evidence of sedentary village life permits us to infer that reliance on domesticated foods had become dominant. Sedentary villages begin to appear all over Mesoamerica (and lower Central America) at this time. The herding of llamas, combined with potatoes and maize agriculture, had a similar early date in the Andes, and is a strategy of human adaptation still widely followed today.

Between 1500 and 1100 B.C., tribal societies in Mesoamerica (Mexico and the northern part of Central America), and the Andes were transformed into the more complex sociopolitical entities of chiefdoms, as described in Chapter 6. For example, archaeological excavations at the sites of La Venta and San Lorenzo, on the tropical east coast of Mexico, revealed giant basalt heads, giant buried masks, and a pyramid in the form of a volcano all within a preplanned plaza. The art style and associated artifacts at these two sites are known as Olmec culture. While both of these sites were ceremonial centers with only small residential areas, enough is now known about Olmec culture to be certain that social stratification and craft specialization were present (Culbert 1983). These are characteristics usually associated with a chiefdom level of sociopolitical organization.

Figure 12.2   **Map Showing Locations of Sites Mentioned in the Chapter**

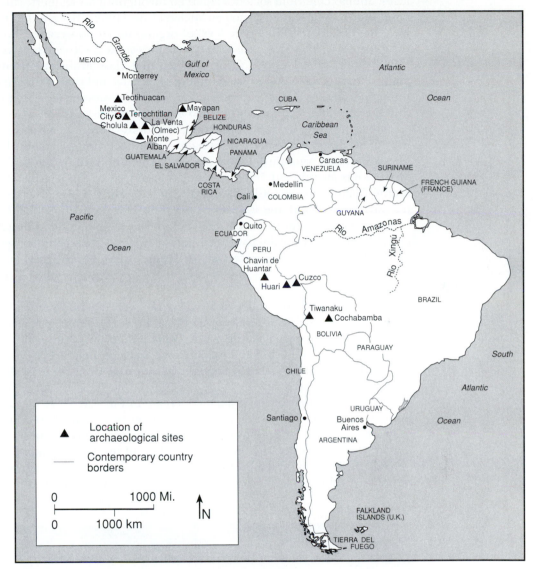

Exotic objects of obsidian and jade found at Olmec sites, as well as Olmec-style art found in the state of Morelos in central Mexico, and also on the southern periphery of Mesoamerica in El Salvador, provide clear evidence that the Olmec were engaged in long-distance trade (Culbert 1983). The site of San Jose Mogote in the valley of Oaxaca, for example, shows strong Olmec influence and evidence of trade between 1100 and 850 B.C. During this period, San Jose Mogote was the largest site in the Oaxaca valley, with more than 80 percent of the population living there, while 20 percent lived in the countryside in small villages. Similar chiefdom societies emerged throughout Mesoamerica at about the same time. Some scholars, such as Michael Coe (1962), believe that the Olmec were the first to develop a state level of organization and were the "mother culture" from which all Mesoamerican civilizations sprang. Others, such as Flannery (1968) and Culbert (1983) favor the idea that class stratification emerged in many places in Mesoamerica at about the same time and that, rather than Olmec influence causing this class stratification, it was the stratification that enhanced widespread trade relations and made Olmec influence possible.

Not long after, as in Mesopotamia, chiefdoms were transformed into states with great drama and speed. This happened not in one place but throughout Mesoamerica at roughly the same period, about 700 B. C. By 500 B. C., San Jose Mogote was abandoned and the population moved to the nearby mountain of Monte Alban, and established another chiefdom on top of it after excavating a flat surface and building a series of temples. The population of the valley increased seven to eight times *after* (not before) the chiefdom of Monte Alban was established, an extraordinary growth rate of about 1.3 percent per year for the Valley. The population growth rate for Monte Alban is calculated at 6 percent per year, two or three times that of modern industrializing countries (Blanton et al. 1981:71).

To the north in the valley of Mexico, the giant city of Teotihuacán grew in an even more explosive fashion. Teotihuacán is the most spectacular site in Mesoamerica, occupying a large portion of the Valley of Teotihuacán (it became the largest city in the world at the time Rome was at its height). However, the city did not evolve slowly; rather it appears that most of the people of the city had once been rural dwellers.

The implications of the dramatic increase in the size of the city and the depopulation of the countryside are enormous because there is no other instance in history where a city grew by suddenly swallowing most of its rural population. In fact, this shift in population flies in the face of most evolutionary and demographic theories about the growth of cities. Cities are supposed to appear when population densities in the countryside pass a certain critical maximum and the

The Zopotec priests of Monte Alban were close to the skies and their gods.

surplus populations develop cities. But it is obvious this process did not occur at Teotihuacán. Some of the population came from outside of the Valley, from cities in Tlaxcala and Puebla. Teotihuacán went through a phase of enormous expansion shortly after its chief rival, Cuicuilco, was destroyed by volcanic lava flows during the first century A.D. From a population between 20 and 30 thousand, it grew to more than 150,000 by about 500 A.D. (Carmack, Gasco, and Gossen 1996:57). On the other hand, the rural population in the basin of Mexico dropped from 100,000 to 15,000. Eighty-five thousand people moved into Teotihuacán! There is no evidence that the move was forced on the rural population. Many of these urban dwellers remained farmers. Abundant natural springs in the area were used to support an elaborate irrigation system that produced abundant agricultural yields.

There is evidence that the city of Teotihuacán was planned before any major building occurred. The Street of the Dead was constructed before construction began on the enormous pyramids. Anyone who has visited Teotihuacán has to be impressed by the planning that went into the design of the city. The city itself is laid out so that the Street of the Dead lies on an axis to a monument found on one of the nearby mountains. The giant city of Teotihuacán, as well as Monte Alban in the highlands of Oaxaca, the lowland Maya states in the region of the southern Yucatán, and the Peten of Guatemala, all collapsed between 600 and 1100 A. D. Teotihuacán was burned in the seventh century A.D. Evidence of selective burning of administrative and religious structures at Teotihuacán argues for internal revolt (Carmack et al. 1996:60). This is the same period in which there is a significant shift towards sea trade around the Yucatán Peninsula and ecological pressures on resources. After the collapse of the theocratic and large states, smaller towns and cities emerged, forming alliances, such as that of Tenochtitlán and its sister cities along ancient Lake Texcoco, or Mayapan and its allies in the northern Yucatán.

By the time the Spaniards arrived in central Mexico, Nahuatl-speaking peoples known as the Aztec had established control over most of the central Mexican highlands and adjacent coastal regions. The saga of the conquest of Tenochtitlán, capital of the Aztecs, is well known. The Aztec emperor, Moctezuma, had visions, portents of the coming of the Spanish. These were confused with the legend of Quetzalcoatl, a mythical ruler–god, reputedly bearded, who, on his departure several hundred years before, declared his eventual return. However, it was really the horse, firearms, and the skillful use of the enemies of the Aztecs that allowed the Spanish their bloody successes, not magic.

The Emergence of Civilizations in the Andes

The transition from hunting and gathering to agriculture in the Andes and adjacent Pacific coast and *montaña* (eastern slopes of the Andes) areas was similar to that in Mesoamerica. By 4200 B.C. there is some evidence of plant domestication along the Peruvian coast. At about the same time, somewhere in the river basins of northern South America, the pattern of root crop agriculture, emphasizing reproduction by cuttings, developed. By 1500 B.C. the pattern of root crop agriculture is fully developed in the Amazon–Orinoco lowlands, and has spread over the Andes to the Pacific coast; the pattern of seed crop agriculture, maize, beans, squash, and chili peppers, but particularly maize, has spread south out of Mesoamerica and is well established in the Andean area. This felicitous conjunction of root crop and seed crop agriculture, combined with such native Andean cultigens as the potato and quinoa (a grain) and a varied climate, led to a rapid expansion of population and rapid development of social organizational complexity.

Stone houses, ceremonial centers, and temples are present by 900 B. C. at the site of Chavin de Huantar, located 16,000 feet above sea level in the northern Peruvian Andes. This spectacular religious center is not unlike La Venta, and authorities have speculated that there may have been contact between the two cultures as early as 800 B. C. Here a stone-sheathed platform containing a maze of narrow passages and galleries surrounded a central plaza where stood an amazing stone pillar. The pillar, called the Lanzon, depicts a mythological jaguar with serpents for hair. The symbolism is strikingly like that of the Olmec culture of Veracruz, Mexico. The Chavin culture dominated the Central Andes for 700 years, and then disappeared about 200 B. C. But the pattern of later states and empires and exploitation had been set.

Chavin was followed by a florescence of small states such as that called Mochica in the Viru Valley of Peru. Thousands of people lived in this and other similar theocratic states located in the coastal river valleys. In the south of Peru, another spectacular civilization evolved called the Nazca. The people of Nazca constructed gigantic stone sketches of a variety of animals and ancestors on the coast of Peru and northern Chile. Most of these were not recognized for what they are until aerial photographs were made of them.

From 600 to 1000 A. D., a classic tributary conquest state emerged known as Tiwanaku (Tiahuanáco in earlier literature), located on the southern shores of Lake Titicaca. It had a ceremonial center of over 20,000 people, massive stone-sheathed courts and platforms, and immense carved stone statues. Tiwanaku controlled a large trade network that spread as far away as Argentina. According to some scholars, a second "twin" empire emerged in northern Peru with similar characteristics, called Huari. Alan Kolata, however, argues that Huari was just a regional center of the once far–flung empire of Tiwanaku that, at its height between 750 and 1000 A.D., had regional centers in coastal Chile, coastal Peru, and the Cochabamba Valley of Bolivia. A significant climate change—a great drought lasting from 1000 to 1400 A.D.—severely affected agricultural production and gradually brought an end to the Tiwanaku empire by 1100 A.D. Smaller, less spectacular, states arose in the coastal river valleys and some of the highland basins (Kolata 1993).

In the fifteenth century, the final pre-Hispanic empire came into existence, that of the mighty Inca. The name *Inca* was given to the ruling family, which could supposedly trace its origins back several centuries, and for those several centuries apparently ruled little more than Cuzco and its immediate environs.

Pachacuti Inca Yapanqui, the ninth Inca, who ruled from 1438–1471 A.D., unified the southern Peruvian highlands, and was succeeded by his son, Topa Inca Yapanqui (1471–1493), who continued to expand the empire in all directions. When his son, Huayna Capac succeeded him, he expanded the Inca realm to its greatest extent, imposing hegemony over an empire that stretched more than 3,000 miles from northern Colombia to central Chile. It included the coastal lowlands, the most inaccessible upper reaches of the Andes up to 15,000 feet, and the upper reaches of the *montaña* (Fagg 1963).

At the peak of his glory, Huayna Capac died in an epidemic in 1527 or 1528. His most probable heir, Ninan Cuyuchi, died in the same epidemic. This left two sons, Huascar Inca by Huayna Capac's Peruvian wife, and Atahualpa Inca by his Ecuadorian wife. Huascar was officially crowned Inca in the southern capital of Cuzco and apparently had the loyalty of the populace. Atahualpa had control of most of the professional army and took over the northern part of the empire, establishing his capital at Quito. After five years of bitter civil war, Atahualpa defeated Huascar, captured him, and before his own death at the hands of the Spaniards, had him killed. On November 15, 1532, Francisco Pizarro and his small band of Spaniards arrived on the plains of Cajamarca, through trickery captured Atahualpa, and held him for ransom for a time. Finally, Atahualpa was accused by the Spaniards of numerous crimes, among them polygyny (which was not a crime in Inca society), usurpation (because he had taken the throne from his brother), fratricide (because he had his brother killed), and idolatry (because he did not worship the Spanish god). As a pagan, he was to be burned at the stake, but at the last minute Father Valverde, the priest who accompanied Pizarro, talked Atahualpa into being baptized, and so he was entitled to be hanged instead—and he was, on July 26, 1533. This was the beginning of the end for the Inca state. But it was not superior force of arms that brought the mighty Inca empire to its knees. It was disease. As Michael Moseley says:

> In 1532, the quintessence of native civilization toppled with the impact of a single European state. The basic impact came neither from advanced technology nor sophisticated corporate organization. The most effective weapons arming the conquistadors were smallpox, measles, and other Old World diseases. These first undermined and later virtually destroyed the demographic foundations of New World society . . . (1983:236).

The Invasion and Its Aftermath

The invasion of Latin America was a staggering event. (The indigenous peoples of Latin America argue that they were invaded but never conquered, so we refrain from using the term "conquest.") It occurred a full century before the English colonies were established in North America. Latin America was the first non-European continental area to be confronted by the forces of Westernization and it was the most dramatically changed. From the very beginning there was a violent and continuous clash of cultures. Christianization of Latin America's Indian populations resulted in the imposition of one set of institutions throughout from Monterrey, Mexico, to Santiago, Chile. The gold and silver mined out of Mexico, Colombia, Bolivia, and Peru paid for several European wars and made the Industrial Revolution possible. New trade routes established to facilitate the mining industry had the consequence of destroying all other trade routes, such as those that existed throughout Latin America in pre-European times. The wealth robbed from Latin America and the imposition of imperialistic institutions condemned its indigenous populations to a future of underdevelopment.

Perhaps the most notable consequence of the invasion, of contact between the Americas and Europe, the consequence with the most far-reaching repercussions for the native cultures of Latin America, was the demographic impact. First to feel the impact were the native populations of the Caribbean islands. Diseases and inhuman working conditions in the mines and plantations resulted in near total extinction within fifty years after initial contact (by 1550). Later, African slaves were brought in to provide a labor force and the islands were economically dominated by cattle ranching and large sugar plantations (Wolf 1982).

As Eric Wolf has pointed out, the invaders and colonists wanted native labor, the crown of Spain wanted native subjects, and the friars wanted native souls. The "conquest" that was to produce utopia instead resulted in the collapse of native cultures and biological catastrophe (Wolf 1959). In Middle America during the first one hundred years after the invasion, native populations declined by as much as 90 percent. While the decline was not this drastic elsewhere in Latin America, most areas did suffer at least a 50 percent decline before recovery began. While in some areas native populations began a slow demographic recovery after 1800, in others the recovery did not begin until a century later.

The litany of reasons for the decline of native populations is long and includes all of the following: excessive labor requirements, excessive tributes, mistreatment in general, drunkenness, starvation, flood, drought, disease, and divine providence. While mistreatment certainly accounts for some deaths, it is no longer seen as the principal cause of population decline. Various European diseases to which the native populations had no initial immunity or resistance were the paramount cause of native deaths. Even a short list of known major epidemics in New Spain presents a grim picture: smallpox epidemics in 1520, 1531, and 1545; typhoid in 1545, 1576, 1735, and twenty nine more times before 1821; a great measles epidemic in 1595; and malaria and yellow fever, apparently from Africa, spread quickly through the Latin American tropics and became endemic (Wolf 1959:196).

Population decline seriously disrupted all aspects of native society and culture in Latin America, but it was not the sole cause of such disruption. The Spanish practice of *reducción,* of concentrating native populations into nucleated villages was especially disruptive for those native populations that were semi-nomadic and those who lived in small, widely dispersed settlements. Inhuman living conditions and brutal treatment did take its toll in areas close to mines and plantations. And mestizoization, a process of biological and cultural blending, while disruptive of native life, produced new cultures neither Indian nor European.

The Colonial Period

By the middle of the sixteenth century, Latin America had three power centers: one at Mexico City, one at Cuzco, Peru, and one in Brazil (which was ruled by Portugal). Later other centers would develop at Buenos Aires, Argentina, and Caracas, Venezuela. As a means to exercise control over the native populations from these centers, the Spanish Crown merged communitarian traditions from Spain with traditional Mesoamerican and Andean ideas of collective landowner-ship. Lands were allocated to Indian communities as collectives, their exploita-tion was carefully regulated, and they could not be sold. The native communities gradually developed internal mechanisms to control this process of domination (see the following section). During the colonial period, the domination of the landscape by Spanish colonial institutions so profoundly altered the human ecol-ogy as to allow us to collapse the two categories of human ecology and political economy into one: political ecology.

Political Ecology: Mines, Haciendas, and Plantations

In previous chapters we have shown how human institutions defined the politi-cal ecology of distinct regions of the world after the development of states, but that underlying state institutions were earlier traditional forms of human adap-tation (that is, human ecology). Nowhere is the outstanding impact of human political institutions on human ecology more clear than in Latin America, be-cause, by 1570, Spain had imposed an entirely new political economy on the whole of Latin America based on centralized bureaucratic cities, haciendas, plantations, and mining. For this reason, in this chapter we combine the cate-gories of human ecology and political economy in the term *political ecology*. By the end of the colonial period, the political ecology of Latin America was de-nominated by the bureaucraticities, the mine, the *hacienda*, and the plantation. The *haciendas* (large agricultural or cattle estates found primarily in the high-lands . . . sometimes the size of small countries) were formed out of former In-dian lands and specialized in growing subsistence goods for local markets, while plantations and mines produced for export (cochineal, cotton, sugar, coffee, sil-ver, gold). The plantations (these are large lowland estates, often run by slave labor in earlier centuries or by indebted peons today) and haciendas were and are interspersed with independent farms called *rancherias* (small farms, usually in cattle or a combination of cattle and maize, or just maíze), also called "open" communities that were owned by Creoles of mixed Spanish–Indian ancestry. In the highlands of both Mesoamerica and the Andes, there were "closed" com-munities with communal lands, owned by vestiges of the original Indian popu-lation. It is in these communities that the religious cargo system flourished (see page 245).

The *rancherias* and *ejidos,* as well as *haciendas,* produced food for local mar-kets—maize, beans, squash, rice, tomatoes, meat. Their members also produced

A descendant of the Zapotec, his home and mule in modern Oaxaca.

household-made objects such as ceramic pots and dishes, candles, rope, woven rugs, and clothing. The difference between *rancherias* and *ejidos* is that the former were usually owned by individual mestizo families, while the latter were collectively owned by Indian villages and/or clans. Sometimes the open and closed communities were in competition for land, and even today tensions exist between the two. To sum up a variety of studies, basically the haciendas relied on labor from the regions of *rancherias* and *ejidos,* although they also depended on those who lived on the larger estates, who were often drawn both from open and closed communities (the resident laborers on plantations or *haciendas* are known as **colonos** in Guatemala). *Colonos* were paid less than subsistence wages, not enough to live on. In some cases, workers were allowed to farm small plots on *hacienda* lands (these plots are often known simply as **milpa,** the same term used for family-owned fields). Ethnographically, it is often difficult to tell when a community was made up of independent ranchero farmers or *colonos,* and often these are so intermarried as to make little difference. In all cases, workers were perpetually in debt to the *hacendado* or to the company store on the plantation. Coffee and cattle were the products of the highland *haciendas.*

Lowland plantations were highly commercial and, through to the mid-twentieth century, had workers who were either slaves or debt peons. Plantations exported cotton, sugar, cochineal, and bananas or other tropical fruits grown on the lowland plantations (Wolf & Mintz 1957).

The traditional literature on Latin American landownership once stressed the difference between the **latifundia** and the **minifundia.** The *latifundia* were the gigantic estates, both plantations and *haciendas,* owned by the elites of Latin America, while the *minifundia* were the *rancherias* and *ejidos.* The two were viewed as separate societies, often contrasted to the manors and peasant estates of Europe in the Middle Ages. However, from studies beginning in the 1960s, there emerges quite a different picture. Rather than forming two separate societies, *latifundistas,* the owners of the large estates, depended on the labor of *mini-*

fundistas, owners of small estates, both Indian *ejido* and mestizo *rancheria* communities. While Spanish bureaucrats, appointed by the Crown of Spain, wielded the power of the Crown from Mexico City, the latifundistas controlled regional power through the election of representatives who were the sole political authorities at the local level. These regional governments, called *ayuntamientos,* made policy for the *municipios* or municipalities. *Municipios* were the primary political divisions during the colonial period and incorporated many towns and villages, usually under the hegemony of a single *cabecera,* a dominant city or town, whose *ayuntamiento* controlled all other public bodies within the municipio. These political bodies led to the development of *caciques,* another name for regional bosses. While the *ayuntamientos* politically controlled the *municipios,* the Indian towns were ruled by their own elders during the colonial period. Minifundistas of either Indian or non-Indian towns and villages were never allowed to serve on the *ayuntamientos.* The result was that the latifundistas gained control over all but national offices prior to the revolutions against Spain. After the revolutions, their power grew to incorporate many, but not all, Indian towns. Those most distant from the *cabeceras* tended to be autonomous until recent times. While the landed elites no longer control power at the local level, regional *caciques* still control much of Mexico and most of Central America.

The type of economic relationship between the two groups has been given the name **debt peonage**. Administrators on large estates would loan out food or money at exorbitant interest (30 percent per year or more was not unusual), and the *minifundistas* would be expected to pay back the sum. Because wages were never enough to pay principal and interest, entire villages of ejiditarios and rancheros were stuck with perpetual debts. It was these debts that spawned the many revolts by the lower classes against their elites from Mexico to Chile.

In recent years, the distinction between plantations and *haciendas,* and between closed and open communities has faded, primarily due to legislation protecting workers, but also due to the fragmentation of the hacienda system through inheritance, or, in the case of Mexico, the redistribution of lands. However, the regions that were originally in plantation or hacienda tenure remain very poor today. Historic and ethnographic data from Mexico and elsewhere show a clear and constant relationship between the existence of large *haciendas* or plantations and regional underdevelopment. It is becoming increasingly clear that not only did plantations and *haciendas* produce poverty instead of wealth, but that they held back the modernization process that might have occurred had the regions in question been allowed to evolve a family farm estate system such as that found in the United States during similar time periods.

The contrast between the Latin American pattern of landownership and that in North America (including Canada) is very revealing. North American farmers were always able to control local town boards and councils. While they might get into debt to banks, they had the political power to fight corporate interests on the East Coast for their own benefit. Most important, the American farmers owned their own land. If the unit of land became too small due to technological innovations, the small farmer could sell out to a large farmer and sell his labor in the small towns. In Latin America, the minifundista was tied to land that he could not own, and to debts he could not pay. No wonder that modern Latin

America has a heritage of rural exploitation that is difficult to overcome. Finally, as the industrial revolution proceeded, in North America efficiencies of rural production drove down the cost of food. The food was purchased by urban workers in greater amounts, and of higher quality as time went by, while farmers continued to produce ever larger harvests. While the price of food went down, the income of farmers went up. With cheaper food, worker salaries stretched further. Finally, farmers could afford to buy what urban workers made, stimulating the urban–rural markets. Both rural and urban workers became progressively more prosperous, buying from each other.

In Latin America, this type of rural–urban market relationship never materialized. Instead, plantations were geared to sell their produce as cheaply as possible to European and American markets, while the hacienda owners were not interested in increasing efficiency because they had all the cheap labor they wanted. Small farmers used most of what they produced to meet their own subsistence needs, and sold their scant surplus in local markets.

The Emergence of Hybrid Cultures and Class Stratification

Underlying Latin American social structure was the political ecology just described. Even though the native populations fell dramatically, especially in the first 100 years after the invasion, they also began to grow again in the centuries that followed. Spanish immigration to Latin America was fairly light, rarely accounting for more than 2 percent of the total population. Spanish men took Indian women as wives, and Indian maids and cooks were forced into concubinage. Sexual unions between Spanish men and Indian women led to the rapid rise of mixed blood or *mestizo* populations. By 1825, about a quarter of the population of Spanish-speaking America was *ladino* (another term for mestizo). By 1950, the ladinos were three-quarters of the population.

The hacienda and plantation social structures of colonial Latin America were highly stratified, with a small number of whites of European descent dominating a pyramid of ladinos, blacks, and Indians until early in the nineteenth century, when the wars with Spain shifted power in favor of upper caste ladinos (usually of light complexion). The ladino population continued to expand and became numerically dominant at the turn of the twentieth century.

Where the Spaniards and Indians mixed cultures and genes, mestizo (ladino) communities arose that have been called "open" communities. The Indian communities were largely "closed." It was and is the open communities that participate in the national political culture of Mexico, Central America, Bolivia, Peru, and Ecuador, while the closed communities by and large have historically not played a role in national political cultures of these same countries.

In those regions where both Indian and ladino populations were substantial, mixed or **syncretic** cultures developed. A syncretic culture is one that combines elements from two or more cultures. An example would be the Tarascans of western Mexico in the state of Michoacan, who maintained their independence during Aztec times and have only incorporated those elements of modern Mexican culture that they wish to adopt. They are expert silversmiths and use their traditional skills to sell in the modern tourist markets. There are many examples of syncretic cultures throughout Mexico. The syncretic cultures, combining important elements of both Indian and Hispanic culture, are concentrated in the highlands of Mexico, but some are found also in lowland regions in southern Mexico and northern Central America, and Andean Bolivia, Peru, and Ecuador. These cultures have usually retained Indian languages. The Spanish Crown allowed the Indians to organize themselves into special Indian towns with their own customs that survived until the late nineteenth century. During the colonial period, Hispanic towns and Indian towns often coexisted in the same regions. For example, Puebla de los Angeles, just south of Mexico City, was built to be specifically Spanish with its own *ayuntamiento* or municipal council governed by the citizens of the city. But it was not able to maintain its Spanish "purity," and like all Mexican cultures is today a blend of the native and Spanish cultures. Only a few kilometers away were the mostly Indian cities of Cholula and Tlaxcala, which were organized and run by Indian *caciques* (chiefs).

The independence of the Indian towns was never complete. Indian priests and caciques were dominated by Spanish institutions, particularly the courts. Churches were forced on Indian towns and the children of elite Indian families were taught the Spanish language and indoctrinated in the Catholic faith. The Catholic faith was universal to most regions of Latin America by the turn of the seventeenth century. The closer the Indian towns were to the Spanish towns, the greater was the acculturation to Spanish norms. Remote Indian towns and villages retained much more of their traditional cultures until relatively late in the nineteenth century when nationalistic political movements precipitated a new wave of acculturation.

The Cargo System   Today in many of the Indian communities of both the highland Andes and Mesoamerica, men must serve their communities by passing through a series of offices that usually involve considerable individual expenditure. This system is known as the **cargo,** or **fiesta *system,*** or the civil–religious hierarchy. Both the structure and the functioning of the system have evolved since colonial times; and there are now, and probably have always been, differences in the system between communities as well. The most detailed description of a modern cargo system is that provided by Frank Cancian for the Maya community of Zinacantan in the highlands of Chiapas, Mexico (1965, 1992). The Spanish term *cargo* means "burden," and basic to all variations of the cargo system is the expenditure of wealth in the sponsorship of religious fiestas in order to accumulate prestige within one's community. The cargo system has been compared to the potlatch of the Northwest Coast and the Big Man redistribution system of the Pacific Islands. Like these other "redistribution" festivals, the cargo system reduced the wealth of all in exchange for status in the community. In the nineteenth century and later, in many Indian communities, there existed a ladderlike arrangement of sets or levels of civil and religious offices, with many positions in the bottom sets and usually only two or a very few in the top sets.

Adult married men were obliged to serve in alternating positions in the civil and the religious hierarchy of offices until they had served in the top sets. The period of service for each office was one year. The lower-level cargos were usually low-status community services such as acting as policemen at the fiestas or sweeping out the church, buying drinks for the elites to be used in celebrations, or, for

A cargo system procession in a highland Guatemalan town.

the women, preparing the clothing of the saints for holy days. The upper-level cargos were those of managing the entire cargo system, and only a handful of men achieved this high status. The elite men usually alternated the religious cargos with civilian political positions, usually ending their careers as **alcaldes** or mayors at the top of a "civilian cargo" system. Considerable expense was involved in fulfilling the obligations of office, so most men did not serve in successive years but "rested" for several years in between cargos. Anthropologists, such as George Foster (1965), theorized that the cargo system acted as a leveling mechanism to make everyone equal (it did not), but also had the impact of producing an "image of limited good" that acted against individuals trying to invest in their land because their profits would have to go into the cargo system. (In Chapter 8 we described how, among the modern Maya, there are political differences between the Catholics who support the old cargo system and the "evangelicals" who do not.)

It has long been thought that the cargo system had its beginnings in the early colonial period when Spanish civil authorities imposed a set of civil offices on Indian communities and the Catholic Church established the *cofradía* (religious brotherhood) system to ensure the proper care of church property and proper celebration of religious holidays. However, this is not a universally accepted view. Many have argued that the cargo system had pre-Hispanic antecedents that combined with the Spanish system imposed in colonial times. In colonial times, positions in the hierarchy of civil offices seem to have been separate from the religious brotherhoods, and the civil offices were usually occupied by the indigenous elites. The brotherhoods were entrusted with the sponsorship of religious fiestas that were supported partly from the yield of corporate properties controlled by the brotherhoods and partly through the contributions of the members. Individual sponsorship of cargos does not appear to have been characteristic of the colonial period (Chance and Taylor 1985). Individual sponsorship emerged as the brotherhoods gradually lost control of corporate community lands in the late colonial period, when the protections provided by the Spanish Crown weakened.

Interestingly, as modern inflation has affected indigenous communities, there has been a return in some communities to more collective forms of sponsorship of religious fiestas. Beverly Chiñas describes this shift for the Isthmus Zapotec of San Juan Evangelista (1973). Chiñas also notes that while, strictly speaking, it is a man who publicly serves a cargo, the Zapotec view is that the man and his wife together fulfill the responsibilities and that the man could not do it alone. For the Peruvian Andes, Catherine Allen notes that a man only accepts a cargo if his wife agrees because it is she who is responsible for providing the elaborate meals and the chicha (corn beer) that must be served on the ritual occasions throughout the year (1988). In Sonqo, the community Allen studied, a man and his wife are not considered to be fully adult members of their community until they have served one cargo.

The Breakdown of the Closed Corporate Community In addition to the different views on the origin and evolution of the cargo system noted above, there have been different interpretations of its function, and it is apparent that these closed communities may be disappearing. Originally, Eric Wolf (1959) argued that the cargo system functioned to redistribute wealth within the Indian community and to protect it from outside forces. But Cancian (1965) conclusively showed for Zinacantan that the cargo system did not level wealth differences, that wealth differences continue to exist, and that it is the well-to-do who can serve the higher-level cargos, with their enormous expenditure requirements for food and drink throughout the year, without going deeply into debt. Studies in many other communities have confirmed that, while the cargo system serves to redistribute some wealth in the community, it does not level wealth differences. Recent writers argue that these communities were never as closed as once thought, and if they were, they have lost their closure in the last two decades. They argue that the cargo system was a means by which the Spanish Crown and the Church and, later, other outsiders exploited indigenous communities. Marvin Harris (1964) contends that the cargo system never protected Indian communities from exploitation by outsiders, that much of what is needed to fulfill cargo obligations, especially alcoholic beverages, must be purchased from outsiders, and that the system thus drained wealth from the community and enhanced the process of domination.

It is also obvious that the revolutionary violence in Guatemala, and economic pressures on the Maya of southern Mexico, have permanently changed whatever once might have been. Modern studies show that, while the cargo system clearly developed as part of a process of domination and exploitation of Indian communities in the highlands of Mesoamerica and the Andes, it has been adapted by the plantation elites as a means to maintain political and economic domination. Research in recent years has shown that the debts developed by Indians as part of their cargo systems were purchased by agents working for lowland plantations, and that members of these communities were subsequently forced to work off their debts on the plantations. It has also come to light that the plantations often owned the lands of the Indian communities, and exchanged the use of these lands for working on the plantations (Smith 1982). Thus, the contrast between the "closed corporate" Indian communities and the "open" Creole *rancherias* is less clear than it once was. It is becoming clear that if these communities were once closed, they are rapidly being opened today by modern elites, plantation owners, and tourists, and that their corporate social structure may be more a part of the past than the present.

The Period of Caudillos in Latin America: 1810–1930

The Wars of Independence in Latin America ushered in the **caudillos**, men of power, who opened the economies to outside market forces (particularly after 1870). This period lasted until the Great Depression of 1929. The economic philosophy of this time period is well illustrated by **Porfirismo**, named after the liberal Mexican dictator, Porfirio Diaz, who ran Mexico from 1876 until the Mexican Revolution of 1910. His point of view was that Latin American countries should open themselves to outside investment, migration, and "scientific knowledge."

Indigenous peoples were viewed as economically backward, openly criticized, and when possible, their lands were taken by elite mestizo landowners who further expanded the hacienda and plantation systems of Latin America. The liberal dictators allowed land to become increasingly concentrated in the hands of the few. Concessions to foreign corporations became common, and in Chile, Peru, and Mexico, the control of mines passed from local families to British and American interests. In Mexico, twenty-nine companies obtained possession of over 27.5 million hectares, about 14 percent of the total land area of the Republic. One-fifth of Mexico was given away in this manner. In Mexico, northern Central America, and the Andean countries, much of the land taken over by haciendas was the former ejido land of Indian corporate communities. Where such estates were not forcibly taken, they were broken up and individual families were given titles to the land. Once the Indians were given individual plots of land, they could be made to sell those lands to pay off debts incurred by community cargo rituals (Wolf 1969:16–17). Many of the landless peasants went to work on the growing railroads, and in the mines and the new factories.

Class and Ritual Kinship

Crosscutting upper and lower classes is a ritual kinship relationship known as **compadrazgo** or godparenthood. This ritual relationship, with its origins in the sacraments of the Catholic Church, requires men and women to assume responsibility for the religious education of their baptized child. In the ritual, men and women are linked by common involvement in the baptism of a child, and call each other **compadre** or **comadre.** Sponsors are chosen by the parents of the child to oversee his or her spiritual growth. However, while the relationship of sponsorship for the child is crucial (the godfather–godchild relationship), the sociologically more important relationship in most of Latin America is that between the parents and the godparents. Between *compadres* (co–fathers) or *comadres* (co–mothers) of the same social class, the relationship may be one of drinking buddies or women helping each other in the harvest or in sewing projects. The tie of coparenthood, then, links the two couples, not just the child and godparents. People who are very popular usually have many *compadres*.

Compadrazgo relationships may be between members of the same class, and as such are symmetrical, or they may be between upper- and lower-class families, in which case the relationship is asymmetrical. In the second type of relationship, called a "patron–client relationship," the upper-class compadre is always the sponsor of a lower-class child. The wealthy compadre is expected to help the family of his *compadre* of the lower class, as well as his godchildren, never the other way around. *Caudillos,* rich landowners, powerful politicians, wealthy industrialists, often have dozens, or hundreds, of *compadres* whom they help out in exchange for political support, forming one of the many patron–client relationships found in Latin America. The help for the lower-class *compadre* and his family (and godson) can be in the form of education, health maintenance, or financial aid during crises. Typically, modern politicians have many *compadres* in the working classes whom they depend on for political support (Wolf & Hansen 1972: 134).

In one study done by Robert Murphy of the rubber-gathering town of Ita at the mouth of the Amazon River, rubber-gatherers, whose lives were very unstable, had storekeepers as their *compadres* or *patrones*. The storekeepers depended on their lower-class *compadres* to gather rubber for them, which they then sold upriver for a profit, and in exchange granted them credit in their stores (which is also a form of debt peonage, cited in Wolf & Hansen 1972). Hacienda owners also typically develop *compadre* relationships with *colonos* living on their estates.

Latin America Sexual Relations: Machismo, Virginity, and Prostitution

In traditional Latin American society, it was common for members of the elite classes to acquire another wife or wives. Once married, a man would become attached to a young woman, usually of a lower social class, and would set her up in another house or apartment, taking care of her financial needs. The man was responsible for taking care of his mistress's children. Thus, polygyny, the marriage of a man to more than one woman, was common, although not legally recognized. Because members of the lower classes could not afford this luxury, this de facto polygyny was primarily an upper-class trait. While the Catholic Church attempted to impose its morality on Latin American men, male chastity was and is ignored and scorned, an attitude that is part of the ***machismo*** complex.

The machismo complex has a second side, however. For, in addition to a man being expected to act like a man by having many mistresses and prostitute lovers, he was also expected to stand up to others who might wish to exploit his own female relatives and friends. His mother and his sister were sacred, beyond reproach, and any insult towards them could be met by pistol duel, knife thrust, or fists. This complex code is expressed in many ***charro*** folk songs in Mexico, in which the women of a man's own class are beyond his grasp, for they must be protected and treated with respect, while the women of the bars and of the night are fair targets. But the women of the lower classes also have their fathers, sons, and male relatives, who must protect them, adding up to codes of behavior that produce, even today, considerable interclass conflict.

Reflecting the feminine side of the machismo complex is what Emilio Willems refers to as the ***virginity complex*** (Willems 1975). This is centered around the upper-class idea that the virginity of unmarried (and upper-class) females should be preserved at all cost through segregation of the sexes, chaperonage, and closely controlled courtship. Men felt that to marry a girl who had lost her virginity would make them appear foolish. After marriage, a woman's behavior was socially restricted by the husband's strict control over her social activities. The wife was expected to remain at home, to raise her children, to reject any advances by other men, and to participate in elite social activities, but remain in the background with other women supervising cooks, maids, and the household staff. But she was also expected to look the other way when her own husband paraded his machismo through the brothels, and had his little affairs with the cook, the maid, and the schoolgirl on the other side of town. These escapades would inevitably produce gossip between networks of upper-class women, and are the subject of many novels and plays. Within the husband's male networks, the same activities brought approval, a clap on the back, and offers of drinks. But, within the man's household, the woman's commitment to family would bring the man's friends to compliment her virtues, emphasizing the theme of the woman as mother.

Lower-class sexual ideas were more relaxed, and lower-class men did not attach the same importance to virginity. Prostitution was and is an answer to the expectations of *machismo* and the virginity complex of the elite and the lower

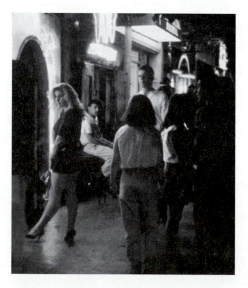

Nighthawk haunts the streets of Juarez . . .

sexual mores of the lower class. The Virginity Complex and the prostitution of lower-class women are a symbolic antithesis, but in curious ways are not really that opposite from each other. From Boys' Town in Matamoros, Mexico, to the red light districts in Medellín, Colombia, and Buenos Aires in Argentina, the practice of prostitution is widespread throughout Latin America, but prostitutes are not viewed as immoral degenerates, as they are in the United States. Americans find the acceptance of prostitution in Latin America to be at odds with their own values, but Latin Americans find the puritanical antiprostitution laws in the United States to be a contradiction to the open sexuality of Americans.

Prostitution has a long and complex history in Spain, Portugal, and in Latin America, and it is not always what it appears to be, for it too is tied to the Virginity Complex. While the prostitute is held in low regard by the elite women of society, in men's songs, especially the Mexican *rancheras* and *corridas* (folk ballads), she is often the emotional and brave antithesis of the coldly virginal daughters of the elite. She is the woman of passion, the fallen but meritorious woman, often standing by her beloved, who may be a revolutionary, warrior, soldier, scoundrel, or general, while the man's calculating wife spends her time trying to trap her amorous husband, or planning ways of moving the status of her family up in the world of social elites. Novels, short stories, and today, *telenovelas* (the Latin American version of the soap opera), tell the stories of women who have fallen on hard times, who are virginal in mind, but must prostitute themselves to make ends meet (thus Bizet's opera about Spain, *Carmen,* with its prostitute cigarette-making heroine). In these stories, women often support their illegitimate children, who are raised by other kinswomen, such as the prostitute's sisters, in distant cities. The mother's shame and her profession is kept a secret, as is her identity, and she is often identified as the maiden aunt.

The ambivalence between men and their wives, and men and their prostitute lovers, is often symbolized by the image of Mary Magdalene, the fallen woman forgiven by Christ, who is also considered a saint, and who washes the body of the dead Christ. The identities of the two Marys are often run together, and the symbolic qualities of prostitutes and virgins have been central themes for centuries. One very famous opera that captures much of the heroics and ambivalence of marriage and loose women, rigid codes and men and women who dare challenge them, is *Don Giovanni,* by Mozart. This tale of an Italian count could take place in Madrid, Mexico City, or Buenos Aires.

While the growing independence of women and their ability to find employment has produced a challenge to machismo, as well as the virginity complex, daily stories in Latin American newspapers of real-life Don Juans, sainted prostitutes, cold wives, and vengeance make one realize that these codes of behavior are not going to disappear overnight. Recently (in early 1997), a chauffeur was arrested in Mexico City for killing his rich employer and wife in retribution for the seduction of his sister, a maid in the rich man's home.

Religion and Community

The values that formed the institutions of religiosity in Latin America from the sixteenth century until today range from the formal hierarchies of the Roman

Catholic Church to the individualistic shamanism of the Amazonian tribalist or highland Andean llama herder or the Candoble of the Bahaian spiritualist. Between these two poles ranged other formal and informal institutions that framed the religious behavior of the peoples of Latin America. The writer, Carlos Fuentes, points to Iberian Catholicism, the religion of the Spaniards who migrated from Spain to Latin America, as the font of religion for Latin societies. It was composed of medieval cults, such as the cult of the saints, the fiesta complex (which resembles the cargo complex, but dates back to medieval times), and religious *sodalities* (associations of men and women that cut across family ties and bound both to the Church). These were transplanted to the Americas, where they found fertile ground. One characteristic of medieval religiosity was the unconditional and spontaneous acceptance of doctrine and sacraments. Impiety, atheism, or agnosticism were inconceivable (Willems 1975).

In addition to the formal hierarchy of the Catholic Church and its doctrines, and perhaps more important, were Iberian folk beliefs such as witchcraft, fear of the evil eye, werewolves, and devil spirits of the cold night. In addition, numerous folk religious beliefs of the Americas and of Africa became part of the syncretic religions of Latin America. In early December 1531, on Tepeyac Hill, near Mexico City, Tonantzin, the Aztec goddess, was transformed into the Virgin of Guadalupe and appeared to the shepherd, Juan Diego, carrying miraculous roses in winter. Nothing has proved as consoling, unifying, and worthy of respect as the figure of the Virgin of Guadalupe in Mexico. She became the Virgin of La Caridad de Cobre in Cuba, and the Virgin of Coromoto in Venezuela. Paralleling the female goddess, Quetzalcoatl, the feathered serpent, the priest of knowledge and self–sacrifice, evolved into Jesus Christ. According to Carlos Fuentes, it is impossible to tell who is being worshipped in the baroque altars of Puebla, Oaxaca, and Tlaxcala: Christ or Quetzalcoatl (Fuentes 1992:146).

Christ, in turn, was transformed into many Christs, just as there were many Quetzalcoatls. There is a Cristo de Entierro, the buried Christ, there is Cristo de Saquipulas or the sacrificed Christ, and there is Christ in heaven. While the Latin American Christs are dead or in agony, the Virgin is surrounded by perpetual glory and adoration. The attitude towards the Virgin Mary is one of celebration, while that toward Christ is more profoundly ambiguous, a combination of suffering, sacrifice, and forgiveness.

The churches were organized around male and female sodalities that handled distinct tasks of the yearly round of fiestas with their spectacular services and processions. Among the middle and upper classes the belief in the cult of the saints was elaborately developed. The effigies of the patron saints, Christ, and the Virgin Mary were carried through the streets of Mexico City, Guatemala City, San Salvador, Bogotá, Medellín, Caracas, and other cities of Latin America on the backs of men and women. To different saints were attributed different powers. *Nuestro Señor de los Temblores* of Lima and Cuzco, who is Jesus Christ of Earthquakes, protected the faithful against the agitations of the mountains (Willems 1975).

The wealthy, fearing for their mortal souls, donated money and property to the Church, and to the associated brotherhoods and sisterhoods (sodalities), and financed the construction of the beautiful temples of Latin America. Hos-

Peace returns to rural Guatemala . . . for how long?

pitals, usually attached to churches, were also financed in this fashion. In this way, the Church became very wealthy, often loaning money out at interest and serving as the premier banking institution.

Church and state were closely linked. During the colonial period, appointments by the crown had to be confirmed by the Vatican. In postcolonial times, highly placed political authorities were closely connected by kinship to Church authorities. There is an old saying in Mexico that in the most aristocratic families one brother was the landowner, one brother was the general, and one brother was the archbishop. The alliance of Church and state was highly developed and both estates reinforced each other except during periods of revolution when the relationships between church and state were severed. There were schisms in the Church that often broke into open conflict. Native-born priests identified themselves with Creole interests, and the wars of revolution produced a conflict between native clergy and Iberian clergy. The Church also engaged in commercial enterprises, and anticlerical factions wanted to confiscate its wealth, as occurred after the revolutions against Spain. The Church only regained its power and prestige in the postrevolutionary years through persuasion and compromise.

In more recent times, the schism in the Church is between the conservative views of the priests, who represent the views of the upper classes, and those who espouse **liberation theology.** (Liberation theology is a largely socialist movement within the Catholic Church, among priests who identify with the human rights needs of the working classes.) Liberation theology argues that the Church should intervene to prevent human rights abuses, while the conservatives argue that the role of the Church is to save human souls, not to interfere in politics—

a blatantly hypocritical position. In very recent years, many Latin Americans have broken with Church doctrine to create new religious movements tied to **evangelical protestantism.** A more conservative movement than liberation theology, evangelicals argue that one should not politicize religion, and that socialism is evil. Evangelical protestantism has become a threat to Church interests, and leaders have been persecuted by government authorities, particularly in Central America.

Dependency, Revolution, and the Rise of State Capitalism

The Depression of the 1930s brought about the disintegration of the power of the liberal *caudillos,* which was based on a coalition of landowning elites who controlled exports, and commercial importers; both benefited from low tariffs. Before the 1930s, the liberal *caudillos* with their patron–client political systems ran Latin America as personal fiefdoms. Attempts to compare these systems to "feudal" European societies are common, but the two systems are not analogous. Latin American societies were not feudal, socialist, or capitalist. They were highly bureaucratic and centralized, like their colonial antecedents, but run by *caudillos* who ruled by the powers of their armies and personalities. One writer, Claudio Veliz (1980), has described these societies as "centralist," and argues that the tradition of centralism dates back to the Spanish colonial period, with its large and expensive bureaucracies. But the one–man, personalistic *caudillo*-based centralism shifted in the 1930s to a new type of political economy, one based on the impersonal technocrat at the head of an enormous state apparatus: state capitalism.

State capitalism was Latin America's response to dependency, much in the same way that socialism in China and Russia were responses to the same threat. But state capitalism is not to be confused with socialism, for it has different roots, as will be described. As the importance of industry increased, trade unions developed power and the industrial working class became a dominant force, particularly in countries with large industrial bases, such as Mexico, Argentina, Chile, Venezuela, Colombia, and Brazil. A wave of political movements, mostly with leftist rhetoric, supporting state corporatist capitalism swept Latin America in the 1930s, but these were not uniform, and were very weak in the countries of Central America and in the Andean countries of Peru, Bolivia, and Ecuador (where the quasi-slave labor of large Indian populations undercut the development of trade unions).

The economies of Latin America, primarily in industrial countries, after the 1930s have been called "corporatist" or "state capitalist." Both terms have roughly the same meaning. The highly centralist "caudillo" governments of the pre-1930s, with their personalized one-man rule, gave way to centralized governments, ostensibly organized by political parties, but really controlled by faceless bureaucrats who remained in power decade after decade while new elections changed the apparent leaders, the presidents and the governors of the states, but really changed little. The state capitalist systems were a response to dependency theory, which was primarily developed by Latin American economists to explain the poverty of the Latin American countries. The *dependistas* (dependency theorists) explained that, as long as Latin America had to compete with European and American corporations, Latin American economies would continue to suffer the trade imbalances fostered by exports of raw materials from haciendas, mines, and plantations.

It is easy to confuse Latin American state capitalism with socialism or Asian systems of the same name. But they differ in certain key respects. One of these is the importance of trade unions, which are often part of the corporatist structures of Latin American societies. Trade unions are often illegal or barely tolerated in capitalist Asian countries, and Asian systems tend not to be corporatist. Latin American political economies are also not socialist because they do not have centralized state planning. The easiest way to conceptualize corporatism is to think of a giant political pyramid with every interest group having a niche, with its own defined rights, ranks, and privileges. The pyramid has cleavages running vertically: church, state bureaucracy, industrialists, the army, trade unions, peasant unions, political parties, all with their specialist interests and privileges informally defined, each one in turn stratified by wealth into a class of elites and nonelites. The corporatist model clearly depends on the colonial model with its social classes and communities, each clearly defined according to royal prerogatives, but this model has been updated to deal with the complexities of the twentieth century, primarily by the addition of the faceless technocrat or bureaucrat. This special class, which is not to be confused with the constantly changing politicians, is a permanent group that runs the economies by adjusting import–export tariffs, duties, borrowed money, taxes, and other aspects of the economies so that they will continue to function decade after decade.

In the corporatist states, trade unions, businessmen, the military, and governments came together, often under one-party states (PRI in Mexico, Peronismo in Argentina) or multiparty "democracies" (Colombia, Venezuela, Brazil, Chile, Venezuela) to protect nascent industries against outside competition. This was done by erecting high tariff walls, Latin America's answer to dependency theory, and giving the control of business organizations to the state. Often the old industrialists of the pre-1930s period became the managers of state-run enterprises in the period that followed. They and their families benefited by the protection of the state and by the many perquisites extended to them, such as free university education in state-run universities for their children. The university students, their jobs secured by their parents and the state, often paraded as Marxists for their few years at the university, and then silently replaced their fathers as leaders in state-run businesses (or as faceless bureaucrats). Business elites married into the families of well-known politicians, and the two groups became indistinguishable through the fifty years during which state capitalism dominated. Outside business groups, such as transnational corporations, were only brought into the state capitalist enterprises to the degree that they agreed to protectionist state policies and to dominant ownership by the state. Thus, we have the curious example of the supposedly German-run Volkswagen of Puebla, Mexico, whose trade unions could strike and close down the city of Puebla with impunity, while the governor of the state would declare that there was nothing he could do, and the managers of the plant would stand around with their hands in their pockets.

Unfortunately, the rural poor, as well as the urban poor, were locked out of the new political machines, or they were manipulated by politicians in standard patron–client relationships. In response, in the 1960s, the disenfranchised poor became involved in radical political movements to overthrow the corporate state and replace it with a socialist state representing all classes. These movements were countered by state terrorism until the early 1980s. By then, most of the radical leaders had "disappeared," the victims of faceless and nameless death squads.

The development of state capitalism cannot be understood as a movement of the left or of the right. In certain countries, leftist trade unions were dominant; in others, rightist business interests. Generally, the more industrial the society, the greater was the influence of the left, and the more agricultural the society, the greater was the influence of the right. The 1930s was a time of seething discontent. New political groups made radical promises and many new political parties developed: Social democrats, communists, syndicalists, business groups, student associations, fascists, and corporatists all attempted to change the structure of society. The elites attempted to accommodate the old to the new. But, in the end, the corporatist state grew larger and more powerful.

Important economic changes occurred during the phase of state corporatism. States expanded to include new industries that became part of state structure. Heavy industry was built up and was subsidized or owned by the state, particularly energy production. Prosperity increased during World War II because the countries of the core shifted to manufacturing war material, and Latin American countries began to make their own goods and brought about the growth of a new industrially oriented middle class. Political instability continued after the war, but so did economic growth. The **Gross Domestic Product** (GDP) rose. There were many changes with important political implications: Literacy went up, life expectancy increased, new transportation was constructed, the middle sectors grew, organized labor became stronger, peasants migrated to cities, the rural proletariat became more organized and more vocal, social problems multiplied, and workers demanded more goods and services. The state grew proportionately to meet the demands of all sectors of society that had been incorporated into the state.

However, state capitalism has not worked well. Latin American countries, borrowing to keep the business enterprises functioning, have approached bankruptcy, and control by elites has led to revolution. Overall, there is a fragmented social order in Latin America—the old corporatist pyramid no longer works well. During the 1960s and 1970s, Latin America became increasingly a conflict–ridden society with numerous groups challenging the power of elites. New elites, with models borrowed from the Asian tigers, are insisting on privatizing industry, introducing real free markets, and reducing the power of the state through democratic reform. Russia is also experimenting with these two transitions toward capitalism and democracy, but from the very different base of state socialism. Mexico is battling to keep the two transitions on course. Threats to the survival of both countries are daily newspaper fare.

From Caudillismo to State Terrorism in Central America

The problems with *caudillos* in Central America were even more severe than in Mexico. Unlike Mexico, there was very little industrialization in Central America until quite late in the 1920s and 1930s, and, even then, industries were limited to clothing, shoes, and concrete. The economies of the Central American countries, particularly Honduras, Guatemala, El Salvador, and Nicaragua, were based on agricultural exports from plantations, many of which were controlled by foreigners or wealthy elites. Communication and transportation systems (telegraph, railroads, and so on) were in foreign hands. Labor organizations were extremely weak and kept that way. The countries tended to be made up primarily of the extremely rich (landowners) and extremely poor (workers of the land and landless workers). There was a small middle class of service personnel, but it tended to identify with the conservative landowners (Woodward 1976). The indigenous peoples of the region were left to fend for themselves when they were not being actively oppressed as in El Salvador in the 1930s.

At a time when Mexico was redistributing agricultural land and expropriating the oil lands of Americans and foreign investors, the elites of the Central American Republics were finding ways to concentrate even more agricultural land and other resources in their own hands. During the first half of this century, the transitions to modernization became increasingly more blocked by the oligarchies. Those arguing for an equitable distribution of resources were accused of being communists and persecuted (Blackman et al.1986).

During the 1930s, the Central American pattern of land-owning *caudillos* dramatically changed due to the world depression. New and powerful labor unions developed in the agricultural sector as the wages of agricultural workers plummeted. A war in Spain between Francisco Franco's fascists and leftist forces alerted the Central American oligarchy to the possibility that radical social movements might occur in the Central American Republics. New right-wing dictators, such as Jorge Ubico in Guatemala, Tiburcio Carías Andino in Honduras, General Maximiliano Hernández Martínez in El Salvador, and Anastasio Somoza in Nicaragua, came to power. In short, in the 1930s, Mexico and the Central American Republics went in opposite political directions: Mexico to the far left and the Central American Republics to the far right (Blackman et al. 1986; Booth 1990; Baloyra 1990; Ebel 1990).

Following World War II, a radical change in Central America in the direction of liberal democracy appeared eminent. In country after country, with the exception of Nicaragua (where the Somoza clan clung to power), the right-wing dictators of the Depression were overthrown. During the late 1940s, labor movements and left-wing political movements grew, infiltrating the universities and the governments. The landed oligarchies found their positions of total control threatened.

The pressing demand of government critics in Central America (and Cuba

BOX 12.1

Case Study: Invention of the Corporatist State in Mexico

The liberal caudillo, Porfirio Diaz, ruled Mexico from 1876 until 1911 when, with the Mexican Revolution a few months old, he resigned and fled to Paris where he died four years later at the age of 85. Before he fled, he stated that the revolutionaries had let a tiger loose. For six years revolutionary armies fought each other and, in the process, destroyed the Mexican economy. The Mexican Revolution had two storm centers, one in the southern region around Morelos. led by Emiliano Zapata, and one centered in the northern state of Chihuahua, led by Doroteo Arango, otherwise known as Pancho Villa. The southern storm center was a region of hacienda agriculture where expanding estates had driven small holders off of their own lands and forced many to become wage workers on lands of the elite (Wolf 1969:27). Villa and Zapata represented claims for revolutionary social change, but more moderate forces became dominant, and a constitutional assembly was called at Queretaro at the end of 1916. The writing of the resulting constitution was dominated by radical General Obregon, who called for secular education, separation of church and state, liquidation of the haciendas and plantations, land reform, wide-ranging labor legislation, and an assertion of the eminent domain of the nation over resources (Wolf l969: 43).

Obregon's Constitution was an explicit statement of state capitalism, but it existed in name only until 1929, when President Plutarco Calles organized the National Revolutionary Party (now known as the Partido Revolutionario Institucional, or PRI, the Institutional Revolutionary Party), which has ruled Mexico since that time. The PRI was founded as a modern mass-based party with a structure radically unlike nineteenth-century parties. Yet, Mexico foundered until 1934 when a new and radically leftist president, General Lázaro Cárdenas, moved the country towards the left and initiated land reform and labor organization on a massive scale. He dismantled the power of the hacienda owners and distributed hacienda lands to the peasantry. Cárdenas nationalized the railroads, the oil fields, and many foreign firms without compensating the foreign-owned corporations. Although he ignored the anticlerical laws of the preceding Calles regime, he

in the Caribbean) was land reform. Most of the land had been alienated from Indian and mestizo farmers, creating a gigantic rural proletariat. Workers in agriculture were reduced to a serf-like existence on the *haciendas* and plantations. Their situation was compared to nineteenth century slavery in the Deep South of the United States by critics.

The owners of the land, like the plantation owners of the Deep South, tended to be absentee landowners. They lived in the central cities and visited maintained a separation of church and state and encouraged the teaching of atheism in the schools. Mexico was the first Latin American society to organize itself explicitly around a corporatist model, and its major symbol became the great pyramid of the sun at Teoti-huacán.

The ability of the PRI to survive was dependent on its ability to reward supporters with jobs in government-run industries, and in government itself (federal, state, and municipal). By 1970, "government" in its many forms accounted for close to 75 percent of all jobs. As long as Mexico was able to borrow money, it was able to expand economically. Until 1980, Mexico's economy grew at rates ranging between 6 to 8 percent per year. But, in the early 1980s, international banks refused to loan more money to Mexico, and its economy went into a tailspin. The rate of inflation soared. The rationale for public support of the PRI was weakened (Purcell 1992: 54). In addition, by 1980 it was apparent that state capitalism was exacerbating the wealth differential between the elites and masses. Despite all of the rhetoric, the rich got richer and the poor got poorer—and Mexico sank deeper and deeper into debt.

President Miguel de la Madrid Hurtado took office in 1982. De la Madrid opened the economy, determined to bring Mexico into the global economy by becoming a signer of the General Agreement on Tariffs and Trade (GATT). He also ended the government's anti–American rhetoric that had dominated Mexico for decades. The immediate impact of his policies was to almost scuttle the 1988 election of his handpicked successor, Carlos Salinas de Gortari. Many former PRI supporters voted for the left-of-center candidate, Cuauhtémoc Cárdenas Solorozano (the son of General Lázaro Cárdenas, the President of Mexico from 1934 to 1940) because of de la Madrid's austerity measures. Cárdenas had created the PRD (the Revolutionary Democratic Party) as a leftist and populist split-off from PRI. Strongly supporting Cárdenas were PRI-affiliated labor union workers whose jobs were threatened (Purcell 1992:54–55).

As we discussed in Chapter 8, well intended reforms, both NAFTA and democratization, are having unintended consequences in the lowlands of Chiapas with the rise of the Zapatista movement. Similar political movements are occurring elsewhere, many of them advocating a restoration of state capitalism or a move toward socialism. The rewards of capitalism and democracy may be long in coming or they may not come at all; the social structure of Mexico has deep roots in exploitation and in class stratification. To change these structures is not going to be an overnight affair. But the changes that are happening in Mexico are widespread in Latin America. At least Mexico no longer has to be concerned about the power structure being in the hands of a landed elite, as is still true in Central America.

their estates every two or three weeks to confer with largely illiterate administrators. They were only interested in profits and invested little in the regions from which they took their livelihood. Many of these lands, particularly on the south coast of Central America, are among the richest agricultural lands in the world. *Colonos* and wandering landless laborers worked the estates of the rich for as little as a dollar a day. The wealthy lived in luxury in Guatemala City, Antigua, Tegucigalpa, Managua, and other large cities (Smith 1982, 1985).

Revolutionary movements broke out after World War II, not unlike those in Mexico two decades before. Rural and urban guerrillas battled right-wing governments for the next half-century. In two instances, Cuba in 1959 and Nicaragua in 1979, revolutionaries came to power. The Cuban revolution is the only one to have survived. The Sandinistas lost the election of 1990 to Violeta Barrios de Chamorro and her party, UNO, in Nicaragua.

Today, without American support for right-wing governments, and without Soviet support for left-wing movements, the violence in Central America has abated. Left-wing political movements and right-wing governments came to uneasy truces, both sides realizing that their goals were not obtainable. But the conditions that produced the conflicts remain. The vast majority of the people of Central America live in grinding poverty. Unemployment remains high, the landless are still landless, crime has increased steadily, and corruption remains a major problem. In addition, there is notable ecological degradation with forests destroyed, land and water poisoned, and soil eroded.

Democratization and Privatization South America

Until the early 1980s, Brazil, Argentina, and Chile, as well as many other South American countries, were dominated by military governments that used state terrorism. They are now moving in a radically new direction, trying to follow Mexico's example and abandon state capitalism. In Brazil, the military returned to the sidelines, and allowed elections, but state capitalism continued under civilian rule for almost another decade. Politicians were big spenders who dramatically boosted public sector pay. Inflation reached 227 percent in 1985, and was brought down by a price freeze. But by 1990 it had reached almost 1500 percent. A spurt of economic growth was brought to a complete standstill, where it stayed for the next three years.

In 1990, Brazil's fortune appeared to improve. On March 15th, a new president, Mr. Fernando Collor, the governor of the tiny state of Alagoas, promised economic and political reforms. He sang the same tune as Salinas de Gortari in Mexico. He had triumphed over Francisco da Lula Silva, a socialist, with an antisocialist campaign, much to the shock of the left. However, halfway through his administration, he was impeached for corruption, and his place taken by his vice president, Itamar Franco. President Franco appointed, as his finance minister, Henrique Cardoso. Mr. Cardoso was famed as one of Latin America's foremost leftist sociologists. Cardoso's early writings were the heart of dependency theory, and his theory was the basis for much of the state corporatist response throughout Latin America. It came as something of a shock when, in 1992, Cardoso pushed through the legislature a set of policies that favored private industry and leveled inflation. He developed a new currency, the *real* (replacing the cruzeiro), and prices, which had been rising at 30–50 percent a month, slowed to single numbers.

Finance minister Cardoso ran for the presidency of Brazil in October of 1994 on an anticorporatist, antistate capitalist platform. His chief opponent was

Francisco de Lula Silva, who clearly expected to win by a landslide with his so-cialist platform. Much to Lula Silva's surprise, Cardoso won easily, with 54 per-cent of the vote, twice Lula's share. Cardoso has rightly singled out formal in-dexation of wages as a major reason for inflation, and it is supposed to be stopped this year, but Cardoso has run into significant opposition by the state corporatist bureaucrats and politicians who run the Brazilian political machine. Brazil remains far behind its neighbors, Chile and Argentina, but they are stim-ulating the Brazilian electorate to examine the economic advances of these two "Latin American tigers."

In Argentina, the military returned the government to the civilians in 1983 after torturing and executing over 25,000 civilians. In the election of 1989, the government decided to allow the Peronist party to compete, and Carlos Saul Menem, leader of the Peronist Justicialist Party, won, but did a very un-Peronist thing. He opened markets, reduced tariffs, and privatized the economy. Basi-cally, Menem jettisoned fifty years of Peronist corporatism. The story in Chile is almost identical to Argentina's. General Pinochet, who overthrew Marxist President Salvator Allende in 1973, had decided to rule in Chile until 1999, but a plebescite in 1989 showed that the majority of the Chilean people were tired of his one-man dictatorship. On December 14, 1989, in a multiparty election, Chile elected Patricio Alwyn as president and state terrorism came to an end. Alwyn, like Saul Menem, decided to follow Mexico's lead. The problems of in-flation, international debt, and the crimes committed by the Pinochet regime against its own people posed major hurdles for the Alwyn administration. How-ever, having finally achieved democracy after a sixteen-year dictatorship, the Chilean people have been moving through the economic and political transi-tions successfully.

Similar changes have occurred in most of the countries of South America. Suddenly, democratic capitalism is bursting out all over. But are the new gov-ernments really democratic? The reason for the state terrorism in the first place was to destroy the left wing, and it was thoroughly destroyed. Are the countries of South America practicing true democracy, or is it a fiction as in the past? At the present time, it appears that elections are open and that mass, participatory democracy is a fact of life. But only time will tell what will happen after the left reorganizes.

Indigenous Strategies of Cultural Survival

As mentioned at the beginning of this chapter, Latin America has more surviv-ing distinct indigenous cultures than any other world region. Within the past twenty-five years there has been a dramatic rise in the formation of indigenous organizations whose purposes are to negotiate with the nation–states of Latin America for various legal rights and protections—especially land rights—and to

BOX 12.2

Ecological Maladaption:
Destruction of the Rain Forest in the Amazon Basin

The Amazon rain forest is the largest in the world. Covering about 7 million square kilometers (about 2.7 million square miles—slightly smaller than the contiguous United States), it makes up about a third of South America. However, new development projects are destroying this rain forest at an alarming rate. During the mid-1990s more than 20,000 square miles of rain forest were being cleared annually to make way for farmland and pastureland for ranches (DeBlij & Muller 1997:255).

The slash-and-burn agriculture traditionally practiced by the indigenous peoples of the area was sustainable because of the small scale of such operations. Temporary stress on one part of the system by small groups of people was followed by long periods of abandonment in which the forest could regenerate itself. These soils cannot support the kind of massive development projects that are now common in the Amazon. Access to these remote areas has been made relatively easy by the rapid expansion of Brazilian highways, which have penetrated the Amazon with a vegenance. Almost 200,000 settlers move into this region annually.

The military rulers of Brazil, who are now out of favor and out of power, decided to open the great Amazon Basin in the 1960s. Brazil borrowed large sums of money in order to invest in the Amazon, particularly in the construction of the Trans-Amazon highway. Farmers were given low-interest loans to move into the Amazon to build farms. Many farmers experimented with expensive fertilizers, pesticides, herbicides, and other chemicals to increase productivity and maintain soil fertility (and continue to do so), putting many into debt. The chemicals do considerable ecological damage, contaminating rivers, streams, and subsurface aquifers.

The process is ongoing, and continues the cycle of exploitation. Settlers move into the Amazon basin, lured by the cheap land prices

protect and preserve, and in some instances rejuvenate, native cultures and traditions. The strengthening of ethnic and cultural identity has become an important universal survival strategy for Latin American indigenous peoples from Mexico to Chile. Native peoples have renewed their efforts to control the processes of domination and exploitation that have beleaguered them for the past 500 years. In many countries, such as Ecuador and Panama, the various indigenous groups have formed country-wide pan-indigenous organizations to promote the welfare of their communities; and some native organizations have formed networks of networks, with their compatriots in other countries, including the United States, and with sympathetic human rights organizations.

and promises of fertile land. However, within two to three years, the soil is depleted and sold to ranchers who can grow pasture grasses for their herds. This leads to a concentration of most of the land in the hands of the large agribusinesses (deBlij and Muller 1997: 255), as the small subsistence farmers keep clearing new areas in search of fertile soil. It has also led to the destruction of the forest habitat of indigenous peoples throughout the Amazon.

In addition to the land development schemes denuding the tropical rain forest, mining and logging concerns are also active in projects throughout the Amazon. The largest and most rapidly developing subregion is the seven States of the Amazon, where population has tripled since 1980 to about 1.5 million. In this region, a huge project, known as the Grande Carajas Project in eastern Pará State, has transformed the environment from a tropical rain forest to an industrial complex. This project was designed to exploit one of the world's largest known deposits of iron ore in the Serra dos Carajás hills. It includes a mining complex, the Tucuruí Dam, and a 535-mile (860 km) railroad to the Atlantic port of São Luís. The infrastructure built for the mining operation, and the workers it has attracted, have led to a related development of the nearby city of Manaus, which is now a major industrial center, specializing in the production of electronic goods (DeBlij and Muller 1997:255).

A second leading development scheme is the Polonoreste Plan located 500 miles to the southwest of Grande Carajas, along the 1500-mile-long highway BR-364 corridor that parallels the Bolivian border. Most of the settlement is within Rondônia State. This project is appealing to plantation workers who have lost their jobs due to mechanization, wealthy ranchers and agribusiness, and subsistence farmers. These groups have been fighting for land in this region, while the Brazilian government is trying to establish some land reform policies.

In the meantime, the rain forest continues to disappear. While this pattern of rain forest destruction is worldwide, the problem is most severe in the Amazon, accounting for over half of all tropical deforestation. Massive rain forest destruction causes the extinction of plant species that could be useful to cure human diseases, alters patterns of rainfall, has a climatic impact worldwide, and exposes fragile tropical soils to massive erosion. It is clear that the development underway in the Amazon is not sustainable and that continued destruction of the tropical forest will indeed have global consequences.

Beyond this, the responses of particular indigenous cultures to renewed oppression from territorial states in the late twentieth century has varied considerably. These varied responses we term strategies for cultural survival. They range from the peaceful—and effective so far—political negotiations of the Kuna with the government of Panama to religious revitalization movements like that of the Ngóbe of Panama in the 1960s to armed rebellion as in the case of the Maya Zapatistas of Chiapas, Mexico (discussed in Chapter 8).

We will examine two cases of cultural survival strategies: beginning on page 446, the Kayapó of Brazil in South America, and beginning on page 449, the Ngóbe of Panama in Central America.

BOX 12.3

■ Case Study: The Drug Trade in Latin America

As revolutions came to an end in Central America and political and economic changes occurred in Brazil, Argentina, and Chile, bringing an end to state terrorism, and ushering in democracy, in other regions of South America drugs, terrorism, and revolution came to be tied together in a complex web, corrupting governments and threatening the way of life of peasants and indigenous peoples.

The smuggling of drugs into the United States is a relatively young enterprise. In the 1960s, the primary drug imported into the United States from Latin America was marijuana. Few hard drugs were smuggled across the Mexican border until the 1970s, when Americans began to import cocaine and other hard drugs. Smuggling has always been a part of life in the Colombian Andes, but since 1979, it has evolved into narcoterrorism, corrupting many officials at a time when the Colombian government is attempting to follow the leadership of Mexico, Brazil, Argentina, and Chile.

The Medellín drug cartel was organized in 1979. Personal armies were organized by the Medellín cartel made up of *sicarios,* hit men, who used motorcycles and small but powerful machine guns to assassinate designated enemies of the cartel. Within a very short time, the city of Cali, in the southern Department of Cauca, de-

veloped its own cartel for largely similar reasons. A third cartel, known as the Atlantic or coastal cartel, also evolved in Cartagena. The three cartels spilled over in their interests, and territorial disputes began to occur. These led to violent confrontations between the *sicarios* of the drug "mafias." Law enforcement personnel began to intervene and became the targets of *sicarios.* Judges, lawyers, and policemen were assassinated. Journalists for Colombian newspapers were also targeted and killed. The Medellín, Cali, and Atlantic drug cartels have acted as brokers in the drug trade; both the drug trade and narcoterrorism have spilled over into neighboring countries, particularly Peru.

Cocaine is a derivative of the coca plant. The coca plants are grown on the lower slopes of the eastern Andean foothills in Peru, Ecuador, and Bolivia, by poor peasant farmers, many of Indian ancestry. Many of the regions where the coca is now grown for the drug trade are traditional coca-growing districts where the crops have been grown for millennia and traded into the highlands. As a result of the new demand, there has been some expansion of coca growing into higher valleys in northern Ecuador and Peru. Less addictive and much less powerful, the leaves of the coca plant have been mixed with lime and chewed by the Indian populations of the Andean highlands for centuries, at least since the time of the Inca.

Coca leaves have been distributed by an internal Indian marketing system until the last twenty years, when the international marketing of cocaine intruded into the local peasant agricultural and marketing system.

Processing plants were set up in the coca-growing areas and the coca leaf is now transformed on the spot into raw coca paste. This is done by adding several chemicals including kerosene, benzene, and acetone. The coca paste must then be transported to more sophisticated laboratories, many of which are located in the Colombian Llanos (eastern plains) and the Magdalena River Valley. Here the raw paste is treated again and turned into cocaine and other coca products. It is then smuggled by plane from these lowland regions in eastern Colombia up to various other distribution points, such as the Cayman Islands, Central America, or Mexico, where it is transhipped to the United States (Gugliotta and Leen 1989).

The coca-growing districts of Ecuador, Peru, and Bolivia were almost entirely in regions that were relatively free of state government control because they were far away from the central capitals and had little to offer the *caudillos* and *caciques*. They developed their own *cacique* elites made up of indigenous leaders. In the mid-to-late twentieth century all of this changed dramatically and the regions attracted the organizational talents of the cartels. The cartels stepped in and offered money and protection to isolated and largely poverty-stricken Indian and mestizo populations. In exchange for the raw coca leaf, the cartels have offered local producers money, goods, and protection, and incorporated the traditional *caciques* as long as they accept control by more powerful *caciques* at the top.

In Northeastern Peru, the *Sendero Luminoso* (Shining Path) revolutionary movement has become a major dealer in drugs and violence with the Medellín and Cali cartels on the receiving end of the drugs. In exchange for "protecting" the local coca growers, the cartel pays the Sendero revolutionaries with weapons.

Because the regions in question are isolated and the jurisdictions of the Peruvian, Bolivian, and Ecuadorian national administrations have not reached them, soldiers and administrators are considered outsiders. American Drug Enforcement Agency (DEA) operatives and others working for the United States, Colombian, Peruvian, Ecuadorian, and Bolivian administrations are alleged to be trying to destroy the peasant drug economies.

The Sendero Luminoso is a relatively unknown revolutionary movement that depends on its ability to terrorize the rural populations, especially in the old Indian regions. It uses extreme violence to intimidate the peasants, the military, and the police. President Alberto Fujimori, put into power through democratic elections, overthrew his own government in order to deal with the Sendero Luminoso but has not had much success until recently when the leader, Anibal Guzman, was captured and jailed.

The most recent American policy is to try to help peasant coca growers find alternative export crops to grow and market. It is hoped that this strategy will take power away from the Shining Path. However, American foreign policy, the demand of the drug cartels, and the brutal policies of the government of Peru have already had a devastating impact on such tribal groups as the Ashaninka (Campa), Peru's largest lowland Indian group.

BOX 12.4

■ Case Study: The Kayapó of Brazil

Brazil's indigenous population, estimated to have been between 3 and 5 million in the early sixteenth century, is now only about 250,000—and even this number represents an increase over the estimated 150,000 to which the population had been reduced by the 1950s. Among the survivors are the Kayapó. Today, many of Brazil's indigenous communities have formed organizations to fight against further encroachment on their territories by outsiders and to protect their human rights. The Kayapó are unusual in that they have successfully appropriated modern technology in their struggle for self-preservation. Anthropologist Terence Turner has conducted research among and worked closely with the Kayapó since the early 1960s and, while not the only source of information on them, his numerous publications are certainly among the most thorough and reliable accounts. Turner (1991, 1995), has carefully documented both traditional Kayapó social organization and their remarkable—and so far successful—struggle for cultural survival against miners, loggers, and the development plans of the Brazilian government.

The Gê–speaking Kayapó live in the southern part of the Brazilian state of Pará on the southern edge of the Amazon rain forest, along tributaries of the middle course of the Rio Xingu. Their population of about 4,000 is divided among 14 villages, the largest of which is Gorotire, with about 1,000 inhabitants. Traditional Kayapó villages are circular with a men's house in the center of a large public plaza that is surrounded by a circle of houses—two or three concentric circles in very large villages. Most villages have between 200–400 people and are usually separated from one another by distances of over 100 kilometers. The villages remain politically autonomous, as they have always been. Kayapó lands have almost all been designated as legal reserves during the past ten years, with a total area of about 100,000 square kilometers (Turner 1995).

Despite recent income from mining and logging concessions, almost all Kayapó continue to rely on their traditional economic activities of slash-and-burn agriculture, hunting, fishing, and gathering as their main source of livelihood. For stretches of several weeks at a time, the Kayapó communities still go on hunting–gathering treks, traveling substantial distances from their base villages.

Family organization is characterized by monogamy and extended family households, with matrilocality being the preferred form of postmarital residence. Young boys around eight years of age are ceremoniously removed from their mothers' households, inducted into an age grade, and reside with their agemates in the men's house until they marry. At marriage, a man takes up residence in his wife's father's household. Kinship is reckoned bilaterally; there are no unilineal descent groups. After the birth of his first child, a man joins one of the men's associations, often that of his wife's father. Women have corresponding associations. It is the men's associations that are responsible for the organization and sponsorship of all ritual and ceremonial activities in a Kayapó village. Each men's association has a leader and it is these men who are the "chiefs" of the village.

Regular contact with outsiders began around the 1850s and was mostly conflictual.

Kayapó men pause for natural refreshments.

More or less peaceful contact with Brazilians began in the 1950s. In the early 1960s, when Terence Turner conducted his initial research among them, the Kayapó had not yet developed the forms of social consciousness that they would later use successfully in their campaigns of political resistance (Turner 1991). But this was soon to come. In the 1970s, recognizing that their cultural survival in the future would depend on their ability to deal successfully with Brazilians, many of the Kayapó village chiefs sent their sons and nephews out for schooling. At the same time, the extended visits of anthropologists and other professionals, who clearly valued Kayapó culture for its own sake, heightened their awareness of "the potential political value of their "culture" in their relations with the alien society" that surrounded them (Turner 1991:301).

In the 1980s, the nature of Kayapó contact with outsiders shifted as miners and loggers in-

vaded the area. After an initial period of armed resistance, the literate young leaders of some of the Kayapó villages established contractual arrangements with the miners and loggers and began to receive a percentage of the profits. At this time, Kayapó lands had not yet been granted official reserve status by the government, although the villages were technically under the protection of Brazil's National Indian Foundation (FUNAI), formerly the Indian Protection Service (SPI).

With funds from the mining and logging concessions, the young leaders were able to make trips to Brasilia to lobby in the halls of government for the Kayapó cause and also to travel abroad and attract the interest and support of humanitarian and environmental organizations. The Brazilian government, under great pressure as a result of the international media coverage of the Kayapó cause, financial and political support from nongovernmental organizations NGOs (both

Brazilian and foreign), and the militancy of the Kayapó themselves, granted a series of reserves to the Kayapó villages in the late 1980s and early 1990s (Turner 1995:103)

After a few years, during which contracts for the extraction of gold and timber continued to be renewed, the Kayapó seemingly had enough of deforestation and severe environmental pollution (mainly from the mercury used in the gold extraction process), cancelled all contracts, and expelled miners and loggers from their reserves. Only a few small mining ventures continue, operated by the Kayapó themselves and a few miners who agreed to teach them. The Kayapó have also begun to explore the possibilities for income from environmentally sustainable activities such as the extraction of Brazil nut oil and ecotourism.

Perhaps the most remarkable aspect of the Kayapó battle for cultural survival has been their use of modern technology, particularly video cameras. They make use of shortwave radios these days to communicate among their distantly scattered villages. Since obtaining their first video camera in 1985, some of the Kayapó have received professional training as cameramen and videotape editors. They have progressed from a "home movie" to a professional level of skill, in large measure due to Terence Turner's Kayapó Video Project, begun in 1990. Turner stresses that the training focused on skills and that the Kayapó editors in particular "retain control of both form and content" (Turner 1992:7). The Kayapó have used video as a medium to document their own cultural practices, particularly their numerous ceremonies, which are spectacular performances with elaborate body painting and colorful feather and fiber costumes and masks. They have become aware of the political power of these external displays of their culture that attract much public interest, particularly at the international level. They have also used video as a means of documenting their political encounters with representatives of the Western world and, as Turner points out (1992:7), they are aware of the international leverage they achieve by having their own photographers filming events that are being covered by the international press, thus assuring that the Kayapó will themselves be a center of media attention. These examples, recounted by Turner, nicely illustrate Kayapó political astuteness in the use of video.

Throughout their continuing struggle for cultural survival, using the technology of the modern Western world to help them achieve their social and political ends, it should be noted that the Kayapó have operated within their own traditional cultural structure of chiefly leadership and authority in politically autonomous villages.

BOX 12.5

■ Case Study: The Ngóbe of Panama

There are over 43 distinct indigenous peoples of Central America with a combined population of between 4 and 5 million. These peoples have been marginalized politically, and, with the exception of the Maya of Guatemala, are largely unknown. El Salvador has more than a half-million Indians, largely silent due to a fear of government reprisals. Other indigenous groups live along the coastal plains of the Caribbean. Among the better known are the Miskito, who became prominent due to their conflict with the Sandinista government in Nicaragua, and the Kuna, of Panama, who are known for their colorful appliqué cloth panels known as *molas* (Miller 1993:218–219).

The indigenous peoples of Central America largely choose to live in rural backlands in relative isolation, preferring a lower standard of living to the loss of their cultural heritage. But isolation is disappearing. Investment schemes, which may help the majority urban populations and are strongly supported by the governments of Central America, often target the natural resources located in the lands of the indigenous peoples. Often looked down upon by Spanish-speaking peasants, whose populations are rapidly expanding (a population of 25 million is projected to double by the year 2010), indigenous peoples are finding there are no places left to retreat to. The remaining forests are being cut down, and native peoples are being displaced and driven into cultural extinction. Two-thirds of Central America's forested lands have been cleared since 1950. Central American peasants look hungrily at the lands of the natives.

What is now the Republic of Panama had an estimated indigenous population *circa* 1500

A.D. of 600,000 to 1,000,000. The impact of the Spanish invasion was disastrous, and within one hundred years many native groups had disappeared altogether and those remaining were greatly reduced in numbers—by as much as 80 percent to 90 percent—and suffered severe disruptions of their lifeways. Population recovery did not begin until the early nineteenth century. Like the Kayapó, the Ngóbe were among the survivors. Their population may have actually reached a low point in the late eighteenth century when the Ngóbe may have numbered as few as 4,000 to 5,000 (Young 1985).

In recent decades their numbers have dramatically increased, so that now the Ngóbe are the second most numerous indigenous group in all of Central America, second only to the Maya. Today there are over 100,000 Ngóbe living within the approximately 11,000 square kilometers of the mountainous region of western Panama that they claim as their remaining traditional territory, and at least another 20,000 living permanently elsewhere in Panama. In the heart of their territory is Cerro Colorado, a mountain containing what may be the world's fourth largest deposit of low-grade copper ore. This copper deposit has figured prominently in Ngóbe struggles for cultural survival since the 1970s, as we will discuss below.

As their numbers have outstripped their resource base, more Ngóbe have permanently moved out of their traditional territory; and many more who have remained have sought to supplement their livelihood with part-time wage labor in a highly inflationary economy with a surplus of unskilled labor and wages that remain well below the inflationary curve. But it is not only the economy of Panama that threatens the survival of Ngóbe culture; the global

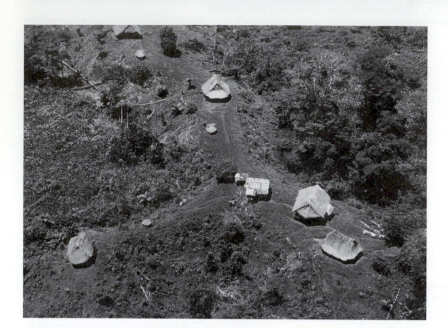

Ngóbe caserío *(hamlet) in Bocas del Toro, Panama. The Ngóbe traditionally live in very small communities of from six to eight houses. These hamlets are usually occupied by members of a single kin group and people who have married into the community.*

economy is affecting them as well. What have been their strategies for cultural survival and how successful have these been to date? In some ways, their story parallels that of the Kayapó; in other ways, it differs.

Even today the majority of Ngóbe depend on slash-and-burn agriculture and the raising of a few cattle and other barnyard animals, supplemented by some hunting and gathering, as their major source of livelihood. They live in small hamlets—most too small even today to be called villages—scattered throughout the mountains at distances of a kilometer and more. Traditionally, each hamlet consisted of the members of a single kin group and in-married women, for the Ngóbe practiced postmarital **virilocality** (residence after marriage on the lands of the husband's kinsmen). Ideally a polygynist, a man often housed his two or more wives and their respective

children in separate dwellings in the same hamlet. Today, many hamlets are occupied by two or more kin groups and this has led to an increase in disputes over land. Land is owned by the kin group as a whole, with both men and women receiving use rights. In theory, this could involve a lot of people using the land because the Ngóbe reckon descent, and thus land use rights, bilaterally, that is, through both mother and father equally. In reality, land use rights are constrained by actual place of residence and generational continuity of use (see Young 1971, Chapter 5, for details).

In the early 1960s, patterns of sharing (reciprocity) of food and labor among kinsmen, near and distant, were still reasonably effective as a means of redistributing goods and services to relieve temporary shortfalls in times of local scarcity, as was the redistribution of food that took place on ritual occasions. However, social and economic strains that had been building up since the 1930s in the context of greater involvement with the agencies and institutions of the outside world were beginning to take their toll. Between the 1930s and the 1970s, the Ngóbe went from marginal involvement with the outside world and its economic system to dependency upon it. The first response to crisis occurred in the early 1960s in the form of a revitalistic religious movement (Young 1971, 1975, 1978).

This social movement came to be known as the religion of Mama Chi (little mother), after the young Ngóbe woman who, in 1961, saw a heavenly vision and received a message from the Christian god. The Ngóbe have been subjected to Christian influence in one form or another since the time of the Spanish invasion, but it would not be accurate to say that very many of them are "Christianized" in the conventional sense of the term. Nonetheless, many Christian elements are incorporated into their belief system. According to Mama Chi, the Ngóbe were to withdraw from contact with the outside world, including the removal of those of their children who were attending outside schools, cease the performance of their traditional rituals and the consumption of alcohol—an integral part of the rituals—and treat each other henceforth as one big family of brothers and sisters. If these teachings were followed, then at the end of a five-year period of trial the Ngóbe would be the recipients of great good fortune; if they were not, then misery and ill fortune was to be their lot. As is often the case with religious prophecy, the nature of both the good fortune and the bad was quite vague.

Although her teachings spread throughout the Ngóbe country, and at its height in the mid-1960s the Mama Chi religion affected all Ngóbe living both within and outside the traditional territory, in the end the movement failed to become an established religion. By the mid-1970s, only a very few followers remained.

Today the Mama Chi religion retains a small number of followers and has the status of what we would call a cult. The Mama Chi religion progressed through a variety of changes and offshoot interpretations before it ceased to be a significant force for change, but its accomplishments in terms of a restructing of Ngóbe internal and external relationships were far-reaching. Later political resistance was born of this revitalistic religious movement.

During 1964–1965, young men with some formal education began to dominate the movement, and within a year the concerns of the movement shifted from predominantly religious to political, from seeking salvation through supernatural means to seeking it through political means. This shift in orientation marks the beginning of a still continuing process of politicization and political restructuring among the Ngóbe. There is no longer any formal connection between the remaining adherents of the Mama Chi religion and the new political organization of the Ngóbe. It is this new political structure that represents the current Ngóbe strategy for cultural survival.

Although Mama Chi's teachings did not succeed as a religion, the movement had an enormous impact on the Ngóbe during its active life. It stimulated a fundamental transformation in social consciousness in at least four important ways. First, by seeking withdrawal from contact with the outside world, the Mama Chi religion forced the Ngóbe into full awareness of the relations of subordination and dependency that existed between them and the outside world. This fostered conscious consideration of alternative means of adaptation to the cash economy.

Second, by ordering the removal of all Ngóbe children from schools, an order that was initially complied with during the early stages of the movement, the Ngóbe quickly realized the importance of knowing Spanish and of literacy as a powerful tool in dealing with government officials, merchants, and other outsiders.

Third, by prohibiting traditional rituals and advocating pan-Ngóbe sister- and brotherhood, the movement forced an assessment of the very foundations of Ngóbe culture as they understood it. This fostered a newfound sense of self-worth, solidarity, and ethnic identity. The Mama Chi religion, as is the case with all indigenous social movements, represented an attempt to restructure relations with the nonindigenous world. In the process, the Ngóbe came to realize that subordination is a state of mind rather than an unalterable condition of life.

Fourth, an emphasis on political autonomy that occurred during one phase of the movement, while even at the time viewed as impractical and unattainable by many, certainly produced in the process a greater appreciation of the potential for using political means to achieve socio-economic ends. However unintentionally, the Mama Chi religion initiated the process of politicization among the Ngóbe.

Prior to the political restructuring that came about within the context of the Mama Chi religion, the Ngóbe had no recognized chiefs. Decisions were made and disputes settled by kin groups. Temporary arbitrators were chosen by kin groups on the basis of their reputations as men who could render judgments that would be acceptable to both sides. Action-oriented decisions were taken by consensus. Ngóbe appointed by the government as *corregidores* (civil judges) in actuality served mainly to record births and deaths in the civil registry. Only if they were known to be good traditional arbitrators did they also serve in that capacity. This system worked well to settle disputes and arrive at decisions internally. It was essentially maladaptive in relations with government agencies and other outside organizations because no one could speak for the Ngóbe as a group.

By 1970, a chief (*cacique*) had been selected to represent each of the three Panamanian provinces in which the Ngóbe claim territory: Bocas del Toro, Chiriqui, and Ver-

aguas. The selection of these men is reported to have occurred at a regional *congreso* (meeting) in Veraguas Province some time in 1968. Each chief appointed local representatives known as *jefes immediators*. By 1970, General Omar Torrijos, then leader of the Panamanian government, had officially acknowledged the three chiefs as the legitimate leaders/representatives of the Ngóbe. However, as late as 1978 many Ngóbe still questioned the authority of the provincial chiefs and were thus still unable to present a united front to outside agencies. But the impending negotiations for an open-pit copper mine at Cerro Colorado were making their need for unity more crucial.

Between 1970 and 1981, three mining companies in succession contracted with the Government of Panama for exploration rights in the Cerro Colorado area. These were Canadian Javelin, Texasgulf, and finally Rio Tinto Zinc. Each company in turn conducted extensive explorations. An access road to Cerro Colorado was constructed through Ngóbe territory from the Pan American Highway, which skirts their territory in Chiriqui Province. During this same period, the Ngóbe were also the object of several national and international development projects. Ignored by the government for most of their history, the Ngóbe now became the object of assimilationist policies disguised as "development" and concern for their welfare.

In the late 1970s, as mining exploration intensified and the opening of a mine looked likely, a group of Ngóbe leaders, some of whom were attending the national university in Panama City, requested and received technical guidance from a Jesuit-affiliated organization known as the Panamanian Center for Study and Social Action regarding the potential social and environmental impacts of a large open-pit copper mine in their territory.

Within this rather ominous context of transnational mining companies and mega-projects, the Ngóbe were still struggling to achieve consensus about the representativeness and scope of authority of their restructured political system. It was not clear, for example, whether the chiefs and their subalterns should concern themselves with internal affairs or only with external affairs, and whether they should supplement or supplant existing forms of authority. Local and regional congresses were held to discuss these matters, as well as to discuss the one issue on which all were agreed—the need to obtain a legally established *comarca* (reservation) from the government. As mining exploration expanded, the issue of the mine also became a widespread concern and was linked by the Ngóbe to legal title to their land.

Gradually, there came to be widespread acceptance of the chiefs and their representatives; and, by unspoken process rather than deliberated decision, the new political structure focused on external affairs. The Ngóbe held their first General Congress with representatives from all three provinces in 1979. At this congress, the Ngóbe were still not of one mind on the issue of the mine. Some believed the government's promises of benefits; others were certain that the mine would bring only social and environmental disaster; still others felt they did not have enough information to make an informed decision. But one clear result of this first General Congress was that the leadership realized that the Ngóbe alone could not control the political dynamics involved in dealing with transnational corporations, and they actively began to seek outside support and use the public media to promote their cause and denounce government and corporate duplicity.

At the second General Congress in 1980, solidarity in opposition to the Cerro Colorado mine was achieved and the Ngóbe leaders publicly declared that they would continue their opposition to the mine until the government grated them their *comarca,* as Torrijos had promised them a decade before. The Ngóbe (with some help from sympathetic Jesuits and other friends) had also drawn international attention to the human rights and environmental issues related to the proposed copper mine. While this strengthened their position, it is not likely that this international outcry alone would have stopped Rio Tinto Zinc had the potential profits been great enough. But high inflation, which dramatically raised initial investment costs, negotiation problems with the Panamanian government, and world market prices of copper that were both low and volatile, combined to force Rio Tinto Zinc in 1981 to suspend plans to open the mine (Gjording 1991).

Throughout the 1980s and early 1990s, the Ngóbe continued to demand legal title to their lands and to openly oppose government development plans. In the 1990s, they added public demonstrations, roadblocks on the Pan American highway, marches to Panama City (a distance of about 500 kilometers), and hunger strikes to their forms of political resistance and as a means of drawing public attention to their plight. They also publish a newsletter, use tape recorders at their meetings, especially those with representatives of government and transnationals, and actively seek support from international environmental and human rights organizations. Despite this, by 1995 the government had granted mining concessions for 80 percent of Ngóbe territory without any consultation with the Ngóbe (Sarsanedas 1995). And, in February of 1996, the government signed an agreement with yet a fourth mining company, Panacobre, a subsidiary of Tiomin Resources, a Canadian corporation, for exploration and exploitation of the copper deposit at Cerro Colorado, again without including the Ngóbe in the process. This precipitated a march to Panama City of more than 100 Ngóbe and a demand for an audience which President Pérez Balladares reluctantly granted. At this meeting the president agreed to submit a proposal to the legislature to demarcate Ngóbe territory as a legal reserve. In late November of 1996, Pérez Balladares did submit the proposal, but it specifies only half the hectares the Ngóbe are claiming and does not suspend the mining contract with Panacobre. The Ngóbe rejected the proposal and continued to protest.

In late January 1997, the Panamanian Legislative Assembly approved the proposal to give the Ngóbe legal title to their land as a *comarca* (reserve); but the government did not rescind the mining contract with Panacobre to exploit the copper deposit at Cerro Colorado.

The long process of learning to use their cultural identity as a political tool in a multicultural world—a process that began with the Mama Chi movement—is now complete. At one of their general congresses about 1992, those present decided on "Ngóbe-Buglé" as their official cultural identification to the outside world, and this is how they are now referenced in the Panamanian daily, *La Presna*; no longer are they referred to as "Guaymí." (The

Buglé are a small indigenous population in Veraguas Province who are culturally related to the Ngóbe.) And they have clearly learned the value of political alliances. In a letter enclosed with the June–July 1996 issue of their newsletter, *Drü*, the letterhead reads "Congreso General Ngóbe–Buglé y Campesino," a public declaration of the fact that they have joined forces with the nonindigenous *campesino* (peasant) population of the region on issues of joint concern. And the letter itself is signed by a Ngóbe who identifies himself as "secretary of international affairs"! The Ngóbe have not yet achieved the success of the Kayapó, and they have had to build an entirely new political structure to deal with external affairs, but, like the Kayapó, they have developed new forms of social consciousness and these have resulted in similar strategies for cultural survival.

Summary

The earliest adaptations of humans in the Americas were those of big game hunting, dating to at least 10,000 B.C. The transformation of these hunting–gathering societies into tribal agricultural societies occurred gradually, between 3000 and 2000 B. C. With great speed, chiefdoms emerged about 1500 B. C., followed by states by 700 B. C. These developments were stimulated, as was true in other world regions, by trade. City-states emerged in both Mesoamerica and the Andes with some remarkable parallels, such as the worship of feline deities.

In the early sixteenth century, the indigenous civilizations of Latin America collapsed as Spanish and Portuguese invaders imposed a political ecology of bureaucratic cities, mines, plantations, and haciendas, while at the same time destroying the indigenous trade connections that had supported millions of people. A population collapse followed that may have destroyed up to 90 percent of the indigenous peoples. The slow population recovery took centuries.

The Spanish Empire, along with that of Portugal, collapsed in the early nineteenth century, and was followed by a century of strong man rule *(caudillos)*. State capitalism replaced *caudillo* rule after the 1930s, in response to the Great Depression and the theory of dependency. State capitalism began as a promise to improve the lot of the poor, but instead made the rich richer and the poor poorer.

In the last decade, state capitalism is being challenged by new forms of political economy that are also appearing in Asia, Africa, and Eastern Europe. These new systems depend on open markets and democracy, but are proving difficult to implement. There is a great fear that these new systems will only mean more poverty and violent social movements. However, there is also hope that Latin America, in the next century, will begin to live up to its promise as a region of prosperous countries, within which indigenous groups and the poorer social classes will gain democratic rights not available to their ancestors.

Key Terms

Alcalde	*Ladino*
Ayuntamiento	**Lanzon**
Cargo (or fiesta) System	*Latifundia*
Caudillo	**Liberation Theology**
Charro	*Machismo*
Colonos	**Mesoamerica**
Comadre	*Mestizo*
Compadrazgo	*Minifundia*
Compadre	**Plantations**
Corregidor	*Porfirismo*
Corrida	*Rancheras*
Debt Peonage	*Sodality*
Ejido	**Syncretic**
Evangelical Protestantism	**Virginity Complex**
Gross Domestic Product (GDP)	**Virilocality**
Hacienda	

chapter

Global Problems, International Development, and Anthropology in the Third Millennium

13

We are leaving so many problems to the next generation . . . poverty, conflict, damage to the environment, abuse of human rights . . . Long term solutions will be possible only when there is better understanding of peoples and communities—the subject-matter of **anthropology** (from a Royal Anthropological Institute advertisement in *Anthropology Today,* vol. 12, no. 6, December, 1996; emphasis in original)

While we will not enter the twenty–first century until January 1, 2001 (contrary to popular belief that this event occurs one year earlier), January 1, 2000 *is* the beginning of the *third millennium A.D.* What are the prospects for humanity on the eve of the third millennium? Will there be widespread Malthusian pestilence, plague, and famine, or prosperity for all? Realistically, the year 2000 will bring neither, but the half-century to century beyond may bring either. It is largely up to us humans to make the choice. If we are to achieve sustainable resource management and thus insure a liveable world for future generations, we must stop abusing nature as we have been most seriously since the beginning of the industrial era. This does not mean that we have to return to a hunting-and-gathering lifestyle, but it may mean that many of us, especially those of us living and doing well in the developed world, will have to change our habits of consumption. Anthropology is one of several sciences that can provide the knowledge to inform policy and personal choices and show the way to prosperity and a sustainable future. The achievement of sustainability in its broadest sense would clearly be the crowning achievement of humankind; but it is difficult to be an optimist in today's world.

In several of the preceding chapters we have examined the historical rise and fall of cultures and civilizations in various regions of the world. We have looked at the factors that influenced cultural evolution in one direction or another in the various regions; we have shown how trade and tribute empires were transformed into territorial states under the influence of economies of scale; and we have examined some of the causes of unrest, conflict, and various other issues within each region. We have suggested that all people everywhere are now being influenced by a growing process of globalization and that at least some of the disharmony evident in the world today is a reaction to this process. We suggest that, as you read what follows, you think about the extent to which the ethnic conflicts in many regions may be politically motivated resource wars.

The desire for economic and political advantage produces policy inconsistencies and distortions that the cynical among us see as giving the lie to supposed humanitarian goals of development. For example, Cuba and China have both been accused of extensive human rights violations. U. S. policy toward Cuba has included an economic blockade for more than three decades. On the other hand, we have granted China "most favored nation" status for purposes of trade. A clear, if macabre, example of radically different interpretations of the same data is the case of human rights violations in El Salvador in the late 1970s. At one point the U. S. Congress was to vote on whether to continue to provide economic (and military) aid to this tiny Central American country. Human rights organizations pointed to the dismal record of human rights violations, including thousands of outright killings by the El Salvadorean government, and lobbied Congress to deny further aid. Those in favor of continuing aid did not dispute the figures on killings and other violations of human rights, but argued that aid should be continued because the total number of killings was less than reported the year before and this showed that the government had improved the human rights situation! Congress voted to continue providing aid.

In this final chapter, our focus will be on two closely interrelated themes that are with us today and that will have a profound influence on the future of human cultures: (1) global environmental issues, particularly as these relate to development; and (2) international development, what it means, its problematic nature, and whether sustainable development is possible. Briefly, **sustainable development** means development that meets current needs without compromising the needs of future generations. More will be said about sustainability below. In the case of both environmental issues and the elusive goal of sustainability, but particularly the latter, we will be looking at how anthropology can contribute to solutions to the world's problems.

Global Problems

No one knows exactly how many different species of life there are on this Earth. About 1.4 million species have been named and described. These are thought to be only a small fraction of the total, and estimates of the total vary from a few million to upwards of 100 million. Likewise, estimates of yearly species extinctions vary from 4,000 to 40,000 (Southwick 1996). Why is this important? For many reasons, but perhaps the two most important practical reasons are that species diversity represents a great storehouse of untapped potential for both human food and medicine. All of our current domesticated foods, both plant and animal, and an overwhelming number of our medicines are refined versions of, or derived from, wild species. To the extent that we diminish the biodiversity of our planet through human action, we decrease the potential for our own well-being in the short term, and that of our descendants in the long term. As Charles Southwick puts it: "Ultimately, good economics will have to involve sound ecology" (1996:4).

In our view, and that of many others, particularly professional ecologists, humans are currently using Earth's renewable resources at unsustainable rates, and contaminating air, land, and water everywhere. That is, renewable resources such as forests and soils are being used more rapidly than nature can replenish them. However, we should point out that not everyone agrees on which resources are most at risk of **depletion** or **degradation,** or on the magnitude of the risk. Even when risks are generally acknowledged, as in the case of deforestation or species extinction, there is little agreement on what might be the best course of action. Many countries have recognized both of these problems and have signed international agreements to work together, but are struggling to establish mutually acceptable goals and policies that will work. The difference between the optimists and the pessimists is reflected in widely varying estimates of such things as food production potential and population growth rates, in strikingly different interpretations of the same data, and in the amount of faith one places in technological innovation as the key to human survival and well-being.

> Most ecologists consider human population growth to be one of the greatest problems in global ecology and a major driving force of environmental degradation. They see excessive consumption as an equally important cause of pollution and environmental deterioration. Most agree that the two factors work hand in hand to threaten the world's ecological integrity (Southwick 1996:159–60).

Pollution of air, land, and water, water scarcity, population growth, agricultural production, energy consumption, and deforestation are among the problems of global scope that humankind faces today. Other problems could be added to this list.

In the following sections we will focus on population, food production, and deforestation. On page 462, we present a case study that examines the complex interrelationships among these factors in the Mexican states of Puebla and Tlaxcala, both bordering the Federal District about thirty miles south of Mexico City. This study also considers the employment needs of the population and the difficulty of balancing these needs with the need to mitigate environmental degradation. This study provides a striking example of the clash between the short-term perceived needs of the people and institutions responsible for environmental degradation and the long-term vision of the institutions responsible for protecting the environment. It also illustrates well the complex links among the political, economic, ecological, and demographic transitions discussed in Chapter 3; and why these transitions are so difficult to achieve.

Population

The world of the rapidly approaching third millennium faces several challenges, global in nature, and all related to the activities of humans in relation to their environment. At the core of these problems is that of population growth. The

Dharvi, India, 370 acre slum—home to one million people, also a major manufacturing center.

human population is rapidly reaching the point, if it has not already been reached, when we will overwhelm the resource base.

Current net worldwide population increase is somewhere between 85 and 90 million persons annually (Southwick 1996; World Resources Institute [WRI] 1996). Net increase means that deaths worldwide have already been subtracted from this total. Deaths worldwide were about 51 million in 1993 (WRI 1996). The human population has gone from about one billion in 1800 to almost 6 billion today. We may believe that we have considerable control over ecosystem dynamics, and we may believe that we can therefore disassociate ourselves from the rest of nature, but, ultimately, we cannot do so. An ecological principle from which we cannot escape is that a species that grows in numbers beyond its available food supply will suffer a reduction in numbers—often a sharp reduction—by starvation and disease. Humanity may be able to postpone such a fate by means of its undeniable genius for technological innovation, but in the end we live in a world of finite resources.

Looking at global population trends is an important way to estimate future demands for food, water, and energy. Projections of the size of the world population by the year 2025 vary from about 7.9 to 11.9 billion, according to the World Resources Institute. The differences in the projections are due largely to different assumptions being made about **fertility rate** trends, as well as mortality rates. The world fertility rate has shown a general decline since the 1960s and currently stands at an estimated three children per woman. Population stability requires a

BOX 13.1

■ Case Study: The Political Ecology of Puebla and Tlaxcala

The central highlands of Mexico consist of fertile basins and valleys separated from each other by forested mountain chains. The small adjacent states of Puebla and Tlaxcala are located in the fertile Puebla basin just south of Mexico City. The basin is surrounded by forested mountains. To the north are the volcanic mountains of Popocatepetl, Ixtaccihuatl, and La Malinche. Ranching, agriculture, lumber, coffee production, mining, and industry, particularly textile and automobile manufacturing, are the chief economic activities in these states. Unfortunately, all are currently creating environmental problems. The Mexican government realizes this and has passed hundreds of laws designed to address these problems.

However, the laws are not enforced and the problems just get worse. In 1987, Smith began the ongoing Puebla–Tlaxcala Project in Political Ecology, which is an attempt to understand why noncompliance is so rampant. The project is one of the few of its kind that focus on the interaction of human institutions and regional ecosystems over an extended time period.

There are 217 *municipios* (municipalities) and, thus, 217 *ayuntamientos* (town halls) throughout the state of Puebla, each with its local construction of *caciques* and connections to local power structures and to the PRI at both state and national levels. The present cacique structure came into being during the presidency of Lázaro Cárdenas (1934–40) and so-

Brick-making leads to deforestation and the excavation of soils two kilometers from modern Cholula.

lidified its power during the term of his successor, Manual Avila Camacho (1940–46). The power structure of each municipio differs depending on the local economy. In some districts, the agricultural ejidos (cooperative farming estates) dominate, in others industrial unions (sindicatos), and in yet others businessmen and industrialists dominate through local chambers of commerce. SARH (the federal and state bureaucracy controlling irrigation and water use), SEDUE (Mexico's Environmental Protection Agency), the governor, the president, and other members of the "elite" government structure must play intricate political games with the various local caciques to achieve minimal public goals.

The state of Puebla, the city of Puebla, the 217 municipalities and their mayors, the governor, the ayuntamientos, and the hundreds of local caciques face two very real problems: the need for economic development to create jobs for a growing population; and the need to mitigate existing environmental problems. At times these two sets of policy goals, job creation and environmental protection, contradict each other at the local level.

Attempts to reform the local power structure have largely failed because the reforms must come from Mexico City down to the local level. Recent reforms by the national PRI have yet to "trickle down" to the local level, and the lack of political and economic reform has blocked any possibility of mitigating ecological problems.

Environmental Issues

Puebla's most serious environmental problems are contamination of the water supply, deforestation, and air pollution. In the northern mountains, particularly in and around the municipality of Huauchinango, there are over 5,000 coffee cultivators who use the local rivers to process coffee, contaminating the water supply. Contamination is so bad that one river, the Arroyo Amarillo or Yellow Arroyo, has been renamed Arroyo Negro or Black Arroyo. The women of the region complain that there is no potable water and that they cannot wash clothing in local rivers because of the bad smell. The San Marcos and Necaxa Rivers are dying and the fishing economy has been killed off (Smith 1994).

Further south, in the fertile Puebla Valley, farmers have turned from growing maize and wheat for local consumption to growing exportable products, such as strawberries and tomatoes, for the U. S. market. These farmers have greatly increased their use of irrigation, fertilizers, herbicides, and pesticides in recent years, at a time when community populations are increasing. More food is being imported to feed people while, at the same time, the water of the region is being contaminated by the agrochemicals used to produce crops for export (Smith 1994).

The textile and automobile industries contribute to regional water pollution. A study of thirty five wells in the municipio of Puebla showed that ground water is contaminated with bacteria, fecal material, and industrial chemicals. The water supply in Lago Valsequillo, once a huge man-made lake formed by the construction of the Valsequillo Dam, has dropped dramatically and the fish in it have died from pollution (Smith 1994).

Deforestation by the peasants living on *ejidos* and by lumber companies is seriously depleting the forests of northern Puebla, especially parks found on the volcanic slopes of Popocatepetl and Ixtaccihuatl. Smugglers steal whole logs and take them out of the state on logging trucks; they are often armed with machine guns. A major cause of deforestation is the cutting of evergreen trees for Christmas. There is a major industry in cutting and smuggling these trees out of state parks where they are supposed to be protected.

The diminished forests no longer absorb rain so that water cascades directly into rivers, significantly increasing rates of soil erosion. This and irrigation agriculture has produced a severe drop in the level of the aquifer, causing shortages of drinking and irrigation water. Potable water is becoming so difficult to obtain for the growing population that it has to be brought in from outside of the region. Millions of pesos are paid for diesel fuel used to truck water. Furthermore, deforestation has led to a reduction in rainfall, which in turn has further reduced the aquifer. (Trees release water vapor into the atmosphere through **transpiration.** Large-scale deforestation can significantly affect rates of precipitation.)

Fueling the environmental problems has been a demographic explosion. People have been leaving rural regions for the last generation and moving into cities. In 1960 Puebla de los Angeles was a city of 700,000; by 1989 its population was over 2,000,000. A million people migrated into the Puebla region in less than five years because of the earthquake in Mexico City in 1985. As is true for all overpopulated cities of the periphery, the air over Puebla is badly polluted as a consequence of industrial and automobile emissions. Over 250,000 automobiles, buses, and trucks contaminate the air of Puebla de Los Angeles. Few of the vehicles have antipollution devices and unleaded gasoline is rare. Two hundred fifty tons of contaminates go into the air each day.

Adding to these already serious environmental problems, in the mid-1980s companies from the northern industrial city of Monterrey began to invade the valley of Puebla, mining river banks for silica sand (used in making glass—for beer bottles) and other minerals. The mining of silica and other minerals has led to further contamination of the rivers of the region.

East of the old Indian city of Cholula (which is next to the largest pyramid in the world), ejido owners have converted thousands of acres of prime agricultural land into a moonscape by mining soils for brick manufacturing.

The bricks are exported to Mexico City and are used locally to house people in the growing fringes of the two cities.

SEDUE as Don Quixote

With this picture of environmental damage in mind, let us examine the relationship between the institutions that attempt to mitigate environmental degradation in the long term and those that are causes of the degradation in the short term.

Mexico has passed hundreds of laws to protect the environment but is unable to enforce them. The one-party political structure means that the party and the government are the same thing. It is thus extremely difficult for the government to punish anyone for breaking its laws. The reason is simple. The lawbreaker is a voter, often a member of the PRI—often a very important member. For the government to move against the PRI is the same as moving against itself.

In the early 1980s, Mexico passed a law to protect the environment called the "law of ecological equilibrium." President Miguel de la Madrid (1982–1988) created a new cabinet-level agency called the Secretariat for Urban Development and Ecology (*Secretaria de Desarrollo Urbano e Ecologia,* or SEDUE). SEDUE was charged with enforcing compliance with the law of ecological equilibrium.

In 1986, de la Madrid appointed an aggressive lawyer to head up the SEDUE branch in Puebla. One of his first acts was to lock up many of the machines (road graders and bulldozers) used to scavenge minerals along the river banks of Puebla. Although he received support from the PRI and local businessmen against the exploiting outsiders from Monterrey, many of these law-breaking outsiders simply pried the locks off of their machines and went back to work.

In 1988, SEDUE officials throughout Mexico decided to attack air pollution. In Puebla, new regulations were passed forcing taxicab and bus drivers to tune their engines and use good fuels.

SEDUE began to irritate local businessmen (who are important contributors to PRI) as it shut down one contaminating local company after another, including several plants of the giant Volkswagen of Mexico, a Chevrolet dealership, and a few textile firms. By 1989, SEDUE had closed down sixty five contaminating businesses including textile, ceramic, and wood manufacturers, grease and oil service stations, and sections of Volkswagen of Mexico. In September of 1989, one textile union leader complained that SEDUE had put forty families out of work by shutting down a textile firm.

Deforestation was tackled with the same energy. SEDUE officials joined with the governor of the state and the president of the city council of Puebla to stop deforestation. Thousands of new trees were planted in parks. One cement factory donated 60,000 trees to the project. But deforestation continued apace as though nothing were being done. The governor appointed a military unit to protect the forests, but little came of this. Peasants belonging to remote mountain-based ejidos publicly complained to the governor that PRI officials were looking the other way when the lumber thieves destroyed the forests.

The attempt to alleviate environmental problems was blocked in Puebla in 1990 due to pressure from a political movement made up of taxicab and truck driver unions, Marxist university students and peddlers (called the October the 26th movement), and local businessmen. Taxicab and truck drivers hijacked trucks and buses that they parked across the interstate running down from Mexico City, effectively paralyzing the city of Puebla. The aggressive SEDUE lawyer from PRI was replaced by a less aggressive lawyer from PRI. By July of 1990, businesses were no longer being shut down for violating pollution laws. Slowly, the movement to protect the environment was stopped by local labor unions and business enterprises as well as Marxist university students. The response of the peasants who had been complaining about the lack of potable water was mixed. The peasant farmers of this region generally side with the leftist students, and many did in this case. However, those living in ejido communities in the forested areas of northern Puebla, which were being illegally logged, remained strongly environmentalist, especially on the issue of preserving local forests, and asked SEDUE for help.

This demonstrates the great difficulty of enforcing national laws at the local level when local power structures are controlled by those who benefit from loose environmental regulation. Local recognition of this problem has led to the emergence of a new political movement called *Patronato Puebla Verde*, a "green" political movement that is trying to force city leaders to comply with national environmental laws. But together SEDUE and the *Patronato Puebla Verde* have been unable to challenge successfully the political machine that runs the city.

The North American Free Trade Agreement (NAFTA) added another dimension to the political ecology of Mexico, but has so far failed to alter the workings of the political machine as far as environmental problems are concerned. American environmentalists initially tried to block NAFTA because of its lack of environmental protection provisions. A side agreement was then added during debates in the U. S. Senate, and this can be considered a part of NAFTA. Thus, the Mexican government is, in theory, bound by NAFTA to enforce environmental regulations similar to those in the United States. However, despite what both U. S. and Mexican environmentalists may want, the Mexican government is still hampered in its enforcement efforts by local politics, as the Puebla–Tlaxcala case illustrates. But with the new international pressure of NAFTA, in particular, the sanctions the U. S. government may impose on businesses that violate environmental regulations, there is some hope. Susan Bilello, a journalist, has recently suggested that the economic pressures produced by NAFTA are forcing a shift in Mexican politics in the direction of the rule of law (1996).

The links among economics, politics, and environmental resources are complex, as the Puebla example shows. The enforcement of environmental laws by an authoritarian government is problematic, as is the enforcement of political or economic laws. NAFTA, an imperfect agreement at best, may nonetheless provide Mexico with the international leverage necessary to move toward compliance with environmental laws that it already has on the books.

rate of two; and even if/when this rate is reached on a worldwide basis, demographic momentum will cause the population of the world to continue to increase for several decades thereafter. Figure 13.1 provides a simple illustration of world fertility rate trends. Figure 13.2 shows projected population growth to the year 2150 A.D. Both show that populations are continuing to increase most rapidly in the poorest countries. This illustrates a relationship between population growth and poverty. What the experts dispute is the direction of the causal arrow. Does poverty cause population growth or does population growth cause poverty? We hope that you realize, having got this far through this book, that such simple formulations mask the complexities and multiple connections of variables in the real world. Anthropology, through an examination of the relationships between values, world views, and the demographic profiles of different cultures, helps us understand that there is more to poverty than simply population growth, and vice versa.

Many scientists believe that if we do not take steps to curb human population growth, nature will do the job for us. Even if it is true that, as the economies improve in those countries where the population is growing most rapidly, the population growth rate will decrease—the view of those who see poverty as the cause of population growth (see discussion of the postulated relationship between wealth and family size in Chapter 3), and there are those who doubt this (some of whom view population growth as the cause of poverty)—it still might be wise for governments to consider population control policies. Such policies would certainly help to hasten the arrival of a sustainable future.

Can the world produce enough food to continue to meet the needs of the growing human population? Let's look at some things that affect agricultural production.

Figure 13.1 **World Fertility Rate Trends**

	1950s	1990s
Developed countries	2.8	1.7
All developing countries	6.2	3.4
Poorest developing countries	—	5.6
WORLD	4.5	3.6

Figure 13.2   **Trends and Projections in World Population Growth, 1750–2150**

Sources:
1. United Nations (U.N.) Population Division. *Long-Range World Population Projections: Two Centuries of World Population Growth. 1950–2150* (U.N., New York. 1992), p. 22.
2. Carl Haub, Director of Information and Education. Population Reference Bureau. Washington, D.C., 1995 (personal communication).

Agriculture and Food Production

Between 1990–1995, only 13 countries out of 157, all in Europe, had reached annual population growth rates close to zero. Only Europe is predicted to reach zero population growth between 2000 and 2005. In all other world regions, population will continue to grow (WRI 1996:190–91). This means, among other things, that the world will need a lot more food. But food production is not just a simple matter of using appropriate—sometimes innovative—agricultural technology to plant and harvest and to increase yields. The agricultural policies of governments also can have a significant impact on production.

In Egypt, for example, until the late 1980s, the agricultural system was completely government controlled. Farmers received their inputs from the government at controlled prices and sold their production to the government at similarly controlled prices. The result was that the government made a fortune and the farmers, who were not benefiting from this system of centralized control, tried to produce as little as possible beyond meeting their own subsistence needs. All this changed in the late 1980s, and now farmers must buy the inputs at market prices and they are likewise free to sell their crops to anyone at whatever prices the market will bear. It is still too soon to say if these new policies have had a significant impact on food production.

However, it is clear that this new freedom for farmers also includes new risks, for example, trying to predict market prices for crops in order to determine what to plant and how much in order to maximize profit. If a farmer guesses wrong, he or she can suffer a substantial loss. The only protection the government currently provides is that floor (minimum) prices are established for certain crops. Thus, if world market prices on such crops (cotton is one, though not a food) drop below the government-established minimum, the government will buy what farmers have to sell, and this reduces (but does not completely eliminate) the risk to farmers (Max Goldensohn, anthropologist and Vice President of Development Alternatives, Inc., personal communication).

The amount of agricultural land annually abandoned globally due to soil exhaustion or loss from erosion currently stands at about 70,000 square kilometers (27,000 square miles). Currently about 86,000 square kilometers of land per year worldwide are lost to desertification, an area about the size of the state of Maine. Deserts now cover 17 percent of the earth's land surface (Southwick 1996:xvii, 85). Soil exhaustion occurs when intensive cropping depletes soil nutrients faster than nature can replace them. The modern solution to this problem has been chemical fertilizers. But these cause watershed pollution problems as well as increasing costs to farmers. Many farmers in the poorer countries of the world cannot afford chemical fertilizers without heavy government subsidies. Thus they must abandon plots after a few years due to sharply declining yields. But soil erosion is a far greater problem.

> The first global survey of soil erosion showed that since World War II, more than 3 billion acres of cropland—an area larger than China and India combined—have been damaged by human activity and will prove costly, if not impossible, to reclaim (*Science News* 1992:215).

Soil erosion on agricultural land was causing an estimated loss of more than 20 billion tons per year in the 1980s. By the 1990s, the loss was estimated to be about 75 billion tons of topsoil per year. Depending on local conditions (temperate, tropical, type of vegetation cover, and so on), it will take between 200 and 1,000 years for one inch of new soil to form. That inch can be lost in as little as ten years. It is estimated that soil in the United States is being lost at seventeen times the formation rate. In Iowa it is being lost at thirty times the formation rate and Iowa had, by 1981, already lost *half* of its original topsoil (Southwick 1996:101). Forty percent of all U. S. cropland currently under production has already eroded to the point of declining productivity (Council on Environmental Quality 1991, cited in Southwick 1996). The relevance of these facts about soil loss and yield declines in the United States becomes evident when we consider that the United States is a major supplier of food grains to developing countries. For example, the U. S. exported more than 84.6 million metric tons of cereal grains annually between 1991–1993, most of it to developing countries. But this is down from 103.6 million metric tons annually exported between 1981–1983—and not all of the difference can be attributed to increased yields and thus declining need for grain imports in the developing countries (WRI 1996:245).

In developing countries, a combination of overgrazing, overcropping, deforestation, and destruction of other vegetational cover is producing massive soil loss. Salination, from flooding and overuse of irrigation, is also a major problem in many watersheds (Southwick 1996:104). The countries of the Middle East suffer from widespread problems of desertification due to overuse and misuse of irrigation and the farming of marginal lands formerly used only for grazing by pastoral nomads (see discussion in Chapter 10). Both Latin America (see Chapter 12) and many countries in Southeast Asia (see Chapter 11), for example, Thailand, the Philippines, and Vietnam, have suffered massive deforestation and consequent soil erosion due to a combination of legal and illegal logging, and the need to open up new agricultural land to keep up with population growth. All three of these Southeast Asian countries, as well as many in Latin America, have enacted strict laws to conserve their forests, but enforcement has been difficult. Africa (Chapter 9) has suffered from numerous large-scale development projects that have focused on export agriculture to the detriment of small farmers. However, development planners are now beginning to recognize the value of local knowledge of the environment in designing projects, so there is some hope new projects will prove more environmentally sound than those of the 1960s and 1970s.

Land provides 99 percent of the food we consume; aquatic systems provide only one percent (Pimental et al. 1995, cited in Southwick 1996:99). Yet only 11 percent of the earth's land surface can be used for agriculture. Worldwide, we are already using about 40 percent of the arable land for crops and pasture (WRI 1996:201). We have no guarantee that the soils and water resources of the other 60 percent will be sufficient to support sustainable agriculture. We must also realize that any additional land brought under cultivation or turned into pasture will be at the expense of existing forest, grasslands, and wetlands. Yet, clearly, massive food production increases will be necessary to feed the rapidly growing human population. Can most of the needed increased yields be gotten from improved agricultural technology? Despite shortcomings and even failure in some areas, the Green Revolution (a combination of improved varieties achieved by genetic engineering and scientifically controlled applications of fertilizers, pesticides, and herbicides) did manage to produce crop yields that kept ahead of population growth from the 1950s through the late 1970s. During the 1980s increased yields from all sources (improved varieties, more intense cultivation, and bringing new land under production) only barely managed to keep apace of population growth. In the 1990s, population growth is beginning to outpace increases in yields.

Currently, many people in the world are undernourished or malnourished. Several million are even worse off; they are quite literally starving. In Mexico, for example, the Latin American Economic Commission estimates that of Mexico's 45 million people living below the poverty line, 9 million have only one-fourth of what is needed to purchase food for a day (*Latinamerica Press* 1996).

Studies by the United Nations Food and Agriculture Organization, the World Bank, and the IFPRI (International Food Policy Research Institute), a part of CGIAR (Consultative Group on International Agricultural Research) are optimistic about the possibility of food production keeping up with population growth, at least up until some time between 2010 and 2020. Lester Brown and Hal Kane of the WorldWatch Institute, on the other hand, count themselves among the pessimists.

They see as serious constraints no recent significant improvements in agricultural technology, declining fisheries productivity, degeneration of rangelands, and steadily increasing water scarcity (WRI 1996). One can certainly add to this list soil loss, resulting in agricultural lands being taken out of production. While worldwide agricultural yields are currently still continuing to show a small increase, they are definitely showing signs of leveling off. And some experts argue that fragile tropical and subtropical environments cannot sustain further production increases.

Most studies agree that agricultural production can continue to meet "effective demand," at least in the near term. But what does this mean? "Effective demand" is the "demand that corresponds to purchasing power irrespective of food needs" (WRI 1996:229). Translated from the unfeeling prose of economics, this means that the hungry poor will continue to go hungry because they do not have the "purchasing power" to buy the food they need. What might be done? Boosting food production *at the household level* would help, but it would not solve the problem of those many urban poor who cannot grow their own food. The World Resources Institute suggests that increasing food production in the developed countries will not meet the food needs of the poor in developing countries (229). Given the recognized constraints, where will the food production increases come from?

According to the FAO, which the World Resources Institutes considers to be optimistic, 66 percent of the increases in developing countries will come from increased yield, 21 percent from expansion of land under cultivation, and 13 percent from greater cropping intensity (meaning the shortening of fallow periods and growing more than one crop per year on lands that currently only produce one yearly crop). Leaving aside the question of whether these sources of increase in agricultural yields represent a realistic scenario, such increases will add to pressures on land and water resources, and contribute to deforestation (at least one-half of the potential agricultural land in developing countries is currently forested). Some of the yield increase will come from an expansion of irrigated lands, adding to the water scarcity and salination problems that already exist in some areas.

Many countries are already facing serious food security problems that are not likely to go away in the near future. "Famines and temporary food deficiencies can result from drought, flood, war, political strife, or poor harvests. Such events are increasing," especially in the developing countries of the world. Africa presents the bleakest picture, with an estimated 175 million undernourished individuals in 1988–1990, which could rise to 300 million by 2010. South Asia is also a problem area (WRI 1996:235).

Production gains can be made by minimizing soil loss, improving the efficiency of water use, reducing post-harvest losses, and generally improving agronomic practices. But will this be enough? High-input agriculture has already proved to have numerous environmental disadvantages. The alternative, integrated farming systems moving toward more organic farming, is certainly much more environmentally friendly. But there is considerable doubt about whether organic farming can produce the required yield increases to meet the needs of the world's growing population. Once again we suggest that policies to control rates of population growth must be a part of the solution, along with a reduction in rates of consumption among the affluent.

The affluent of the world must learn to consume not only less food, but less energy in general. While rates of energy consumption are difficult to calculate and will always be approximations, it is still instructive to compare such "relative" rates by country. Energy consumption is often calculated in gigajoules (gJl), approximately the equivalent of 6.9 gallons of oil, and based on use of electricity, petroleum products and other fossil fuels, and other energy sources of significance in particular countries, both commercial and domestic. Without going on at length about the need for the most developed nations to reduce energy consumption if we are to move toward worldwide sustainability of resource use, we offer a simple comparison to demonstrate the point: Energy consumption in the United States is more than five times that of Mexico, almost 15 times that of Brazil and China, 35 times that of Indonesia, 40 times that of India, and an astounding 140 times that of Haiti and Bangladesh, the poorest nations in the world (Southwick 1996:271).

Deforestation

Charles Southwick, an ecologist, estimates that forests in 1990 covered about 4.3 billion hectares (28.7 percent) of the earth's land surface. As he also points out, forests covered an estimated 45.5 percent of the earth's land surface about 10,000 years ago, when the transition from food extraction (hunting and gathering) to food production (agriculture and animal husbandry) began (1996:117). Rates of deforestation steadily increased from 1960 to 1990 in the developing countries of the world, and fully one-fifth of all natural tropical forest cover was lost during those three decades. Asia lost 33 percent while Africa and Latin America each lost about 18 percent. Between 1980 and 1990 alone 8 percent (163 million hectares) of natural tropical forest cover was lost (World Resources Institute,

The tropical forests are the lungs of nature: A Brazilian farmer ponders his work.

1996). There is no sign that rates of tropical deforestation are significantly decreasing during the 1990s.

What drives this process of deforestation? Population growth and poverty are the usual suspects. The poor do contribute to deforestation by clearing land for agriculture and because wood is their chief—often their only—source of fuel for cooking. But, compared to other sources of tropical deforestation, the damage done by the poor is minuscule. And it is also true that, at least in an indirect sense, population growth contributes to deforestation. As many developing countries struggle to keep food production apace with population growth, governments establish policies that encourage the conversion of tropical forests to agricultural use. The tragedy of this solution to the food problem is that most tropical forest soils are thin and not well suited to prolonged or permanent use for agriculture or pasture. The indigenous peoples who inhabit these forests in places like the Amazon basin of South America have understood the limitations of these lands for centuries and have evolved sustainable forms of shifting cultivation (also called swidden or slash-and-burn cultivation), utilizing tiny plots scattered throughout the forest and interspersing root crops, seed crops, and tree crops to duplicate in some way the natural biological diversity of the tropical forest itself. Attempts at permanent agriculture on these same lands becomes economically nonviable after just a few short years. Unfortunately, by the time such plots are abandoned, there is little chance that the forest will return.

Logging, cattle ranching, and commercial-scale export agriculture are the major causes of tropical deforestation (Southwick 1996). About 60 percent of tropical forest loss in Mexico is due to ranching (Renner 1997), and much of the beef does not feed Mexicans but is exported. The timber trade has argued for years that its role in deforestation is negligible and that land-clearing and fuelwood collection are the chief causes. A new study by the World Wide Fund for Nature (WWF), which assesses illegal as well as legal logging, comes to the conclusion that the international timber trade is the primary cause of forest loss and degradation, not just in the tropics but worldwide (1996). It is the industrial nations of the world that are the major consumers of lumber and timber products.

While the spotlight has recently been on tropical deforestation, the situation is not much better in the temperate forests of the developed countries. The United States, for example, lost 1.1 percent of its remaining forest between 1980 and 1990 (World Resources Institute 1996), and this forest is, like that of other developed countries, already less than half of what it was in the seventeenth century. In the United States and most of Europe, remaining forests are second growth and plantations. Very little old growth forest remains.

In 1989 the U. S. Forest Service, charged with the management and conservation of forests representing 8.2 percent of the nation's land area, opened approximately 2.6 million acres to timber cutting. In the same year, the U. S. Forest Service reforested only 148,600 acres through tree planting programs (*Report of the U. S. Gen. Accounting Office, 1990*). Thus, over 17 times more acreage of Forest Service land was used for deforestation than for reforestation (Southwick 1996:121).

Ineffective management policies, coupled with the desire for short-term gains and a certain amount of corruption, raise the prospect of massive cutting of Siberia's extensive forests (WRI 1996). Illegal logging is already underway in some areas.

"Forests, not floods" was the chant being repeated at a street demonstration on the University of Oregon campus, January 13, 1997, following the disastrous floods of December, 1996, throughout the Northwest and California. Decades of clear-cutting have left many steep slopes in the Northwest unstable, causing massive mud slides and exacerbating flooding throughout many watersheds, despite the numerous dams constructed for flood control by the U. S. Army Corps of Engineers. While some believe that damming of major watersheds has contributed to the problem, in the aftermath of the greatest floods of this century others are arguing for more dams.

Beyond the wood and nonwood products they provide for human use, forests serve many ecologically beneficial purposes. Natural forests are complex ecosystems containing many species. Great biodiversity is especially true of tropical forests. Forests capture and slowly release water, thus protecting watersheds and keeping rates of soil erosion low. Through transpiration, forests also release great quantities of water into the air that eventually returns as rain or snow. Forests release oxygen and lock up carbon dioxide gas (CO_2), considered to be a major contributor to the greenhouse effect. Some ecologists and climatologists believe that the massive deforestation in the tropics since the 1950s is causing global warming. Forests are essential to the health of our global ecosystem and to the well-being of all cultures and nations. Thus, deforestation, currently taking place on a massive scale in the tropics, as well as forest degradation, an all too common phenomenon in the developed countries of the temperate zone, are global problems that must be addressed. Forest degradation occurs as a result of air pollution that produces acid rain, and also through reduction in natural species diversity due to logging and then replanting forests with only one kind of tree so that they can be easily logged again in a few years.

Sustainable forest management is essential to the health of the planet. Anthropologists and ecologists are aware that indigenous peoples in Latin America, North America, and throughout Asia and Southeast Asia have practiced sustainable forest management for centuries. The Kayapó of Brazil (see Chapter 12) and the Guaraní of Paraguay are just two examples. Their model has always been that of agroforestry, a model that incorporates the use of the nontimber products of the forest interspersed with their subsistence plots. In recent years, some groups, such as the Guaraní, have been able to sell rubber, yerba mate, and other forest products commercially without damaging the forests on which they depend (Reed 1997). Studies have shown that the sustained yields of forest products that do not require damaging the trees are economically much more beneficial in the long term than are the short-term gains realized from selling the logs. The modern world has much to learn about forestry from the indigenous world.

International agreements have been in place since 1994 that specify that by the year 2000 all forest products in both the tropical and temperate forests should come only from forests that are being sustainably managed (WRI 1996:212). Will these agreements be honored? Only time will tell. The problem may be one of convincing developing countries, which are being asked to sustainably manage their tropical forests, that the developed countries are sustainably managing their domestic forests.

International Development and Development Anthropology

The post-World War II phenomenon of international development aid was supposed to eliminate poverty and result in general economic well-being for the countries of the underdeveloped Third World. Almost a half-century of development, economic and technological, has had the opposite effect and has produced many of the problems that we face today and that will be with us for the foreseeable future. Development aid has produced the seeming paradox of increased poverty. To understand why this is so is not an easy matter, and experts do not agree on the relationship between causes and consequences. Anthropology can contribute to an understanding of these problems, dealing as it does in interrelationships and cross-cultural comparisons; but it will require the collective knowledge of many disciplines and many cultures, and the political will in policy-making of many nations, to solve these problems, for they are truly global in scope. Policy failures have certainly contributed significantly to current problems.

International Development Aid

According to the tenets of capitalism, the only healthy economy is a growing, expanding economy. In other words, economic growth is the engine that drives us toward, greater prosperity. Since the end of World War II, the First World has provided, through bilateral and multilateral agencies, an enormous amount of financial, material, and technical aid to the so-called underdeveloped or lesser developed countries of the Third World. Economic development was (and for many economists and politicians still is) seen as the force that would produce social development (often phrased as an improvement in the quality of life, especially for the poor) and political development (which, for the countries of the First World, unequivocally meant a transition to democracy). But for a period much longer than the fifty years since the end of World War II, economic growth, despite its benefits, has led to the destruction of thousands of life-sustaining ecosystems on all parts of the planet, and the growth of poverty rather than the alleviation of it. Many scientists—ecologists and anthropoligists in particular—are concerned that the current process of economic globalization is exacerbating existing environmental and social problems and, if not checked, may result in global ecological collapse and the end of life as we know it.

While the early goals of development aid were to stimulate the economies of the lesser developed countries (LDCs), to alleviate poverty, and to improve the

Large families in Somalia prevent the transition to prosperity and add to political volatility.

standard of living in general for the peoples—especially the poor—of the LDCs, the overall effect of five decades of development projects, mostly in the Third World countries of Africa, Asia, and Latin America, has been the opposite. Poverty has increased. The rich have got richer and the poor poorer in relative terms; that is, while in some countries the standard of living of the poor may be somewhat better than it was a half-century ago, the gap between the rich and the poor has increased. In some countries, for example Rwanda and Somalia in Africa, the poor are poorer now than they were fifty years ago in *absolute* terms. And throughout much of the world the percentage of the population living in poverty has increased rather than decreased. This is even true in the United States.

A later rephrasing of the goals of development stressed improvement in the "quality of life" but, given the value-laden nature of this concept, it would seem impossible to use it as a cross-culturally valid measure. How, exactly, would one go about measuring the "quality of life" when the concept itself means different things in different cultures, depending on what is valued? The United Nations Development Programme has developed what is called the *Human Development Index*. This index is supposed to assess progress in a way that is more relevant to sustainable development than strictly economic indicators such as **Gross National Product (GNP)** and **Gross Domestic Product (GDP).** Particular attention is given to issues of equity, poverty, and gender. The HDI is an aggregate indicator based on national life expectancy, educational attainment, and GDP measured in terms of purchasing power parity (WRI 1996:160, 176). While it provides a basis for comparison of countries in terms of "progress," it is, like all other such indices, culturally insensitive and does not measure the quality of life from different cultural perspectives. "Progress" is defined strictly in terms of the goals of the Western (First) world.

Sustainable Development

Today the focus of development aid is on sustainable development. But what exactly does this mean and how much is being done to achieve it, assuming that it is a worthwhile goal? There is also talk, mostly among politicians, economists, and some businesspersons, of sustainable growth. But this is clearly wrong-headed, for growth cannot continue indefinitely, that is, cannot be sustained, in a world of finite resources. However, as anthropologists we must attempt to understand the social and cultural context of this kind of thinking and work to engender other, more sensible, modes of thought. Our life quite literally depends on it. Herman Daly (1996), formerly an economist with the World Bank and currently a professor at the University of Maryland, has repeatedly said that the oft-used phrase "sustainable growth" is an oxymoron, a contradiction in terms. But among economists, Daly is a lone voice crying in the wilderness. Most economists, as we have said, believe that the only healthy economy is a growing economy, and most equate growth with development. But this need not be so. Development can be defined as the realization of potential (Brooks 1990), which does not necessarily imply continuous economic growth. In fact, given that the resources of the Earth are finite, though many are renewable, successful development, that is, sustainable development, cannot possibly mean continuous economic growth. Sustainable development must mean something other than economic growth.

What do we mean by sustainable development? And what would it take to achieve it? Many scholars in various disciplines—anthropologists, ecologists, economists, political scientists, sociologists—as well as development planners, policy-makers, politicians, and bureaucrats, have commented on the first question, or attempted to answer it. But no matter how they have defined it, few have proposed a plan to achieve sustainable development. Indeed, it was only in the late 1980s, in the World Commission on Environment and Development report, *Our Common Future* (1987), that a basic definition of sustainable development was proposed. In this report, sustainable development was defined as "development that meets the needs of the present without compromising the ability of future generations to meet their own needs." Today, sustainable development has become the buzzword and the most popular concept in the field of international development.

In our view, sustainable development should, at a minimum, be defined as development that is

- **Environmentally sustainable,** that is, ecosystems and resources are maintained in a healthy state over a long period of time, biodiversity is preserved, and the natural capacity of ecosystems is protected;
- **Economically sustainable,** net benefits over costs are realized in the long term; and

- **Socially sustainable,** which includes cooperation of resource users, institutional capacity, and political will, among other things (Young 1991:27–28).

David Brooks defines sustainable development in terms of five broad requirements: "integration of conservation and development; satisfaction of basic human needs; achievement of equity and social justice; provision for social self-determination and cultural diversity; [and] maintenance of ecological integrity" (1990:24).

These two ways of defining what sustainable development is, or should be, are not all that different. To achieve sustainable development requires working closely with the intended beneficiaries of development at the local level, and taking local cultural context and local knowledge into account in project design. Anthropologists working in development have been advocating this approach for a long time.

Development Anthropology and the Anthropology of Development

An oversimplified but still useful way to characterize what cultural anthropologists do is to divide them into those who do basic research, most of whom are employed in academic institutions, and those who do applied work, most of whom are employed outside of academe (with the caveat that some anthropologists do both during the course of their careers). A substantial number of anthropologists of both kinds currently concern themselves with the processes and problems of international development. Again oversimplifying, we can say that those inclined toward basic research focus on the anthropological analysis of the processes, projects, and outcomes of international development. In other words, they do the anthropology of development. Some of those who call themselves applied anthropologists (remember that applied anthropology can be defined as the application of anthropological knowledge to the solution of contemporary human problems, and it encompasses much more than just international development) do development anthropology. They are actually employed on development projects, by public and private agencies that provide development assistance, in a variety of capacities ranging from short-term consulting to project management to regional oversight responsibilities.

Those concerned with the anthropology of development tend to be hypercritical of development both as process and product. Some, for example Arturo Escobar (1995), focus on development as a profoundly colonial discourse, as a contrived reality designed to perpetuate the economic domination and subordination of the Third World by the First. It follows that they are also very critical of development anthropology, that is, of the active involvement of anthropologists in the development process. As the number of anthropologists working in development has increased since the mid–1970s, the critique has become more strident. The agendas of development agencies are seen as ethnocentric, as having policies and programs that link progress to capitalism, industrialization, and modern technology (Warren and Bourque 1991). This is considered a very one-sided and very "Western" view that fails to take account of differences in cultural perspectives about what is valued. Development anthropologists do not necessarily disagree. As Moreno–Black and Young have pointed out:

> There is no escaping the fact that . . . in development agencies [there is] no shortage of officials and technicians who hold ethnocentric viewpoints, although there are also many who do not. Anthropologists who work within the development establishment know in more detail than their critics the sins of the establishment. But they believe they can be effective in countering ethnocentric biases and that they can have a positive impact on the process of development . . . [Development] anthropologists have chosen to confront the dragon while their critics apparently prefer to hide from it in the hope that it will go away (1992:84).

Two points on which both development anthropologists and their critics agree is that development project planners have generally not given sufficient (if any) attention to the importance of cultural differences and their potential (or actual) impact on project outcomes, and have generally not sought the active involvement of the intended beneficiaries early on in the project design stage, much less in prior consultations to determine whether development is desired at all and, if so, what kinds of projects are wanted. Small nongovernmental organizations (NGOs) have a much better record in this regard than bilateral and multilateral aid agencies such as USAID and the World Bank.

The case of the fish processing plant at Lake Turkana (see Box 13.2) in Kenya provides an example of development gone wrong. More important, it shows how the failure to incorporate existing anthropological knowledge into project planning and implementation can have disastrous consequences.

The Turkana are often oblivious to western development specialists.

The Employment of Anthropologists in Development

Large funding agencies, such as the World Bank, the United Nations, and the Agency for International Development have in the past been reluctant to have anthropologists participate in development projects other than as troubleshooters when something goes wrong. But the attitudes of these agencies have been changing and more and more anthropologists are being hired both as permanent employees and as consultants who work as part of a project team from the early design phase of a project. There has been a realization that the anthropologist can supply a perspective and a type of technical expertise not normally found among economists, agronomists, engineers, or other technically trained individuals. The perspective includes the knowledge that an understanding of the local culture is essential to project success, and that the local culture must be understood in its own terms (cultural relativism), as well as in the context of the regional and the national, and often the international (cultural dynamics). It also includes a focus on thinking small, that is, taking a bottom-up approach. The technical expertise of anthropologists varies, but, for those working in development, it includes methods for arriving at an understanding of local (or indigenous) knowledge systems and methods for building project activities on such local knowledge. Local or indigenous knowledge has always been at the core of ethnography; only recently has it become a popular topic in the world of international development (see, for example, Warren, Slikkerveer, and Brokensha 1995, for a recent selection of essays on the topic).

The reason people are poor usually has little to do directly with a lack of knowledge about how to improve their economies. It has a lot to do with the institutions that govern their lives, particularly those at the national level. If the anthropologist cannot change the national rules, and he or she usually cannot, then it is smarter to work on small projects, particularly those that may initiate change from the ground up. In other words, the reason most people in the periphery are poor has a lot to do with the political economy of the world and the institutions within the peripheral nation–state. Up until very recently, the political economy of the world allowed the core to monopolize wealth. Under such circumstances, massive aid projects were unlikely to achieve positive results. While this is changing, there is still not a great deal that massive aid projects can achieve, as illustrated by the Turkana fish project and many other massive development projects around the world. The environmental and social costs of many large projects often outweigh the economic benefits, despite favorable environmental impact assessments and social soundness analyses (both required for all USAID projects) at the project design stage.

A far better approach is to suggest small changes. For example, Peter Little, a development anthropologist with the Institute for Development Anthropology, did a study of Somalia cattle markets and recommended that cattle herders in Somalia would do better if they sold their cattle across the border in Kenya rather than on the overseas market. He argued that just a few traders in Mogadishu controlled the profits of trade to their own benefit (Little 1988). Unfortunately, Somalia descended into a civil war shortly after Little published his report on his study of cattle markets, and his idea could not be implemented.

Patricia Vondal's research on Indonesian duck farming, conducted be-

BOX 13.2

■ Case Study: The Frozen Fish Plant in the Desert

In the early 1970s, Norwegian developers became concerned about the lack of available high-protein food among the Turkana pastoral nomads who live just south of the Sahara desert in the Sahel in northern Kenya. A project was formulated that was designed to catapult the Turkana out of susceptibility to drought and protein scarcity and into a commercially viable venture that would utilize a renewable, environmentally safe, high-protein, low-cholesterol resource, namely fish. It would also settle the Turkana in permanent villages. According to the United Nations Food and Agriculture Organization (FAO), pastoral nomadism threatened the fragile ecosystems of the Sahel, and settling nomadic pastoralists into permanent communities would address this problem. The British government published a handbook on rangeland management that argued, "since the ecologically unsound dependence on milk is at the root of [the pastoralists'] problem, that is the most obvious point of attack. Reduce the dependence on the milk diet, and the battle is at least part won" (Harden 1990:178).

There happened to be a gargantuan natural fish tank in Turkana territory in northwest Kenya called Lake Turkana, which teemed with Nile perch as well as *tilapia*, a delicious whitefish. The perch can grow to four feet and longer. The Kenya Fisheries Department confidently predicted huge catches every year for decades. Norwegian developers took up the challenge to convert the Turkana pastoralists into fish farmers. A severe drought in the 1960s had killed 11 thousand head of Turkana cattle, and many herders had turned to fishing. Norway, through its development agency, Norad, tried to systemize the conversion (Harden 1990).

Salaried Norad fishing experts arrived in 1972 with twenty fiberglass boats, four motorboats, and the *Iji*, a thirty–six foot research vessel that had been trucked overland more than 700 miles. It was determined that the most desirable product would be frozen fish fillets. Consultants recommended the construction of an "ice–making, freezing, and cold storage plant." The government of Kenya liked the idea and Norad invested two million dollars in the construction of a fish plant that looks like an upscale Lutheran church according to

tween 1981 and 1983 (Vondal 1989) illustrates how local innovations can have desirable regional consequences and how the anthropologist's holistic approach can reveal not just what happened but how it happened and what the important interconnections are. Vondal's work is a good illustration of how basic anthropological research can inform the development process by providing a systematic account of local knowledge, practice, and innovation.

Blaine Harden, a journalist who studied the history of the project. Harden writes:

> Although it was surrounded by tin-roof shacks, desert scrub, and the odd camel, it would not have looked out of place in the upper-middle-class suburbs of Oslo or Washington or Los Angeles. The Norwegians also built a road connecting the remote fish plant to Kenya's highway system and to Nairobi. That cost $20 million. The idea was for the Turkana Fishermen's Cooperative Society to sell quick-frozen fish fillets in Kenya's cities and abroad (Harden 1990:180).

When the plant was completed in 1981, the Norwegians discovered that chilling the fish from 100 degrees to below freezing using diesel-powered generators cost more than the fillets were worth. Production also demanded more clean water than Turkana District had. The plant only operated for a few days before its freezers were turned off. "It became Africa's most handsome, most expensive dried fish warehouse" (Harden 1990:180).

Then, as happens every thirty years, part of Lake Turkana disappeared when the Omo, the major river that feeds the lake, ran low because of drought. Twenty thousand Turkana, whom the Norwegians had lured to the lake to become fishermen, were stuck without fish. And their livestock were dying due to overcrowding on the barren, overgrazed banks of the lake. In addition, nearly every tree near the lake had been chopped down for firewood. To top things off, the research vessel became stranded in the middle of the lake.

According to Harden, the Norwegians could have driven thirty-five miles to the town of Lodwar where colonial records would have shown that the lake had dried up once before, in 1954:

> No one checked. Nor did Norad take the trouble to learn—from mountains of available anthropological studies—that the Turkana people consider fishing to be the last resort of an incompetent who cannot handle his livestock. Unless they are very hungry, they do not eat fish. They consider as beneath contempt those who are forced to survive as fishermen without livestock (Harden 1990:181).

Norad had attempted in good faith to help the Turkana. But ignorance of local climatic conditions and fluctuations made the project ecologically unsustainable; ignorance of local cultural values made it culturally unsustainable; and overconfidence in modern technology made it economically unsustainable. High-technology answers to problems of poverty are common, and they are very attractive to government officials. Such projects come with a lot of money that can be siphoned off for relatives and political cronies of the bureaucrats. There is little doubt in these cases that once the developers leave, the projects will collapse. Anthropologists are quite wary of large-ticket, high-tech approaches to the transformation of poor societies.

BOX 13.3

■ Case Study: The Duck Farmers of Borneo

Present-day Indonesia is a kaleidoscope of 300 languages and more than 100 ethnic groups. While primarily Muslim, and with a small minority of Christians, many of its people believe in animism or nature worship. About 75 percent of the population live in rural areas, and more than one-half engage in fishing and small-plot rice and vegetable farming.

After enduring centuries of control by Portuguese and then Dutch colonists, and being ravaged by the Japanese army during World War II, Indonesia won its independence in the 1950s. Its revolutionary president, Sukarno, tried to move the country towards socialism but he was overthrown by Army General Suharto in 1966. Suharto institutionalized capitalistic re-

form measures that are beginning to transform Indonesia into a modern market-oriented nation–state.

Patricia Vondal, a development anthropologist with the Agency for International Development, studied changes that had taken place in Indonesian duck farming. Her study on the marketplace economy of South Kalimantan province in Indonesian Borneo showed how improved economic conditions, which were the consequence of a stable government, led to entrepreneurial innovations in duck farming (Vondal 1989). The traditional farm management strategy of the farmers of Southeastern Borneo's interior swamplands was to produce duck eggs in combination with the exploitation of forest, swamp, and riverine resources, as well

Duck farming: Sustainable development is possible when farmers have a knowledge of ecological processes and access to markets.

as traditional rice and vegetable farming. Duck farming was a specialization in a seasonally flooded riverine and swampland ecosystem in which rice and vegetable farming are limited to the dry season. Duck eggs are a major alternative to fresh food in the diets of the people of South Kalimantan during the rainy season. The eggs are held in high regard as a healthy food that promotes strength and are favored in baking many types of pastries that are a product of the region.

Traditional flock management strategies were determined by the availability of resources used for duck feed. These included freshwater snails and fish, swamp vegetation, and sago palm. The ducks were herded to forage in the rivers and swamplands, and the farmers supplemented this feed with additional fish that they caught. However, the annual depletion of fish in the dry season severely disrupted duck farming. Freshwater fish breed at the beginning of the rainy season, in November. During the rainy season, floods spread out from the rivers, and fish densities also increase, which benefits the ducks. Towards September and October, however, the dry season reduces the water supply and fishing sharply increases, depleting stocks. Available fish exceed local demand, and much is salted, dried, and sold in the provincial capital of Banjarmasin. As the dry season progressed, however, lack of fresh fish forced most farmers to sell their duck flocks and turn to other occupations, such as trading or timbercutting, both of which take them away from their families for periods up to half a year. A sudden change in diet causes ducks to stop laying for six to eight weeks.

With the improved economy of Southeastern Borneo in recent years, more people have been able to afford duck eggs, and the price for these has risen. And, as the human population grew, there was also an increased demand for duck eggs. Duck eggs are not the food of the poor, but of a growing middle class that places a high value on this form of food. Thus, duck farming has become increasingly more attractive, but the limitation placed on the farmers by the depletion of fish in the dry season appeared insurmountable.

One of the most important points of Vondal's work is that she showed that with stable (or expanding) markets these peasant farmers searched for alternatives to fresh fish as a food source for their ducks. A few duck farmers began experimenting with the use of slightly rotted dried fish not fit for human consumption and with dried fish purchased from the local market. Local traders were quick to respond. Fish that were too old or too small for human consumption were increasingly sold at local markets to duck farmers.

The discovery of how dried fish could be used for duck feed had a dramatic impact on egg production. Villagers could now duck farm on a year-round basis and hold production relatively constant by manipulating the type and amount of fish, either dried or fresh, that they gave to their mature flocks, thus breaking the environmental and biological constraints that had limited duck farming to a part-year activity. In addition, saltwater fishermen found a new market for their dried fish stocks, selling to duck farmers, thus further increasing the regional economic impact of this innovation in duck farming.

Vondal's research demonstrates that under conditions of market predictability, due in large part to a stable government ensuring a lack of corruption, transaction costs are low and offer the opportunity for people to experiment. Innovative experimentation, which always involves a certain amount of risk, becomes economically feasible under such low-risk conditions. The anthropologist, with her holistic approach, can offer valuable insights for the design of small-scale development projects and a reasonable account of the conditions that will enhance their likelihood of success. The unanswered question in this case is what environmental impact year-round duck farming is likely to have.

Summary

There exists much tension between the short-term needs of the growing human population and the need to achieve sustainable resource management on a worldwide basis if the needs of future generations are to be adequately met. Among the requirements to achieve sustainable development will be policies that serve to eventually reduce the size of the human population and policies that serve to reduce rates of consumption among the overly affluent.

Throughout this book, we have explored the processes that have influenced the rise and fall of nations and civilizations. In this last chapter, we have examined some—but by no means all—of the global environmental problems facing humankind as we approach the third millennium A.D. International development, intended to alleviate poverty and create worldwide economic well-being, has instead lead to greater poverty and environmental degradation in the process. Economic growth, despite its benefits for some, has served as the engine of resource depletion and environmental contamination. Human population growth has contributed to resource depletion as food production technologies struggle to keep apace of our growing numbers, often at the expense of existing natural forests and grasslands.

Anthropologists working in development have stressed the need to understand the processes involved within their varied cultural contexts and the need to integrate local knowledge in development planning. Anthropology does not have definitive answers to the global problems facing humanity—nor does any other scientific discipline. But we are certain that any viable solutions will have to incorporate an understanding of cultural values and cultural context, and in this sense we are certain that an anthropological perspective can contribute, indeed *must* contribute, to a better future for humankind.

We have met the enemy and they are us.—Pogo

Key Terms

Degradation	**Gross National Product (GNP)**
Depletion	**Purchasing Power Parity**
Fertility Rate	**Sustainable Development**
Gross Domestic Product (GDP)	**Transpiration**

Glossary

A-cosmic The belief in principles or forces that are not cosmic, such as the basic principles (Ten Commandments) of the three monotheistic religions.

Acephalous Headless tribes; social structures in which there are no apparent leaders; decision-making depends on egalitarian relationships.

Achieved Status Status in a society that is determined by virtue of accomplishing those things that the society values.

Allophones Sound variations of a single phoneme due to the context of other sounds in which they occur.

Alterative Movement A social movement with the limited goal of changing some aspect of the individual (partial change of the person, not the society).

Amratian This is the second stage following the Badarian, producing the first decorated pottery; burials show increased stratification but this is still a tribal society. This site is also from Upper Egypt near Abydos and is dated to between 4000 to 3500 B.C.

Anthropology The study of humankind and all its manifestations in all times and places.

Applied Anthropology The use of the knowledge anthropology and related disciplines have accumulated in attempts to find solutions to contemporary human problems.

Articulation The connection (articulation) between increasing levels of efficiency in production and financial rewards to the workers found in Western Europe and the United States.

Artifacts All objects that have been systematically altered by human manufacture or use.

Ascribed Status Status in a society that is determined by birth.

Assimilation The surrender of ethnic markers or identity (or culture) to a dominant ethnic group. Assimilation may be forced or voluntary.

Astrolabe An instrument used in navigation to measure the positions of the sun or stars.

Atman The Hindu term for the soul, which is reborn every generation.

Authoritarian Structural power found in state capitalist societies. Some degree of authority is given to nonelite or nongovernment groups as long as they do not challenge the means of authority of the elites.

Badarian This is the first of three stages of the predynastic period in Egypt, dating to 5,000 B.C. These tribal farmers and gatherers lived in mud huts and practiced burials in wooden tombs, probably tied to an ancestor cult much like the cultures of Dynastic Egypt.

Bands Peoples of the peripheries of ancient and modern states and chiefdoms who practiced hunting and food-gathering, had egalitarian societies, and were largely nomadic. Bands are characterized by a family level of sociopolitical organization. Band societies probably preceded the development of tribes, chiefdoms, and states. Property rights are public.

Bound Morphemes Minimal units of meaning in a language that must occur attached to some other morpheme. Suffixes and prefixes in English are examples of bound morphemes.

Brahmans The caste of priests in India, usually considered the highest caste.

Brideprice Common in societies practicing patrilineal descent, wealth is paid to the family or clan of the bride in recognition of her status and the loss she represents to her family of orientation and clan.

Caste Rank and status distinction made in hegemonic societies in which members of the same caste are expected to marry one another (castes are, in theory, endogamous) and practice the same occupation. Rank and status are inherited, usually through the father, and are coupled to rituals and ceremonies established by religion, such as the Hindu religion in India.

Caste Endogamy Marriage to a member of one's own caste.

Caste System There are four basic Indian castes: Brahman (priests), Kshatriyas (warriors), Vaisyas (merchants), and Sudras (laborers or peasants); these are subsequently subdivided and can be considered "supercastes" or overranking categories. Into the four castes are ranked thousands of castes, each of which is an endogamous group practicing a specific profession. In addition, there is a fifth "class" of untouchables, those generally not considered part of the four-caste system and "outside" of society.

Caudillo Spanish term for a man of power or authority, supreme commander, a head of state, a political boss.

Charismatic Phase The first phase in a redemptive movement when followers believe in their messianic or charismatic leader. The leader is believed to have special knowledge of the word of God, the meaning of nature, or the future revealed by history. The term *charismatic* refers to the special powers he/she appears to have.

Chiefdoms Chiefdoms are ranked (but not usually stratified) societies in which descent is often traced from a founding ancestor, and rank is based on one's relationship to this ancestor. The "chief" is usually the highest-ranking individual because he/she can claim the most direct line of descent from the founding ancestor. Property rights are controlled by the chief, and trade is central to chiefdom development. Sociopolitical organization is at the multi-village level.

Chou The first state or empire in China, dated to between 1100 B.C. and A.D. 220. Ironworking was common, as were mass burials and extensive warfare. Confucius taught his message, and Buddhism spread through China; the Great Wall was built to keep nomads out.

Clan A descent group in which every member believes him- or herself to be descended from a common ancestor in the distant past, but the genealogical links to the ancestor are not precisely known.

Class This is a social category used for modern industrial societies and refers to ranking of the population into distinct levels based on wealth or achievement. Most modern societies have a three-class system composed of upper, middle, and lower classes. In modern states the majority of the people belong to the middle class.

Cognatic Descent Descent traced through any combination of male and female links to a common ancestor.

Cognitive Science An interdisciplinary science, primarily made up of psychology, psychiatry, biology, linguistics, and anthropology, that studies how cognition occurs in the human brain.

Colono In Guatemala, a resident laborer on a corporate plantation.

Comadre A comother; the female sponsor of one's child, for example, at baptism.

Compadre A cofather or a coparent generally; usually a wealthy relative, neighbor, or friend.

Comparative Linguistics Focuses on the origins of different languages and the genetic relationships among languages; also called historical linguistics.

Comparison Looking at cultural features across a sample of cultures in an attempt to determine if the features regularly co-occur; also referred to as the comparative method or the method of controlled comparison.

Complementary Opposition A process whereby groups with distinct interests at a low level are tied to each other by common membership in a higher-level category that draws their cooperation.

Compradors The commercial elites in the Middle East who were enriched by links to European colonial governments, usually as importers of European goods. The children of this class often became the revolutionaries driving out colonial governments.

Connectivity The contextual relations of cultures to each other.

Conquistadores The Conquerors, a Spanish term, referring to the first wave of colonists to the Americas (which included soldiers and nonsoldiers alike) whose actions were based on mercantilist beliefs. The interest of Spanish colonists was the capture of wealth, not its creation.

Contratistas Agents who buy the debts of plantation workers and then force them to pay the debts by working on plantations; a form of debt peonage.

Corporate Ownership Rights to the use of a resource are limited to those who are members of a group and are much more specific, in contrast to public ownership. In tribal societies, lineages or clans or other groups based on a principle of descent may be corporate owners of property.

Corporations In capitalist societies, corporations are fictions based on the extension of private property rights from individuals to groups or associations of individuals. This protects the rights of any one member by distributing liabilities to all.

Corporatism This means the same thing as state capitalism, except that the society is conceptualized as formed into a giant pyramidlike corporation.

Corregidor The political position of civil judge; a ceremonial post in the traditional cargo system with no real power. Within an *ayuntamiento* the same term is applied to positions analogous to councilman or alderman.

Cosmic A form of polytheism very common to non-monotheistic peoples who believe that the forces of the cosmos are supernatural beings (winds, rains, stars, sun). Roman and Greek Hellenism is a cosmic religion.

Crusades Any of the military expeditions undertaken by the Christians of Europe in the eleventh, twelfth, and thirteenth centuries to recover the Holy Land from various Islamic states.

Cultural Evolution The long-term process of culture change, usually resulting in greater complexity of social institutions and technology. The labels *band, tribe, chiefdom,* and *state* are often used to designate stages or levels of increasing cultural complexity.

Cultural Materialism A theory of culture change stating that cultures are primarily the products of adaptations to the material bases of life. Marvin Harris is the most forceful proponent of this theory.

Cultural Relativism The view that there is an internal rationale to the beliefs, behaviors, and practices of all cultures and that as anthropologists we should attempt to understand each belief, behavior, or practice in its own cultural context without judging it to be right or wrong, good or bad, by our own cultural or moral or ethical standards.

Culture Shared knowledge, beliefs, and patterns for behavior, the resulting behavior, and the resulting material products.

Debt Peonage Debt slavery; workers are loaned food, clothing, and other goods at high interest rates and are then trapped by their debt, often as near-slaves. Supposedly outlawed after World War II, it is still common in remote rural regions.

Degradation A human-induced reduction in the *quality* of natural resources, such as soil, water, and air, that reduces the capacity of these resources to support life. Contamination of soil with toxic waste is an example of soil degradation.

Deity A supernatural being, a god; that is, a being with powers that are beyond those of nature.

Dependency Theory The theory that traditional cultures cannot modernize because they are caught in a dependency relationship with rich societies, which keeps them poor.

Depletion A human-induced reduction in the *quantity* of a natural resource; for renewable resources such as forests, a reduction at a rate greater than the natural rate of regeneration or replacement. Erosion is an example of soil depletion.

Descriptive Linguistics The synchronic analysis of the structures of languages into agreed-on components and categories in order to provide descriptions that permit the comparison of languages.

Dharma A person's essential quality or character or destiny according to Buddha.

Diaspora This term refers to several different occasions when the Jewish peoples were dispersed from their homelands, the first of which occurred after the Babylonian destruction of Jerusalem in 597 B.C. Another disapora was the expulsion of the Jews from Spain in the late fifteenth century A.D. The same term is often applied to Palestinians driven out of Palestine at various times, beginning with the 1948 creation of Israel.

Diffusionism A nineteenth-century theory, often conceptualized as in opposition to the theory of unilineal evolution, in which culture traits originate in only one or a few places (such as Egypt) and diffuse to other world regions.

Disarticulation The lack of a connection between efficiency in the workplace and wages.

Dispersed clan A clan whose members live in many villages.

Divination (scapulamancy) The use of ox and other scapulae to foretell the future. Symbols, which later became Chinese writing, were painted on the scapula and then these were heated and the future was "read" by studying cracks in the symbols.

Doi Moi Vietnamese parallel to the Russian word *perestroika,* meaning to open markets or restructure the economy away from closed socialist practices.

Dowry Often confused with brideprice, this is wealth given by the family of orientation of the bride as an endowment to the groom or to compensate the bride for her loss of rights when she marries out.

Ecological Circumscription A theory developed by Robert Carneiro, who argues that agricultural societies evolve because growing populations are prevented from migrating due to mountains, deserts, or jungles. The growing populations produce increased conflict because of land limitations, which is resolved by developing hierarchy and castes or classes based on the wealth of the landowning group.

Economic Anthropology The comparative study of economic systems.

Economic Liberalization The transformation of state capitalist or state socialist societies into democratic capitalist societies. In general, it refers to the introduction of free or open markets to societies that have closed markets.

Ecosystem An arbitrarily defined spatial unit of interacting biological organisms and their nonliving environment. Ecosystems are subunits of the entire living system of Earth, which is called the biosphere.

Ecosystem Approach The approach, when used by anthropologists, that emphasizes the adaptations between human communities and their biophysical habitat. This approach directs attention to biological, physical, and behavioral–cultural factors.

Ejido A term used mainly in Mexico for a collective estate, usually owned by Indian communities and found mostly in the highland regions of Latin America.

Emic The insider or native point of view (as opposed to *etic*).

Emic Analysis Using for purposes of analysis the categories or features of the culture in which they occur, as understood by the members of that culture (see also *etic analysis*).

Encomiendas Rights given to the Conquistadores and their immediate descendants to the labor of Indians, but not to their lands. The right to the exploitation of Indian labor led to a population collapse and to the opening of lands, which became the *haciendas*.

Enculturation or **Socialization** The process whereby children learn what their parents and others around them know.

Endogamy Marriage within a specified group like a clan or a lineage. Clan endogamy is more common than lineage endogamy.

Entrepots Trade centers (see *Treaty Ports*).

Ethnicity Regional or national identity based on language, religion, or heritage. Specific ethnic identities are usually identifiable by self-defined "ethnic markers," such as flags, speech patterns, costumes, beliefs, or other criteria that separate one ethnic group from another.

Ethnocentrism The view that the ways of one's own culture are superior to those of any other and are, in fact, the only "correct" ways.

Ethnocide The destruction of the ethnic markers, ethnic identity, or culture of an ethnic group or groups.

Ethnographer The label given to an anthropologist when he/she is doing field research in order to write an ethnography.

Ethnographic Present A fiction used in ethnographic writing whereby the writer places all events and descriptions in the present, even though the information may encompass a considerable span of time.

Ethnography A descriptive account of a culture or subculture; the description and analysis of a cultural scene; the task of producing such a description.

Ethnohistory This is a special field of cultural anthropology that attempts to understand the lifeways of past populations through judicious, if tedious, analysis and interpretation of a combination of historical records and archaeological data.

Ethnolinguistics Also known as **ethnosemantics,** this is the study of the ways in which people of different cultures use their language to organize, categorize, and classify everything that makes up their world.

Ethnology Means very much the same thing as "cultural anthropology" in its generalizing, comparative study of culture with a big "C." As a contrast, ethnography would be the specific study of a Caribbean plantation community while the study of plantation systems in general and their impact on people would be ethnology.

Ethnonationalism Separatist social movements that are transformative and redemptive at the same time.

Ethnoscience Also known as cognitive anthropology, the systematic study of the systems of classification in different cultures; the study of folk taxonomies of plants and animals or the systems of classification of relatives (kin), for example.

Etic The outsider or observer point of view, usually following a set of descriptive categories agreed upon in the observer's discipline.

Etic Analysis The use of categories or features for comparison that are devised or decided on by the researcher. Such analytic categories are often those agreed on by the discipline as a whole.

Evangelical Protestantism A religious movement in Latin America that offers an alternative to the Catholic Church in the form of Protestantism; often has a conservative political perspective, the opposite of liberation theology.

Exogamy Marriage outside of some specified group like a lineage or clan. In societies with descent groups, marriage must usually be with someone who is not a member of one's own descent group. In societies with only bilateral kin groups, marriage must usually be with someone who is not a close relative, or who does not share the same surname.

Family of Orientation The family into which one is born.

Family of Procreation The family one creates.

Family Realm A cross-generational set of relationships based on the sexual bonding of two consenting adults.

Female Infanticide Causing the death of a female infant either through ritual murder or through neglect. In societies where this occurs, it is usually permitted because sons are considered more valuable than daughters.

Feminism A political movement based on the ideological commitment to the equality of women.

Fertility Rate The average number of living children that a woman will have in her lifetime.

Feudalism In general, refers to the manorial system of Western Europe and differs significantly from the tributary systems found in Asia. Feudal societies are not highly centralized, and while a king or queen can demand tribute from the manorial lords, he/she cannot count on them for political support.

Filial Piety (*hsiao*) The devotion of the child to the father and the father to the emperor in the Confucian religion of China.

Finca A Latin American term for almost any type of farm, ranging from a large plantation to a small farm.

Five pillars The five major expectations of those who practice Islam.

Food Extraction Hunting and food-gathering; taking the food resources that nature provides.

Food Production The deliberate propagation of domesticated plants or animals for use as food.

Footbinding The mark of male control over the female in the Mandarin classes; infant girls had their feet bound while young, crippling them as adults; the grown-in foot was considered a sign of beauty; generally not practiced by the peasant class.

Forensic Anthropology A specialized subdiscipline of biological anthropology dealing with law, particularly the identification of victims of crime and causes of death.

Free Morphemes The minimal units of meaning in a language that can stand alone. In English, most free morphemes are what we commonly call words.

Functionalism A twentieth-century theory based on the idea that the characteristics of human institutions are based on the functions of those institutions. An alternative, and broader, theory known as structural-functionalism reduced all functions to one of solidarity.

Gaucho An Argentine cowboy, usually of Indian descent (Araucanian), who specialized in cattle herding on the great cattle haciendas (called *estancias*).

Genocide The physical destruction of an ethnic group or nationality.

Gentry The wealthiest and most powerful upper segment of the Chinese clan; it was the group from which the Mandarins were recruited.

Gerzean Gerzean culture probably represents a chiefdom society and rose out of the preceding Amratian. It was widespread, found in both Upper and Lower Egypt between 3500 B.C. and 3100 B.C. when Egypt was unified.

Globalization The integration of the world economy through computer and telecommunication technologies for the benefit of financial interest groups.

Grammar The basic rules of a language that determine the structure of phrases and sentences.

Gross Domestic Product (GDP) The value of all final goods and services produced within the borders of a country, usually calculated on the basis of a common currency such as the U.S. dollar (but see *Purchasing Power Parity,* below).

Gross National Product (GNP) GDP plus net income from abroad.

Guru A spiritual leader among Buddhists.

Haciendas Traditionally, large Latin American estates, somewhat similar to the manors of Western Europe, that grew out of the *encomiendas,* granted to the Conquistadores in exchange for their loyalties to the Hispanic and Portuguese crowns. The control of land became the most important single vehicle for wealth in Latin America.

Hegemonic Cores The heartland of tributary empires, usually tribute-taking states (or cities) that control a periphery made up of tributary states.

Historical Archaeology Using archaeological excavation techniques to study the sites where literate societies, that is, those for which there is some written record, once existed.

Holism The view that we must attempt to understand whatever features of culture we are examining within the larger context in which they occur.

Hominids This zoological classification refers to modern *Homo sapiens sapiens* (humans) and their direct ancestors.

Human Ecology The study of the relationship of cultural systems to physical habitats; also known as cultural materialism in its more environmentally or technologically deterministic forms. An alternative term is cultural ecology, which means approximately the same thing.

Hypoglycemia An abnormally low level of glucose in the blood.

Ideal Culture What people think they ought to do.

Ideal Type An abstract perfect or idealized form of something, such as a nuclear family, that may seldom, if ever, occur in reality (see *Ideal Culture*).

Il Rah An invisible road followed by pastoral nomads that is often compared to a giant carpet laid over the landscape of grasses and water.

Incest taboo A prohibition against sex with a close relative.

Indigenismo Initially, in the early twentieth century, a transformative movement in Latin America to liberate the communities of Indians but later a means of co-opting Indian communities within conservative and state capitalist political parties.

Indigenous Refers to contemporary reformative social movements, not to be confused with *indigenismo,* which seek to restore rights to the original inhabitants of various world regions ranging from Malaysia to Latin America.

Infix A bound morpheme that occurs within another morpheme, in contrast, for example, to a prefix that is bound to the beginning of another morpheme. Infixes are common in some American Indian languages like Navaho.

Infrastructural Level The level of materialistic systems within an overall sociocultural system, that is, those systems that have to do directly with production and reproduction.

Ingenio In Latin America, a giant processing plant for sugarcane.

Institutions The sets of rules governing human behavior. Institutions can be simple (rules governing kinship) or extremely complex (the modern state or corporation).

Intepretivism A theory that rejects materialism and argues that cultures are best understood through the humanistic and symbolic interpretation of ethnographic descriptions. Clifford Geertz is the foremost proponent of this theory.

Islam The religious system of Allah according to his Prophet Muhammad.

Jajmani A redistribution economy focused on the role of the *jajman,* usually a member of the elite Brahman landowning caste, who collected the surplus production of members of distinct castes as taxes and distributed them back; the nonagricultural castes were given grain in exchange for products or services.

Karma One's destiny within the Hindu religion.

Kerese A shallow well dug vertically to tap an aquifer; there are usually horizontal tunnels at the bottom of the well; can be controlled by a single clan.

Khan The hereditary chief or leader of a clan or chiefdom among pastoral nomads, but also applied to the chiefs of settled towns throughout the Middle East and Inner Asia.

Kibbutz Collective farms in Israel organized during the early or Zionistic phase of Israeli history with roots in socialist philosophy.

Kshatriya The second level caste of warriors and rulers.

Kulturkreise The German variant of diffusion theory, which thought traits diffused out from several different civilizations; these were the central places or circles (*kreise*).

Ladang The term used in Indonesia to refer to swidden plots (see *Swidden*).

Ladino Spanish term used in Guatemala meaning the same thing as *mestizo* or *creole.*

Laissez Faire This is a both an economic theory and a political philosophy that emphasizes a lack of restraints on economic transactions, particularly by the state, in order to reduce transaction costs.

Lanzon A temple at the site of Chavin de Huantar in the Peruvian Andes depicting a feline deity, dated to about 800 B.C.

Late or **Upper Paleolithic** The last phase of the "Stone Age," also known as Upper Paleolithic, coinciding with the appearance of biologically modern humans (*Homo sapiens sapiens*), and lasting from 40,000 to 9000 B.C.

Latifundia Term used for *haciendas* or plantations; large, elite-owned estates.

Legal Anthropology The comparative study of law, although often it means just the study of non-Western legal systems.

Lexicon A list of all of the morphemes of a language.

Liberation Theology A political movement within the Catholic Church in Latin America supporting the interests of the poor; often associated with a socialist point of view.

Lineage A unilineal descent group in which all members can trace their relationship to a common ancestor by known (or presumed) links through either a line of females (a matrilineage) or a line of males (a patrilineage).

Linguistic Anthropology One of the four major subdisciplines of anthropology; linguistics is the science of the study of language.

Lungshan A Chinese early chiefdom that appeared between 4000 and 2000 B.C. Of particular importance is evidence for shamanism and ancestor worship in the form of scapulamancy.

Machismo The Latin American expectations that a man will exploit those women he can and protect those he must. Based on the term *macho,* which means strong male.

Mahayana Buddhism Buddhist tradition found in Tibet, China, Vietnam, Korea, and Japan.

Mana A Polynesian word that is used in anthropology to refer to a powerful magical force that can be manipulated by humans who have the appropriate ritual knowledge.

Mandarin Those from the gentry who passed the state exam (usually based on Confucian philosophy) and became the bureaucracy in China. This class was ideally separate from the Chinese aristocracy or ruling class, an ideal that was often broken.

Manorial System Dating back to Roman rule in Western Europe, the manorial system consisted of large landed estates (manors) ruled by lords who were under the tributary control of a single king/queen and his/her clan or lineage. The lords of the manors did not own them but were granted the right to use them in exchange for tribute to the king (the manorial system is a tributary state).

Mansabdars The Muslim upper caste in India, which controlled both the army and bureaucracy.

Mantrayana Buddhism Stresses the relationship of a *guru* to his followers.

Mastabas Cut stone tombs with flat roofs housing mummies, these predynastic monuments presaged the development of Egyptian pyramids in the Dynastic period.

Matrifocal Literally, focused on the mother. In anthropology, this term is used to describe a household formed or headed by one or more adult women and their children. Adult male partners of these women are not permanent residents in these households.

Matrilineal Descent Descent traced through a line of females. Both women and men acquire membership in a matrilineal descent group from their mothers, but only women can pass membership in the group on to their children.

Medical Anthropology Applied biological anthropology; the study of the interrelationships between medical beliefs and practices in a society and other aspects of its culture.

Menghirs, Dolmens, and Passage Graves These are similar types of burial monuments, usually associated with chiefdom-level social structures. They are found in Western Europe for the Mesolithic and Neolithic. They are also found in Asia; usually consisting of three vertically placed rocks overlaid by a fourth "roof," these monuments are thought to have been the burial sites of chiefs.

Mercantilism This economic philosophy determined European international policies during the colonial period and was based on the idea that wealth was limited and could only be divided, not created. A further characteristic was the idea that money (specie) was the store of wealth, particularly in the form of silver and gold,

Meroe A chiefdom or state that arose directly south of Egypt between 1500 B.C. and 350 A.D. Meroe has very Egyptian characteristics.

Mesoamerica The cultural hearth of prehistoric Mexico and northern Central America, containing the high civilizations of the Aztec and Maya and their antecedents. Mesoamerica encompasses approximately the southern two-thirds of Mexico, all of Guatemala, and the northern one-third of El Salvador and Honduras.

Mesolithic The Middle Stone Age, the period during which the domestication of plants and animals took place, generally characterized by microlithic tools, dating from about 9000 to 7000 B.C. The period following is called the Neolithic, or New Stone Age.

Messianic Term used to refer to transformative or charismatic movements led by a leader or leaders who promise deliverance or redemption.

Mestizo Originally meant mixed blood, hybrid, usually of Indian and Spanish descent; often the term is used instead of *creole*, which refers to a hybrid language. Today the term means anyone of Indian and Spanish heritage.

Microblade A type of implement found in European Mesolithic cultures, formed by snapping a blade into smaller pieces and forming them into composite tools; also called a microlith.

Millet Under the Ottoman Empire, a millet was a religious and political unit defined by its adherence to a religion and granted certain rights and privileges. The Islamic millet had the highest rank, while Christians, Jews, and members of other communities were granted lower ranks. Nonetheless, non-Islamic communities or ethnic groups were allowed to keep their practices as long as they did not contradict the Islamic state.

Milpa The term used in Mesoamerica to refer to swidden plots (see *Swidden*).

Minifundia Small estates, usually owned by independent farmers whose labor is used by large estates.

Modernization The process whereby traditional societies borrow the technology and institutions of modern societies and, thereby, lose their traditional characteristics and become "modern."

Modernization Theory The theory that traditional cultures can modernize by borrowing the technologies of advanced capitalist societies.

Modes of Production The major forms of systemic organization in culture for the production of goods. The way production is organized determines how the systems of a society are organized according to Marxist theory.

Moiety A division of society into two social groups, usually based on a rule of unilineal descent. In other words, all of the lineages or clans in a society will belong to one or the other of these two moieties. Usually, the lineages or clans belonging to a moiety share descent from a common (usually mythical) ancestor in the distant past.

Moksha The ultimate release from samsara, according to Hindu belief.

Monotheism The doctrine or belief that there is a single high God; this is the belief of the "People of the Book" or Old Testament: Jews, Christians, and Arabs.

Morphemes The minimal units of language that have meaning.

Morphology The study of morphemes, the technical term that is used to define minimal units of meaning in a language. Many English morphemes are what we call words, but many words consist of more than one morpheme. For example, *boy* is a word and a single morpheme; *boys* is also a word but consists of two morphemes, *boy* and the plural marker morpheme *s*.

Multiculturalism A reformative social movement with the objective of granting distinct ethnic groups the right to retain some or all of their heritage (markers, identity, culture). In general, multiculturalism can be considered a type of civil rights movement that goes beyond the demand for equality before the law and seeks a degree of recognition from the larger society of its distinct heritage.

Municipio Spanish term for a political division that is the equivalent of a township.

Neolocal Residence The type of residence commonly associated with nuclear families; the husband and wife both leave their families of orientation (the ones they were born into) to form independent families of procreation (the ones in which they produce children).

Nirvana The Hindu idea of escape from the caste system and of birth and rebirth or *samsara*.

Nuclear Family An ideal type composed of a husband and wife who are the parents of the children of the marriage.

Paleoanthropology That aspect of biological anthropology that studies the origins and physiology of the ancestors of modern *Homo sapiens sapiens*.

Paleoecology A subdiscipline of archaeology specializing in the reconstruction of ancient physical habitats and human adaptations.

Paradigm A body of belief or values, facts, and definitions that serves as the overall framework within which data are interpreted in any scientific discipline; a supermodel.

Paramount Chief The central office of a chiefdom; it is an ascribed role that is inherited by either the oldest or most talented of a set of offspring who can claim descent from the founding ancestor of the chiefdom.

Patrilineal Descent Descent traced through a line of males. Both men and women acquire membership in a patrilineal descent group from their fathers, but only men can pass membership in the group on to their children.

Patrilineality Descent traced through a line of male ancestors.

Patrilocality Residence after marriage in the house of the husband's father. Sometimes also used to mean residence after marriage on the land of the husband's kin (but see *virilocality*).

Patron In Latin America, the boss or benefactor, usually a member of the elite class.

Peasant The lowest classes, ranks, or castes of the *tsu* or clan; those who worked the land as distinct from the Mandarin or merchant classes.

Perennial Irrigation More complex irrigation/well/tunnel structures requiring state support.

Phonemics The study and classification of the meaningful contrastive units of sound (phonemes) of a language and their variation. Phonemes are sounds that make a difference in meaning in a given language. For example, in English /b/ and /p/ are phonemes because they provide the contrast between such words as *ban* and *pan,* which have different meanings.

Phonetics The study and classification of all the sounds of a language, which are called phones.

Phratry A grouping of two or more lineages or clans into a larger group based on a belief in common descent; like a moiety, except that the lineages or clans form more than two groups, called phratries.

Physiological Anthropology That aspect of biological anthropology that studies the functional adaptations of *Homo sapiens sapiens.*

Plantations Similar to *haciendas* but organized for the production of export commodities such as sugar, cotton, or hemp (for cordage); they tend not to be self-sufficient but depend on local farmers for food.

Political Anthropology The study of the emergence and development of public policy; the comparative study of political systems.

Political Ecology A theoretical perspective that combines the interests of political economy in the links between productive activity and the distribution of power with the interests of human (or cultural) ecology in the interactions between humans and their bio-physical environments.

Political Economy The study of how institutions influence the distribution of wealth and power.

Polygyny Marriage between one male and two or more females forming multifamily social structures.

Polytheistic The doctrine or belief in many gods or powers.

Porfirismo The "liberal" philosophy articulated by Porfirio Dias, the dictator of Mexico from 1873 to 1911, of industrializing rapidly by opening countries to outside investment.

Potlatch A redistribution feast, traditional among some Native peoples of Northwestern North America, in which an individual gives away wealth in order to achieve prestige or higher status.

Prebendalism A political system based on a ruler giving offices to his followers as gifts, rewards, or stipends for political support.

Primatology The specialized study of the closest relatives of *Homo sapiens sapiens:* the great apes (chimpanzees, gorillas, orangutans, and gibbons) belonging to several related disciplines (biological anthropology, biology more properly zoology, and psychology).

Process The systematic series of actions leading to adaptations or maladaptations by individuals or communities.

Proletariat Those without property; the rural proletariat are those without land and the urban proletariat are those without wealth or the opportunity to acquire wealth.

Property Rights The culturally defined ownership of natural resources and human-made goods. The possibilities are: public ownership (all have access to resources), collective (only members of a group own resources), state (ownership by a public authority), and individual or private ownership (access to resources restricted to a person with rights to those resources).

Public ownership Rights to the use of a resource belong to anyone; analogous to the use of highways or parks in Western culture.

Purchasing Power Parity The amount of a common "market basket" of goods and services that can be purchased locally, using local currency, including goods and services not traded internationally. GDP adjusted on the basis of purchasing power parity is often significantly higher than GDP calculated solely on the basis of U.S. dollars.

Qanats Horizontal wells dug into hills or mountains to tap aquifers (subterranean pools of water); can be controlled by a single clan.

Quran The Koran, the sacred scripture of Islam, believed by orthodox Mohammedans to be the revealed word of God spoken in Arabic.

Real Culture What people actually do.

Reciprocity Economic transactions between individuals or groups in which exchange is based on trust that the person to whom something is given will be equally willing to give in return (moral relationships). Generalized reciprocity occurs among close kinsmen; there is no expectation that something of equal value will be returned and there is no expectation that the return will take place within a specified period of time. The only expectation is that at some time something will be given back. Balanced reciprocity occurs among close and more distant kinsmen, and sometimes among good friends. There is the expectation that something of equivalent value will be given within an agreed-on period of time. Reciprocity is the opposite of market exchange, which is based on profit (amoral relationships).

Redemptive Movement A social movement with the goal of completely changing the individual (changing the state of the person, not the society). Generally, redemptive movements are religious or psychological in nature.

Redistribution A form of economy in which goods are given to a central figure or group and then given back (redistributed) in some form.

Reference Group The social environment of a movement made up of other people (reference) who are used as a contrast or a basis for comparison to establish relative deprivation.

Reformative Movement A social movement that has goals limited to targeting certain aspects of society for change (change is to the social system, not the self).

Relative Deprivation A social science theory explaining the motivation of people involved in social movements. Motivation is found in the feeling of alienation by a people who feel that they are illegitimately deprived of status, property, power, or worth.

Renaissance The period marking the transition from the medieval to the modern world, roughly from the fourteenth through the sixteenth centuries, when the arts and philosophies of the ancient world, particularly Greece and Rome, were rediscovered and made the basis for a "new birth" of European culture.

Resource Mobilization The resources a group must control in order to succeed in its goals. It is not enough that a group is deprived; it must also have the capacity to succeed (one block to success is structural power, see Chapter 7).

Resource Utilization The transformation of natural resources into cultural goods.

Role What one does within a society in relation to others. Father, judge, and governor are all roles within our society for example, as are daughter, defendant, and citizen.

Salinization Irrigation water in deserts dissolves salts from basic soils and deposits them again in concentrated form so that after several generations of use the soils lose their fertility.

Samsara The Hindu belief in reincarnation.

Samurai The Japanese military aristocracy during the feudal period.

Satori The flash of insight that distinguishes Zen from other Buddhist schools.

Sectarian This means the opposite of secular; movements that have a religious basis.

Semantics The study of the meaning of words, phrases, sentences, and even larger units of discourse.

Seppeku One of the ritual codes of Bushido requiring the Japanese warrior to commit suicide if he could not complete a mission.

Sexual Bonding Sexual relations leading to the creation of family groups.

Shaman A religious specialist, male or female, who is able to communicate with and control natural and supernatural forces and mediate between humans and these nonhuman forces.

Shogun The Japanese commander in chief, supreme military ruler during the feudal period.

Sinified The process of enculturation whereby non-Chinese people learned Chinese culture; often used to refer to Munghal invaders who took over the Chinese state but became Chinese.

Social Darwinism Another nineteenth century evolutionary theory that proposed that human culture evolves through a process of natural selection, competition, and survival of the fittest, analogous to Darwinian biological evolution.

Social Movement An attempt by people to organize themselves to effect change in the face of resistance.

Social Structure The rules (institutions) governing social relationships and organization in human societies. In bands and tribes, these relationships are based on kinship. In modern societies they are based on kinship and broader community relationships defined by expected roles and statuses.

Society A population separated from surrounding populations and having a distinctive culture; people who live in a common territory, share a common language and culture, and interact on a regular basis.

Sociolinguistics The study of language variation in social contexts. Sociolinguists study, for example, the ways in which language use serves to mark status distinctions in a society.

Socionatural Systems According to John W. Bennett (1993:14), all interactions between human activity and the environment constitute socionatural systems. We broaden this definition to encompass the interaction of human societies with each other, as well as with their biophysical environments.

Sodality An association based on common interest; in tribal society it crosscuts clans and other unilineal lineages; in modern society, any type of fraternity or sorority based on common interest, such as male or female groups in Latin America supporting the Catholic Church and its religious celebrations.

Solidarity The social bond between individuals; thought to be the glue that holds society together.

State Capitalism Often confused with democratic capitalism in Latin America, state capitalism is nondemocratic and tends to be characterized by state ownership of industrial capital (but not land, which is often in the hands of the elite).

States Stratified and centralized societies that occupy a territory controlled by a central authority. States usually consist of at least two classes, an elite, or gentry, and a lower class, with the elite in control of the bureaucracy. In this text, states are the central points of hegemony over trade, and rights to property are controlled by the state through the king or other maximal leader. States and chiefdoms differ by degree, and are often so similar as to be distinguishable only in scale and not in organizational structure.

State Socialism Often confused with communism, state socialist societies tend to be nondemocratic (although they often claim lofty democratic goals), and are characterized by state ownership of industrial capital and land (all means of production). State socialist societies differ from state capitalist in having neither free markets nor private property rights, but have centrally controlled and managed economies. Communist and socialist societies differ in the myth that the former are owned by the working class while the latter are controlled by bureaucratic managers. In fact, most socialist or Communist societies are state socialist.

Status One's position in a social structure (for example, elite, commoner, middle class, lower class); the variables used to determine status vary among cultures.

Stratified The primary characteristic of states in which status relationships fall into a minimum of two stratified classes (but often many more) also known as political classes or as social classes. In tributary states (also known as primitive states) status relationships are ascribed and the upper class (aristocracy) is endowed with power, while the lower class (peasantry) is not. In modern industrial societies, status relations are achieved (in theory).

Structural Power Structural power is control over the political process by the elites who control state capitalist or state socialist economies; it is also the residual control over power by former elites once an economic system no longer exists.

Subculture A division within a complex culture that is based on recognized differences such as ethnicity, religion, or occupation. Subcultures share some, but not all, of the elements of the larger culture of which they are a part.

Sumptuary Laws Laws found in chiefdoms and hegemonic states that specify privileges of the elite or nobility and simultaneously prohibit commoners from exercising the same privileges.

Supernatural A belief in principles or forces that are not part of the natural universe but are beyond; found among the Peoples of the Book.

Sustainable Development Development or improvement in the quality of human life that is economically viable (benefits are greater than costs), socially and culturally acceptable, and ecologically viable (resources are used at a rate equal to or less than the rate of renewal); a strategy designed to meet current needs without compromising the needs of future generations.

Swidden Shifting agriculture dependent on cutting down and burning a small patch of forest, planting crops on the plot for two or three years, and then allowing the plot to lie fallow (remain unused) for a number of years until the forest has grown back.

Symbolic Anthropology An intepretivist approach that emphasizes meaning and the importance of symbols in the interpretation of ethnographic data.

Syncretic The blending of elements of two or more distinct traditions; it may refer to religion, music, other aspects of culture, or culture as a whole.

Syntax The study of the organization of words into phrases and sentences.

Teleological An argument or logical position that ascribes goals to a system. Teleological also means to ascribe *telos* or historical goals to "things."

Territorial Clan A clan that claims ownership of a territory in which its members are concentrated.

Theocracy A form of government in which a sacred diety is viewed as the supreme ruler.

Theravada Buddhism Early school of Buddhism found in Burma, Sri Lanka, and elsewhere in Southeast Asia.

Thick Description A highly detailed ethnographic account interlaced with emic interpretation that emphasizes the understanding of a culture from the point of view of its members.

Ti Also, T'i or Shang-ti, a superior being in the Chinese pantheon of gods during the Lungshan period.

Totalitarian Structural power found in socialist or communist societies. No political autonomy is allowed to nongovernment or nonelite groups.

Trade The exchange of natural or human-made goods between individuals, communities, and cultures.

Trade/Raid Nexus These are the two sides of the coin of pastoral nomadic adaptations; when the tribe succeeds in protecting its herd and has a surplus of animals, it trades with settled town dwellers. When it is not successful, it raids.

Transformative Movement A social movement that has as its goals the radical and total change of the social order (the system outside the self).

Transhumance Herding Transhumance herding is often viewed as the opposite of settled farming, with herders driving cattle, camels, horses, or goats over a changing landscape, dependent on their knowledge of local ecosystems, for survival. But settled farming and transhumance herding are tied together symbiotically. The markets of the farmer are supplied by goods carried by the drover, and both exchange the appropriate goods with each other (grain for meat, and vice versa). Transhumance herders have a permanent base village, unlike true pastoral nomads who do not.

Transpiration A loss of water vapor into the air by plants. This water vapor eventually returns to the earth as precipitation (rain or snow).

Treaty Ports Also known as ports-of-trade, these were *entrepots* or trade centers where European traders were protected by the state as long as they did not interfere in politics.

Tribes In general, a type of society that is in between egalitarian bands and more hierarchical chiefdoms or states. Tribes are found in the peripheries of states and chiefdoms, but tend to have access to richer resources than bands do. Tribes tend to have minimal levels of hierarchy and political organization and can be characterized as having a village level of sociopolitical organization. Property rights are collective.

Tributary Economy A type of economy in which goods are provided as tribute to a central figure who embodies the authority of the state. A tribute is distinct from a tax in that tribute is based on the hereditary right of an elite.

Tributary Empires This is another name for premodern "world systems" (Wallerstein 1974). Tributary empires are based on hegemonic cores controlling trade and warfare and receiving tribute from those societies in the periphery, which they dominate.

Tributary States These are states found in the peripheries of hegemonic empires that pay tribute to the cores of empire. Also known as theater states, often they are not distinguishable from chiefdoms.

Tsu The traditional multigenerational Chinese clan or extended family based on patrilineal descent; incorporated the elite Mandarin as well as peasant lower classes.

Ulema A council of men who are experts on Islamic religion and law.

Unilineal Descent Descent traced from a founding ancestor through either a line of females (matrilineal descent) or a line of males (patrilineal descent) to determine one's membership in a unilineal descent group.

Unilinear Evolution A type of evolutionary theory common in the nineteenth century in which all cultures were thought to evolve through a fixed series of stages, such as those of savagery, barbarism, and civilization as postulated by Lewis Henry Morgan.

Untouchable This is a social category in the Indian caste system made up of those people whose occupations are considered ritually unclean, such as leatherworkers, those who dispose of dead animals, those who handle the dead, those who clean latrines, and so on. Since only the four central castes were considered acceptable aspects of Indian society, the Untouchables were considered a fifth category outside of the social system.

Vaisya The third-level caste of landholders and merchants.

Varnas The term for the four Indian castes.

Vedas The sacred scriptures of Hinduism; there are four Books of Wisdom: Rig-Veda, Yajur-Veda, Sama-Veda, and Atharva-Veda.

Villein The peasants living on the manors who worked the land and were at the bottom of the manorial status pyramid.

Virginity Complex The Latin American expectation that women will maintain their virginity at all cost; found primarily among the elite classes.

Virilocality Residence after marriage on the lands of the husband's kin.

Whorfian Hypothesis The Whorfian hypothesis states that there is a close relationship between the way members of a culture perceive their world and the way they use their language to communicate their perceptions (their world view). It is the view that the categories of one's language structure one's perception of the world.

World Systems Theory A type of dependency theory that expands the dependency argument from the relationship between a rich colonial country and a poor colonized country to all rich core countries and all poor "peripheral countries." This theory accounts reasonably well for relations under conditions of colonialism and neo-colonialism, but fails to explain current changes around the world due to globalization.

Yang-shao The first neolithic, probably tribal, culture of China, circa 6000 to 5000 B.C., characterized by partially subterranean houses, domesticated rice, millet, pigs, dogs, chickens, and water buffalo; they made stone sickles, mortars, pestles, and ceramics, probably practiced slash-and-burn agriculture.

Zamindars The Hindu elite under the control of the *mansabdars* during the first phase of British colonialism.

Zen Buddhism A form of Buddhism that stresses personal enlightenment; found in Korea and Japan.

Zionism The plan to colonize Palestine with Hebrews outlined in the Balfour Declaration of November 2, 1917. Also, Jewish nationalism.

References

ABERLE, DAVID F. (1991). *The Peyote Religion among the Navaho*. Norman: University of Oklahoma Press.

ACHESON, JAMES M. (1996). Household organization and budget structures in a Purepecha pueblo. *American Ethnologist* 23(2):331–351.

ACHESON, JAMES M. (1995). Coase among the Purepechas: Transaction costs and institutional change in a Mexican Indian pueblo. *Journal of Institutional and Theoretical Economics* 151(2):3–43.

ACHESON, JAMES M. (1986). Social organization of the Maine lobster market. In S. Plattner (Ed.), *Markets and Marketing* (pp. 105–132). Monographs in Economic Anthropology, No. 4. Lanham, MD: University Press of America.

ACHESON, JAMES M. (Ed.) (1994). *Anthropology and Institutional Economics*. Monographs in Economic Anthropology, No. 12. New York: University Press of America.

ACHESON, JAMES M., AND JAMES A. WILSON (1996). Order out of chaos: The case for parametric fisheries management. *American Anthropologist* 98(3):579–594.

ADAMS, ROBERT MC. (1975). The emerging place of trade in civilization studies. In J. A. Sabloff & C. C. Lamberg–Karlovsky (Eds.), *Ancient Civilization and Trade* (pp. 451–464). Albuquerque: University of New Mexico Press.

ADAMS, ROBERT MC. (1974). Anthropological perspectives on ancient trade. *Current Anthropology* 15(3):239–258.

AL KHALIL, SAMIR (1989). *Republic of Fear*. New York: Pantheon Books.

ALGAZE, GUILLERMO (1991). *The Uruk World System*. Chicago: University of Chicago Press.

ALLEN, CATHERINE J. (1988). *The Hold Life Has: Coca and Cultural Identity in an Andean Community*. Washington, DC: Smithsonian Institution Press.

Anthropology Today (1996). 12(6). [Advertisement].

ARENSBERG, CONRAD (1961). The community as object and as sample. *American Anthropologist* 63:241–264.

ARENSBERG, CONRAD, AND SOLON T. KIMBALL (1972). *Culture and Community*. Gloucester, MA: Peter Smith.

ARMSTRONG, G. PATRICK (1989). Gorbachev's nightmare. *Crossroads* 29:21–30.

BALOYRA, ENRIQUE (1990). El Salvador. In Howard Wiarda and H. F. Kline (Eds.), *Latin American Politics and Development*, 3rd ed. (pp. 183–197). Boulder, CO: Westview Press.

BARFIELD, THOMAS (1993). *The Nomadic Alternative*. Englewood Cliffs, NJ: Prentice-Hall.

BARNETT, HOMER (1953). *Innovation: The Basis of Cultural Change*. New York: McGraw-Hill.

BARTH, FREDRIK (1961). *Nomads of South Persia: The Baseri Tribe of the Khamseh Confederacy*. Boston: Little, Brown.

BARTH, FREDERIC (Ed.) (1969). *Ethnic Groups and Boundaries*. Boston: Little, Brown.

BASHAM, A. L. (1959). *The Wonder That Was India*. New York: Grove Press.

BAXTER, CRAIG (1992). Bangladesh: A parliamentary democracy if they can keep it. *Current History* 91(563):132–137.

BELLAH, ROBERT, ET AL. (1985). *Habits of the Heart*. New York: Harper & Row.

BENEDICT, RUTH (1946). *The Chrysanthemum and the Sword*. Boston: Houghton Mifflin.

BENJAMIN, MEDEA (Trans. & Ed.) (1989). *Don't Be Afraid Gringo: A Honduran Woman Speaks from the Heart. The Story of Elvia Alvarado*. New York: Harper Collins.

BENNETT, JOHN W. (1993). *Human Ecology as Human Behavior*. New York: Transaction Publishers.

BENNETT, JOHN W. (1985). The micro–macro nexus: typology, process and system. In Billie R. DeWalt and Pertti J. Pelto (Eds.), *Micro and Macro Levels of Analysis in Anthropology: Issues in Theory and Research* (pp. 23–54). Boulder, CO: Westview.

BENNETT, JOHN W. (1976). *The Ecological Transition*. Chicago: Aldine.

BENNETT, JOHN W. (1969). *The Northern Plainsmen*. Chicago: Aldine.

BENNETT, JOHN W. (1958). Economic aspects of a boss-henchman system in the Japanese forestry industry. *Economic Development and Cultural Change* 7:13–30.

BERNARD, H. RUSSELL (1995). *Research Methods in Anthropology: Qualitative and Quantitative Approaches*, 2nd ed. Walnut Creek, CA: Altamira Press.

BERTHRONG, DONALD J. (1948). La Crosse, a Case Study in Social History, 1900–1910. Unpublished MA Thesis, Department of History, University of Wisconsin, Madison.

BILELLO, SUZANNE (1996). Mexico: The rise of civil society. *Current History* 95(598):82–87.

BLACKMAN, MORRIS J., WILLIAM M. LeoGRANDE, AND KENNETH E. SHARPE (Eds.) (1986). *Confronting Revolution: Security through Diplomacy in Central America*. New York: Random House.

BLANTON, RICHARD, AND GARY FEINMAN (1984). The Mesoamerican World System. *American Anthropologist* 86:673–682.

BLANTON, RICHARD E., STEPHAN A. KOWALEWSKI, GARY FEINMAN, AND JILL APPEL (Eds.) (1981). *Ancient Mesoamerica*. Cambridge: Cambridge University Press.

BLOCK, MAURICE (1994). Language, anthropology, and cognitive science. In Robert Borofsky (Ed.), *Assessing Cultural Anthropology* (pp. 276–282). New York: McGraw-Hill.

BODLEY, JOHN H. (1982). *Victims of Progress*. Menlo Park, CA: Cummings Publishing.

BOHANNEN, PAUL, AND P. CURTIN (1995). *AFRICA AND AFRICANS*. Prospect Heights, IL: Waveland.

BOORSTIN, DANIEL J. (1983). *The Discoverers*. New York: Random House.

BOOTH, JOHN A. (1990). Nicaragua: Revolution under siege. In Howard Wiarda and H. F. Kline (Eds.), *Latin American Politics and Development*, 3rd ed. (pp. 467–482). Boulder, CO: Westview.

BOROFSKY, ROBERT (Ed.) (1994). *Assessing Cultural Anthropology*. New York: McGraw-Hill.

BOURGOIS, PHILIPPE (1996). Confronting anthropology, education, and inner–city apartheid. *American Anthropologist* 98(2):249–265.

BROOKS, DAVID (1990). Beyond catch phrases: What does sustainable development really mean? *International Development Research Centre Reports* 19(1):24–25.

BROWN, LESTER R., NICHOLAS LENSSEN, AND HAL KANE, ET AL. (1996). Vital Signs 1996: *The Trends That Are Shaping Our Future*. New York: W. W. Norton.

BRUMFIEL, ELIZABETH (1994). *The Economic Anthropology of the State*. Monographs in Economic Anthropology, No. 11. Lanham, MD: University Press of America.

BURG, STEVEN (1993). Why Yugoslavia fell apart. *Current History* 92(577):353–354.

BURGOS-DEBRAY, ELIZABETH (see Menchu, Rigoberta).

BUSBY, ANNETTE (1995). Kurds. In J. Middleton and A. Rassam (Eds.), *Africa and the Middle East* (pp. 174–177). Encyclopedia of World Cultures, Vol. 9. Boston: G. K. Hall & Co.

BUXBAUM, EDWARD (1967). The Greek–American group of Tarpon Springs, Florida: A study of ethnic identification and acculturation. Unpublished Ph. D. Dissertation, Department of Anthropology, University of Pennsylvania.

CALHOUN, CRAIG, DONALD LIGHT, AND SUZZANE KELLER (1994). *Sociology*, 6th ed. New York: McGraw–Hill.

CAMPBELL, JOHN (1964). *Honour, Family, and Patronage*. Oxford: Clarendon Press.

CANCIAN, FRANK (1965). *Economics and Prestige in a Maya Community*. Stanford: Stanford University Press.

CANCIAN, FRANK (1992). *The Decline of Community in Zinacantan*. Stanford: Stanford University Press.

CARMACK, ROBERT M., JANINE GASCO, AND GARY H. GOSSEN (1996). *The Legacy of Mesoamerica: History and Culture of a Native Civilization*. Upper Saddle River, NJ: Prentice–Hall.

CARNEIRO, ROBERT L. (1973). Slash-and-burn cultivation among the Kuikuru and its implications for cultural development in the Amazon Basin. In Daniel Gross (Ed.), *Peoples and Cultures of Native South America* (pp. 98–123). New York: Doubleday.

CARNEIRO, ROBERT L. (1970). A theory of the origin of the state. *Science* 169:733–738.

CARROLL, JOHN B. (Ed.) (1956). *Language, Thought, and Reality: Selected Writing of Benjamin Lee Whorf*. Cambridge, MA: MIT Press.

CARTER, GWENDOLEN M., AND P. O'MEARA (1986). *African Independence: The First Twenty-Five Years.* Bloomington: Indiana University Press.

CHAGNON, NAPOLEON (1968). *Yanomamo: The Fierce People.* New York: Holt, Rinehart and Winston.

CHAGNON, NAPOLEON (1974). *Studying the Yanomamo.* New York: Holt, Rinehart and Winston.

CHANCE, JOHN K., AND WILLIAM B. TAYLOR (1985). Cofradias and cargos: An historical perspective on the Mesoamerican civil-religious hierarchy. *American Ethnologist* 12(1):1–26.

CHANG, K. C. (1975). Ancient trade as economics or as ecology. In J. A. Sabloff and C. C. Lamberg-Karlovsky (Eds.), *Ancient Civilization and Trade* (pp. 211–224). Albuquerque: University of New Mexico Press.

CHAO, PAUL (1977). *Women under Communism: Family in Russia and China.* Bayside, NY: General Hall.

CHIÑAS, BEVERLY L. (1973). *The Isthmus Zapotecs: Women's Roles in Cultural Context.* New York: Holt, Rinehart and Winston.

CLAESSEN, HENRI J. M., AND PIETER VAN DE VELDE (Eds.) (1991). *Early State Economies.* New Brunswick, NJ: Transaction Books.

CLIFFORD, JAMES, AND GEORGE E. MARCUS (Eds.) (1986). *Writing Culture: The Poetics and Politics of Ethnography.* Berkeley: University of California Press.

COATSWORTH, JOHN (1979). Obstacles to economic growth in nineteenth-century Mexico. *American Historical Review* 39:939–960.

COATSWORTH, JOHN (1974). Railroads, landholding, and agrarian protest in the early Porfiorato. *Hispanic American Review* 54:48–71.

COE, MICHAEL D. (1962). *Mexico.* New York: Praeger.

COE, MICHAEL D., DEAN SNOW, AND ELIZABETH BENSON (1986). *Atlas of Ancient America.* New York: Facts on File.

COHEN, THEODORE (1987). *Remaking Japan: The American Occupation as New Deal.* New York: Free Press.

COHEN, YEHUDI (Ed.) (1968). *Man in Adaptation: The Cultural Present.* Chicago: Aldine.

COLLIER, GEORGE A. (1994). Roots of the rebellion in Chiapas. *Cultural Survival Quarterly* 18(1):14–18.

COLLINGWOOD, DEAN (1991). *Japan and the Pacific Rim.* Sluice Dock, Guilford, CT: Dushkin Publishing Group.

COMAROFF, JOHN (1994). Democracy, fried chicken and the anomic bomb. *Cultural Survival Quarterly* 18(2/3):34–39.

COMMINS, STEPHEN K., MICHAEL F. LOFCHIE, AND RHYS PAYNE (Eds.) (1986). *Africa's Agrarian Crisis: The Roots of Famine.* Boulder, CO: Lynne Rienner.

CONKLIN, HAROLD C. (1961). The study of shifting cultivation. *Current Anthropology* 2(1):27–61.

COSSALI, PAUL, AND CLIVE ROBSON (1986). *Stateless in Gaza.* London: Zed Books.

CRAMER, CHRISTOPHER (1994). Rebuilding South Africa. *Current History* 93(583):208–212.

CRESSEY, GEORGE B. (1963). *Asia's Lands and Peoples.* New York: McGraw–Hill.

CULBERT, T. PATRICK (1983). Mesoamerica. In Jesse D. Jennings (Ed.), *Ancient North Americans* (pp. 495–555). San Francisco: W. H. Freeman.

CUNLIFFE, BARRY (1974). *Iron Age Communities in Britain.* London: Routledge & Kegan Paul.

DALY, HERMAN (1996). *Beyond Growth: The Economics of Sustainable Development.* Boston: Beacon Press.

DE BLIJ, H. J., AND PETER O. MULLER (1997). *Geography: Realms, Regions, and Concepts*, 8th ed. New York: John Wiley and Sons.

DE JANVRY, ALAIN (1981). *The Agricultural Question in Latin America.* Baltimore, MD: John Hopkins University Press.

DE TOCQUEVILLE, ALEXIS (1957). *Democracy in America.* New York: New American Library.

DE WAAL, ALEX (1996). In the disaster zone. In William Haviland and Robert J. Gordon (Eds.), *Talking About People*, 2nd ed. (pp. 241–251). Mountain View, CA: Mayfield.

DE WAAL, ALEX (1994). Genocide in Rwanda. *Anthropology Today* 10(3):1–2.

DEAN, WARREN (1969). *The Industrialization of São Paulo, 1880–1945.* Austin: University of Texas Press.

DES FORGES, ALISON (1994). Burundi: Failed coup or creeping coup. *Current History* 93(583):203–207.

DIVALE, WILLIAM, AND MARVIN HARRIS (1976). Population, warfare, and the male supremicist complex. *American Anthropologist* 78(3):521–538.

DOUGLAS, MARY (1966). *Purity and Danger.* London: Routledge & Kegan Paul.

DOWNS, JAMES F. (1971). Spirits, power, and man. In Y. Cohen (Ed.), *Man in Adaptation: The Institutional Framework* (pp. 187–194). New York: Aldine.

DRENNAN, ROBERT D. (1976). Religion and social evolution in formative Mesoamerica. In Kent Flannery (Ed.), *The Early Mesoamerican Village* (pp. 345–368). New York: Academic Press.

DREWAL, MARGARET THOMPSON (1992). *Yoruba Ritual.* Bloomington: Indiana University Press.

Duncan, Kenneth, and I. Rutledge (1977). *Land and Labor in Latin America.* Cambridge: Cambridge University Press.

Earle, Timothy (1987). Chiefdoms in archaeological and ethnohistorical perspective. *Annual Reviews of Anthropology* 16:299–308.

Ebel, Roland (1990). Guatemala: The politics of unstable stability. In Howard Wiarda and H. F. Kline (Eds.), *Latin American Politics and Development,* 3rd ed. (pp. 498–518). Boulder, CO: Westview.

Economist, The (1996). August 31.

Economist, The (1995). April 8.

Economist, The (1992). October 19.

Eickelman, Dale (1981). *The Middle East: An Anthropological Approach.* Englewood Cliffs, NJ: Prentice–Hall.

Eiseley, Loren (1958). *Darwin's Century.* Garden City, NY: Doubleday.

Elashmawi, Fared, and Philip R. Harris (1993). *Multicultural Management.* Houston, TX: Gulf Publishing.

Ensminger, Jean (1992). *Making a Market: The Institutional Transformation of an African Society.* Cambridge: Cambridge University Press.

Eschleman, J. Ross (1994). *The Family.* Boston: Allyn & Bacon.

Escobar, Arturo (1995). *Encountering Development: The Making and Unmaking of the Third World.* Princeton, NJ: Princeton University Press.

Esman, Milton J., and Itamar Rabinovich (Eds.) (1988). *Ethnicity, Pluralism, and the State in the Middle East.* Ithica, NY: Cornell University Press.

Etzioni, Amitai (1993). *The Spirit of Community.* New York: Crown.

Evans-Pritchard, E. E. (1940). *The Nuer.* Oxford: Clarendon Press.

Fagan, Brian (1995). *People of the Earth: An Introduction to World Prehistory,* 8th ed. New York: Harper Collins.

Fagan, Brian (1989). *People of the Earth: An Introduction to World Prehistory.* Glenview, IL: Scott Foresman.

Fage, J. D. (1995). *A History of Africa,* 3rd ed. London: Routledge.

Fagg, John E. (1963). *Latin America: A General History.* New York: Macmillan.

Fei, Hsiao-tung. (1981). *Toward a People's Anthropology.* Beijing: New World Press.

Fishlow, A. (1965). *American Railroads ad the transformation of the antebelllum economy.* Cambridge: Hardvard University Press.

Flannery, Kent (1968). The Olmec and the Valley of Oaxaca: A model for interregional interactions in formative times. In Elizabeth P. Benson (Ed.), *Dumbarton Oaks Conference on the Olmec* (pp. 79–110). Washington, DC: Dumbarton Oaks Research Library.

Flannery, Kent V., and Joyce Marcus (1983). The growth of site hierarchies in the valley of Oaxaca, Part 1. In Kent Flannery and J. Marcus (Eds.), *The Cloud People* (pp. 53–64). New York: Academic Press.

Fogel, Robert W. (1964). *Railroads and American Economic Growth.* Baltimore: Johns Hopkins University Press.

Foster, George M. (1965). Peasant society and the image of limited good. *American Anthropologist* 67: 293–315.

Frank, Andre Gunder (1979). *Dependent Accumulation and Underdevelopment.* New York: Monthly Review Press.

Frank, Andre Gunder (1969). *Latin America: Underdevelopment or Revolution.* New York: Monthly Review Press.

Frank, Andre Gunder (1967). *Capitalism and Underdevelopment in Latin America.* New York: Monthly Review Press.

Frankfort, Henri (1956). *The Birth of Civilization in the Near East.* New York: Doubleday.

Freeman, Charles (1993). *The World of the Romans.* New York: Oxford University Press.

French, Rebecca R. (1994). Tibetans. In Paul Friedrich and Norma Diamond (Vol. Eds.), *Encyclopedia of World Cultures, Volume VI: Russia and Eurasia/China* (pp. 493–496). Boston: G. K. Hall.

Fuentes, Carlos (1992). *The Buried Mirror: Reflections on Spain and the New World.* Boston: Houghton Mifflin.

Gasco, Janine, and Barbara Voorhies (1989). The ultimate tribute: The role of the Soconusco as an Aztec tributary. In Barbara Voorhies (Ed.), *Ancient Trade and Tribute: Economies of the Soconusco Region of Mesoamerica* (pp. 287–303). Salt Lake City: University of Utah Press.

Gearing, Frederick O. (1971). The structural poses of 18th-century Cherokee villages. In Y. Cohen (Ed.), *Man in Adaptation: The Cultural Present* (pp. 181–187). New York: Aldine.

Geertz, Clifford (1996). *After the Fact: Two Counties, Four Decades, One Anthropologist.* Cambridge: Harvard University Press.

Geertz, Clifford (1968). *Islam Observed.* New Haven, CT: Yale University Press.

GEERTZ, CLIFFORD (1963). *Agricultural Involution.* Berkeley: University of California Press.

GERNET, JACQUES (1996). *A History of Chinese Civilization.* Cambridge: Cambridge University Press.

GILBERT, MARTIN (1993). *The Dent Atlas of Jewish History.* London: J. M. Dent.

GILBERT, MARTIN, (Ed.) (1990). *The Illustrated Atlas of Jewish Civilization: 4000 Years of Jewish History.* New York: Macmillan.

GIVENS, DAVID B., AND TIMOTHY JABLONSKI (1995). 1995 survey of anthropology PhDs. In *The AAA Guide: A Guide to Departments, A Directory of Members* (pp. 306–317). Arlington, VA: American Anthropological Association.

GIVÓN, TALMY (1979). *On Understanding Grammar.* New York: Academic Press.

GJORDING, CHRIS N. (1991). *Conditions Not of Their Choosing: The Guaymí Indians and Mining Multinationals in Panama.* Washington, DC: Smithsonian Institution Press.

GLAZER, NATHAN, AND DANIEL P. MOYNIHAN (1975). *Ethnicity: Theory and Experience.* Cambridge: Harvard University Press.

GLAZER, NATHAN, AND DANIEL P. MOYNIHAN (1970). *Beyond the Melting Pot.* Cambridge: MIT Press.

GOLDMAN, MINTON F. (1992). *Commonwealth of Independent States and Central/Eastern Europe.* Sluice Dock, Guilford, CT: Dushkin Publishing Group.

GOLDSCHMIDT, ARTHUR (1983). *A Concise History of the Middle East.* Boulder, CO: Westview.

GOLDSCHMIDT, WALTER (1978). *As You Sow: Three Studies in the Social Consequences of Agribusiness* [orig. 1947]. Montclair, NJ: Allenheld, Osmun.

GOSSEN, GARY (1994). Comments on the Zapatista movement. *Cultural Survival Quarterly* 18(1):19–21.

GROVE, DAVID (1981). The formative period and the evolution of complex culture. In J. Sabloff (Vol. Ed.), *Archaeology. Supplement to the Handbook of Middle American Indians,* Vol. 1 (pp. 373–391). Austin: University of Texas Press.

GUGLIOTTA, GUY, AND JEFF LEEN (1989). *Kings of Cocaine.* New York: Harper & Row.

HALL, EDWARD, AND MILDRED HALL (1990). *Understanding Cultural Differences.* Yarmouth, ME: Intercultural Press.

HALLIDAY, FRANK E. (1989). *England: A Concise History.* New York: Thames & Hudson.

HARDEN, BLAINE (1990). *Africa: Dispatches from a Fragile Continent.* Boston: Houghton Mifflin.

HARDGRAVE, ROBERT L. (1992). After the dynasty: Politics in India. *Current History* 91(563):106–112.

HARRIS, MARVIN (1994). Cultural materialism is alive and well and won't go away until something better comes along. In Robert Borofsky (Ed.), *Assessing Cultural Anthropology* (pp. 62–76). New York: McGraw-Hill.

HARRIS, MARVIN (1992). Distinguished lecture: Anthropology and the theoretical and paradigmatic significance of the collapse of Soviet and East European Communism. *American Anthropologist* 94(2):295–303.

HARRIS, MARVIN (1979). *Cultural Materialism: The Struggle for a Science of Culture.* New York: Random House.

HARRIS, MARVIN (1968). *The Rise of Anthropological Theory.* New York: Thomas Crowell.

HARRIS, MARVIN (1964). *Patterns of Race in the Americas.* New York: Walker.

HARRIS, PHILIP R., AND ROBERT T. MORAN (1987). *Managing Cultural Differences,* 2nd ed. Houston: Gulf Publishing.

HARRISON, SELIG S. (1992). South Asia and the United States: A chance for a fresh start. *Current History* 91(563):97–106.

HATCH, ELVIN (1985). Culture. In Adam Kuper and J. Kuper (Eds.), *The Social Science Encyclopedia* (pp. 178–180). London: Routledge & Kegan Paul.

HEADLAND, THOMAS, KENNETH PIKE, AND MARVIN HARRIS (Eds.) (1990). *Emics and Etics: The Insider/Outsider Debate.* Newbury Park, CA: Sage.

HEGEL, GEORG W. F. (1956). *The Philosophy of History.* New York: Dover.

HERRNSTEIN, RICHARD J., AND CHARLES MURRAY (1994). *The Bell Curve: Intelligence and Class Structure in American Life.* New York: Free Press.

HIMMELSTEIN, HAL (1984). *Television, Myth, and the American Mind.* New York: Free Press.

HOBSBAWM, E. J. (1962). *The Age of Revolution 1789–1948.* New York: Mentor.

HOCKETT, CHARLES F. (1960). Logical considerations in the study of animal communication. In W. E. Lanyon and W. N. Tavolga (Eds.), *Animal Sounds and Communication* (pp. 392–430). Washington, DC: American Institute of Biological Sciences, Publication No. 7.

HOLLOWAY, THOMAS (1977). The coffee colonos of Sao Paulo Brazil: Migration and mobility. In K. Duncan and I. Rutledge (Eds.), *Land and Labor in Latin America* (pp. 301–321). Cambridge: Cambridge University Press.

HOMANS, GEORGE [1941] (1968). English villagers of the thirteenth century. In Y. Cohen (Ed.), *Man in Adaptation: The Cultural Present* (pp. 466–477). Chicago: Aldine.

HOURANI, ALBERT (1991). *A History of the Arab Peoples.* Cambridge: Cambridge University Press.

HOWELL, NANCY (1990). *Surviving Fieldwork.* Washington, DC: American Anthropological Association.

HUGHES, JOHNATHAN (1987). *American Economic History.* Glenview, IL: Scott Foresman.

HUNT, SHANE (1973). Growth and guano in nineteenth century Peru. Discussion Paper no. 34, Princeton, University.

HUNTINGTON, SAMUEL P. (1996). *The Clash of Civilizations and the Remaking of World Order.* New York: Simon & Schuster.

HUNTINGTON, SAMUEL P. (1993). Democracy's third wave. In L. Diamond and M. F. Plattner (Eds.), *The Global Resurgence of Democracy* (pp. 3–25). Baltimore: Johns Hopkins University Press.

HUTCHINSON, SHARON (1996). *Nuer Dilemmas: Coping with Money, War, and the State.* Berkeley: University of California Press.

JANNEDY, STEFANIE, ROBERT POLETTO, AND TRACEY L. WELDON, (Eds.) (1994). *Language Files: Materials for an Introduction to Language & Linguistics,* 6th ed. Columbus: Ohio State University Press.

JENNINGS, JESSE D. (Ed.) (1983a). *Ancient North Americans.* San Francisco: W. H. Freeman.

JENNINGS, JESSE D. (Ed.) (1983b). *Ancient South Americans.* San Francisco: W. H. Freeman.

JOHNSON, ALLEN W., AND TIMOTHY EARLE (1987). *The Evolution of Human Societies: From Foraging Group to Agrarian State.* Stanford, CA: Stanford University Press.

JOHNSON, GREGORY (1973). Locational exchange and early state development in Southwestern Iran. University of Michigan Museum of Anthropology, Anthropology Papers #51.

JOSEPH, RICHARD (1996). Nigeria: Inside the dismal tunnel. *Current History* 95(601):193–200.

KAPUR, RAJIV (1986). *Sikh Separatism: The Politics of Faith.* London: Allen & Unwin.

KARNOW, STANLEY (1983). *Vietnam: A History.* New York: Viking.

KEDDIE, NIKKI (1981). *Roots of Revolution: An Interpretive History of Modern Iran.* New Haven, CT: Yale University Press.

KEESING, ROGER (1981). *Cultural Anthropology.* New York: Holt, Rinehart, Winston.

KEESING, ROGER M. (1976). *Cultural Anthropology: A Contemporary Perspective.* New York: Holt, Rinehart and Winston.

KEHOE, ALICE (1981). *North American Indians.* Englewood Cliffs, NJ: Prentice-Hall.

KIMBALL, SOLON, AND W. PARTRIDGE (1979). *The Craft of Community Study: Fieldwork Dialogues.* Gainesville: University of Florida.

KIMMERLING, BARUCH, AND J. S. MIGDAL (1994). *Palestinians: The Making of a People.* Cambridge: Harvard University Press.

KNIGHT, VIRGINIA C. (1992). Zimbabwe: The politics of economic reform. *Current History* 91(565): 219–223.

KOLATA, ALAN (1993). *The Tiwanaku: Portrait of an Andean Civilization.* Cambridge, MA: Blackwell.

KRADER, LAWRENCE (1968). *Formation of the State.* Englewood Cliffs, NJ: Prentice-Hall.

KROEBER, ALFRED (1948). *Anthropology.* New York: Harcourt Brace.

KROEBER, ALFRED (1917). The superorganic. *American Anthropologist* 19:163–213.

KROEBER, ALFRED (1909). Clasificatory systems of relationship. *Journal of the Royal Anthropological Institute* 39:77–84.

KROEBER, ALFRED, AND CLYDE KLUCKHOHN. (1952). *Culture: A Critical Review of Concepts and Definitions.* New York: Vintage Books.

LA LONE, DARRELL E. (1994). An Andean world system: Production transformations under the Inka empire. In Elizabeth Brumfiel (Ed.), The Economic Anthropology of the State (pp. 17–41). Monographs in Economic Anthropology, No. 11. New York: University Press of America.

LACEY, ROBERT (1981). *The Kingdom: Arabia and the House of Sa'ud.* New York: Avon.

LANTERNARI, VITTORIO (1963). *The Religions of the Oppressed: A Study of Modern Messianic Cults* (Trans. from the Italian by Lisa Sergio.). New York: Mentor.

LAPIDUS, IRA M. (1988). *A History of Islamic Societies.* Cambridge: Cambridge University Press.

LARSON, GERALD J. (1995). *India's Agony over Religion.* Albany: State University of New York Press.

LASKY, HAROLD (1948). *The American Democracy, a Commentary and Interpretation.* New York: Viking.

LATINAMERICA PRESS (1996). Mexico: Restless poor are hungry. Vol. 28, no. 34 (Sept. 19), pp. 1, 8.

LAUGHLIN, ROBERT (1995). Sna Jtz's'ibajom, the house of the writer. *Cultural Survival Quarterly* 19(2):9.

LEACH, EDMUND (1954). *Political Systems of Highland Burma.* Boston: Beacon Press.

LEACH, EDMUND (1961). *Pul Eliya: A village in Ceylon.* Cambridge: Cambridge University Press.

LEE, RICHARD (1984). *The Dobe !Kung.* New York: Holt, Rinehart and Winston.

LEE, RICHARD (1972). *The Dobe !Kung.* New York: Holt, Rinehart and Winston.

LEFF, MARION (1969). Long-term Brazilian development. *Journal of Economic History* 29:473–93.

LEIBENSTEIN, HARVEY (1957). *Economic Backwardness and Economic Growth.* New York: Wiley.

LEMARCHAND, RENE (1994). *Burundi: Ethnocide as Discourse and Practice.* New York: Cambridge University Press.

LEMOINE, JACQUES (1989). Ethnicity, culture and development among some minorities of the People's Republic of China. In Chien Chiao and Nicholas Tapp (Eds.), *Ethnicity and Ethnic Groups in China* (pp. 1–9). Hong Kong: Don Bosco Printing Co., Ltd.

LEVY JR., MARION J. (1966). *Modernization and the Structure of Societies.* Princeton, NJ: Princeton University Press.

LEWIN, ROGER (1992). *Life at the Edge of Chaos.* New York: Macmillan.

LEWIS, BERNARD (1995). *The Middle East.* New York: Scribner's Sons.

LIEBERMAN, DEVORAH, AND MEL GURTOV (Eds.) (1992). *Revealing the World: An Interdisciplinary Reader for International Studies.* Dubuque, IA: Kendall/Hunt Publishing Co.

LITTLE, PETER (1988). Preliminary observations of rural-urban linkages in southern Somalia. Development Anthropology Network. *Bulletin of the Institute for Development Anthropology* 6(1):4–10.

LODGE, GEORGE C. (1990). *Perestroika for America.* Boston: Harvard Business School.

LOFCHIE, MICHAEL F. (1986). Africa's agricultural crisis: An overview. In Stephen K. Commins, Michael F. Lofchie, and Rhys Payne (Eds.), *Africa's Agrarian Crisis: The Roots of Famine* (pp. 3–18). Boulder, CO: Lynne Rienner.

MACDONALD, CHARLES (1989). The Kurdish challenge and revolutionary Iran. *Journal of South Asian and Middle Eastern Studies* 13(1/2):52–68.

MAGNARELLA, PAUL J. (1993). *Human Materialism.* Gainesville: University of Florida Press.

MAIR, LUCY (1974). *African Societies.* Cambridge: Cambridge University Press.

MALINOWSKI, BRONISLAW [1944] (1960). *A Scientific Theory of Culture and Other Essays.* New York: Oxford University Press.

MALOTKI, EKKEHART (1983). *Hopi Time: A Linguistic Analysis of the Temporal Concepts in the Hopi Language.* Berlin: Mouton.

MANGO, ANDREW (1979). The multiple crisis in Turkey. *Asian Affairs* 10:125–31.

MARCUS, GEORGE E., AND MICHAEL M. J. FISCHER (1986). *Anthropology as Cultural Critique: An Experimental Moment in the Human Sciences.* Chicago: University of Chicago Press.

MARX, KARL (1936). *Capital, a critique of political economy.* New York: The Modern Library.

MASTERS, WILLIAM H., AND VIRGINIA E. JOHNSON (1966). *Human Sexual Response.* Boston: Little, Brown.

MASUDA, SHOZO, ISUMI SHIMADA, AND CRAIG MORRIS (Eds.) (1985). *Andean Ecology and Civilization: An Interdisciplinary Perspective on Andean Ecological Complementarity.* Papers from the Wenner-Gren Foundation for Anthropological Research Symposium No. 91. Tokyo: University of Tokyo Press.

MAYBURY-LEWIS, DAVID (1997). *Indigenous Peoples, Ethnic Groups, and the State.* Boston: Allyn & Bacon.

MAYBURY-LEWIS, DAVID (1992). Millenium. New York: Viking.

MCCORKLE, CONSTANCE M. (1989). The context of the cotton/cereal equation in Burkina Faso. In S. Smith and E. Reeves (Eds.), *Human Systems Ecology* (pp. 81–106). Boulder, CO: Westview.

MCGRANAHAN, CAROLE (1993). Tibetans. In Marc S. Miller (Ed.), *State of the Peoples: A Global Human Rights Report on Societies in Danger* (pp. 125–126). Boston: Beacon Press.

MCGREAVY, WILLIAM (1971). *An Economic History of Colombia, 1845–1930.* Cambridge: Cambridge University Press.

MCLEOD, W. H. (1989). *The Sikhs.* New York: Columbia University Press.

MCNEILL, WILLIAM (1974). *The Shape of European History.* New York: Oxford University Press.

MCNEILL, WILLIAM (1963). *The Rise of the West.* Chicago: University of Chicago Press.

MEGGERS, BETTY J. (1971). *Amazonia: Man and Culture in a Counterfeit Paradise.* Chicago: Aldine.

MENCHU, RIGOBERTA (1984). *I, Rigoberta Menchu.* (Elizabeth Burgos-Debray, ed.; Ann Wright, trans.) London: Verso.

MICHAEL, ROBERT T., JOHN H. GAGNON, EDWARD O. LAUMANN, AND GINA KOLATA (1994). *Sex in America: A Definitive Survey.* Boston: Little, Brown.

MIDDLETON, JOHN (1995). Introduction to Africa. In John Middleton and Amal Rassam (Eds.), *Encyclopedia of World Cultures, Volume IX, Africa and the Middle East* (pp. xxiii–xxxiv). Boston: G. K. Hall.

MIGDAL, JOEL S. (1996). Society-formation and the case of Israel. In Michael Barnett (Ed.), *Israel in Com-*

parative Perspective: Challenging the Conventional Wisdom (pp. 173–198). Albany, NY: SUNYPress.

MILLER, MARC S. (and Cultural Survival staff) (1993). *State of the Peoples: A Global Human Rights Report on Societies in Danger.* Boston: Beacon Press.

MILLER, ROBERT (1959). A History of La Crosse, Wisconsin, 1900–1959. Unpublished Ph.D. Dissertation, Peabody College.

MINTZ, SIDNEY (1985). *Sweetness and Power.* New York: Viking Penguin.

MINTZ, SIDNEY [1960] (1974). *Worker in the Cane.* Westport, CT: Greenwood Press.

MOORE, SALLY FALK (1994). *Anthropology and Africa: Changing Perspectives on a Changing Scene.* Charlottesville & London: University Press of Virginia.

MORAN, EMILIO (1982). *Human Adaptability: An Introduction to Ecological Anthropology.* Boulder, CO: Westview.

MORAN, EMILIO (Ed.) (1990). *The Ecosystem Approach in Anthropology.* Ann Arbor: University of Michigan Press.

MORENO-BLACK, G., AND PHILIP YOUNG (1992). Anthropology and international development in the late twentieth century. In Devorah Lieberman and Mel Gurtov (Eds.), *Revealing the World: An Interdisciplinary Reader for International Studies* (pp. 53–91). Dubuque, IA: Kendall/Hunt.

MORGAN, L. H. (1877). *Ancient Society.* New York: World Publishing Society.

MORGAN, L. H. (1870). *Systems of Consanguinity and Affinity of the Human Family.* Washington, DC: Smithsonian Institute.

MOSELEY, MICHAEL E. (1992). *The Incas and Their Ancestors.* London: Thames & Hudson.

MOSELEY, MICHAEL E. (1983). Central Andean civilization. In Jesse D. Jennings (Ed.), *Ancient South Americans* (pp. 179–239). San Francisco: W. H. Freeman & Co.

MURDOCK, GEORGE P. (1967). *Ethnographic Atlas.* Pittsburgh, PA: University of Pittsburgh Press.

MUSLIH, MOHAMMED (1994). Jericho and its meaning: A new strategy for the Palestinians. *Current History* 93(580):72–77.

NASH, JUNE (1994). Global integration and subsistence insecurity. *American Anthropologist* 96(1): 7–30.

NASH, MANNING (1989). *The Cauldron of Ethnicity in the Modern World.* Chicago: University of Chicago Press.

NIEHOFF, ARTHUR, AND CONRAD ARENSBERG (1963). *Technical Cooperation and Cultural Reality.* Washington DC: Department of State and Agency for International Development.

NORTH, DOUGLAS (1990). *Institutions, Institutional Change and Economic Performance.* Cambridge: Cambridge University Press.

NORTH, DOUGLAS (1981). *Structure and Change in Economic History.* New York: W. W. Norton.

NOTAR, BETH E. (1994). Hani. In Paul Friedrich and Norma Diamond (Vol. Eds.), *Encyclopedia of World Cultures, Volume VI: Russia and Eurasia/China* (pp. 449–452). Boston: G. K. Hall.

OGBURN, WILLIAM F. (1938). *Machines and Tomorrow's World.* New York: Public Affairs Committee.

OGDEN, SUZANNE (1991). *China.* Guilford, CT: The Dushkin Publishing Group.

OLIVER, SYMMES (1962). Ecology and cultural continuity as contributing factors in the social organization of the Plains Indians. *University of California Publications in American Archaeology and Ethnology* 48:13–49. Reprinted in Yehudi Cohen (Ed.), *Man in Adaptation: The Cultural Present.* Chicago: Aldine.

OVERBEEK, JOHANNES (1974). *History of Population Theories.* Rotterdam: Rotterdam University Press.

PARK, KYEYOUNG (1996). Use and abuse of race and culture: Black-Korean tensions in America. *American Anthropologist* 98(3):492–499.

PARK, ROBERT E. (1936). Human ecology. *American Journal of Sociology* 42:3–49.

PARK, ROBERT E., E. W. BURGESS, AND R. D. MCKENZIE (1925). *The City.* Chicago: University of Chicago Press.

PEHRSON, ROBERT (1966). *The Social Organization of the Marri Baluch.* Chicago: Aldine.

PELETZ, MICHAEL G. (1995). Kinship studies in late twentieth-century anthropology. *Annual Review of Anthropology* 24:343–72.

PERETZ, DON (1977). *The Palestinian State.* Port Washington, NY: Kinniket Press.

PIKE, KENNETH (1954). *Language in Relation to a Unified Theory of the Structure of Human Behavior,* Vol. 1. Glendale, CA: Summer Institute of Linguistics.

PILCHER, WILLIAM (1972). *The Portland Longshoremen.* New York: Holt, Rinehart and Winston.

PIMENTAL, D., ET AL. (1995). Environmental and economic costs of soil erosion and conservation benefits. *Science* 267:1117–1123.

PINAULT, DAVID (1992). *The Shiites: Ritual and Popular Piety in a Muslim Community.* New York: St. Martin's Press.

POLANYI, KARL [1944] (1962). *The Great Transformation: The Political and Economic Origins of Our Time.* New York: Beacon Press.

PORTES, ALEJANDRO, AND J. WALTON (1976). *Urban Latin America*. Austin: University of Texas Press.

PRUNIER, GERARD (1995). *The Rwanda Crisis: History of a Genocide*. New York: Columbia University Press.

PURCELL, SUSAN KAUFMAN (1992). Mexico's new economic vitality. *Current History* 91(563):123–127.

RAPPAPORT, ROY A. (1994). Humanity's evolution and anthropology's future. In R. Borofsky (Ed.), *Assessing Cultural Anthropology* (pp. 153–165). New York: McGraw-Hill.

RAPPAPORT, ROY A. (1979). *Ecology, Meaning and Religion*. Berkeley, CA: North Atlantic Books.

RASSAM, AMAL (1995). Introduction to the Middle East. In John Middleton and Amal Rassam (Eds.), *Encyclopedia of World Cultures, Volume IX, Africa and the Middle East* (pp. xxxv–xxxix). Boston: G. K. Hall.

REDFIELD, ROBERT (1941). *The Folk Culture of Yucatan*. Chicago: University of Chicago Press.

REDFIELD, ROBERT, RALPH LINTON, AND MELVILLE J. HERSKOVITS (1936). A memorandum on acculturation. *American Anthropologist* 38:149–152.

REDMAN, CHARLES (1978). *The Rise of Civilization*. San Fransisco: W. H. Freeman.

REED, RICHARD (1997). *Forest Dwellers, Forest Protectors: Indigenous Models for International Development*. Boston: Allyn & Bacon.

REEVES, ED (1989). Market places, market channels, market strategies: Levels for analysis of a regional system. In Sheldon Smith and Ed Reeves (Eds.), *Human Systems Ecology* (pp. 58–80). Boulder, CO: Westview.

REICH, ROBERT B. (1991). *The Work of Nations*. New York: Alfred Knopf.

REISCHAUER, EDWIN O. (1988). *The Japanese Today*. Cambridge: Cambridge University Press.

RENFREW, COLIN (1979). *Problems in European Prehistory*. New York: Cambridge University Press.

RENFREW, COLIN, AND J. M. WAGSTAFF (Eds.) (1982). *An Island Polity: The Archaeology of Exploitation in Melos*. Cambridge: Cambridge University Press.

RENNER, MICHAEL (1997). Chiapas: An uprising born of despair. *World Watch* 10(1):12–24.

RIESMAN, DAVID (1950). *The Lonely Crowd: A Study of the Changing American Character*. New Haven, CT: Yale University Press.

ROSENBERG, NATHAN, AND L. E. BIRDZELL, JR. (1986). *How the West Grew Rich*. New York: Basic Books.

ROY, SARA (1994). The Gaza Strip: Past, present, and future. *Current History* 93(580):67–71.

ROYAL ANTHROPOLOGICAL INSTITUTE (1951). *Notes and Queries on Anthropology*. London: Routledge & Kegan Paul.

RUST, WILLIAM, AND R. J. SHARER (1988). Olmec settlement data from La Venta, Tabasco, Mexico. *Science* 242:102–104.

SABLOFF, JEREMY A., AND DAVID F. FRIEDEL (1975). A model of a pre-Columbian trading center. In Sabloff and Lamberg-Karlovsky, *op cit*.

SABLOFF, J. A., AND C. C. LAMBERG-KARLOVSKY (Eds.) (1975). *Ancient Civilization and Trade*. Albuquerque: University of New Mexico Press.

SAHLINS, MARSHALL (1994). Goodbye to tristes tropes: Ethnography in the context of the modern world. In Robert Borofsky (Ed.), *Assessing Cultural Anthropology* (pp. 377–393). New York: McGraw-Hill.

SAHLINS, MARSHALL (1977). Culture and environment: The study of cultural ecology. In Sol Tax and Leslie G. Freeman (Eds.), *Horizons in Anthropology*, 2nd (revised) edition (pp. 215–231). Chicago: Aldine.

SAHLINS, MARSHALL (1972). *Stone Age Economics*. Chicago: Aldine.

SAHLINS, MARSHALL (1968). *Tribesmen*. Englewood Cliffs, NJ: Prentice–Hall.

SAHLINS, MARSHALL (1961). The segmentary lineage: An organization of predatory expansion. *American Anthropologist* 63:322–345.

SAHLINS, MARSHALL, AND E. R. SERVICE (Eds.) (1960). *Evolution and Culture*. Ann Arbor: University of Michigan Press.

SANFORD, ALBERT, AND H. J. HERSHEIMER (1951). *A History of La Crosse, Wisconsin*. La Crosse, WI: La Crosse Historical Society.

SARSANEDAS, JORGE (1995). Basta Ya! *Drü* 8(44):2.

SCHNEIDER, DAVID M. (1980). *American Kinship: A Cultural Account*, 2nd ed. Chicago: University of Chicago Press.

Science News (1992), No. 141, p. 215.

SCOTT, SHAUNNA L. (1995). *Two Sides to Everything*. Albany, NY: State University of New York Press.

SERVICE, ELMAN (1966). *The Hunters*. Englewood Cliffs, NJ: Prentice-Hall.

SERVICE, ELMAN (1962). *Primitive Social Organization*. New York: Random House.

SHILLINGTON, KEVIN (1989). *History of Africa*. New York: St. Martin's Press.

SHUBANE, KHEHLA (1992). South Africa: A new government in the making? *Current History* 91(565):202–207.

SINOPOLI, CARLA (1994a). Political choices and economic strategies in the Vijayanagara Empire. In Elizabeth Brumfiel (Ed.), *The Economic Anthropology of the State* (pp. 223–242). Monographs in Economic Anthropology, No. 11. Lanham, MD: University Press of America.

SINOPOLI, CARLA (1994b). The archaeology of empires. In W. H. Durham, E. V. Daniel, and B. Schieffelin (Eds.), *Annual Review of Anthropology*, vol. 23 (pp. 159–180). Palo Alto, CA: Annual Reviews, Inc.

SKLAR, RICHARD L. (1986). The colonial imprint on African political thought. In Gwendolen M. Carter and Patrick O'Meara (Eds.), *African Independence: The First Twenty-Five Years* (pp. 1–30). Bloomington: Indiana University Press.

SMITH, RICHARD (1974). Los Cafeteros. Unpublished Ph. D. Dissertation. Department of Anthropology, University of Oregon.

SMITH, ROBERT (1988). *Kingdoms of the Yoruba*. Madison: University of Wisconsin Press.

SMITH, SHELDON (1995). *World in Disorder: An Anthropological and Interdisciplinary Approach to Global Issues*. Lanham, MD: University Press of America.

SMITH, SHELDON (1994). Politics and ecology in Puebla. In Elizabeth Brumfiel (Ed.), *The Economic Anthropology of the State* (pp. 325–348). Monographs of the Society for Economic Anthropology, No. 11. Lanham, MD: University Press of America.

SMITH, SHELDON (1993). *World in Disorder: An Interdisciplinary Approach to Global Issues*. Lanham, MD: University Press of America.

SMITH, SHELDON (1985). The re-establishment of community: The emerging festival system of the American Midwest. *Journal of American Culture* 8(3):91–100.

SMITH, SHELDON (1982). Human ecology, socionatural systems, and the central-satellite plantation system of Guatemala and Colombia. *Studies in Comparative International Development* 17(1):3–21.

SMITH, SHELDON, AND RICHARD L. SMITH (1989). Horizontal and vertical linkages in highland Antioquia, Colombia: The architecture of the landscape. In S. Smith and E. Reeves (Eds.), *Human Systems Ecology: Studies in the Integration of Political Economy, Adaptation, and Socionatural Regions* (pp. 170–201). Boulder, CO: Westview.

SMITH, SHELDON, AND ED REEVES, (Eds.) (1989). *Human Systems Ecology: Studies in the Integration of Political Economy, Adaptation, and Socionatural Regions*. Boulder, CO: Westview.

SMITH-AYALA, EMILIE (1991). *The Granddaughters of Ixmucané: Guatemalan Women Speak*. Toronto, Canada: Women's Press.

SNEIDER, DANIEL (1992). The Soviet 'ecocidal' legacy. *Christian Science Monitor*. June 11.

SO, ALVIN (1990). *Social Change and Development*. London: Sage.

SOUTHWICK, CHARLES H. (1996). *Global Ecology in Human Perspective*. New York & Oxford: Oxford University Press.

SOWELL, THOMAS (1981). *Ethnic America: A History*. New York: Basic Books.

SPENCER, ROBERT F. (1959). The North Alaskan Eskimo: A study in ecology and society. *Ethnology Bulletin* 171. Washington: Smithsonian Institution Bureau of America.

SPOONER, BRIAN (1982). *Desertification and Development*. London: Academic Press.

STAPLES, ROBERT (1985). Changes in Black family structure: The conflict between family ideology and structure conditions. *Journal of Marriage and the Family* 47:1005–1013.

STAVRIANOS, L. S. (1982). *The World since 1500*. Englewood Cliffs, NJ: Prentice-Hall.

STEWARD, JULIAN H. (1968). The Great Basin Shoshonean Indians: An example of a family level of sociocultural integration. In Y. Cohen (Ed.), *Man in Adaptation. The Cultural Present* (pp. 101–115). Chicago: Aldine.

STEWARD, JULIAN H. (1955). *Theory of Culture Change*. Urbana: University of Illinois Press.

STEWARD, JULIAN H. (1951). Levels of sociocultural integration: An operational concept. *Southwestern Journal of Anthropology* 7:374–390.

STEWARD, JULIAN H. (1949a). South American cultures: An interpretive summary. In J. H. Steward (Ed.), *Handbook of South American Indians*, vol. 5 (pp. 669–772). Smithsonian Institution, Bureau of American Ethnology, Bulletin 143. Washington, DC: U. S. Government Printing Office.

STEWARD, JULIAN H. (1949b). Cultural causality and law: A trial formulation of the development of early civilizations. *American Anthropologist* 51:1–27.

STEWARD, JULIAN H. (Ed.) (1967). *Contemporary Change in Traditional Societies* (3 vols.). Urbana: University of Illinois Press.

STEWARD, JULIAN (Ed.) (1956). *The People of Puerto Rico*. Urbana: University of Illinois Press.

STONE, IRVING (1977). British direct and portfolio investments in Latin America before 1914. *Journal of Economic History* 37:690–722.

STONICH, SUSAN (1993). *I Am Destroying the Land: The Political Ecology of Poverty and Environmental Destruction in Honduras*. Boulder, CO: Westview.

SULLIVAN, JO (1989). *Africa*. Guilford, CT: Dushkin Publishing Group.

SULLIVAN, LAWRENCE R. (1995). The Three Gorges project: Dammed if they do? *Current History* 94(593): 266–269.

TAMBIAH, STANLEY J. (1994). The politics of ethnicity. In Robert Borofsky (Ed.), *Assessing Cultural Anthropology* (pp. 430–442). New York: McGraw-Hill.

TASKER, PETER (1987). *The Japanese*. New York: E. P. Dutton.

Temu, Arnold and Bonaventure Swai (1981). *Historians and Africanist History: A Critique*. London: Zed Press.

THORNTON, ARLAND (1989). Changing attitudes towards family issues in the United States. *Journal of Marriage and the Family* 51:873–893.

THUROW, LESTER (1992). *Head to Head: The Coming Economic Battle among Japan, Europe, and America*. New York: William Morrow.

TISHKOV, VALERY A. (1994). Inventions and manifestations of Ethno-Nationalism in Soviet academic and public discourse. In Robert Borofsky (Ed.), *Assessing Cultural Anthropology* (pp. 443–453). New York: McGraw-Hill.

TOOKER, DEBORAH (1993). The Hani of China. In Marc S. Miller (Ed.), *State of the Peoples: A Global Human Rights Report on Societies in Danger* (pp. 118–119). Boston: Beacon Press.

TURNER, TERENCE (1995). An indigenous people's struggle for socially equitable and ecologically sustainable production: The Kayapó revolt against extractivism. *Journal of Latin American Anthropology* 1(1):98–121.

TURNER, TERENCE (1992). Defiant images: The Kayapó appropriation of video. *Anthropology Today* 8(6):5–16.

TURNER, TERENCE (1991). Representing, resisting, rethinking: Historical transformations of Kayapó culture and anthropological consciousness. In George W. Stocking, Jr. (Ed.), *Colonial Situations: Essays on the Contextualization of Ethnographic Knowledge, History of Anthropology*, vol. 7 (pp. 285–313). Madison: University of Wisconsin Press.

TYLOR, EDWARD B. [1871] (1958). *The Origins of Culture*. Part I of *Primitive Culture*. New York: Harper & Brothers.

VAN BUREN, MARY (1996). Rethinking the vertical archipelago: Ethnicity, exchange, and history in the South Central Andes. *American Anthropologist* 98(2): 338–351.

VAN WILLIGEN, JOHN (1993). *Applied Anthropology: An Introduction*. Westport, CT: Bergin & Garvey.

VANSTONE, JAMES W. (1974). *Athapaskan Adaptations: Hunters and Fishermen of the Subarctic Forests*. Chicago: Aldine.

VELIZ, CLAUDIO (1980). *The Centrist Tradition of Latin America*. Princeton, NJ: Princeton University Press.

VONDAL, PATRICIA (1989). The ecology of farm management in a swampland region of Indonesia. In Sheldon Smith and Ed Reeves (Eds.), *Human Systems Ecology* (pp. 107–123). Boulder, CO: Westview.

WALDROP, M. MITCHELL (1992). *Complexity: The Emerging Science at the Edge of Order and Chaos*. New York: Simon & Schuster.

WALLERSTEIN, IMMANUEL (1988). Development: Lodestar or illusion. *Economic and Political Weekly* 23(39): 2017–2023.

WALLERSTEIN, IMMANUEL (1979). *The Capitalist World-Economy*. New York: Cambridge University Press.

WALLERSTEIN, IMMANUEL (1974). *The Modern World System: Capitalist Agriculture and the Origins of the European World Economy in the Sixteenth Century*. New York: Academic Press.

WARNER, W. LLOYD (1949). *Democracy in Jonesville: A Study of Quality and Inequality*. New York: Harper.

WARNER, W. LLOYD, AND PAUL S. LUNT (1942). *The Status System of a Modern Community*. New Haven, CT: Yale University Press.

WARREN, D. MICHAEL, L. JAN SLIKKERVEER, AND DAVID BROKENSHA (Eds.) (1995). *The Cultural Dimension of Development: Indigenous Knowledge Systems*. London: Intermediate Technology Publications.

WARREN, K., AND D. BOURQUE (1991). Women, technology, and international development ideologies: Analyzing feminist voices. In M. di Leonardo (Ed.), *Gender at the Crossroads of Knowledge. Feminist Anthropology in the Postmodern Era* (pp. 278–311). Berkeley: University of California Press.

WEBER, MAX [1930] (1958a). *The Protestant Ethic and the Spirit of Capitalism*. New York: Scribner.

WEBER, MAX (1958b). *The Religion of India*. Glencoe, IL: Free Press.

WEBER, MAX (1951). *The Religion of China*. Glencoe, IL: Free Press.

WEBER, MAX (1949). *The Methodology of the Social Sciences*. (Trans. & Ed. by Edward H. Shills and Henry A. Finch). Glencoe, IL: Free Press.

WEEKS, DENNIS (1992). The AIDS pandemic in Africa. *Current History* 91(565):208–213.

WEINER, ANNETTE B. (1988). *The Trobrianders of Papua New Guinea*. New York: Holt, Rinehart and Winston.

WHITE, LESLIE (1959). *The Evolution of Culture*. New York: McGraw-Hill.

WHITE, LESLIE (1949). *The Science of Culture*. New York: Grove Press.

WHORF, BENJAMIN L. [1936] (1956). An American Indian Model of the Universe. In John B. Carroll (Ed.), *Language, Thought, and Reality* (pp. 57–64). Cambridge, MA: MIT Press.

WILLEMS, EMILIO (1975). *Latin American Culture: An Anthropological Synthesis*. New York: Harper & Row.

WILSON, WILLIAM J. (1996). *When Work Disappears*. New York: Alfred A. Knopf.

WILSON, WILLIAM J. (1991). Studying inner-city social dislocations: The challenge of public agenda research. *American Sociological Review* 56(1):1–14.

WILSON, WILLIAM J. (1987). *The Truly Disadvantaged: The Inner City, The Underclass, and Public Policy*. Chicago: University of Chicago Press.

WITTFOGEL, KARL (1957). *Oriental Despotism*. New Haven, CT: Yale University Press.

WOLCOTT, HARRY F. (1994). *Transforming Qualitative Data: Description, Analysis, and Interpretation*. Thousand Oaks, CA: Sage.

WOLF, ERIC (1994). Facing power, old insights, new questions. In Robert Borofsky (Ed.), *Assessing Cultural Anthropology* (pp. 218–228). New York: McGraw-Hill.

WOLF, ERIC (1982). *Europe and the People without History*. Berkeley: University of California Press.

WOLF, ERIC (1969). *Peasant Wars of the 20th Century*. New York: Harper & Row.

WOLF, ERIC (1959). *Sons of the Shaking Earth*. Chicago: University of Chicago Press.

WOLF, ERIC, AND E. C. HANSEN (1972). *The Human Condition in Latin America*. London: Oxford University Press.

WOLF, ERIC, AND S. MINTZ (1957). Haciendas and plantations in Middle America and the Antilles. *Social and Economic Studies* 6:380–412.

WOLFE, ALVIN (1977). The supranational organization of production: An evolutionary perspective. *Current Anthropology* 18:615–635.

WOODWARD, RALPH (1976). *Central America*. New York: Oxford University Press.

WORLD COMMISSION ON ENVIRONMENT AND DEVELOPMENT (1987). *Our Common Future*. New York & Oxford: Oxford University Press.

WORLD RESOURCES INSTITUTE, UNITED NATIONS ENVIRONMENTAL PROGRAMME, UNITED NATIONS DEVELOPMENT PROGRAMME, AND WORLD BANK (1996). *World Resources 1996–97*. New York & Oxford: Oxford University Press.

WORLD WIDE FUND FOR NATURE (1996). The timber trade and global forest loss. WWF article at URL http://www.panda.org/tda/forest/forest2.htm.

WORSLEY, PETER (1968). *The Trumpet Shall Sound: A Study of Cargo Cults in Melanesia*. New York: Schocken.

WRIGHT, ANN (see Menchu).

YAMAMURA, KOZO (1987). Behind the 'made in Japan' label. In M. Hyoe and J. Hirschmeir (Eds.), *Politics and Economics in Contemporary Japan* (pp. 127–142). Tokyo: Japan Cultural Institute.

YERGIN, DAVID (1991). Oil: The strategic prize. In Micah Sifry and C. Cerf (Eds.), *The Gulf War Reader* (pp. 21–26). New York: Random House.

YOUNG, PHILIP D. (1991a). Conceptual frameworks, sustainable development, and the management of fragile lands. In Philip D. Young (Ed.), *Fragile Lands Management in Latin America and the Caribbean: A Synthesis* (pp. 21–58). Bethesda, MD: Development Alternatives.

YOUNG, PHILIP D. (1985). Guaymí socionatural adaptations. In William G. D'Arcy and Mireya D. Correa (Eds.), *The Botany and Natural History of Panama La Botánica e Historia Natural de Panamá* (pp. 357–365). St. Louis: Missouri Botanical Garden.

YOUNG, PHILIP D. (1978). La trayectoria de una religión: El movimiento de Mama Chi entre los Guaymíes y sus consecuencias sociales. *La Antigua* 11:45–75. Panama: Universidad Santa María La Antigua.

YOUNG, PHILIP D. (1975). Guaymí nativism: Its rise and demise. *Proceedings of the XLI International Congress of Americanists*, vol. 3 (pp. 93–101). Mexico, DF: Instituto Nacional de Antropología Historia.

YOUNG, PHILIP D. (1971). *Ngawbe: Tradition and Change Among the Western Guaymí of Panama*. Illinois Studies in Anthropology, No. 7. Urbana: University of Illinois Press.

YOUNG, PHILIP D. (Ed.) (1991b). *Fragile Lands Management in Latin America and the Caribbean: A Synthesis*. Bethesda, MD: Development Alternatives.

Name Index

Subject Index